Two year olds of 2008

STEVE TAPLIN

Raceform

A **RACING POST** COMPANY

Published in 2008 by Raceform
Compton, Newbury, Berkshire, RG20 6NL

A catalogue record for this book is available from the British Library.

ISBN 978-1-905153-91-6

Cover designed by Adrian Morrish
Interiors designed by Fiona Pike

Printed by Creative Print and Design, Wales

Contents

Foreword

Steve Taplin's Two Year Olds Guide for the season is a superbly informative publication. Now in its 24th year it has proved invaluable to any keen student of the turf. Whether you are an owner, trainer, breeder, bloodstock agent, racegoer or punter, the analysis of the pedigrees combined with the trainer's comments are a fascinating insight to the new crop of young horses in each year.

Comments from around sixty trainers shows Steve has earned our respect and we are more than willing to give up our time and hopefully some accurate statements to help Steve with his publication.

An example of the worth of the book is evident in Jim Bolger's comments in the 2007 edition when he said the following about the subsequent champion two year old New Approach: "a lovely, big horse, he'll be a 2yo for the mid-to-back-end and he goes very well. A quality horse and we won't rush him."

I can assure you there is not a trainer who is not wiser about their own team from the pedigree summary, having read this wonderfully researched publication.

John Gosden

Introduction

Welcome to the 24th edition of *Two Year Olds* which aims to point horse racing fans in the general direction of the best young racehorses in Britain and Ireland. I have to say a big thank you once again to all the trainers (and their very helpful secretaries and assistant trainers) who have contributed by once again allowing me to interview them this spring. Within these pages you'll find comments from 74 trainers (surpassing my previous record tally of 67) who were only too pleased to assist me in making this book a worthwhile publication. In particular I must thank John Gosden for kindly writing the foreword, for welcoming me to his Clarehaven Stables and for painstakingly discussing all his two-year-olds with me. Over the years I've been fortunate to have most of England's top trainers recommend my book and John's position in the ranks of English trainers is second to none.

It's always nice to introduce fresh faces and those trainers appearing for the first time this year are Marco Botti, Simon Callaghan, Jeremy Gask, David Lanigan, David Murray-Smith, Jon Portman, Alan Swinbank, Tom Tate, Ed Vaughan and Nicky Vaughan.

The book has established a reputation for selecting stacks of winners, including many of the top two year olds from each crop, but it's important not to discard the book when the turf season is over in November. For example in last year's book Lambourn trainer John Hills was insistent that his late developing Tri Nations was 'as nice a horse as we have in the yard ... he's beautiful.' Twelve months later his belated debut was in Division 1 of the Wood Ditton Stakes, which he won at the rewarding odds of 40-1. Just for good measure Jeremy Noseda's Fanjina – also given a good report in *Two Year Olds of 2007* – won Division 2 of the same event.

The purchase prices of the two year olds you will find in the book show that vast sums continue to be spent on those horses that attract the eyes of the big players, but also evident is the fact that many of them are either sold for relatively modest sums or not sold at all. Considering the horses in this book hopefully represent the best of the bunch, what about the thousands that haven't met the standards expected of them and have therefore failed to find a place in *Two Year Olds*?

By and large, stallion fees have declined slightly over the past three years, tempting breeders to send increasing numbers of mares to the breeding shed, resulting in record numbers of foals. The obvious exceptions to those decreases in stud fees are at Coolmore, Banstead Manor and Cheveley Park – due to the fee increases for Galileo, Montjeu, Danehill Dancer, Dansili and Pivotal.

The record prices seen at the bloodstock sales over the past couple of years may, at first glance, seem to have continued in 2008. After all, the mare Playful Act was sold for $10.8 million, a Sadler's Wells yearling filly went for 2,500,000 Guineas and there was the 3,400,000 Guineas purchase of the Group 1 winning filly Satwa Queen. All three acquisitions were world records. The bottom end of the market tells a different story, however. Large crops of foals, the result of breeders crossing their fingers that the market will continue to rise, can only result in those fingers getting burnt. That said, along with many other people I couldn't resist the temptation to dive in and purchase a foal last year. Hope springs eternal!

The Darley-Coolmore battle continued in 2007, with the emphasis shifted away from yearling sale skirmishes and towards the acquisitions of tried and tested racehorses, particularly – and spectacularly – by Sheikh Mohammed. The Epsom and Kentucky Derby winners (Authorized and Street Sense), the outstanding Manduro and the champion two year olds of 2006 and 2007 (Teofilo and New Approach) were the most significant of a large number of such purchases. The last two were trained by Jim Bolger of course and given good reviews in *Two Year Olds*. As if that wasn't enough, Sheikh Mohammed has since spent an unprecedented £200 million for the land and horses belonging to Woodford Stud in Australia. A staggering amount of money by anyone's standards.

From my point of view, 2007 was a very good year for my Living Legend Racing Partnership. Our two fillies, Morinqua and La Chicaluna, won five races and almost £50,000 between them. Morinqua was particularly consistent and we were pleased she got some black type in the Land O'Burns Stakes.

The following is a rough guide to my description of the ability of family members mentioned in the pedigree assessment of every two year old, based upon professional ratings. Please note that these descriptions are standard throughout the book in the vast majority of cases, but there are instances where I rely upon my own judgement of the horse's rating.

Below 60 = moderate
60 - 69 = modest
70 - 79 = fair
80 - 89 = quite useful
90 - 99 = fairly useful
100 - 107 = useful
108 - 112 = very useful
113 - 117 = smart
118 - 122 = very smart
123 - 127 = high-class
128 – 134 = top-class
135 and above = outstanding

The two year olds in this book are listed under their trainers and I have carefully selected those horses most likely to perform well this year. There are several 'horses to follow' lists, such as the chapters called Fifty To Follow and Star Two Year Olds. These are always useful for those who want to follow a select number of horses. The chapter entitled Bloodstock Experts Mark Your Card is a particularly fruitful section for pin-pointing winners. Note also that many trainers suggest their 'bargain buy'. My only stipulation is that the horse should have cost less than 25,000 guineas at the yearling sales.

My friends at Raceform have helped ensure that the book is comprehensively indexed.

The book is divided into the following sections:

(a) Fifty to Follow
(b) Ten to Follow in Ireland
(c) Star Two Year Olds. This system gives an instant appraisal of the regard in which a horse is held.
(d) The Bloodstock Experts Mark Your Card. Bloodstock agents and stud managers suggest potentially smart two-year-olds bought or raised by them.
(e) Two-Year-Olds of 2008. The main section of the book, with each two year old listed under the trainer. Trainers' comments (when given) appear after the pedigree assessments. Readers should bear in mind that all the trainers' comments come from my interviews, which took part between late March and mid-April.
(f) Stallion Reference. This details the racing and stud careers of sires with more than two two year olds in the book.
(g) Racing Trends. This is a statistical analysis of those juvenile events that regularly highlight the stars of the future. It includes a list of three year olds to follow this season.
(h) Statistical Review

There are inevitably some unnamed horses in the book, but please access my website www.stevetaplin.co.uk throughout the season for updates on those horses named after the book was published.

Finally, I must offer my thanks to Hilda Marshall whose help with research during the hectic weeks in April ensured the book was completed on time.

Researched and compiled
by Steve Taplin BA (Hons).

Fifty to follow

Here is a choice selection of two year olds from the book for you to follow.

ADORING (IRE)
'A tall filly, she's done well and moves well ... one for the mid-summer, she's had a bit of a break and has done well for it. A tall filly and a good mover.'
William Haggas

ALMIQDAAD
'He's a nice colt and from what we've seen of him we like him. He's got a bit of quality and he'll make a two year old, probably around July time over six furlongs.'
Michael Jarvis

ALSALAAL
'A nice horse and nice mover, he's a big, strong colt that goes well.'
John Gosden

ARCHIE RICE (USA)
'I like him a lot, he's got a beautiful way of going, has a lovely temperament and is very well-balanced. He could be ... a really nice horse.'
William Jarvis

ART CONNOISSEUR (IRE)
'He's very sharp...a real precocious type, he'll start at five furlongs but should stay six on pedigree.'
Michael Bell

AWINNERSGAME (IRE)
'I'm happy with him and he's a six furlong horse that will hopefully be running in mid-May. I think he's a two year old that will win his races.'
Jeremy Noseda

BALLYALLA
'A gorgeous filly, she could be a real nice one. She's big and she moves really well. I trained the dam and this filly won't be early but she's one to look forward to.'
Richard Hannon

BLACK KAT (IRE)
'A very nice colt, he'll be ready before the end of May and he's probably a six furlong two year old. Looks very sharp.'
Brian Meehan

BLOWN IT
'I love this horse and mark my words you'll be hearing a lot more about him ... I think he's a very smart colt.'
Jamie Osborne

CECILY
'She's bred to go early ... the dam, grandam, great-grandam and her half-sister Violette all came to hand early. The family are all quick and if she's any good she will be too!'
Sir Mark Prescott

COOL ART (IRE)
'This is a good horse – a real athlete ... shows us lots of ability and he has the potential to be running in Group races later in the year. A really nice colt.'
Simon Callaghan

CORNISH ROSE
'This filly is a natural and has looked that way from day one ... hopefully she'll be out in May. She goes well, has plenty of scope and she should mature as the year goes on.'
Mark Tompkins

DREAM DATE (IRE)
'A very nice filly, she's strong, sharp and keen to please ... when I put this filly upsides for the first time she was the one that caught my eye.'
William Haggas

DUNES QUEEN (USA)

'She could win the Guineas this year if I wanted her to! A smashing, big filly, she's got everything going for her. A filly with size and scope, she's very nice.'
Mick Channon

EDDIE BOY

'A lovely, scopey colt, he's a very good mover and has plenty of presence – he's quite a striking horse.'
Michael Bell

EMIRATES CHAMPION

'A very nice, attractive horse, he's a very easy mover with a good temperament and we'd like to see him out around June/July time.' Godolphin

FINJAAN

'He'll be an early two year old and he shows bags of promise, I'm quite excited by him and I like him a lot. If we're going to have a little team that might make it to Ascot he'll be one of them.'
Marcus Tregoning

FLORENTIA

The family all run at two, we've had them all and they've won 27 races for us – nearly all as two year olds.'
Sir Mark Prescott

HESKETH

'If he's forward enough he might be the sort of horse we could aim at the Chesham Stakes. We loved him as a yearling and he's turning into the horse we thought he'd be.'
Ralph Beckett

HIMALYA

'A nice horse, a good mover and an early July type two year old. He'd be a horse I like and is one to follow.'
Jeremy Noseda

HONESTLY (USA)

'She's doing very well ... she'll be out in May and she looks talented.'
Brian Meehan

HONIMIERE (IRE)

'She's a lovely filly – a superstar! Probably one of the best fillies we've ever had, she's very straightforward and learned very quickly.'
Alan Swinbank

JAZACOSTA (USA)

'He'll have a run over five furlongs in early May before I step him up to six. A big, strong, robust type of two year old ... I like him a lot.'
Amanda Perrett

JOHNNY ROOK (GER)

'This is a strong, powerful horse that will be a two year old, I like him and he looks to go nicely.'
Ed Dunlop

KINGSGATE STORM (IRE)

'He's a big, strong, solid sort and although it's a bit early to say he's another Kingsgate Native he's a very similar type. I'm very pleased with him and he'll make a proper two year old.'
John Best

KONKA (USA)

'I like this filly a lot. The dam won a stakes race at two, this filly looks very sharp, she's quite well-grown and there's a lot to like about her.'
Ed Vaughan

LOVE TO CHAT (USA)

'He'll be one of my best horses ... a real fine two year old, he's my favourite and he's got loads of gears.'
Stan Moore

LUXURIA (IRE)

'She hasn't stopped improving since she came in. A lovely filly and she looks like replacing her good half-sister Sweepstake.'
Richard Hannon

MAFAAZ

'A very good-looking Medicean colt, he moves very well and has a good, powerful stride on him ... He'll be one for mid-season.'
John Gosden

MAJESTIC LADY
'She's grown recently and has done really well. We're delighted with her and it looks like she's going to be fast.'
Barry Hills

MATTAMIA (IRE)
'A big, strong horse ... he's very similar to a nice horse I had called Lord Kintyre. He's strong, good tempered and I'd expect him to be one of my nicer horses.'
Rod Millman

MRS KIPLING
'One of my real picks of the fillies ... shows lots of speed, has a great outlook and is a filly we really like. Potentially a stakes filly – she could be a very exciting horse.'
Simon Callaghan

OASIS KNIGHT (IRE)
'I particularly like this colt, he's really nice ... a lovely-moving horse and ... this is the nicest foal the mare has had since High Accolade.'
Marcus Tregoning

OUQBA
'He's certainly going to make a two year old, he has a great temperament and you wouldn't know you had him in the yard. He's done one bit of work ... and he did it great.'
Barry Hills

OVERACHIEVER (IRE)
'This filly is nice and early and will be running before the end of May ... she seems to have plenty of speed and looks a sharp sort.'
Pat Eddery

PROWL
'A big, scopey filly, she was very well bought and she's a lovely, strong filly that moves extremely well. She looks nice.'
Ed Dunlop

RIO CARNIVAL (USA)
'A filly with a good attitude, she moves along nicely and does everything right. Like her mother, I wouldn't want to rush her and so August/ September time should be right for her. I'll probably start her over seven furlongs but she's a lovely, quality filly.'
John Gosden

ROMANTICIZE
'This is a filly I'm cracking on with, she's very, very sharp ... she'd win over five furlongs but she'll be better over six. One of my early ones – definitely.'
Peter Chapple-Hyam

ROSE DIAMOND
'A good, tough filly that'll be suited by six furlongs in May or June. She looks quite precocious ... she shows plenty of speed and it's so far so good with her.'
Roger Charlton

RUSSIAN JAR (IRE)
'He's a big colt from a very good family and he's a lovely horse. He could make a nice two year old and hopefully he'd have enough pace to go six furlongs.'
Michael Jarvis

SILVER GAMES (IRE)
'A very nice filly, she's done particularly well and we're just starting to do some more serious work with her. A filly with a bit of size and scope about her, she could be anything and might be really nice.'
Mick Channon

SWINDLER
'He looks pretty special I must say. It surprises me that for a probable middle-distance horse he has plenty of dash ... at this moment in time I'd say he's just about the pick of my two year olds.'
Andrew Balding

SWISS DIVA
'She looks like a two year old ... has a good temperament. She's precocious and has a good pedigree, so she has every chance.'
David Elsworth

TAARAB
'This colt has an excellent temperament and is loving everything he does. He has class and should be one for seven furlongs in mid-summer.'
Godolphin

TROPICAL PARADISE (IRE)
'A stunning filly and as soon as she come in her coat she's be racing ... I really like her and she's a very nice sort.'
Peter Winkworth

UNNAMED
b.f. Dansili – Achieve (Rainbow Quest)
'She's probably the pick of my fillies. She does everything so very easily for a big filly and just cruises against the other two year olds ... she could probably win over six furlongs and then need further in time ... I like this filly a lot.'
Peter Chapple-Hyam

UNNAMED
b.c. Noverre – Mandragore (Slew O'Gold)
'He's lovely – the apple of my eye at the moment. I think he's a bit special – you find one every now and again...he has bags of pace and is a lovely horse to have around ... he has enough toe to win over five and he'll go on to be a nice six/seven furlongs colt.'
George Margarson

UNNAMED
ch.c. Galileo – Safeen (Storm Cat)
'He just floats over the ground and if I had to choose just one horse this is it. I think he's lovely and he does everything so easily ... I just love him.'
Peter Chapple-Hyam

UNNAMED
b.c. Kheleyf – Sewards Folly (Rudimentary)
'He's a lovely horse who goes very well and he'll start in May with a view to going to the Coventry Stakes. He'd be better at six furlongs than five.'
Peter Chapple-Hyam

UNNAMED
b.c. King's Best – Tegwen (Nijinsky)
'The nicest colt I've got, he's got an awful lot of quality about him ... he shows a tremendous amount of speed ... a very likeable, mature, attractive horse.'
David Simcock

Ten to follow in Ireland

ARAZAN (IRE)
'He's a particularly nice colt, very mature, well-forward and he's a possible runner in late May. The dam bred Azamour along with a number of other colts that didn't do a lot. I'm hopeful that this fellow will be better than the disappointing ones. At the moment he looks that way.'
John Oxx

BRAZILIAN SPIRIT (IRE)
'She goes nicely and we like her a lot. She's typical of the other two out of the dam we trained. She isn't a big filly, but she's very muscular and six furlongs should suit her.'
Kevin Prendergast

KAMADO
'A real sharp, racey colt, he's growing a bit on me at the moment. He was a small tank and now he's medium-sized and he's just got to strengthen back up again. He's doing his work very impressively, which is what you'd expect being bred the way he is, he'll be a sprinter and I expect it'll be a 'Goodbye starter – hello Judge' job!'
Eddie Lynam

MY TOPAZ (IRE)
'A sharp colt, he goes well and he'll be a six furlong horse beginning in May. A nice horse and one to note.'
Dermot Weld

OHIYESA (IRE)
'I looked at every Noverre at the Sales since the nice horse I trained by him called Summit Surge but I didn't buy any of them until this one – and I love her. She's very speedy, could be anything, has a great attitude and she thinks she's a colt. I'd be disappointed if she's not a smart sprinter.'
Ger Lyons

OPTIMAL POWER (IRE)
'A nice, big, strong colt by Verglas, I've had luck with this family already and I like him a lot. He's getting his act together now, he should be out over six furlongs in May and he'll probably end up getting a mile. A very good-looking horse.'
Eddie Lynam

ROCKFIELD LADY (IRE)
'This is the filly! She's absolutely gorgeous; she's just gone through a little stage of growing and has a lovely action and a very good attitude. You'd be looking at starting her off over six furlongs in mid-summer and if you saw her in the string she stands out.'
Michael Grassick

SILVER SHOON (IRE)
'A sharp filly, I could see her starting over five furlongs in May. It's a fast family, she goes well and shows a lot of potential.'
Dermot Weld

TANOURA (IRE)
'A very nice filly, very well put together and sharp-looking. She's seems a quick learner and she goes well so I expect her to show us plenty as a two year old. The dam was quite speedy, so even though she's by Dalakhani I wouldn't be surprised if this filly had the speed for six furlongs.'
John Oxx

WANNA (IRE)
'A fine, big, scopey filly, she's very good-bodied and is one for the second half of the season. A filly with a good action, she looks quite exciting.'
Tommy Stack

Star Two Year Olds

The stars placed alongside the names of each two year old in the main section of the book give the reader an instant appraisal of the regard in which each horse is held. Stars are awarded for the following:

- A particularly glowing statement from the trainer, stud manager or bloodstock agent.
- A pedigree that suggests a two year old win is very much on the cards.
- A son or daughter of either a successful sire or else a first-season sire about whom the trainers have given me very good reports.
- A trainer associated with successful two year olds.
- My personal endorsement, based on how high I feel the horse could climb this year.

As you can see, the highest rating a horse can attain is five stars and clearly this is a very firm statement of the high regard in which the horse is held. The Five Star two year olds are listed below for quick reference.

FIVE STARS ★★★★★

AFRICA'S STAR Michael Jarvis

AKRISRUN Dermot Weld

ARAZAN John Oxx

ART CONNOISSEUR Michael Bell

ASPRO MAVRO John Gosden

BURJ DUBAI Saeed bin Suroor

DANEHILL DESTINY William Haggas

DUNES QUEEN Mick Channon

FANTASY LAND Brian Meehan

FATHER TIME Henry Cecil

GLAMOROUS SPIRIT Jeremy Noseda

HOSANNA Brian Meehan

INHIBITION Andrew Balding

LIFFEY DANCER Luca Cumani

MYSTIKA Tommy Stack

OSTAADI Michael Jarvis

PENINSULA GIRL Mick Channon

RIO CARNIVAL John Gosden

SEA THE STARS John Oxx

SHIMAH Kevin Prendergast

SILVER SHOON Dermot Weld

TIANTAI Henry Cecil

b.f. Dansili – Achieve Peter Chapple-Hyam

ch.c. Galileo – Safeen Peter Chapple-Hyam

b.c. Giant's Causeway – Spiritual Air Simon Callaghan

b.c. Kheleyf – Sewards Folly Peter Chapple-Hyam

The Bloodstock Experts Mark Your Card

In this section, Bloodstock Agents and Stud Managers suggest two year olds to follow, pointing out some of the nicest horses they have dealt with either as foals or yearlings.

The Top Tipster title for 2007 was won by Highclere Thoroughbred Racing's Harry Herbert, whose five selections yielded four winners – pretty impressive! Beaten by a neck into second were the trio Will Edmeades, David Redvers (each with three winners from four) and Angus Gold (three from five, including the listed winner Janina). I should also mention in despatches David McGreavy (two from three, including the smart colt Berbice), Kirsten Rausing (two winners, including 20-1 shot Lady Jane Digby), Tom Goff (who tipped the excellent Winker Watson) and Amanda Skiffington (her tip Stimulation recently won the listed Free Handicap).

Please note that most of the following two year olds are in the main section of the book listed under their trainers and are highlighted by the symbol ♠

JAMES DELAHOOKE

BLUE NYMPH Ralph has done really well with the produce of Julian and Sarah Richmond-Watson's Lawn Stud. This big backward Selkirk filly is probably all wrong for this book, but I am sure she will make her mark in due course. Trained by Ralph Beckett.

JAZACOSTA Guy Harwood and I used to stay at Hermitage Farm outside Louisville on our way to Keeneland. Warner L. Jones Jr. was the owner, a real character (sadly no longer with us) and his then manager Bill Landes bred this Dixieland Band colt which cost $165,000. Trained by Amanda Perrett.

MAYOLYNN (USA) A lovely Johannesburg filly purchased in Keeneland for Bob and Pauline Scott, who are building a new stud in Essex. The former chairman of Corals fulfils a lifelong ambition by having a horse with Henry Cecil.

UNNAMED *gr. f. Mr Greeley – Silver Kestrel* This filly was sold for 65,000 guineas at Tattersalls and reappears there on 17 April in the Two-Year-Old sale. Bred by Dominic Burke, the breeder of Katchit. She has always looked very sharp. *Author's note:* This filly was sold in the Two-Year-Olds Sale for no less than 540,000gns!

PETER DOYLE

DANES WORLD A filly by Danehill Dancer, she comes from a lovely family that has been very lucky for Richard.

HELIODOR A colt by Scrimshaw, he's very racey looking and Richard thinks a lot of him (all these are trained by Richard Hannon).

RED HEAD A filly by Redback (the sire of Gilded) and out of a half sister to Lady Links (the dam of Selinka) and closely related to Bold Edge. A Richard Hannon marque.

SOUL CITY A colt by Elusive City out of Savage. I also bought her dam as a yearling and she was a top two year old in Germany.

ROSS DOYLE

DOUGHNUT A very sharp filly by Acclamation, not overly big, but built to do the job as she did at Folkestone on her debut. All these are trained by Richard Hannon.

NOBLE JACK A lovely, big, strong colt by Elusive City (a stallion that could make it) and out of a fast family.

VERLEGAN A classy looking filly by Royal Applause, a half sister to Rag Top & Red Top, a family that team Hannon and Doyle have had a lot of luck with. Hopefully this filly will continue the trend.

UNNAMED A very nice colt by Marju out of a mare called Night Owl, he could be a very nice horse for later in the year.

WILL EDMEADES
Four nice colts – all in training with Richard Hannon.

APPRAISAL A really nice colt from the family of Red Clubs, Petong etc., who does everything effortlessly. He was bought for The Waney Racing Group, who enjoyed much success with another chestnut son of Mark Of Esteem in Redback.

BONNIE CHARLIE A racey son of Intikhab related to Averti and Reesh, who is improving physically every day. Hopefully, he will be an early scorer for Thurloe Thoroughbreds.

GLOBAL A cheap 'spec' buy for the trainer, who seems pleased with him. A good moving colt with a nice outlook, he too should come to himself fairly soon.

RIO DEL ORO A strong sharp type with an American dirt pedigree, who will race for The Waney Racing Group. He is doing everything asked of him and should be early.

ANGUS GOLD
ALKHAFIF b.c. Royal Applause – My First Romance
A very obvious type on breeding, a Royal Applause half brother to two Queen Mary winners - although he has plenty of scope he has done everything right so far and I will be surprised if he didn't make a two year old. Trained by Ed Dunlop.

FINJAAN b.c. Royal Applause – Alhufoof
Another colt by Royal Applause out of a Dayjur mare who won as a two year old – he has always looked a sharp type and Marcus feels he will be one of his earliest two year olds. Trained by Marcus Tregoning.

MASAMAH (IRE) gr.c. Exceed & Excel – Bethesda.
A March foal by Exceed & Excel from a fast family, he certainly looks the type to make a two year old. With Ed Dunlop.

OUQBA b.c. Red Ransom – Dancing Mirage
A sharp little colt by Red Ransom who was bought at Doncaster Sales - he has done a bit of work already and will not be long in running and the trainer is happy with the way he goes. Trained by Barry Hills.

TAAZUR b.c. Needwood Blade - Mouches le Nez
He was bought at Tattersalls Part 2 and looks to go well so far and has a bit of scope to him. Trained by Mark Johnston.

CHARLIE GORDON-WATSON
AWINNERSGAME Very closely related to the Irish 1000 Guineas winner Saoire and showing signs of being earlyish. I like the sire and we have had previous success with the same connections with Arabian Gleam. Trained by Jeremy Noseda.

DUBAI ECHO I have not seen this horse for a while but he was one of the first two year olds to go into the yard and what I have heard is favourable. He is an athletic Mr Greeley colt with a bit of class about him. Trained by Sir Michael Stoute.

KINGSHIP SPIRIT A real neat type of two year old by the right sire in Invincible Spirit, he is meant to be fairly forward and definitely looks the part. Trained by Jeremy Noseda.

SRI PUTRA *colt by Oasis Dream – Wendylina*
A striking, most good looking Oasis Dream colt who was expensive but showing all the right signs, I would not have thought would be particularly early but hopefully mid-season. Interestingly this name was originally given to a now 3 year old but is going to be changed as they consider this horse better. Trained by Michael Jarvis

BRIAN GRASSICK

JA ONE *b.f. Acclamation – Special Dancer (Shareef Dancer)*
Purchased at Goffs Million Sale for €105,000, she is out of a winning half sister to the very useful Cajarian and the dam of Group 1 winner Caradak. A tall, scopey filly with a great attitude and looks as if she might be an early type despite her size. Trained by Barry Hills.

UNNAMED *ch.f. Pivotal – Lurina (Lure)*
A half-sister to Centennial, a very useful two year old in 2007 from a Group placed half-sister to the top broodmare Alidiva from a top family. Bred and raised at Newtown Stud on behalf of W Lazy T Ltd. A very attractive filly with a very good action, she looks to the type to be suited by good ground and should be out mid-summer. Trained by Michael Grassick.

UNNAMED *b.f. Rock of Gibraltar – Quiet Mouse (Quiet American)*
Purchased at Goffs Million Sale for €270,000, she is a half-sister to the high-class filly Ugo Fire from the family of Pearly Shells. A lengthy filly with a great way of going and a nice temperament. She looks likely to be out late Summer. Trained by Michael Grassick.

UNNAMED *b.f. Smarty Jones – Djebel Amour (Mt Livermore)*
Purchased at Keeneland September Sale for $300,000 she is out of a winning daughter of the champion filly Sayyedati, from the family of Dubian. She is a very sharp, precocious filly and looks a very early type. Trained by Tommy Stack.

HARRY HERBERT

HARBINGER *b.c. Dansili – Penang Pearl*
This was our most expensive yearling purchase last year but was a John Warren 'must have' horse! He is beautifully balanced and he is one of those horses who really hold themselves well. He appears well liked by Sir Michael and his team and he looks the type to make into a late July or early August two year old. Trained by Sir Michael Stoute.

PRINT *b.c. Exceed And Excel – Hariya*
A well grown two year old who is now beginning to fill to his very substantial frame. He is one of those immature, somewhat leggy types who carry themselves in the manner of a well above average two year old. I love this horse and he could be on the track some time in late July or early August. Trained by Mick Channon.

ORATORY *b.c. Danehill Dancer – Gentle Night*
This is a really strong mature colt who could just turn into a Royal Ascot type if good enough. He moves well and looks to have an excellent temperament. Provided he takes his faster work without any hiccups then a late May or early June start is possible. Richard Hughes has already claimed him as 'his' ride so that can be added to the positive list! Trained by Richard Hannon.

HOSANNA *b.f. Oasis Dream – Rada's Daughter*
This filly has just moved into fast work and could be a really precocious type. She has a very strong physique and she is likely to be our first two-year-old runner. She has found everything asked of her very easy so far and the trainer could not be happier with her progress. Trained by Brian Meehan.

TIGER EYE *b.f. Danehill Dancer – Pink Stone*
This filly, trained by Peter Chapple-Hyam, could be very good. She is one of those that has gone from weak and immature to strong and imposing in an astonishingly short period of

time. She floats over the ground and will hopefully be an early July starter. Peter reports that all who ride her like her enormously and from the side of the gallops she is hard to fault. All in all a really exciting filly who could be anything! Both Danehill Dancers look very well bought by John Warren!

DAVID McGREAVY

UNNAMED *Kheleyf – Assigh Lady*
He is from the family of Dan Marino who we raced and he looked a real two year old type at the sales, the trainer is very pleased with his progress so fingers crossed. Trained by Mick Channon.

GEMINI JIVE *Namid – Pearl Bright*
A half sister to Berbice who did so well last year, she is a fine, strong sort who is well balanced and swings along nicely. A real quality filly. Trained by Mick Quinlan.

UNNAMED *Bachelor Duke – Isadora Duncan*
A very early lot at Tattersalls Ireland, who was bought for €6,500, the sire's average is 38,000gns and he looks to have sired some really good sorts in his first crop. She is a Christian, has never put a foot wrong and although a May foal already looks to have ability. Trained by Mick Quinlan.

JOHNNY McKEEVER

RAGGLE TAGGLE *b.f. Tagula – Jesting (Muhtarram)*
A sharp, early filly who should win some early season contests. Trained by Ralph Beckett.

LIGHT THE FIRE (IRE) *b.c. Invincible Spirit – Rouge Noir (Saint Ballado)*
Brian Meehan is pleased with this Invincible Spirit colt we purchased for Joe Allbritton.

OVERACHIEVER *b.f. Exceed And Excel – Panglossian (Barathea)*
Pat Eddery likes what he sees of her. I bought her for Con Wilson at Tatteralls last October.

KIRSTEN RAUSING

AESTIVAL *b.c. Falbrav -– Summer Night (Nashwan)*
A half-brother to Black Type winners Songerie (Group winner at two), Souvenance and Soft Morning, this colt was purchased by those fillies' trainer Sir Mark Prescott for 100,000gns as a yearling at Tattersalls Oct (1) sales. The trainer also has this colt's 2007 two year old half-sister Sourire, rated 96p by Timeform after her two wins last year. Aestival may well turn out to be a notable representative for Falbrav in that stallion's only European crop. Trained by Sir Mark Prescott.

ALANBROOKE *gr c. Hernando – Alouette (Darshaan)*
A half-brother to the dual Champion Stakes winner Alborada and German Horse of the Year, Triple Group 1 winner Albanova, as well as an own brother to Alakananda, a useful winner and herself dam of Derby second Dragon Dancer. This colt was bred by Lanwades and sold by our yearling division, Staffordstown, for 380,000gns to Mark Johnston at the Tattersalls October Sales (1). He has always been a very forward colt with great conformation and a willing temperament, as well as a particularly good mover. All being well, I would not be surprised to see him run by the early to middle part of Summer. He is a most promising and interesting prospect. Trained by Mark Johnston.

FAME AND GLORY *b.c. Montjeu – Gryada (Shirley Heights)*
A lovely colt who is bred well enough to be a Derby winner in 2009. Purchased by Coolmore interests as a foal from the Lanwades consignment at the 2006 Tattersalls December Sales. Trained by Aidan O'Brien.

GASSIN *ch.c Selkirk – Miss Riviera Golf (Hernando)*
An imposing colt, bred (as was his dam and granddam) at Lanwades for owner/breeder Mr J.L.C Pearce. This colt's dam (and her own sister) both won listed races in France. His dam's first three foals are all useful winners, including the

listed winner Hotel du Cap and now four-year-old The Carlton Cannes. Gassin could be a class horse in the making with his noticeably good action, though do not expect to see him much before Goodwood in August. Trained by Geoff Wragg.

JANE EYRE gr.f. .Sadler's Wells – Albanova (Alzao)
This filly was the highest priced yearling of either sex ever sold in Ireland, selling to Coolmore interests for €2.4million at the 2007 Goffs Million Sale. She was an outstanding physical specimen with a great temperament then, and, if she has continued to develop in a similar way, she should definitely be one to watch (though no doubt at short odds) when making her debut in the second half of the season. Her dam won her only start at two and the dam's own-sister, Alborada, was a Group winner at The Curragh at two. Trained by Aidan O'Brien.

PATRONNE b.f. Domedriver – Pat Or Else (Alzao)
A smallish filly, she is a homebred, repre-senting a currently underrated sire. She could well be one of the trainer's first two year olds to come to hand. Her dam never won but is already the dam of five winners, including the 2007 listed stakes winning two year old Triskel (the only stakes winner by her sire, in a large crop). The next dam bred dual Group 1 winners My Emma and Classic Cliche. Beautifully bred, this filly only needs to win a race (or two) to greatly enhance her value. Trained by Sir Mark Prescott.

DAVID REDVERS
BLOWN IT b.c. More Than Ready – Short Shadow
A proper early season two year old who has been showing Jamie loads of boot and very typical of what we look for as a typical 'Donnie type'. Hopefully this lad will be good enough for Ascot.

HESKETH b.c. Nayef – Agony Aunt
A gorgeous quality colt who could be anything but will not be running early. Trained by Ralph Beckett.

SPRITUAL HEALING b.c. Invincible Spirit – Tarbela
This filly looks a real rocket and has been showing a good bit at home.

TROPICAL PARADISE gr.f. Verglas – Lady Ladylisandra)
A really sharp quality filly who looks sure to fly the Peter Winkworth flag in some nice races this summer.

ROBIN SHARP
KINGSGATE STORM gr.c. Mujadil – In The Highlands
Sold by Houghton Bloodstock (UK) Ltd at the Doncaster St Leger Sales for 65,000gns to John Best. He looked a real two year old with a great temperament.

ROYAL EXECUTIONER b.c. Royal Academy – Guillotine
A real hardy colt bought by an excellent new client of ours. He has had the forethought to go to a trainer that does really well with the stallion, Peter Chapple-Hyam. Watch out for this colt.

WIGAN PIER b.f. Gulch – Kiralik
The first foal of a really super mare, this filly has quality written all over her. She is in training with Tim Easterby and is sure to give her enthusiastic owners some pleasure.

AMANDA SKIFFINGTON
CARNABY HAGGERSTON gr.c. Invincible Spirit – Romanylei
This was a horse I paid a lot of money for as a foal; I thought he was gorgeous, and he looked a sharp sort when I last saw him. The trainer apparently likes him a lot, and hopefully he will be a good one. Trained by Kevin Ryan

ZERO MONEY *ch.c. Bachelor Duke – Dawn Chorus*
Having just spoken to Roger, he tells me this horse does everything right and moves really well. Probably a second half of the season two year old. Trained by Roger Charlton.

IVOR NOVELLO *b.c. Noverre – Pearly Brooks*
Looked a very sharp sort when I bought him at Doncaster last year – hopefully just the type to do well at two. Trained by Alan Swinbank.

LARRY STRATTON

ANN BIRKETT *b.f. Beat Hollow - Blue Gentian*
A half-sister to the useful and tough Bavarica with same trainer Julia Fielden. By an underrated sire and looks to have her sister's toughness.

BALLADIENE *b.f. Noverre – Kinnego*
A sharp sort bought as a foal, the first foal of a half-sister to a Pretty Polly winner. Owned by a partnership of mainly Irishmen who don't expect to be waiting around long for her to run. Trained by Mark Tompkins.

ANTHONY STROUD

LADY TRISH *b.f. Red Ransom – Artifice (Green Desert)*
A lovely filly we purchased at the Tattersalls October Yearling Sale. She is from the family of Sir Gerry, who we purchased last year and went on to win the Group 2 Gimcrack Stakes and like Sir Gerry, this filly is also owned by the Galligan Family. She has done everything right in her work so far and we have high hopes for her this year. She should develop into an exciting three year old for next season as well. Trained by James Fanshawe.

GLAMOROUS SPIRIT *b.f. Invincible Spirit – Glamorous Air (Air Express)*
A fast and precocious filly we purchased at the Goffs Kempton Breeze-Up Sale for The Searchers Syndicate, who had so much success last year with our purchase Fleeting Spirit, who had a similar profile to this filly, as they were both consigned by leading breeze-up consignor Con Marnane of Bansha House Stables. She looked very fast in her breeze, so much so that the rider was unable to pull her up. We hope she will be an early sort with ambitions of Royal Ascot. Trained by Jeremy Noseda.

UNNAMED *b.c. Fasliyev – Ziffany (Taufan)*
This colt was purchased as a foal at the 2006 Goffs November Foal Sale. He was one of the standouts of that sale and we very much hope that he will follow in the footsteps of his illustrious siblings, Majors Cast and Jessica's Dream. Trained by Jeremy Noseda.

UNNAMED *ch.c. Proud Citizen – Near Mint (Dehere)*
A classy colt purchased at the Keeneland September Yearling Sale by an up-and-coming young sire, Proud Citizen. This colt has shown lots of quality in his early work and looks just the sort to make a good two year old. Trained by Walter Swinburn.

Two Year Olds of 2008

ERIC ALSTON

1. BALLARINA ★★★

b.f. Compton Place – Miss Uluwatu (Night Shift)
February 23. First living foal. €40,000Y.
Tattersalls Ireland. Sue Alston. The dam, a fair
10f winner, is a half-sister to four winners
including the Irish two year old 5f winner and
6f listed-placed Joyce. The second dam, Miss
Kinabalu (by Shirley Heights), was placed twice
at up to 1m and is a half-sister to four minor
winners here and abroad including Miss Ranjani
(dam of the Group winners Asian Heights and St
Expedit) and to the unraced dam of the very
smart Group 3 6f Prix de Meautry winner
Andreyev. (Mrs P O Morris).
'She ran in the Brocklesbury but it was a non-
event as far as we were concerned because she
split from the rest and ran on her own on the far
side. She'll want fast ground and I'm giving her a
break now because the race wound her up a bit,
but she's a nice filly that can motor a bit. Five
furlongs is fine for her.'

2. IMPRESSIBLE ★★★

b.f. Oasis Dream – Imperial Bailiwick
(Imperial Frontier)
April 4. Half-sister to the fair 2007 two year old
5f winner (on her only start) Quiet Elegance
(by Fantastic Light), to the high-class sprinter
Reverence (by Mark Of Esteem), winner of the
Haydock Park Sprint Cup and the Nunthorpe
Stakes, the very useful two year old listed 6f
Chesham Stakes winner and 1m Britannia
Handicap second Helm Bank (by Wild Again),
the modest 6f winner Fortress (by Generous),
the modest 10f winner Sedgwick (by Nashwan)
and a winner at up to 7.5f in Italy by Efisio. The
dam was a useful winner of three races at
around 5f including the Group 2 Flying Childers
Stakes, was placed in the Molecomb Stakes and
the Prix du Petit-Couvert and is a half-sister to
three winners in France (all over 1m+). The
second dam, Syndikos (by Nashua) was second
six times in the USA and is a half-sister to five
minor winners. (Mr & Mrs G Middlebrook).
'A half-sister to Reverence, this filly is sharpish but
very small so I'll be trying to crack on with her.
Hopefully I'll get her out before mid-season.'

3. STAR ADDITION ★★

b.c. Medicean – Star Cast (In The Wings)
January 18. Third foal. 18,000Y. Tattersalls
October. W Hutchinson. Half-brother to the
fair 5f winner of four races Princess Ellis (by
Compton Place) and to the moderate 5f winner
That's Blue Chip (by Namid). The dam, a minor
11f and 12f winner, is a half-sister to seven
winners. The second dam, Thank One's Stars (by
Alzao), is an unraced half-sister to five winners.
(John & Marie Thompson).
'A lovely colt, he's one for the back-end of the
season despite being an early foal. He really is
nice and the dam seems to breed speedy types.'

DAVID ARBUTHNOT

4. BADERRA BOY ★★★

ch.c. Needwood Blade – Roonah Quay
(Soviet Lad)
March 5. Fifth foal. €32,000Y. Tattersalls
Ireland. D Arbuthnot. Half-brother to the quite
useful two year old 5f winner Makila King (by
Wizard King), to the fair 7f all-weather winner
Compton Quay (by Compton Place). The dam is
an unplaced half-sister to eight minor winners.
The second dam, Piney Lake (by Sassafras), is a
placed half-sister to ten winners. (Mr Paul
Claydon).
'He's coming on alright and he'll be reasonably
early. The sire was a tough horse and when he
went to America he won over a mile. This colt
might get that far next year but as a two year
old she'll be suited by six/seven furlongs.'

5. PLACE THE DUCHESS ★★★

b.f. Compton Place – Barrantes
(Distant Relative)
February 12. First foal. 25,000Y. Tattersalls
October 2. D Arbuthnot. The dam, a listed-
placed winner of five races from 5f to 7f, is a
half-sister to four winners. The second dam, Try
The Duchess (by Try My Best), a two year old
listed winner, is a half-sister to three winners.
(Mr & Mrs George Ward).
'She'll be reasonably early and she's a very nice-
natured filly. A typical sprinting type so she'll be
a five/six furlong type from May.'

6. RUMBLE OF THUNDER (IRE) ★★

b.c. Fath – Honey Storm (Mujadil)
March 11. Third foal. 15,000Y. Tattersalls October 2. D Arbuthnot. Half-brother to the fair 7f and 1m winner of three races Coalpark (by Titus Livius). The dam won over 1m and is a half-sister to nine winners including the Group 3 winner and Group 2 placed Compton Bolter. The second dam, Milk And Honey (by So Blessed), won twice at two years and is a half-sister to nine winners including the Group 3 winner Beeshi. (Mr F Ward & Mr A Ward).
'Very forward both physically and mentally, he'll start off at seven furlongs.' TRAINER'S BARGAIN BUY

7. UNNAMED ★★

ch.c. Compton Place – Simply Sooty (Absalom)
January 25. Eleventh foal. 16,000Y. October 2. D Arbuthnot. Half-brother to the very smart Group 3 7.3f Horris Hill Stakes and Group 3 7f Craven Stakes winner Umistim, to the quite useful dual 1m winner Just Tim (both by Inchinor), the modest 1m and hurdles winner Cursum Perficio (by Tagula) and a winner in Denmark by First Trump. The dam, a fair two year old dual 5f winner, is a half-sister to two minor winners. The second dam, Classical Vintage (by Stradavinsky), won once at two years and is a half-sister to 11 minor winners.
'A very nice horse, he'll be a mid-season two year old and I expect he'll turn out to be a miler. The dam's getting on a bit but he doesn't look like the produce of an old mare at all, in fact he's nice and strong.'

ALAN BAILEY

8. ASPEN DARLIN (IRE) ★★★

b.f. Indian Haven – Manuka Magic (Key Of Luck)
March 20. First foal. €10,000Y. Tattersalls Ireland. A Bailey. The dam is an unraced half-sister to three winners. The second dam, Magic Garter (by Precocious), is an unraced half-sister to seven winners and to the unraced dam of Grand Lodge. (Indian Haven Syndicate).
'She's only a small filly but she's all heart and very genuine. She won her first start at Warwick and will definitely get six furlongs, maybe seven. All she wants to do is please you.'

9. FUAIGH MOR (IRE) ★★★

ch.f. Dubai Destination – Marl (Lycius)
March 14. €6,000Y. Tattersalls Ireland. Phil Buchanan. Half-sister to the fair 2007 two year old dual 7f winner Relinquished, to the fairly useful two year old 6f winner Marching Song (both by Royal Applause), the fairly useful two year old 6f winner Medley (by Danehill Dancer), the fairly useful three-year-old 7f and 1m winner Green Line (by Green Desert), the fair two year old 6f winner Flower Market (by Cadeaux Genereux) and the modest 6f winner Snow Bunting (by Polar Falcon). The dam, a fairly useful two year old 5.2f winner, is a half-sister to several winners including the very useful 1999 two year old listed 5f National Stakes winner Rowaasi. The second dam, Pamela Peach (by Habitat), a half-sister to the Jersey Stakes second Dawson Place, was a sprint winner at four years in the USA. (P Buchanan).
'She won a seller at Warwick and she'll improve a hell of a lot for the run. She was a cheap purchase, but when I bought her she looked like a hat rack! I like that sort because at least you know you can improve them. I think she'll get a mile and she's very genuine. I like fillies – they've done well for me over the years and this one will be a nice, big filly when she furnishes.'

10. MYTTONS MAID ★★★

b.f. Bertolini – The In-Laws (Be My Guest)
February 24. Seventh foal. 15,000Y. Doncaster St Leger. A Bailey. Half-sister to the French 10f winner Risky Nizzy (by Cape Cross), to the quite useful two year old 1m winner Lady Mytton (by Lake Coniston) and the fair 10f winner Prince Vector (by Vettori). The dam, a fairly useful two year old 7f winner, is closely related to the fairly useful 7f winner Mrs Fisher and a half-sister to six winners. The second dam, Amboselli (by Raga Navarro), was placed over 5f at two years and is a half-sister to nine winners. (G Mytton).
'This is a lovely filly, she's just done her first bit of work this morning, she did well and she's really nice. I can see her wanting seven furlongs this

year, so she'll be one for the mid-season onwards. She's looking a picture now and I'm sure she'll be alright.'

11. OMEGA WOLF (IRE) ★★
b.c. Spartacus – Brave Cat (Catrail)
March 13. Fifth foal. €34,000Y. Tattersalls Ireland. Phil Buchanan. Half-brother to the fairly useful 2007 two year old 5f winner Eileen's Violet (by Catcher In The Rye) and to the Italian winner of 7 races from 5f to 1m from two to four years Revovegas (by Revoque). The dam is an unraced half-sister to four minor winners here and abroad. The second dam, Flimmering (by Dancing Brave), is an unraced half-sister to seven winners. (P Buchanan).
'I like him a lot but he's split a pastern. He'll be OK and he wasn't going to be an early sort anyway. I see him being a miler much later on in the year.'

12. UNNAMED ★★★
b.f. Shinko Forest – Bo' Babbity (Strong Gale)
May 1. Half-sister to 11 winners including the useful sprint winner of five races Blue Iris (by Petong) and the quite useful triple 6f winner Abbajabba. The dam, a fair two year old 5f winner, is a half-sister to the high-class Group 3 5f King George Stakes winner Anita's Prince.
'She's really nice, she's only just arrived and won't run until August, but she's a bit classy and I'm sure she'll win races this year and be a better three year old.'

ANDREW BALDING
13. BELLA ROWENA ★★★
b.f. Kyllachy – Luxurious (Lyphard)
February 2. Fourteenth foal. Half-sister to the ten winners including the US Grade 2 San Luis Obispo Handicap winner and Grade 1 placed Persianlux (by Persian Bold), the French winner of 16 races and listed-placed Luxurious Dancer (by Dancehall), the fairly useful 7f to 12f winner Luberon (by Fantastic Light), the French two year old 1m winner Lucid (by Kris), the quite useful 1m winner Mushajer (by Linamix) and the German winner of four races from two to four yrs Lusty Boy (by Shining Steel). The dam is a placed half-sister to five winners including the

Group 3 10f Prix La Force winner The Scout. The second dam, Tropicaro (by Caro), won the Group 1 1m Prix Marcel Boussac, was second in the Group 1 10f Prix Saint-Alary and is a half-sister to five winners. (Horses For Causes).
'She goes nicely. She's not a big, robust filly but more of a neater type and a very good mover. Very much a two year old type.'

14. BEN'S DREAM ★★★
b.c. Kyllachy – Kelso Magic (Distant View)
April 12. Third foal. €38,000Y. Tattersalls Ireland. Brieryhill Bloodstock. 46,000 two year old Kempton Breeze-up. A Balding. Half-brother to the fairly useful 2007 Irish two year old dual 6f winner Jopau and to the quite useful two year old 7f and subsequent winner Fongtastic (both by Dr Fong). The dam, a useful two year old dual 5f winner, is a half-sister to the US winner of three races and Grade 2 placed Proceeded. The second dam, Bowl Of Honey (by Lyphard), is an unraced half-sister to four winners including the Group 3 Prix Exbury winner Nero Zilzal and the Group 1 Premio Parioli second Golden Mintage.
'We bought him from the breeze up sales. He'd breezed very nicely and we'd got word previously that he was alright. We haven't worked him since he came in but he looks every inch a two year old. He'll be out in early May and he's a neat, athletic horse, certainly not over-big and not particularly robust but a good mover.'

15. BRIEF ENCOUNTER (IRE) ★★★
b.br.c. Pyrus – Just One Look (Barathea)
January 27. First foal. 32,000Y. Doncaster St Leger. Will Edmeades. The dam, a fair two year old 6f winner, is a half-sister to two winners including the Group 2 German St Leger second Western Devil. The second dam, Western Sal (by Salse), a fair 10f and 12f winner, is a half-sister to seven winners including the dual Group 3 winner and 2,000 Guineas third Redback. (Thurloe Thoroughbreds XXII).
'A strong, butty, two year old type. He's done a bit upsides and looks like being out in early April. He's certainly got enough speed for five and he'll do plenty of racing. One we'll crack on with.'

16. CAVERA (USA) ★★★

b.f. Not For Love – Spelling (Alphabet Soup)
May 7. Second foal. The dam, a stakes-placed winner of five races in the USA and Grade 2 placed, is a half-sister to five winners including the Leopardstown Derby Trial winner Port Bayou. The second dam, Mrs K (by Dixieland Band), a US stakes-placed winner of three races, is a half-sister to eight winners. (Mr G Strawbridge).
'The owner is very excited about this filly. He's taken a shine the stallion and he bought the mare because she was tough and consistent. She's a fairly late foal but a two year old type.'

17. CELESTIAL DREAM (IRE) ★★★★

b.f. Oasis Dream – Lochangel (Night Shift)
February 13. Fifth foal. Half-sister to the quite useful three year old 7f winner Star Pupil (by Selkirk). The dam, a very smart winner of the Group 1 5f Nunthorpe Stakes, is a half-sister to the champion sprinter Lochsong. The second dam, Peckitts Well (by Lochnager), was a fairly useful winner of five races at two and three years from 5f to 6f. (Mr J C Smith).
'She's the nicest of the Jeff Smith two year old's we have and also far and away the nicest produced by the dam. A two year old type, she was held up by one or two little niggles but she should be out in late May or early June over five furlongs.'

18. CELTIC SPUR (IRE) ★★★

b.c. Celtic Swing – Kart Star (Soviet Star)
April 18. 12,000Y. Tattersalls October 2. Half-brother to the quite useful 2007 7f to 9f placed two year old Admiral Barry (by Kalanisi). The dam, a winner of four races in France including the listed 1m Prix Coronation, is a half-sister to the listed winner Karmifira. The second dam, Karmiska (by Bikala), won the Group 3 10f Prix de la Nonette and is a full or half-sister to six winners including the French listed 12f winner Karmichah. (Mick & Janice Mariscotti).
'He looked pretty poor at the sales but he's done very well since. He won't be out until the mid-summer but he looks every inch a racehorse.'
TRAINER'S BARGAIN BUY

19. CHIBERTA KING ★★★★

b.c. King's Best – Glam Rock (Nashwan)
February 27. Third foal. 30,000Y. Tattersalls October 1. A Balding. Half-brother to the unraced 2007 two year old Cheeky Download (by Fasliyev). The dam, a useful 10f winner and third in the Group 3 Princess Royal Stakes, is a half-sister to five winners including the very useful Group 3 6f Cherry Hinton Stakes winner Applaud and the useful listed 10.2f winner Sauterne. The second dam, Band (by Northern Dancer), is a placed half-sister to five winners including the US Grade 3 9f New Orleans Handicap winner Festive. (Pink Hat Partnership).
'I'm delighted with him, he's a lovely horse. A big, scopey colt with a good action and he goes nicely at this moment in time. I'll probably wait for the seven furlong maidens with him but he could be more forward if we wanted him to be. A very nice animal.'

20. COUNTESS ZARA (IRE) ★★

b.f. Xaar – Lochridge (Indian Ridge)
February 7. First foal. The dam, a smart listed 6f winner of five races, is closely related to the useful listed 5f winner Loch Verdi. The second dam, Lochsong (by Song), a champion sprinter and winner of the Prix de l'Abbaye (twice), the Kings Stand Stakes and the Nunthorpe Stakes, is a half-sister to the Nunthorpe Stakes winner Lochangel. (J C Smith).
'I trained the dam who was very good and this is her first foal. She's rather like another of my two year old's King's Siren in that she wouldn't be particularly early but she's just a nice filly.'

21. DER ROSENKAVALIER (IRE) ★★★

b.c. Captain Rio – Brooks Masquerade (Absalom)
March 10. Eighth foal. 30,000Y. Tattersalls October 2. A Balding. Half-brother to the quite useful 6f (at two years) and 9.5f winner Fiveoclock Express (by Woodborough) and to three minor winners abroad by Daggers Drawn, Woodborough and Midyan. The dam is an unplaced half-sister to eight winners including the dual listed Two Clubs (herself dam of the Group 1 Haydock Park Sprint Cup winner Red

Clubs). The second dam, Miss Cindy (by Mansingh), a fairly useful 5f to 7f winner of six races, is a sister to the Vernons Sprint Cup winner and useful sire Petong. (D Brownlow).
'He's a nice, good, solid two year old type. Hopefully he'll be ready to run in early June and he's a straightforward two year old.'

22. DEYA'S DREAM ★★
b.f. Clodovil – Dream On Deya (Dolphin Street)
April 20. Sixth foal. 24,000Y. Ascot November Sales. Not sold. Half-brother to the fairly useful 7f winner of four races (including at two years) and listed-placed Norisan (by Inchinor), to the quite useful winner of four races over 1m Dream Tonic (by Zafonic) and the quite useful two year old 7f winner Wavertree Dream (by Dushyantor). The dam ran once unplaced and is a half-sister to seven winners including the dual Group 3 winner Proud Native. The second dam, Karamana (by Habitat), is an unraced half-sister to six winners. (Miss A V Hill).
'A nice filly, she's going well at this stage and should make a two year old.'

23. GEORGINA MACRAE ★★★
b.f. Bahamian Bounty – Sadly Sober (Roi Danzig)
January 1. Ninth foal. 25,000Y. Tattersalls October 2. A Balding. Half-sister to Half One (by Kyllachy), unplaced in two starts in Ireland at two years in 2007, to the fairly useful 7f and 1m winner Ettrick Water (by Selkirk), a winner in Hong Kong by Charnwood Forest and a bumpers winner by Halling. The dam, a modest 6f to 10f placed maiden, stayed 10f and is a half-sister to seven winners including the Grade 2 American Derby winner Overbury and the dam of the Irish Oaks winner Vintage Tipple. The second dam, Overcall (by Bustino), a winning Irish middle-distance stayer, is a half-sister to nine winners including the dam of the Melbourne Cup winner Vintage Crop. (Mr E Sutherland).
'We had a setback with her but it shouldn't stop her from being ready by mid-summer, she's big and strong and I've had a bit of luck with Bahamian Bounty's in the past. She looks a good, solid two year old type.'

24. INHIBITION ★★★★★
br.f. Nayef – Spurned (Robellino)
April 28. Half-sister to the very smart Group 2 1m Oettingen-Rennen and Group 3 8.5f Diomed Stakes winner Passing Glance (by Polar Falcon), to the smart Group 3 7f Prix de Palais-Royal and European Free Handicap winner Hidden Meadow, the smart listed 11f winner Scorned (both by Selkirk), the useful 6f (at two years) and listed 1m winner Kingsclere (by Fairy King), the fairly useful sprinter Overbrook (by Storm Cat), the fairly useful 12f winner Casual Glance (by Sinndar) and the modest 9.7f winner Jona Holley (by Sharpo). The dam, a fairly useful two year old 7f winner, later stayed 10f. The second dam, Refill (by Mill Reef), was placed over 6f here before winning over 11f in the USA. (KRC).
'A lovely filly, she's really athletic and I love her. She's not going to be early and I've just turned her out at the moment. She's the most straightforward out of the mare so far and by far the nicest filly she's had. I'm very happy with her.'

25. KING'S SIREN ★★
b.f. King's Best – Blue Siren (Bluebird)
April 11. Half-sister to the useful two year old listed 5.2f winner and Group 2 Flying Childers Stakes third Speed Cop, to the fairly useful dual 5f winner (including at two years) Siren's Gift (both by Cadeaux Genereux) and the fair 6f winner Indiana Blues (by Indian Ridge). The dam, a very useful winner of three races from 5f to 7f, was disqualified from first place in two more, notably the Group 1 5f Nunthorpe Stakes (the winner on merit) and is a half-sister to several winners including the quite useful 9f winner Northern Habit. The second dam, Manx Millenium (by Habitat), was placed over 1m and is a half-sister to several winners. (Mr J C Smith).
'She'll make a two year old by mid-summer and she's quite straight forward but not as far forward or racey looking as most of the mare's offspring were. More of a rangy, three year old type but time will tell.'

26. PERFECT SECRET ★★★

b.f. Spinning World – Sharp Secret
(College Chapel)
February 6. The dam, a modest winner of six races from 6f to 1m, is a half-sister to numerous winners. The second dam, State Treasure (by Secretariat), won in the USA and is a half-sister to a Group 3 winner. (Mr J & Dr B Drew).
'She's looks just what you'd want in terms of the make and shape of a two year old and she's done a couple of bits of work and looks to go alright.'

27. PRINCE SIEGFRIED ★★★

b.c. Royal Applause – Intrum Morshaan
(Darshaan)
March 24. Fourth foal. 38,000Y. Tattersalls October 1. A Balding. Half-brother to the fair 9f winner Peking Beauty (by Kendor) and to the modest all-weather dual 11f winner Zed Candy (by Medicean). The dam, a fairly useful 2m winner, is a half-sister to three winners including the useful Irish two year old listed 6f and subsequent US Grade 3 winner Coney Kitty. The second dam, Auntie Maureen (by Roi Danzig), a fair Irish 9f and 10f winner, is a half-sister to three minor winners. (D Brownlow).
'A lovely, big horse. I loved him as a yearling and he's grown a lot since then. He's just going through an awkward stage at the moment but I'd still be hopeful he'd be ready to run over six furlongs in early June. A nice horse, we've already established he's got a bit of an engine and he goes alright.'

28. PRIVATE ICE ★★

br.f. Pivotal – Midnight Air (Green Dancer)
March 30. Half-sister to the Grade 2 Long Island Handicap, Group 3 May Hill Stakes and Group 3 Prestige Stakes winner Midnight Line (by Kris S), to the quite useful 1m winner L'Amour, the fair 9.3f all-weather winner Westerly Air (both by Gone West), the fair 11.6f winner Thinking Positive (by Rainbow Quest) and the modest 8.5f all-weather winner Midnight Watch (by Capote). The dam won the Group 3 1m May Hill Stakes at two years and is a half-sister to five minor winners and to the dam of the Group 1 5f Prix de l'Abbaye winner Imperial Beauty. (Mr. G Strawbridge).
'An enormous filly but she's quite athletic and she should make a two year old at the back-end, probably over seven furlongs.'

29. RAPID WATER ★★

b.c. Anabaa – Lochsong (Song)
April 26. Brother to the fair 6f all-weather winner Lochstar, closely related to the useful listed 5f winner Loch Verdi (by Green Desert) and half-brother to the smart listed 6f winner of five races Lochridge (by Indian Ridge). The dam, a champion sprinter and winner of the Prix de l'Abbaye (twice), the Kings Stand Stakes and the Nunthorpe Stakes, is a half-sister to the Nunthorpe Stakes winner Lochangel. The second dam, Peckitts Well (by Lochnager), was a fairly useful winner of five races at two and three years from 5f to 6f. (J C Smith).
'A full brother to the three year old Lochstar who I think a lot of but has been tough to keep sound. This colt goes well and he's more likely to make the track this year than his brother ever was but it won't be until the backend.'

30. REGAL BLUSH ★★★

b.f. Bachelor Duke – Royale Rose (Bering)
May 5. Seventh foal. 48,000Y. Tattersalls October 1. Dwayne Woods. Half-sister to the Group 3 10.5f Prix Fille de l'Air winner Antioquia (by Singspiel), to the modest 8.5f winner Lady Hen (by Efisio) and the modest 12f and 2m all-weather winner Vin du Pays (by Alzao). The dam, a fair 1m winner at three years, is a half-sister to two winners including the French listed winner Rouen. The second dam, Rose Blanche (by Nureyev), won over 8.5f in France and is a half-sister to five winners. (Horses For Causes).
'A nice, athletic filly, we wouldn't be in a hurry with her and she'll be ready by late summer. She moves nicely but we haven't done much with her so far. A good advert for her first season sire.'

31. SET THE TREND ★★★

b.br.c. Reset – Masrora (Woodman)
March 3. Third foal. 7,000Y. Tattersalls December. Bobby O'Ryan. Half-brother to the modest two year old 7f winner Daisy Bucket (by

Lujain). The dam, placed from 10f to 12f, is a half-sister to one winner. The second dam, Overseas Romance (by Assert), is an unraced half-sister to the Irish 1,000 Guineas winner Trusted Partner (dam of the high-class filly Dress To Thrill) and to the Group 2 Premio Legnano winner Easy To Copy (the dam of three stakes winners). (Favourites Racing).

'He's a nice, big, deep-girthed colt with a long stride on him. He should be ready to run in June and he's a nice colt.'

32. SIR COOL (IRE) ★★★

b.c. Selkirk – Legend Has It (Sadler's Wells)
February 27. First foal. 130,000Y. Tattersalls October 1. A Balding. The dam, a quite useful 9f and 12f winner, is a half-sister to one winner. The second dam, Magical Cliché (by Affirmed), was placed four times at up to 1m and is a sister to several good winners including the Group 2 Premio Legnano winner Easy To Copy and the Irish 1,000 Guineas winner Trusted Partner (dam of the high-class filly Dress To Thrill). (George Strawbridge Jnr).

'He's just had a little setback but he looked real nice until then. One for the middle of the season, he's a close-coupled two year old type as opposed to the usual rangy Selkirk type. I loved him at the sales and I still do.'

33. SWINDLER ★★★★

b.c. Sinndar – Imitation (Darshaan)
March 15. Seventh foal. 65,000Y. Tattersalls October 1. T Noonan. Half-brother to the fairly useful 12f winner Forged (by Peintre Celebre), to the quite useful 12f winner Stealing Beauty (by Sadler's Wells) and the fair triple 10f winner Hurry Up Helen (by In The Wings). The dam is an unraced sister to the Group 2 Sea World International Stakes winner and Group 1 placed Darnay and a half-sister to 3 winners. The second dam, Flawless Image (by The Minstrel), a two year old winner and third in two Group 3 events over sprint distances in Ireland, is a half-sister to eight winners in the USA. (Mr P C McMahon).

'He looks pretty special I must say. It surprises me that for a probable middle-distance horse he has plenty of dash. He'll appear over seven furlongs

in mid-summer and at this moment in time I'd say he's just about the pick of my two-year-olds. I wouldn't swap him!'

34. TASMAN GOLD ★★★

ch.c. Piccolo – Silken Dalliance (Rambo Dancer)
February 14. Sixth foal. 30,000Y. Doncaster St Leger. A Balding. Half-brother to the modest 2007 9f placed two year old Oceana Blue (by Reel Buddy), to the fair 7f (at two years) to 1m winner Oceana Gold (by Primo Valentino) and the modest 7f (two year old seller) and 12f winner Snake Skin (by Golden Snake). The dam was a fairly useful 6f and 1m winner of four races at three years. The second dam, A Sharp (by Sharpo), was unraced. (The C H F Partnership).

'He looks a real two year old type. I've had all of them out of the mare and he's by far the most attractive to look at. More likely to make up into a decent two year old than the others were.'

35. THE DESERT SAINT ★★★★

b.c. Dubai Destination – Maria Theresa (Primo Dominie)
April 8. Fourth foal. 37,000Y. Tattersalls October 1. A Balding. Half-brother to the fair 2007 6f placed two year old Fervent Prince (by Averti), to the very useful 5f and 6f winner of four races (including at two years), Intrepid Jack (by Compton Place) and the quite useful 1m and 10f winner Pagan Crest (by Indian Ridge). The dam is an unraced half-sister to the Group 2 Sandown Masai Mile and Group 2 Premio Emilio Turati winner Nicobar. The second dam, Duchess Of Alba (by Belmez), a fair 13.8f winner, is a half-sister to seven winners including four listed winners. (A Taylor).

'A proper two year old, he's doing everything very easily at this moment in time. He's a bit behind the others because he had a bit of a setback early on but I hope he'll be out by the middle of May and I'm delighted with him. A nice colt that would have the speed for five furlongs.'

36. WARRANT'S ATTENTION (IRE) ★★★

b.c. Fruits Of Love – Irish Lover (Irish River)
March 17. Fourth foal. 16,000Y. Doncaster Festival. A Balding. Half-brother to a winner

abroad by Mujadil. The dam won once over 10f in Italy and is a half-sister to four winners including the Group 2 winner Lowther Stakes and Group 2 Queen Mary Stakes winner Flashy Wings. The second dam, Lovealoch (by (by Lomond), a very useful 7f (at two years) and 9f winner here and placed in the Group 2 Falmouth Stakes and the Group 2 Premio Lydia Tesio, subsequently won once in the USA and is a half-sister to seven winners. (R Parry).

'A smashing little colt, he's a real good sort and goes very well at this point in time. A two year old type and I'm very happy with him.'

37. YEOMAN BLAZE ★★★
b.c. Needwood Blade – Gymcrak Flyer
(Aragon)
March 18. Fourth foal. 24,000Y. Doncaster Festival. Half-brother to the two year old 5f seller winner Bob's Flyer (by Lujain). The dam, a fair winner of 12 races from 6f to 1m and from three to eight yrs, is a half-sister one winner. The second dam, Intellect (by Frimley Park), ran three times unraced at two years and is a full or half-sister to six winners. (Yeoman Homes Ltd).

'He looks every inch a two year old and would have been our first two year old runner but for a little setback.'

38. UNNAMED ★★★
b.br.c. Ten Most Wanted – Miss Orah
(Unfuwain)
February 24. Third foal. 25,000Y. Tattersalls October 3. Emerald Bloodstock. The dam, a fairly useful two year old 7f here, subsequently won at 4 yrs in the USA and is a half-sister to nine winners including the Canadian Grade 2 and 7f listed winner of seven races Vanderlin and the French 7.5f and 1m winner Monaiya (dam of the listed Pretty Polly Stakes winner Musetta). The second dam, Massorah (by Habitat), a very useful winner of the Group 3 5f Premio Omenoni and second in the Group 3 5f Prix du Gros-Chene, is a half-sister to four minor winners abroad. (Calzaghe Partnership).

'He goes real nice and he comes from the same family as Vanderlin who was trained here. He's very different than him but he goes very nicely and I would hope he'd be out in May.'

39. UNNAMED ★★★
b.f. Reset – Mountain Ash (Dominion)
April 19. Ninth foal. 30,000Y. Tattersalls October 1. Not sold. Half-sister to the quite useful 2007 two year old 1m winner Whistledownwind (by Danehill Dancer), to the useful 1m Britannia Stakes winner Analyser, the fairly useful 7f winner and listed 10f Lupe Stakes second Musical Treat (by Royal Academy and dam of the champion two year old filly Finsceal Beo), a winner in Greece by Danehill and two minor winners abroad by Fairy King and Fasliyev. The dam won over 7f twice at two years and subsequently was a very useful Italian Group 3 and listed winner over 7f and 1m. She is a half-sister to seven winners including the very useful 1m to 10.5f winner New Berry and the 2,000 Guineas Trial winner Lidhame. The second dam, Red Berry (by Great Nephew), a listed winner of four races, was second in the Cheveley Park Stakes and is a half-sister to nine winners. (Mrs P Grimes).

'A sweet filly, she's neat and I haven't done much with her yet. I'd like to see her put on a bit of condition but she'll be fine. She'll start off at six furlongs in Jun eand build up to seven.'

40. UNNAMED ★★
b.c. Pursuit Of Love – Society Rose
(Saddlers' Hall)
February 16. Sixth foal. 40,000Y. Doncaster St Leger. A Balding. Half-brother to the fair 2007 7f placed two year old Society Venue (by Where Or When) and to the fair 9f winner Sociable (by Danehill). The dam, a fairly useful two year old 7f winner, is a half-sister to six winners including the Group 1 6f Cheveley Park Stakes winner Regal Rose and to the Japanese stakes winner over 10f Generalist. The second dam, Ruthless Rose (by Conquistador Cielo), ran twice unplaced and is a half-sister to nine winners including the high-class miler Shaadi. (Mr & Mrs W Clifford).

'A nice sort of horse, he's a back-end type but I'm very happy with him so far.'

DAVID BARRON

41. DANTE DEO (USA) ★★★

b.f. Proud Citizen – Best Feature (El Gran Senor)
April 3. $65,000Y. Keeneland September. Harrowgate Bloodstock. Half-sister to three winners including the US stakes-placed Angel Smoke (by Smoke Glacken) and a minor US winner by Conquistador Cielo. The dam is an unraced sister to the listed winner Amwag and a half-sister to the Australian Grade 1 winner Istidaad. The second dam, Mazzei Mood (by Roberto), a minor three year old winner, is a full or half-sister to three stakes winners. (R G Toes).
'A big, strong filly, she's nice but wouldn't be ready until mid-season. She goes nicely.'

42. DARK LANE ★★★

b.c. Namid – Corps de Ballet (Fasliyev)
January 31. First foal. 46,000Y. Doncaster St Leger. D Armstrong. The dam, a fairly useful 5f (at two years) and 6f winner, is a half-sister to seven winners including the prolific Hong Kong winner of eight races and over £500,000 Quick Action and the listed winners Doowaley and Misraah. The second dam, Dwell (by Habitat), a fairly useful three year old 1m winner, was listed-placed and is a half-sister to the dams of the South African Grade 2 winner Gleaming Sky and the smart winner of the Cambridgeshire Cap Juluca. (D W Armstrong).
'A good sort of horse but sore shins have delayed him for a couple of weeks. He's a good sort and when we started with him he looked a fairly mature horse. He'll be a sprinting type two year old.'

43. INGLEBY KING (USA) ★★★

b.br.c. Doneraile Court – Smart Lady Too (Clever Trick)
April 10. Fourth foal. $32,000Y. Keeneland September. Harrowgate Bloodstock. Half-brother to a minor US winner by Saint Ballado. The dam is an unraced half-sister to 12 winners and to the unraced dam of the US Grade 1 winner Roamin Rachel. The second dam, Pia's Lady (by Pia Star), ran unplaced twice. (D Scott).
'We bought him to be a colt we could get on with but unfortunately he's had a touch of sore shins

so he's having a break for now. He should still be out before mid-season and is a sprinting type.'

44. NOBLE HEART (IRE) ★★★

b.f. Acclamation – Toldya (Beveled)
April 28. Second foal. 26,000Y. Doncaster St Leger. D Armstrong. Half-sister to Feeling Lucky (by Namid), unplaced in one start at two years in 2007. The dam, a fairly useful 5f and 6f winner of 6 races from three to five years, is a sister to the listed Oak Tree Stakes winner Moon Over Miami and a half-sister to four winners. The second dam, Run Amber Run (by Run The Gantlet), a minor US five year old winner, is a half-sister to six winners. (D W Armstrong).
'A very nice filly, she wasn't that well-grown when we got her but she's done extremely well and has grown tremendously. She's back in work now and if she continues the way she going she'll be out before long. At present she's showing quite a bit of toe, so I'd be quite hopeful with her.'

45. RAFFANETTI (IRE) ★★★

b.c. Raphane – Proud Boast (Komaite)
May 28. The dam, a useful sprint winner of six races including a listed event, is a half-sister to four winners. The second dam, Red Rosein (by Red Sunset), won nine races over sprint distances including the Wokingham Handicap and is a half-sister to five winners. (P Savill).
'A nice sort of colt but he's a late foal so we haven't pressed any buttons with him yet. We're only just getting moving with him now and if he's any good he'll be quick, judging by his pedigree.'

46. UNNAMED ★★★

b.f. Arch – Marketplace (Relaunch)
April 20. Ninth foal. $10,000Y. Keeneland September. Harrowgate Bloodstock. Half-sister to four winners including the US stakes winner and Grade 2 placed Package Store (by Mister Baileys). The dam is an unraced sister to a US stakes-placed winner and a half-sister to six winners. The second dam, Supplier (by Irish River), is a placed half-sister to four stakes winners.
'She's not going to be that early but she's getting

herself organised and is working now. I'd imagine she'll be out in late May or early June and if the produce of this sire are any good they're usually quick. It's possible we might have pinched this filly.' TRAINER'S BARGAIN BUY

RALPH BECKETT

47. AMEN TO THAT (IRE) ★★

b.f. Acclamation – In Time (Generous)
March 4. Sixth foal. €47,000Y. Goffs Million. D Redvers. Brother to the unplaced 2007 two year old Force And Motion and half-brother to the minor French 7f winner Lucky In Time (by Key Of Luck), the Italian two year old winner Sin Verguenza (by Royal Anthem) and a three year old winner in the USA by Tactical Cat. The dam, placed twice at two years, is a half-sister to six winners including the Group 3 Jersey Stakes winner River Deep. The second dam, Affection Affirmed (by Affirmed), won four races at five years in the USA and a full or half-sister to six winners including the dam of the dual Group 1 winner Zoman. (R A Pegum).
'A sharp filly that looks like a two year old. I think she's slightly hiding her light under a bushel and she's a good, hard-knocking filly that we'll just have to feel our way with.'

48. ASAINT NEEDS BRASS (USA) ★★★★

b.br.c. Lion Heart – British Columbia (Selkirk)
January 23. Third foal. 24,000Y. Doncaster St Leger. D Redvers. Half-brother to the quite useful two year old 6f all-weather winner Crumbs Of Comfort (by Pulpit) and to the French two year old 7.5f winner Becky Moss (by Red Ransom). The dam is an unplaced sister to two winners and a half-sister to the two year old Group 1 National Stakes winner Heart Of Darkness. The second dam, Land Of Ivory (by The Minstrel), a very useful winner over 7f (at two years) and 1m, was placed in the Prix Cleopatre and Lupe Stakes. She is a half-sister to the high-class middle-distance colt Gold and Ivory. (Mrs I M Beckett).
'He'll probably have won before you book is out. He's a real two year old, very forward and I don't think he's just an early two year old. We should be able to campaign him throughout the summer as well. He'll win a maiden alright.' Ralph was correct – this colt won first time out!

49. BLUE NYMPH ★★★ ♠

ch.f. Selkirk – Blue Icon (Peintre Celebre)
March 30. Half-sister to the fair 2007 7f placed two year old Red Icon (by Red Ransom). The dam, a winner over 11f in France, is a half-sister to several winners including the Group 1 10f Prix de l'Opera winner Bright Sky. The second dam, Bright Moon (by Alysheba), won three Group 2 races over middle-distances in France. (J H Richmond-Watson).
'A huge Selkirk filly but she's coping very well with her work and I should think she'll be ready by the second half of the season. She finds it all very easy and I like her.'

50. BOTHY ★★★

ch.c. Pivotal – Villa Carlotta (Rainbow Quest)
March 5. Half-brother to the fairly useful 10f winner Shela House (by Selkirk) and to the quite useful 10f winner Villa Sonata (by Mozart). The dam, a smart 12f listed winner of four races, is a half-sister to the fairly useful 10f winner Seeyaaj. The second dam, Subya (by Night Shift), was a very useful winner of five races from 5f (at two years) to 10f including the Lupe Stakes, the Masaka Stakes and the Milcars Star Stakes (all listed events). (J H Richmond-Watson).
'A really nice horse, he's going to take some time but I do think he'll make a two year old. He has a very similar shape to a Pivotal horse we had a few years ago that was second in the German Guineas called Johnny Jumpup. He has a similar character to him too. He might turn into a nice two year old in the second half of the season.'

51. CONCLUSIVE ★★★★

b.c. Selkirk – Never A Doubt (Night Shift)
February 19. Third foal. 100,000Y. Tattersalls October 1. D Redvers. Half-brother to the useful 2007 two year old 5f and 7f winner and Group 2 7f Rockfel Stakes third Royal Confidence (by Royal Applause). The dam, a very useful two year old Group 2 5.5f Prix Robert Papin winner, is a half-sister to two winners. The second dam, Waypoint (by

Cadeaux Genereux), a fairly useful 6f and 7f winner (including on the all-weather), is a half-sister to five winners including the Group 2 6f Diadem Stakes winner Acclamation. (Thurloe Thoroughbreds XXIII).

'He's a big, solid horse and although Selkirk's often need a bit of time I'm not sure this horse does. I'm pretty sure he's done most of his growing and I like him. I think he's a really nice individual and hopefully by the end of August I'll be able say 'I told you he'd be a nice horse!' We'll look to winning a maiden and go on from there but I'd hope he'd be more than a handicapper. I'd love to have a really nice horse for Thurloe as they've been big supporters of mine over the years.'

52. DREAMWALK (IRE) ★★★

b.c. Bahri – Celtic Silhouette (Celtic Swing)
April 24. Second foal. 50,000Y. Tattersalls October 2. Not sold. Half-brother to the very useful 7f (at two years) and Group 3 1m Premio Dormello winner Celtic Slipper (by Anabaa). The dam, placed four times at four and five years in France, is a sister to the listed winner and Group 2 Dante Stakes second Celtic Silence and a half-sister to the listed winner Royal And Regal. The second dam, Smart 'n Noble (by Smarten), won the Group 2 Barbara Fritchie Handicap and is a half-sister to seven winners. (P D Savill).

'He's similar to the nice half-sister we had last year, Celtic Slipper, although he's a bit more backward. He's a bit leaner than she was at this stage but he's a very good-moving, athletic horse. He'll make a two year old and he could be really nice but he needs to settle a bit as he's inclined to argue with his riders. But he gives the impression that it'll all come to him at some point.'

53. FINNEGAN McCOOL ★★★

b.c. Efisio – Royal Jade (Last Tycoon)
January 19. Eighth foal. 40,000Y. Tattersalls October 3. D Redvers. Half-brother to the fairly useful 6f winner of five races (including at two years) Million Percent, to the fair triple 5f winner Scottish Exile (both by Ashkalani), the quite useful two year old 6f all-weather winner Mullion (by Reprimand), the fair dual 6f winner Exmoor (by Cape Cross) and the fair 6f to 1m all-weather winner Xaloc Bay (by Charnwood Forest). The dam, a fairly useful 7f winner, is a half-sister to six winners including the Group 3 5f King George Stakes winner Averti. The second dam, Imperial Jade (by Lochnager), a useful sprint winner of four races and second in the Group 2 Lowther Stakes, is a sister to the triple Group 3 winning sprinter Reesh. (Lawrence & Wilkinson).

'A sharp colt, he's already done a couple of pieces of work and I should think he'll be out before the end of April. He's from a really good family and he's all two year old. Although he's by Efisio and many of them need soft ground he doesn't look like he wants it slow. I'd say he'll be a good ground horse and I should be able to find a slot for him. I'm hoping he'll be an early winner for us.'

54. GILBERTIAN ★★★

b.c. Sakhee – Fudge (Polar Falcon)
February 20. Half-brother to the useful 5f (at two years) to 7f winner of four races and Group 2 third Gloved Hand (by Royal Applause), the fair 10f and all-weather 12f winner Jackie Kiely (by Vettori) and the moderate 7f and 1m winners Rigat (by Dansili) and Magroom (by Compton Place). The dam is an unraced half-sister to seven winners including the quite useful 1m to 10f winner Summer Fashion (herself dam of the Group winners Definite Article, Salford City and Salford Express). The second dam, My Candy (by Lorenzaccio), is a placed half-sister to seven winners including the Ballymoss Stakes and Royal Whip Stakes winner Candy Cane. (The Turf Club).

'The dam ran for me when she was in-foal. Although she wasn't easy, being in-foal really suited her and she became more and more straightforward as the year went on and she ended up being second in a Group 3. This colt looks like making a two year old and he has a bit of quality about him although he's a bit of a thug at the moment. I'd be hopeful that we'll have some sport with him this year. He flipped over as a yearling and banged his head and as

a consequence he carries his head to one side, which is why he never went to the sales.'

55. HESKETH ★★★★ ♠
b.c. Nayef – Agony Aunt
(Formidable)
February 26. Sixth foal. €72,000Y. Goffs Million. D Redvers. Half-brother to the fairly useful 6f winner of four races here and in the UAE winner Doctor Hilary (by Mujahid), to the quite useful all-weather 6f winner Cool Tune, the modest 5f to 7f winner of 7 races Only If I Laugh (both by Piccolo), the moderate 1m all-weather winner Disabuse (by Fleetwood) and the modest 11f winner Miss Havisham (by Josr Algharoud). The dam, a quite useful 10f winner, is a half-sister to one winner. The second dam, Loch Clair (by Lomond), is an unplaced half-sister to six winners including the Group 1 winner Wind In Her Hair (herself dam of the champion Japanese horse Deep Impact). (R A Pegum).
'Although he's by Nayef he's an early foal and there's a couple of winning two year old's in the family. He's done a couple of half-speeds and we'll move him along. If he's forward enough he might be the sort of horse we could aim at the Chesham Stakes. We loved him as a yearling and he's turning into the horse we thought he'd be.'

56. IT'S TOAST (IRE) ★★★★
b.f. Diktat – Kapria
(Simon du Desert)
March 25. Third foal. €60,000Y. Deauville August. D Redvers. Half-sister to the useful 2007 two year old 6.5f St Leger Sales race winner Dream Eater (by Night Shift) and to the modest 1m all-weather winner Tremelo Pointe (by Trempolino). The dam, a dual French 11f winner and third in the Group 3 Prix Penelope, is a half-sister to two winners out of the minor French four year old winner Sheer Drop (by Kenmare), herself a half-sister to five winners. (The Sunday Club).
'A really nice, strong filly, she's sharp and will be one of our hopes for the season. She's done a couple of easy bits of work and I see her being out in early summer.'

57. KIMBERLEY ROCKS ★★★★
b.f. Intikhab – Kalimar (Bigstone)
April 3. Fourth foal. €65,000Y. Goffs Million. D Redvers. Half-sister to the unraced 2007 two year old Sambelucky (by Barathea), to the fair dual 10f winner Kindlelight Blue (by Golan) and the modest dual 12f winner Tibouchina (by Daylami). The dam is an unplaced half-sister to three winners including the dam of the Group winners Kasthari and Karasta. The second dam, Karlafsha (by Top Ville), won twice in France at three years including the listed 1m Prix des Lilas, was fourth in the Group 2 9.2f Prix de l'Opera and is a half-sister to five winners. (P K Gardner).
'We bought her on spec and we wouldn't normally do that with a €65,000 yearling! But I did love her and we had her half-sister Tibouchina who had plenty of ability but wouldn't always show it. This filly is much more businesslike and although she's taking time to lose her winter coat she's one I'm looking forward to. I think she's a really nice filly and she'll be one of our big hopes for the season.'

58. MR UDAGAWA ★★★
b.c. Bahamian Bounty – Untold Riches
(Red Ransom)
March 3. Second living foal. 28,000Y. Tattersalls October 1. D Redvers. Half-brother to the 10f seller winner Ciccone (by Singspiel). The dam, a fairly useful 1m and 9f winner of three races, is a half-sister to five winners in the USA. The second dam, Asdaf (by Forty Niner), won once over 7f at three years and is a half-sister to nine winners. (Mr B R Ingram).
'A big, tall, lanky horse and a real athlete. He's laid-back, he covers the ground well and he does everything easily. I think he's a nice horse but because he's so tall I'm still waiting for him to strengthen up.' Apparently devotees of the TV soap Neighbours will know who Mr Udagawa is!

59. OLYNARD (IRE) ★★★
b.c. Exceed And Excel – Reddening
(Blushing Flame)
May 7. Fourth foal. €52,000Y. Goffs Million. D Redvers. Half-brother to the unraced 2007 two

year old Red Planet and to the very useful two year old 6f and 7f winner and Group 1 Nunthorpe Stakes third Pivotal Flame (both by Pivotal). The dam, a fairly useful 2m winner, is a sister to the Italian winner and Group 3 placed Musical Score and a half-sister to five winners. The second dam, Music In My Life (by Law Society), a modest 7.5f and 1m placed three year old, is a half-sister to four winners. (Mr R J Roberts).

'A nice horse, he's quite leggy and he needs to strengthen up so I haven't done much with him. He shows enough to show we'll have some sport with him this year and his half-brother Pivotal Flame got better with age so I would hope he would as well.'

60. PERFECT AFFAIR (USA) ★★
b.c. Perfect Soul – Caribbean Affair (Red Ransom)
April 18. Sixth foal. 37,000Y. Tattersalls October 3. D Redvers. Half-brother to the minor US stakes winner No Place Like It (by Real Quiet) and to two minor winners in the USA by Conquistador Cielo and Miesque's Son. The dam is an unplaced half-sister to the US stakes winner Stellar Affair. The second dam, Fawn And Hahn (by Grey Dawn II), a minor winner in the USA, is a half-sister to seven winners. (I J Heseltine).

'The sire won a Grade 2 over 12 furlongs in Canada and ended up winning the Grade 1 Shadwell Mile. This colt is huge but he's very well balanced and light on his feet for such a big horse. He finds his work easy and we should be able to campaign him at some point this year.'

61. PICK A PURSE ★★★
ch.c. Piccolo – Silver Purse (Interrex)
April 12. Seventh foal. 9,000Y. Doncaster St Leger. D Redvers. Half-brother to the fair 2007 two year old 5f winner Only In Jest (by Averti), to a winner in Greece by Robellino, a two year old winner in Japan by Mister Baileys and a minor two year old winner abroad by Piccolo. The dam, a modest two year old 5.7f winner, is a half-sister to six winners here and abroad. The second dam, Money Supply (by Brigadier

Gerard), is an unraced sister to the Irish listed winner Senior Citizen.

'A very good-moving horse, he'd want fast ground, he points his toe and he was only nine grand at the sales because he was quite small. He's filled out a lot now and he looks terrific value.' TRAINER'S BARGAIN BUY

62. POYLE MEG ★★
b.f. Dansili – Lost In Lucca (Inchinor)
January 22. Fourth foal. 35,000Y. Tattersalls October 3. Not sold. Half-sister to the quite useful two year old dual 5f winner Another True Story (by Piccolo) and to a dual four year old winner in Germany by Lujain. The dam, a fair 12f winner, is a half-sister to three winners including the Group 2 Lowther Stakes winner Jemima. The second dam, Poyle Fizz (by Damister), is an unraced full or half-sister to four winners. (C Wiggins).

'A neat filly and she's quite forward but I haven't done much with her yet and she's just cantering away because she had a few niggling problems. She's nice but she is a bit on the small side and I would think she'd be a six furlong filly.'

63. RAGGLE TAGGLE ★★★ ♠
b.f. Tagula – Jesting (Muhtarram)
February 24. Fourth foal. 15,000Y. Doncaster Festival. McKeever St Lawrence. Half-sister to three winners abroad by Definite Article (two) and Revoque. The dam is an unraced half-sister to six winners out of the Galtres Stakes winner Sans Blague (by The Minstrel). (Lady Marchwood).

'She worked well this morning, she wasn't very expensive but she's very solid and very professional. A hardy filly and she should be capable of winning a maiden before going on from there. I like the way she does everything, she just gets on with it and enjoys her work.'

64. ROYAL SUPERLATIVE ★★★
b.f. King's Best – Supereva (Sadler's Wells)
January 10. First foal. The dam, an Italian winner of five races, is a half-sister to several winners. The second dam, Final Farewell (by Proud Truth), ran once unplaced and is a half-

sister to three winners and to the dam of Danehill. (Duchess of Cornwall).

'She'll make a two year old, her temperament is good despite being a King's Best and I would think six furlongs on fast ground in mid summer should suit her. Not a big filly, so we'll look to campaign her this year.'

65. RUSSIAN ART ★★★

b.c. Johannesburg – Sweet Deimos
(Green Desert)
February 22. First foal. 50,000Y. Tattersalls October 2. D Redvers. The dam, a useful Irish 6f (at two years) and 7f winner and third in the Group 3 Debutante Stakes, subsequently won and was Grade 3 placed in the USA and is a half-sister to three minor winners. The second dam, Bint Zamayem (by Rainbow Quest), a fairly useful three year old 10f winner, was listed-placed over 10f and is a half-sister to the Group 3 Prix Chloe winner Rouquette. (M R Green).

'He's a real two year old, very sharp, not a big horse and he's not going to grow much more. He bustles along all the time as if he can't wait to get to the bottom of the gallop, so he's very keen on his work and it looks like we'll be able to belt on with him early. A solid, compact sort of horse and he'll have a chance.'

66. TOP TOWN GIRL ★★★

b.f. Efisio – Halland Park Girl (Primo Dominie)
February 17. Fifth foal. 47,000 foal. Tattersalls December. R Frisby. Half-sister to the quite useful 5.2f and 6f winner Lindbergh and to the modest 7f all-weather two year old winner Hallandale (both by Bold Edge). The dam won five races at two years including the listed Doncaster Stakes and is a half-sister to two minor winners. The second dam, Katsina (by Cox's Ridge), a useful two year old 7f winner, was placed in two listed events and is a half-sister to nine winners including the listed 10f Virginia Stakes winner Rambushka. (Landmark Racing Ltd).

'A nice filly, she's a real Efisio in that she has a plain head and is quite stocky. Quite small when she arrived but she's growing at the moment and she'll make a two year old. I like her and she

should be ready sometime in the middle of May. You know what you're getting with Efisio because he's a good sire of fillies, they tend to be very straightforward with no real temperament issues and although they're not oil paintings they are runners.'

67. WETHERBY PLACE (IRE) ★★

ch.f. King's Best – Summer Sunset
(Grand Lodge)
April 19. First foal. €55,000Y. Deauville August. D Redvers. The dam, a fairly useful two year old 1m winner, was listed placed twice and is a half-sister to six winners including the listed winner Rolo Tomasi. The second dam, Elegant Bloom (by Be My Guest), won once at two years in Ireland and is a half-sister to 12 winners. (R A Pegum).

'A sweet, scopey, leggy filly, she's a longer term prospect than some of the others but there's quite a lot of quality about her. I'm hoping that it'll all fall into place with her one day, she's pretty straightforward and I like her.'

68. UNNAMED ★★

b.f. Tobougg – Barakat (Bustino)
April 1. Twelfth foal. 72,000Y. Tattersalls October 1. Not sold. Sister to Killcara Boy, unplaced in one start at two years in 2007 and half-sister to the 10.3f and US stakes winner and Grade 2 placed Mabadi (by Sahm), to the useful 10f winner and listed-placed Ta Awun (by Housebuster), the fairly useful 10f winner Mudalal (by Dixieland Band), the fairly useful middle-distance winner Mumaris (by Capote), the quite useful 11.7f winner Mabrooka (by Bahri), the fair 8.5f winner Tadawul (by Diesis) and the fair 7f winner Fakih (by Zilzal). The dam, a fairly useful 14.6f winner, is a half-sister to the Group 1 winners Ibn Bey and Roseate Tern. The second dam, the useful 7.5f and 1m winner Rosia Bay (by High Top), herself a half-sister to the Queen Elizabeth II Stakes and Budweiser Arlington Million winner Teleprompter. (D B Clark).

'A very nice filly, I thought she was going to be very backward and I'd have to send her home because she grew very fast and went weak, but *in the last few weeks she's really come to hand. Although she has a ten furlong pedigree we should be able to race her this year. She's a very attractive filly and there's a bit of quality about her.'*

69. UNNAMED ★★

b.br.c. Golden Missile – Brady's Best (Wild Again)

February 5. Third foal. $25,000Y. Keeneland September. Peter Doyle. 15,000 two year old. Kempton Breeze-up. R Beckett. The dam is an unraced sister to the US Grade 1 Hopeful Stakes winner Wild Escapade and a half-sister to the US Grade 2 winner Mazel Trick. The second dam, Mazaleca (by Ramahorn), won the Grade 3 Red Bank Handicap in the USA.

'He came from the breeze up sales and he's still for sale! A nice horse and one to start in auction races before stepping him up.'

MICHAEL BELL

70. ADVISOR ★★★

gr.c. Anabaa – Armilina (Linamix)

April 24. Fourth foal. €120,000Y. Deauville August. John Warren. Half-brother to the French two year old winner Aliyeska (by Fasliyev). The dam won twice at three years, was Group 3 placed and is a sister to the Group 3 Prix Berteux winner Artistique and a half-sister to three winners. The second dam, Armarama (by Persian Bold), won the Group 2 Ribblesdale Stakes and is a half-sister to Kalaglow. (Royal Ascot Racing Club).

'Being out of a Linamix mare he probably wouldn't do much in the first half of the season, but he's a nice, big, scopey horse. He'll be trained very much with his three year old career in mind but he looks a very nice prospect.'

71. ART CONNOISSEUR (IRE) ★★★★★

b.c. Lucky Story – Withorwithoutyou (Danehill)

March 20. First foal. 55,000Y. Tattersalls October 2. Kern/Lillingston. The dam, a quite useful two year old 7f winner, is a half-sister to one winner. The second dam, Morningsurprice (by Future Storm), is an unraced half-sister to five winners including the dam of the Oaks and

Irish Derby winner Balanchine and the Group two winners Romanov and Red Slippers. (Mr Richard Green).

'He's very sharp and will be racing in April. A real precocious type, he'll start at five furlongs but should stay six on pedigree.' This colt won impressively on his debut a week after I'd spoken to Michael and then again at the Craven meeting!'

72. ASSIGNMENT ★★★

b.c. Barathea – Urgent Liaison (High Estate)

April 1. Sixth foal. 110,000Y. Tattersalls October 2. John Warren. Closely related to the fairly useful 12.3f winner Qudraat (by In The Wings) and half-brother to the fairly useful 10f winner and listed third Imoya (by Desert King) and the South African winner at three and four yrs Jahazi (by Green Desert). The dam is an unraced half-sister to five winners including the very smart Group 2 9f Budweiser International Stakes winner Great Dane. The second dam, Itching (by Thatching), is an unraced half-sister to seven winners including the dual Group 1 winner Croco Rouge and Alidiva (dam of the Group 1 winners Sleepytime, Ali Royal and Taipan). (Highclere Thoroughbred Racing (Munnings).

'A handsome individual, he had a little setback in February but that was no bad thing. He's a big, fine, strong horse and a good mover. He'll be brought back into work with a view to running in the second half of the season. A big, imposing horse and very much a two year project.'

73. AUNT NICOLA ★★★★

b.f. Reel Buddy – Night Gypsy (Mind Games)

March 6. Fourth foal. 31,000Y. Doncaster St Leger. Kern/Lillingston. Half-sister to the fair 5f winner of four races at two and three years Safari Mischief (by Primo Valentino). The dam, a fair two year old 5f winner, is a sister to the listed two year old winner On The Brink and a half-sister to the useful two year old triple 6f winner Blue Tomato. The second dam, Ocean Grove (by Fairy King), a quite useful two year old 6f winner, is a half-sister to five winners here and abroad. (Mr R P B Michaelson & Mr John Thompson).

'She's from a fast family whose progeny tend to do well as two year old's – especially the fillies. She's a real two year old type, with a good temperament and she's eager to please. Looks every inch a two year old.'

74. BALLANTRAE (IRE) ★★★

b.f. Diktat – Badawi (Diesis)

March 24. Sister to the useful two year old 7f winner and Group 3 7f Vintage Stakes third Fox and half-sister to the very useful two year old 6f winner and Group 1 Cheveley Park Stakes third Badminton (by Zieten), the useful 6f and 7f winner and Group 3 Nell Gwyn Stakes second Cala (by Desert Prince), the useful all-weather 7f winner Rafferty (by Lion Cavern), the fairly useful three year old 1m winner Badagara (by Warning), the quite useful all-weather 7f to 9f winner Saguaro, the fair dual winner at around 7f Balfour (both by Green Desert). The dam was a useful 1m and 9f winner of four races. The second dam, Begum (by Alydar), is an unraced half-sister to seven winners including the US Grade 3 winner and good broodmare Old Goat. 'A big, scopey filly, she'll probably not be out that early. One for the second half of the season, she has plenty of scope and she'll be nice but we haven't pressed her yet.'

75. BATTLE OF HASTINGS ★★★★

b.c. Royal Applause – Subya (Night Shift)

March 15. Tenth foal. 62,000Y. Tattersalls October 2. M Bell. Half-brother to six winners including the smart 12f listed winner Villa Carlotta (by Rainbow Quest), the fairly useful 7f winner and listed-placed Subyan Dreams (by Spectrum) and the fairly useful 10f winner Seeyaaj (by Darshaan). The dam was a very useful winner of five races from 5f (at two years) to 10f including the Lupe Stakes, the Masaka Stakes and the Milcars Star Stakes (all listed events). The second dam, Ashshama (by Arctic Tern), a quite useful 10f winner, is a half-sister to four winners including the German listed winner and Group 3 placed Shine Share. (Mr R Green). 'He got the name because he was Lot No. 1066 in the catalogue! He's a nice, precocious sort that's done some work so I imagine he'll have

run before this book is out. He's still a bit green but he's goes OK. A two year old type, he's a nice horse in the making and like a lot of Royal Applause's he's not very big, but he does cover the ground.'

76. BIN END ★★

b.c. King's Best – Overboard (Rainbow Quest)

March 2. Third foal. 8,000Y. Tattersalls October. Not sold. Half-brother to the modest 2007 all-weather 7f placed two year old Sea Admiral (by Sinndar). The dam, placed over 12f, is a half-sister to four winners including the Group 3 6f Coventry Stakes winner Red Sea and the useful 7f (at two years) and Italian Group 3 12f winner Sailing. The second dam, Up Anchor (by Slip Anchor), won four races including the Group 3 12f St Simon Stakes, was third in the Italian Oaks and is a half-sister to five winners including the triple US Grade 3 winner at around 8.5f Just Class. (The Hon. Mrs J M Corbett & Mr C Wright). 'He's very nice but he didn't make a bid at the Sales (hence the name!) He goes very nicely, is stoutly bred and will be out at the back-end of the season. A big, strong horse that'll give his owners plenty of fun.'

77. BRAE HILL ★★★

b.c. Fath – Auriga (Belmez)

March 27. Eighth foal. 32,000Y. Tattersalls October 3. D Redvers. Half-brother to the quite useful two year old 6f winner Sylvan and to the fairly useful 6f (including at two years) and 7f winner of 6 races Morse (both by Shinko Forest), the fair two year old 6f and 7f winner Good Wee Girl (by Tagula), the four year old 1m seller winner Forest Air (by Charnwood Forest) and a winner in the Czech Republic by Barathea. The dam, a fair 6f and 7f placed two year old, is a half-sister to eight winners including the listed Blue Riband Trial Stakes winner Beldale Star and the listed winner and smart broodmare Moon Drop. The second dam, Little White Star (by Mill Reef), is an unplaced half-sister to five winners. (Thurloe Thoroughbreds). 'He's a nice horse, not particularly fashionably bred but the dam has bred a couple of good

ones. He's a hard-knocking two year old type
and he'll give his owners plenty of fun.'

78. BRIGHT WIRE ★★★
b.c. Elusive City – Alinga (King's Theatre)
**March 14. Third foal. €95,000Y. Goffs Million.
R Frisby.** The dam, a useful two year old dual 6f
and subsequent US stakes winner, is a half-sister
to one winner. The second dam, Cheyenne Spirit
(by Indian Ridge), a useful winner of seven races
including a listed event over 6f, is a half-sister to
five winners including the dam of the Group
winners Ashdown Express and Hoh Buzzard. (T
G N Burrage).
'A strong, precocious type, I trained his mother
who was useful. He was bought at Goffs and his
season will be centred around the Goffs Million
race. He's a nice, mature colt and he looks like
being a two year old.'

79. BUBSES BOY ★★★
ch.c. Needwood Blade – Welcome Home (Most
Welcome)
**April 5. Seventh foal. 27,000Y. Tattersalls
October 3. R Frisby.** Closely related to the useful
two year old dual 7f winner, dual listed-placed
and subsequent US stakes winner Joint
Aspiration (by Pivotal). The dam, a 12f all-
weather winner at three years, is a half-sister to
seven winners including the 5f Windsor Castle
Stakes winner and Group 1 Phoenix Stakes third
Gipsy Fiddler and the listed Doncaster Stakes
winner Two Clubs. The second dam, Miss Cindy
(by Mansingh), a fairly useful 5f to 7f winner, is
a sister to the Vernons Sprint Cup winner and
useful sire Petong. (Mr C Gershinson).
'A good advertisement for his sire, he's a strong,
well-made individual and he's ready to stride
along a bit now. I think he'll do himself justice
this year, probably over six and seven furlongs.'

80. BUSSEL ALONG ★★★★
b.f. Mujadil – Waaedah (Halling)
**February 8. First foal. 28,000Y. Tattersalls
October 3. Charlie Gordon-Watson.** The dam,
a quite useful two year old 7f winner, is a sister
to one winner and a half-sister to three winners
including the useful two year old 7f and 1m

winner Setteen. The second dam, Agama (by
Nureyev), won once at three years in France and
is a half-sister to six winners.
'Her dam won over seven furlongs as a two year
old and the sire gets plenty of two year old
winners. This filly is willing to please and I'm
viewing her as a sort of six/seven furlongs two
year old from the middle of the season onwards.'

81. CAUGHT ON CAMERA ★★★
b.f. Red Ransom – Colorsnap (Shirley Heights)
April 26. Twelfth foal. Half-sister to the very
useful two year old 5f and 7f Italian listed winner
and Group 2 1m Falmouth Stakes second Croeso
Cariad (by Most Welcome), to the Irish listed 12f
winner and Coronation Stakes and Irish Oaks
third Mona Lisa (by Giant's Causeway), the Irish
two year old listed 7f Debutante Stakes winner
Photogenic (by Midyan), the fairly useful 12f
winner Ishtak (by Nashwan), the German three
year old winner Flashing Green (by Green
Desert) and the fair two year old dual 1m winner
General's Star (by Night Shift). The dam is an
unraced half-sister to Colorspin (winner of the
Irish Oaks and dam of the Group 1 winners
Opera House, Kayf Tara and Zee Zee Top), Bella
Colora (winner of the Prix de l'Opera and dam of
the very smart colt Stagecraft) and the Irish
Champion Stakes winner Cezanne. The second
dam, Reprocolor (by Jimmy Reppin), won the
Lingfield Oaks Trial and the Lancashire Oaks.
(Helena Springfield).
'A well-bred filly, she's similar on looks to her half-
sister Croeso Cariad who we trained. She came
in relatively late so we're only just getting to
know her, but she's a good "grubber", has a good
temperament and so far so good.'

82. CHIC RETREAT (USA) ★★★
b.f. Elusive Quality – Saraa Ree (Caro)
May 7. Half-sister to the two year old 6f to 1m
winner and subsequent US Grade 1 Eddie Read
Handicap winner Sarafan (by Lear Fan), to the
very useful 1m to 12f and dual listed winner
Hagwah (by Dancing Brave), the quite useful
10f winner Swains Bridge (by Swain) and the fair
1m all-weather winner Shanghai Crab (by
Manila). The dam, a useful 7f winner, is a half-

sister to three winners. The second dam, Star River (by Riverman), won twice in France and is a sister to the top-class miler and sire Irish River. (Mr C Wright).

'She's a May foal so we won't be rushing her although she looks like being a two year old. She gets up Warren Hill easily for one who hasn't done a lot and we're hopeful that once we get after her she'll show us all the right signs.'

83. DOVE MEWS ★★★★

b.f. *Namid – Flying Fulmar (Bahamian Bounty)*
February 24. The dam, a quite useful 5f, 6f (both at two years) and 7f winner, is a half-sister to a multiple winner from two to five years in Norway. The second dam, West Humble (by Pharly), a fairly useful 7f winner, is a half-sister to four winners including the Group 3 5f Premio Omenoni winner Leap For Joy. (Sir Thomas Pilkington).

'I trained the dam who was pretty useful at two and it's a good two year old family. This filly is stronger than her dam was and she'll certainly pay her way this season.'

84. EARTHSHINE (IRE) ★★★

b.f. *Red Ransom – Painted Moon (Gone West)*
April 6. First foal. 24,000Y. Tattersalls October. Not sold. The dam is an unplaced half-sister to numerous winners including the high-class Irish 1,000 Guineas, Coronation Stakes and Nassau Stakes winner Crimplene and the smart Group 3 12.3f Chester Vase winner Dutch Gold. The second dam, Crimson Conquest (by Diesis), a quite useful two year old 6f winner, is a half-sister to the US stakes winner at around 1m Sword Blade. (Marwan Al-Maktoum).

'A small, but racey filly. She goes nicely and for a small filly she really covers the ground and I can see her being effective over six furlongs.'

85. EDDIE BOY ★★★★

b.c. *Tobougg – Maristax (Reprimand)*
May 3. Sixth foal. 80,000Y. Tattersalls October 1. Kern/Lillingston. Brother to the two year old 7f and listed 1m winner and Group 3 Musidora Stakes second Sweet Lilly and half-brother to the useful 10.4f winner Ofaraby (by Sheikh

Albadou), The dam, a fair two year old 7f winner, is closely related to the useful two year old listed 5f winner Four-Legged-Friend and a half-sister to six winners including the dual US Grade 3 winner Superstrike and the dam of the Group 1 winning sprinters Goodricke and Pastoral Pursuits. The second dam, Marista (by Mansingh), ran twice unplaced at two years and is a half-sister to three winners. (Mr C Gershinson).

'A lovely, scopey colt, he's a very good mover and has plenty of presence – he's quite a striking horse. He'll probably start over seven furlongs and he's a nice colt.'

86. HALFWAY HOUSE ★★★

b.c. *Dubai Destination – Zanzibar
(In The Wings)*
March 10. Third foal. 43,000Y. Tattersalls October 1. Kern/Lillingston. Half-brother to the fair 2007 1m placed Celtic Dragon (by Fantastic Light) and to the very useful 10f and 12f winner and listed-placed Spice Route (by King's Best). The dam, winner of the Group 1 11f Italian Oaks, is a half-sister to two winners. The second dam, Isle Of Spice (by Diesis), a fair three year old 9.7f winner, is a half-sister to five winners.

'He's a good-bodied, athletic colt and the mare has been quite successful so far. This is a late summer two year old type and he won't be rushed.'

87. HARTY BOY (USA) ★★★

ch.c. *Stravinsky – Peanut Gallery
(Mister Baileys)*
March 21. Second foal. 45,000Y. Tattersalls October 1. Kern/Lillingston. The dam, a stakes-placed winner of five races from 2 to five years in the USA, is a half-sister to two winners. The second dam, Baggywinkle (by Devil's Bag), is an unplaced half-sister to eight winners. (Bamber, Barnett, Cole, Hart, Manasseh, King).

'A straightforward horse to deal with, he's a good mover and we haven't really pressed any buttons with him but he looks like having the makings of a summer two year old. A colt with a very good attitude.'

88. LA ADELITA (IRE) ★★★★

b.f. Anabaa – Aiming (Highest Honor)
April 11. Second foal. 140,000Y. Tattersalls October 1. BBA (Ire). Half-sister to the fairly useful 2007 two year old dual 6f winner Easy Option (by Danehill Dancer). The dam was placed over 7f (at two years) and 1m and is a half-sister to four winners including the very smart dual listed 5f winner Watching. The second dam, Sweeping (by Indian King), a useful two year old 6f winner, is a half-sister to ten winners. (Mrs M Bryce).
'A nice filly that goes well, she's very active – always on the go. I imagine she'll be alright over six furlongs and she's quite high up on our pecking order.'

89. LOCHAN MOR ★★★★

b.c. Kyllachy – Bright Moll (Mind Games)
February 13. First foal. The dam, a fairly useful two year old 5f and 6f winner, is a half-sister to three winners. The second dam, Molly Brown (by Rudimentary), a fairly useful 5f (at two years) and 6f winner, is a half-sister to two winners including the listed 1m Premio Nearco winner Stato King. (Mr Andrew Buxton).
'The dam came to hand very early as a two year old and this colt looks as though he'll be precocious. I like him, he's very genuine and looks as though he's got plenty of speed.'

90. MONEYCANTBUYMELOVE ★★★

b.f. Pivotal – Sabreon (Caerleon)
February 8. Third living foal. 75,000Y. Tattersalls October 1. Not sold. Half-sister to the quite useful 1m winner Pillar Of Hercules (by Rock Of Gibraltar) and to a minor winner in Japan by Mozart. The dam, a quite useful 10.2f winner, is a half-sister to five winners including the French 2,000 Guineas and Grade 1 Keeneland Turf Mile Stakes winner Landseer and the very smart listed 10f winner and Group 1 placed Ikhtyar. The second dam, Sabria (by Miswaki), is an unraced half-sister to four winners including the very useful Grand Criterium third King Sound. (M L W Bell Racing Ltd).
'A strong, well-made filly. Pivotal's don't tend to

be early but she looks as though she'll certainly be able to do herself justice in the second half of the season. A filly with a bit of an attitude – which is something I quite like.'*

91. NIGHT KNIGHT ★★★

b.c. Bachelor Duke – Dark Albatross (Sheikh Albadou)
March 13. Third foal. €44,000Y. Goffs Million. R Frisby. The dam, a fair two year old 6f winner, is a half-sister to six winners including the Irish 1m and 9f listed winner Unusual Heat. The second dam, Rossard (by Glacial), won 1four races in Scandinavia and the USA including the Grade 1 10f Flower Bowl Handicap and is a half-sister to four winners. (Scotney, Asplin, Symonds, Ball & Chelingworth).
'He's done extremely well since we bought him but we haven't done much with him yet. I don't imagine we'll have him out much before July time but he's a handsome individual.'

92. PIQUANTE ★★

b.f. Selkirk – China (Royal Academy)
February 8. Fourth foal. 65,000Y. Tattersalls October 1. John Warren. The dam was placed twice over 14f and is a half-sister to the very smart Group 1 Grand Prix de Paris winner Grape Tree Road, to the smart Group 2 Geoffrey Freer Stakes winner Red Route and the smart Queens Vase and Northumberland Plate winner Windsor Castle. The second dam, One Way Street (by Habitat), a winner of four races including the Group 3 12f Princess Royal Stakes, is a full or half-sister to six winners. (Highclere Thoroughbred Racing (Persimmon).
'A stoutly-bred filly by Selkirk, she's good-looking and a good mover. I won't rush her because she has a middle-distance pedigree and she'll be trained with next year in mind.'

93. RED HORSE (IRE) ★★★

ch.c. Bachelor Duke – Miss Childrey (Dr Fong)
March 20. First foal. 65,000Y. Tattersalls October 2. Kern/Lillingston. The dam, an Irish two year old listed 6f winner, is a half-sister to five winners. The second dam, Blazing Glory (by

Glow), won three races over 5f and is a full or half-sister to six winners. (R I Morris).

'He's neater than my other horse by the same sire, Bachelor Duke, his dam was a decent two year old and although we haven't done much with him at this stage I would hope he'd do himself justice as a two year old. He looks a two year old type and a hardy horse.'

94. RED ZOE (USA) ★★★

b.br.f. Danehill Dancer – Starbourne (Sadler's Wells)
March 22. Second foal. 80,000Y. Tattersalls October 1. Kern/Lillingston. The dam, a useful Irish listed 1m winner, was third in the Irish 1,000 Guineas and is a sister to the Irish 12f winner and listed-placed Starrystarrynight and a half-sister to two winners. The second dam, Upper Circle (by Shirley Heights), ran twice unplaced and is a sister to the dam of the Oaks winner Lady Carla. (T Neill).

'A well-bred filly, she's backward and we've just turned her out for some spring grass. She'll just need a bit of time but she's very attractive and I did expect her to be more precocious than she actually is. We'll get her back in with a view to an autumn campaign.'

95. SECRET SOCIETY ★★★★

b.c. Exceed And Excel – Shady Point (Unfuwain)
April 18. Fifth foal. Half-sister to the fairly useful 6f to 9f winner at two and three years Mastership (by Best of The Bests). The dam was a fair 1m all-weather winner. The second dam, Warning Shadows (by Cadeaux Genereux), won the Group 2 10f Sun Chariot Stakes and was second in the Irish 1,000 Guineas. (Marwan Al Maktoum).

'He's a nice horse, the sire seems to be very popular and this chap goes well. I should imagine he'll be running in May over six furlongs.'

96. SICILIANDO ★★★

b.c. Bertolini – Donna Vita (Vettori)
February 2. First foal. 20,000Y. Tattersalls October 3. Charlie Gordon-Watson. The dam, a fairly useful two year old 7f winner, was fourth

in a listed event over 11f at three years and is a half-sister to three winners including the Group 1 placed Reduit. The second dam, Soolaimon (by Shareef Dancer), is a placed half-sister to four winners including the French Group 3 winner Audacieuse. (Mr W Gredley).

'A relatively inexpensive colt, this is a nice horse. He's doesn't look that sharp and he moves as if he's going to want six or seven furlongs. maybe even further in time. He's a good, strong, robust colt with a lovely temperament and he could be quite a nice horse.'

97. SOFONISBA ★★★★

b.f. Rock Of Gibraltar – Lothlorien (Woodman)
March 4. 22,000Y. Tattersalls October 2. A Brambilla. Closely related to the fair 7.5f winner Lorien Hill and to the minor Japanese winner Daisy Do (both by Danehill) and half-sister to the fair 207 7f placed two year old Dream Express (by Fasliyev) and the moderate 14f to 2m winner Miss Devious (by Dr Devious). The dam, a quite useful 1m winner, is a sister to the useful 1m (at two years) to 10f winner Monsajem and to the US two year old winner Mellifont and a half-sister to six winners. The second dam, Fairy Dancer (by Nijinsky), a winner over 6f in Ireland at two years, is closely related to four winners by Northern Dancer, notably the top-class racehorse and outstanding sire Sadler's Wells, the high-class sire Fairy King and the two year old Group 1 winner Tate Gallery. (Marco & Sarah Moretti).

'She was inexpensive as a yearling but it looks money well spent and her pedigree goes back to possibly the best family in the book. She'll certainly be paying her way as a two year old at around six or seven furlongs.' TRAINER'S BARGAIN BUY

98. STEEL FREE (IRE) ★★★

b.f. Danehill Dancer – Candelabra (Grand Lodge)
January 21. Second foal. €150,000Y. Goffs Million. R Frisby. Half-sister to the unraced 2007 two year old Eneyda (by Cape Cross). The dam, a fairly useful dual 7f winner, is a half-sister to two two year old winners. The second dam,

Chatterberry (by Aragon), a modest two year old 5f winner, is a sister to the Group 3 Cornwallis Stakes and Group 3 King George Stakes winner Argentum and a half-sister to seven winners. (T G N Burrage).

'A spunky filly with a bit of an attitude – which is no bad thing. She'll be targeted at the Goffs Fillies race and she's quite a live wire. She could be quite nice and she'll probably have the speed for six furlongs as it's a fast family.'

99. UNNAMED ★★★

ch.f. Dr Fong – Merewood (Woodman)
January 22. First foal. The dam, a fair 9f and 10f placed maiden, is a half-sister to several winners including the high-class sprinter Reverence (winner of the Haydock Park Sprint Cup and the Nunthorpe Stakes) and the very useful two year old listed 6f Chesham Stakes winner and 1m Britannia Handicap second Helm Bank (by Wild Again). The second dam, Imperial Bailiwick (by Imperial Frontier), was a useful winner of three races at around 5f including the Group 2 Flying Childers Stakes, was placed in the Molecomb Stakes and the Prix du Petit-Couvert and is a half-sister to three winners in France (all over 1m+). (Mr & Mrs G Middlebrook).

'She's quite a strong, well-made filly, very athletic and I can see her running around June/July time over six or seven furlongs. Quite an attractive filly and a good mover.'

100. UNNAMED ★★★

b.f. Alhaarth – Pilgrim's Way (Gone West)
March 12. Fifth foal. €90,000Y. Goffs Million. R Frisby. Half-sister to Miss Rochester (by Montjeu), unplaced in one start at two years in 2007. The dam, a quite useful 7f and 1m winner at three years, is a sister to the smart 6f and 1m winner Mugharreb and a half-sister to three winners. The second dam, Marling (by Lomond), winner of the Cheveley Park Stakes, the Irish 1,000 Guineas, the Coronation Stakes and the Sussex Stakes, is a half-sister to the Group 1 National Stakes winner and Irish 2,000 Guineas second Caerwent. (M B Hawtin).

'A filly with a nice pedigree, we haven't done much with her yet but I think she was quite well-

bought. She won't be rushed and we'll see how we get on but I think she's quite nice.'

101. UNNAMED ★★

b.f. One Cool Cat – Termania (Shirley Heights)
May 9. Fifth foal. €140,000Y. Goffs Million. Demi O'Byrne. Half-sister to the minor French 12f and 15f winner Rotation (by Galileo) and to the minor French 15f winner Castle Howard (by Montjeu). The dam was placed over 13f in France and is a half-sister to six minor winners. The second dam, Bubbling Danseuse (by Arctic Tern), won once and was second in the Group 3 1m Prix de Sandringham and is a half-sister to six winners. (Mr M Tabor).

'Quite a spunky filly, we've just got to win her round, I think there's quite a lot of Shirley Heights in her because she's not the most straightforward to deal with. But certainly she's neat and athletic.'

102. UNNAMED ★★★

b.br.f. Highest Honor – Zither (Zafonic)
February 7. Second foal. 32,000Y. Tattersalls December. Not sold. Half-sister to the unraced 2007 two year old Themwerethedays (by Olden Times). The dam, a fairly useful 6f (at two years) and 7f winner, is a half-sister to the useful two year old listed 6f winner Dowager and the useful 1m (at two years) and 10f winner Dower House. The second dam, Rose Noble (by Vaguely Noble), a modest three year old 11.5f winner, is a half-sister to six winners including the champion two-year-old and high-class sire Grand Lodge, winner of the St James's Palace Stakes and the Dewhurst Stakes. (Mr Luke Lillingston, Mr B Burrough & Mr J Root).

'She's a big, scopey filly that's grown significantly over the winter and so we won't rush her. But she has a good attitude, she moves well and in time I'm sure she'll be alright.'

ALAN BERRY

103. GRISSOM (IRE) ★★

b.c. Desert Prince – Misty Peak (Sri Pekan)
April 20. Fifth foal. €16,000Y. Tattersalls Ireland. Alan Berry. Half-brother to the Italian winner of four races (including at two years) and listed-placed Penthouse Serenade (by Val

Royal), to the quite useful 5f and 6f winner of five races (including at two years) Katie Boo (by Namid). The dam was placed four times from 5f to 7f in Ireland at two and three years including when third in the listed 6f Silver Flash Stakes and is a half-sister to one winner. The second dam, Miss Declared (by Alleged), is an unraced half-sister to nine winners in the USA. (Jim & Helen Bowers).

'He seems quite a sharp, strong colt and is a little bull of a horse, so hopefully he'll make a nice two year old.'

104. POLLISH ★★★
b.f. Polish Precedent – Fizzy Fiona (Efisio)
February 20. 2,500Y. Doncaster October. Lord Crawshaw. Half-sister to four winners including the fair 5f winner of seven races Frascati (by Emarati) and the minor two year old winners Birikina (by Atraf) and Blue Marble (by Fraam). The dam is an unraced half-sister to one winner. The second dam, A sharp (by Sharpo), is an unraced half-sister to four minor winners. (Lord Crawshaw).

'She's a half-sister to Frascati – a filly we had a bit of luck with. She's a bit bigger than that filly was and seems to know which way to go, so she'll be alright when she gets a bit of sun on her back. Despite being by Polish Precedent she gets sharpness from the mother.'

105. THAT BOY RONALDO ★★★
b.f. Pyrus – Red Millennium (Tagula)
March 16. Third foal. 10,000Y. Doncaster Festival. Alan Berry. The dam won five races over 5f including a listed event and wa Group 3 placed twice. The second dam, Lovely Me (by Vision), is a placed half-sister to four minor winners. (Sporting Kings).

'She's a nice filly and seems quite sharp. Athletic-looking just like her mother who did well for us, she'll be a sprinter.'

106. UNNAMED ★★★
br.g. Mull Of Kintyre – Capetown Girl (Danzero)
February 14. First foal. €7,000Y. Tattersalls Ireland. Alan Berry. The dam, a modest 6f winner, is a half-sister to two other minor

winners. The second dam, Cavernista (by Lion Cavern), is a placed half-sister to nine winners including the Group 1 Prix du Cadran winner Give Notice.

'A really nice horse, he's been gelded, he's big and strong and I can see him turning into a really nice type. We won't rush him because he's quite a big horse so he needs a bit of time to fill out, but six furlongs should be fine for him. He's open to inspection if anyone's interested in owning him!'

JOHN BEST

107. DIAMOND TWISTER (USA) ★★
b.c. Omega Code – King's Pact (Slewacide)
April 6. $72,000Y. Ocala August. Newmarket/Best. Half-brother to the 2007 US two year old stakes winner Thoroughly (by Full Mandate) and 2 minor US winners by Chester House and Montbrook. The dam is an unplaced half-sister to five winners including the US Grade 1 winner Coup de Fusil. The second dam, Cult (by Dr Fager), is a placed half-sister to three stakes winners. (J Griffin & Owen Mullen).

'A nice, big, strong colt, not an early type but he moves well and at the moment he's doing everything right. He's a really good-looking horse and the owner came along with me to the Sales at Ocala and picked him out. I think he made a wise choice because I expect him to be a nice horse.'

108. FLASH MANS PAPERS ★★★★
b.c. Exceed And Excel – Franglais (Lion Cavern)
March 4. Third foal. 38,000Y. Doncaster St Leger. Highflyer Bloodstock. Half-brother to the 2007 7f placed two year old Temple Of Thebes (by Bahri). The dam won three races from 6f to 1m at three and four years in Germany and is a half-sister to three winners including the Grade 1 E P Taylor Stakes winner Fraulein. The second dam, Francfurter (by Legend Of France), was a quite useful three year old dual 10f winner.

'He has no real pedigree on the dam's side but Exceed And Excel is a pretty sought-after sire. He's not over over-big but he's mature both physically and mentally and he'll be one of our

first runners I should think. He's been showing a lot of pace and I'd be hopeful for him as a two year old, particularly as he reminds me of two nice horses we had called Steely Dan and Desert Spirit.'

109. GOOD BUY DUBAI (USA) ★★

b.br.c. Essence Of Dubai – Sofisticada (Northern Jove)

March 2. Eighth foal. $35,000Y. Ocala August. Newmarket/Best. Half-brother to the US stakes winners Color Of Smoke (by American Standard) and Cousins Lew (by Slew Gin Fizz) and a US stakes-placed winner by Mr Greeley. The dam, unplaced in one start, is a half-sister to eight winners including the US Grade 3 winner Lyphard Line. The second dam, Line Item Two (by Crimson Satan), a minor winner at two and three years, is a half-sister to the US Grade winner Annihilate 'Em. (Mr J A Keaty).

'He's not going to be one of the earlier ones. He needed to fill out a bit so we gave him a bit of time and he's filled out really well. We've just started to do a little bit more with him now and I'm thrilled to bits with him. He moves really well, if I was being critical about him he's a little bit hotheaded at the moment but I think he'll calm down from that fairly quickly. One for June or a bit later perhaps and he's going to want seven furlongs this year.'

110. GREAT BOUNDER (CAN) ★★

b.br.c. Mr Greeley – Jo Zak (Vilzak)

March 27. Seventh foal. $140,000Y. Keeneland September. Not sold. Half-brother to four winners including the US Grade 2 9f Bonnie Miss Stakes winner Jill Robin L and the US stakes winner Zak's Precocious (both by Precocity). The dam is an unraced half-sister to a US stakes placed winner. The second dam, Jo's Princess (by Temerity Prince), won seven minor races in the USA and is a half-sister to three stakes winners. (Mr D Gorton).

'He certainly won't be early but he's the classiest-looking one we've got in the yard. He's by a proper sire and I'm very hopeful for him although he's much more of a three year old type.'

111. KINGSGATE STORM (IRE) ★★★★ ♠

gr.c. Mujadil – In The Highlands (Petong)

April 21. Eighth foal. 65,000Y. Doncaster St Leger. Highflyer Bloodstock. Half-brother to the 2007 7f placed two year old Trust In Me (by Spartacus), to the quite useful two year old 5f and 6f winner Glenmorangie (by Danzig Connection), the modest 6f winner Strathmore (by Fath) and a winner in Jersey by Missed Flight. The dam is an unplaced full or half-sister to five winners. The second dam, Thevetia (by Mummy's Pet), is a placed half-sister to seven winners. (J H Mayne).

'He was the only Mujadil in the St Leger sale and it was just after Kingsgate Native had won the Nunthorpe, so that probably doubled his price. He's a big, strong, solid sort and although it's a bit early to say he's another Kingsgate Native he's a very similar type. I'm very pleased with him and he'll make a proper two year old.'

112. MULLIONMILEANHOUR ★★★★

b.c. Mull Of Kintyre – Lady Lucia (Royal Applause)

February 10. First foal. 26,000Y. Doncaster St Leger. Highflyer Bloodstock. The dam, a moderate maiden, was placed fourth twice over 5f and 7f at two years and is a half-sister to one winner. The second dam, Inventive (by Sheikh Albadou), a quite useful two year old dual 5f winner, is a half-sister to three winners. (Kent Bloodstock).

'No real pedigree on the dam's side, I found myself having to buy my yearlings on looks because the good pedigrees were very expensive. I'm hopeful he'll turn out OK, mentally and physically he's pretty mature and he's quite a strong colt.' This colt won quite impressively on his debut at Kempton.

113. YALDAS GIRL (USA) ★★★

gr.f. Unbridled's Song – Marina de Chavon (Exploit).

March 20. First foal. $200,000Y. Fasig-Tipton Kentucky July. Simmstown Manor. The dam, a stakes winner of four races in the USA at two and three years, is a half-sister to the stakes winner and Grade 2 placed The Lady's Groom.

The second dam, T K O Lady (by Two Punch), is an unraced sister to the triple US Grade 2 winner Punch Line. (Mr D Gorton).
'She's an early type, shows a lot of speed for an Unbridled's Song and she's sharp enough. She moves really well, covers a lot of ground and she's quite a flashy filly. In time she'll want a bit more of a trip but she could be sharp enough to win over five or six.'

114. UNNAMED ★★★
b.c. Kheleyf – Bezant (Zamindar)
April 18. First foal. 19,000Y. Doncaster St Leger. Highflyer Bloodstock. The dam, placed once at three years over 1m, is a half-sister to two winners including the Group 2 Beresford Stakes third Sant Jordi. The second dam, Foresta Verde (by Green Forest), is a placed half-sister to eight winners.
'A horse that's going to need a bit of time but he's a big, strong colt that's just starting to do a bit more work, he's a good mover and I'm very pleased with what he's doing. The damline isn't very strong but Kheleyf has had a cracking start as a sire. A really nice-looking horse, he was a little bit light when we got him and needed to fill out, but he's done that now.'

115. UNNAMED ★★★
b.br.c. Officer – Morganza (Clever Trick)
April 14. Second foal. $165,000Y. Keeneland September. Kern/Lillingston. The dam is an unplaced half-sister to 11 winners including the US stakes winner and Grade 2 placed Catahoula Parish. The second dam, Dancing Proud (by Proud Clarion), was a Canadian stakes winner of six races. (Kent Bloodstock).
'Probably the nicest of the Kent Bloodstock syndicate horses. I think Officer is a pretty decent sire and the dam's side is good as well. This colt looks really well but his knees are a bit immature so we'll give him some time and bring him out in the latter part of the season. He'll be a really nice back-end two year old with next year in mind.'

116. UNNAMED ★★
b.c. Noverre – Zanoubia (Our Emblem)
April 2. Third foal. $70,000Y. Keeneland September. Kern/Lillingston. Half-brother to the fair 2007 two year old 6f winner Hunt The Bottle (by Bertolini). The dam won at two years in France and was listed-placed and is a half-sister to four winners including a US stakes winner. The second dam, Broadcast (by Broad Brush), a minor US three year old winner, is a sister to the Grade 1 Breeders Cup Classic winner Concern and to the US Grade 3 winner Tennis Lady. (Kent Bloodstock).
'This colt came over from America as if he needed time but he filled out very quickly so I would expect him to run in mid-summer. Probably the biggest improver we have in the yard.'

MICHAEL BLANSHARD

117. BRAD'S LUCK (IRE) ★★★
ch.g. Lucky Story – Seymour (Eagle Eyed)
April 15. Third foal. 39,000Y. Tattersalls October 2. J M Beever. Half-sister to the fairly useful 5f and 6f winner (including at two years) Charles Darwin (by Tagula). The dam, placed twice over 5f in Ireland at two years, is a half-sister to seven winners including the Group 1 7f Prix de la Foret winner Mount Abu. The second dam, Twany Angel (by Double Form), is a placed half-sister to six minor winners abroad. (J M Beever).
'He's a big horse, but he'll be alright over six furlongs in May. He'll be a better three year old because he's big but that won't stop him and he goes well.'

118. JAQ'S SISTER ★★★
b.f. Bertolini – Polly Golightly (Weldnaas)
March 14. Half-sister to the modest 2007 8.7f placed two year old Miss Bouggy Wouggy (by Tobougg) and to the fair two year old 5f winner Paper Lily (by Piccolo). The dam, a tough and quite useful winner of 10 races over 5f, including at two years, is out of the modest sprint maiden Polly's Teahouse (by Shack). (Mr D Sykes).
'She's sharp and a bit like her mother, so she's going to be alright. Not very big, but very tough, she's sharper then her three year old half-sister and should be out over five furlongs in May.'

119. MOSSY ROSE ★★★
br.f. Diktat – Milly Fleur (Primo Dominie)
February 2. 20,000Y. Tattersalls October. J C Fretwell. Half-sister to the fairly useful 2007 two year old 6f winner and listed-placed Bespoke Boy (by Acclamation). The dam was a modest 6f winner at three years. The second dam, My Cadeaux (by Cadeaux Genereux), a fairly useful dual 6f winner, is a half-sister to five winners including the Group 2 5f Prix du Gros-Chene winner Millyant, the Group 2 5f Flying Childers Stakes and Group 3 5f Palace House Stakes winner Prince Sabo and the dam of the Gimcrack Stakes winner Abou Zouz. (John Gale & Partners).
'She wants six furlongs, she's a lovely mover and will be out in May.'

120. WINTERBOURNE ★★★★
ch.f. Cadeaux Genereux – Snowing (Tate Gallery)
March 6. Eighth foal. Half-sister to the 2007 Irish two year old 5f winner and listed-placed Shivering (by Royal Applause), to the very smart Group 2 Prix du Gros-Chene and dual Group 3 sprint winner The Trader (by Selkirk) and the useful two year old dual 5f winner Molly Moon (by Primo Dominie). The dam, a quite useful dual 5f winner at three years, is a half-sister to two minor winners. The second dam, Biding (by Habat), a fairly useful dual 5f winner at three years, is a half-sister to 11 winners including the dams of the Group winners Bassenthwaite, Glancing, Hadeer, Bay Street and Monassib. (Lady Bland).
'She's very nice, has a bit of class about her and I'm just taking my time with her, she'll be alright over six furlongs and will be running by the end of May.'

JIM BOLGER
121. AARONESS (USA) ★★★
b.f. Distorted Humor – Diamonds For Lil (Summer Squall)
April 24. Second foal. $550,000Y. Keeneland September. BBA (Ire). The dam, a minor US two year old winner, is a half-sister to five winners including the minor US stakes winner Lovat's

Lady. The second dam, Lady Lady (by Little Current), is an unraced half-sister to 5 stakes winners including the US Grade 1 winners Al Mamoon and La Gueriere.

122. ABAMA LADY (CAN) ★★★
ch.f. Mr Greeley – Schonbrunn (Val de l'Orne)
April 10. Eleventh foal. $360,000Y. Keeneland September. BBA (Ire). Half-sister to the US stakes winner and Grade 2 placed Nymphenburg (by San Romano), to the minor US stakes winner La Habitant Time (by Iskandar Elakbar) and to three minor winners by Cool Victor, Schossburg and Forest Wildcat. The dam, a minor US three year old winner, is a sister to the champion Canadian filly La Lorgnette (herself the dam of Hawk Wing). The second dam, The Temptress (by Nijinsky), was a minor US two year old winner.

123. ABIGAIL'S AUNT ★★★
ch.f. Efisio – Rohita (Waajib)
May 3. Eleventh foal. 185,000Y. Tattersalls October 1. Blandford Bloodstock. Half-brother to the useful 5f (at two years) and listed 7f winner Kalindi (herself dam of the Irish Group 3 winner Abigail Pett), to the quite useful two year old 6f winner Addeyll (both by Efisio), the useful 6f and 7f winner (including at two years) Mahmoom, the fair 2006 two year old 6f winner Movethegoalposts (both by Dr Fong) and a winner in Japan by Fantastic Light. The dam, a fairly useful two year old 5f and 6f winner, was third in the Group 3 6f Cherry Hinton Stakes and is a half-sister to five winners. The second dam, Ruby River (by Red God), ran once unplaced and is a half-sister to six minor winners.

124. AFRICAN SUNDANCE (USA) ★★★
b.f. Johannesburg – Mystery Rays (Nijinsky)
March 1. Fourteenth foal. $290,000Y. Keeneland September. BBA (Ire). Half-sister to the Group 3 7f Craven Stakes and US Grade 3 winner King Of Happiness (by Spinning World), to the French listed winner and German Group 3 placed Anani (by Miswaki), the French two year old 1m winner and three year old listed 1m

placed Metaphor (by Woodman), to the minor US winner John Irving (by Mr Prospector) and minor winners abroad by Bering and Devil's Bag. The dam won three races in France including the Group 3 12f Prix Minerve and Group 3 10.5f Prix Fille de l'Air, is closely related to the German Group 2 6f winner Robin des Pins and a half-sister five winners including the Group 3 1m Beresford Stakes winner Ahkaam. The second dam, Rare Mint (by Key To The Mint), was unplaced.

125. BEAUTY FLASH ★★★
b.f. Oasis Dream – Pie High (Salse)
February 12. Second foal. 35,000Y. Tattersalls October 1. Blandford Bloodstock. Half-sister to the fair 2007 two year old 1m all-weather winner Crosstar (by Cape Cross). The dam, a fairly useful 7f winner of four races, is a half-sister to five winners including the Group 3 5f Premio Omenoni winner and Group 2 Diadem Stakes second Leap For Joy. The second dam, Humble Pie (by Known Fact), a fairly useful two year old 6f winner, is a half-sister to four winners including the high-class sprinter College Chapel.

126. BLAS CEOIL (USA) ★★★
b.br.f. Mr Greeley – Extraterrestral (Storm Bird)
January 1. Eighth foal. Closely related to the minor US stakes winner Alienated and to a stakes-placed winner in Japan (both by Gone West) and half-sister to the Japanese stakes winner Exhaust Note (by A P Indy) and a US stakes-placed winner by Grand Slam. The dam, a minor US three year old winner, is a half-sister to five winners including the triple US Grade 1 winner Judge Angelucci and the US Grade 1 winners Peace and War. The second dam, Victorian Queen (by Victoria Park), was a champion grass horse and champion mare in Canada. This filly ran fourth of seven on her debut at Dundalk in mid-April.

127. BRUINNEALL (IRE) ★★★★
b.c. Galileo – Speirbhean (Danehill)
February 9. Fourth foal. Sister to the champion two year old colt and Group 1 Dewhurst Stakes and Group 1 National Stakes winner Teofilo and to the fairly useful Irish 10f winner Senora Galilei. The dam, an Irish listed 1m winner, is a half-sister to numerous winners including the Irish listed 9f winner Graduated. The second dam, Saviour (by Majestic Light), won three races at two and three years and is a half-sister to five winners including the triple US Grade 1 winner Judge Angelucci and the US Grade 1 winners Peace and War.

128. CEAPADOIR (USA) ★★★
b.c. Mr Greeley – Hardly Fair (Wolf Power)
February 10. First foal. $500,000Y. Keeneland September. Tom Gentry. The dam is an unraced half-sister to the dam of the US Grade 1 winner Whywhywhy and the US Grade 2 winner Spellbinder. The second dam, Very Fair (by Honest Pleasure), a minor US winner at three and four years, is a half-sister to the multiple US Grade 1 winner Make Change.

129. DANCING BANDIT (USA) ★★★
b.f. Dixieland Band – Dancing Gulch (Gulch)
April 7. Second foal. $360,000Y. Keeneland September. Tom Gentry. The dam, a US stakes winner of seven races and Grade 2 placed, is a half-sister to the US dual Grade 2 winner and sire Distorted Humor. The second dam, Danzig's Beauty (by Danzig), won the Grade 2 Gardenia Stakes and was Grade 1 placed.

130. FAILTE ISTEACH (IRE) ★★★
b.f. Galileo – Affianced (Erins Isle)
May 16. Fourth foal. Sister to the 1m (at two years) and Group 1 Irish Derby, Group 2 Prix Niel and Group 2 Prix Noailles winner Soldier Of Fortune and to the smart 7f (at two years) and Group 3 10f Meld Stakes winner Heliostatic. The dam, a useful 7f listed (at two years) and 10f winner in Ireland, is a half-sister to the Group 1 1m Gran Criterium winner Sholokhov and a half-sister to 4 other stakes horses. The second dam, La Meillure (by Lord Gayle), a listed winner and Group 3 placed in Ireland, is a half-sister to eight winners.

131. GAN AMHRAS (IRE) ★★★
b.c. Galileo – All's Forgotten (Darshaan)

January 14. Second foal. €145,000Y. Goffs Million. Jim Bolger. The dam, a fair Irish 8.5f winner, is a half-sister to the UAE listed winner and Group 2 Godolphin Mile second Parole Board. The second dam, Forget About It (by Be My Guest), a winner over 7f and 1m at three years in Ireland, is a half-sister to seven winners including the Group 3 Railway Stakes winner Camargo.

132. GREANNMHAR (USA) ★★
ch.f. Distorted Humor – Copano Bay (Seattle Slew)
February 13. Third foal. $300,000Y. Keeneland September. Tom Gentry. Half-sister to a stakes-placed winner in the USA by Hennessy. The dam is an unraced sister to the multiple US Grade 1 winner Lakeway. The second dam, Milliardaire (by Alydar), a minor US four year old winner, is a sister to the Grade 1 Del Mar Futurity Stakes winner Saratoga Six.

133. INTENSE FOCUS (USA) ★★★
b.c. Giant's Causeway – Daneleta (Danehill)
February 24. Second foal. €340,000Y. Goffs Million. Jim Bolger. The dam, a two year old 7f winner, was listed placed and is a sister to the Group 3 12f Noblesse Stakes winner Danelissima and a half-sister to four winners. The second dam, Zaveleta (by Kahyasi), a useful dual listed 7f winner, is a half-sister to numerous winners including the two year old Group 1 1m Gran Criterium winner Sholokov and the dam of the Irish Derby winner Soldier Of Fortune.

134. LATIN CONNECTION (IRE) ★★★
b.c. Soviet Star – Via Verbano (Caerleon)
February 21. Seventh foal. €52,000Y. Tattersalls Ireland. BBA (Ire). Half-brother to the Irish two year old 7f winner Ambika (by Danehill Dancer), the 1m to 12f winner of five races Addario, the quite useful Irish two year old 5f winner Latin Walk (by Lil's Boy), the Irish two year old 1m winner Armanatta and the Irish two year old 7f winner Solid Gold (all by Spectrum). The dam won four races from 6f (at two years) to 1m and is a half-sister to five winners including the very useful Irish two year old listed 6f Tyros Stakes winner and subsequent US dual Grade 2 winner Via Lombardia. The second dam, Closette (by Fabulous Dancer), won in France over 1m and in Ireland over 7f.

135. NANCY ROCK (IRE) ★★★
b.f. Rock Of Gibraltar – Patrimony (Cadeaux Genereux)
January 16. First foal. €180,000Y. Goffs Million. Jim Bolger. The dam is an unraced half-sister to the very useful two year old listed 6f winner and Group 1 6f Cheveley Park Stakes second Suez. The second dam, Repeat Warning (by Warning), a fair 8.3f placed three year old, is a half-sister to nine winners including the high-class winners Bella Colora (dam of the Prince Of Wales's Stakes winner Stagecraft), Colorspin (dam of the Group 1 winners Zee Zee Top, Opera House and Kayf Tara) and Cezanne.

136. NELLIE FINLAY (IRE) ★★★
b.f. Rock Of Gibraltar – Bon Expresso (Spectrum)
March 26. First foal. €65,000Y. Goffs Million. BBA (Ire). The dam, an Irish listed 7f winner and third in the Group 3 7f Athasi Stakes, is a half-sister to three winners including the Irish two year old 6f winner and listed-placed Princess Nutley. The second dam, Queen Leonor (by Caerleon), won three races at four years in France and was listed-placed and is a half-sister to three minor winners.

137. SCANDAL SHEET (IRE) ★★★
b.f. Galileo – Sandrella (Darshaan)
April 12. Sixth foal. 70,000Y. Tattersalls October 1. BBA (Ire). Sister to the fairly useful 2007 two year old 1m winner Kitty Hawk Miss and half-sister to the fair 12f and 2m winner San Hernando (by Hernando) and the modest 12f all-weather winner Vivacita (by Medicean). The dam is an unraced half-sister to five winners including the Champion Stakes and dual US Grade 1 winner Storming Home. The second dam, Try To Catch Me (by Shareef Dancer), won once over 1m at three years in France and is a half-sister to eight winners including the Group 2 Criterium de Maisons-Laffitte winner Bitooh.

138. SCRIBONIA (IRE) ★★★

b.f. Galileo – Scribonia (Danehill)
March 25. First foal. The dam is an unraced half-sister to six winners including the very useful two year old listed 6f winner and dual Group 1 placed Luminata and the very useful dual 6f winner (including at two years) and Group 3 placed Aretha. The second dam, Smaoineamh (by Tap On Wood), an Irish 6f winner at two years and useful at up to 14f, is a half-sister to the champion sprinter Double Form and the Lupe Stakes winner Scimitarra.

139. SIODUIL (IRE) ★★★

b.f. Oasis Dream – Indian Belle (Indian Ridge)
February 28. First foal. 130,000Y. Tattersalls October 1. BBA (Ire). The dam, a fairly useful Irish 10f winner, is a half-sister to two winners. The second dam, Abyat (by Shadeed), is an unraced half-sister to eight winners including the Group 1 Middle Park Stakes winner Hayil.

140. SKY MYSTIC (IRE) ★★★

b.f. Galileo – Raghida (Nordico)
January 1. Half-sister to the fairly useful 2007 Irish two year old 6f winner and Group 3 fourth Rock Moss (by Rock Of Gibraltar) and to the very useful Irish two year old 5f to 1m winner Marionnaud (by Spectrum). The dam, a fairly useful Irish two year old dual 5f winner, was second in the Group 3 5f Curragh Stakes and the Group 3 Molecomb Stakes and is a sister to the useful 6f to 7f winner and Group 3 placed Nordic Fox and a half-sister to seven winners including the Group 1 Gran Criterium winner Sholokhov. The second dam, La Meilleure (by Lord Gayle), a quite useful listed 1m winner in Ireland at three years, is a half-sister to six winners.

141. SOLASAI (USA) ★★★

b.br.f. Malibu Moon – Twin Sails (Boston Harbor)
April 10. Fourth foal. €105,000Y. Goffs Million. Jim Bolger. Half-sister to a minor US two year old winner by Cat Thief. The dam, a minor US two year old winner, is a half-sister to five winners including the Group 3 Derby Trial third Desert Warrior. The second dam, Navajo Pass (by Secretariat), won twice at three years in the USA and is a sister to the US Grade two winners Pancho Villa and Terlingua (the dam of Storm Cat) and a half-sister to Royal Academy.

142. SOLAS NA GEALAI (IRE) ★★

b.c. Galileo – Lunar Lustre (Desert Prince)
March 12. Third foal. €435,000Y. Goffs Million. Jim Bolger. Half-brother to the unraced 2007 two year old Glitz (by Hawk Wing). The dam ran twice unplaced and is a half-sister to eight winners including the Group 2 Prix du Conseil du Paris winner Majorien and the Group 2 Prix de Malleret winner America. The second dam, Green Rosy (by Green Dancer), a French 10f winner and listed-placed, is a full or half-sister to ten winners including the US Grade 3 winner Rose Bouquet.

143. SEACHANTACH (USA) ★★★

b.c. Elusive Quality – Subtle Breeze (Storm Cat)
February 20. First foal. $410,000Y. Keeneland September. Tom Gentry. The dam, placed once over 7f at three years, is closely related to the top-class Irish Derby and Epsom Oaks winner Balanchine and a half-sister to the Group 2 Jockey Club Stakes winner Romanov and the Group 2 Sun Chariot Stakes winner Red Slippers. The second dam, Morning Devotion (by Affirmed), a useful two year old 6f winner, was placed in the Hoover Fillies Mile and the Lancashire Oaks.

144. SWAY ME NOW (USA) ★★

b.br.f. Speightstown – Disrupt (Deputy Minister)
March 9. First foal. $340,000Y. Keeneland September. BBA (Ire). The dam, a minor US three year old winner, is a half-sister to 3 other minor winners. The second dam, Dispute (by Danzig), won four Grade 1 events in the USA and is a half-sister to the US Grade 1 winners Adjudicating and Time For A Change.

145. TARRIP (USA) ★★★

b.f. Green Desert – Spinnette (Spinning World)
April 1. Third foal. $400,000Y. Keeneland September. Barouche Stud. Sister to the fairly useful French dual 1m winner (including at two

years) Green Lyons. The dam, a smart 10f winner and third in the Group 2 Sun Chariot Stakes, is a half-sister to the French two year old 1m winner and Group 3 Prix Vanteaux second Naissance Royale. The second dam, Net Worth (by Forty Niner), won two races over 8.5f and 9f in the USA at three years and is a half-sister to six other minor winners.

146. VOCALISED (USA) ★★★
b.c. Vindication – Serena's Tune (Mr Prospector)
May 30. Fourth foal. $560,000Y. Keeneland September. Tom Gentry. Half-brother to the minor US stakes winner Serena's Cat (by Storm Cat). The dam, a stakes winner of seven races in the USA, is a half-sister to the Group 1 Coronation Stakes winner Sophisticat and the US Grade two winners Grand Reward and Harlington. The second dam, Serena's Song (by Rahy), was an outstanding US winner of 11 Grade 1 events and is a half-sister to the US Grade 3 Golden Rod Stakes winner Vivid Imagination.

147. ZAVAALA (IRE) ★★★
ch.f. Rock Of Gibraltar – Zavaleta (Kahyasi)
April 16. Ninth foal. €72,000Y. Tattersalls Ireland. Edward Daly. Half-sister to the Group 3 12f Noblesse Stakes winner Danelissima , to the Irish two year old 7f winner and listed placed Daneleta (both by Danehill), the fairly useful Irish two year old 1m winner and listed placed Simonetta (by Lil's Boy), the Irish three year old 6.5f winner and listed-placed Benicio (by Spectrum) and a winner in Japan by Caerleon. The dam a useful dual listed 7f winner, is a half-sister to numerous winners including the two year old Group 1 1m Gran Criterium winner Sholokov and the two year old listed 7f winner Affianced (herself dam of the Irish Derby winner Soldier Of Fortune). The second dam, La Meilleure (by Lord Gayle), a listed winner in Ireland, was Group 3 placed.

MARCO BOTTI
148. CALLING VICTORY (FR) ★★★
b.f. Vettori – Calling Card (Bering)
March 1. Fourth foal. €45,000Y. Deauville August. De Burgh/Farrington. Half-sister to the

minor Italian three year old winner Daily Call (by Daylami). The dam, a useful French 10.5f winner, was listed-placed and is a half-sister to five winners. The second dam, Cheeky Charm (by Nureyev), ran unplaced twice and is closely related to the listed winners Theatrical Charmer and Mohaajir and a half-sister to seven winners. (Mrs R J Jacobs).
'She's a nice, big filly with plenty of scope and a very good mover. She's quite big and I think she'll be a filly for the second half of the season over seven furlongs, but we think a lot of her.'

149. DENICES DESERT ★★
b.f. Green Desert – Denice (Night Shift)
March 17. Fourth foal. 100,000Y. Doncaster St Leger. Hugo Merry. Half-sister to the unplaced 2007 two year old Victoria Valentine (by Royal Applause). The dam, a winner at two years in Germany and second in the Group 2 German 1,000 Guineas, is a half-sister to two winners. The second dam, Despoina (by Aspros), won in Germany and is a full or half-sister to six winners. (Mrs R J Jacobs).
'A well-bred filly, she still looks a bit backward so we've been easy with her. She's moves well and should be another one for the second half of the season.'

150. HOLAMO (IRE) ★★★★
b.br.f. Montjeu – Holy Nola (Silver Deputy)
January 21. Fifth foal. 110,000Y. Tattersalls October 1. Not sold. Half-sister to the US Grade 2 San Felipe Stakes and dual Grade 3 winner Preachinatthebar (by Silver Charm) and to the minor French three year old winner and Italian listed placed Nolas Lolly (by Lomitas). The dam, a stakes winner of five races in the USA, is a half-sister to five winners including the triple US Grade three winners Bare Necessities. The second dam, Shrewd Vixen (by Spectacular Bid), a listed-placed winner of six races, is a half-sister to three winners. (Mrs R J Jacobs).
'A very smart filly that comes from a good family, she's in full work but obviously because she's by Montjeu we aren't in a hurry with her. Not a big filly, but she's one for the seven furlong races later on.'

151. KHESKIANTO ★★
b.f. Kheleyf – Gently (Darshaan)
April 3. Second foal. 9,000Y. Doncaster St Leger. Marco Botti. Half-sister to the quite useful 2007 Irish two year old 7f winner Man With A Plan (by Dr Fong). The dam is an unraced half-sister to four winners. The second dam, Germane (by Distant Relative), a useful winner of the Group 3 7f Rockfel Stakes and placed in two listed events, is a half-sister to seven winners including the very useful German 10f winner Fabriano.
'She's still in pre-training in Italy. I know she's going well and should be a sharp two year old. If the owner wants her to race there later on then she needs to start her career there, before coming over to England sometime in the beginning of May.'

152. KITTY ALLEN ★★★
b.f. One Cool Cat – Aly McBe (Alydeed)
April 10. Third foal. 9,000Y. Tattersalls October 3. Not sold. Half-sister to the modest 5f and 6f winner Music Box Express (by Tale Of The Cat). The am is an unraced half-sister to four winners including the dam of the US Graded stakes winners Tour Of The Cat and Cat On Tour. The second dam, Mother Cat (by Banquet Table), is an unraced half-sister to eight winners including the US Grade 1 winner Field Cat. (Dachel Stud).
'I think she'll be our first two year old runner. She has plenty of speed and she's very straight-forward.' TRAINER'S BARGAIN BUY

153. KIYARI ★★★
b.f. Key Of Luck – Ashford Castle (Bates Motel)
March 16. Fifth foal. 23,000Y. Doncaster St Leger. M Botti. Half-sister to the quite useful 12f winner Aspasias Tizzy (by Tiznow). The dam, a minor stakes winner of six races from 6f to 8.5f, was Grade 3 placed twice and is a half-sister to eight winners including the US dual Grade 1 winner Strategic Maneuver. The second dam, Prayer Wheel (by Conquistador Cielo), a listed-placed winner in Canada, is a half-sister to seven winners. (El Catorce).
'I bought her from Doncaster, she's a small filly and won't grow much more but she looks racey

and should be an early type. Maybe not a five furlong filly, but she should be ready for six furlongs in June.'*

154. LOST IN THE DESERT ★★
b.c. Nayef – Desert Harmony (Green Desert)
February 9. Third foal. The dam won three races at three and four years in Italy and is a half-sister to two winners including the US stakes winner Thihn. The second dam, Hasana (by Private Account), is an unraced sister to the South African Grade 1 winner Flying Snowdrop and a half-sister to the Group 2 Child Stakes winner Magic Gleam.
'He's quite a big, strong horse and being by Nayef he'll be one for the second half of the year. He should be an interesting horse.'

155. UNNAMED ★★★
b.br.c. Johannesburg – Rock Salt (Selkirk)
January 30. First foal. 25,000Y. Tattersalls December. E Bulgheroni. The dam, placed twice at three years in France, is a sister to the very smart Group 2 10f Prix Eugene Adam and Group 3 9f Prix de Guiche winner Kirkwall and a half-sister to three winners. The second dam, Kamkova (by Northern Dancer), a placed middle-distance stayer, is a half-sister to ten winners including the top-class US middle-distance colt Vanlandingham.
'A nice horse, he's very tall but he goes well and shows ability. I don't think he'll be a five furlong runner but it shouldn't be long before we run him.'

CLIVE BRITTAIN

156. KAABARI (USA) ★★★
b.br.f. Seeking The Gold – Cloud Castle (In The Wings)
Closely related to the modest 9.7f winner Samdaniya (by Machiavellian) and half-sister to the fairly useful 6f (at two years) and 1m winner Queen's Best (by King's Best) and the French 12f winner and Group 3 Prix de Royaumont third Reverie Solitaire (by Nashwan). The dam was a very smart winner of the Group 3 Nell Gwyn Stakes and was placed in the Group 1 Yorkshire Oaks and the Group 1 Prix Vermeille. She is a

half-sister to five winners including the high-class middle-distance horses and multiple Group 1 winners Warrsan and Luso. The second dam, Lucayan Princess (by High Line), a very useful winner of the listed 6f Sweet Solera Stakes at two years, was third in the 12.3f Cheshire Oaks and is a half-sister to seven winners. (Saeed Manana).

157. TOO MANY TEARS (IRE) ★★★
ch.f. Diesis – Westernize (Gone West)
February 28. First foal. 40,000Y. Tattersalls October 1. Rabbah Bloodstock. The dam was placed once at three years in the USA. The second dam, Palme d'Or (by Sadler's Wells), won the Group 3 10.5f Prix de Flore and is a half-sister to six winners including the dual Group 1 winner Pistolet Bleu. (Saeed Manana).

158. UNNAMED ★★★
b.f. Kheleyf – Baalbek (Barathea)
April 12. Fifth foal. 36,000Y. Tattersalls October 3. Rabbah Bloodstock. Half-sister to the fair 2007 two year old 7f winner Brave Mave (by Daylami), to the fairly useful 9f and 10f winner Silca Key (by Inchinor) and the fairly useful triple 1m winner Cross The Line (by Cape Cross). The dam, a fair three year old 1m winner, is a half-sister to four winners. The second dam, Temple Row (by Ardross), is an unraced half-sister to ten winners including the Group winning two year old's Long Row and Colmore Row. (Saeed Manana).

159. UNNAMED ★★★
b.f. Oasis Dream – Bedazzling (Darshaan)
April 25. Fifth foal. 50,000Y. Tattersalls October 1. Rabbah Bloodstock. Half-sister to the 2007 two year old 7f winner Broken Moon (by Galileo), to the modest dual 10f winner Don Pasquale (by Zafonic) and the Italian two and three year old winner Sbrufun (by Barathea). The dam, a dual 7f winner and fourth in the Group 2 1m Falmouth Stakes, is a sister to the listed 10f winner and Group 2 12f Great Voltigeur Stakes fourth Bustan and a half-sister to three winners. The second dam, Dazzlingly Radiant (by Try My Best), a quite useful winner

of three races over 6f, is a half-sister to three winners including Dance By Night (dam of the French 1,000 Guineas winner Danseuse du Soir). (Saeed Manana).

160. UNNAMED ★★
b.br.f. Dixieland Band – Be Fair (Fast Gold)
January 24. Third foal. $160,000Y. Keeneland September. Rabbah Bloodstock. Half-sister to the minor stakes-placed winner Both Sides (by Stravinsky). The dam, a triple Grade 1 winner in Brazil, is a half-sister to another Brazilian triple Grade 1 winner Virginie. The second dam, Misty Moon (by Baronius), was a minor winner at three years in Brazil. (Saeed Manana).

161. UNNAMED ★★★
ch.c. Cadeaux Genereux – Crescent Moon (Mr Prospector)
March 15. Fifth foal. 50,000Y. Tattersalls October 2. Charlie Gordon-Watson. Brother to the quite useful 2007 two year old dual 6f winner La Chicaluna. The dam was placed five times at up to 10.5f in France and is a three-parts sister to the French 10f and 11f winner and Group 2 Prix Niel placed Gulf News. The second dam, Balanchine (by Storm Bird), a top-class winner of four races from 7f (at two years) to 12f including the Epsom Oaks and the Irish Derby, is closely related to the Jockey Club Stakes and Rose Of Lancaster Stakes winner Romanov and to the Sun Chariot Stakes winner Red Slippers. (Saif Ali & Saeed H Altayer).

162. UNNAMED ★★★
b.f. Green Desert – Darling Flame (Capote)
May 7. Eighth foal. 30,000Y. Tattersalls October 1. Rabbah Bloodstock. Half-sister to the fair 2007 1m placed two year old Clovis, to the fair two year old 6f winner Catherine Howard (both by Kingmambo), the French 7f listed winner Bezrin (by Danzig), the Irish 7.5f winner and Group 3 placed Flamelet (by Theatrical), the fair Irish 6f winner Richelieu and the minor Australian winner Firemaid (both by Machiavellian). The dam, a useful 6f (at two years) and 7f winner, is a half-sister to seven winners including the very smart Japanese

Group 1 winning miler Heart Lake. The second dam, My Darling One (by Exclusive Native), a high-class winner at up to 9f, won the Grade 1 Fantasy Stakes in the USA. (Saeed Manana).

163. UNNAMED ★★

ch.f. Nayef – Ermine (Cadeaux Genereux)
May 10. Fifth foal. 40,000Y. Tattersalls October 2. Rabbah Bloodstock. Half-sister to the fairly useful 5.7f (to two years) to 7f winner Hoh Bleu Dee (by Desert Style) and to the quite useful 7f winner of four races at four and five years Carnivore (by Zafonic). The dam, a quite useful three year old 1m winner, is a half-sister to five winners including the very smart 1m (at two years) and Group 3 10f Brigadier Gerard Stakes winner and 2,000 Guineas and Derby third Border Arrow. The second dam, Nibbs Point (by Sure Blade), a useful winner of the listed 12f Galtres Stakes, was second in the Group 3 Park Hill Stakes and is a half-sister to nine winners. (Saeed Manana).

164. UNNAMED ★★★

b.f. Acclamation – Flag (Selkirk)
April 9. Fourth foal. 40,000Y. Tattersalls October 1. Rabbah Bloodstock. Half-sister to the fair 2007 5f placed two year old Liberty Ship (by Statue Of Liberty), to the quite useful 5f winner of three races (including at two years) Azygous (by Foxhound) and the modest 5f winner Twosheetstothewind (by Bahamian Bounty). The dam is an unraced half-sister to three winners including the Italian listed winner Armenian Dancer. The second dam, Flower Arrangement (by Lomond), is an unraced half-sister to five winners including the Kentucky Derby second Bold Arrangement. (Saeed Manana).

165. UNNAMED ★★★

b.f. Elusive City – Frond (Alzao)
February 6. Seventh foal. 30,000Y. Tattersalls October 1. Rabbah Bloodstock. Half-sister to the fair 2007 7f placed two year old Addikt (by Diktat), to the useful two year old 7f and listed 1m winner Streets Ahead (by Beat Hollow), the fairly useful two year old 6f winner and listed-

placed Ridder (by Dr Fong), the German 10f winner Portcullis (by Pivotal) and the Scandinavian 1m and 10f winner Azolla (by Cadeaux Genereux). The dam, a quite useful two year old 7f winner, is a half-sister to six winners. The second dam, Fern (by Shirley Heights), a useful 12f winner and third in the listed 10f Lupe Stakes, is a half-sister to the Group 1 Fillies Mile winner and Oaks second Shamshir. (Saeed Manana).

166. UNNAMED ★★

b.f. Fasliyev – Kyda (Gulch)
March 21. Second foal. 20,000Y. Tattersalls October 1. C Brittain. The dam, a modest 9f winner, is a half-sister to three minor winners. The second dam, Trampoli (by Trempolino), won six Graded stakes events and is a half-sister to eight winners including the US Grade 1 winner Roi Normand. (C Brittain).

167. UNNAMED ★★★

ch.f. Almutawakel – My American Beauty (Wolfhound)
April 24. Second foal. 32,000Y. Tattersalls October 2. Rabbah Bloodstock. Half-sister to the fair 2007 6f placed two year old Dome Rock (by Domedriver). The dam, a fairly useful 5f and 6f winner of seven races from two to five years, is a half-sister to two winners including the US dual Grade 3 winner Desert Lady. The second dam, Hooray Lady (by Ahonoora), a fairly useful winner of six races at around 1m, is a half-sister to seven winners. (Saeed Manana).

168. UNNAMED ★★★

b.f. Dubai Destination – Nasaieb (Fairy King)
April 20. Fifth foal. 35,000Y. Tattersalls October 1. Hillview Bloodstock. Half-sister to the 2007 6f placed two year old Luminous Gold (by Fantastic Light), to the useful two year old 5f winner and Group 2 5f Flying Childers Stakes third Kissing Lights (by Machiavellian) and to the minor French two year old winner Nilassiba (by Daylami). The dam, a fairly useful two year old 5f winner, was third in the listed 5f National Stakes and is a half-sister to five winners including the Group 3 7f Solario Stakes winner

Raise A Grand. The second dam, Atyaaf (by Irish River), is an unplaced half-sister to eight winners including the listed John Of Gaunt Stakes winner Weldnaas. (Saeed Manana).

169. UNNAMED ★★★★
b.f. *Oasis Dream – Presto Vento (Air Express)*
March 14. Second foal. 62,000Y. Tattersalls October 1. Rabbah Bloodstock. Half-sister to the fair 2007 two year old 5f winner Presto Levanter (by Rock Of Gibraltar). The dam was a useful two year old 5f listed and three year old 7f listed winner. The second dam, Placement (by Kris), is an unraced half-sister to four winners including the Group 2 Sun Chariot Stakes winner Danceabout and the French dual Group 3 winner Pole Position. (Saeed Manana).

170. UNNAMED ★★★
b.f. *King's Best – Sadinga (Sadler's Wells)*
February 4. Third foal. 32,000Y. Tattersalls October 3. Rabbah Bloodstock. Half-sister to the fair two year old 5f winner Cool Judgement (by Peintre Celebre). The dam, a quite useful Irish 12f winner, is a half-sister to seven winners including the Group 1 Moyglare Stud Stakes winner Priory Belle. The second dam, Ingabelle (by Taufan), won the Group 3 Phoenix Sprint Stakes and is a half-sister to four winners. (Saeed Manana).

171. UNNAMED ★★★
b.f. *Diktat – Shining Vale (Twilight Agenda)*
January 31 Fifth foal. 42,000Y. Tattersalls October 1. Rabbah Bloodstock. Half-sister to the German two year old winner and Italian Group 3 placed Mrs Snow (by Singspiel) and to a minor Italian two year old winner by Lomitas. The dam is an unraced half-sister to the German and Italian Group 2 winner Walzerkoenigin. The second dam, Great Revival (by Keen), is an unplaced half-sister to eight winners including the Group 1 winners Play It Safe and Providential. (Saeed Manana).

172. UNNAMED ★★★
ch.f. *Needwood Blade – Silent Tribute (Lion Cavern)*
April 14. Sixth foal. 27,000Y. Tattersalls October

2. Rabbah Bloodstock.
Half-sister to Stoneacre Ma (by Dubai Destination), unplaced in one start at two years in 2007. The dam, a useful 6f winner here, won a 1m listed event in Italy (both at two years) and is a half-sister to four winners. The second dam, Tribal Rite (by Be My Native), a fairly useful Irish two year old listed 6f and three year old 10f winner, is a half-sister to the Middle Park Stakes winner Balla Cove, the US stakes winner Burning Issue and the Irish listed winner Blasted Heath. (Saeed Manana).

173. UNNAMED ★★★
b.f. *Tobougg – Skew (Niniski)*
January 27. Fourth living foal. 32,000Y. Tattersalls October 2. Rabbah Bloodstock. Half-sister to the fair two year old 7f winner Sketch (by Perugino), to the French 13f winner Art and the moderate 2m winner Skit (both by In The Wings). The dam is an unraced half-sister to the Group 3 12f John Porter Stakes and Group 3 Lancashire Oaks winner Spout, to the French listed winner Mon Domino and the smart middle-distance performers Aldwych (by In The Wings) and Dombey. The second dam, Arderelle (by Pharly), a quite useful three year old 10f winner, is a half-sister to eight winners including the Group 2 Prix Greffulhe winner Arokar. (Saeed Manana).

MEL BRITTAIN
174. CARANBOLA ★★★
br.f. *Lucky Story – Ladywell Blaise (Turtle Island)*
March 17. 2,000Y. Doncaster October. M Brittain. The dam, a modest 6f to 7f winner of four races, is a sister to a stakes-placed winner in the USA and a half-sister to four winners. The second dam, Duly Elected (by Persian Bold), is a placed sister to the Group 1 Phoenix Stakes winner King Persian.
'She'll have her first run in mid-April and I'll be disappointed if she doesn't run a big race. A lovely, big, strong filly, she'll start at five furlongs but should stay further.'

175. FALBRINA ★★★
ch.f. *Falbrav – Haniya (Caerleon)*
March 22. Ninth foal. 8,000Y. Tattersalls

October. **Not sold.** Half-sister to six winners including the fairly useful 7.6f (at two years) to 10f winner Zulfaa (by Bahri), the quite useful two year old 7f winner Atwaar (by Woodman), the quite useful dual 10f all-weather winner Ameeq (by Silver Hawk) and the fair three year old 7f winner Musawah (by Gulch). The dam, a fairly useful 12f winner, is a half-sister to seven winners including the US Grade 2 Bernard Baruch Handicap winner and Grade 1 Rothmans International and Group 1 Prix de la Salamandre placed Volochine. The second dam, Harmless Albatross (by Pas de Seul), won the Group 3 1m Prix des Chenes (at two years) and is a half-sister to the Group two winners Fortune's Wheel and Libertine.
'She's bred to get middle-distances actually but she has shown a bit of speed. I ran her yesterday and unfortunately it was too soft, she lost a shoe and she's come back with a sore shin. She'll be back and although she'll be progressive she might win at a stiff five furlongs and she'll be better over six.'

176. ROSSETT ROSE (IRE) ★★★
ch.f. Rossini – Sabaah Elfull (Kris)
March 8. Seventh foal. €7,500Y. Tattersalls Ireland. M Brittain. Half-brother to the UAE four year old 6f and 7f winner Outlaw (by Danehill), to the quite useful two year old 5f winner Oh Dara (by Aljabr) and the fair 12f all-weather winner Cry Presto (by Street Cry). The dam, a modest three year old 5f winner, is closely related to the smart French Group 3 6f Prix de Meautry winner Pole Position and a half-sister to the Group 2 Sun Chariot Stakes winner Danceabout. The second dam, Putupon (by Mummy's Pet), a fairly useful two year old 5f winner, is a sister to the Gimcrack Stakes winner Precocious and a half-sister to the Japan Cup winner Jupiter Island and the Queen Mary Stakes winner Pushy.
'A two year old type, I haven't done too much with her yet but she'll be running soon and she's sharp enough. A big, strong filly and a good sort.'

177. SANDIES SISTER ★★
ch.f. Bertolini – Nijmah (Halling)
March 15. 2,200Y. Tattersalls October. Half-sister to the unplaced 2007 two year old Sandies Choice (by Tobougg). The dam was placed at two years and is a half-sister to nine winners including the Group 2 Sandown Mile second On The Ridge. The second dam, Star Ridge (by Storm Bird), is an unraced half-sister to the US Grade 1 winner Bee A Scout.
'She'll be a two year old and she'll be running soon, starting off at five furlongs but she'll be better at six. A nice sort of filly, very correct.'

178. UNNAMED ★★
ch.c. Falbrav – Irish Light (Irish River)
March 19. 8,200Y. Doncaster October. M Brittain. Half-brother to the fair 2007 two year old 7f winner Carnival Queen (by Carnival Dancer), to the useful 5f and 6f winner (including at two years) and Group 1 6f Phoenix Stakes third Polar Force (by Polar Falcon) and the fairly useful 1m and 8.3f two year old winner Harnour (by Desert King). The dam, a fairly useful dual 1m winner at three years, is a half-sister to five winners including the US stakes winner and Grade 3 placed Solar Bound. The second dam, Solar Star (by Lear Fan), a fairly useful two year old 6f winner, is a half-sister to five winners including Gold Land, a winner of three Grade 3 stakes in the USA.
'I see him as a July type two year old and I'll maybe start him off at six or seven furlongs at Newcastle. We had a hold up with him so he wasn't broken until quite late, so I haven't rushed him because he's a lovely horse. I don't name these horses because I own them all and if someone comes along to buy one they can choose the name themselves.'

179. UNNAMED ★★
b.c. Xaar – Love Of Silver (Arctic Tern)
April 17. Eleventh foal. 3,000Y. Tattersalls October. Not sold. Half-brother to the fairly useful 8.3f winner and listed-placed Silver Bracelet (by Machiavellian), to the quite useful 10f and 12f winner Horseford Hill (by In The Wings) and the modest 2m winner Taxman (by

Singspiel) and the placed dam of the Italian Group 3 winner Kuiacoss. The dam, a very useful filly, won two races at two years over 6f and 7f including the Group 3 Prestige Stakes, was third in the Group 1 Prix Marcel Boussac and is a half-sister to six winners. The second dam, Silver Clover (by Secretariat), won three races at up to 9f at 4 yrs in the USA and is a half-sister to six winners.
'We had a bit of a hold up due to an infection in his foot, there's nothing seriously wrong and he'll be OK but obviously it's set us back a bit. He's a lovely build of a horse – a real two year old type.'

180. UNNAMED ★★
ch.c. Tobougg – Sabrata (Zino)
February 27. €11,000Y. Tattersalls Ireland. M Brittain. Half-brother to the quite useful two year old dual 7f winner Receivedwiththanx (by Celtic Swing), to the fair 10f to 12f and hurdles winner Goose Island (by Kahyasi) and the 7f seller winner Head Scratcher (by Alhijaz). The dam won at two years in France and is a half-sister to a winner in Japan. The second dam, Sulmona (by Miswaki), a winner in France and second in the listed Prix Zeddaan, is a half-sister to eight winners.
'A lovely horse, he'll probably want a bit more time but we're getting there. Maybe late May will suit him as a starting date and he's probably a six furlong type two year old.'

181. UNNAMED ★★
b.f. Xaar – Talah (Danehill)
March 30. Fifth foal. 3,500Y. Tattersalls October. M Brittain. Half-sister to the useful 7f and 8.5f winner Ceremonial Jade and to the modest 6f winner Sea Rover (both by Jade Robbery). The dam, a fairly useful second over 6f at two years on her only start, is a sister to the listed winner and French 1,000 Guineas second Firth Of Lorne and a half-sister to five winners including the smart two year old 6f winner and Group 3 placed Shmoose. The second dam, Kerrera (by Diesis), a smart winner of the Group 3 Cherry Hinton Stakes and second in the 1,000 Guineas, is a half-sister to the high-class two year old Rock City.

'A nice filly and a half-sister to a horse we have called Sea Rover. She'll be racing in May, she's a little bit "up behind" and needs to grow a touch, but she's a typical two year old.'

SIMON CALLAGHAN
182. ALEXANDER NEWSTALK ★★★★
b.f. Choisir – National Ballet
(Shareef Dancer)
April 16. Tenth foal. 32,000Y. Tattersalls October 2. Blandford Bloodstock. Half-sister to the quite useful 2007 Irish two year old 6.3f winner Melanesia (by Chevalier), to the very useful two year old Group 3 7f Rockfel Stakes and listed 7f winner Name Of Love (by Petardia and herself dam of the US Grade 3 winner Perilous Pursuit), the useful 7f winner (at two years) and 9f listed placed Annapurna (by Brief Truce), the minor French dual three year old winner Sallwa (by Entrepreneur) and a winner over hurdles by Blues Traveller. The dam is an unraced half-sister to seven winners including four listed winners. The second dam, Britannia's Rule (by Blakeney), won the Lupe Stakes and was third in the Oaks.
'She only arrived in March but she's a really natural, forward-going filly and a real two year old type. The family has produced lots of sprinters and she's a filly with a really low action, she goes very well and she'll be making her mark in early season two year old races.'

183. CELTIC REBEL (IRE) ★★★
b.c. Bahri – Farjah (Charnwood Forest)
April 16. Fourth foal. 60,000Y. Doncaster St Leger. Blandford Bloodstock. Half-brother to the 2007 5f placed two year old (on his only start) Taine (by Invincible Spirit) and to the fairly useful two year old 6f winner and listed-placed Celtic Sultan (by Celtic Swing). The dam, a French two year old 5.5f winner, is a half-sister to four winners. The second dam, Anam (by Persian Bold), won twice at three years and is a half-sister to five winners. (P M Cunningham).
'A really forward colt from quite a precocious family on the dam's side. He's a horse that shows lots of speed and we really like him. He's should be out by the time of the Guineas meeting.'

184. COOL ART (IRE) ★★★★
b.c. One Cool Cat – Fee Faw Fum (Great Commotion)
April 9. Sixth foal. 100,000Y. Tattersalls October 2. Blandford Bloodstock. Half-brother to the Italian winner of six races from two to four years Fabled Bully (by Northern Flagship) and to the Italian three year old winner of two races Full Power (by Elnadim). The dam won three minor races at two and three years in Italy and is a half-sister to nine winners. The second dam, Fourth Of July (by Free Round), won once at two years in France.
'This is a good horse – a real athlete and he'd be one of my picks. He'll probably be running by the time of the Guineas meeting and he shows us lots of ability, he's done a bit of work and he has the potential to be running in Group races later in the year. A really nice colt.'

185. ECHO DANCER ★★
br.c. Danehill Dancer – Entail (Riverman)
April 29. Fifth foal. 50,000Y. Tattersalls October 3. Blandford Bloodstock. Half-brother to the useful two year old 6f winner Let Us Prey (by Hawk Wing), to the fair two year old 6f winner Entailment (by Kris) and the French two year old 10f winner Grandretour (by Grand Lodge). The dam, a fairly useful winner of three races from 7f to 1m at four years, is a half-sister to three minor winners. The second dam, Estala (by Be My Guest), won once at two years in France and was listed-placed and is a half-sister to five winners including the Group three winners Vortex, Prove and Danefair (dam of the Group 3 winner Trade Fair). (Mr D F O'Rourke).
'A late foal and a half-brother to a pretty decent horse we trained last year called Let Us Prey, he's going to be very much one for the back-end of the season. Quite a raw horse, he's going to need time, but he's a horse that I like and he's a nice mover.'

186. ELUSIVE RONNIE (IRE) ★★★
b.c. One Cool Cat – Elusive Kitty (Elusive Quality)
February 6. The dam, a modest 1m and 9f placed maiden, is a half-sister to the two year old 5f and 7f and subsequent US Grade 3 8.5f winner Southern Africa. The second dam, Al Fahdi (by Be My Chief), a fairly useful 6f (at two years) to 1m winner, was third in the Group 3 Prestige Stakes and is a half-sister to six winners. (Woodcote Stud).
'A really typical, precocious two year old, he'll probably have run before your book is out and he's the sort of horse that could break his maiden the second time out and he'll certainly be making his mark in the early season two year old races. He's not a star but he's a really mature, precocious horse.'

187. GOLDEN POOL (IRE) ★★★
b.f. Danetime – Miss Megs (Croco Rouge)
February 6. First foal. 28,000Y. Tattersalls October 2. Blandford Bloodstock. The dam, a fair 9f and 11f winner in Ireland, is a half-sister to four winners including the listed winner Santa Isobel. The second dam, Atlantic Record (by Slip Anchor), is an unraced half-sister to four winners. (Lord Clinton & Mr M Green).
'This is a lovely big filly, she shows lots of natural ability and she'll be running in mid-summer. A filly we really like, she's by a decent stallion and out of a mare that won three races. I think she was a really good buy.'

188. MRS KIPLING ★★★★
b.f. Exceed And Excel – Quinzey (Carnegie)
January 31. Third foal. 55,000Y. Tattersalls October 2. Blandford Bloodstock. Half-sister to the fair two year old 1m all-weather winner Stanley George (by Noverre). The dam is an unraced half-sister to two winners. The second dam, Quinpool (by Alydar), won three races in the USA and was third in the Grade 1 Kentucky Oaks and is a half-sister to seven winners. (Sangster Family & M Green).
'One of my real picks of the fillies, she's a real natural and shows lots of speed, has a great outlook and is a filly we really like. Potentially a stakes filly. she could be a very exciting horse. She was given the name because of the 'exceedingly good cakes'!'

189. ROSE OF ZOLLERN ★★★

b.c. War Chant – Rose Of Zollern
(Seattle Dancer)
March 18. Third foal. 45,000Y. Tattersalls October 2. Blandford Bloodstock. Half-brother to the fairly useful two year old dual 7f all-weather winner and subsequent German listed placed Flor Y Nata (by Fusaichi Pegasus) and to the fair all-weather 6f and 7f winner Rosa De Mi Corazon (by Cozzene). The dam won nine races including the German 1,000 Guineas and a stakes event in the USA and is a half-sister to three winners. The second dam, Kalisha (by Rainbow Quest), is an unraced half-sister to the Dewhurst Stakes winner Kala Dancer. (Mr Y M Nasib).
'A lovely, big colt out of a good mare. He won't be running before the seven furlong maidens start because of his size, but he could potentially be a decent horse. He's a really athletic colt, he looks great and although we haven't done any fast work with him I really like this guy.'

190. SIR DAY STAR (USA) ★★★

b.c. Five Star Day – Sir Harriett
(Sir Harry Lewis)
April 10. Seventh foal. $140,000 two year old. Fasig-Tipton Calder two year old's-in-training. Newmarket / Merry / Callaghan. Brother to the US stakes winner of five races Sir Five Star and half-brother to three winners including the US stakes winner Overpass (by Slavic). The dam, a minor US three year old winner, is a daughter of the minor winner of five races Buenas Neches (by Hagley), herself a half-sister to five winners. The sire, a son of Carson City and the winner of a Grade 2 stakes, has bred ten stakes winners including the US Grade 2 winner Dance Daily.
'He's only just arrived and was a horse I loved in America where he breezed very well and he's a full-brother to a decent sprinter. I think he's the sort of horse we can continue with and he'll be a pretty precocious two year old.'

191. SPIRITUAL ART ★★★

b.f. Invincible Spirit – Oatey (Master Willie)
April 14. Sixth foal. 130,000Y. Doncaster St Leger. Blandford Bloodstock. Half-sister to the quite useful two year old 5f winner Alternative (by Dr Fong) and to the fair three year old 1m all-weather winner Jomus (by Soviet Star). The dam, a modest dual 5f winner at three years, is a half-sister to ten winners including the smart Group 3 Lingfield Derby Trial winner Munwar and the smart Irish middle-distance listed winner Hateel. The second dam, Oatfield (by Great Nephew), was placed at two years. (N A Callaghan).
'A really nice filly, she'll start off in late April/ early May and shows lots of natural speed. We really like her.'

192. UNNAMED ★★★

b.c. Chevalier – Cappuchino (Roi Danzig)
March 23. Tenth foal. 26,000Y. Tattersalls October 2. Blandford Bloodstock. Closely related to a winner in Saudi Arabia by Danetime and half-brother to the moderate 2007 6f and 7f placed two year old Redbackcappuchino (by Redback), the useful two year old 7f winner Blue Bolivar (by Blues Traveller), the fair three year old 5f winner Cayman Expresso (by Fayruz) and the moderate 6f banded winner Mister Becks (by Beckett). The dam, a moderate three year old 7f winner on the all-weather, is a half-sister to seven winners including the listed winner Chookie Heiton. The second dam, Royal Wolff (by Prince Tenderfoot), won twice over sprint distances in Ireland and is a half-sister to the Group 2 Premio Melton winner Gaius. (N A Callaghan).
'A nice big horse, he's going to be a mid-to-late summer horse and we picked him up pretty cheaply. He's a really good-looking horse and one that we really like, he just needs a bit of time to grow into his frame.' TRAINER'S BARGAIN BUY

193. UNNAMED ★★★★

b.c. Proud Citizen – Endless Reward (End Sweep)
February 2. Third foal. €110,000Y. Goffs Million. Not sold. 88,000 two year old. Kempton Breeze-Up. Merry/Callaghan. Half-brother to the minor US winner at two and three years Capo d'Oro (by Capote). The dam is

a placed sister to the US stakes winner Cox's Sweep and a half-sister to the US dual Grade 3 winner Valid Bonnet. The second dam, Miss Cox's Hat (by Cox's Ridge), a winner in the USA and third in the Grade 1 Matron Stakes, is a half-sister to nine winners.

'A lovely horse that stands at about 16.1, he's a real big, long-striding colt and later in the year he's a horse we'll hear plenty of. He shows us a lot of ability and he has a great attitude. He's certainly going to be going seven furlongs, possibly a mile and he was my pick of the Kempton breeze-up. A colt I really like.'

194. UNNAMED ★★★
ch.f. Monsieur Bond – Feeling Blue (Missed Flight)
March 25. First foal. 40,000Y. Doncaster St Leger. Blandford Bloodstock. The dam, a moderate winner over 5f at three years, is a half-sister to three winners. The second dam, Blues Indigo (by Music Boy), won over 6f and was second in the Group 3 Palace House Stakes and is a half-sister to five winners. (M R Green).

'She needs a bit of time. Although the sire was fast he was a horse that improved with age. This filly will be a sprinter, I like her and she's got a great attitude. I'm sure that later in the year when she strengthens up she'll be a nice filly.'

195. UNNAMED ★★★
ch.f. Johannesburg – Game Player (Drumalis)
February 1. Fourth foal. 70,000Y. Tattersalls October 1. Not sold. Half-sister to two winners in the USA including the stakes-placed Game Of Skill (by Wild Again). The dam won five minor races in the USA and is a sister to the stakes winner Playinaround and a half-sister to four winners. The second dam, Playing Through (by Messenger Of Song), won eight minor races in the USA and is a full or half-sister to eight winners. (Mrs E O'Leary).

'A really nice filly, she'll really tough with a good outlook and a good attitude. A six/seven furlong filly, she has an American pedigree so whether she'll be one that might appreciate the dirt I don't know, but she's a filly that I like.'

196. UNNAMED ★★★
ch.f. El Prado – Hatoof (Irish River)
March 12. Eighth foal. $300,000Y. Keeneland September. Tony Nerses. Half-sister to four winners including the French 10.5f winner and listed-placed Mighty Isis (by Pleasant Colony) and the fairly useful 12f winner Prospects Of Glory and the UAE 8.5f winner Dubai Edition (both by Mr Prospector). The dam, a high-class filly and winner of seven races notably the 1,000 Guineas, the Champion Stakes and the Prix de l'Opera, is a half-sister to the US Grade 1 winner Irish Prize and the French listed winners Fasateen and Insijaam. The second dam, Cadeaux d'Amie (by Lyphard), won over 1m at two years and 10f at three years in France, was third in the Group 3 Prix d'Aumale and is a half-sister to the champion two year old filly and Prix Vermeille winner Mrs Penny. (Saleh Al Homeizi & Imad Al Sagar).

'She's quite a leggy filly and will need a bit of time, but she's really athletic and a huge-striding filly. I really like her, she has a nice way of going.'

197. UNNAMED ★★★★
b.f. Medicean – Lady Donatella (Last Tycoon)
January 23. Fifth foal. 42,000Y. Tattersalls October 2. Blandford Bloodstock.
Half-sister to the quite useful 2007 two year old 7f winner Maxwil (by Storming Home) and to the modest 6f and 7.6f winner Dark Moon (by Observatory). The dam, a modest 12f placed maiden, is a half-sister to seven winners including the very useful Group 3 Earl of Sefton Stakes winner Right Wing. The second dam, Nekhbet (by Artaius), a fair 5f to 7f placed two year old, is a half-sister to seven winners including the Irish St Leger winner M-Lolshan. (Countrywide Steel & Tubes Ltd).

'This is a really tough filly, she's got plenty of character and likes to give her rider a difficult time in the mornings. A January foal, she's very early and mature and I imagine she'll be running by the end of April. A strong, mature, two year old type with a good action. We like her.'

198. UNNAMED ★★

ch.f. Danehill Dancer – Lilissa (Doyoun)
April 28. Ninth foal. 210,000Y. Tattersalls October 1. Demi O'Byrne. Half-sister to the Irish and US winner of nine races and Group 1 second Livadiya (by Shernazar), to the French three year old 9f winner and Group 3 placed Liska (by Bigstone), the useful 10f and 12f winner and smart broodmare Lidakiya (by Kahyasi), the fairly useful 10f winner Lishtar (by Mtoto), the modest dual 2m winner Leo McGarry (by Fantastic Light) and the modest 10f winner Foxilla (by Foxhound). The dam, a French 9f and 10.5f winner, is a half-sister to five winners including the Group 3 12f Prix Minerve winner Linnga. The second dam, Lisana (by Alleged), won twice at three years in France. (M Tabor).
'A nice, long-striding filly, being out of a Doyoun mare she's going to need a bit of time and the family do improve with age. She's just doing two canters at the moment, she's a filly we like but she's just going to take time.'

199. UNNAMED ★★★

b.f. Danetime – Naraina (Desert Story)
February 17. Second foal. 42,000Y. Tattersalls October 2. Blandford Bloodstock. Sister to the fair 2007 two year old 6f winner Outside Edge. The dam is an unraced half-sister to four winners including the Group 3 12f Princess Royal Stakes winner Narwala (herself the dam of 4 stakes winners). The second dam, Noufiyla (by Top Ville), is a placed half-sister to five winners. (Countrywide Steel & Tubes Ltd).
'She's probably going to be one of the first of our fillies to run. She's small, strong and robust, she shows lots of speed and she's a real two year old type that should start her career in April.'

200. UNNAMED ★★★

b.f. Pivotal – Pietra Dura (Cadeaux Genereux)
March 11. Third foal. 380,000Y. Tattersalls October 1. Blandford Bloodstock. The dam, an Irish two year old 7f winner, was listed-placed and is a half-sister to one winner. The second dam, Bianca Nera (by Salse), a smart two year old winner of the Group 1 7f Moyglare Stud Stakes and the Group 2 6f Lowther Stakes, is

half-sister to four winners including the Moyglare Stud Stakes second Hotelgenie Dot Com (herself dam of the dual Group 1 winner Simply Perfect). (M Tabor).
'A really nice filly, she's grown quite a lot since we bought her and is probably a filly that has a lot of Pivotal in her. So she'll need a bit of cut in the ground and more time than I originally thought. But she's a real quality filly with a lot of presence about her and I would imagine that later in the year she could be a decent filly.'

201. UNNAMED ★★

b.f. Catcher In The Rye – Rainbow Java (Fairy King)
February 13. Fifth foal. 35,000Y. Doncaster St Leger. Blandford Bloodstock. Half-sister to the quite useful Irish 5f listed-placed New Spirit (by Invincible Spirit), to the Italian two year old winner Meciapino (by Glen Jordan). The dam, a 5f winner at three years in Italy, is a half-sister to five winners including the Ascot Gold Cup winner Mr Dinos. The second dam, Spear Dance (by Gay Fandango), won twice at three years and is a half-sister to eight winners including the Group three winners Rasa Penang and Darcy's Thatcher. (N A Callaghan).
'A very laid-back filly and although originally we thought she'd be early she's gone a bit weak and grown, so we're going easy with her at the moment. But she has a good attitude and is a nice type of filly.'

202. UNNAMED ★★★★★

b.c. Giant's Causeway – Spiritual Air (Royal Applause)
January 22. First foal. 250,000Y. Tattersalls October 1. Demi O'Byrne. The dam, a fairly useful two year old 6f winner, subsequently won at four years in the USA and is a half-sister to two winners including the very useful two year old 5f winner and Group 2 6f Mill Reef Stakes second Mystical Land. The second dam, Samsung Spirit (by Statoblest), a fair dual 6f winner (including at two years), is a half-sister to seven winners and to the placed dam of the Group 2 6f Mill Reef Stakes winner Indian Rocket. (M Tabor/M R Green).

'This is a very nice colt – I really like him. He's a big, long-striding colt with a lot of quality and presence about him. He'll probably start over six furlongs, he has a really good attitude for a Giant's Causeway and a good way of going.'

203. UNNAMED ★★★★

b.c. Kyllachy – Succumb (Pursuit Of Love)
April 25. Second foal. 92,000Y. Tattersalls October 2. Blandford Bloodstock. The dam is an unraced half-sister to seven winners including the useful On Call, a listed winner of seven races at up to 2m. The second dam, Doctor Bid (by Spectacular Bid), is an unraced half-sister to nine winners including the smart Group 3 Prix Thomas Bryon winner Glory Forever and the dam of the Group winners Verglas and Cassandra Go. (M R Green).
'This is a horse we bought from Cheveley Park, the same people we bought Excellent Art from. He's a really nice colt and a very strong, mature horse that will definitely be making his mark in two year old races. The sire as a rule gets horses that need a bit of cut in the ground but this guy has a great action, he's done two bits of work and shows plenty of ability. We really like him.'

204. UNNAMED ★★

b.f. Invincible Spirit – To The Woods (Woodborough)
March 9. Third foal. 50,000Y. Doncaster St Leger. Blandford Bloodstock. The dam, a fairly useful 5f and all-weather 7f winner, is a half-sister to the two year old 6f winner and Group 2 6f Lowther Stakes fourth Valjarv and the 5f and 6f (at two years) winner and listed-placed Ikan. The second dam, Iktidar (by Green Desert), a quite useful Irish 1m placed maiden, is a half-sister to five winners. (J R Crickmore).
'Although this filly is by Invincible Spirit she just needs a bit of time. Her dam stayed seven furlongs and I'd say she'll be racing from the middle of the season onwards. A filly with a great attitude and a nice mover, but we'll take our time with her at the moment.'

HENRY CANDY

205. AMOUR PROPRE ★★

ch.c. Paris House – Miss Prim (Case Law)
March 13. 1,500Y. Doncaster October. Henry Candy. The dam is an unplaced half-sister to two minor winners. The second dam, Calamanco (by Clantime), won two races at three and four years and is a sister to the dam of the Group 1 Golden Jubilee Stakes winner Cape Of Good Hope. (Simon Broke & Partners). *'You can see by the purchase price that she isn't out of the ordinary but I wouldn't be surprised if she won, especially if she continues to improve the way she has done since the Sales.'* TRAINER'S BARGAIN BUY

206. BENDED KNEE ★★★★

b.f. Refuse To Bend – Flavian (Catrail)
February 16. Half-sister to the moderate two year old 6f and 7f winner Young Flavio (by Mark Of Esteem). The dam, a fairly useful 6f (at two years) and 7f winner, is a half-sister to six winners including the useful triple 7f winner Mata Cara (herself the dam of a French listed winner) and the fairly useful 10f winner Refugio. The second dam, Fatah Flare (by Alydar), won over 6f (at two years) and the Group 3 10.5f Musidora Stakes at three years. She is a half-sister to eight winners including Sabin, a dual US Grade 1 winner over 9f and 10f. (Major M G Wyatt).
'A very nice filly, she's one for the second half of the year, she's big, well-grown and a good mover. One for September time over six furlongs.'

207. DARK MISCHIEF ★★★

b.c. Namid – Syrian Queen (Slip Anchor)
February 25. Seventh foal. 34,000Y. Tattersalls October 3. H Candy. Half-brother to the modest 9f winner Sham Sharif (by Be My Chief) and to 2 minor French winners by Oscar and Croco Rouge. The dam, a quite useful 10f winner, is a half-sister to eight winners including the Cherry Hinton Stakes winner and 1,000 Guineas second Kerrera and the Coventry, July, Gimcrack, Greenham and Criterion Stakes winner Rock City. The second dam, Rimosa's Pet (by Petingo), won the Group 3 8.5f Princess

Elizabeth Stakes (at two years) and the Group 3 10.5f Musidora Stakes and is a half-sister to five winners. (First of Many Partnership).
'A nice horse, he's big, well-grown and very scopey. He'll make a two year old around June time over five furlongs.'

208. EASILY FORGIVEN ★★★★
b.c. Kyllachy – Cutpurse Moll (Green Desert)
March 11. Eighth foal. 17,000Y. Tattersalls October 3. H Candy. Half-brother to the smart listed winning sprinter Colonel Cotton, to the modest 6f all-weather winner Comrade Cotton (both by Royal Applause), the fairly useful 6f winner Cyclone Connie (by Dr Devious), the quite useful 7f (at two years) and 12f winner Lola Sapola (by Benny The Dip), the modest two year old 7f seller winner Inch Pincher (by Inchinor) and the moderate all-weather 8.6f to 11f winner Lake Diva (by Docksider). The dam, a fair 7f winner at three years, is a half-sister to the dual listed winner Polka Dancer. The second dam, Pretty Pol (by Final Straw), won the Group 3 10f Premio Carlo Porta and is a half-sister to the smart 1m to 10f colt Wylfa.
'Small and very strong, she moves well and will start faster work in May. She looks the part and will be an out-and-out five furlong horse.'

209. LADY MASTER ★★★
b.f. Kheleyf – Syzygy (Entrepreneur)
March 3. First foal. 6,000Y. Doncaster Festival. The dam is an unraced half-sister to one winner. The second dam, Theano (by Thatching), won four races at 3 and four years, was third in two Group 3 events in Ireland and is a half-sister to three winners. (Fighttheban Partnership VI).
'A sharp filly, she'll be doing some faster work in April and she's strong. A good mover, she'll be suited by five furlongs.'

HENRY CECIL
210. APPLE CHARLOTTE ★★★
b.f. Royal Applause – Maid Of Camelot (Caerleon)
March 13. Sixth foal. 82,000Y. Tattersalls October 1. De La Warr Racing. Half-sister to Arthur's Girl (by Hernando), unplaced in her only

start at two years in 2007 and to the fair two year old 7f all-weather winner Messiah Garvey (by Lear Fan). The dam was a useful winner of the listed 10f Lupe Stakes and is a half-sister to two winners. The second dam, Waterfowl Creek (by Be My Guest), a quite useful three year old dual 1m winner, is a full or half-sister to seven winners including the very useful Inchmurrin (a winner of six races including the Group 2 Child Stakes and herself dam of the very smart colt Inchinor) and the two year old Group 2 6f Mill Reef Stakes winner Welney. (De La Warr Racing).
'An active filly.'

211. AT A GREAT RATE (USA) ★★★
b.f. Arch – Glia (A P Indy)
April 5. The dam won the listed Prix Imprudence and a minor stakes event in the USA and was second in the Grade 2 Revere Stakes and the Group 2 Prix Miesque. She is a sister to the US triple Grade 3 winner Snake Mountain, closely related to the Group 3 Prix de Cabourg winner Loving Kindness and a half-sister to the Group 1 Prix Marcel Boussac winner Denebola and to the dam of the 'Arc' winner Bago. The second dam, Coup de Genie (by Mr Prospector), won the Group 1 6f Prix Morny and the Group 1 7f Prix de la Salamandre winner and is a sister to the champion two year old and top-class sire Machiavellian and a half-sister to the high-class miler Exit To Nowhere. (Exors of the late Stavros Niarchos).
'This is a nice filly and she should make a two-year-old.'

212. BOUVARDIA ★★★
b.f. Oasis Dream – Arabesque (Zafonic)
March 19. Fourth foal. Half-sister to Sligo (by Sadler's Wells), unplaced in two starts in Ireland at two years in 2007 and to the smart listed 6f winner Camacho (by Danehill). The dam, a useful listed 6f winner, is a sister to two winners including the useful 5f and 6f winner Threat. The second dam, Prophecy (by Warning), was a very useful winner of the Group 1 6f Cheveley Park Stakes and was second in the Group 3 7f Nell Gwyn Stakes. (Khalid Abdulla).
'A nice filly that will make a two-year-old later on.'

213. BRIEF LOOK ★★★
b.f. Sadler's Wells – Half Glance (Danehill)
February 16. The dam won three races including the two year old Group 3 1m May Hill Stakes and is a half-sister to the Irish Derby, St Leger and Turf Classic placed Tycoon. The second dam, Fleeting Glimpse (by Rainbow Quest), a 10f winner in France, was second in the Group 1 10f Prix Saint-Alary and is a half-sister to the 1,000 Guineas winner Wince (herself dam of the Group 1 Yorkshire Oaks winner Quiff). (K Abdulla).
'This is a nice filly and worth mentioning, but she needs time.'

214. CLOUDY START ★★★
b.c. Oasis Dream – Set Fair (Alleged)
March 10. Half-brother to the very useful listed 7f (at two years) and listed 11.4f Cheshire Oaks winner Valentine Girl (by Alzao), to the fairly useful 12.3f winner Solitary (by Sanglamore) and a minor winner in Germany by Polish Precedent. The dam, a French 10f winner, is a sister to the smart Group 2 winning stayer Non Partisan and a half-sister to the Grade 3 Canadian stakes winner Jalaajel and the useful dual two year old 7f winner and Group 3 Prix d'Aumale third Suntrap (herself dam of the Group/Grade 1 winners Raintrap and Sunshack). The second dam, Sunny Bay (by Northern Bay), won 3 stakes events in the USA and was second in the Grade 1 Sorority Stakes. (Khalid Abdulla).
'A likeable filly.'

215. CONCIOUSNESS ★★
ch.f. Pivotal – Sacred Song (Diesis)
March 4. Half-sister to the Group 2 10f Prix Guillaume d'Ornano winner Multidimensional (by Danehill). The dam won four races from 6f (at two years) to 12f including the Group 3 Princess Royal Stakes and the Group 3 Lancashire Oaks and is a half-sister to the dual Canadian Grade 2 winner Strut The Stage. The second dam, Ruby Ransom (by Red Ransom), won over 1m in Canada and is a half-sister to the Grade 1 Breeders Cup Turf winner Chief Bearheart. (Exors of the late S S Niarchos).
'A small filly out of a mare that I like.'

216. DOGGERBANK (IRE) ★★★
b.f. Oasis Dream – Discreet Brief (Darshaan)
April 15. Second foal. 95,000Y. Tattersalls October 1. Not sold. The dam won the Group 3 Park Hill Stakes, was Group 3 placed in Italy and is a half-sister to two winners. The second dam, Quiet Counsel (by Law Society), won once at three years and is a half-sister to seven winners including the Group 1 Yorkshire Oaks winner Key Change. (Mr G Schoeningh).
'This filly needs a bit of time but she could be alright.'

217. FATHER TIME ★★★★★
b.c. Dansili – Clepsydra (Sadler's Wells)
January 28. Fifth foal. Brother to the Group 1 10f Criterium de Saint-Cloud (at two years) and Group 3 10.3f Musidora Stakes winner Passage Of Time (by Dansili) and half-brother to the fairly useful 10f winner Sandglass (by Zafonic). The dam, a quite useful 12f winner, is a half-sister to several winners including the useful listed 10.5f winner Double Crossed. The second dam, Quandary (by Blushing Groom), a useful winner of four races from 9f to 10f including the listed James Seymour Stakes at Newmarket, is a half-sister to the Group 1 Prix du Moulin winner All At Sea. (Khalid Abdulla).
'An attractive colt, a good mover and very likeable. He could have a touch of class.'

218. HALLINGDAL BLUE (UAE) ★★★
b.f. Halling – Blue Melody (Dayjur)
March 11. 16,000Y. Tattersalls October. Mallalieu Bloodstock. The dam, a useful two year old 5f winner Blue Melody, is closely related to the smart Group 1 6f Middle Park Stakes and Group 2 7f Challenge Stakes winner Zieten and the Group 1 6f Cheveley Park Stakes and Group 3 5f Queen Mary Stakes winner Blue Duster. The second dam, Blue Note (by Danzig), won five races from 5f to 7f in France including the Group 2 Prix Maurice de Gheest and the Group 3 Prix de le Porte Maillot. (The Sticky Wicket Syndicate II).
'A fine-looking filly, she just needs a bit of time.'

219. HONEST QUALITY (USA) ★★★
b.f. Elusive Quality – Honest Lady (Seattle Slew)
January 26. Half-sister to the US winner and dual Grade 1 placed First Defence (by Unbridled's Song), to the French listed 1m winner and listed-placed Phantom Rose (by Danzig) and the French two year old 5f winner Documentary (by Storm Cat). The dam, winner of the Grade 1 Santa Monica Handicap, is a half-sister to the US triple Grade 1 winner Empire Maker and the Grade 1 Arlington Million winner Chester House. The second dam, Toussaud (by El Gran Senor), a 6f and 7f winner here, subsequently won a Grade 1 in North America. (K Abdulla).
'A nice filly, she could make a two year old.'

220. KING'S TROOP ★★★
ch.c. Bertolini – Glorious Colours (Spectrum)
April 5. Third foal. 25,000Y. Tattersalls October 2. Highflyer Bloodstock. Half-brother to the unraced 200 two year old Royal Soverin (by Royal Applause). The dam, a modest 1m placed maiden, is a half-sister to four winners including the high-class 7f to 11f winner Hawksley Hill. The second dam, Gaijin (by Caerleon), a useful two year old 6f winner, is a full or half-sister to five winners including Thousla Rock, winner of the Group 3 Premio Umbria. (W H Ponsonby).
'A racey colt that should make a two year old.'

221. MAYOLYNN (USA) ★★★ ♠
ch.f. Johannesburg – Civilynn (Lost Code)
March 13. Fourth foal. $250,000Y. Keeneland September. James Delahooke. Half-sister to a minor US winner by Banker's Gold. The dam won at two years in the USA and was Grade 3 placed and is a half-sister to seven winners including the dam of the two year old dual Group 2 winner Flashy Wings). The second dam, Civility (by Shirley Heights), a very useful 12f winner, is a half-sister to four winners including the smart two year old Piney Ridge. (B Scott).
'A good mover, she needs to furnish.'

222. MIDDAY ★★★
b.f. Oasis Dream – Midsummer (Kingmambo)
March 21. Second foal. Half-sister to the unraced 2007 two year old Spring Season (by Dansili). The dam, a quite useful 11f winner and listed-placed over 12f, is a half-sister to numerous winners including the Oaks and Fillies Mile winner Reams of Verse, the Eclipse Stakes and Phoenix Champion Stakes winner Elmaamul. The second dam, Modena (by Roberto), is an unraced half-sister to the smart two year old 7f winner and Queen Elizabeth II Stakes third Zaizafon. herself the dam of Zafonic. (Khalid Abdulla).
'A nice filly from a family I know well.'

223. ON OUR WAY ★★★
b.c. Oasis Dream – Singed (Zamindar)
February 6. Second foal. 55,000Y. Tattersalls October 1. Henry Cecil. Half-brother to the unplaced 2007 two year old Egregius Max (by Royal Applause). The dam won once at around 1m in France and is a half-sister to the French listed winner and Group 3 placed Inhabitant. The second dam, Infringe (by Warning), won once at three years in France and is a half-sister to seven winners including the Group three winners Ecologist, Green Reef and Infrasonic. (J R May).
'A tall colt and a good mover that needs time.'

224. RARE VIRTUE (USA) ★★★
b.f. Empire Maker – Heat Haze (Green Desert)
February 10. The dam, winner of the Grade 1 Matriarch Stakes and the Grade 1 Beverly D Stakes, is closely related to the Coronation Stakes, Prix Jacques Le Marois and Breeders Cup Filly & Mare Turf winner Banks Hill, to the Grade 1 Matriarch Stakes winner Intercontinental, the US dual Grade 1 winner Cacique and the French Group 2 1m winners Dansili and Champs Elysees. The second dam, Hasili (by Kahyasi), won over 5f at two years and stayed a mile. (Khalid Abdulla).
'She's very nice but like all the family she'll need time. A very good mover with plenty of scope.'

225. ROSE MAYLIE (USA) ★★★
b.br.f. Grand Slam – Katherine Seymour (Green Desert)
February 7. Second foal. $140,000Y. Keeneland September. Anthony Stroud. The dam, a very

useful two year old 7f winner and third in the Group 2 7f Rockfel Stakes, is a half-sister to two winners. The second dam, Sudeley (by Dancing Brave), a modest 11.5f winner, is a half-sister to the high-class middle-distance colts Peacetime and Quiet Fling, to the Cambridgeshire winner Intermission (herself dam of the good sprinter Interval) and to the dams of the Group/Graded stakes winners Wandesta, De Quest and Flaming Torch. (Mark & Sue Harniman).
'A nice filly.'

226. TIANTAI (USA) ★★★★★

b.br.c. Storm Cat – Coup de Genie
(Mr Prospector)
April 21. Brother to the Group 1 Prix Marcel Boussac winner and Group 1 7f Prix de la Foret second Denebola and half-brother to the listed Prix Imprudence and minor US stakes winner and Grade 2/Group 2 second Glia, the US triple Grade 3 winner Snake Mountain (both by A P Indy), the Group 3 Prix de Cabourg winner Loving Kindness (by Seattle Slew) and to the dam of the 'Arc' winner Bago. The dam was a smart winner of the Group 1 6f Prix Morny and the Group 1 7f Prix de la Salamandre and was third in the 1,000 Guineas. She is a sister to the champion two year old Machiavellian and a half-sister to the high-class miler Exit To Nowhere, the smart miler Hydro Calido and the unraced dam of the Grand Criterium winner Way Of Light. The second dam, Coup de Folie (by Halo), won the Group 3 1m Prix d'Aumale at two years and is out of an unraced half-sister to Northern Dancer. (Exors of the late Stavros Niarchos).
'A nice colt that should make a two year old.'

227. TINAR (USA) ★★★★

b.f. Giant's Causeway – Seattle Tac (Seattle Slew)
April 27. First foal. $400,000Y. Keeneland September. McKeever St Lawrence. The dam, a minor US winner at two and three years, is a half-sister to the champion two year old colt One Cool Cat. The second dam, Tacha (by Mr Prospector), a minor US three year old winner, is a sister to the US Grade 2 winner and French 1,000 Guineas second Sha Tha. (F Nass).
'This is a nice filly. I like her, but she needs time.'

228. TOMINTOUL STAR ★★

gr.f. Dansili – Lixian (Linamix)
February 8. First foal. 26,000Y. Tattersalls December. Henry Cecil. The dam, placed at two and three years in France, is out of the useful 11.6f and 12f winner and Group 3 12f Princess Royal Stakes second New Abbey (by Sadler's Wells), herself a half-sister to the Irish Oaks winner and good broodmare Wemyss Bight. (Angus Dundee Distillers plc).
'A nice filly that needs time.'

229. UNWAVERING (IRE) ★★★

b.c. Refuse To Bend – Archipova
(Ela-Mana-Mou)
May 9. Half-brother to the smart triple Group 3 winner at 1m and 9f Autumn Glory (by Charnwood Forest), to the quite useful 10f all-weather winner Rose Street (by Noverre) and the fair two year old 1m winner Oddsmaker (by Barathea). The dam won twice at up to 15f at four years in Italy and is a half-sister to four winners including the useful 10.2f winner and Group 2 12.5f Prix de Royallieu third Abyaan. The second dam, Anna Comnena (by Shareef Dancer), a fair 10f placed three year old, is a sister to the useful middle-distance winner Atlaal and a half-sister to the German Group 3 winner Anno Luce and to the dams of the Group winners Annus Mirabilis, Anna of Saxony, Annaba and Pozarica. (Mr J McKeon).
'A nice mover but a big colt that will need time.'

230. WEMYSS BAY ★★★

b.f. Sadler's Wells – Wemyss Bight
(Dancing Brave)
February 19. Sister to the 1m (at two years) and Group 1 10f Grand Prix de Paris winner Beat Hollow and to the quite useful 10f winner Ancient Culture and half-sister to the useful 10f winner Yaralino (by Caerleon). The dam, a very smart filly, won five races including a maiden race over 9f (at two years), the Group 1 12f Irish Oaks, the Group 2 12f Prix de Malleret, the Group 3 10.5f Prix Cleopatre and the Group 3 10.5f Prix Penelope. The second dam, Bahamian (by Mill Reef), a very useful winner of the Group 3 Lingfield Oaks Trial and placed in the Prix de

l'Esperance (disqualified from first place), the Prix de Pomone, the Park Hill Stakes and the Princess Royal Stakes. (K Abdulla).
'A nice filly that needs time.'

231. WINGWALKER ★★★★
b.c. Dansili – Emplane (Irish River)
February 5. Brother to the two year old Group 3 7f Prix la Rochette winner and Group 1 placed Early March (by Dansili) and half-brother to the fairly useful French 10f winner Itinerary (by Dr Fong), the quite useful 7f winner Painted Sky (by Rainbow Quest) and the minor French 11f winner Coach Lane (by Barathea). The dam, a useful three year old 1m winner, is a sister to the useful two year old 1m winner Boatman and a half-sister to the quite useful two year old 7f winner Palisade. The second dam, Peplum (by Nijinsky), a useful winner of the listed 11.3f Cheshire Oaks, is a half-sister to the top class filly Al Bahathri, winner of the 1,000 Guineas and the Coronation Stakes. (K Abdulla).
'A very nice colt and a good mover.'

232. YOUNG STAR GAZER ★★★
ch.c. Observatory – Ash Glade (Nashwan)
May 8. Ninth foal. 24,000Y. Tattersalls October 4. Henry Cecil. Brother to a two year old winner in Greece and half-brother to the quite useful 5f and 6f winner of nine races Magic Glade (by Magic Ring), to a hurdles winner by Zilzal and a winner in Greece by Inchinor. The dam is an unraced half-sister to five winners including the 1,000 Guineas and Group 3 Fred Darling Stakes winner Wince. The second dam, Flit (by Lyphard), a fair three year old 10f winner, is a sister to Skimble (dam of the US Grade 1 winner Skimming) and closely related to the Grade 1 Washington Lassie Stakes winner Contredance. (Pkd Partnership).
'A very nice mover, he's slightly backward and immature.'

233. ZA ZA ★★★
br.f. Barathea – Madiyla (Darshaan)
April 17. Half-sister to the fair 2007 1m placed two year old Burn The Breeze (by Barathea), to the French listed winner and Group 2 1m Prix

de Sandringham second Lethals Lady (by Rudimentary), to the fairly useful two year old 7f winner Giving (by Generous), the quite useful 12f winner Silver City (by Unfuwain) and a minor winner in France and the USA by Ezzoud. The dam, a fair 12f winner, is a half-sister to six winners including the two year old Group 1 National Stakes winner Manntari. The second dam, Manntika (by Kalamoun), a fair 10f winner in Ireland, is a half-sister to the dam of the Group 3 Prix La Rochette winner Fine Fellow. (Bloomsbury Stud).
'A nice filly, she's done very well and could make a two year old later on.'

234. UNNAMED ★★★
b.c. Xaar – Darabela (Desert King)
January 25. First foal. The dam, an Irish three year old 7f winner, is a half-sister to the smart Group 2 Goodwood Cup winner Darasim. The second dam, Dararita (by Halo), a winner in France over 12.5f at three years, is a half-sister to the Group 2 12.5f Prix Maurice de Neiuil winner Darazari, the listed 10.5f and 12f winner Dariyoun, the smart King Edward VII Stakes second Kilimanjaro and the two year old 8.2f winner and French Derby third Rhagaas.
'An active colt that should make a two year old.'

235. UNNAMED ★★★
b.br.f. Storm Cat – Rafina (Mr Prospector)
April 22. Sister to the Irish two year old 7f winner and Group 3 Acomb Stakes third Lucifer Sam and half-sister to the two year old Group 2 1m Royal Lodge Stakes winner and Group 3 10.3f Dee Stakes winner Admiralofthefleet (by Danehill), the useful two year old 8.5f winner Canberra and the minor French 14f winner Gallo's Wells (both by Sadler's Wells). The dam was placed three times in France and is a sister to the champion European two year old Machiavellian and to the smart Group 1 Prix Morny and Group 1 Prix de la Salamandre winner Coup de Genie, closely related to the Group 2 1m Prix d'Astarte winner Hydro Calido and a half-sister to the Group 1 Prix Jacques le Marois winner Exit to Nowhere. The second dam, Coup de Folie (by Halo), won four races

from 6f to 10f including the Group 3 1m Prix d'Aumale and was stakes placed in the USA. (Tabor/Magnier/ Niarchos).
'A backward filly that needs time.'

236. UNNAMED ★★★★
ch.f. Dalakhani – Slap Shot (Lycius)
January 17. First foal. 150,000Y. Tattersalls October 1. C de Moubray. The dam won six races in Italy including the Group 3 Gran Premio Citta di Napoli and was second in the Group 1 5f Prix de l'Abbaye and is a half-sister to two winners in Turkey. The second dam, Katanning (by Green Desert), is a placed half-sister to one winner. (Ammerland Verwaltung Gmbh & Co.KG).
'Very active and likeable, he should make a two year old in the second half of the season.'

237. UNNAMED ★★★★
b.c. Bahri – Woodren (Woodman)
February 7. Fifth foal. 35,000Y. Tattersalls October 3. Guy Stephenson. Half-brother to the Swedish winner of nine races from three to five years Wings Of A Dove (by Hernando). The dam, a 2m winner in Ireland, is a half-sister to five winners including the UAE stakes winner Resplendent Star. The second dam, Whitethroat (by Artaius), is an unplaced half-sister to the French Derby winners Assert and Bikala and to the Irish St Leger winner Eurobird. (G Stephenson).
'A nice colt, he's a good mover with plenty of size and scope.'

MICK CHANNON
238. ARABIAN FLAME (IRE) ★★★★
b.c. King's Best – Frappe (Inchinor)
February 26. Sixth foal. 58,000Y. Tattersalls October 2. Gill Richardson. Half-brother to the quite useful 2007 two year old 7f all-weather winner Applauded (by Royal Applause), to the 7f (at two years) and Group 2 12f Ribblesdale Stakes winner Thakafaat (by Unfuwain) and the fairly useful 10f winner Quantum (by Alhaarth). The dam, a fairly useful two year old 6f winner, is a half-sister to the 2,000 Guineas winner Footstepsinthesand. The second dam, Glatisant (by Rainbow Quest), winner of the Group 3 7f Prestige Stakes, is a half-sister to eight winners and to the placed dam of the very smart two year old Superstar Leo. (Jaber Abdullah).
'A nice King's Best colt, he's one for the middle of the season onwards. He's just cantering at the moment so I don't know an awful lot about him, but he's a lovely colt.'

239. BAROOD (IRE) ★★★
b.c. Xaar – Radiant Energy (Spectrum)
February 25. Second foal. 22,000Y. Tattersalls October 3. Gill Richardson. Half-brother to Solaria (by Desert Prince), placed in a seller on her only start at two years. The dam, a 1m winner at three years, is a half-sister to five winners. The second dam, Blaine (by Lyphard's Wish), is a placed half-sister to seven winners including the dam of the dual Group 1 winner Croco Rouge. (Jaber Abdullah).
'A nice, big, strong horse. We won't be hanging about with him, he's quite forward and although he doesn't seem to be one of our nicest two year old's he'll be alright.'

240. CANWINN (IRE) ★★★★
b.c. Refuse To Bend – Born To Glamour (Ajdal)
March 9. Tenth foal. 90,000Y. Tattersalls October 2. Gill Richardson. Half-brother to the 2007 Irish two year old 5.8f winner Lady Meagan (by Val Royal), the useful two year old 5f winner and Group 2 6f Gimcrack Stakes second Sailing Shoes (by Lahib), the fairly useful Irish 10f winner Tarbaan, the Italian three year old winner Dazzeling Dawn (both by Nashwan), the quite useful two year old 6f winner Encanto (by Bahhare), the Irish two year old 7f and subsequent US winner Hot Trotter (by Halling) and the quite useful 6f and 7f winner Pawan (by Cadeaux Genereux). The dam, a winner over 6f in Ireland at two years, is a half-sister to eight winners including the French listed winner North Haneena. The second dam, the French winner Haneena (by Habitat), was fourth in the Cheveley Park Stakes and is a half-sister to six winners including the Jersey Stakes winner Gwent. (Sheikh Ahmed Al Maktoum).

'A lovely colt, he'll be a six furlong two year old to start with before stepping up in distance.'

241. CONAKRY ★★★
ch.c. Imperial Dancer – Ajig Dancer (Niniski)
February 17. Sixth foal. 15,000Y. Doncaster Festival. Gill Richardson. Half-brother to the fairly useful 2007 two year old 5f winner and Group 2 Norfolk Stakes fourth Silver Guest (by Lujain), to the very useful two year old 5f and German Group 2 6f winner Ajigolo (by Piccolo) and the fairly useful two year old dual 5f winner and listed-placed Indiannie Star (both by Fraam). The dam, a quite useful 7f winner of four races, is a half-sister to two winners. The second dam, Gloire (by Thatching), is an unraced sister to the smart sprinter Puissance, winner of the Group 3 Greenlands Stakes. (Capital).
'A smashing little horse, everything out of the family wins and he'll be no different. He's not very big and hence we got him quite cheap. He'll be running by the end of April.'

242. DAANAAT (IRE) ★★★★
b.f. Kheleyf – Belle Argentine (Fijar Tango)
May 2. Eighth foal. Half-sister to the smart two year old Group 3 5f Cornwallis Stakes winner Alzerra (by Pivotal), to the useful three year old 6f and 7f winner and Group 3 7f Solario Stakes third Matloob (by Halling) and the quite useful three year old 1m winner Saaryeh (by Royal Academy). The dam won the listed 1m Prix La Camargo in France, was third in the French 1,000 Guineas and fourth in the 10.5f Prix de Diane. The second dam, Jarlina (by Pharly), is an unraced half-sister to the Group 2 Prix d'Harcourt winner Lovely Dancer. (Sheikh Ahmed Al-Maktoum).
'Not very big, I trained the half-sister Alzerra and this filly looks quite sharp. A five furlong type, we'll get on with her and it won't be long before she's out.'

243. DANIDH DUBAI (IRE) ★★★★
b.f. Noverre – Dani Ridge (Indian Ridge)
March 28. Second foal. €28,000Y. Tattersalls Ireland. Gill Richardson. Half-sister to the modest 2008 two year old 6f winner Ridge Wood Dani (by Invincible Spirit). The dam, a

quite useful triple 6f winner, is a sister to the Group 3 Diomed Stakes winner Blomberg. The second dam, Daniella Drive (by Shelter Half), won 12 minor races at two to five years in the USA. (Jaber Abdullah).
' A very nice filly, she'll be racing in May and then we'll see if she's good enough for Ascot. I like her.'

244. DUBAI GEM ★★★
b.f. Fantastic Light – Reflectance (Sadler's Wells)
January 25. First foal. 30,000Y. Tattersalls October 2. Gill Richardson. The dam ran once unplaced and is a half-sister to one minor winner. The second dam, Spain Lane (by Seeking The Gold), a smart French sprinter, won the Group 2 Prix du Gros Chene and the Group 3 Prix de Seine-et-Oise and is closely related to the very smart US Grade 1 9f and 10f winner Marquetry and a half-sister to six winners. (Jaber Abdullah).
'A lovely horse but she's going to need time and won't be seen out until around Goodwood time. She's quite mature in as much as she's not weak and backward, so she'll definitely make a two year old later on.'

245. DUBAI'S GAZAL ★★★★
b.f. Fraam – Dakhla Oasis (Night Shift)
January 5. The dam, winner of the Group 2 German 1,000 Guineas, is a sister to two winners including the Group 3 6f Prix de Seine-et-Oise and German Group 3 6f Benazet-Rennen winner Dyhim Diamond and a half-sister to the US two year old Grade 1 8.5f Starlet Stakes winner Creaking Board (herself dam of the US Grade 3 winner Crowd Pleaser). The second dam, Happy Landing (by Homing), was placed twice in France at three years and is a half-sister to four minor winners. (Jaber Abdullah).
'Very nice, she's a little bit backward in her coat but I think she's a really nice filly and she could be anything.'

246. DUNES QUEEN (USA) ★★★★★
b.f. Elusive Quality – Queen's Logic
(Grand Lodge)
January 1. Half-sister to the quite useful two year old 1m winner Go On Be A Tiger (by Machiavellian). The dam, a champion two year

old filly and winner of the Group 1 6f Cheveley Park Stakes and the Group 2 6f Lowther Stakes, is a half-sister to the top-class multiple Group 1 winner Dylan Thomas. The second dam, Lagrion (by Diesis), was placed five times in Ireland and stayed 12f and is a full or half-sister to three winners. (Jaber Abdullah).

'She could win the Guineas this year if I wanted her to! A smashing, big filly, she's got everything going for her. A filly with size and scope, she's very nice.'

247. FANTASTIC DUBAI (USA) ★★★★
b.c. Storm Cat – Shy Lady (Kaldoun)
May 4. Sixth foal. $400,000Y. Keeneland September. Charlie Gordon-Watson. Half-brother to the high-class Group 1 1m St James's Palace Stakes and Group 2 6f Mill Reef Stakes winner Zafeen (by Zafonic) and to the useful two year old Group 3 7f Prix du Calvados winner Ya Hajar (by Lycius). The dam, winner of a listed event over 6f in Germany, was fourth in the Group 2 6f Moet and Chandon Rennen and is a half-sister to four winners. The second dam, the minor French three year old winner Shy Danceuse (by Groom Dancer), is a half-sister to the dual Group 3 winner Diffident. (Jaber Abdullah).

'I've had all the half-brothers and sisters and it's a great family. He needs a bit more time than the others, but he's a May foal and he'll be OK later on.'

248. IMPERIAL HOUSE ★★★
b.c. Imperial Dancer – Cotton House (Mujadil)
February 24. Third foal. 45,000Y. Tattersalls October 2. Gill Richardson. Half-brother to the fair 2007 6f placed two year old Cotton Reel (by Cape Cross). The dam, a useful listed sprint winner of five races and fourth in the Group 2 Temple Stakes, is a half-sister to two winners. The second dam, Romanovna (by Mummy's Pet), is an unplaced half-sister to three minor winners here and abroad. (Mohammed Jaber).

'A big, strong colt, I don't think he'll be early and he's likely to be ready in mid season. I'll wait for six furlongs with him and he's got a bit of size and scope about him.'

249. INTHAWAIN ★★★
br.f. Bertolini – Ambassadress (Alleged)
March 2. Seventh foal. €25,000Y. Goffs Million. Gill Richardson. Half-sister to the Italian winner of ten races Golden Lagoon (by Lahib) and to three other minor winners abroad by Shareef Dancer, Efisio and Polar Falcon. The dam is an unraced half-sister to six winners including Rami (Group 3 Concorde Stakes), Crack Regiment (Group 3 Prix Eclipse) and La Grand Epoque (second in the Group 1 Prix de l'Abbaye). The second dam, Ancient Regime (by Olden Times), won the Group 1 Prix Morny and is a sister to the Prix Maurice de Gheest winner Cricket Ball. (Jaber Abdullah).

'A nice filly, she's just going to need a bit of time and I haven't really asked anything serious of her, but she goes nicely.'

250. KARRIAKOU (IRE) ★★★★
b.f. Cape Cross – Karri Valley (Storm Bird)
April 8. Thirteenth foal. €90,000Y. Goffs Million. Gill Richardson. Half-sister to the fairly useful 1m winner Kamari, to the Irish listed winner and Irish Derby fourth Campo Catino, the minor French five year old winner Taglioni (all by Woodman), the smart hurdler Giacomo (by Indian Ridge), the fairly useful Irish 12f winner Trebizond (by Sadler's Wells) and the fair Irish two year old 1m winner Grand Corniche (by Machiavellian). The dam, unplaced in one start, is closely related to the two year old Group 1 1m National Stakes winner Fatherland. The second dam, Lisadell (by Forli), won the Coronation Stakes and the Athasi Stakes and is a half-sister to Thatch and to the dam of Nureyev. (Mr Nigel Bunter).

'A very nice filly, but she's a Cape Cross that's going to need seven furlongs or a mile. A great mover, I like her.'

251. KESSRAA (IRE) ★★★★
b.c. Kheleyf – Safe Care (Caerleon)
March 10. Fifth foal. €150,000Y. Goffs Million. John Ferguson. Half-brother to the fair 2007 two year old 7f winner Dhhamaan (by Dilshaan). The dam is an unraced sister to seven winners including the dual Group 3 winning sprinter

Lugana Beach. The second dam, Safe Haven (by Blakeney), is an unplaced half-sister to 1five winners, notably Mtoto. (Sheikh Ahmed Al Maktoum).

'He's a nice, big, strong horse. The sire is definitely going to be alright. he has some very nice two year old's.'

252. LA CRÈME (IRE) ★★★

b.f. Clodovil – Dawiyda (Ashkalani)
May 3. First foal. €100,000Y. Goffs Million. Gill Richardson. The dam is an unraced half-sister to five winners. The second dam, Dawala (by Lashkari), a minor winner in France over 12f, is closely related to the top-class French Derby winner Darshaan and a half-sister to numerous winners including the top-class Prix Vermeille winner Darara and the Prix de Royallieu winner Dalara. (G & J Smith).

'A lovely big filly with plenty of size and scope. She's shows a bit already, she's definitely a two year old and although she's a first foal she doesn't look it. She's got something about her and she'll be even better once she gets a bit of sun on her back – like a lot of them will.'

253. LA DIANA (USA) ★★★

gr.f. Johannesburg – La Samanna (Trempolino)
March 24. Fifth foal. 36,000Y. Tattersalls October 2. Gill Richardson. Half-sister to the US stakes-placed two year old winner Madison Dollie (by Forest Wildcat). The dam, a minor winner at three and four years in the USA, is a half-sister to five winners. The second dam, Jewel Of The Mile (by Spectacular Bid), is an unraced half-sister to five winners.

'I like her, she's a nice filly, a great mover and I'm very pleased with her. I think she's a nice sort of filly.'

254. LADY GENEROUS ★★

b.f. Sakhee – Principessa (Machiavellian)
April 5. First foal. 24,000Y. Tattersalls October 3. G Howson. The dam, a fair 1m (at two years) to 12f placed maiden, is a sister to three winners including the Group 2 6.5f Criterium des 2 Ans and Group 2 5f Prix du Gros-Chene winner and sire Titus Livius and a half-sister to four winners.

The second dam, Party Doll (by Be My Guest), a very useful winner of four races in France including 3 listed events from 5f to 1m, was Group 3 placed twice and is a half-sister to ten winners. (Derek & Jean Clee).

'A sweet filly, but you won't see her until the back-end of the season, probably over seven furlongs.'

255. LAHALEEB (IRE) ★★★

b.f. Redback – Flames (Blushing Flame)
April 28. Fourth foal. 70,000Y. Tattersalls October 2. Hugo Merry. Half-sister to Dawn Storm (by City On A Hill), unplaced in one start at two years in 2007 and to the fairly useful dual 6f (at two years) and listed 1m Masaka Stakes winner Precocious Star (by Bold Fact). The dam is an unraced half-sister to four winners including the listed winner Dance Partner. The second dam, Dancing Debut (by Polar Falcon), is a placed half-sister to four winners. (M Al-Qatami & K Al-Mudhaf).

'She came in quite late but she's going the right way now and she's a very nice filly. A really nice individual, but because she was late in she's still behind the others in her work.'

256. LASSO THE MOON ★★★

b.c. Sadler's Wells – Hotelgenie Dot Com (Selkirk)
January 18. Fourth foal. 180,000Y. Tattersalls October 1. Gill Richardson. Half-brother to the unplaced 2007 two year old Rimrock (by Royal Applause) and to the Group 1 Fillies' Mile and Group 1 Falmouth Stakes winner Simply Perfect (by Danehill). The dam, a 7f winner at two years and second in the Group 1 7f Moyglare Stud Stakes, is a half-sister to four winners including the Moyglare Stud Stakes and the Group 2 6f Lowther Stakes winner Bianca Nera. The second dam, Birch Creek (by Carwhite), was placed five times including when third in the Group 3 1m Premio Royal Mares and is a half-sister to seven winners including the useful Group 3 winning sprinter Great Deeds. (Derek & Jean Clee).

'I trained the dam and of course the half-sister was good too. He's one for the back-end of the year and next season, but he's alright and he's cantering away.'

257. LHASHAN (GB) ★★★
b.f. *Green Desert – Society Lady*
(Mr Prospector)
April 10. Sister to the high-class Group 2 6f Lowther Stakes and Group 3 5f Queen Mary Stakes winner Bint Allayl and to the smart 5f and 6f (at two years) and Group 3 7f Jersey Stakes winner Kheleyf and half-sister to the fairly useful two year old 6f winner and listed-placed Nasmatt (by Danehill), the fairly useful 7f and 1m winner Laa Rayb, the fair UAE 7f and 1m winner Mannjal (both by Storm Cat), the fairly useful two year old 7f winner Wardat Allayl and the fair UAE 1m winner Binsina (both by Mtoto). The dam, a fair 6f and 7f placed two year old, is a sister to a minor winner and a half-sister to several others including the useful French two year old 5.5f winner Kentucky Slew. The second dam, La Voyageuse (by Tentam), won 26 races in Canada where she was a champion filly. (Sheikh Ahmed Al Maktoum).
'Not in the yard by early April.'

258. MANAGUA ★★★★
br.c. *Kaldounevees – Teresa Balbi (Master Willie)*
March 14. Third foal. 50,000Y. Tattersalls October 2. Gill Richardson. Half-brother to the 2007 Italian two year old winner Isoline Royal (by Fantastic Light). The dam, a two year old 1m and subsequent French listed 10f winner, is a half-sister to four winners. The second dam, Pondicherry (by Sir Wimborne), a modest 7f winner, is a full or half-sister to 13 minor winners. (Capital).
'He's a smashing horse. He'll win over five, six, seven furlongs – whatever! Definitely a winner, he's quite forward and seems ready to win a race already.'

259. MESYAAL ★★★
ch.c. *Alhaarth – Rowaasi (Green Desert)*
March 25. The dam, a very useful two year old listed 5f National Stakes winner, is a half-sister to several winners including the fairly useful two year old 5.2f winner Marl. The second dam, Pamela Peach (by Habitat), a half-sister to the Jersey Stakes second Dawson Place, was a sprint winner at four years in the USA. (Sheikh Ahmed Al Maktoum).
'Quite a nice colt, he's done everything I've asked but he's just had a couple of niggles that have set him back. He's doing well now and he's one you'd want to get on with. A nice horse, he goes well and he'll be out around May time.'

260. MOHANAD (IRE) ★★★★
b.c. *Invincible Spirit – Irish Design (Alhaarth)*
April 24. Second foal. 70,000Y. Tattersalls October 2. Gill Richardson. The dam ran once unplaced and is a half-sister to four winners including Idris, a winner of four Group three races in Ireland. The second dam, Idara (by Top Ville), won twice in France and was third in the Group 2 Prix de Pomone. (Sheikh Ahmed Al Maktoum).
'He's got plenty of speed, he seems to do everything right and he'll win. How good he's going to be it's hard to say but time will tell and he is a nice colt.'

261. NOTHING TO WORRY (IRE) ★★★★
b.c. *Noverre – Rahika Rose (Unfuwain)*
April 28. Fifth foal. 20,000Y. Tattersalls October. Gill Richardson. Half-brother to the useful two year old Group 3 7f Superlative Stakes and four year old listed 1m winner and Group 2 placed Kings Point (by Fasliyev) and to the modest dual 7f winner Lordship (by King's Best). The dam won three races over 7f and 1m in Ireland and was third in the listed 7f Athasi Stakes. She is a half-sister to three minor winners out of the two year old 5f winner and Group 3 7f C L Weld Park Stakes second Rahik (by Wassl), herself a half-sister to five winners. (Jaber Abdullah).
'For some reason he was a little bit behind the others but he's going the right way now. Quite a nice little colt, he hasn't grown much but he's a nice horse and hopefully I can get on with him now.'

262. PENINSULA GIRL (IRE) ★★★★★
b.f. *Cape Cross – Rio de Jumeirah*
(Seeking The Gold)
February 16. First foal. 150,000Y. Tattersalls October 1. Gill Richardson. The dam, a quite

useful listed-placed 10f winner, is a half-sister to five winners including the Group 1 Fillies Mile and Group 3 May Hill Stakes winner Teggiano. The second dam, Tegwen (by Nijinsky), a quite useful 10f winner, is a half-sister to four winners. (G & J Smith).

'A very nice filly, she could be anything, she does everything really nicely and I get all the right vibes from her. Five, six or seven furlongs – I don't think it would matter to her. She seems to have plenty of boot and she has a great pedigree to go with it.'

263. PLEASE SING ★★★★

b.f. Royal Applause – Persian Song (Persian Bold)
February 16. Tenth foal. 70,000Y. Tattersalls October 1. R Frisby. Half-sister to the very useful 7f (at two years) to 10f winner and Group 1 National Stakes third Mountain Song, to the fairly useful two year old 6f winner and Group 3 6f Princess Margaret Stakes third Raindancing (both by Tirol), the fairly useful 7f (at two years) and dual 10f winner Barney McCall (by Grand Lodge), the quite useful Irish two year old 1m winner Rock Lily (by Rock Of Gibraltar), the quite useful 1m to 10.3f winner Zandeed (by Inchinor), the fair two year old 6f winner Border Minstral and the fair 10f winner Zagaleta (both by Sri Pekan). The dam is an unplaced sister to the Solario Stakes winner Bold Arrangement (placed in seven Group/ Grade 1 races including the Kentucky Derby). The second dam, Arrangement (by Floribunda), is a placed half-sister to the Cheveley Park Stakes winner Lindsay. (Mrs Ann Black).

'A big filly, she was a bit late coming in but she's going the right way now and she's very nice. I think she'll need six furlongs at least but she's got everything in place and I'm in no rush with her.'

264. PRINCABILITY (IRE) ★★★

b.c. King's Best – Harmonic Sound (Grand Lodge)
March 19. Fourth foal. 60,000Y. Tattersalls October 2. Gill Richardson. The dam is an unraced half-sister to seven winners including the listed winner Army Of Angels and the Group

2 Lowther Stakes second Seraphina. The second dam, Angelic Sounds (by The Noble Player), a minor two year old 5f winner, is a half-sister to six winners including the Group 1 Prix de la Foret winner Mount Abu. (Jon & Julia Aisbitt).

'A lovely horse, we won't see him until Goodwood time but he's done everything right and he'll tell me when he's ready.'

265. PRINT (IRE) ★★★ ♠

b.c. Exceed And Excel – Hariya (Shernazar)
March 17. Second foal. €100,000Y. Goffs Million. John Warren. The dam, a fairly useful Irish 10f winner, is a half-sister to four winners including the US Grade 3 winner Harghar. The second dam, Harouniya (by Siberian Express), won once at three years and is a half-sister to ten winners including the dual Group 1 winning two year old Hittite Glory. (Highclere Thoroughbred Racing).

'A lovely horse but backward and one for later in the year. He's a big horse that needs time.'

266. RAIMOND RIDGE (IRE) ★★

b.br.c. Namid – Jinsiyah (Housebuster)
April 18. Sixth foal. €70,000Y. Goffs Million. Gill Richardson. Closely related to the smart listed 5f and 6f winner of 13 races Indian Maiden (by Indian Ridge) and half-brother to the unplaced 2007 two year old Kingsdalemillenium (by Hawk Wing), the quite useful Irish dual 7f winner Kingsdale Orion (by Intikhab) and the fair 7f and 10.5f winner Neqaawi (by Alhaarth). The dam, a useful two year old 7f winner, is a half-sister to five winners including the fairly useful dual 1m winner Bintalshaati. The second dam, the fair staying maiden Minifah (by Nureyev), is a placed half-sister to the Kentucky Derby winner Winning Colors. (Box 41).

'He's ready to run, he's sharp and although he isn't a star he should win. Five or six furlongs will suit him.'

267. REACTION ★★★

ch.c. Alhaarth – Hawas (Mujtahid)
April 16. Seventh foal. 37,000Y. Tattersalls October 2. John Warren. Half-brother to the

quite useful 2007 Irish 5f placed two year old La Sylvia (by Oasis Dream), to the two year old listed 7f Prix Herod winner and smart hurdler Power Elite (by Linamix) and the fair 1m winner Nans Best (by Rock Of Gibraltar). The dam, a 1m winner at three years in Ireland, is a sister to the listed winner Mutakarrim and a half-sister to five winners including the listed winner Nafisah. The second dam, Alyakkh (by Sadler's Wells), a fair three year old 1m winner, is a full or half-sister to six winners including the Champion Stakes and 2,000 Guineas winner Haafhd. (Highclere Thoroughbred Racing).
'I feel that if I can get on with him he'll be alright but he's had a few niggling problems. We'll have to take our time with him but he'll be OK.'

268. ROYAL MUWASIM ★★★
b.f. Reset – Millitrix (Doyoun)
March 29. Fifth foal. 10,000Y. Tattersalls October 3. Gill Richardson. The dam was placed over 7f (at two years) and 1m and is a half-sister to the Group 3 winner and Group 1 placed Royal Millennium. The second dam, Galatrix (by Be My Guest), won over 1m and is a half-sister to six winners including the dual Group 1 winner Croco Rouge and the outstanding broodmare Alidiva (dam of the Group 1 winners Ali-Royal, Sleepytime and Taipan). (Jaber Abdullah).
'A nice horse this, she looks like she needs a lot of time but actually she's not as backward as she looks. She's done everything alright and come the end of May we might see a different horse.'

269. SILCA MEYDAN (GB) ★★★
b.c. Diktat – Golden Silca (Inchinor)
March 13. Third foal. 20,000Y. Tattersalls October 1. Not sold. Half-brother to the moderate 1m placed two year old Silca Destination (by Dubai Destination). The dam, a smart Group 2 6f Mill Reef Stakes and German Group 2 winner, was second in the Group 1 Coronation Stakes and the Group 1 Irish 1,000 Guineas and is a half-sister to six winners including the smart two year old Group 1 6f Prix Morny winner Silca's Sister and the very useful 5f and 6f winner of ten races (including at two

years) Green Manalishi. The second dam, Silca-Cisa (by Hallgate), a fairly useful dual 5f winner, was listed placed over 5f at four years and is a half-sister to one winner. (Aldridge Racing Partnership).
'A big horse. I've trained most of the family and he won't be real early but when he comes he'll be alright. A big, strong colt.'

270. SILVER GAMES (IRE) ★★★★
gr.f. Verglas – Mise (Indian Ridge)
February 26. Second foal. €70,000Y. Deauville August. Gill Richardson. Half-sister to the 2007 two year old Group 2 6f Lowther Stakes winner Nahoodh (by Clodovil). The dam is an unraced half-sister to five winners including the listed winner Minoa. The second dam, Misbegotten (by Baillamont), a French listed 1m Prix Finlande winner, was second in the Group 2 Prix de l'Opera and is a half-sister to four winners. (Box 41).
'A very nice filly, she's done particularly well and we're just starting to do some more serious work with her. A filly with a bit of size and scope about her, she could be anything and might be really nice.'

271. SKY HIGH KID (IRE) ★★★★
b.c. One Cool Cat – Market Hill (Danehill)
January 17. Second foal. €70,000Y. Goffs Million. Gill Richardson. Half-brother to the unraced 2007 two year old Perikal (by Peintre Celebre). The dam, a modest three year old 6f winner, is a half-sister to the very smart two year old 1m winner and 2,000 Guineas second Tamburlaine. The second dam, Well Bought (by Auction Ring), a poor 7f and 1m placed maiden, is a half-sister to six winners including the Group 2 12f King Edward VII Stakes winner Open Day and the Group 3 1m Prix La Rochette winner River Knight. (Box 41).
'Goes well, he's quite strong and he's a nice horse that's ready to rock 'n' roll. He'll be alright and he should win. We'll start him over five but he'll probably be better over six.'

272. TOO MUCH TROUBLE ★★★
b.c. Barathea – Tentpole (Rainbow Quest)

April 4. Fourth foal. 80,000Y. Tattersalls October 1. Gill Richardson. Half-brother to Tepee (by Halling), a modest fourth over 7f at two years in 2007. The dam, an Irish 14f winner, is a half-sister to three winners. The second dam, Polent (by Polish Precedent), a minor French 13f and 15.5f winner, is a half-sister to six winners including the Oaks winner Snow Bride (herself dam of the Derby, King George and 'Arc' winner Lammtarra). (Jaber Abdullah).
'He's going to be one for later in the year, but for a big horse he's not at all weak. He's definitely going to make a two year old, but later on.'

273. WOHAIDA (IRE) ★★★
b.f. Kheleyf – Cambara (Dancing Brave)
March 11. Half-sister to the fairly useful two year old 7f and 10f winner Dubai On (by Daylami), to the useful 7f (at two years) and 1m winner and Group 3 7f Horris Hill Stakes second Samhari (by Indian Ridge), the quite useful four year old 1m winner Habshan (by Swain) and the UAE 6f winner Afreet (by Kris). The dam was a useful winner of three 1m events at three years and is a half-sister to the good French 6f to 1m winner Pluralisme, the very useful 10f Virginia Stakes winner Singletta, the very useful 11f Grand Prix Prince Rose winner Classic Tale, the useful 1m winners Only and Cambrian and to the 10f winner Ghislaine. herself dam of the high-class miler Markofdistinction. The second dam, Cambretta (by Roberto), won over 9f in Ireland and is a sister to the high-class middle-distance colt Critique. (Sheikh Ahmed Al Maktoum).
'A big filly, but she's not weak or backward and she's quite nice. She won't be early as I haven't done an awful lot with her, but she's OK.'

274. UNNAMED ★★★
b.c. Poliglote – Ciena (Gold Away)
January 30. First foal. 60,000Y. Tattersalls October 1. Gill Richardson. The dam, placed over middle-distances in France, is a half-sister to a listed winner in France. The second dam, Silwana (by Nashwan), a French two year old 1m winner, is a half-sister to seven winners including the French Group 2 winner Silver Fun. (Mr John Livock & Mr M Channon).

'A lovely horse, a great mover and I like him. One for later in the year.'

275. UNNAMED ★★★★
b.f. Dansili – Evening Promise (Aragon)
February 18. Third foal. €145,000Y. Goffs Million. Bobby O'Ryan. Half-sister to the moderate 6f all-weather two year old winner Lovers Kiss (by Night Shift). The dam won seven races from 6f to 1m at two to four years including three Grade 3 events in the USA and the listed Firth Of Clyde Stakes. She is a half-sister to six winners out of Rosy Sunset (by Red Sunset), herself an unplaced half-sister to ten winners including the very smart middle-distance colt Bandari. (Mr Liam Mulryan).
'She's a big, strong filly that reminds me of Silver Touch. She has a lot of ability and she goes real nice. By May time she should be telling us if she's ready.'

276. UNNAMED ★★
b.f. Hawk Wing – Holly Blue (Bluebird)
April 18. Sixth foal. 50,000Y. Tattersalls October 1. Gill Richardson. Half-sister to Blue Jeans (by Royal Applause), a modest 5f and 6f placed two year old here and subsequently a winner in Denmark. The dam, a useful 1m listed winner, is a half-sister to six minor winners. The second dam, Nettle (by Kris), a useful listed 7f winner, is a half-sister to five winners. (Mrs Tania Trant).
'A lovely filly that just needs a bit of sun on her back and she'll probably need seven furlongs anyway.'

277. UNNAMED ★★
br.f. Anabaa – Jubilee Treat
(Seeking The Gold)
February 20. First foal. 60,000Y. Tattersalls October 2. Gill Richardson. The dam, a quite useful 10f winner, is a half-sister to four winners. The second dam, Dance Treat (by Nureyev), won the Group 3 10f La Coupe and the Group 3 10.5f Prix de Flore and is a half-sister to four winners. (Saif Ali & Saeed H Altayer).
'A well grown filly that needs a bit of time and six or seven furlongs.'

278. UNNAMED ★★★
b.c. Chevalier – Kathy Tolfa (Sri Pekan)
April 16. First foal. 50,000Y. Tattersalls October
3. Gill Richardson. The dam is an unraced sister
to the Italian listed winner of ten races Kathy
Pekan and a half-sister to two winners including
the Group 3 5f Premio Omenoni winner of 11
races Kathy College. The second dam, Katy
Guest (by Be My Guest), won at two and three
years in Italy and is a half-sister to three winners.
(Saif Ali & Saeed H Altayer).
'He's nice. When he comes in his coat he'll be
alright because he's quite strong and shows a bit
of dash. A nice horse.'

279. UNNAMED ★★★★
b.c. Cape Cross – Mennetou (Entrepreneur)
February 4. First foal. 175,000Y. Tattersalls
October 1. Gill Richardson. The dam is an
unraced half-sister to five winners including the
Prix de l'Arc de Triomphe winner Carnegie, the
Group 2 10f Prix Guillaume d'Ornano winner
Antisaar and the Group 3 St Simon Stakes
winner Lake Erie. The second dam, Detroit (by
Riverman), won the Prix de l'Arc de Triomphe
and is a half-sister to the Cheveley Park Stakes
winner Durtal.
'He could be anything, I haven't done a lot with
him yet but hope he'll be good enough to go
somewhere nice. He's a smashing individual with
a great temperament that goes real well. One to
follow I expect.'

280. UNNAMED ★★★
b.f. King's Best – Moonlight Wish
(Peintre Celebre)
February 27. Second foal. €45,000Y. Goffs
Million. Gill Richardson. Half-sister to Jonquille
(by Rock Of Gibraltar), unplaced in two starts at
two years in 2007. The dam is an unraced sister
to the Group 1 Prix de Diane second Millionaia
and a half-sister to four winners. The second
dam, Moonlight Dance (by Alysheba), winner of
the Group 1 10f Prix Saint-Alary, is a half-sister
to four winners including the Dante Stakes
winner Claude Monet. (Mrs Maggie Findlay &
Mr M Channon).
'A sweet little filly, she hasn't grown much but I

think she's going to need six or seven furlongs.
She's nice but I can't say a lot more at this stage.'

281. UNNAMED ★★★★
b.c. Danehill Dancer – Mountain Law
(Mountain Cat)
February 9. Second foal. €270,000Y. Goffs
Million. Gill Richardson. The dam is an unraced
half-sister to seven winners including the smart
Group 3 7f Hungerford Stakes winner With
Reason and the useful Group 3 1m Curragh
Futurity Stakes and 7f Sweet Solera Stakes
winner Jural. The second dam, Just Cause (by
Law Society), is an unraced half-sister to five
winners out of the Group 1 Prix Saint-Alary
winner Tootens. (Mrs Maggie Findlay & Mr M
Channon).
'A very nice horse that could be anything. A big
horse with bags of size and scope, he goes well
and we'll see him in May over six furlongs. I'm
very pleased with him.'

282. UNNAMED ★★★★
b.c. Bahamian Bounty – Pascali (Compton Place)
February 25. First foal. €63,000Y. Tattersalls
Ireland. Gill Richardson. The dam, a modest 6f
winner, is a half-sister to two winners. The
second dam, Pass The Rose (by Thatching), is an
unraced half-sister to four winners including the
smart filly Pass The Peace, winner of the Group
1 6f Cheveley Park Stakes and herself dam of
the Group 1 winners Embassy and Tarfshi. (Mrs
Maggie Findlay).
'He's a smashing colt that goes really well. He'll
be ready for winning by May time and he's got
bags of speed. Very nice.'

283. UNNAMED ★★★
b.c. King's Best – Tee Cee (Lion Cavern)
February 25. Fifth foal. 42,000Y. Tattersalls
October 2. Equine Services. Half-brother to the
useful two year old triple 6f winner and listed
placed Yajbill (by Royal Applause), to the quite
useful two year old 7f winner Bold Crusader (by
Cape Cross) and the fair 7f all-weather winner
Fantastic Cee (by Noverre). The dam, a fair three
year old 7f winner, is a half-sister to five winners
including the useful 7f and 1m winner Bishr. The

second dam, Hawayah (by Shareef Dancer), a modest two year old 7f winner, is a half-sister to six winners. (Mr Tim Corby).
'A bit backward but he's a nice colt and like a lot of King's Best horses he's just in need of a bit of time.'

PETER CHAPPLE-HYAM

284. ABULHARITH ★★★
b.c. Medicean – Limuru (Salse)
April 15. Fourth foal. 38,000Y. Tattersalls October 2. Andrew Sime. Half-brother to the modest 2007 7f placed two year old Shanzu (by Kyllachy) and to the fair two year old 10f winner Shimoni (by Mark Of Esteem). The dam is an unraced sister to the US Grade 1 and Italian Group 1 winner Timboroa. The second dam, Kisumu (by Damister), is an unraced half-sister to five winners including the Group 1 winners Efisio and Mountain Bear. (Z A Galadari).
'He's never stopped growing since he came here but he's coming back to the way he was as a yearling now. A big horse, I like him but he's one for August onwards and seven furlongs.'

285. ACADEMY OF WAR (USA) ★★★
b.br.c. Royal Academy – Lover Come Back (Dynaformer)
March 11. First foal. 55,000Y. Tattersalls October 2. Blandford Bloodstock. The dam, placed once at four years in the USA, is a half-sister to two winners including the US stakes winner Shareefa (herself dam of the US Grade 1 winner Vergennes). The second dam, Foolish Beauty (by Foolish Pleasure), won once at two years in the USA and is a half-sister to five winners including the US dual Grade 1 winner Nijinsky's Secret. (Mrs V E Mercer).
'He'll be better at six furlongs than five and the plan would be to get him out in May. He's a horse I like a lot, he has a good action and would want fast ground. I expect he'll get further in time.'

286. AZTEC RULER ★★★★
b.c. Galileo – Guaranda (Acatenango)
January 28. The dam, a fairly useful 10f and 12.3f, was listed-placed and is a half-sister to

two winners. The second dam, Gryada (by Shirley Heights), a fairly useful two year old 7f and 8.3f winner, was third in the Group 3 1m Premio Dormello and is a full or half-sister to four winners. (Plantation Stud).
'He's quite forward for a Galileo, strong and although he's going to want a trip based on his pedigree he's got a lot of speed and I think he'll be out at the July meeting. He's a horse I like a lot and he's one of my picks.'

287. BAARIQ ★★★
b.c. Royal Applause – Second Of May (Lion Cavern)
March 7. First foal. 56,000Y. Tattersalls October 2. Andrew Sime. The dam, a modest three year old 1m winner, is a half-sister to three winners including the Group 3 Brigadier Gerard Stakes winner Take A Bow. The second dam, Giant Nipper (by Nashwan), ran once unplaced and is a half-sister to two winners. (Z A Galadari).
'Quite a big horse and he's going to want a bit of time. I see him wanting seven furlongs, hopefully around the July meeting. He moves well and does everything nicely.'

288. BURNING FLAME ★★★
ch.f. Pivotal – Red Flame (Selkirk)
January 23. Second foal. Sister to the unraced 2007 two year old Singe. The dam is an unplaced half-sister to the useful dual listed 6f winner of five races Falcon Hill. The second dam, Branston Jewel (by Prince Sabo), a fairly useful two year old dual 5f winner, was second in the Group 3 5.5f Prix d'Arenberg and is a half-sister to nine winners including the Group Sandown Mile winner Desert Deer and the very useful and tough mare Branston Abby. (Cheveley Park Stud).
'A filly that's going to take a bit of time but she's doing well now and she comes from a fast family. She's grown a lot recently but she's one that I like and I wouldn't knock her.'

289. CHARGER ★★★★
b.c. Rock Of Gibraltar – Ruthless Rose (Conquistador Cielo)
March 23. Closely related to the Group 1 6f

Cheveley Park Stakes winner Regal Rose and to the Japanese 10f stakes winner Generalist (both by Danehill) and half-brother to the smart 1m (at two years) to 14f winner and St Leger fourth Regal Flush (by Sakhee), the fairly useful two year old 7f winner Society Rose (by Saddlers' Hall), the quite useful 10f winner Regal Velvet (by Halling), the fair two year old 6f winner Delta Downs (by Deputy Minister) and a winner in Japan by Green Desert. The dam ran twice unplaced and is a half-sister to nine winners including the high-class miler Shaadi. The second dam, Unfurled (by Hoist The Flag), won once in the USA. (Cheveley Park Stud).

'His half-brother was fourth in the St Leger last year and he's a colt that looks like taking time. But I don't mind him at all, he's got a great attitude, he's a great mover and he does everything very easily along with the other colts. If I had to pick a couple of colts he'd be one of them. A big colt and 'on the leg' still, he'll probably be starting off at seven furlongs.'

290. COUNTRYWIDE CITY ★★★★
b.c. Elusive City – Handy Station (Desert Style)
April 10. First foal. €36,000Y. Tattersalls Ireland. Allan Bloodlines. The dam is an unplaced half-sister to five winners including the useful sprinter Damalis. The second dam, Art Age (by Artaius), is an unraced half-sister to nine winners. (Countrywide Steel & Tubes Ltd).

'He's not the biggest horse but he's more than useful and he goes really well. He'll be my first two year old runner for sure and hopefully he can win and go on from there. He's good enough to go to Royal Ascot without necessarily being good enough to win but he's a handy little horse that'll run quite a lot. He'll be even better when we step him up to six furlongs.'

291. DIAMOND GIFT (USA) ★★★
ch.f. Johannesburg – Granulette (El Gran Senor)
April 20. Seventh foal. 67,000Y. Tattersalls October 2. Cheveley Park Stud. Half-sister to the US stakes winner Moomtazz (by Rhythm) and to two minor winners in the USA and Canada by Pleasant Tap and Distant View. The dam is an unraced half-sister to three winners.

The second dam, Tuca Tuca (by Miswaki), won seven races in Italy and is a half-sister to three winners. (Cheveley Park Stud).

'She's quite a sharp little thing and I'm just about to start kicking along with her. She's probably had too easy a time because she's quite fat, but everything is fine with her and she should be OK.'

292. EAGLES CALL (USA) ★★★★
ch.c. Johannesburg – Golden Flyer (Machiavellian)
January 20. First foal. 100,000Y. Doncaster St Leger. Peter Chapple-Hyam. The dam is an unraced half-sister to five winners including the Irish Group 3 placed Gee Kel. The second dam, Shir Dar (by Lead On Time), won the US Grade 2 Palomar Handicap and is a half-sister to nine winners. (Sangster Family & Matthew Green).

'He's another one that's quite sharp, he'll be better over six furlongs than five and I'm planning to aim him for Royal Ascot. I think he's more than useful. A very nice horse, I don't think he's quite as good as my Bahamian Bounty two year old Skid Solo but he's not far off.'

293. EXCEPTIONAL ART ★★★★
ch.c. Exceed And Excel – Only In Dreams (Polar Falcon)
March 4. Seventh foal. 40,000Y. Doncaster St Leger. Blandford Bloodstock. Half-brother to the very useful two year old 5f and 6f winner and Group 2 July Stakes second Cape Fear (by Cape Cross) and to the moderate three year old 1m seller winner If I Can Dream (by Brief Truce). The dam, a fair two year old 7f winner, is a half-sister to four other minor winners. The second dam, Dream Baby (by Master Willie), was unplaced on her only start and is a half-sister to nine winners. (M R Green).

'He's coming on really well and has done some bridle work nicely. He just needs to develop more and strengthen up. He'll start off over six furlongs in May, he's more than useful and he goes well.'

294. GIBB RIVER (IRE) ★★★★
ch.c. Mr Greeley – Laurentine (Private Account)
March 16. Seventh foal. 170,000Y. Tattersalls October 1. Blandford Bloodstock. Half-brother

to the useful 12f and jumps winner Goblet Of Fire (by Green Desert) and a minor winner abroad by Red Ransom. The dam, a listed-placed 12f winner in France, is a half-sister to four winners including the Oaks winner Love Divine (herself dam of the St Leger winner Sixties Icon). The second dam, La Sky (by Law Society), a useful 10f winner and second in the Lancashire Oaks, is closely related to the Champion Stakes winner Legal Case. (Favourites Racing Ltd).

'He's a big horse and he does everything really well. He's out of a slightly staying type mare but I could start working him now and he'd probably do well. But I'm going to wait and he'll probably be out around June time over six or seven furlongs. Definitely a horse with plenty of potential.'

295. HYDRANT ★★

b.c. Haafhd – Spring (Sadler's Wells)
May 14. Eleventh living foal. 125,000Y. Tattersalls October 1. John Warren. Half-sister to the smart listed 1m and 10f winner Inglenook (by Cadeaux Genereux), to the fairly useful 10f winner Double Aspect (by Dr Fong), the quite useful 9f winner Puffin (by Pennekamp) and two minor winners abroad by Hector Protector and Cadeaux Genereux. The dam, a very useful winner of three races from 12f to 14f including a Group 3 event in Italy, was placed in several other Group races and is closely related to the top-class colt Pentire, winner of the King George VI and Queen Elizabeth Diamond Stakes and a half-sister to six winners. The second dam, Gull Nook (by Mill Reef), a smart winner of the Group 2 12f Ribblesdale Stakes, is closely related to the Group 3 12f Princess Royal Stakes winner Banket and a half-sister to the Group 3 13.5f Ormonde Stakes winner Mr Pintips. (Highclere Thoroughbred Racing (Admiral Rous)).

'He's a late foal out of a staying family and he's going to want some time. He'll be a staying horse next year but not a slow stayer! He'll start off at seven furlongs this year, he's shown me so far that he's not a complete waste of time and he'll tell us when he's ready.'

296. LIGHT SLEEPER ★★★★

b.c. Kyllachy – Snoozy (Cadeaux Genereux)
March 23. Sixth foal. 45,000Y. Tattersalls October 1. J Fretwell. Half-brother to the quite useful Irish 6f (at 2years) and 1m winner Bermeco (by Dr Fong) and to a winner in Sweden by Inchinor. The dam is an unraced sister to a listed winner abroad. The second dam, Quiet Week-End (by Town And Country), won the listed Chesham Stakes and is a half-sister to seven winners including the Moyglare Sus Stakes winner Lemon Souffle and the Falmouth Stakes and Nassau Stakes winner Caramba. (J C Fretwell).

'He seems to go along nicely and he's coming together pretty well. Everything he does comes easy to him, he'll be along in June or July time and he's a horse I like a lot. He's real nice.'

297. MAXWELL HAWKE ★★★★

br.c. Rock Of Gibraltar – Twice The Ease (Green Desert)
March 31. Fifth foal. 130,000Y. Tattersalls October 1. Blandford Bloodstock. Closely related to the useful 2007 two year old 5f winner Achilles Of Troy (by Danehill Dancer) and half-brother to the quite useful 5f and 6f winner Oranmore Castle (by Giant's Causeway). The dam ran twice unplaced and is a sister to the Irish two year old listed 6f winner Desert Ease and a half-sister to five winners including the triple Group 3 winner Two-Twenty-Two. The second dam, Easy To Copy (by Affirmed), a useful winner of five races from 1m to 12f in Ireland and Italy including the Group 2 Premio Legnano, was subsequently Grade 2 placed in the USA and is a sister to the Irish 1,000 Guineas winner Trusted Partner (dam of the US Grade 1 winner Dress To Thrill). (Comic Strip Heroes).

'He's a really nice horse but he's taking a bit of time to come together even though his brother Achilles Of Troy was very sharp. This horse will want six furlongs and hopefully I'll be able get him ready for May time. He's alright.'

298. MONITOR CLOSELY (IRE) ★★★

b.c. Oasis Dream – Independence (Selkirk)
April 13. Fourth foal. 140,000Y. Tattersalls

October 1. Blandford Bloodstock. Half-brother to the unraced 2007 two year old Stone Of Scone (by Pivotal), to the two year old Group 1 1m Criterium International winner Mount Nelson (by Rock Of Gibraltar) and the quite useful 9.5f winner Off Message (by In The Wings). The dam won four races at three years from 7f to 1m including the Group 2 Sun Chariot Stakes and the Group 3 Matron Stakes and is a half-sister to one winner. The second dam, Yukon Hope (by Forty Niner), a fair maiden, is out of a half-sister to Reference Point. (Mr L J Inman).
A big horse and quite a late foal, he'll want time but he's pulling himself together and he's doing well now. He'll want seven furlongs to start with in mid-summer and he's alright.'

299. NICKY NUTJOB ★★★
b.c. Fasliyev – Natalie Too (Irish River)
February 20. Fourth living foal. 52,000Y. Doncaster St Leger. Blandford Bloodstock. Half-brother to a jumps winner by Theatrical. The dam, a Peruvian Grade 1 winner, is a half-sister to four winners. The second dam, Likely Split (by Little Current), is a placed half-sister to six winners including the very smart French sprinters Ancient Regime (dam of three good sprinters herself) and Cricket Ball and the US stakes winners Mug Punter and Olden. (Comic Strip Heroes).
'He's grown quite a bit but he does everything quite nicely. I'm more than happy with him and he's coming on well. He's going to be a six/ seven furlong horse in mid-season.'

300. QUEEN OF VENUS ★★★
b.f. Kyllachy – Dust (Green Desert)
April 6. Sixth foal. 32,000Y. Doncaster St Leger. Blandford Bloodstock. Half-sister to the quite useful two year old dual 5f winner Princess Sofie (by Efisio) and to the modest 5f all-weather winner Desert Dust (by Vettori). The dam, a modest dual 1m all-weather winner, is a half-sister to four winners. The second dam, Storm Warning (by Tumble Wind), a very smart sprinter, won four races including the Group 3 Premio Omenoni and the listed Scarbrough

Stakes and is a half-sister to seven winners.
'She's just starting to come along a bit, she's start off at six furlongs and everything she does is nice. I couldn't be happier with her.'

301. RAYVIN MAD ★★★★
b.c. Bahamian Bounty – Poppy's Song (Owington)
April 21. Fourth foal. 20,000Y. Tattersalls October 2. C McCormack. Half-brother to the unplaced 2007 two year old Tittle (by Tobougg). The dam, a fair dual 5f winner (including at two years), is a half-sister to nine winners including the top-class Group 1 5f Nunthorpe Stakes winner and sire Kyllachy. The second dam, Pretty Poppy (by Song), a modest two year old 5f winner, stayed 7.6f and is a half-sister to four winners including the Criterium de Maisons-Laffitte winner Corviglia.
'He goes really well actually and both my Bahamian Bounty's are sharp. He's very strong, very mature and he's just started working now. He'll be ready in May and he has plenty of ability.' TRAINER'S BARGAIN BUY

302. RIVALRY ★★★★
ch.f. Medicean – Fearless Revival (Cozzene)
March 30. Thirteenth foal. Half-sister to the high-class Group 1 5f Nunthorpe Stakes winner and sire Pivotal (by Polar Falcon), to the fairly useful dual 1m winner Brave Revival (by Dancing Brave) and the fairly useful 10f winner Revival (by Sadler's Wells). The dam, a useful winner two year old 6f and 7f winner and second in the Group 3 Rockfel Stakes, was listed placed over 10f at three years. The second dam, Stufida (by Bustino), won the Group 1 10f Premio Lydia Tesio. (Cheveley Park Stud).
'A beautifully bred filly, she's quite sharp and she's done a bit of work already. She does everything well and I'd love to consider her for Royal Ascot but whether she's quite precocious enough or not I don't know. A filly I like a lot, she's very useful.'

303. ROMANTICIZE ★★★★
b.f. Kyllachy – Romancing (Dr Devious)
January 31. Third foal. Sister to the modest 2007 7f all-weather winner Romantic Verse. The

dam, a fair 10f placed maiden, is a sister to the listed 6f winner Irresistible. The second dam, Polish Romance (by Danzig), a minor 7f winner in the USA, is a sister to the US stakes winner Polish Love and a half-sister to three minor winners. (Cheveley Park Stud).
'This is a filly I'm cracking on with, she's very, very sharp. She's a little madam in the box – she won't half kick you! She'd win over five furlongs but she'll be better over six. One of my early ones – definitely.'

304. SEE THAT GIRL ★★★
b.f. Hawk Wing – Hampton Lucy (Anabaa)
March 22. Second foal. 150,000Y. Tattersalls October 2. Allan Bloodlines. Sister to Polmaily, a fair 6f and 1m placed two year old on his only two starts in 2007. The dam, a modest 6f all-weather winner, is a half-sister to seven winners including the Group 3 7f Prix du Calvados winner Shigeru Summit and to the French listed winner of six races Okabango. The second dam, Riveryev (by Irish River), is a placed half-sister to five winners. (David Allan).
'She seems to go along very well but she needs to grow a bit which is slightly unusual for a Hawk Wing. She looks like a proper two year old but one for June or July time, probably over seven furlongs. She's alright and I wouldn't knock her.'

305. SKID SOLO ★★★★
ch.c. Bahamian Bounty – Amaniy (Dayjur)
May 7. Ninth foal. 40,000Y. Doncaster St Leger. Blandford Bloodstock. Closely related to the useful 7.2f (at two years) and 10f winner Tabadul (by Cadeaux Genereux) and half-brother to the fair 1m (at two years), 14f and hurdles winner Duroob (by Bahhare) and the modest four year old 6f all-weather winner Ikbal (by Indian Ridge). The dam, a useful two year old 5f and 6f winner, is a half-sister to five winners including the US Grade 2 7f winner Kayrawan. The second dam, Muhbubh (by Blushing Groom), won the Group 3 6f Princess Margaret Stakes, was second in the Group 2 6f Lowther Stakes and is a half-sister to Mathkurh (dam of the Group 2 Cherry Hinton Stakes winner Asfurah and the US dual Grade 3

winner Istintaj). (The Comic Strip Heroes).
'He may be a May foal but he's very precocious, he looks like a bull and against my normal train of thought he's going to start at Newbury in April before he's actually two. He's just so forward, so naturally strong and he's ready to go. He's Royal Ascot bound, everything comes easy to him and he's just a machine.'

306. SUNSHINE ALWAYS (IRE) ★★★★
gr.c. Verglas – Easy Sunshine (Sadler's Wells)
April 3. Third foal. 80,000Y. Tattersalls October 1. Cheveley Park Stud. Half-brother to the unraced 2007 two year old Second Glance (by Lemon Drop Kid). The dam, an Irish three year old 7f winner and third in the two year old Group 3 7f C L Weld Park Stakes, is a sister to the Irish 6f (at two years) and 10f winner and listed-placed Unique Pose and a half-sister to two winners. The second dam, Desert Ease (by Green Desert), an Irish two year old listed 6f winner, is a half-sister to five winners including the Group 3 Tetrarch Stakes and Group 3 7f Concorde Stakes winner Two-Twenty-Two. (Cheveley Park Stud).
'He goes very well and does everything asked of him. I did a bit of work with him the other day and he just worked a bit flat because he's going through a growing phase, so I'll wait for the six furlong races in May. I like him a lot and he's still a possible Royal Ascot horse. I haven't had a Verglas before but people tell me they're often a bit hot.'

307. SUPER FLIGHT ★★★★
b.c. Exceed And Excel – Strings (Unfuwain)
February 22. First foal. €140,000Y. Goffs Million. Jurgen Albrecht. The dam is an unraced half-sister to five winners including the French 2,000 Guineas winner Victory Note. The second dam, Three Piece (by Jaazeiro), an Irish placed two year old, is a half-sister to eight winners including Orchestration (Group 2 Coronation Stakes) and Welsh Term (Group 2 Prix d'Harcourt). (Miss A Shaykhutdinova).
'A nice big horse and strong, he's growing a bit at the moment. I like him a lot, the sire has done well in Australia and I wish I'd bought more of

his yearlings. Whether this colt is going to be one for Royal Ascot I don't know, but he'll start off at six furlongs and we'll take it from there. He's a lovely horse with a big, galloping stride and he does everything so easily.'

308. TIGER EYE ★★★★ ♠

b.f. Danehill Dancer – Pink Stone (Bigstone)
February 12. Fourth foal. 82,000Y. Tattersalls October 1. John Warren. Half-sister to the quite useful two year old 8.3f winner Alright My Son (by Pennekamp) and to a minor winner abroad by Agnes World. The dam was placed three times in France and stayed 10f and is a half-sister to eight winners including the triple Group 3 winner Pink and to the French listed winners Ring Pink and Lypink. The second dam, Pink Valley (by Never Bend), won the listed Prix d-Aumale and is a half-sister to 12 winners including the French 2,000 Guineas winner and sire Green Dancer. (Highclere Thoroughbred Racing, VC2).
'She's going to want a bit of time because she's a very big filly but she does everything very easily and in time she's going to be a lovely filly. There are no problems with her whatsoever, she'll start at seven furlongs and she'll want further later on. A nice filly.'

309. TIMELESS DREAM ★★★★

b.f. Oasis Dream – Simply Times (Dodge)
May 13. Seventh foal. Sister to the 2007 two year old maiden and Group 3 7f Horris Hill Stakes fourth Brave Prospector and half-sister to the Group 2 7f Hungerford Stakes and Group 3 6f Bentinck Stakes winner Welsh Emperor (by Emperor Jones), the very useful listed 5f winner Majestic Times (by Bluebird), the fairly useful 5f (at two years) to 7f winner Forever Times (by So Factual), the quite useful 5f and 6f winner Distant Times (by Orpen) and the modest 6f all-weather winner Elegant Times (by Dansili). The dam ran twice unplaced at two years and is a half-sister to five winners including the US two year old stakes winner Bucky's Baby. The second dam, Nesian's Burn (by Big Burn), was a stakes-placed winner at up to 1m in the USA and is a half-sister to nine winners. (Times Of Wigan).

'She's a nice filly but she's a late foal and will need a bit of time. She does everything nicely though and it looks like she'll need six or maybe seven furlongs. I like her a lot.'

310. WEST WITH THE WIND (USA) ★★★★

b.f. Gone West – Opera Aida (Sadler's Wells)
February 18. Second foal. $220,000Y. Saratoga August. Blandford Bloodstock. The dam is an unplaced half-sister to five winners. The second dam, State Crystal (by High Estate), winner of the Group 3 12f Lancashire Oaks and placed in the Yorkshire Oaks and the Prix Vermeille, is a half-sister to 3 Group winners including the Group 1 Fillies' Mile winner Crystal Music. (Miss K Rausing).
'Another one of my sharper ones, she'd be better at six furlongs than five but she's a very nice filly and I'll be trying to get her to Royal Ascot. I like her.'

311. WHOOSKA (USA) ★★★★

b.f. Smart Strike – Bushra (Danzig)
February 16. Third foal. $70,000Y. Keeneland September. Blandford Bloodstock. The dam, a minor US four year old winner, is a sister to the US stakes winners Lech and Crimson Guard and a half-sister to the US Grade 3 stakes winner Savina. The second dam, Wedding Reception (by Round Table), a US stakes-placed winner, is a full or half-sister to three stakes winners. (C G P Wyatt).
'A nice filly, she'll want seven furlongs but she's up there with the best of my fillies, I like her a lot and she does everything really nicely.'

312. UNNAMED ★★★★★

b.f. Dansili – Achieve (Rainbow Quest)
February 23. Third foal. 300,000Y. Tattersalls October 1. BBA (Ire). The dam is an unraced sister to the Derby and Hollywood Turf Handicap winner Quest For Fame and to the Group 3 Queens Vase second Silver Rainbow and a half-sister to the Grade 2 Long Island Handicap winner and Prix Vermeille second Yenda. The second dam, Aryenne (by Green Dancer), was a high-class winner of the French 1,000 Guineas and the Criterium des Pouliches

and is a half-sister to three winners. (Lady Bamford).

'She's probably the pick of my fillies. She does everything so very easily for a big filly and just cruises against the other two year old's. She wouldn't be Royal Ascot bound but she'll be one for something big later on I hope. Although she's out of a Rainbow Quest mare she's quite speedy and she could probably win over six furlongs and then need further in time. Dansili is as good a sire as there is at the moment and I like this filly a lot.'

313. UNNAMED ★★★

b.c. Clodovil – Cape Flattery (Cape Cross)
February 28. First foal. 32,000Y. Doncaster St Leger. Blandford Bloodstock. The dam, a modest Irish 11f winner, is a half-sister to two winners. The second dam, Ayers Rock (by In The Wings), won two races over 10f and 12f in Ireland and is a half-sister to two winners. (Mr M Daffey).

'He's doing everything really well, he's more of a seven furlong type from July onwards and he's a horse that I like. There's nothing wrong with him.'

314. UNNAMED ★★★

b.c. Kyllachy – Exhibitor (Royal Academy)
April 3. Third foal. 26,000Y. Doncaster St Leger. Blandford Bloodstock. Half-brother to the modest 2007 7f placed two year old Locum (by Dr Fong). The dam, a modest 10f winner, is a half-sister to four winners including the French listed winner and smart broodmare Aka Lady. The second dam, Akadya (by Akarad), a listed winner in France, is a full or half-sister to eight winners. (M R Green).

'He came in late but he's going along nicely now and cantering well. I couldn't be happier with him, he's one for six or seven furlongs in early summer.'

315. UNNAMED ★★★

b.f. Kyllachy – Halland Park Lass (Spectrum)
March 2. Second foal. 480,000Y. Tattersalls October 1. Half-sister to the two year old Group 1 Middle Park Stakes and Group 1 Prix Morny winner Dutch Art (by Medicean). The dam ran 3 times unplaced and is a half-sister to the Scandinavian Group 3 winner King Quantas. The second dam, Palacegate Episode (by Drumalis), won 11 races including the Group 3 Premio Omenoni and the listed St Hugh's Stakes and is a half-sister to the listed winners Palacegate Jack and Another Episode. (A W Black).

'She's just going through a bit of a growing phase at the moment but she's done a little bit of work and has done it nicely. She'll start off very small just to get a win and then we'll step her up.'

316. UNNAMED ★★★★

b.c. One Cool Cat – Passe Passe (Lear Fan)
April 7. Sixth foal. 68,000Y. Tattersalls October 1. Blandford Bloodstock. Half-brother to La Troupe (by King's Best), placed fourth over 7f on her only start at two years in 2007, to the fairly useful 7f (at two years) and 10f winner Cabinet (by Grand Lodge), the quite useful two year old 5f winner Ryedale Ovation (by Royal Applause) and the fairly useful 10.2f and 12f winner and Australian Grade 2 placed Magic Instinct (by Entrepreneur). The dam, a fair 7f to 12f placed maiden, is a half-sister to the Irish listed winner and French Group 2 placed Windermere. The second dam, Madame L'Enjoleur (by L'Enjoleur), a two year old stakes winner in the USA, was placed in two Grade 1 events over 8.5f and is a half-sister to the Grade 1 9f Hollywood Derby winner Labeeb and the Grade two winners Fanmore and Alrassam. (M R Green).

'He goes along very well and I like this horse a lot. I'm more than happy with him, he'll want six furlongs in either May or June, he goes well and he's got a good engine.'

317. UNNAMED ★★★★★

ch.c. Galileo – Safeen (Storm Cat)
March 12. Third foal. $600,000Y. Keeneland September. Tony Nerses. The dam is an unraced half-sister to the listed winner and Italian Group 3 winner Revere. The second dam, Bint Pasha (by Affirmed), won the Prix Vermeille, the Yorkshire Oaks and the Group 2 Pretty Polly Stakes. (Saleh Al Homeizi & Imad Al Sagar).

'We'd better mention this colt! He's not been here

long but he just floats over the ground and if I had to choose just one horse this is it. I think he's lovely and he does everything so easily. I would hope to run him over seven furlongs (maybe the Haynes, Hanson and Clark at Newbury) and then go for the Dewhurst, but whether it'll come off or not I don't know! I just love him.'

318. UNNAMED ★★★★★
b.c. Kheleyf – Sewards Folly (Rudimentary)
April 1. Fourth foal. 200,000Y. Tattersalls October 1. Tony Nerses. Half-brother to the modest 2007 7.5f placed two year old Honour The World (by Tobougg) and to the useful Group 3 5f Cornwallis Stakes winner and Group 2 Flying Childers Stakes second Hunter Street (by Compton Place). The dam was placed at two years and is a half-sister to six minor winners. The second dam, Anchorage (by Slip Anchor), won twice at three years and is a half-sister to six winners including the Group 3 Ormonde Stakes winner Brunico. (Saleh Al Homeizi & Imad Al Sagar).
'He's a lovely horse who goes very well and he'll start in May with a view to going to the Coventry Stakes. He'd be better at six furlongs than five and he's got more quality than his half-brother Hunter Street who was an out-and-out sprinter.'

319. UNNAMED ★★★★
b.c. Monsieur Bond – Song Of Skye (Warning)
March 31. Fourth foal. 54,000Y. Doncaster St Leger. DeBurgh/Farrington. Half-brother to the quite useful 5f (at two years) and 7f winner and listed-placed Skyelady (by Dansili). The dam, a quite useful 5f (at two years) and 7f winner, is a half-sister to five winners. The second dam, Song Of Hope (by Chief Singer), a useful two year old 5f winner, was second in the listed Firth of Clyde Stakes and is a half-sister to ten winners. (S Harris).
'This is a horse that I like, he goes along quite nicely and I won't run him over five furlongs because he'll be better at six. He does everything he's asked to do very well, he's moves nicely and has a good attitude. He's definitely alright.'

ROGER CHARLTON
320. AFFLUENT ★★★★
b.f. Oasis Dream – Valencia (Kenmare)
February. Sixth foal. Half-sister to the useful two year old 6f winner and Group 3 7f placed Cantabria (by Dansili), to the useful two year old 5f and listed 6f winner Deportivo (by Night Shift), the useful two year old listed 5f winner Irish Vale (by Wolfhound), the fairly useful two year old 7f and 7.6f winner La Coruna (by Deploy) and the fair 7f winner Subadar (by Zamindar). The dam, placed over 1m at two years on her only start, is a half-sister to numerous winners including the dual US Grade 1 winner Wandesta, the Group 2 12f winner De Quest and the smart 10f to 15f winner Turners Hill. The second dam, De Stael (by Nijinsky), a fairly useful dual 7f winner at two years, is a sister to the high-class middle-distance colts Peacetime and Quiet Fling. (Khalid Abdulla).
'A sharp, small, strong filly that should be early and is bred to be speedy.'

321. ALL ABOUT YOU (IRE) ★★★★
b.c. Mind Games – Expectation (Night Shift)
April 23. Seventh foal. 120,000Y. Tattersalls October 1. Charlie Gordon-Watson. Brother to the two year old Group 2 6f Richmond Stakes winner and Group 1 6f Prix Morny third Always Hopeful and to the fairly useful 6f and 1m winner Extraterrestrial and half-brother to the useful two year old 6f winner and listed-placed Nacho Libre (by Kyllachy), the quite useful two year old dual 6f winner Enford Princess (by Pivotal) and the quite useful three year old dual 1m winner Polly Plunkett (by Puissance). The dam, a modest 6f placed two year old, is a half-sister to four minor winners here and abroad. The second dam, Phantom Row (by Adonijah), is a poor half-sister to ten winners including the Horris Hill Stakes winner Long Row and the Norfolk Stakes winner Colmore Row. (Mountgrange Stud).
'He's from a very good family and is bred to be speedy but he's a big, strong colt with plenty of scope. Unlikely to stay more than six furlongs, he could be running in May or June. The dam has consistently produced good horses.'

322. BLOCK PARTY ★★★
b.c. Dansili – Mylania (Midyan)
March 22. Fourth foal. 140,000Y. Tattersalls October 2. Charlie Gordon-Watson. The dam, placed over a mile as a three year old, is a half-sister to two winners. The second dam, Appelania (by Star Appeal), won twice over 1m at three years and is a half-sister to the dam of the high-class Hong Kong horses Mensa and Firebolt. (Mountgrange Stud Ltd).
'He's grown quite a lot since the sales and he'll need time. A nice horse, he's a bit light on pedigree but is one for the second half of the year.'

323. BORDER PATROL ★★★
b.c. Selkirk – Ffestiniog (Efisio)
April 17. Half-brother to the fairly useful 2007 two year old 6f winner Harlech Castle (by Royal Applause), to the smart sprint winner of 11 races (including the Group 3 Prix de Meautry) Eisteddfod (by Cadeaux Genereux), to the useful two year old 5f to 7f winner Brecon Beacon (by Spectrum), the useful dual 7f (at two years) and UAE Group 3 1m winner Boston Lodge (by Grand Lodge), the quite useful two year old dual 7f winner Tredegar (by Inchinor) and the quite useful 5f and 6f winner Oceans Apart (by Desert Prince). The dam, a fairly useful two year old listed 7.3f and three year old 1m winner, is a half-sister to several winners. The second dam, Penny Fan (by Nomination), was placed once over 5f at three years, is closely related to the listed 5f Scarborough Stakes winner Rivers Rhapsody and a half-sister to the Group 3 5f Prix d'Arenburg winner Regal Scintilla. (Elite Racing Club).
'Only arrived in training quite late and he's not as precocious as the rest of his family but he's a nice, quality two year old – probably for the middle to back end of the season.'

324. BROAD CAIRN ★★★
b.c. Green Desert – Celtic Cross (Selkirk)
January 28. Fourth foal. Half-sister to the quite useful 9f and 10f winner Maclean (by Machiavellian) and to the quite useful 10f, 14f and hurdles winner Fretwork (by Galileo). The

dam, a useful 1m winner, is a half-sister to the useful 9f and 10f winner New Assembly, to the useful two year old 7f winner Right Approach and the useful stayer Temple Way. The second dam, Abbey Strand (by Shadeed), a fair Irish 10f winner, is a half-sister to numerous winners including the very useful two year old Group 3 1m Prix La Rochette winner Grand Chelem and the smart two year old Group 3 1m winner Splendid Moment. (The Queen).
'A solid colt with a good temperament. He'll be ready by July onwards and he looks OK.'

325. CLASSICALLY ★★
b.c. Indian Haven – Specifically (Sky Classic)
March 29. Eighth foal. 200,000Y. Tattersalls October 1. Kern/Lillingston. Half-sister to the 1,000 Guineas and Group 2 Rockfel Stakes winner Speciosa (by Danehill Dancer), to the US Grade 3 stakes winner of 11 races and Grade 1 placed Major Rhythm (by Rhythm), the minor US winner of six races Bold Classic (by Pembroke), the fair 9.7f and 10f winner Thundermill (by Thunder Gulch) and the modest all-weather 5f and 6f winner Shadow Jumper (by Dayjur). The dam won once at two years in the USA and is a half-sister to seven winners including the Group 1 Champion Stakes, Grand Prix de Saint-Cloud and Hong Kong Cup winner Pride. The second dam, Specificity (by Alleged), a useful winner of the listed 12.2f George Stubbs Stakes, is a half-sister to the ten winners including the St Leger and Irish St Leger winner Touching Wood. (J P Smith).
'He's a big horse with a quality pedigree. The sire was big and although you'd hope this colt might win for his owner this year he's likely to be a better three year old.'

326. DREAM RUNNER ★★
b.c. Oasis Dream – La Coruna (Deploy)
January 28. First foal. The dam, the fairly useful two year old 7f and 7.6f winner, is a half-sister to the useful two year old 6f winner and Group 3 7f placed Cantabria, to the useful two year old 5f and listed 6f winner Deportivo and the useful two year old listed 5f winner Irish Vale. The second dam, Valencia (by Kenmare), placed

over 1m at two years on her only start, is a half-sister to numerous winners including the dual US Grade 1 winner Wandesta, the Group 2 12f winner De Quest and the smart 10f to 15f winner Turners Hill. (Khalid Abdulla).
'He hasn't arrived here yet (late March).'

327. FAULT ★★★
b.c. Bahamian Bounty – Trundley Wood (Wassl)
February 15. Sixth foal. 48,000Y. Tattersalls October 2. Charlie Gordon-Watson. Half-brother to the fairly useful three year old dual 7f winner River Royale (by Royal Applause), the minor Italian winner of 16 races Squanto (by Prince Sabo) and the minor German 1m (at two years) and 10f winner Flaviatore (by Deploy). The dam, a modest two year old 7f winner, is out of the quite useful 6f (at two years) and 1m winner Tharwat (by Topsider), herself a half-sister to seven winners. (J W Livock).
'He looks a neat, two year old type and hopefully from May onwards he'll make a two year old, probably over six furlongs.'

328. FIANCEE (IRE) ★★★
b.f. Pivotal – Name Of Love (Petardia)
April 8. Half-sister to Angel Pie (by Diesis), unplaced in two starts at two years in 2007, to the US Grade 3 8.5f placed Perilous Pursuit and the fair all-weather 9.5f winner Almavara (both by Fusaichi Pegasus). The dam, a very useful two year old Group 3 7f Rockfel Stakes and listed 7f Oh So Sharp Stakes winner, is a half-sister to three winners including the useful 7f winner (at two years) and 9f listed placed Annapurna. The second dam, National Ballet (by Shareef Dancer), is an unraced half-sister to seven winners including the listed winners Broken Wave, Guarde Royale, Clifton Chapel and Saxon Maid. (Lady Rothschild).
'She hasn't arrived in training yet (late March) but I've seen her and she's an attractive filly and not too big.'

329. GOING FOR GOLD ★★
b.f. Barathea – Flash Of Gold (Darshaan)
February 1. Second foal.
The dam, a fair 12f placed maiden, is a half-sister to four winners including the smart Group 2 12f Ribblesdale Stakes and Group 2 13.3f Geoffrey Freer Stakes winner Phantom Gold. The second dam, Trying For Gold (by Northern Baby), was a useful 12f and 12.5f winner at three years. (The Queen).
'A scopey filly that moves well but she needs time.'

330. LA TIZONA (IRE) ★★★
b.c. Alhaarth – Rosse (Kris)
May 20. Fifth foal. 36,000Y. Tattersalls October 1. Not sold. Half-brother to the quite useful 2007 two year old 6f winner Upton Grey (by Dalakhani) and to the modest 7f winner Lasso (by Indian Ridge). The dam, a useful dual 7f winner, is a half-sister to eight winners including the high-class Group 1 1m Coronation Stakes winner Rebecca Sharp and the smart Group 3 11.5f Lingfield Derby Trial winner Mystic Knight. The second dam, Nuryana (Nureyev), was a useful winner of the listed 1m Grand Metropolitan Stakes and is a half-sister to five winners. (A E Oppenheimer).
'Although a late foal, he looks a two year old type. A neat horse and if you didn't know his pedigree or birth date you'd say he'd be one of those to be racing in May.'

331. LITTLE CONKER ★★★
b.f. Red Ransom – Bedara (Barathea)
February 6. Sixth foal. Half-sister to the useful 1m winner of three races Mutajarred (by Alhaarth), to the fairly useful 7f (at two years) and 1m winner Arm Candy (by Nashwan) and the quite useful two year old 1m winner Mozafin (by Zafonic), subsequently a winner in Austria at three years. The dam, a quite useful 10.5f winner, was listed-placed and is a half-sister to two minor winners abroad. The second dam, Cutting Reef (by Kris), a staying winner of two races in France including a listed event at Maisons-Laffitte, is a half-sister to seven winners. (Duchess of Roxburghe).
'A small, neat filly, she's quite a character and has been a difficult ride. Judging by her size we'll have to get on with it because she needs to make it by the summer.'

332. MULTIPLICATION ★★★
b.f. Marju – Lunda (Soviet Star)
February 24. Ninth foal. 110,000Y. Tattersalls October 2. Norris/Huntingdon. Half-sister to the useful 2007 Group 3 7f placed two year old Bazergan, to the fair 7f winner Jakarta (both by Machiavellian), the very useful 1m to 10f winner and Italian Derby third Lundy's Lane, the very smart 1m (at two years) and dual Group 3 middle-distance winner Blue Monday (both by Darshaan), the 1m (all-weather) and 10f winner Dancing Tsar (by Salse) and the modest 7f all-weather winner Zamhrear (by Singspiel). The dam ran three times unplaced at three years and is a half-sister to six winners including the high-class middle-distance horses Luso (winner of the Aral-Pokal, the Italian Derby and the Hong Kong International Vase) and Warrsan (Coronation Cup and Grosser Preis von Baden). The second dam, Lucayan Princess (by High Line), won the listed 6f Sweet Solera Stakes at two years, was third in the 12.3f Cheshire Oaks and is a half-sister to seven winners. (D G Hardisty).
'She's light on her feet, shows a bit of speed and more likely to make a two year old than a three year old. The family normally take longer, but this filly is one to get on with I think.'

333. PERCEPTION (IRE) ★★
b.f. Hawk Wing – Princesse Darsha (Darshaan)
April 27. Fourth foal. €70,000Y. Deauville August. Amanda Skiffington. Half-sister to a winner in Germany by Silvano. The dam is an unplaced half-sister to seven winners including the German Group three winners Piranga and Prince Firebird. The second dam, Princesse d'Espoir (by Sensitive Prince), is an unplaced half-sister to nine winners. (De La Warr Racing).
'Only just arrived, she's attractive and moves well. A big filly, she's not going to be early and is one for the mid-summer.'

334. RAISE THE BET ★★
b.c. Haafhd – Shanty (Selkirk)
May 4. Fourth foal. 120,000Y. Tattersalls October 1. Charlie Gordon-Watson. The dam, a fairly useful two year old 1m winner, is a half-sister to the very useful filly Nightbird, a winner of five races from 5f to 7f including 2 listed events. The second dam, Pippa's Song (by Reference Point), a fair 12f winner, is a half-sister to eight winners including the Group 3 Prestige Stakes winner Glatisant (herself dam of the 2,000 Guineas winner Footsteps-inthesand) and to the placed dam of the champion two year old filly Superstar Leo. (Mountgrange Stud Ltd).
'He's grown a lot since the sales and he looks a bit immature at the moment. A nice mover, he definitely needs time and probably a bit of distance.'

335. ROSE DIAMOND ★★★★
gr.f. Daylami – Tante Rose (Barathea)
January 31. First foal. The dam, a winner of five races including the Group 1 Haydock Park Sprint Cup, the Group 4 7f Fred Darling Stakes and Group 3 6f Summer Stakes, is a half-sister to several winners including the Sweet Solera Stakes winner Bay Tree. The second dam, My Branch (by Distant Relative), a winner of two listed races over 6f (at two years) and 7f, was placed in the Cheveley Park Stakes and the Irish 1,000 Guineas and is a half-sister to five winners. (B E Nielsen).
'A nice filly, she's the first and sadly the only foal out of the mare. A good, tough filly that'll be suited by six furlongs in May or June. She looks quite precocious and although she's by Daylami so was her three-parts sister Bay Tree and she did alright as a two year old. She shows plenty of speed and it's so far so good with her.'

336. SPLENDORINTHEGRASS ★★★
ch.c. Selkirk – Portelet (Night Shift)
April 22. Eighth foal. 185,000Y. Tattersalls October 1. Charlie Gordon-Watson. Half-brother to the unplaced 2007 Irish two year old Isabelle's Dream (by Domedriver), to the very smart two year old Group 2 7f Champagne Stakes winner Etlaala, the useful 7f and 1m winner and listed-placed Selective and the modest 5f winner Come What May and half-brother to the useful 6f and 7f winner Overspect (by Spectrum) and the fair dual 7f winner Marmooq (by Cadeaux Genereux). The dam, a

fairly useful 5f winner of four races, is a half-sister to four winners. The second dam, Noirmont (by Dominion), is an unraced half-sister to the Group winners Braashee, Adam Smith and Ghariba. (Mountgrange Stud Ltd).
'A nice horse, well-related and he'll hopefully run from July onwards. The family have all been six/seven furlong horses and he'll probably be much the same.'

337. TRADING NATION (USA) ★★
b.c. Tiznow – Nidd (Known Fact)
April 3. Half-brother to five winners including the useful two year old dual 7f winner Fifteen Love (by Point Given), to the fairly useful 7f winner Expected Bonus (by Kris S), the quite useful four year old 5f winner Charengo (by Danzig), the quite useful two year old 5f winner Clove and the minor US 5.5f winner Guise Cliff (both by Distant View). The dam won three races in France and the USA including the Group 3 7f Prix de la Porte Maillot and is a half-sister to numerous winners including the Breeders Cup Classic winner Skywalker, the US Grade 2 7f Malibu Stakes Pac Mania and the French listed 6.5f winner and US Grade 2 placed Danzante. The second dam, Bold Captive (by Boldnesian), won ten races in the USA including a 9f stakes event. (Khalid Abdulla). The sire won the Breeders Cup Classic.
'Probably not as forward as his half-brother Fifteen Love was, he's more immature. He moves well and will hopefully be out by the mid-summer.'

338. TRULY ASIA ★★
b.c. Acclamation – Tasha's Dream (Woodman)
February 6. Second foal. 160,000Y. Tattersalls October 2. Charlie Gordon-Watson. Brother to the fairly useful 2007 Irish two year old 7f winner Unquenchable Fire. The dam is a placed sister to the Group 3 Tetrarch Stakes winner Major Force and a half-sister to seven winners including the Peruvian Grade 2 winner Dancing Action and the Group 3 Curragh Cup winner Quality Team. The second dam, Ready For Action (by Riverman), won at three years and is a half-sister to four winners. (HRH Sultan Ahmad Shah).

'A lengthy, slightly plain horse that looks like he'll need a bit of time. He doesn't strike me as a fast horse yet, even though he ought to be, so we'll see how we get on with him.'

339. ZERO MONEY ★★★ ♠
ch.c. Bachelor Duke – Dawn Chorus (Mukaddamah)
March 6. Sixth foal. 180,000Y. Tattersalls October 2. A Skiffington. Half-brother to the useful Irish 7f winner and listed-placed Dangle (by Desert Style), to the Irish 7f (at two years) to 10f and subsequent Hong Kong stakes winner Solid Approach (by Definite Article), the quite useful Irish 5f winner Divert (by Averti), the quite useful Irish 7f winner Devious Diva (by Dr Devious) and the quite useful two year old dual 6f winner La Campanella (by Tagula). The dam is an unraced half-sister to five winners including Barrier Reef, a winner of eight races and second in the Group 3 Beresford Stakes. The second dam, Singing Millie (by Millfontaine), won twice in Ireland at three years and is a half-sister to seven winners. (Ms G F Khosla).
'He looks quite precocious and shows a bit of speed. You'd hope that he'd be able to run by early summer over six furlongs.'

PAUL COLE
340. ALTIMATUM (USA) ★★★
ch.c. Rahy – Aldiza (Storm Cat)
February 6. Fourth foal. $260,000Y. Keeneland September. Paul Cole. Half-brother to the US stakes-placed winners Alchemist and Altesse (both by A P Indy). The dam, a US Grade 1 winner of six races, is a half-sister to the Grade 2 winner Atelier. The second dam, Aishah (by Alydar), won the Grade 2 Rare Perfume Stakes and is a sister to the multiple Grade 1 winner Althea. (Mr D S Lee).

341. ALYSTAR (IRE) ★★★
ch.f. Rock Of Gibraltar – Arpege (Sadler's Wells)
March 3. Third foal. €200,000Y. Goffs Million. Paul Cole. The dam is an unraced sister to the smart German Group 2 8.5f and Italian Group 2 1m winner Crimson Tide, closely related to the US Grade 2 and Group 3 Prix de

Sandringham winner Pharatta and a half-sister to the US stakes winner and Group 1 Prix Marcel Boussac fourth La Vida Loca. The second dam, Sharata (by Darshaan), is an unraced half-sister to the Derby and Irish Derby winner Shahrastani. (Mr S A Smith).

342. CLODOLINE ★★

b.f. *Clodovil – Esquiline (Gone West)*
February 12. Seventh foal. 45,000Y. Tattersalls October 3. Paul Cole. Half-sister to the useful 6f to 8.2f and subsequent US stakes winner Wixoe Express (by Anabaa), to the fair two year old 7f winner Aspen Falls (by Elnadim) and the French 11f winner Coppet (by Pennekamp). The dam is an unplaced half-sister to five minor winners in France. The second dam, Ville Eternelle (by Slew O'Gold), won three races in France and is a half-sister to nine winners including Mill Native (Grade 1 10f Arlington Million) and the French Group three winners French Stress, Sporades and American Stress. (A H Robinson).

343. DESIRE TO EXCEL (IRE)

b.c. *Desert Style – Sanpala (Sanglamore)*
March 12. Fifth foal. 150,000Y. Tattersalls October 2. P Cole. Half-brother to the Group 3 7f Criterion Stakes and listed 7f winner Silver Touch (by Dansili). The dam ran once unplaced in France and is a half-sister to seven winners including the Group three winners Danefair, Prove and Vortex. The second dam, Roupala (by Vaguely Noble), a fair three year old 1m winner, is a half-sister to five winners and to the dams of the Group/Graded stakes winners Bad Bertrich Again, Prolix and Daros. (HRH Sultan Ahmad Shah).

344. DREAM IN WAITING

b.f. *Oasis Dream – Lady In Waiting (Kylian)*
March 16. Fourth foal. Half-sister to the quite useful two year old 7f all-weather winner Wait For The Light (by Fantastic Light). The dam won six races including the listed 6f Empress Stakes (at two years) and the Group 2 10f Sun Chariot Stakes and was Group placed four times. She is closely related to the 7f (at two years) and

Group 3 15f Prix du Lutece winner Savannah Bay and a half-sister to three winners. The second dam, High Savannah (by Rousillon), a fair middle-distance placed maiden, is a half-sister to six winners including the useful sprinters Maid For The Hills and Maid For Walking (herself dam of the US Grade 1 winner Stroll). (Pegasus Racing Ltd).

345. ELECTRIC FLIGHT (USA) ★★★

b.c. *Elusive Quality – Famously (Sadler's Wells)*
February 16. First foal. 90,000Y. Tattersalls October 1. Oliver Cole. The dam won 3 minor races in France and is a sister to the Group 2 Prix de Royallieu winner and US Grade 3 winner Moon Queen and to the very useful dual 12f winner and Group 2 placed Rostropovich, closely related to the Group 3 1m Premio Dormello winner Barafamy and half-sister to very useful listed 10f and 12f and subsequent US Grade 2 winner Innuendo. The second dam, Infamy (by Shirley Heights), a very smart 10f to 12f filly, won the Grade 1 Rothmans International, the Group 2 Sun Chariot Stakes and the Group 3 Gordon Richards Stakes and is a half-sister to three winners. (Miss A Shaykhutdinova).

346. HERRING SENIOR (IRE) ★★

b.br.c. *Kheleyf – Karenaragon (Aragon)*
March 26. Sixth foal. 38,000Y. Tattersalls October 2. P Cole. Half-brother to James Dean (by Clodovil), second over 7f on the all-weather on his only start at two years in 2007, to the moderate 10f winner Zain and the minor French two year old winner Sugrila (both by Alhaarth). The dam, a moderate 5f placed two year old, is a sister to the useful sprinter and US triple Grade 3 winner Evening Promise and a half-sister to six winners. The second dam, Rosy Sunset (by Red Sunset), is an unplaced half-sister to ten winners including the triple Group 2 middle-distance winner Bandari. (P F I Cole Ltd).

347. INDIAN VIOLET (IRE) ★★★

b.c. *Indian Ridge – Violet Spring (Exactly Sharp)*
March 5. Fourth foal. 155,000Y. Tattersalls October 1. Paul Cole. Half-brother to the very

useful two year old Group 2 6f Richmond Stakes winner Carizzo Creek (by Charnwood Forest) and to the fair 7f (at two years) and 6f winner Violet Ballerina (by Namid). The dam, unraced until five years when she won over 2m in Ireland, is a half-sister to three other minor winners and to the placed dam of the US Grade 3 winner Doc Holiday. The second dam, Violet Somers (by Will Somers), is an unraced sister to the smart sprinters Balidar (winner of the Prix de l'Abbaye) and Balliol (winner of the Cork and Orrery Stakes). (Mrs L Spencer).

348. KAYFIAR (USA) ★★★
ch.c. Lion Heart – Ivor Jewel (Sir Ivor)
January 21. Ninth foal. €100,000Y. Goffs Million. Paul Cole. Half-brother to five winners including the US stakes winner and Grade 3 placed Water Street (by Storm Bird) and minor US winners by Theatrical and Gulch. The dam, a two year old winner in France and Group 3 placed twice, is a half-sister to six winners. The second dam, Adlibber (by Never Bend), was a stakes winner of nine races in the USA and was Grade 3 placed. (Mrs S A Smith).

349. MEYDAN ★★★
b.f. Reset – In The Groove (Night Shift)
April 3. Half-sister to the fairly useful two year old 5f and 6f winner Incarvillea (by Mr Prospector) and to the quite useful two year old 7f winner Cote d'Argent (by Lujain). The dam was a top-class middle-distance filly and won seven races, notably the Irish 1,000 Guineas, the Juddmonte International, the Dubai Champion Stakes and the Coronation Cup. all Group 1 events. She is a half-sister to four winners, including the fairly useful miler Spanish Pine, out of the quite useful dual 12f winner Pine Ridge (by High Top). herself out of the minor 12f and 14f winner Wounded Knee (by Busted). (Bigwigs Bloodstock).

350. MILIEMIL ★★★
*b.f. Acclamation – Lady Betambeau
(Grand Lodge)*
January 19. Second foal. 44,000Y. Doncaster St Leger. P Cole. Half-sister to the 2007 French two

year old winner Caprice des Bleus (by Kyllachy). The dam is an unplaced sister to the listed Atalanta Stakes winner Lady Bear. The second dam, Boristova (by Royal Academy), a minor Irish two year old 9f winner, is a half-sister to six winners. (Mr D S Lee).

351. MONS CALPE (IRE) ★★★
*b.c. Rock Of Gibraltar – Taking Liberties
(Royal Academy)*
May 8. Eighth foal. 110,000Y. Tattersalls October 1. Paul Cole. Closely related to Double Duty (by Danehill Dancer), unplaced in one start at two years in 2007, to the listed 1m winner Troubadour and the fair two year old 6f all-weather winner Danapali (both by Danehill) and half-brother to the fair 1m to 10f winner Eccollo, the French two year old winner and 5f listed-placed Agapimou (both by Spectrum), the quite useful five year old dual 1m winner Saponi and the minor French dual winner Tosca's Impulse (both by Indian Ridge). The dam ran once unplaced and is a sister to the Irish two year old Group 3 1m Futurity Stakes winner Equal Rights and a half-sister to six winners including the Australian Grade 3 winner Freedom Fields. The second dam, Lady Liberty (by Noble Bijou), won the Grade 1 12f South Australian Oaks and is a half-sister to four winners. (HRH Sultan Ahmad Shah).

352. STAN'S COOL CAT (IRE) ★★★
*b.f. One Cool Cat – Beautiful France
(Sadler's Wells)*
February 10. Eleventh foal. €75,000Y. Goffs Million. Paul Cole. Half-sister to seven winners including the Irish 9f winner Beautiful Hill (by Danehill), to the Irish two year old winner, Group 3 placed and subsequent Hong Kong winner Beautiful Fire (by Selkirk), the Irish two year old 6f and subsequent US winner Beauty Go Leor (by Cadeaux Genereux), the dual Irish 1m and subsequent US winner French Smile (by Indian Ridge) and the US winner of three races Fureur France (by Brief Truce). The dam, an Irish 9f winner, is a half-sister to seven winners including the Irish listed 9f winner Rimpa and to the unraced dam of the St Leger winner

Scorpion and the US Grade 2 winner Memories. The second dam, Thistlewood (by Kalamoun), is an unraced half-sister to the top-class middle-distance stayer Ardross. (Wansdyke Farms).

353. STAN'S SMARTY GIRL (USA) ★★★
gr.f. Smarty Jones – Terre Haute (Caro)
April 16. Ninth foal. $100,000Y. Keeneland September. Paul Cole. Half-sister to the US Grade 1 Hollywood Futurity winner Tactical Cat and to the Group 2 placed winner Storm Passage (both by Storm Cat). The dam, a US stakes winner and Grade 3 placed, is a half-sister to seven winners. The second dam, Mia Dancer (by Marshua's Dancer), a minor US stakes winner, is a half-sister to the US Grade 1 winner Skip Trial. (Wansdyke Farms). The sire won the Kentucky Derby and the Preakness Stakes.

354. STORM MIST (IRE) ★★★
ch.c. Giant's Causeway – Madeira Mist (Grand Lodge)
January 17. First foal. €200,000Y. Goffs Million. Paul Cole. The dam won eight races in the USA and Canada including the Grade 3 Dance Smartly Handicap and is a half-sister to five winners including the Irish listed winner Misty Heights. The second dam, Mountains Of Mist (by Shirley Heights), a quite useful 10f winner, is a half-sister to seven winners including the Group 2 Lowther Stakes winner Enthused. (Mrs L Spencer).

355. SULTAN'S WAY (IRE) ★★★
b.c. Indian Ridge – Roses From Ridey (Petorius)
May 14. Sixth foal. €140,000Y. Goffs Million. Oliver Cole. Half-brother to the fair 2007 7f placed two year old Tense (by Invincible Spirit) and to the useful two year old Group 2 6f July Stakes second Armigerent (by In The Wings), subsequently a winner abroad. The dam ran twice unplaced at two years and is a half-sister to six winners including the German and Italian Group 1 winner Kutub and two listed winners in Ireland. The second dam, Minnie Habit (by Habitat), an Irish four year old 9f winner, is closely related to the dual Group 3 sprint winner Bermuda Classic (herself dam of the Coronation

Stakes winner Shake The Yoke and the Phoenix Sprint Stakes winner Tropical). (HRH Sultan Ahmad Shah).

356. THUNDEROUS MOOD (USA) ★★★★
b.br.c. Storm Cat – Warm Mood (Alydar)
March 1. Eighth foal. $575,000 two year old. Fasig-Tipton Calder two year old's-in-training. Paul Cole. Brother to the Leopardstown 1,000 Guineas Trial Stakes winner Royal Tigress and half-brother to the useful two year old listed 6f winner Miguel Cervantes (by Danzig), the smart two year old Group 3 6f Norfolk Stakes winner Warm Heart and the minor US winner of four races Archdiesis (both by Diesis). The dam won four races at up to 9f in the USA and is a half-sister to a stakes winner in Japan. The second dam, Summer Mood (by Raja Baba), a winner of 1seven races and a champion sprinter in Canada, is a half-sister to the multiple Graded stakes winner Present Value.

357. TRESSWAY (IRE) ★★
b.f. Giant's Causeway – Chantress (Peintre Celebre)
April 20. First foal. 85,000Y. Tattersalls October 1. Paul Cole. The dam, a fairly useful 9.3f and 10.3f winner, was listed-placed and is a half-sister to three winners including the Group 3 6f Coventry Stakes winner Red Sea and the useful 7f (at two years) and Italian Group 3 12f winner Sailing. The second dam, Up Anchor (by Slip Anchor), won four races including the Group 3 12f St Simon Stakes, was third in the Italian Oaks and is a half-sister to five winners including the triple US Grade 3 winner at around 8.5f Just Class. (Mr D S Lee).

LUCA CUMANI
358. AUSONIUS ★★★
b.c. Kyllachy – Baileys Silver (Marlin)
March 30. Third foal. 80,000Y. Tattersalls October 2. Charlie Gordon-Watson. Half-brother to the quite useful two year old 5f winner Bahama Baileys (by Bahamian Bounty). The dam is an unraced half-sister to two winners including the Group 3 Nell Gwyn Stakes second Zaheemah. The second dam, Port Of Silver (by

Silver Hawk), a US two year old stakes winner, is a half-sister to five winners. (Robert Tullett & Partners).

'A good-looking horse, medium-sized and fairly strong. I see him possibly wanting seven furlongs or a mile even as a two year old and in the second half of the season.'

359. BOURNE ★★
gr.c. Linamix – L'Affaire Monique (Machiavellian)
March 29. Third foal. 60,000Y. Tattersalls October 1. Not sold. The dam, a useful 10f winner, is a full or half-sister to 11 winners including the Group 2 Princess Of Wales's Stakes winner Little Rock and the Group 2 Prix de Pomone winner Whitewater Affair and the Group 3 Musidora Stakes winner Short Skirt. The second dam, Much Too Risky (by Bustino), won twice at two years and is a half-sister to the Group 1 winners Arctic Owl and Marooned. (Aston House Stud).

'Linamix is not known for siring two year old's but this is a smallish sort of horse, fairly well-made and well put together. He could have a run or two at the back-end.'

360. BURMA ROCK (IRE) ★★★
b.c. Danehill Dancer – Burmese Princess (King Of Kings)
April 14. Third foal. 68,000Y. Tattersalls October 1. Charlie Gordon-Watson. Brother to Shoot Pontoon, unplaced in two starts at two years in 2007 and half-brother to the minor Italian three year old winner of three races Vegas Star (by Spinning World). The dam, a modest 6f placed two year old, is a placed half-sister to six winners including the smart Group 3 7f Jersey Stakes winner Gneiss. The second dam, Rangoon Ruby (by Sallust), won seven races including the Group 3 Baroda Stud Phoenix Sprint and was placed in a Grade 3 event in the USA. (Drones Racing).

'He'll make a two year old, he's strong and forward and he should be a horse to look forward to running from August onwards.'

361. CYGNET ★★★
b.c. Dansili – Ballet Princess (Muhtarram)
February 9. Third foal. 150,000Y. Tattersalls October 1. Charlie Gordon-Watson. The dam is an unraced half-sister to four winners including the Australian Grade 2 winner Rasheek and the Group 3 September Stakes winner Burooj. The second dam, Princess Sucree (by Roberto), was placed over 6f and 8.5f in the USA at four years and is a half-sister to the Kentucky Derby winner Cannonade, to the top-class broodmare Kennelot (dam of the Grade 1 winners Stephans Odyssey and Lotka) and to the smart winners Circle Home, Del Sarto and Wassl Touch. (Lady Milford Haven & The Hon. Mrs Steel).

'A good-looking horse, Dansili's seem to get better with age but this colt will hopefully make a nice two year old. He's forward enough to run from mid-summer and over seven furlongs.'

362. DAY OF THE EAGLE (IRE) ★★★
b.c. Danehill Dancer – Puck's Castle (Shirley Heights)
May 14. Eighth foal. €100,000Y. Goffs Million. Charlie Gordon-Watson. Half-brother to the useful listed 5f winner and Group 2 5f Flying Childers Stakes second Emerald Peace (by Green Desert and herself dam of the two year old listed winner Vital Statistics), to the Irish two year old 1m winner and listed placed Cobra and the Irish 12f winner Down Mexico Way (both by Sadler's Wells). The dam, a fairly useful two year old 1m winner and third in the listed 10f Zetland Stakes, is a half-sister to the champion two year old filly and Cheveley Park Stakes winner Embassy and to the Group 2 Pretty Polly Stakes winner Tarfshi. The second dam, Pass The Peace (by Alzao), won five races including the Cheveley Park Stakes, was second in the French 1,000 Guineas and is a half-sister to three winners. (Mr Chris Wright & Mr Andy Macdonald).

'This is a backward colt and he has a lot of growing to do, but I like him, he's a very likeable horse and a good mover.'

363. FANTASIA ★★★
b.f. Sadler's Wells – Blue Symphony (Darshaan)
February 10. Second foal. Half-sister to the fair 2007 two year old 7f winner Blue Rhapsody (by

Cape Cross). The dam, a fair 10f winner, is a half-sister to one winner. The second dam, Blue Duster (by Danzig), winner of the Group 1 6f Cheveley Park Stakes and the Group 3 5f Queen Mary Stakes, is a sister to the smart Group 1 6f Middle Park Stakes and Group 2 7f Challenge Stakes winner Zieten and a half-sister to several other winners. (Fittocks Stud & Mr A Bengough). *'A good-looking filly, she's a bit on the small side but her mother is quite small. Being by Sadler's Wells and out of a Darshaan mare you wouldn't expect her to be early despite the fact that it's a fast family. She's a nice filly, very well put together and hopefully she'll be out from August onwards this year.'*

364. FENOMEN ★★★

ch.c. Pivotal – Sispre (Master Willie)
March 26. Half-brother to the two year old Group 2 9f Premio Guido Berardelli winner and Italian Derby third Fisich, to the Italian 12f winner and listed placed Fa A Mezz (both by Halling) and the quite useful dual 12f and hurdles winner Furmigadelagiusta (by Galileo). The dam, a 6f to 1m winner, is a half-sister to seven winners including the Group 2 6f Gimcrack Stakes winner Chilly Billy and the US Grade 3 placed Mister Approval. The second dam, Sweet Snow (by Lyphard), won over an extended 10f in France and is a half-sister to nine winners including the US stakes winners Windansea and Sing And Swing. (Scuderia Rencati Srl).
'I like him, he's good-looking and he'll make a two year old over seven furlongs plus.'

365. FREE FALLING ★★★

ch.f. Selkirk – Free Flying (Groom Dancer)
February 10. Second foal. Half-sister to the fair 2007 two year old 7f winner Sky Dive (by Dr Fong). The dam ran unplaced twice and is a half-sister to numerous winners including the Group 1 Fillies Mile winner and Oaks second Shamshir. The second dam, Free Guest (by Be My Guest), won nine races including the Group 2 Sun Chariot Stakes (twice) and the Group 2 Nassau Stakes and is a half-sister to seven winners including the Group 2 12f Blandford

Stakes winner and Oaks second Royal Ballerina. (Fittocks Stud).
'Her half-brother by Dr Fong won as a two year old so let's hope the dam is imparting a bit of precocity. She'll be one for the second half of the season.'

366. FURIOUS ★★

b.c. Montjeu – Frottola (Muhtarram)
January 15. Half-brother to Falcativ (by Falbrav), unplaced on his only start at two years in 2007. The dam won numerous races at around 1m and 9f in Italy and is a half-sister to the useful 10f to 12f winner Windy Britain. The second dam, For My Love (by Kahyasi), is an unraced half-sister to the useful winners Be Fresh (sprinter) and How Long (up to 1m). (Scuderia Rencati Srl).
'A very good-looking horse, I'm a great fan of Montjeu's but despite this colt having an early foaling date he's not going to be a precocious two year old.'

367. ITALIAN CONNECTION ★★★★

b.f. Cadeaux Genereux – Bianca Nera (Salse)
April 27. Seventh foal. 180,000Y. Tattersalls October 1. Meon Valley Stud. Sister to the Irish two year old 7f winner and listed placed Pietra Dura and half-sister to the modest 5f to 7f winner of five races Glencairn Star (by Selkirk). The dam, a smart two year old winner of the Group 1 7f Moyglare Stud Stakes and the Group 2 6f Lowther Stakes, is half-sister to four winners including the very useful Group 1 Moyglare Stud Stakes second Hotelgenie Dot Com (herself dam of the dual Group 1 winner Simply Perfect. The second dam, Birch Creek (by Carwhite), was placed five times including when third in the Group 3 1m Premio Royal Mares and is a half-sister to seven winners. (Helena Springfield Ltd).
'She's a nice filly, well put together and has grown a lot but without losing her strength. Amongst the fillies she'll be one of the first to appear and I expect her to run around July time.'

368. LIFFEY DANCER (IRE) ★★★★★

b.f. Sadler's Wells – Brigid (Irish River)
March 21. Eighth foal. 2,500,000Y. Tattersalls

October 1. Charlie Gordon-Watson. Sister to the Group 1 7f Moyglare Stud Stakes winner Sequoyah, to the 2007 two year old Group 1 Fillies' Mile winner Listen and the fair 7f winner Clara Bow and half-sister to the Irish listed 5.6f winner and Group 3 7f placed Oyster Catcher (by Bluebird). The dam, a minor French three year old 1m winner, is a sister to the French listed 7f winner Or Vision (herself dam of the Group/Grade 1 winners Dolphin Street, Insight and Saffron Walden) and a half-sister to six winners. The second dam, Luv Luvin' (by Raise a Native), won two races in the USA and was stakes-placed. (Merry Fox Stud).

'We call her 'two point five' because of her purchase price! She's got a pedigree to die for, she's really well, looks very nice and is well put together. We haven't done much with her but she's doing well and will hopefully be racing from July onwards.'

369. MABAIT ★★★★
b.c. Kyllachy – Czarna Roza (Polish Precedent)
March 1. First foal. 70,000Y. Tattersalls October 2. L Cumani. The dam is an unraced half-sister to eight winners including the dam of the Group 2 Queen Mary Stakes winner Elletelle. The second dam, Nemesia (by Mill Reef), a very useful 10.2f and four year old 13.4f listed winner, is a full or half-sister to eight winners including the smart Tattersalls Rogers Gold Cup winner Elegant Air. (Sheikh Mohammed Obaid Al Maktoum).

'He's a precocious type, a bit on the small side but well put together. Quite cheeky and full of energy, he should be one of my early two year old's, probably from June or July onwards, starting at six furlongs.'

370. MAGALING (IRE) ★★★★
ch.c. Medicean – Fling (Pursuit Of Love)
March 15. First foal. 110,000Y. Tattersalls October 2. L Cumani. The dam, a quite useful listed-placed 10f winner, is a sister to one winner and a half-sister to eight winners including the useful 6f (at two years) and 9f winner Rudimental. The second dam, Full Orchestra (by Shirley Heights), a quite useful

10f winner at three years, is a half-sister to 11 winners including the US Grade 3 winner Cat Attack. (Sheikh Mohammed Obaid Al Maktoum).

'He should be one of those horses I hope to race from June or July onwards. He's a bit on the small side but full of spirit and an excellent mover. He'll start off at six before moving up to seven furlongs.'

371. MAJOR PHIL ★★★
b.c. Captain Rio – Choral Sundown (Night Shift)
March 13. Ninth foal. 32,000Y. Doncaster St Leger. G Howson. Half-brother to smart two year old 7f and 1m winner and Group 2 12f King Edward VII Stakes second Snowstorm (by Environment Friend), to the useful 7f to 12f winner of eight races Celestial Welcome, the quite useful 1m winner of four races here and subsequent Swedish winner Night Chorus, the quite useful two year old 6f winner Rouge Etoile (all by Most Welcome) and the fair 1m winner Malech (by Bahhare). The dam, a quite useful winner of four races at up to 12f, is a half-sister to five winners. The second dam, Choir (by High Top), is an unplaced full or half-sister to nine winners. (L Marinopoulos).

'A nice little colt, he's a bit on the small side but he does everything nicely and he could be among my early brigade. He's bred to be a six furlong horse.'

372. MASWERTE (IRE) ★★★
b.c. Fraam – Rose Chime (Tirol)
February 24. Seventh foal. 48,000Y. Tattersalls October 2. L Cumani. Half-brother to the quite useful 2007 two year old listed 5f placed Rose Rouge (by Kyllachy), to the modest all-weather dual 1m winner Tiger Tops (by Sabrehill) and the modest 7f winner Plum (by Pivotal). The dam, a modest two year old 6f and 7f winner, is a half-sister to five winners including the Irish listed winner Rosie's Mac. The second dam, Repicado Rose (by Repicado), is a placed half-sister to five winners. (Sheikh Mohammed Obaid Al Maktoum).

'A very good-looking horse, he's huge and therefore a bit weak but beautifully put together.

Once he finds his strength he could be a horse that will do something this year.'

373. PAISLEY ★★

ch.f. Pivotal – Pongee (Barathea)
February 21. First foal. The dam, a very useful Group 2 12f Lancashire Oaks winner, is a half-sister to the very useful 10f (at two years) and 11f winner and listed-placed Pukka. The second dam, Puce (by Darshaan), a very useful listed 12f winner, is a half-sister to seven winners. (Fittocks Stud).

'The dam developed and improved a lot from three to four, so although she's nice whatever this filly does this year will be a bonus.'

374. PRIMERA VISTA ★★

b.c. Haafhd – Colorvista
(Cadeaux Genereux)
March 27. Sixth foal. 48,000Y. Tattersalls October 1. Not sold. Half-brother to Island Vista (by Montjeu), placed second over 7f on his only start at two years in 2997, to the very useful two year old dual 7f winner and Group 1 Racing Post Trophy second Mudeer (by Warning), the fairly useful 13f and 14.6f winner Durable, the Japanese winner of seven races Step Forward (both by Caerleon), the quite useful 12f to 2m all-weather winner Amir Zaman (by Salse) and the Japanese two year old winner Christian Name (by Cadeaux Genereux). The dam is an unraced half-sister to Colorspin (winner of the Irish Oaks and dam of the Group 1 winners Zee Zee Top, Opera House and Kayf Tara), Bella Colora (winner of the Prix de l'Opera and dam of the very smart colt Stagecraft) and the Irish Champion Stakes winner Cezanne. The second dam, Reprocolor (by Jimmy Reppin), was a very useful winner of the Group 3 12f Lingfield Oaks Trial and the Group 3 12f Lancashire Oaks. (Castle Down Racing).

'He was a little bit backward and took time to come together but he's going the right way now. It's still too early to say when he'll be ready to run but hopefully it'll be sometime in the second half of the season.'

375. RAGLAN (IRE) ★★

ch.c. Night Shift – Intellectuelle (Caerleon)
May 3. Seventh foal. 52,000Y. Tattersalls October 2. H Howson. Half-brother to the quite useful two year old 6f winner Montaquila (by Hawk Wing), the fair Irish 10f winner Strike One (by Danehill Dancer), the French 6f winner Fastidia (by Fasliyev) and a bumpers winner by Spinning World. The dam, a minor French two year old winner, is a half-sister to the Group 3 10.5f Prix de Flore winner Audacieuse and the Irish listed 14f winner Lord Jim. The second dam, Sarah Georgina (by Persian Bold), a quite useful two year old 6f winner, is a half-sister to ten winners including the French 1,000 Guineas winner Danseuse du Soir. (L Marinopoulos).

'This is a big colt and I didn't expect that when he was bought. He's quite weak at the moment and the next 3 months will tell us where we are with him. Night Shift's usually make two year old's but this colt is out of a Caerleon mare, so we'll just have to wait and see.'

376. SPLASHDOWN ★★★★

ch.f. Falbrav – Space Time (Bering)
February 25. Half-sister to the listed 10f winner Cosmodrome (by Bahri), to the fairly useful two year old 8.2f winner Muscida (by Woodman) and the US triple turf winner at around 1m and 9f Tadreeb (by Theatrical). The dam was placed over 7f at two years in France and is a half-sister to three minor winners. The second dam, Space Ritual (by Top Ville), won at two years in France and is a half-sister to the Canadian Grade 2 winner Calista. (Fittocks Stud).

'A very, very good-looking filly, one of the best lookers in the yard. She goes well, does everything nicely and although she's bigger than her half-sister Cosmodrome she'll be one for the middle of the season onwards and I like her.'

377. SWIFT FLIGHT ★★★★

ch.c. Kyllachy – Starfleet (Inchinor)
April 29. Fourth foal. 95,000Y. Tattersalls October 2. Charlie Gordon-Watson. Half-brother to the useful two year old 7f winner and subsequent US Grade 3 third Mr Napper Tandy (by Bahamian Bounty) and to the quite useful

1m and 9f winner Wind Star (by Piccolo). The dam, a modest maiden, was placed over 7f and 10f and is a half-sister to six winners including the listed National Stakes winner Pool Music. The second dam, Sunfleet (by Red Sunset), is a placed half-sister to seven winners including the Group 3 Curragh Stakes winner Peace Girl. (Saeed Suhail).

'This is a fairly precocious colt, he's well put together, appears to be fairly speedy and he'll probably start off at six furlongs in mid-summer.'

378. THIEF ★★
b.c. Falbrav – Eurolink Raindance (Alzao)
March 2. Third foal. Half-brother to the quite useful 2007 6f and 7f placed two year old House (by Elusive Quality). The dam, a useful two year old 6f and 7f and subsequent US Grade 3 winner, is a half-sister to the smart 7f (at two years) and 10f winner Bonecrusher and the Group 3 10f winner Mango Mischief. The second dam, Eurolink Mischief (by Be My Chief), a quite useful three year old 12f winner, is a half-sister to the useful middle-distance colt and listed Glorious Stakes winner Duke Of Eurolink. (The Antoniades Family).

'He hasn't been in long so I don't know much about him yet, but he's a biggish horse that moves well and he should be alright.'

379. TOO TALL ★★★★
b.c. Medicean – Embark
(Soviet Star)
April 28. First foal. 145,000Y. Tattersalls October 1. Charlie Gordon-Watson. The dam ran once unplaced and is a sister to the dual Group 1 Lockinge Stakes winner Soviet Star and a half-sister to four winners. The second dam, Shore Line (by High Line), a very useful 7f winner, was fourth in the Oaks and is a sister to the Group two winners Ancholia and Quay Line (grandam of the Oaks winner Pure Grain). (S.B.C Ltd).

'He's going through a growing stage at the moment, he's very "up behind" but I like him, he's a very good mover and he seems to have the right attitude. I'm very hopeful he'll be running from the mid-summer onwards.'

380. UNNAMED ★★★★
b.c. Danehill Dancer – Model Queen
(Kingmambo)
March 17. Fourth foal. 350,000Y. Tattersalls October 1. Ed Dunlop. Half-brother to the quite useful dual 7f winner Regal Parade (by Pivotal) and to the minor French 10f winner Sister Sylvia (by Fantastic Light). The dam, a fair three year old 7f winner, is a half-sister to five winners including the French listed 1m winner Arabride. The second dam, Model Bride (by Blushing Groom), is an unraced half-sister to six winners including the smart Queen Elizabeth II Stakes third Zaizafon (herself the dam of Zafonic) and to the unraced Modena (the dam of Elmaamul and Reams Of Verse). (Lady C Warren & The Hon. Mrs H Herbert).

'A very good-looking horse, he's a big colt and he's still growing but I like him. Hopefully one for July onwards over seven furlongs.'

MICHAEL DODS
381. COMPTON FORD ★★
ch.c. Compton Place – Coffee Time (Efisio)
April 21. Third foal. 25,000Y. Doncaster St Leger. J Brummitt. Half-brother to the fair triple 5f winner (including at two years) Cuppacocoa (by Bertolini). The dam was placed 19 times at two to four years, including in the listed Hilary Needler Stakes at two years and is a half-sister to three winners. The second dam, Petula (by Petong), won the listed St Hugh's Stakes at two years and is a half-sister to six winners including the Group 3 Ballycorus Stakes winner Naahy. (Septimus Racing Group).

'He's sharp and wants fast ground – he didn't like the going on his debut at Newcastle. He's not the biggest horse, so we'll be aiming to win with him this year.'

382. CUTTING COMMENTS ★★★
b.c. Acclamation – Razor Sharp (Bering)
April 10. Second foal. 45,000Y. Doncaster St Leger. J Brummitt. Half-brother to the two year old 8.6f seller winner Gold Response (by Intikhab). The dam won over 11f in France and is a half-sister to two winners. The second dam, Navarazi (by Arazi), is an unraced half-sister to

Dancing Brave and the dual Group 1 winner Jolypha. (Mr A Dick).

'He'll be racing in May, he's very sharp and I'll start him off over five furlongs but he'll get six. A forward type, with a bit of scope and definitely a two year old type.'

383. EMBRACING THE KING ★★

b.f. King's Best – All Embracing (Night Shift)
March 5. First foal. €32,000Y. Goffs Million. Jeremy Brummitt. The dam, a quite useful 7f winner, is a half-sister to numerous winners including the very smart 6f and 7f (at two years) and Group 2 10f Prix Guillaume d'Ornano winner Highdown and the Group 2 12f King Edward VII Stakes second Elshadi. The second dam, Rispoto (by Mtoto), a modest 12f winner, is a half-sister to seven winners including the Group 3 10f Royal Whip Stakes winner Jahafil.

'Quite a nice filly but she certainly won't be out before September over seven furlongs. It's a late-maturing pedigree so we'll just go steady with her.'

384. HEY UP DAD ★★

b.c. Fantastic Light – Spanish Quest (Rainbow Quest)
April 23. Third foal. 14,000Y. Tattersalls October 2. Michael Dods. The dam is an unraced half-sister to the listed winner Spanish Don. The second dam, Spanish Wells (by Sadler's Wells), won at three years in France and is a sister to two winners and a half-sister to the Irish Oaks winner Wemyss Bight.

'He probably won't run until there's a mile race for him but he's a very nice horse and for 14,000 Guineas he was for nothing.' TRAINER'S BARGAIN BUY

385. JIMWIL (IRE) ★★★

b.c. One Cool Cat – Vulnerable (Hector Protector)
February 4. First foal. 35,000Y. Tattersalls October 2. Dwayne Woods. The dam won over 7f at three years in France. The second dam, Beleaguer (by Rainbow Quest), a winner at four years, is a sister to the Group 1 Racing Post Trophy winner Armiger and a half-sister to four

winners. (Bill Nelson & Jim Mahony).

'He'll be running towards the end of May. Quite sharp, he'll be quite a nice two year old.'

386. MISTER BOMBASTIC (IRE) ★★★

ch.c. Monsieur Bond – Sheen Falls (Prince Rupert)
March 7. Seventh foal. €48,000Y. Goffs Million. J Brummitt. Half-brother to the Irish 7f to 9f winner and listed placed Provosky (by Polish Patriot), to the fairly useful two year old 1m all-weather winner Strikeen (by Intikhab), the quite useful Irish 11f winner Glandore (by Persian Bold), the modest 10f winner Wednesdays Boy (by Alhaarth) and the Italian three year old winner of three races Lord Royce (by Mujtahid). The dam, a quite useful Irish 11f winner, is a half-sister to two winners including the Irish listed placed Amethyst. The dam was placed at two years and is a half-sister to seven winners including the Group 2 Pretty Polly Stakes winner Noora Abu. The second dam, Ishtar Abu (by St Chad), won at three years and is a half-sister to five winners. (Mr W A Tinkler).

'A big horse, he'll probably start off over a stiff six furlongs, or maybe seven, from July onwards and he's quite a nice, striking individual.'

387. MISTER FANTASTIC ★★

ch.c. Green Tune – Lomapamar (Nashwan)
March 21. First foal. 35,000Y. Tattersalls October 3. J Brummitt. The dam, a fair three year old 10f winner, is a half-sister to five winners including the two year old Group 2 1m Royal Lodge Stakes winner Mons and the Irish Oaks third Inforapenny. The second dam, Morina (by Lyphard), won over 11f in France and is a half-sister to eight winners. (Mr W A Tinkler).

'He's quite a nice horse but it's a late maturing pedigree, so we'll start him off from August onwards over seven furlongs.'

388. MISTER TINKTASTIC (IRE) ★★

ch.c. Noverre – Psychic (Alhaarth)
March 14. Second living foal. 50,000Y. Tattersalls October 2. Dwayne Woods. Half-brother to the minor French dual three year old winner Barapsy (by Barathea). The dam, a fair

three year old 5f winner, is a half-sister to four winners including the two year old winners and listed-placed Hurricane Floyd and Best Side. The second dam, Mood Swings (by Shirley Heights), a fair two year old 6f winner, is a sister to the listed two year old Sweet Solera Stakes winner Catwalk and a half-sister to five winners. (Mr W A Tinkler).

'He'll start off at six furlongs in June or July, he's quite big and a nice type of horse that'll be sharp later on.'

389. UNNAMED ★★★
ch.g. Haafhd – Mall Queen (Sheikh Albadou)
March 30. 18,000Y. Tattersalls October 3. D Neale. The dam won the listed 6f Prix Yacowlef at two years and is closely related to the two year old 6f listed Criterium d'Evry winner Sheer Reason and a half-sister to the useful Group 3 11.5f Lingfield Oaks Trial winner Munnaya and the useful two year old 6f winner Balla Jidaal. The second dam, Hiamm (by Alydar), a very useful filly, won the Group 3 6f Princess Margaret Stakes at two years and listed events over 7.6f and 1m at three years. She is a half-sister to the champion Canadian three year old Key to the Moon, the dual US Grade 1 winner Gorgeous and the Grade 1 Kentucky Oaks winner Seaside Attraction. herself dam of the Cherry Hinton winner Red Carnival and the US Grade 1 winner Golden Attraction. (D Neale).

'His knees are a bit open so we haven't got on with him yet. A strong, stocky horse, he'll be a quick horse when he's ready.'

ANN DUFFIELD
390. CAMELOT COMMUNION (IRE) ★★★★
b.f. Elusive City – Second Prayer (Singspiel)
January 9. Third foal. €65,000Y. Goffs Million. Gill Richardson. Half-sister to the modest 2007 5f placed two year old Miss Clonyn (by Statue Of Liberty) and to the fair Irish 7f (at two years) and UAE 1m winner First Empire (by Desert Prince). The dam is an unraced half-sister to five winners including the listed Galtres Stakes winner Firecrest. The second dam, Trefoil (by Blakeney), won three races in France and is a half-sister to six winners including the French

Group 2 winner First Prayer, the US Grade 3 winner Water Lily (herself dam of the Grade 1 winner Talinum) and the dam of the Melbourne Cup winner Jeune. (Middleham Park Racing XXIV).

'The sire has had a couple of winners already from his first crop and this is quite a nice filly, we like her and we paid a fair bit for her. A very good-looking filly, she's just how you would want a filly to look. a beautiful head, great conformation, strong-bodied and nice bone. A good mover, she carries her jockey's well and although she has got some pace, being by Singspiel I think she'll be better over six furlongs than five and she'll progress.'

391. HEL'S ANGEL (IRE) ★★
b.f. Pyrus – Any Dream (Shernazar)
April 3. €5,500Y. Tattersalls Ireland. Gil Richardson. Half-sister to the modest two year old dual 7f winner Dreaming Diva (by Whittingham) and to the moderate five year old 9.5f winner Rem Time (by Fraam). The dam won over 13f and is a half-sister to three winners including the Irish Group 3 winner Tarry Flynn. The second dam, Danzig Lass (by Danzig) won at two years and is a sister to a stakes winner and a half-sister to the US Grade 2 winner Jade Flush. (Mrs H L Baines).

'She's grown a lot and is now quite tall, so she won't be out too early. But she goes really well and she's very game.'

392. LADY LUACHMHAR ★★
br.f. Galileo – Radhwa (Shining Steel)
April 13. Fourth foal. €220,000Y. Goffs Million. Gill Richardson. Half-sister to the fair 2007 7f placed two year old Dr Livingstone (by Dr Fong). The dam won the listed 7f Prix Herod at two years. The second dam, Iguassu (by Fabulous Dancer), is a placed half-sister to nine winners including the Group 2 winner Shir Dar. (Mrs H Steel).

'A very good-looking filly, she was always big and she's grown even more. She won't until the back-end of the season and again, anything she does this year will be a bonus. A nice, quality filly but very much a three year old type.'

393. PACIFIC BAY (IRE) ★★★
b.br.f. Diktat – Wild Clover (Lomitas)
February 3. First foal. €50,000Y. Goffs Million. Not sold. The dam, a French 9f winner, is a half-sister to four winners including the very useful 7f and 1m winner Three Graces and the French 12f listed winner Trefula. The second dam, Trefoil (by Kris), was a very useful listed winner over 10.5f in France. She is a full or half-sister to 12 winners including the smart middle-distance winners Maysoon, Richard of York, Three Tails (dam of the high-class middle-distance colts Sea Wave and Tamure) and Third Watch. (Mrs H Steel).
'She was ready to run but we're giving her a bit more time. She's got a bit of pace and we like her. A tough, genuine and good-looking filly, we'd be happy to start her off at five furlongs.'

394. SMOKE ME A KIPPER (IRE) ★★★
gr.f. Verglas – Anoukit (Green Desert)
January 20. Fourth foal. 10,000Y. Tattersalls October 2. Gill Richardson. Half-sister to the French two year old 5f and 6f winner Ingoe (by Bahhare). The dam won 3 minor races at three years in France, including over 10f, and is a half-sister to three winners in France and Spain. The second dam, Amal (by Top Ville), won five races from 3 to 6 years in France and was listed-placed 4 times and is a half-sister to seven winners. (Reavey Gough Racing Partnership).
'She's grown so we backed off her bit and she's just started to do a bit of quicker work now. She's nice, goes quite well and was very cheap. She isn't tall but she's quite lengthy and very correct. She looks like her Dad and has a bit of a knee action.'

395. STAR OF SOPHIA (IRE) ★★
b.f. Hawk Wing – Sofia Aurora (Chief Honcho)
March 12. Fourth foal. €33,000Y. Tattersalls Ireland. Gill Richardson. Half-sister to the modest 6f to 1m winner Outrageous Flirt (by Indian Lodge) and to the two year old 6f seller winner Queen Of Bulgaria (by Imperial Ballet). The dam, a minor two year old winner in Italy, is a half-sister to five winners including the smart hurdler Mixsterthetrixster. The second dam,

Parliament House (by General Assembly), a minor winner in the USA is a half-sister to numerous winners including Molesnes (Group 1 Prix du Cadran). (Middleham Park Racing XVII).
'A little bit weak at the moment, we've backed off her for now but she's a good-looking filly that will want a trip.'

396. STREVELYN ★★★
br.c. Namid – Kali (Linamx)
February 19. First foal. 18,500Y. Doncaster Festival. Gill Richardson. The dam, a fair three year old 7f winner, is a half-sister to two winners. The second dam, Alkarida (by Akarad), won over 1m at three years in France and is a half-sister to seven winners. (Mr C L Stirling).
'He goes really nicely, he's not a sharp and early two year old but hopefully he'll be one for May or June onwards. He'll want six or seven furlongs and might even stay a mile, being out of a Linamix mare. He goes well and although he'll be better as a three year old he'll be alright this year and we do like him.' Having already given me her 'Bargain Buy', Ann asked George for his opinion and this is the one he came up with! TRAINER'S BARGAIN BUY

397. SUNSET CREST ★★
b.f. Reel Buddy – Day Star (Dayjur)
March 13. Fifth foal. 12,000Y. Doncaster St Leger. Ann Duffield. Half-sister to the unraced 2007 two year old Babel (by Xaar) and to the quite useful two year old 6f winner Tractor Boy (by Mind Games). The dam, a fair three year old 6f winner, is a half-sister to numerous winners including the French 1,000 Guineas winner Rose Gypsy and the fairly useful 7f winners Egoli and Crystal Cavern. The second dam, Krisalya (by Kris), a fairly useful 10.4f winner, is a half-sister to 12 winners including the high-class Group 1 9.3f Prix d'Ispahan winner Sasuru, the high-class Challenge Stakes and Jersey Stakes winner Sally Rous, the listed winners Sossus Vlei and Little Bean, the Group 3 Park Hill Stakes second The Faraway Tree and the Ascot Gold Cup third Chauve Souris. (Mr T Holdcroft & Mrs G Garrity).
'She's alright and is coming along nicely. We're only just doing some faster work with her, so

we're a bit behind yet. A good-looking filly, she's quite big, we like her and she looks like a sprinter.'

398. THE PROPER GURU ★★
b.f. Ishiguru – Aloma's Reality (Proper Reality)
January 19. Second foal. Sister to the fair 2007 two year old 5f winner The Real Guru. The dam was unplaced in two starts in the UAE and is out of the multiple US sprint winner Palinode (by Pall Mall). (Adrian & Alison Parry).
'She's a big, backward filly, she was one of the last to be broken and brought in, so although she's cantering every day she's behind most of the others. But once she gets her act together she'll be a nice filly and the pedigree says she'll be a two year old.'

399. VENETIAN LADY ★★★
b.f. Tobougg – Perfect Partner (Be My Chief)
February 10. Fourth reported foal. 20,000Y. Tattersalls October 2. Gill Richardson. Half-sister to the unplaced 2007 two year old Top Vision (by Medicean) and to the modest two year old 6f winner Molly Dancer (by Emarati). The dam is an unraced half-sister to six winners including the 6f Ayr Gold Cup and Washington Singer Stakes winner Funfair Wane and to the Italian listed 7.5f winner Cabcharge Striker. The second dam, the fairly useful listed two year old 6f winner Ivory Bride (by Domynsky), is a half-sister to the useful listed 8.5f and listed 10f winner Putuna and the useful sprinter Lochonica. (Mr S I Dalziel).
'A very big filly, she's also been very gross so she's taken a lot of time to come to hand. She's making progress now and she's a lovely filly otherwise – strong, well-built and looks like a sprinter.'

400. WHAT A FELLA ★★★
b.c. Lujain – Fred's Dream (Cadeaux Genereux)
February 17. Third foal. 8,000Y. Tattersalls October 3. Gill Richardson. The dam, placed once over 1m at three years in a seller, is a half-sister to two winners. The second dam, Vaguar (by Vaguely Noble), a listed-placed winner in France, is a half-sister to three winners.
'A forward going colt, he's big and strong and it

won't be long before he's out. One of our earlier types, he's really good-looking, a decent mover and is just a nice size.' TRAINER'S BARGAIN BUY

ED DUNLOP
401. ALKHAFIF ★★★ ♠
b.c. Royal Applause – My First Romance (Danehill)
March 8. Ninth foal. 180,000Y. Tattersalls October 2. Shadwell Estate Co. Half-brother to the fairly useful 2007 6f placed two year old Romantic Destiny (by Dubai Destination), to the Group 3 5f Queen Mary Stakes winners Romantic Myth (by Mind Games) and Romantic Liason (by Primo Dominie), the useful two year old 5f winner Power Packed (by Puissance), the fairly useful dual 5f winner Zargus (by Zamindar), the quite useful two year old 7f winner Wedaad (by Fantastic Light) and the fair two year old 5.5f winner Chance For Romance (by Entrepreneur). The dam ran twice unplaced and is a half-sister to six minor winners here and abroad. The second dam, Front Line Romance (by Caerleon), won once and was Group 3 placed over 1m at two years in Ireland and is a full or half-sister to ten winners including Knight Line Dancer, a winner of four Group 3 events in Italy. (Hamdan Al Maktoum).
'This is quite a tall horse, not as sharp and precocious as you'd expect from the pedigree but he's a good mover and has a good attitude for a Royal Applause. I think he'll be alright later in the season.'

402. ANDHAAR ★★★
b.br.c. Bahri – Deraasaat (by Nashwan)
January 27. The dam, a quite useful two year old 8.2f winner, is a sister to the useful two year old 1m and listed 9f placed Wahchi, closely related to the smart Group 2 14.6f Park Hill Stakes winner Ranin and a half-sister to numerous winners including the very useful 7f and 1m winner Ghalib. The second dam, Nafhaat (by Roberto), a fairly useful 12f winner, stayed 15f. (Hamdan Al Maktoum).
'A good-moving colt with a good attitude but despite being an early foal he's probably one for later in the year.'

HERNANDO

Sire of 34 individual 3-y-o winners and 12 individual 2-y-o winners in 2007

Fee: **£12,000** (1st October Special Live Foal)

NORTHERN DANCER Sire Line

New at Lanwades for 2008

PICCOLO

Sire of unbeaten 2007 top 2-y-o WINKER WATSON

Fee: **£5,000** (1st October Special Live Foal)

IN REALITY Sire Line

SELKIRK

Sire of 10 individual Gr.1 winners and a leading broodmare sire

Fee: **£35,000** (1st October)

NATIVE DANCER Sire Line

First Season 2008

SIR PERCY

Unbeaten Champion 2-y-o and Derby Winner

Fee: **£8,000** (1st October Special Live Foal)

NEVER BEND Sire Line

First European yearlings 2008

WITH APPROVAL

80% winners to runners in UK and Ireland in 2007

Fee: **£5,000** (1st October Special Live Foal)

GREY SOVEREIGN Sire Line

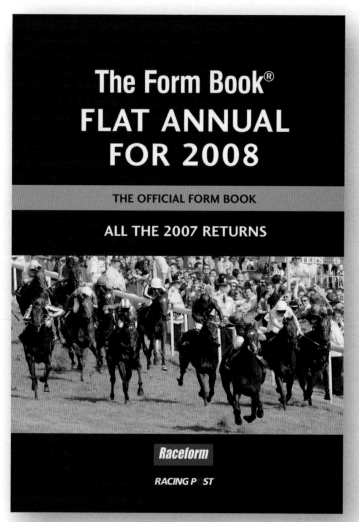

403. ARCTIC FREEDOM ★★★
b.br.f. *War Chant – Polar Bird (Thatching)*
March 23. Twelfth foal. 52,000Y. Tattersalls December. Charlie Gordon-Watson. Half-sister to the useful 2007 two year old listed 6f winner Polar Circle, to the smart two year old listed 7f winner and Group 2 6f Gimcrack Stakes second Fokine, to the fairly useful 6f winner Arctic Burst (all by Royal Academy), the Group 2 6f Prix Robert Papin winner and Group 1 1m Coronation Stakes second Ocean Ridge (by Storm Bird) and the fairly useful 5f winner Alpine Twist (by Seattle Dancer). The dam, a very useful winner of six races here and in the USA including two year old Group 3 5f Debutante Stakes, is a half-sister to six winners. The second dam, Arctic Winter (by Briartic), a winner at three years in Germany, is a sister to the Canadian Grade 1 winner Son Of Briartic and a half-sister to ten winners including the dam of the Canadian Grade 1 winner Halo's Princess. (Sangster Family).
'A very nice filly, she's good-moving, racey and attractive.'

404. AZWA ★★★
b.f. *Haafhd – Shahaamah (Red Ransom)*
February 17. Second foal. Half-sister to the fairly useful 2007 two year old 7f winner Zakhaaref (by Daylami). The dam is an unraced half-sister to four winners including the very useful two year old 6f winner and Group 2 6f Lowther Stakes second Khulan and the useful 7f (at two years) and 1m winner Thajja. The second dam, Jawlaat (by Dayjur), a fairly useful dual 6f winner, is closely related to the July Cup winner Elnadim and a half-sister to the Irish 1,000 Guineas winner Mehthaaf. (Hamdan Al Maktoum).
'I've got two Haafhd's and they're both small. This one looks racey, she's about to do some faster work and so far so good. She's got a nice pedigree and she looks OK.'

405. COME ON TOBY ★★★★
b.c. *Piccolo – Fleeting Moon (Fleetwood)*
February 3. First foal. 40,000Y. Tattersalls October 3. Blandford Bloodstock. The dam, a modest 11f all-weather winner, is a half-sister to four minor winners. The second dam, Aunt Judy (by Great Nephew), is an unplaced half-sister to eight winners including five listed winners. (Old Road Securities plc).
'He's done some faster work and he looks like a six furlong type two year old. He's nice, he goes well and will be out in May.'

406. CRYSTAL MOMENTS ★★★
b.f. *Haafhd – Celestial Choir (Celestial Storm)*
February 24. Fourth foal. 32,000Y. Tattersalls October 2. Blandford Bloodstock. Half-sister to a minor winner abroad by So Factual and a hurdles winner by Key Of Luck. The dam, a quite useful 7f to 12f winner of nine races on the flat, also won seven races over jumps and is a half-sister to five winners. The second dam, Choir (by High Top), is an unplaced half-sister to nine winners. (Mohammed Jaber).
'I like this filly, she's racey and has done some work. She wasn't very expensive to be honest and she's a solid, strong, neat filly that goes OK.'

407. DEMEANOUR (USA) ★★★★
ch.f. *Giant's Causeway – Akuna Bay*
(Mr Prospector)
March 30. Fifth foal. 130,000Y. Tattersalls October 1. John Warren. Half-sister to the useful 2007 two year old 5f and 6f winner and Group 3 Solario Stakes third Gaspar Van Wittel (by Danehill Dancer), to the quite useful 10f winner Sugar Ray (by Danehill) and a minor winner abroad by King Of Kings. The dam, a two year old 7f winner, is a half-sister to three winners including the Ribblesdale Stakes second Gothic Dream. The second dam, Dark Lomond (by Lomond), won the Irish St Leger and is a half-sister to five winners including the Irish Group winners South Atlantic and Forlene. (Highclere Thoroughbred Racing (Eclipse)).
'This is a pretty filly that cost a fair bit and she has a pedigree. She'll be nice, probably over six or seven furlongs.'

408. DERBAAS (USA) ★★
b.c. *Seeking The Gold – Sultana (Storm Cat)*
February 26. Second foal. Half-brother to

the quite useful 1m winner Jaleela (by Kingmambo). The dam is an unraced sister to the high-class Group 1 7f Prix de la Salamandre and Group 1 1m Sussex Stakes winner Aljabr. The second dam, Sierra Madre (by Baillamont), a very smart winner of the Group 1 1m Prix Marcel Boussac and the Group 1 12f Prix Vermeille, is a half-sister to several minor winners. (Hamdan Al Maktoum).
'Still in Dubai in early April.'

409. FAREER ★★★
ch.c. Bahamian Bounty – Songsheet (Dominion)
April 29. Fifth living foal. 160,000Y. Tattersalls October 1. Shadwell Estate Co. Half-brother to the fairly useful 5f and 6f (at two years) and subsequent US stakes winner Monsieur Boulanger (by Compton Place) and the modest 12f all-weather winner Bond Casino (by Kyllachy). The dam, a fair 5f winner of five races from three to five years, is a half-sister to eight minor winners. The second dam, Songstead (by Song), a fairly useful 6f winner of four races at two and three years, is a half-sister to three winners. (Hamdan Al Maktoum).
'A nice, good-looking horse. He moves well and cost a lot of money for a Bahamian Bounty. A colt with plenty of size and scope, I like him but he'll be a seven furlong horse I'd say.'

410. HUKBA (IRE) ★★
b.f. Anabaa – Banaadir (Diesis)
February 21. Half-sister to the quite useful 9f winner Jidaar (by Grand Lodge). The dam was placed over 10f and is a half-sister to one winner. The second dam, Treble (by Riverman), won the Group 1 Prix Saint-Alary and is a half-sister to two winners. (Hamdan Al Maktoum).
'A nice filly but she's going to want some time.'

411. JOHNNY ROOK (GER) ★★★★
b.c. Dashing Blade – Just Zoud (Ezzoud)
February 4. First foal. The dam is a minor winning half-sister to several winners including the US Grade Cinema Handicap winner Just Wonder. The second dam, Just Fky (by Capote), won five races and is out of a half-sister to the

US Grade 1 winners Stella Madrid and Tis Juliet. (The Serendipity Partnership).
'He was bought for me in Germany and his sire is pretty successful over there. This is a strong, powerful horse that will be a two year old, I like him and he looks to go nicely.'

412. LARAFFELLE (GR) ★★★
ch.f. Bertolini – Holgera (Winged Love)
February 26. First foal. €20,000Y. Goffs Million. Blandford Bloodstock. The dam, a minor dual winner in Germany at four years, is a half-sister to three winners including the German listed winner Homita. The second dam, Honcera (by Salmon Leap), is an unraced half-sister to eight winners. (J Weatherby, Champneys).
'I nicked this filly! The dam wasn't particularly good but she's looks a strong, racey individual and we're just doing some faster work with her.'

413. LITTLE CALLA (IRE) ★★★★
ch.f. Indian Ridge – Queen Of Palms (Desert Prince)
April 1. First foal. €145,000Y. Goffs Million. Blandford Bloodstock. The dam, an Irish listed 7.5f three year old winner, is a half-sister to the Irish listed winners Artistic Blue and Cool Clarity. The second dam, Tapolite (by Tap On Wood), won the listed 7f Tyros Stakes, is a sister to the two year old Group 3 1m Killavullen Stakes winner Sedulous and a half-sister to four winners. (St Albans Bloodstock LLP).
'This is a nice filly. She's racey, has done some fast work and has got some size. She wasn't very big when we bought her but she's filled out. I worked her on the grass the other day and she seemed to like it. I like her.'

414. MASAMAH (IRE) ★★★★ ♠
gr.c. Exceed And Excel – Bethesda (Distant Relative)
March 19. Third living foal. 60,000Y. Doncaster St Leger. Shadwell Estate Co. Half-brother to the fair two year old 5f all-weather winner Fluttering Rose (by Compton Place). The dam, a fairly useful 5.7f and 6f winner at four years, is a half-sister to four winners including the Group 1 6f Middle Park Stakes winner Fard. The second

dam, Anneli Rose (by Superlative), a plating-class winner of one race over 6f on the all-weather at three years, is a half-sister to the Middle Park Stakes and Flying Childers Stakes winner Gallic League. (Hamdan Al Maktoum).

'Everyone seems to be excited about this new sire Exceed And Excel. This looks a nice horse, I thought he was going to be very early but he's grown, which is good, and he's going to be a nice, big horse. He looks a racey, fast type of horse.'

415. MOONBURST ★★★

gr.f. Dalakhani – Moon Goddess
(Rainbow Quest)

March 10. Third foal. The dam, a fairly useful 1m winner, is a half-sister to the Group 1 Eclipse Stakes and Group 1 Lockinge Stakes winner and sire Medicean. The second dam, Mystic Goddess (by Storm Bird), a fairly useful winner of the listed 7f Sweet Solera Stakes at two years, was placed in the Queen Mary Stakes, the Cherry Hinton Stakes and the Rockfel Stakes and is a half-sister to the smart Group 1 Gran Criterium winner Sanam and to the South African Grade 2 winner Shaybani. (Cheveley Park Stud).

'A small, neat, strong filly, she's only little and on pedigree she should stay but maybe there's speed coming from the second dam. She looks OK and has done a couple of half-speeds.'

416. NASEMAH (IRE) ★★★

ch.f. Sakhee – Nafhaat (Roberto)

May 12. Fifteenth foal. Half-sister to the smart Group 2 14.6f Park Hill Stakes winner Ranin (by Unfuwain), to the very useful 7f and 1m winner Ghalib (by Soviet Star), the useful 6.5f (at two years) to 7f winner Qhazeenah (by Marju), the useful two year old 1m and listed 9f placed Wahchi, the quite useful two year old 8.2f winner Deraasaat (both by Nashwan), the quite useful 6f (at two years) and 1m winner Mihnah (by Lahib) and the quite useful 7.6f and 10f winner Hadeel (by Polish Precedent). The dam, a fairly useful 12f winner, stayed 15f. The second dam, Distant Horizon (by Exclusive Native), is a lightly raced sister to the US Grade 1 12f turf winner Sisterhood. (Hamdan Al Maktoum).

'I like her, she was quite weak when she came in and I've just sent her for a holiday. She'll be a nice filly later on.'

417. NORTHERN HERO (IRE) ★★★★

b.c. Hawk Wing – Bona Dea (Danehill)

January 21. Second foal. 75,000Y. Tattersalls October 2. Charlie Gordon-Watson. Half-brother to Simone Martini (by Montjeu), placed fourth once over 1m at two years in 2007. The dam is an unraced sister to four winners including the French listed winner Darina. The second dam, Sweet Justice (by Law Society), won once at three years in France and is a half-sister to seven winners.

'This colt is small and racey, he'll be a two year old and has done some faster work. He'll start in the six furlong maidens and he goes well.'

418. PARTNER SHIFT (IRE) ★★★

b.c. Night Shift – What A Picture
(Peintre Celebre)

February 22. First foal. €100,000Y. Deauville August. Charlie Gordon-Watson. The dam is an unplaced half-sister to the Group 1 Gran Criterium winner Night Style and the listed Prix d'Automne winner Maid Of Dawkins. The second dam, Style For Life (by Law Society), won two races in France over middle-distances, was listed-placed and is a half-sister to six winners including the Irish Derby winner Grey Swallow. (Mr P Lassen).

'We paid quite a lot of money for him, he's a three-parts brother to Night Style who I trained. He's a strong, scopey horse, good-looking but a little bit backward in his coat so he's behind some of them, but he seems to go OK.'

419. POLEMICA (IRE) ★★★

b.f. Rock Of Gibraltar – Lady Scarlett
(Woodman)

February 22. Fourth foal. 90,000Y. Tattersalls October 2. Will Edmeades. Half-sister to the fairly useful 6f (at two years) and 5f winner and listed placed Sunrise Safari (by Mozart). The dam is an unraced half-sister to five winners including the listed Sha Tin Trophy winner and Irish Derby third Desert Fox and the US Grade

three winners Poolesta and Home Of The Free. The second dam, Radiant (by Foolish Pleasure), won once at three years and is a half-sister to the triple Grade 1 winner Gold And Ivory and to the dams of the Group/Graded stakes winners Heart Of Darkness, Anees, Elusive Quality and Rossini. (Thurloe Thoroughbreds XXIII).
'A nice filly, she's strong, powerful and a good mover. Looks fairly early.'

420. PORTOBELLO PARK (USA) ★★★★
b.c. Montjeu – Bayberry (Bering)
April 12. First foal. The dam, a fairly useful 10f winner, was listed placed and is a half-sister to three winners including the Group 3 1m Prix d'Aumale winner Birthstone. The second dam, Baya (by Nureyev), a very useful Group 3 1m Prix de la Grotte winner, was second in the Group 1 10.5f Prix de Diane. (Ballygallon Stud Ltd).
'This is a nice horse, he's not going to be early but he's not huge and backward, I like him and he has a good attitude so far. He'll be nice.'

421. PROWL ★★★★
b.f. One Cool Cat – Go Supersonic (Zafonic)
March 7. First foal. 38,000Y. Tattersalls October 2. John Warren. The dam, placed fourth over 1m and 10f on both her starts, is a half-sister to the Oaks winner Lady Carla. The second dam, Shirley Superstar (by Shirley Heights), a fairly useful two year old 7f winner, is a half-sister to two winners. (Highclere Thoroughbred Racing (St Simon)).
'A big, scopey filly, she was very well bought and she's a lovely, strong filly that moves extremely well. She looks nice.'

422. RAPID LIGHT ★★★
ch.f. Tobougg – La Coqueta (Kris)
February 5. Third foal. 26,000Y. Tattersalls October 2. Cheveley Park Stud. The dam is an unraced half-sister to three German Group winners including Laverco (German Derby) and Laveron (German St Leger). The second dam, La Virginia (by Surumu), won twice at three years in Germany and is a sister to the dam of the triple Group 1 winner Lomitas. (Cheveley

Park Stud).
'A good-looking filly, she's strong, moves well and looks to go OK.'

423. SATWA LAIRD ★★★★
b.c. Johannesburg – Policy Setter (Deputy Minister)
March 28. Fifth foal. 150,000Y. Tattersalls October 1. D Metcalfe. Half-sister to three minor winners in the USA by Coronado's Quest, Pulpit and Dixieland Band. The dam, a minor winner in the USA, is a half-sister to five winners including the Grand Criterium second and Coronation Cup third Blush Rambler. The second dam, Romanette (by Alleged), a US stakes winner and Grade 2 placed, is a half-sister to six winners. (The Lamprell Partnership).
'Probably the most precocious of all my two year old's, he's strong, neat, powerful and he'll be running in May. He seems to go well.'

424. SATWA STAR (IRE) ★★★★
b.c. King's Best – Sheppard's Watch (Night Shift)
March 28. Second foal. 30,000Y. Tattersalls October 1. Not sold. The dam, a very useful 6f (at two years), Group 3 7.5f Concorde Stakes and dual listed winner, is a full or half-sister to two winners. The second dam, Sheppard's Cross (by Soviet Star), a quite useful 7f winner, is a half-sister to five winners. (The Lamprell Partnership).
'I nicked this one as well! I bought him privately, he's quite a tall horse but he goes well land he's got speed.'

425. SPRING ADVENTURE ★★★
b.f. Dr Fong – Yavari (Alzao)
February 26. The dam, a quite useful all-weather dual 1m winner, is a half-sister to the Group 1 6f Prix Morny, Group 3 6f July Stakes and Group 3 7f Supreme Stakes winner Tagula. The second dam, Twin Island (by Standaan), ran once unplaced and is a half-sister to the Group 3 C.L. Weld Park Stakes winner Jolly Saint (herself dam of the Breeders Cup Mile winner Da Hoss). (Mrs S M Roy).
'A strong, powerful filly that hasn't been in the yard as long as some, she moves well and will be a two year old.'

426. TAE KWON DO (USA) ★★★★

b.c. Thunder Gulch – Judy's Magic
(Wavering Monarch)
**March 18. Sixth foal. $140,000Y. Keeneland
September. Blandford Bloodstock.** Half-
brother to the US winner and Grade 1 Go For
Wand Handicap second She's Got The Beat (by
Sultry Song). The dam, a minor US two year old
winner, is a sister to a stakes winner and a half-
sister to eight winners. The second dam, Mary
Roland (by Relaunch), a minor US three year old
winner, is a half-sister to eight winners.
'The sire's stock generally have a preference for
dirt, but this is a strong, powerful horse. He looks
to go well.'

427. TOLL ROAD ★★

b.f. Dubai Destination – Endorsement
(Warning)
May 10. Fourth foal. Half-sister to the Group 3
10f Ballysax Stakes and Group 3 12f Ballyroan
Stakes winner Mores Wells (by Sadler's Wells),
to the fairly useful dual 12f winner and Group 3
2m Queens Vase third Galient (by Galileo) and
the quite useful two year old 7f winner Road
Rage (by Giant's Causeway). The dam, a useful
winner of the Group 3 2m Queen's Vase, is a
half-sister to three winners. The second dam,
Overdrive (by Shirley Heights), winner of the
Queen Alexandra Stakes, is closely related to the
Lingfield Oaks Trial winner Mill On The Floss and
a half-sister to the Lancashire Oaks second
Shadywood (dam of the smart Park Hill Stakes
winner Madame Dubois). (Cliveden Stud).
'A nice filly, we gave her a bit of a break and she's
a strong filly but a late foal so she's not going to
be early. A very well-bred filly.'

428. YOKOZUNA ★★★

b.c. Efisio – Celt Song (Unfuwain)
**April 27. 12,500Y. Tattersalls 3. Charlie Gordon-
Watson.** Half-brother to the smart two year old
listed 7f Sweet Solera Stakes winner and 1,000
Guineas, Coronation Stakes and Nassau Stakes
placed Princess Ellen (by Tirol) and to numerous
maidens. The dam is an unraced half-sister to
three minor winners. (Pims Partnership).
'A typical Efisio, he's strong, compact and racey.

The dam hasn't bred anything apart from
Princess Ellen who I bought for virtually nothing.'
TRAINER'S BARGAIN BUY

429. ZAFFAAN ★★★★

ch.c. Efisio – Danceabout (Shareef Dancer)
**February 18. 150,000foal. Tattersalls
December. Shadwell Estate Co.** The dam won
the Group 2 Sun Chariot Stakes and the listed 7f
Oak Tree Stakes and is a half-sister to four
winners including the Group 3 6f Prix de
Meautry winner Pole Position. The second dam,
Putupon (by Mummy's Pet), a fairly useful two
year old 5f winner, is a full or half-half-sister to
ten winners including the good horses Jupiter
Island (Japan Cup), Pushy (Queen Mary Stakes)
and Precocious (Gimcrack Stakes). (Hamdan Al
Maktoum).
'I like this colt. He's strong, small and a typical
Efisio. A powerful colt that's done a couple of bits
of faster work and seems to go OK. He'll be an
earlyish two year old.'

430. UNNAMED ★★★

br.f. Galileo – Common Knowledge
(Rainbow Quest)
**January 31. Third foal. 145,000Y. Tattersalls
October 1. Ed Dunlop.** The dam is an unraced
half-sister to six winners including the Group 2
12f Jockey Club Stakes and dual US Grade 2
winner Blueprint and the listed 10f winner Fairy
Godmother. The second dam, Highbrow (by
Shirley Heights), a very useful two year old 1m
winner, was second in the Group 2 12f
Ribblesdale Stakes, is closely related to the good
middle-distance colt Milford and a half-sister to
the Princess of Wales's Stakes winner Height of
Fashion. herself the dam of Nashwan, Nayef and
Unfuwain. (St Albans Bloodstock LLP).
'Not an obvious two year old but she's a lovely
filly. A nice, strong, robust filly and one for later
on but she looks nice.'

431. UNNAMED ★★★

b.f. Royal Applause – Desert Royalty (Alhaarth)
**March 5. First foal. 48,000Y. Tattersalls October
3. Charlie Gordon-Watson.** The dam, a fairly
useful winner of four races from 1m to 12f, was

listed-placed twice and is a half-sister to two winners. The second dam, Buraida (by Balidar), a modest three year old 6f winner, is a sister to the smart sprinter Carol's Treasure and a half-sister to four winners.

'I trained the dam and this is a strong, powerful type. The pedigree is a bit of a mixture because the dam was a staying filly, but we loved her as a yearling so we bought her. She still requires an owner.'

432. UNNAMED ★★★
b.f. Galileo – Palacoona (Last Tycoon)
April 13. Sixth foal. 220,000Y. Tattersalls October 1. John Warren. Half-sister to the very useful 1m winner Diamond Tycoon (by Johannesburg). The dam, a French listed 1m winner, was Group 3 placed and subsequently won in the USA and is a half-sister to six winners. The second dam, Palavera (by Bikala), a listed-placed winner in France, is a half-sister to five winners including the French Derby winner Polytain. (St Albans Bloodstock LLP).

'This is a nice, big, scopey filly, but she's a mid-April foal by Galileo and she's not screaming to be early. A good mover, she'll be nice in time.'

HARRY DUNLOP
433. ARRIVEDERLA ★★
b.f. Acclamation – Alwiyda (Trempolino)
March 14. Sixth foal. €70,000Y. Goffs Million. Blandford Bloodstock. Half-sister to the fair 10f and hurdles winner Reaching Out (by Desert Prince), to the Italian winner of four races at two and three years Zartwyda (by Mozart) and the French 12f winner Qudrah (by Darshaan). The dam, a minor three year old winner in France, is a half-sister to six minor winners. The second dam, Alimana (by Akarad), a fair two year old 9f winner, is a half-sister to eight winners including the disqualified Oaks winner Aliysa (herself dam of the Group 3 winner Desert Story). (W J Armitage).

'She's a very good-looking filly, but quite backward and big and she'll take a bit of time. One for the back-end of the season over seven furlongs.'

434. BY PRECEDENCE (USA) ★★★
b.br.c. Johannesburg – Episode (Kris S)
April 4. Tenth foal. 100,000Y. Tattersalls October 2. Charlie Gordon-Watson. Half-brother to the Canadian Grade 3 winner and US Grade 2 placed Vestrey Lady (by Vicar) and to 2 minor three year old winners in the USA by Coronado's Quest and Unbridled. The dam won once in the USA and is a half-sister to seven winners including the US Grade 3 winner and sire Mr Greeley. The second dam, Long Legend (by Reviewer), won four races and is out of the Group 1 Prix Jacques le Marois winner Lianga. (Prince A A Faisal).

'A horse I like a lot, he's not going to be an early type but he's quite a big, strong, stocky two year old. He'll want seven furlongs in mid-summer.'

435. CAT PATROL ★★★
b.f. One Cool Cat – Ambrosine (Nashwan)
April 2. Second foal. Half-sister to Rosentraub (by Dansili), unplaced in two starts at two years in 2007. The dam, a quite useful 10f and 12f winner, is a half-sister to the useful 9f and 12f winner Camrose. The second dam, Tularosa (by In The Wings), won over 11f in France and is a half-sister to the top-class middle-distance colt Most Welcome and the useful middle-distance winners Top Guest and Bourbon Topsy. (Normandie Stud).

'A few people are a bit nervous about the temperaments of the One Cool Cat two year old's but this filly has been very good. She's quite small and she'll be out when the six furlong races start. A bonny little filly and hopefully she'll have some speed too.'

436. FONDANT FANCY ★★★
b.f. Falbrav – Foodbroker Fancy (Halling)
May 2. Half-sister to the smart 7f (at two years), listed 10f and subsequent US Grade 3 12f winner Dalvina (by Grand Lodge) and to the very useful 7f (at two years) and listed 10f winner Soft Centre (by Zafonic). The dam, a smart 6f (at two years) and dual listed 10f winner, is a half-sister to the useful listed two year old 6f winner Femme Fatale. The second dam, Red Rita (by Kefaah), a fairly useful four year old 6f winner,

was second in the Group 3 6f Cherry Hinton Stakes and the Group 3 6f Princess Margaret Stakes at two years and is a half-sister to three minor winners. (Normandie Stud).

'Quite a late foal. I like her a lot but she'll take a bit of time and is probably one for the middle of the year. She hasn't been here long but what I've seen of her I like. She isn't the biggest (and her half-sister Dalvina wasn't huge either) and she still looks quite immature at the moment. I would think she'd be one for seven furlongs although it's very early days yet.'

437. FORGOTTEN DREAMS (IRE) ★★★

b.f. Olden Times – Jawaher (Dancing Brave)
February 23. Eighth foal. 45,000Y. Tattersalls October 1. Not sold. Half-sister to Zomaradah (by Deploy), a winner of six races including the Group 1 Italian Oaks and herself dam of the high-class miler Dubawi, to the quite useful 12f, 14f and hurdles winner Nichol Fifty (by Old Vic) and two minor winners abroad by Dihistan and Water Cay. The dam was placed over 1m and 9f and is a half-sister to the Derby winner High Rise out of the winning stayer High Tern (by High Line), herself a half-sister to Group 1 winner High Hawk (the dam of In The Wings). (Prince A A Faisal).

'Quite a tall filly, she's one I like a lot. She had a bit of a setback so having originally thought she'd be ready when the six furlong races start she's now going to be a bit later than that. She's attractive and it's a good family.'

438. KEY TO LOVE (IRE) ★★★

b.f. Key Of Luck – Ski For Me (Barathea)
March 27. Third foal. Half-sister to the fair 2007 two year old 7f winner Night Skier (by Night Shift). The dam, a quite useful two year old 1m winner, is a half-sister to two winners. The second dam, Ski For Gold (by Shirley Heights), a fair two year old 7f winner, stayed 2m and is a half-sister to the very useful 6f (at two years) and subsequent Grade 1 10f Santa Barbara Handicap winner Bequest. (Anamoine Ltd).

'She looks like a filly we can get on with, she's not huge and looks to have some speed. Hopefully she'll be one for six furlongs in May.'

439. PETER GRIMES (IRE) ★★★

ch.c. Alhaarth – Aldburgh (Bluebird)
March 28. Fifth foal. 18,000Y. Tattersalls October 1. Harry Dunlop. Half-sister to the quite useful two year old 1m winner Montreaux (by Jade Robbery) and to a three year old winner in Japan by Timber Country. The dam ran once unplaced and is a half-sister to four winners and to the dam of the high-class filly Attraction. The second dam, Eastern Shore (by Sun Prince), is a placed half-sister to seven winners. (Be Hopeful Partnership).

'I like him quite a lot, he's definitely going to want seven furlongs as he's a big, strong colt that'll need a bit of time, but a bit later on we should have some fun with him.'

440. THREE MOONS (IRE) ★★★

b.f. Montjeu – Three Owls (Warning)
January 22. Fourth foal. Half-sister to the useful two year old 5f winner Black Velvet (by Inchinor). The dam, a fair 1m winner, is a half-sister to five winners including the French listed 7f winner Thames. The second dam, Three Terns (by Arctic Tern), won over 9f in France and is a half-sister to three winners including the Group 3 1m Prix des Reservoirs winner Three Angels. (Mrs Ben Goldsmith).

'I like her very much, she's a big, strong, solid filly. I had the half-sister last year who basically wanted seven furlongs or a mile as a three-year-old and I think this filly would want at least that much. Temperament-wise these Montjeu's can be a bit hot so one has to be a bit careful with them. July or August time over six or seven furlongs would be a good start for her.'

441. UNNAMED ★★★

b.f. Diktat – Bayleaf (Efisio)
March 10. Fifth living foal. 5,000Y. Tattersalls October 3. Highflyer Bloodstock. Half-brother to the useful 5f and 6f (at two years) and dual 10f winner and Group 3 5f Molecomb Stakes third Folio (by Perugino). The dam, a useful two year old 5f winner, was listed-placed and is a sister to the fairly useful two year old 5f winner, Group 3 Molecomb Stakes third and subsequent US winner of three races at up to 6f

Baize (herself dam of the US Grade 1 Del Mar Oaks winner Singhalese). The second dam, Bayonne (by Bay Express), a dual 5f winner at three years, is a half-sister to seven winners. (J F Jarvis).

'Quite a tall filly, she's just having a break but she shows some speed and I would think six or seven furlongs would suit her. She was very cheap and yet she's from a good family. The sire's done alright with his fillies and this filly will be out around August-time.'

JOHN DUNLOP

442. ALBAHER ★★★

b.c. Oasis Dream – Dance Sequence (Mr Prospector)

March 30. Eighth foal. 150,000Y. Tattersalls October 2. Shadwell Estate Co. Half-brother to the fairly useful 10f and 12.3f winner Sequential (by Rainbow Quest), to the fairly useful two year old dual 5f winner Dance On (by Caerleon) and the quite useful two year old 6f winner Hornpipe (by Danehill). The dam, a very useful winner of the Group 2 6f Lowther Stakes, is a sister to the US dual Grade 2 winner Souvenir Copy and to the Japanese Grade 2 1m winner Shake Hand. The second dam, Dancing Tribute (by Nureyev), a very useful 6f and 1m winner and second in the Cheveley Park Stakes, is closely related to the dam of the Cherry Hinton Stakes winner Dazzle. (Hamdan Al Maktoum).

'This colt has a precocious pedigree but he's backward and won't be seen out until the mid-season on later.'

443. ALHUDHUD (USA) ★★

b.c. Swain – Wasnah (Nijinsky)

March 11. Ninth foal. Half-brother to the top-class colt Bahri, a winner over 6f (at two years) and the Group 1 1m St James's Palace Stakes and Group 1 1m Queen Elizabeth II Stakes, to the fair 12f winner Winsa (both by Riverman), the very smart Bahhare (by Dayjur), winner of the Group 2 7f Laurent Perrier Champagne Stakes and third in the Champion Stakes and the fair 1m winners Amwaal (by Seeking The Gold) and Ashwaaq (by Gone West). The dam, a fairly useful maiden, was placed five times from

7f (at two years) to 10.5f. She is closely related to the Group 3 Tetrarch Stakes winners Dance Bid and Northern Plain and a half-sister to the US Grade 2 winner Winglet. The second dam, Highest Trump (by Bold Bidder), won the Group 2 5f Queen Mary Stakes at Royal Ascot. (Hamdan Al Maktoum).

'Currently in Dubai.'

444. ANAASHEED ★★★

b.f. Cape Cross – Kahalah (Darshaan)

February 12f. The dam, a fair 12f winner, is a half-sister to numerous winners including the very useful Irish listed 10f winner Nafisah, the very useful Irish 1m and 9f winner Bawaader and the useful Irish listed 12f and jumps winner Mutakarrim. The second dam, Alyakkh (by Sadler's Wells), a fair three year old 1m winner, is a half-sister to the very useful Irish three year old 1m listed stakes winner and Group 1 Coronation Stakes second Hasbah. (Hamdan Al Maktoum).

'She's progressing well and should make a two year old in the second half of the season.'

445. FALLEN IN LOVE ★★★

b.f. Galileo – Fallen Star (Brief Truce)

March 8. Third foal. Half-sister to the unraced 2007 two year old Star Of Gibraltar (by Rock Of Gibraltar). The dam, a listed 7f winner and Group 3 placed twice, is a half-sister to six winners including the Group 1 7f Lockinge Stakes winner Fly To The Stars. The second dam, Rise And Fall (by Mill Reef), is an unplaced full or half-sister to seven winners including the listed winners Special Leave, Spring To Action and Laughter. (Normandie Stud).

'A filly that should make a two year old in the second half of the season.'

446. GOOD FOR HER ★★★

b.f. Rock Of Gibraltar – Tyranny (Machiavellian)

February 26. Half-sister to the unplaced 2007 two year old Danvers (by Cape Cross). The dam, a fairly useful dual 7f winner, is a half-sister to the listed 1m and subsequent US Grade 2 winner Spotlight. The second dam, Dust Dancer (by Suave Dancer), won four races including the

Group 3 10f Prix de la Nonette and is a half-sister to six winners including the Group 3 7.3f Fred Darling Stakes winner Bulaxie (herself dam of the Group 2 winner Claxon) and the dual French listed winner Zimzalabim. (Normandie Stud).
'This filly is quite sharp and will hopefully be racing from July onwards.'

447. GOODWOOD CHIMES (IRE) ★★★
b.c. Elnadim – Cloche du Roi (Fairy King)
March 14. Seventh foal. 28,000Y. Tattersalls October 2. R Frisby. Half-brother to the moderate 7f all-weather winner Tirana (by Brief Truce), to the minor French winner at three and four years Rinocerose (by Ali-Royal) and a winner abroad by Lend A Hand. The dam, placed once at three years in France, is a half-sister to the Group 2 Prix de l'Opera winner Clodora. The second dam, Cloche d'Or (by Good Times), won the Group 3 Princess Margaret Stakes and is a half-sister to five winners. (Goodwood Racehorse Owners Group (Fifteen)).
'A big horse, he'll make a two year old in the second half of the season.'

448. GYR (IRE) ★★★★
ch.c. Pivotal – Rafha (Kris)
March 2. Thirteenth foal. 180,000Y. Tattersalls October 1. Larry Stratton. Half-brother to the Group 1 6f Haydock Park Sprint Cup winner Invincible Spirit (by Green Desert), to the smart Group 3 John Porter Stakes and Group 3 Ormonde Stakes winner Sadian (by Shirley Heights), the Group 3 12f Princess Royal Stakes winner Acts Of Grace (by Bahri), the very useful 11f winner Aquarius (by Royal Academy), the useful listed 6f winner Massarra, the quite useful 1m winner Kodiac (both by Danehill), the useful 14f and 2m winner Fnan (by Generous) and the useful dual 1m (at two years) and 11.8f winner Al Widyan (by Slip Anchor) and the modest dual 12f winner Jafaru (by Silver Hawk). The dam, a very smart winner over 6f (at two years) and the Group 1 10.5f Prix de Diane, the Group 3 Lingfield Oaks Trial and Group 3 May Hill Stakes, is a half-sister to nine winners. The second dam, Eljazzi (by Artaius), a fairly useful two year old 7f

winner, is a half-sister to eight winners including the good miler Pitcairn. (Prince A A Faisal).
'This is a nice colt and a good mover.'

449. HOBOOB (USA) ★★
ch.f. Seeking The Gold – Bint Salsabil (Nashwan)
April 6. Seventh foal. Closely related to the UAE 1m winner Mutawaged (by Gulch) and the fair 7f all-weather winner Alsaleet (by Mr Prospector) and half-sister to the useful two year old 7f winner Mukafeh (by Danzig) and the quite useful 9f winner Alhaitham (by Storm Cat). The dam, a very useful winner of four races from 6f to 10f including the Group 3 Rockfel Stakes, is a half-sister to several winners including the 10f winner Alabaq and the two year old 6f and 7f winner Sahm (both very useful). The second dam, Salsabil (by Sadler's Wells), won two of her three races as a two-year-old (notably the Group 1 1m Prix Marcel Boussac) and trained on to become a top class three year old, winning the 1,000 Guineas, the Irish Derby, the Epsom Oaks and the Prix Vermeille. all Group 1 events. She is a half-sister to the high-class colt Marju, winner of the St James's Palace Stakes and the Craven Stakes and to the very useful Prix de Psyche winner Danse Royale. (Hamdan Al Maktoum).
'Currently in Dubai.'

450. HOWARD ★★★
ch.c. Haafhd – Dolores (Danehill)
March 10. Second foal. The dam, a listed 1m winner and second in the Group 2 1m Sun Chariot Stakes, is a half-sister to one winner. The second dam, Agnus (by In The Wings), a winner twice in Belgium, is a half-sister to 4 other winners abroad including Wavy Run, a winner of 13 races in Spain, France and the USA including the US Grade 2 San Francisco Mile Handicap. (Normandie Stud).
'This colt is progressing well but he won't be seen out until the second half of the season.'

451. IMAAM ★★★★
ch.c. Pivotal – Khulood (Storm Cat)
January 30. Second foal. Half-brother to the

quite useful 2007 two year old 5f winner Kashoof (by Green Desert). The dam, a useful listed 7f (at two years) and Group 3 7f Nell Gwyn Stakes winner, is a half-sister to numerous winners including the Irish 1,000 Guineas winner Mehthaaf and the July Cup winner Elnadim. The second dam, Elle Seule (by Exclusive Native), a very smart winner of the Group 3 1m Prix d'Astarte, also won over 10.5f and is a half-sister to the Group/Grade 1 winners Fort Wood, Hamas and Timber Country and to the Group winners Northern Aspen, Colorado Dancer and Mazzacano. (Hamdan Al Maktoum).
'A quality individual and an early foal.'

452. IN SECRET ★★★
b.f. Dalakhani – Conspiracy (Rudimentary)
March 8. Half-sister to the quite useful 2007 two year old 7f winner Presbyterian Nun (by Daylami), to the useful 10f to 11.6f winner In Disguise (by Nashwan), the fairly useful two year old triple 7f winner Jedburgh (by Selkirk) and the fairly useful two year old 7f winner Impersonator (by Zafonic). The dam, a useful two year old listed 5f winner, is a half-sister to seven winners including the Group 2 10f Sun Chariot Stakes winner Ristna and the dual listed winner Gayane. The second dam, Roussalka (by Habitat), won seven races at up to 10f including the Coronation Stakes and the Nassau Stakes (twice) and is a half-sister to the Fillies Triple Crown winner Oh So Sharp (herself dam of the Prix Saint Alary winner Rosefinch). (The Earl Cadogan).
'His sire suggests stamina, but nevertheless he could make a two year old.'

453. ITLAAQ ★★★★
b.c. Alhaarth – Hathrah (Linamix)
March 25. Second foal. The dam, winner of the listed 1m Masaka Stakes and third in the 1,000 Guineas, is a half-sister to five winners including the smart Group 2 12f Premio Ellington winner Ivan Luis and the French/German listed winners Amathia and Zero Problemo. The second dam, Zivania (by Shernazar), a useful Irish winner of four races from 1m to 9.5f, is a half-sister to the Group 3 Prix Gontaut Biron winner Muroto.

(Hamdan Al Maktoum).
'A likeable colt with a touch of quality.'

454. KING OF WANDS ★★★★
b.c. Galileo – Maid To Treasure
(Rainbow Quest)
February 7. First foal. The dam, a fair 7f (at two years) and 10f placed maiden, is a half-sister to numerous winners including the useful 7f (at two years) and 10f winner Maid To Perfection and the useful two year old 7f winner Artistic Lad. The second dam, Maid For The Hills (by Indian Ridge), was a useful two year old and won twice over 6f including the listed Empress Stakes and is a half-sister to five winners including the Group 3 6f Princess Margaret Stakes second Maid For Walking. (Normandie Stud).
'A classy colt with scope.'

455. KYLE OF BUTE ★★★
ch.c. Kyllachy – Blinding Mission (Marju)
March 8. Fifth foal. 32,000Y. Tattersalls October 1. J Dunlop. Half-brother to the fair 7f and subsequent Spanish winner Langston Boy and to a minor winner abroad by Danehill Dancer. The dam, a fair 9f placed maiden, is a full or half-sister to four winners. The second dam, Blinding (by High Top), ran unplaced twice and is a half-sister to the triple Group 3 winner Hadeer. (Mrs H I Slade).
'A colt that should make a two year old.'

456. MEJALA (IRE) ★★★
b.f. Red Ransom – Wissal (Woodman)
February 12. Half-sister to the useful 7f (at two years) and 1m winner and listed-placed Sudoor (by Fantastic Light). The dam is an unraced sister to the high-class two year old Group 2 7f Laurent Perrier Champagne Stakes Bahhare and a half-sister to the Group 1 1m St James's Palace Stakes and Group 1 1m Queen Elizabeth II Stakes winner Bahri. The second dam, Wasnah (by Nijinsky), a fairly useful maiden, was placed at up to 10.5f and is a half-sister to the Group/Graded stakes winners Dance Bid, Northern Plain and Winglet. (Hamdan Al Maktoum).
'A nice type, but one for the back-end of the season.'

457. MERDAAM ★★★
ch.c. Dubai Destination – Faydah (Bahri)
February 2. Third foal. Half-sister to the unplaced 2006 two year old Lanehaya (by Cape Cross). The dam, unplaced in two starts, is closely related to the top-class Group 1 1m Queen Elizabeth II Stakes and Group 2 1m Queen Anne Stakes winner Lahib and to the useful 10f winner Eshtiaal and a half-sister to the smart two year old 6f winner and Group 3 1m Craven Stakes third Nwaamis, the useful 7f (at two years) and listed 1m winner Hawriyah, the very useful US miler Maceo and the fairly useful 7f and 1m winner Sajjaya. The second dam, Lady Cutlass (by Cutlass), won three races from 5f to 7f in the USA and was stakes placed. (Hamdan Al Maktoum).
'A good-moving colt, but backward at the moment.'

458. NAIZAK ★★★
ch.f. Medicean – Sunny Davis (Alydar)
February 24. Eleventh foal. 110,000Y. Doncaster St Leger. Shadwell Estate Co. Half-sister to the useful 6f (at two years) to 1m (in Sweden) winner Warming Trends, to the Italian winner of six races Dawing (both by Warning), the quite useful 12f winner Sunny Chief (by Be My Chief), the quite useful 10f winners Roborant (by Robellino) and Dance In The Sun (by Halling), the fair 6f (at two years) to 1m winner Davis Rock (by Rock City) and the Italian two year old winner Golden Aviance (by Generous). The dam, a fair two year old 7f winner, is out of the minor US winner Goldie Hawn (by Northern Dancer), herself a sister to the Grade 2 winner Larida (dam of the Coronation Stakes winner Magic Of Life) and a half-sister to the champion US filly Miss Oceana. (Hamdan Al Maktoum).
'A strong filly.'

459. SHAWQ ★★★
b.f. Noverre – Ashwaaq (Gone West)
April 28. First foal. The dam, a fair 1m winner, is a half-sister to the top-class colt Bahri, a winner over 6f (at two years) and the Group 1 1m St James's Palace Stakes and Group 1 1m Queen Elizabeth II Stakes and to the very smart Bahhare (by Dayjur), winner of the Group 2 7f Laurent Perrier Champagne Stakes and third in the Champion Stakes. The second dam, Wasnah (by Nijinsky), a fairly useful maiden, was placed five times from 7f (at two years) to 10.5f. She is closely related to the Group 3 Tetrarch Stakes winners Dance Bid and Northern Plain and a half-sister to the US Grade 2 winner Winglet. (Hamdan Al Maktoum).
'A smallish filly, she should be a two year old.'

460. SAIRAAM (IRE) ★★★
b.br.f. Marju – Sayedati Eljamilah
(Mr Prospector)
May 1. Fifth foal. Half-sister to the fair 2007 7f placed two year old Sayedati Elhasna (by Alhaarth), to the quite useful two year old 6f winner Motarassed, the fair two year old 6f winner Nudrah (both by Green Desert) and the fair 11f winner Mujahaz (by Act One). The dam, unplaced in two starts, is a half-sister to numerous winners including the Derby winner Erhaab and the very useful Group 2 10f Premio Lydia Tesio winner Oumaldaaya. The second dam, Histoire (by Riverman), won once in France over 10.5f and is a half-sister to the Group 3 7f Prix de la Porte Maillot winner Hamanda. (Hamdan Al Maktoum).
'A strong, wide filly.'

461. SOLAR GRAPHITE (IRE) ★★★
b.c. Rock Of Gibraltar – Solar Crystal (Alzao)
April 8. Eighth foal. 45,000Y. Tattersalls October 2. Angie Sykes. Half-brother to the smart 2007 two year old 6f winner and Group 1 Racing Post Trophy third Feared In Flight (by Hawk Wing), to the useful two year old 7f winner, listed-placed and hurdles winner Lunar Crystal (by Shirley Heights) and the quite useful 10f winner Crystal (by Danehill). The dam, a smart two year old, won the Group 3 1m May Hill Stakes, was third in the Group 1 1m Prix Marcel Boussac and is a half-sister to six winners including the Group three winners Dubai Success and State Crystal. The second dam, Crystal Spray (by Beldale Flutter), a minor Irish four year old 14f winner, is a half-sister to eight winners including the Group 2 winner

Crystal Hearted. (Gail Brown Racing Partnership). *'A colt that should make a two year old in the second half of the season.'*

462. TACTIC ★★★★

b.c. Sadler's Wells – Tanaghum (Darshaan)
May 16. Second foal. The dam, a useful listed-placed 10f winner, is a half-sister to four winners including the smart Group 2 10f Premio Lydia Tesio winner Najah. The second dam, Mehthaaf (by Nureyev), won the Irish 1,000 Guineas, the Tripleprint Celebration Mile and the Nell Gwyn Stakes and is closely related to the Diadem Stakes winner Elnadim and to the French two year old 7.5f winner Only Seule (herself dam of the Group 1 7f Prix de la Foret and Group 1 6.5f Prix Maurice de Gheest winner Occupandiste). (Hamdan Al Maktoum).
'A late foal but a very nice colt for later in the season.'

463. WAAHEJ ★★★★

b.c. Haafhd – Madam Ninette (Mark Of Esteem)
January 23. Second foal. 130,000Y. Tattersalls October 1. Shadwell Estate Co. Half-brother to the unplaced 2007 two year old No No Ninette (by Oasis Dream). The dam is an unraced half-sister to nine winners including the very smart King's Stand Stakes and Temple Stakes winner Bolshoi and the useful sprinters Mariinsky, Great Chaddington and Tod. The second dam, Mainly Dry (by The Brianstan), is an unraced half-sister to four winners. (Hamdan Al Maktoum).
'An early foal, this colt is bred to be quick.'

464. ZAAQYA ★★★★

b.f. Nayef – Classical Dancer (Dr Fong)
February 13. First foal. 300,000Y. Tattersalls October 2. Shadwell Estate Co. The dam, a fairly useful 8.3f winner, was listed-placed twice and is a half-sister to three winners including the Group 1 Premio Roma winner Imperial Dancer. The second dam, Gorgeous Dancer (by Nordico), an Irish three year old 1m winner and third in the listed Irish Oaks Trial, is a half-sister to three winners. (Hamdan Al Maktoum).
'A nice filly and a good mover.'

PAT EDDERY

465. CITIZENSHIP ★★★

b.c. Beat Hollow – Three More (Sanglamore)
February 11. Half-brother to the useful two year old 7f winner and Group 2 6f Richmond Stakes fourth Trilogy (by Grand Lodge). The dam is a half-sister to the very smart 9f Feilden Stakes and 10f Mecca Bookmakers' Classic winner Kefaah, to the smart two year old 7f Somerville Tattersall Stakes winner and Group 2 Criterium de Maisons Laffitte second Tertian and the useful Tote-Ebor Handicap winner Primary. The second dam, Tertiary (by Vaguely Noble), was second over 10.5f in France, is a sister to the Prix Saint-Alary and Washington DC International winner Nobiliary and a half-sister to the Prix de la Foret and Prix Jacques le Marois winner and top class sire Lyphard. (Khalid Abdulla).
'A nice colt that's been working and potentially he's a nice horse. He won't be too early but he should be a two year old from mid-summer onwards over six/seven furlongs.' It was good to discuss these horses with Simon Double, the manager of Pat Eddery Racing.

466. MILLWAY BEACH ★★★★

b.c. Diktat – Cape Cod (Unfuwain)
April 13. 17,000Y. Doncaster Festival. Pat Eddery. Half-brother to the unplaced 2007 two year old Jemiliah (by Dubai Destination). The dam was placed over 6f at three years and is a sister to two winners including the listed-placed Abeyr and a half-sister to three winners including the useful two year old 7.3f Radley Stakes winner Boojum. The second dam, Haboobti (by Habitat), is an unplaced half-sister to six winners including the US stakes winner and Grade 3 placed Aerturas. (Pat Eddery Racing (Toulon)).
'He'll be racing from June onwards and he seems to have a touch of class. He's always looked the business ever since he was broken in, looks a little bit weak at the moment to be racing straight away but he's very professional and knows his job already. A very nice colt.'

467. OLIVE GREEN (USA) ★★

b.f. Diesis – Zaghruta (Gone West)

March 23. Fourth foal. The dam is an unraced sister to the champion two year old and three year old Zafonic, winner of the 2,000 Guineas, the Dewhurst Stakes, the Prix de la Salamandre and the Prix Morny and to the smart Group 3 6f Prix de Cabourg winner Zamindar. The second dam, Zaizafon (by The Minstrel), won twice over 7f at two years and was placed in the Group 1 1m Queen Elizabeth II Stakes and the Group 3 1m Child Stakes. She is a half-sister to the unraced Modena, herself dam of the Eclipse Stakes and Phoenix Champion Stakes winner Elmaamul. (Khalid Abdulla).
'She's a full-sister to Gifted Leader, a colt that hasn't run yet but we think he's nice. This is quite an athletic filly, she won't be rushed but seems to have ability and she'll make a two year old later on.'

468. OVERACHIEVER (IRE) ★★★★ ♠
b.f. Exceed And Excel – Panglossian (Barathea)
May 3. Second foal. 115,000Y. Tattersalls October 1. McKeever St Lawrence. The dam, a modest 11f and 12f placed maiden, is a half-sister to seven winners including the Grade 2 America Derby winner Overbury. The second dam, Overcall (by Bustino), a winning Irish middle-distance stayer, is a half-sister to nine winners including the dam of the Melbourne Cup winner Vintage Crop. (F.C.T Wilson).
'This filly is nice and early and will be running before the end of May, probably over six furlongs. She seems to have plenty of speed and looks a sharp sort.'

469. PRIVATE PASSION (IRE) ★★★
b.c. Captain Rio – Victoria's Secret (Law Society)
April 7. Eighth foal. 30,000Y. Doncaster St Leger. P Eddery. Half-brother to the useful 6f (at two years) and 7f winner of 12 races Master Robbie, to the Italian 7f (at two years) and 1m winner of seven races Small Secret (both by Piccolo), the fair 7f winner Grand Opera (by City On A Hill) and the modest 1m winner of six races Legal Lover (by Woodborough). The dam, a fair 12f winner, is a half-sister to five winners. The second dam, Organdy (by Blakeney), a quite useful three year old 1m winner, is a full or half-sister to nine winners. (Pat Eddery Racing (Lomond)).
'He'll be out in May, he's a nice colt and we'll try and aim him at the St Leger Sales race. He's always shown ability and he's a sharp sort that wants six furlongs to start with. A very athletic-looking colt and quite professional.'

470. SPRING QUARTET ★★
b.c. Captain Rio – Alice Blackthorn (Forzando)
March 1. First foal. 19,000Y. Doncaster St Leger. P Eddery. The dam, a fair 6f (at two years) and 7f winner, is a half-sister to the smart Group 3 5.2f and 6f Wokingham Handicap winner Ratio. The second dam, Owdbetts (by High Estate), a fair 7f to 10.2f winner of four races, is a half-sister to three minor winners. (Pat Eddery Racing (Qtr 6)).
'He's been working and although he's quite green at the moment he does have ability and he'll make a two year old for sure. The penny hasn't dropped yet but early summer should be about right for him and he's quite nice.'

471. SQUAD ★★
ch.c. Choisir – Widescreen (Distant View)
March 18. Fourth foal. The dam is an unraced half-sister to the champion two year old and three year old Zafonic, winner of the 2,000 Guineas, the Dewhurst Stakes, the Prix de la Salamandre and the Prix Morny and to the smart Group 3 6f Prix de Cabourg winner Zamindar. The second dam, Zaizafon (by The Minstrel), won twice over 7f at two years and was placed in the Group 1 1m Queen Elizabeth II Stakes and the Group 3 1m Child Stakes. She is a half-sister to the unraced Modena, herself dam of the Eclipse Stakes and Phoenix Champion Stakes winner Elmaamul. (Khalid Abdulla).
'Not the biggest colt in the world, but he looks a sharp sort although there are no plans for him at the moment. On size you'd think he'd be a two year old.'

472. UNNAMED ★★
b.c. Prince Sabo – Pieta (Perugino)
May 1. Third foal. 13,000Y. Doncaster Festival. Pat Eddery. Half-brother to the modest 6f

winner Mister Always (by Titus Livius). The dam, a 6f seller winner at four years, is a half-sister to three winners. The second dam, Auction Maid (by Auction Ring), is an unraced half-sister to five winners.

'The sire isn't particularly fashionable these days and despite the fact he's a May foal I think he was definitely a bargain. He should be out from late May/June onwards, he's developed physically really well since we bought him and looks an uncomplicated, two year old type with scope.' TRAINER'S BARGAIN BUY

DAVID ELSWORTH

473. FAST FLOW ★★★
b.f. Fasliyev – Premier Prize (Selkirk)
April 21. Second foal. Half-sister to the unraced 2007 two year old Win On Red (by Red Ransom). The dam, a useful 7f (at two years) and listed 10f winner, was third in the Group 2 Sandown Mile and is a half-sister to four winners including the Group 2 15f Prix Kergorlay winner Gold Medallist. The second dam, Spot Prize (by Seattle Dancer), a useful filly, won over 5f at two years and was fourth in the Oaks. (J C Smith).
'I'd be disappointed if she isn't a nice filly, she's quite scopey and a home-bred of Jeff Smith's.'

474. FLEURON ★★★★
b.br.f. Diktat – Forthwith (Midyan)
March 20. Eighth foal. 58,000Y. Tattersalls October 1. D Elsworth. Sister to the useful two year 7f winner, Group 2 7f Rockfel Stakes second and Group 3 7f Nell Gwyn Stakes third Favourita and the fair 6f winner Fleuret and half-sister to the very useful 12f winner and Group 3 12f Gordon Stakes second Time Zone (by Shirley Heights), the quite useful two year old 7f winner Forthright (by Cadeaux Genereux) and the German 9f and 10f and subsequent all-weather 9.4f winner Sinjaree (by Mark Of Esteem). The dam, a useful 7f (at two years) and 10f listed winner, was third in the Group 2 Premio Lydia Tesio and is a half-sister to the quite useful 8.5f winner Forum. The second dam, Top Society (by High Top), is an unraced half-sister to two minor winners. (Wyck Hall Stud Ltd).

'She's a precocious type and I expect her to be fairly early. If she shows up well enough she could be an Ascot filly but realistically I haven't done enough with her to say. But if I could one pick that might be early enough, then she'd be one of three to choose from (along with Izzi Mill and Swiss Diva). She looks like she's ready to run and is an athletic little filly that looks like she wants to get on with it'

475. HIGHLAND RIVER (IRE) ★★★
b.c. Indian Creek – Bee One (Catrail)
April 18. Half-brother to the fair triple 1m winner Highland Harvest (by Averti). The dam was placed over 5f and 6f and is a half-sister to several winners. The second dam, Ruwy (by Soviet Star) won over 1m. (J Wotherspoon).
'I trained both the sire (who won the Hardwicke Stakes) and the dam and I think this colt is a very nice individual. I like him a lot and you mustn't leave him out of the book. He's not a speedy horse but he's precocious enough and he should make a two year old later in the year.'

476. IZZI MILL (USA) ★★★★
gr.f. Lemon Drop Kid – Lets Get Cozzy (Cozzene)
April 12. Fifth foal. 37,000Y. Tattersalls October 1. Not sold. Half-sister to the minor US two year old winner Sweet Roberto (by Red Ransom). The dam won five races and was Grade 3 placed in the USA and is a half-sister to four winners. The second dam, Sweet Lassie (by Posse), a listed-placed winner of five races in France, is a half-sister to four winners.
'She's quite precocious, quite sharp and an attractive little filly that looks like a two year old.'

477. MAID OF STONE ★★
ch.f. Rock Of Gibraltar – Gold Flair (Tap On Wood)
March 26. €18,000Y. Goffs Million. Suzanne Roberts. Half-sister to six winners including the Italian listed placed Mambostar (by Common Grounds) and the minor two year old winners Duball Remy (by Roi Danzig) and Conquistadores (by Bachir). The dam, placed at two and four years, is a sister to the Group 2 Great Voltigeur

Stakes winner Nisnas and a half-sister to five winners. The second dam, Suemette (by Danseur), was unraced.

'A big, tall filly that moves with style and elegance and shows an unprompted competitive nature.'

478. NEWLYN ART ★★★
ch.c. Compton Place – Miss Rimex (Ezzoud)
February 14. Fifth foal. 65,000Y. Tattersalls October 1. Not sold. Brother to the Hong Kong Group 3 7f winner Flaming Lamborgini and half-brother to the fair Irish 1m winner Baileys Best (by Mister Baileys). The dam, a quite useful 6f (at two years) and 1m winner, is a half-sister to seven winners including the dam of the stakes winners Guys And Dolls and Pawnbroker. The second dam, Blue Guitar (by Cure The Blues), a fairly useful winner of two races over 1m and 8.3f, is a half-sister to two listed winners including the dam of the Group three winners Guest Performer and Sojourn. (M R Green).

'He should be precocious and he's a particularly attractive colt. He's the sort of horse that wouldn't look out of place in a yard specialising in early two-year-olds. He's just had a minor setback, but he'll be alright and you'd like him because he's a good-looking colt.'

479. OUSTER ★★
b.c. Lomitas – Odabella's Charm (Cadeaux Genereux)
February 18. Second foal. 55,000Y. Tattersalls October 2. Suzanne Roberts. The dam, a quite useful 8.3f winner at three years, is a half-sister to ten winners. The second dam, One Life (by L'Emigrant), is an unraced half-sister to five winners including the outstanding filly and broodmare Miesque. (Mr R Tooth).

'Full of style, he's powerfully built but an active colt and the sort of horse you're wishing your life away with because you're dying to see him in six months time! He could be our Derby horse.'

480. RED MARGARITA ★★
ch.f. Dalakhani – Red Bartsia (Barathea)
March 19. Third foal. 24,000Y. Tattersalls October 3. D Elsworth. Half-sister to the

unraced 2007 two year old Red Rock Prince (by Rock Of Gibraltar). The dam, an Irish 12f winner at three years, is a sister to one winner and a half-sister to eight winners including the high-class and multiple winning stayer Persian Punch and the Group 3 7f Solario Stakes winner Island Magic. The second dam, Rum Cay (by Our Native), a fair 14.6f winner, is a half-sister to three winners. (Huggins, McGrath & Elsworth).

'A few of us have bought this filly to win the Melbourne Cup – so she might not be an obvious candidate for your book Steve! But she's a quality filly and was cheap for a Dalakhani. She isn't that backward and is one for the end of the season.'

481. SALFORD SPIRIT ★★★
b.c. Desert Sun – Cribella (Robellino)
April 10. Fourth living foal. 145,000Y. Tattersalls October 2. D Elsworth. Half-brother to the useful three year old listed 10f winner Ruby Wine (by Kayf Tara). The dam, a fair all-weather dual 12f winner, is a half-sister to two winners. The second dam, Crinoline (by Blakeney), won once at three years and is a full or half-sister to nine winners. (Mr A J Thompson).

'A very nice colt and I had to pay a lot of money for him. He's a class act but won't make a two year old until the autumn. He's an elegant and classy individual.'

482. SNOQUALMIE GIRL ★★★
b.f. Montjeu – Seattle Ribbon (Seattle Dancer)
February 7. Sister to the smart listed 10f winner and Group 2 Dante Stakes third Snoqualmie Boy (by Montjeu) and half-sister to the quite useful two year old 6f winner Robocop, the modest 9f and 10f winner Seattle Robber (both by Robellino) and the fair 7f and 10f winner Seattle Express (by Salse). The dam, placed over 9f and 10f at three years, is a sister to the two year old Group 1 1m winner Seattle Dancer. The second dam, Golden Rhyme (by Dom Racine), was a quite useful three year old 7f winner. (J C Smith).

'Not as big and imposing as her full brother was at this stage but she goes well. She's neat, looks relatively precocious and should make a two year old.'

483. SONNING GATE ★★
b.c. Desert Sun – Sunley Scent (Wolfhound)
March 4. Third foal. 34,000Y. Tattersalls October 2. D Elsworth. Half-brother to the fairly useful two year old all-weather 5f and 6f winner and listed placed Resplendent Alpha (by Best Of The Bests). The dam, a quite useful 6f and 7f winner of three races at three and four years, is a half-sister to seven minor winners. The second dam, Brown Velvet (by Mansingh), is an unplaced half-sister to two winners including the Group 3 Child Stakes winner Stumped (herself dam of the Irish 1,000 Guineas winner Sonic Lady).
'A big horse and he's nice but again he's one for the end of the season and next year.'

484. SWISS DIVA ★★★★
br.f. Pivotal – Swiss Lake (Indian Ridge)
February 4. Second foal. Half-sister to Swiss Franc (by Mr Greeley), a smart 2007 two year old 5f winner and Group 2 three times. The dam, a dual listed 5f winner (including at two years), is a half-sister to the useful two year old dual 5f winner and listed placed Dubai Princess. The second dam, Blue Iris (by Petong), a useful winner of five races over 5f and 6f including the Weatherbys Super Sprint and the Redcar Two-Year-Old Trophy, is a half-sister to nine winners. (Lordship Stud).
'She looks like a two year old, seems similar to the three year old half-brother Swiss Franc and has a good temperament. She's precocious and has a good pedigree, so she has every chance.'

485. UNNAMED ★★★
ch.f. Intikhab – Blazing Glory (Glow)
May 1. Ninth foal. €45,000Y. Goffs Million. R Fabrizius. Half-sister to the Irish two year old listed 6f winner Miss Childrey (by Dr Fong), to the fairly useful 5f and 6f winner La Piazza (by Polish Patriot), the quite useful 5f and 6f winner Prince Dome (by Prince Sabo), the quite useful 5f winner (at two years) Brimstone (by Ballad Rock), the minor Irish 1m winner Arboreta (by Charnwood Forest) and a winner in Germany by Lahib. The dam won three races over 5f and is a full or half-sister to six winners. The second

dam, Salvationist (by Mill Reef), won four races at three years in France and is a half-sister to eight winners including the Group 2 King Edward VII Stakes winner Marquis de Sade. (Oak Lodge Stud).
'I expect her to be a winning two year old, she had a bit of a setback and so I had to leave her for a bit, but she's back now and she'll probably be running by June time.'

486. UNNAMED ★★
b.c. Lomitas – Zacchera (Zamindar)
January 14. Second foal. 25,000Y. Tattersalls October 3. Gordon Li. Half-brother to the unplaced 2007 two year old Oriental Girl (by Dr Fong). The dam, a quite useful 6f winner, is a half-sister to numerous winners including the high-class Group 1 July Cup winner Sakhee's Secret, the smart listed winner of six races from 5f to 7f Palace Affair and the very useful 6f to 8.3f winner Duke Of Modena. The second dam, Palace Street (by Secreto), a useful winner over 6f and 7f including the listed Cammidge Trophy, is a half-sister to the Extel Handicap winner Indian Trail and the Italian Group 3 winner Sfriss. (G W Y Li).
'Quite an attractive horse, I expect him to be out in the second half of the year and be a three year old.'

JAMES EUSTACE
487. BLUE ARCTIC ★★★
b.f. Bertolini – Bogus Mix (Linamix)
February 3. 8,000Y. Tattersalls October 2. James Eustace. Half-sister to the two year old 7f seller winner Dispol Shabama (by Bahamian Bounty) and to a winner in Macau by Petong. The dam is an unplaced half-sister to three minor winners. The second dam, La Kermesse (by Storm Bird), a modest 7f winner, is a half-sister to three minor winners. (Blue Peter Racing 8).
'She was a cheap purchase but well bought I hope! She's quite a nice filly and I like her, she will be a two year old and will probably want six furlongs rather than five. She's done a bit of work already and gone nicely.' TRAINER'S BARGAIN BUY

488. GENEVA GEYSER ★★★★
b.c. One Cool Cat – Genevra (Danehill)
January 1. Half-brother to Girl Of Panagea (by Soviet Star), placed second over 1m on her only start at two years in 2007, to the quite useful two year old 6f winner Granato (by Cadeaux Genereux), the quite useful 9f and 10f winner Gigondas (by Octagonal) and the Italian dual 1m winner Guantanamera. The dam, a useful German two year old miler, is a half-sister to numerous winners. (J C Smith).
'A nice, big, scopey horse. He won't be sharp and early but I like to think he'll make up into a nice individual. He really looks the part – a big, good-looking horse. He doesn't strike you as being quick because he's a long-striding horse, but he does strike you as being a nice horse and is the one I'd have the highest hopes for at the moment.'

489. INTEGRIA ★★★
b.c. Intikhab – Alegria (Night Shift)
March 11. Third foal. Brother to the quite useful dual 6f winner (including at two years) Fast Bowler. The dam, a fairly useful dual 6f winner (including at two years), is out of the fair middle-distance placed maiden High Habit (by Slip Anchor), herself a half-sister to the smart sprinter Blue Siren. (J C Smith).
'The nicest produced by the dam so far. Her half-brother Fast Bowler won twice but sadly started bleeding and the next foal just wasn't an athlete at all. This one is a nicer colt than Fast Bowler – to look at anyway. He's quite athletic, he'll be a two year old alright and I do like him.'

490. MISTER STANDFAST ★★★
b.c. Haafhd – Off The Blocks (Salse)
April 22. Ninth foal. 30,000Y. Tattersalls October 2. James Eustace. Half-brother to the Italian two year old 7.5f winner and listed-placed Gulfstream Park (by Barathea), to the fairly useful two year old 1m winner Jaad, the fairly useful three year old 1m winner We'll Come (both by Elnadim) and two minor winners in Italy by Groom Dancer and Prince Sabo. The dam was placed at up to 1m and is a half-sister to four winners including the Sweet Solera Stakes second The Jotter and the Group 1 Gran Criterium second Line Dancer. The second dam, Note Book (by Mummy's Pet), a fairly useful 6f winner, is a sister to the Norfolk Stakes winner Colmore Row and a half-sister to eight winners including the Horris Hill Stakes winner Long Row. (The MacDougall Partnership).
'A nice horse and I know the family because I was an assistant to William Jarvis and he's trained most of the family. I liked a lot of yearlings by Haafhd and was able to afford this one. He's a decent sized colt so he won't be early and I think he'll be one for the second half of the season.'

491. PENPERTH ★★★
b.f. Xaar – Penelewey (Groom Dancer)
April 7. Second foal. Half-sister to the fairly useful 2007 two year old 1m winner Jedediah (by Hernando). The dam, a useful 6f and 7f winner of three races, is a half-sister to five winners here and abroad. The second dam, Peryllys (by Warning), is a placed half-sister to six winners. (Major M G Wyatt).
'A nice filly, she'll be a two year old but she wasn't ridden away until quite late on so she's not going to be too early. She looks quite sharp and five or six furlongs should suit her. Her half-brother was a nice two year old last year and he's not by an obvious two year old sire, unlike Xaar.'

492. TURKISH LOKUM ★★★
b.f. Bertolini – Malabarista (Assert)
February 5. 17,000Y. Tattersalls October 2. James Eustace. Half-sister to the quite useful 10f winner Spirit Of The Fen (by Pivotal), to the quite useful 7f (at two years) and dual 1m winner Capulette (by Grand Lodge), the French 7f winner of three races Epouvantail (by Spectrum) and the Italian 10f and 11f winner of six races Basista (by Barathea). The dam won once over 12.5f in France and is a half-sister to three listed winners and to the dams of 5 Group or listed winners. The second dam, Karosa (by Caro), won once in France and was second in the Group 3 5f Prix d'Arenburg. (Mr Y Gelgin).
'This filly is sharp and early, she's working already and she'll be quick enough for five furlongs. She'll be racing in April, she has a bit of speed and I do like her.'

JEREMY GASK

Jeremy trains at Sutton Veny in Wiltshire for a group of investors (collectively known as Horses First Racing Ltd) who purchased yearlings for the first time in 2007 having already had older horses in training. Over the past five years Jeremy has trained around 300 winners in South West Australia and he was 'head-hunted' to lead this team of relatively expensive, well-bred horses. After I interviewed him he was pleased to show me around the place and he explained that a lot of investment has been put into this yard, and boy how it shows! The whole place looks great and there are a variety of gallops with the centrepiece being an oval track placed in a natural bowl in the landscape which is absolutely beautiful. Jeremy pointed out that these horses have been bought with a long-term plan in place and they won't all necessarily be at their best this season.

493. HANTA YO (IRE) ★★★

ch.c. Alhaarth – Tekindia (Indian Ridge)
March 31. Fourth foal. 105,000Y. Doncaster St Leger. John Warren. Half-brother to the fair 12f all-weather winner Reciprocation (by Singspiel). The dam won once over 7f at three years in France and is a half-sister to six winners including the US stakes winner and Grade 2 third Thé Key Rainbow. The second dam, Te Kani (by Northern Dancer), won once in France and is a half-sister to seven winners including the US triple Grade 1 winner Ogygian. (Horses First Racing Ltd).
'He'll make a two year old alright and if I was willing to have a bet he'd be the first two year old to make the track for us. He's done a few bits of faster work, he's quite a compact colt and he's a fairly forward going type.'

494. JOSHUA BLOOM ★★★

b.c. Royal Applause – Joking Apart (Rainbow Quest)
January 26. First foal. 24,000Y. Doncaster St Leger. Oaks Farm. The dam ran once unplaced and is a half-sister to Fantastic Light, winner of six Group/Grade 1 events including the Breeders Cup Turf, the Prince of Wales's Stakes and the Irish Champion Stakes and to the listed

Pretty Polly Stakes winner Hi Dubai. The second dam, Jood (by Nijinsky), ran just twice but was quite useful, being placed over 7f at two years and over 10f at three years. She is a half-sister to the Grade 1 Ashland Stakes and Grade 1 Hollywood Oaks winner Gorgeous, the Grade 1 Kentucky Oaks winner Seaside Attraction (herself dam of the Cherry Hinton Stakes winner Red Carnival), the Canadian dual Grade 3 winner Key to the Moon and the Group 3 Princess Margaret Stakes winner Hiaam. (Horses First Racing Ltd).
'He was bought privately and is a nice colt that originally was being prepared for the breeze-ups. He should be racing fairly early.'

495. MEDICEAN MAN ★★

ch.c. Medicean – Kalindi (Efisio)
March 31. Fifth foal. 80,000Y. Tattersalls October 1. Angie Sykes. Brother to the useful two year old Group 3 6f Round Tower Stakes winner and Group 2 7f Rockfel Stakes third Abigail Pett and half-brother to the quite useful all-weather dual 7f winner (including at two years) Autograph Hunter (by Tobougg) and the modest 5f and 6f all-weather winner of eight races Mambazo (by Dansili). The dam, a useful 5f (at two years) and listed 7f winner, is a full or half-sister to four winners. The second dam, Rohita (by Waajib), a fairly useful two year old 5f and 6f winner, was third in the Group 3 6f Cherry Hinton Stakes and is a half-sister to five winners. (Horses First Racing Ltd).
'He's currently in pre-training after having had a slight accident coming home from the sales. So he's a bit behind the rest but he's a nice type.'

496. SUTTON VENY (IRE) ★★★

gr.f. Acclamation – Carabine (Dehere)
March 14. Fourth foal. 52,000Y. Doncaster St Leger. John Warren. Half-sister to the fair 5f, 6f (both at two years) and 9.5f winner Fiore Di Bosco (by Charnwood Forest) and to the modest Irish 7f winner Glorificamus (by Shinko Forest). The dam is an unraced half-sister to eight winners including the 2,000 Guineas winner Mystiko. The second dam, Carracciola (by Zeddaan), was placed four times in France

and is a half-sister to ten winners including the Group 2 Prix de Malleret winner Calderina. (Horses First Racing Ltd).

'I love her. We decided to give her a bit of a break just so she could mature physically. There's a bit of scope about her and I'd expect to have her out from mid-season onwards.'

497. UNNAMED ★★
b.g. Tobougg – Alexander Ballet (Mind Games)
April 2. Second foal. 50,000Y. Doncaster St Leger. Angela Sykes. The dam, an Irish three year old 5f winner, is a half-sister to other two minor winners. The second dam, Dayville (by Dayjur), a quite useful triple 6f winner, is a half-sister to four winners including the Grade 1 Yellow Ribbon Handicap winner Spanish Fern. (Horses First Racing Ltd).

'A scopey horse, he needed to be gelded just because of his attitude but it won't hold him up that much. He'll be a mid-season two year old and a nice type that should get middle-distances next year.'

498. UNNAMED ★★
ch.g. Haafhd – Decision Maid (Diesis)
April 6. Fourth foal. 50,000Y. Tattersalls October 1. Angie Sykes. Half-brother to the useful 2007 two year old 7f winner and dual listed placed Latin Lad (by Hernando) and to the quite useful 1m and 10f winner Shake On It (by Lomitas). The dam, a quite useful two year old 7f winner, is a half-sister to five winners including the listed 7f winner Miss Ivanhoe. The second dam, Robellino Miss (by Robellino), won seven races at up to 9f in the USA, was stakes-placed and is a half-sister to the listed winners Grangeville and Palana. (Horses First Racing Ltd).

'He was getting too heavy so we decided to geld him. In pre-training now, he's due back in soon and is a very mature, strong horse. I wouldn't be surprised if he came along quite quickly because he's quite strong and looks physically capable.'

499. UNNAMED ★★★
b.f. Proud Citizen – Divine Diva (Theatrical)
March 19. Third foal. 32,000 two year old.

Kempton breeze-up. Horses First Racing. Half-sister to the fair 2007 two year old 6f winner Eager Diva (by More Than Ready) and to the minor US stakes winner Organ Pipe (by Stormy Atlantic). The dam is an unplaced sister to the US Grade 3 winner Sing For Free and a half-sister to nine winners. The second dam, Dumdedumdedum (by Star de Naskra), won six races including the Grade 3 Barbara Fritchie Handicap and is a half-sister to the dual Grade 2 winner Nepal. (Horses First Racing Ltd).

'A tall, scopey filly, she's one for the back-end of the season but I was really impressed with the way she breezed up for a filly you wouldn't expect to be early.'

500. UNNAMED ★★★
ch.f. King's Best – Pretty Sharp (Interrex)
April 25. Eighth foal. 50,000Y. Tattersalls October 1. Angie Sykes. Half-sister to the moderate 2007 6f placed two year old Twilight Belle (by Fasliyev), to the Group 3 5f Duke Of York Stakes winner Twilight Blues (by Bluebird), the quite useful two year old 7f winner Sharp As A Tack (by Zafonic), the quite useful two year old 5f winner and listed 5f placed Incise (by Dr Fong), the quite useful two year old 7f winner Mobsir (by Mozart), the modest Irish 8.5f winner Sagittate (by Grand Lodge) and a winner abroad by Pivotal. The dam, a modest 7f placed two year old, is a half-sister to six winners including the quite useful 6f (at two years) to 10f winner Kings Assembly. The second dam, To The Point (by Sharpen Up), a fairly useful two year old 5f winner, is a half-sister to five winners. (Horses First Racing Ltd).

'I'd expect her to be pretty sharp, she's in work and I think she'll be out fairly soon. Quite a speedy filly but being by King's Best she'll hopefully have some scope as well.'

501. UNNAMED ★★★
b.c. Danetime – Tumbleweed Pearl (Aragon)
April 28. Fifth foal. 62,000Y. Tattersalls October 2. Angie Sykes. Half-brother to the two year old Group 2 5f Queen Mary Stakes winner Gilded (by Redback) and to the modest four year old 6f winner Jasmine Pearl (by King Of Kings). The

dam, a fairly useful 5.7f (at two years) and 6f winner, is a half-sister to five winners including the Group 3 Horris Hill Stakes, Ballycorus Stakes and Prix de la Porte Maillot winner and Gimcrack Stakes second Tumbledown Ridge. The second dam, Billie Blue (by Ballad Rock), is a placed half-sister to four minor winners. (Horses First Racing Ltd).

'He moves nicely and was looking like being fairly early but he had a slight setback and he's now going to be one for the middle of the season onwards. He's lightly framed, not over-big and it'll be interesting to see what sort of a trip he gets.'

JAMES GIVEN

502. BENYW (IRE) ★★
b.f. Noverre – Abington Angel (Machiavellian)
January 27. First foal. 24,000Y. Tattersalls October 2. Allan Bloodlines. The dam, a fair 12f winner, is a half-sister to five winners including the very useful Group 3 6f Cherry Hinton Stakes winner Applaud, the useful listed 10.2f winner Sauterne and the useful 10f winner and Group 3 placed Glam Rock. The second dam, Band (by Northern Dancer), is a placed half-sister to five winners including the US Grade 3 9f New Orleans Handicap winner Festive. (Mr R S G Jones & Mr B Coulhard).

'She's a first foal and looks that way a bit, but she's strong for her size. It's a good family and she looks like being a two year old by the middle of the summer. It's been such a long winter that I'm further behind with my two year old's than ever.'

503. BITZA BAILEYS ★★★★
b.f. Zamindar – Hamsah (Green Desert)
April 17. Seventh living foal. 20,000Y. Tattersalls October 2. Allan Bloodlines. Half-sister to the fairly useful two year old dual 5f winner and Group 3 5f Queen Mary Stakes third Sharplaw Star (by Xaar), to the fairly useful Irish two year old 5f winner and listed placed Sparkling Outlook (by College Chapel) and the quite useful two year old triple 5f winner Promenade (by Primo Dominie). The dam, a quite useful two year old dual 5f winner, was listed-placed and is a half-sister to the Irish

2,000 Guineas winner Wassl and to the dam of the Queen Mary Stakes winner On Tiptoes. The second dam, Hayloft (by Tudor Melody), a very useful winner of three races including the Group 3 Molecomb Stakes, is a half-sister to five winners. (G R Bailey Ltd).

'Zamindar is a fine sire of fillies and his stud fee went up this year. This filly does look exactly as you'd expect a sprinting-type two year old to look like. She has a nice, big, strong back-end and hails from a family of the Limestone Stud's upon whose land I train. She's one of those I feel most pleased at having bought because she's an exciting prospect.' TRAINER'S BARGAIN BUY

504. CYFLYMDER (IRE) ★★★
b.c. Mujadil – Nashwan Star (Nashwan)
April 11. Second foal. €55,000Y. Goffs Million. Allan Bloodlines. The dam, placed from 7f to 12f at three years, is a half-sister to five winners including the Group 1 1m Queen Elizabeth II Stakes winner Air Express. The second dam, Ibtisamm (by Caucasus), a fair three year old 1m winner, is a half-sister to four winners including the Grade 3 British Columbia Oaks winner Au Printemps (herself dam of the US Grade 1 winners Success Express and Greenwood Lake). (Mr R S G Jones & Mr B Coulhard).

'He looks very much a two year old type and he could be one of our first two year old runners. He's by Mujadil (a decent sire of early two year old's) out of a Nashwan mare and he seems to take more after the sire.'

505. DR SPEED ★★★
br.c. Dr Fong – Bimbola (Bikala)
April 2. Fourth foal. 23,000Y. Tattersalls October 2. Allan Bloodlines. The dam won seven races including the Group 2 Prix de Pomone and the Group 3 Premio Legnano and is a half-sister to four minor winners. The second dam, Agnes Lily (by Raise A Cup), is a placed full or half-sister to six winners. (Mr R S G Jones & Mr B Coulhard).

'He's a nice, big, scopey colt and a good mover. One for a bit later in the season and we've made a provisional entry for him in the Derby. He's just a lovely looking horse and we didn't pay a lot for him. At the time of the sale he just had a bruised foot and couldn't be shown, so I think we got him cheaply. Seven furlongs will suit him to start with.'

506. ELEGANTA (IRE) ★★★

b.f. Desert Style – Cover Girl
(Common Grounds)
March 5. Third foal. 35,000Y. Tattersalls October 2. Allan Bloodlines. Sister to the useful two year old 5f and 5.7f winner, Group 3 Cornwallis Stakes third and subsequent US Grade 3 placed Shermeen and half-sister to the modest 2007 1m placed two year old Luxie (by Acclamation). The dam, a fair two year old 6f and 7f and subsequent Scandinavian listed winner, is a half-sister to two winners. The second dam, Peace Carrier (by Doulab), was placed over 12f in Ireland and is a placed half-sister to six winners including the listed winner Sandhurst Goddess – herself dam of the Molecomb Stakes and Anglesey Stakes winner Lady Alexander. (Mr N Collins).
'The half-sister Shermeen is still performing well on the west coast of the USA and has recently been Grade 2 placed. This filly is having a break because she's growing a lot so despite the look of speed in the pedigree she's going to take some time.'

507. HIGH TENSILE ★★

b.f. Diktat – Shifty Mouse (Night Shift)
February 21. Sixth foal. 4,000Y. Tattersalls December. James Given. Sister to the fairly useful two year old 5f and 6f winner Mimi Mouse and half-sister to the modest 2007 5f placed two year old Linnet Park (by Compton Place) and a winner in Hungary by Eagle Eyed. The dam is an unplaced half-sister to nine winners out of Top Mouse (by High Top), herself a sister to the Nassau Stakes winner and good broodmare Triple First. (R Walker).
'I thought she was a nice purchase. she was so cheap. She's a very different animal to her full-sister Mimi Mouse who was a sprinter type. This filly is taller, longer-striding and scopier. She'll make a two year old in mid-season, probably over six furlongs.'

508. LOOKAFTERNUMBERONE (IRE) ★★★

gr.c. Verglas – Septieme Face (Lit de Justice)
February 27. First foal. 32,000Y. Tattersalls October 2. Allan Bloodlines. The dam, unplaced in France at two years, is a half-sister to three minor winners. The second dam, Secret Form (by Formidable), winner of the Group 2 Prix de l'Opera, was second in the French 1,000 Guineas and the French Oaks and is a half-sister to seven winners. (Cavan Pickering & Stewart Whitehead).
'A first foal but he isn't small, he's got a good attitude and is nice and strong. Quite forward and with a good way of going, I'm expecting him to be a six/seven furlong horse.'

509. MARJURY DAW (IRE) ★★

b.f. Marju – The Stick (Singspiel)
February 27. First foal. 17,000Y. Doncaster St Leger. Peter Swann. The dam, placed fourth once over 7f from 10 starts, is a sister to one winner and a half-sister to six winners. The second dam, Fatah Flare (by Alydar), won over 6f (at two years) and the Group 3 10.5f Musidora Stakes at three years. She is a half-sister to eight winners including Sabin, a dual US Grade 1 winner over 9f and 10f. (Danethorpe Racing Partnership).
'She's a first foal but doesn't really look it. She'll want some ease in the ground but has a nice way of getting on with her job. One for the second half of the season.'

510. PRIMA LAUREA ★★★

b.f. Royal Applause – First Degree (Sabrehill)
March 24. Fourth foal. €36,000Y. Tattersalls Ireland. Allan Bloodlines. Sister to Royal Degree, a promising second on both his starts (including over 5f at two years in 2007) and half-sister to the quite useful 7f and 10f winner Keel (by Carrowkeel) and the quite useful 1m all-weather and 10f winner Zelos (by Mujadil). The dam is an unplaced half-sister to the Group 2 6f Richmond Stakes winner Mister Cosmi and the listed 6f Ripon Champion two year old Trophy winner Auditorium (both by Royal Applause). The second dam, Degree (by Warning), a quite useful four year old 1m winner, is a sister to the

German listed winner Dark Marble. (Living Legend Racing Partnership).

'She had a little setback which necessarily enforced a break on her and now she's returned she's grown a bit and is taking her time getting fit again. Nevertheless she does look like a two year old type and the mix of Royal Applause with this family seems very successful. She should make her debut over five furlongs sometime from mid-May onwards.'

511. REAL DANDY ★★★

b.g. Bahamian Bounty – You Make Me Real (Give Me Strength)
March 1. Tenth foal. 26,000Y. Doncaster St Leger. Not sold. Half-brother to the Group 3 6f Railway Stakes and subsequent US winner Camargo (by Brief Truce), to the fairly useful 9f to 12f winner Chinkara (by Desert Prince), the quite useful 12f winner Protective (by Hector Protector), the Irish 7f and 1m winner Forget About It, the Irish 9f, 14f and hurdles winner Real Guest, the hurdles winner Dip's Guest (all by Be My Guest), the fair 11f winner Natural (by Bigstone) and a winner in Italy by Cadeaux Genereux. The dam, a sprint winner of four races in the USA, is a half-sister to seven winners including the US stakes winner Wonderloaf. The second dam, Icy Dial (by Banderilla), won 11 races in the USA including a minor stakes and is a half-sister to the dam of the US Grade three winners Gala Spinaway and Power Play. (Mr P Onslow & Mr I Henderson).

'He was naughty both as a foal and a yearling, so not surprisingly he's been gelded. But that's done the trick and he's much better behaved now. He should be a two year old sprinter and start off before mid-season.'

512. ROYAL TROOPER (IRE) ★★

b.c. Hawk Wing – Strawberry Roan (Sadler's Wells)
February 22. Seventh foal. €100,000Y. Goffs Million. Allan Bloodlines. Half-brother to the Irish 10f winner Portsmouth (by Fusaichi Pegasus). The dam, an Irish 7f and 1m listed winner, was second in the 1,000 Guineas and is a sister to the Irish 1,000 Guineas and Epsom Oaks winner Imagine and a half-sister to Generous, winner of the Derby, the Irish Derby, the King George VI and Queen Elizabeth Diamond Stakes and the Dewhurst Stakes. The second dam, Doff The Derby (by Master Derby), is an unraced half-sister to the Prix Ganay winner Trillion (herself dam of the out-standing racemare Triptych). (Mr J A Barson).

'If this colt could produce the goods he has a stallion's pedigree. I see him as a seven furlong two year old, he's a nice, big, scopey, strong horse.'

513. SENSACION SENSUAL ★★★

b.f. Josr Algarhoud – Charlie Girl (Puissance)
May 6. Sixth foal. 17,000Y. Doncaster Festival. Peter Swann. Sister to the useful two year old dual 6f winner and listed-placed Josh and half-sister to the quite useful 2007 two year old 6f winner Russian Reel (by Reel Buddy), the fair 5f (including at two years) and 6f winner Feelin Foxy (by Foxhound) and the two year old 5f seller winner Gone To Ground (both by Foxhound). The dam, a two year old 5f winner, is a half-sister to four winners. The second dam, Charolles (by Ajdal), is a placed half-sister to the French dual Group 1 winner Creator. (Danethorpe Racing Partnership).

'She isn't that backward for a May foal, although she isn't going to be running until the middle of the season. She gets on with her job and she'll make a two year old over six and seven furlongs.'

514. TRICKY SITUATION ★★

b.f. Mark Of Esteem – Trick Of Ace (Clever Trick)
February 22. Sixth foal. 26,000Y. Doncaster October. James Given. Half-sister to the Group 3 12f Princess Royal Stakes winner of seven races and Group 1 Yorkshire Oaks third Trick Or Treat (by Lomitas) and to the modest three year old 10f winner Trickstep (by Imperial Ballet). The dam, a stakes-placed winner of four races in the USA over 1m or more, is a half-sister to three winners including the US Grade 2 La Prevoyante Handicap winner Prospectress. The second dam, Seductive Smile (by Silver Hawk), is an unraced half-sister to six winners including the Group 1 Premio Roma winner Nizon, the US Grade 3

winner Don Roberto and the South African Grade 3 winner Lord Balmerino. (Mr P Onslow & Mr I Henderson).

'A half-sister to our best horse last year in Trick Or Treat. This filly is bigger than Trick Or Treat was at this stage and I doubt her doing anything until the back-end of the season because she's quite backward.'

515. VEROON (IRE) ★★★

b.c. Noverre – Waroonga (Brief Truce)
February 2. Fifth foal. 32,000Y. Doncaster St Leger. P Swann. Half-brother to the fairly useful dual 5f winner (including at two years) Foursquare (by Fayruz) and to the modest 5f and 6f winner Lord Of The Reins (by Imperial Ballet). The dam is an unraced half-sister to five winners. The second dam, Water Spirit (by Riverman), is an unraced half-sister to nine winners. (Danethorpe Racing Partnership).

'A nice, big, strong horse, the sire gets plenty of two year old winners and he could be racing by June over six furlongs. A colt with a nice way of going.'

516. ZELOS DIKTATOR ★★★

br.c. Diktat – Chanterelle (Indian Ridge)
February 8. First foal. 12,000Y. Tattersalls October 2. Allan Bloodlines. The dam, a fair two year old 6f winner, is a half-sister to the minor French 1m winners Chanteline and Pochettino. The second dam, Chantereine (by Trempolino), a minor winner at three years in France, is a half-sister to three winners including the Cheveley Park Stakes second Line Of Thunder (herself dam of the Kentucky Derby and Belmont Stakes winner Thunder Gulch). (Mr M J Beadle & Mr I Booth).

'He's a good size for a first foal and is a good, scopey Diktat. He'll make a two year old by mid-season.'

517. UNNAMED ★★★

b.c. Fath – Solas Abu (Red Sunset)
March 27. Seventh foal. 20,000Y. Tattersalls October 2. Allan Bloodlines. Half-brother to the quite useful two year old 6f winner Shannon Dore (by Turtle Island) and to a winner in

Holland by Dolphin Street. The dam, a quite useful 9f and 10f winner in Ireland, is a half-sister to two winners. The second dam, Curie Abu (by Crofter), won once at four years and is a half-sister to six winners including the Group 2 Pretty Polly Stakes winner Noora Abu. (The One Stop Partnership).

'He's a good-looking horse but we have to try and steady him because he's quite keen in his work. He's quite forward and I suspect he'll be out by the middle of the summer at the latest.'

518. UNNAMED ★★

b.f. Sakhee – Thracian (Green Desert)
March 31. Sixth living foal. 5,500Y. Tattersalls October 3. James Given. Half-sister to the quite useful dual 2m winner Trilemma (by Slip Anchor), to the fair two year old 7f winner Thrasher (by Hector Protector), the fair two year old 5f winner Sunley Gift (by Cadeaux Genereux) and a winner in Japan by Zafonic. The dam, a fairly useful two year old 6f and 7f winner, is a half-sister to 12 winners including the Group 2 12f Ribblesdale Stakes winner Third Watch, the Group 3 Prix Foy winner Richard of York, the Group 2 Premio Dormello winner Three Tails (herself dam of the high-class colts Tamure and Sea Wave), the Group 3 Fred Darling Stakes winner Maysoon and the dams of the Group winners Lend A Hand and Talented. The second dam, Triple First (by High Top), won seven races including the Sun Chariot Stakes, the Nassau Stakes and the Musidora Stakes. (Moonfleet Racing).

'She was very cheap – given away I think – and she'll be off a very low weight in median auctions. The dam was rated 105 and it's such a strong family. She's been a bit backward and is still growing although she's not going to be big, just a decent size. She hasn't done anything wrong yet.'

JOHN GOSDEN

519. ALSALAAL ★★★★

b.c. Sakhee – Recherchee (Rainbow Quest)
March 4. Twelfth foal. 78,000Y. Tattersalls October 1. Gill Richardson. Half-sister to the useful two year old listed 7f Superlative Stakes

winner and Group 2 Futurity Stakes second Recondite, to the fair 10f and 12f winner Freedom Quest (both by Polish Patriot), the fair dual 12f and hurdles winner Celtic Star and the 10f winner Absolutelythebest (by Anabaa). The dam is an unraced half-sister to three winners including the listed stakes winner Nordica. herself dam of the Group 3 Fred Darling Stakes winner Sueboog and the listed winner Marika. The second dam, Princess Arabella (by Crowned Prince), won at three years and is a half-sister to the Oaks and Irish Oaks winner Fair Salinia and to the US Grade 2 winner Rambo Dancer.

'A nice horse and nice mover, he's a big, strong colt that goes well.'

520. ANJUNA ★★★

b.br.f. El Corredor – Red Dot (Diesis)
January 23. First foal. 70,000Y. Tattersalls October 1. Hugo Lascelles. The dam is an unraced half-sister to four winners including the Grade 1 9f Kentucky Oaks and the Grade 1 10f Alabama Stakes winner Flute. The second dam, Rougeur (by Blushing Groom), a winner over 10f in France and 12f in the USA, was Grade 2 placed and is a half-sister to the Park Hill Stakes winner and good broodmare Eva Luna.

'A sweet filly, she's sharp and I'll be moving along with her in May. Goes nicely.'

521. ASPRO MAVRO (IRE) ★★★★★

b.c. Spartacus – Alexia Reveuse (Dr Devious)
May 13. Third living foal. 40,000Y. Tattersalls October 2. Blandford Bloodstock. Closely related to the useful listed 1m winner of four races Deauville Vision (by Danehill Dancer). The dam is an unraced half-sister to three minor winners. The second dam, Marienthal (by Top Ville), is a placed sister to the Group 1 Prix Royal Oak winner Top Sunrise.

'This is a nice horse that moves well and goes nicely. I'm very pleased with him indeed, he's grown, has a nice attitude and is a lovely mover. One I'll be moving along with.'

522. BAWAARDI (IRE) ★★★

b.c. Acclamation – Global Trend (Bluebird)
January 26. First foal. 130,000Y. Doncaster St

Leger. Shadwell Estate Co. The dam is an unraced half-sister to three winners including the French and US stakes winners Night Chapter. The second dam, Context (by Zafonic), is a placed half-sister to five winners including the US Grade 2 winner Bon Point.

'He's going nicely and he'll be working upsides in mid-April. He's moving along just fine and is a quick actioned horse that looks like being a top of the ground type. Bred like he is you'd expect him to be a speed horse.'

523. BRUTON STREET (USA) ★★★★

b.br.c. Dynaformer – Fit For A Queen
(Fit To Fight)
April 29. Fourteenth foal. $500,000Y. Keeneland September. J Gosden. Half-brother to seven winners including the US stakes winners and Grade 1 and Grade 2 placed Royal Assault (by Kris S), the US Grade 2 placed Kingsland (by Mr Prospector). The dam, a two year old winner over 6f here, subsequently won five Graded stakes events in the USA.

'A neat, well-made and well-balanced individual, he's not particularly typical of the sire. He goes very nicely at this stage but is obviously a horse you'd want to be bringing out for seven-furlong maidens. So I wouldn't be inclined to run him at six but I'd be happy with him at this stage.'

524. CLOCKMAKER (IRE) ★★★

b.c. Danetime – Lady Ingabelle (Catrail)
March 27. Second foal. 130,000Y. Tattersalls October 2. John Gosden. Brother to the modest 6f to 10f placed maiden Takanewa. The dam, a modest fourth over 10f, is a half-sister to seven winners including the two year old Group 3 July Stakes winner Mister Links. The second dam, Lady Anna Livia (by Ahonoora), won twice in Holland and is a half-sister to nine winners.

'A big, rangy, Danetime colt, there's not much pedigree on the dam's side but he's a nice mover. He's immature in his forelegs at the moment and I'll be taking my time with him. But he's a nice character and he goes well. He cost a lot of money but it was the last crop of Danetime and I think everybody wanted one.'

525. CLOSE ALLIANCE ★★★★
b.c. Gone West – Shoogle (A P Indy)
January 24. Half-brother to the fair 2007 two year old 6f winner Moral Duty (by Silver Deputy) and to the quite useful French 1m winner Cross Purposes (by Distant View). The dam, a quite useful two year old 7f winner, is closely related to the US Grade 1 winner Sleep Easy and a half-sister to the US Grade 1 winner Aptitude and the smart 6f (at two years) to 8.5f (in the USA) winner Electrify. The second dam, Dokki (by Northern Dancer), is an unraced half-sister to the US Grade 1 winners Coastal and Slew O'Gold. (Khalid Abdulla).
'A nice sort of horse, with a good mind on him for a Gone West. He moves well, he's strong and he'd be one of our more precocious types. I wouldn't have any hesitation I getting him ready for six furlong maidens in May if he goes the right way.'

526. COMMENDATION ★★★
b.f. Royal Applause – Ring Of Love (Magic Ring)
February 18. Fifth foal. 38,000Y. Tattersalls October 2. Cheveley Park Stud. Half-sister to the very useful 6f (at two years) and 1m dual listed winner and Group 2 placed Bahia Breeze (by Mister Baileys). The dam, a fair 5f winner of four races (including at two years), is a half-sister to seven winners including the useful two year old 5f and 6f winner Gold Desert. The second dam, Fine Honey (by Drone), a fairly useful two year old 5f winner, is a half-sister to seven winners.
'A neat filly, we'll get on with her early.'

527. CONGREGATION ★★
b.c. Cape Cross – Have Faith (Machiavellian)
January 20. First foal. The dam, a quite useful two year old 7f winner, is a sister to the useful UAE winner of seven races Opportunist and a half-sister to the Group 2 1m Matron Stakes winner Favourable Terms. The second dam, Fatefully (by Private Account), a smart winner of four races including a listed event over 1m, is a half-sister to two minor winners.
'He's a first foal and on the small side. A neat little guy that just needs to get a little more strength and shape about him, but he's done nothing wrong at this stage and is just cantering.'

528. DEBUSSY (IRE) ★★★
b.c. Diesis – Opera Comique (Singspiel)
February 26. First foal. The dam, a two year old Irish 9f winner and third in the Group 3 7f C L Weld Park Stakes, is a half-sister to numerous winners including the top-class King George VI and Queen Elizabeth Diamond Stakes, Great Voltigeur Stakes and Chester Vase winner Belmez. The second dam, Grace Note (by Top Ville), a fairly useful 10f Chepstow winner and second in the Group 3 12f Lingfield Oaks Trial, is a half-sister to the dams of the high-class 10.5f Prix de Diane winner Lypharita and the very useful winners Arousal and In Focus.
'A straightforward filly, she'd want to be out for the seven furlong maidens and she moves well. One for the second half of the season.'

529. DONAVITUM ★★★
gr.c. Cadeaux Genereux – Miss Universe (Warning)
March 2. Fifth living foal. 120,000Y. Tattersalls October 1. John Ferguson. Brother to the useful two year old 7f winner Tasdeed and half-brother to the two year old 8.6f and subsequent dual US Grade 3 winner Worldly (by Selkirk), the quite useful 2007 two year old 1m winner Comeback Queen (by Nayef) and the fairly useful 8.3f, 10f and hurdles winner Day To Remember (by Daylami). The dam, a useful two year old 6f winner and third in the Group 3 Solario Stakes, is a half-sister to five winners including the useful German 7f (at two years) to 11f winner Silver Sign and the fairly useful 1m and 9f winner Everest. The second dam, Reine d'Beaute (by Caerleon), a fairly useful 1m and 9f winner on her only starts, is a half-sister to eight winners including the Group 3 May Hill Stakes winner Intimate Guest.
'Quite a tough character, I moved along with him quite early on as he was quite full of himself. He goes fine and on pedigree he'd want to start at seven furlongs, I don't really intend to go six with him. but you never know. When they start the

seven furlong maidens in June at Sandown I like to have something ready and he looks to me that type of horse.'

530. DREAMCOAT ★★★★

ch.c. Pivotal – Follow A Dream (Gone West)
April 25. Third living foal. 120,000Y. Tattersalls October 1. Not sold. Half-brother to the smart 1m to 10f winner Pipedreamer (by Selkirk). The dam, a fairly useful maiden, was placed five times at up to 8.3f at two and three years and is a half-sister to the useful middle-distance winner of four races Elusive Dream. The second dam, Dance a Dream (by Sadler's Wells), a smart winner of the Cheshire Oaks and second in the Epsom Oaks, is a sister to the 2,000 Guineas winner and Derby fourth Entrepreneur and to the very useful middle-distance listed winner Sadler's Image and a half-sister to numerous winners including the Coronation Stakes winner Exclusive.
'A nice individual, he had a big, heavy middle on him when he arrived but he's tightened up well. A good mover, I would see him coming out in mid-season on the July course. I'd be happy with him and he has a very nice attitude.'

531. EUSTON SQUARE ★★★★

b.c. Oasis Dream – Krisia (Kris)
March 15. Half-brother to the Group 1 July Cup and Group 1 Prix de l'Abbaye winner Continent (by Lake Coniston), to the French three year old 5.5f winner Risiafon (by Zafonic) and the fair 6f winner Keys Of Cyprus (by Deploy). The dam won over 12f and is a half-sister to the French listed 10.5f and 12f winner Short Pause. The second dam, Interval (by Habitat), won the Group 2 Prix Maurice de Gheest, was third in the 1,000 Guineas and is a half-sister to the very useful 1m and 10f winner Interim and to the unraced Welcome Break. dam of the Hoover Fillies Mile winner Invited Guest. (Khalid Abdulla).
'A very attractive horse, it's interesting to see the dam won over a mile and a half – that rather puts me off as I never like to see that in a sprinter. But I like this horse, he's well-balanced, goes well and he's the type of horse I'd be running from mid-May onwards.'

532. FAVOURS BRAVE ★★★★

b.c. Galileo – Tuning (Rainbow Quest)
March 12. Half-brother to the smart 10.5f winner and Group 2 10.4f Dante Stakes second Tuning Fork (by Alzao), to the quite useful French two year old 1m winner Prototype (by Beat Hollow) and the modest 10f and 12f winner Mixing (by Linamix). The dam, a smart winner of the 14f Ebor Handicap, is a sister to the fairly useful French 12f winner Raincloud and a half-sister to the useful Group 3 7f Rockfel Stakes second Clog Dance. The second dam, Discomatic (by Roberto), a French 9f winner, is a half-sister to the Phoenix Stakes winner Digamist. (Khalid Abdulla).
'A nice sort of horse, he's filled out and strengthened behind since he came here, which is a lot of help to us. He moves very well.'

533. FLINTLOCK (IRE) ★★

b.g. Oasis Dream – Finity (Diesis)
March 21. Second foal. 62,000Y. Doncaster St Leger. R O'Gorman. Half-brother to the unraced 2007 two year old Rock Exhibition (by Rock Of Gibraltar). The dam, a useful two year old 7f winner, was third in the Group 3 7f C L Weld Park Stakes and is a half-sister to two winners. The second dam, Silversword (by Highest Honor), a winner at three years in France and Group 3 placed, is a full or half-sister to six winners.
'He shows some attitude and apparently his mother was that way. I've gelded him and I'll get on with him.'

534. FLOODLIT ★★★★

b.f. Fantastic Light – Westerly Air (Gone West)
March 8. Second foal. The dam, a fair 9.3f winner, is a half-sister to four winners including the Grade 2 Long Island Handicap, the Group 3 May Hill Stakes and Group 3 Prestige Stakes winner Midnight Line. The second dam, Midnight Air (by Green Dancer), won the Group 3 1m May Hill Stakes at two years and is a half-sister to five minor winners and to the dam of the Group 1 5f Prix de l'Abbaye winner Imperial Beauty.
'A nice-moving, very elegant filly. She has a lovely action, is very light on her feet and would want

top of the ground. I'll introduce her in a seven furlong maiden in July/August time.'

535. FROSTED ★★★

ch.f. Dr Fong – Arctic Air (Polar Falcon)
May 15. Sixth foal. 170,000Y. Tattersalls October 1. Cheveley Park Stud. Sister to the triple listed winner and Group 2 6f Gimcrack Stakes second Andronikos (by Dr Fong) and half-sister to the quite useful two year old 6f winner Arctic Cape (by Cape Cross) and the moderate 7f winner Selkirk Sky (by Selkirk). The dam, a quite useful two year old 7f winner, is a sister to the useful listed 7f winner Arctic Char and a half-sister to six winners including the Group two winners Barrow Creek and Last Resort and the dam of the Group 2 winner Trans Island. The second dam, Breadcrumb (by Final Straw), a very useful 6f and 7f winner, is a half-sister to four winners including the Group 2 Prix Maurice de Gheest winner College Chapel.
'A nice Dr Fong filly, she has a strong, aggressive attitude and goes well. I wouldn't be trying to sprint her over six, she's the type for seven furlong maidens and she looks strong and solid.'

536. GERTRUDE BELL ★★★

b.br.f. Empire Maker – Script (Storm Cat)
February 22. Fourth foal. $75,000Y. Keeneland September. Blandford Bloodstock. The dam, a minor US three year old winner, is a half-sister to the US Graded stakes winners Academy Award, Good Mood and Statuette (herself dam of the Group 1 Dewhurst Stakes second Tomahawk) and to the placed dam of the US Grade 1 winner Well Chosen. The second dam, Mine Only (by Mr Prospector), a minor US three year old winner, is a full or half-sister to three stakes winners.
'A nice filly and a good mover, she's elegant and the sire has done well with two-year-olds when you wouldn't necessarily expect him to. She should be a nice filly in the second half of the season. This filly is owned by my wife.'

537. GREEN BERET (IRE) ★★★

b.c. Fayruz – Grandel (Owington)
February 16. Fourth foal. 120,000Y. Doncaster St Leger. J Gosden. Brother to the very

promising 2007 two year old 5f winner Inxile and half-brother to the very smart Group 3 5f Prix du Petit Couvert and Group 3 5f Palace House Stakes winner Tax Free (by Tagula). The dam is an unraced half-sister to three minor winners. The second dam, Fernlea (by Sir Ivor), was listed-placed in Ireland and is a half-sister to three winners.
'A strong horse that goes nicely, he has a little bit of an eye for the fillies and he needs to iron that out of his system fast, but he moves well. He goes promisingly, he has a good attitude when he's concentrating and I'll get him ready to run in May.'

538. HALLIWELL HOUSE ★★★

ch.f. Selkirk – Dusty Answer (Zafonic)
February 10. Third foal. 105,000Y. Tattersalls October 1. Cheveley Park Stud. Half-sister to the fair 2007 7f and 8.5f placed two year old Counterclaim (by Pivotal). The dam, a quite useful two year old 7f winner, was listed placed over 1m and is a half-sister to three winners including the listed 1m and subsequent US Grade 2 winner Spotlight. The second dam, Dust Dancer (by Suave Dancer), won four races including the Group 3 10f Prix de la Nonette and is a half-sister to six winners including the Group 3 7.3f Fred Darling Stakes winner Bulaxie (herself dam of the Group 2 winner Claxon).
'A little immature but she's a Selkirk, very much a seven furlong filly with a great attitude. She wants to give all in the mornings and I'll just bring her along for the maidens at that time of year.'

539. KANSAI SPIRIT (IRE) ★★★

ch.c. Sinndar – Daanat Nawal (Machiavellian)
March 24. Eighth foal. 30,000Y. Tattersalls December. Norris/Huntingdon. Half-brother to the smart 6f (at two years) and 1m listed winner and dual Group 2 placed Babodana (by Bahamian Bounty) and two winners abroad by Zilzal and Petong. The dam is an unraced half-sister to five minor winners. The second dam, Negeen (by Danzig), a quite useful 5f (at two years) and 7f winner, is a half-sister to ten winners including the US dual Grade 1 winner Smile.

'A big, powerful galloping type and the sort to see out in seven furlong or mile maidens. He goes well and is a big, raw-boned horse, very much for September or October time.'

540. LAKE LADOGA ★★★
b.f. Green Desert – Viz (Kris S)
March 31. Ninth living foal. Sister to the very useful listed 7f (at two years) and 1m winner Secret Charm and half-sister to the smart two year old listed 7f winner and Oaks third Relish The Thought, the quite useful 10f and 12f winner Miss Particular (both by Sadler's Wells), the quite useful 12.4f winner Valiant Effort (by In The Wings) and the fair 10f winner Mandragola (by Machiavellian). The dam, a US two year old 1m winner, was third in the Grade 1 1m Hollywood Starlet Stakes and is a sister to the US stakes winner and Grade 2 placed Mistress S. The second dam, Shapiro's Mistress (by Unpredictable), a stakes winner at two years in the USA, is a half-sister to the Breeders Cup Juvenile and Santa Anita Derby winner Brocco. 'A nice little filly with a sharp action, she goes about her business and is the type I'll try to get out in May or early June.'

541. LONDON BRIDGE ★★
b.c. Beat Hollow – Cantanta (To Ville)
January 12. Half-brother to five winners including the French Group 3 12f Prix de Royaumont winner Cantilever (by Sanglamore), the French listed 12f winner Tailfeather (by In The Wings), the fairly useful 9.7f winner Bowstring (by Sadler's Wells) and the French two year old 1m winner Welcome (by Be My Guest). The dam won over 2m at three years and is a sister to the Irish Oaks winner Princess Pati and a half-sister to numerous winners out of Sarah Siddons (by Le Levanstell). (Khalid Abdulla).
'A big, strong horse, he's doing no more than one canter at the moment but he goes very nicely.'

542. MAFAAZ ★★★★
ch.c. Medicean – Complimentary Pass (Danehill)
January 10. Fifth foal. 400,000Y. Tattersalls

October 1. Shadwell Estate Co. Half-brother to the useful two year old 7f winner and Group 3 7f Acomb Stakes second Gweebarra (by Lomitas) and to the modest 1m and 10f winner Spunger (by Fraam). The dam, a quite useful 1m placed maiden, is a half-sister to five minor winners. The second dam, Capo Di Monte (by Final Straw), a smart 6f (at two years), dual 10f listed and subsequently a Grade 3 11f winner in the USA, is a half-sister to five winners including the Group 1 12f Aral-Pokal winner Wind In Her Hair (herself dam of the Japan Cup winner Deep Impact). (Hamdan Al Maktoum).
'A very good-looking Medicean colt, he moves very well and has a good, powerful stride on him. His knees are a bit immature yet but he's a nice sort of horse. He'll be one for mid-season and would be quite capable of racing over six furlongs'

543. MAYAALAH ★★★
b.f. Cape Cross – Chater (Alhaarth)
March 29. The dam is an unraced half-sister to three winners including the 1,000 Guineas and Group 2 7f Rockfel Stakes winner Lahan. The second dam, Amanah (by Mr Prospector), a useful 1m winner, is a half-sister to two winners including the fairly useful two year old winners Alhufoof and Habub. (Hamdan Al Maktoum).
'She's a nice sort of filly, but she's small and is one I ought to try and move along with. I'll try and get her out in May because there's not a lot of scope there.'

544. MOOAKADA ★★★
gr.f. Montjeu – Sulaalah (Darshaan)
April 18. First foal. The dam is an unraced half-sister to two winners. The second dam, Bint Shadayid (by Nashwan), a very useful winner of the Group 3 7f Prestige Stakes, was placed in the 1,000 Guineas and the Fillies Mile. (Hamdan Al Maktoum).
'A rangy, attractive filly with a good action. I definitely wouldn't want to run her under seven furlongs. I like this filly, she shows quite a bit of fieriness about her which seems to be the pattern with Montjeu fillies.'

545. MORAL MAZE (IRE) ★★★
ch.c. Indian Ridge – Scruple (Catrail)
March 6. Fourth foal. 150,000Y. Tattersalls December. John Gosden. Half-brother to the quite useful three year old 7f all-weather winner Critic (by Fasliyev). The dam is an unraced half-sister to the smart triple listed winner over 6f and 7f Hot Tin Roof. The second dam, No Reservations (by Commanche Run), a quite useful listed-placed 6f (at two years) and 7f winner, is a half-sister to five winners including the very useful sprinters Hanu and Sanu.
'A strong horse with a good action, he takes a good grip and looks very racey. A mid-season horse, I trained the dam and although she was unraced she had ability. This colt is alright, he goes well.'

546. MURAWEG (IRE) ★★★
b.c. Kheleyf – Lady Moranbon (Trempolino)
April 14. Twelfth foal. 90,000Y. Doncaster St Leger. Shadwell Estate Co. Half-brother to the fairly useful 9.5f, 10f and hurdles winner Diego Cao (by Cape Cross), to the fairly useful 10f winner Space Cowboy (by Anabaa), the quite useful 5f and 6f two year old winner Lady Le Quesne (by Alhaarth), the fair dual 7f winner Sweet Gale (by Soviet Star), four winners in France by Pistolet Bleu, Homme de Loi, Slip Anchor and Sillery and a winner of six races in Italy by Bering. The dam won twice over 9f and 10f at four years in France and is a half-sister to six winners. The second dam, Brigade Speciale (by Posse), won a listed event in France and is a half-sister to the Group 2 Royal Lodge Stakes winner Gairloch.
'A nice horse, he's grown a lot and I like him (but not the broodmare sire). A nice, solid sort of horse that moves well.'

547. NEHAAM ★★★
b.c. Nayef – Charm The Stars (Roi Danzig)
March 1. Seventh foal. 200,000Y. Tattersalls October 1. Shadwell Estate Co. Half-brother to the very useful Group 3 14f winner Astrocharm (by Charnwood Forest), the quite useful 8.2f winner Astronomical (by Mister Baileys) and the quite useful 12.3f winner Sand And Stars (by Dr

Devious). The dam ran twice unplaced and is a half-sister to two minor winners. The second dam, Deloraine (by Pharly), is a placed half-sister to six winners including the Breeders Cup Turf winner Northern Spur.
'An attractive colt, he has a good action on him. He's a little bit tense but he's a lovely mover that needs a good, quiet rider but he seems to shows a bit of class and definitely wants seven furlong maidens.'

548. NO BRAINER ★★★
b.c. Falbrav – On The Tide (Slip Anchor)
February 2. Seventh living foal. 60,000Y. Tattersalls October 1. John Gosden. Half-brother to the useful 1m and 10f winner Tier Worker (by Tenby), the fairly useful two year old 6f winner Surf The Net (by Cape Cross), the quite useful dual 10f winner Mingling (by Wolfhound), the quite useful dual 12f and hurdles winner Top The Charts (by Singspiel) and the quite useful 1m winner Hareer (by Anabaa). The dam, a fair three year old 1m winner, is a half-sister to eight winners including the high-class Gimcrack Stakes winner Rock City and the smart Cherry Hinton Stakes winner Kerrera. The second dam, Rimosa's Pet (by Petingo), a very useful winner from 6f to 10.5f including the Group 3 Musidora Stakes and the Group 3 Princess Elizabeth Stakes, is a half-sister to five winners.
'A strong colt, he's a good mover and is just going to take a bit of time. You wouldn't expect these Falbrav's to be early. He goes well.'

549. PERGAMON (IRE) ★★
b.c. Dalakhani – Pinaflore (Formidable)
April 22. Twelfth foal. 130,000Y. Tattersalls December. John Gosden. Half-brother to eight winners including the two year old Group 3 1m Prix la Rochette winner Pinmix, to two minor winners in France (all by Linamix), the US Grade 2 winner Pinfloron (by Caerleon) and the Group 3 Prix Thomas Bryon winner Pinakaral (by Akarad). The dam won three races at two and three years in France including the listed Prix de Lieurey and is a half-sister to nine winners. The second dam, Pink Satin (by Right Royal), a

winner and Group 3 placed in France, is a half-sister to the French 2,000 Guineas winner Blue Tom and the Prix Morny winner Amber Rama. 'A very likeable horse, he's very open of his knees and I'm going to be very patient with him, so you won't be seeing him until September time.'

550. PLEASANT CAPE ★★★

b.f. Cape Cross – Felicity (Selkirk)
January 24. The dam, winner of the Group 3 10f Golden Daffodil Stakes, is a half-sister to the Group 3 7f Hungerford Stakes winner Sleeping Indian, US stakes winner Spanish Spur and the useful 10f winner Jalisco. The second dam, Las Flores (by Sadler's Wells), a useful 10f winner, was second in the Lingfield Oaks Trial and third in the Italian Oaks and is a full or half-sister to five winners including the Group 2 Royal Whip Stakes winner Bach. (George Strawbridge).
'She'll be coming in to us late, but she's a nice type of filly with a bit of quality about her. We had the mare and won a Group 3 with her. She looks quite nice.'

551. PURITY ★★★★

ch.f. Pivotal – Virtuous (Exit To Nowhere)
May 7. Sister to the quite useful 10f winner Virtuosity, closely related to the very smart two year old Group 2 6f Coventry Stakes winner and Group 1 6f Middle Park Stakes third Iceman (by Polar Falcon) and half-sister to the quite useful 10f winner Peace (by Sadler's Wells) and the fair two year old 6f winner Liberty (by Singspiel). The dam, a fairly useful two year old 1m winner, was third in the listed 11.5f Oaks Trial. The second dam, Exclusive Virtue (by Shadeed), a fairly useful two year old 7f winner, stayed 12f and is a half-sister to eight winners including the 2,000 Guineas winner and Derby fourth Entrepreneur and the Coronation Stakes winner Exclusive. (Cheveley Park Stud).
'An attractive, neat, quality filly with a nice shape to her. She's a little bit weak at the moment and so isn't going to emulate Iceman and win at Royal Ascot, but she's a nice sort of filly for mid-season.'

552. RED SPIDER ★★★★

b.c. Red Ransom – Lane County (Rahy)
March 26. First foal. The dam is a half-sister to the Irish 7f (at two years) and 1m winner Egyptian. The second dam, Link River (by Gone West), won the Grade 1 9f John A Morris Handicap in the USA.
'A nice horse that stands over plenty of ground he has a good action and is a good mover. One I'll start moving along soon and I like him.'

553. REPORTAGE (USA) ★★★★

b.c. Elusive Quality – Journalist (Night Shift)
March 27. Half-brother to the useful two year old 6f winner and Group 3 Firth Of Clyde Stakes third La Presse (by Gone West) and to the useful 7f and 1m winner Paper Talk (by Unbridled's Song). The dam, a useful two year old 6f winner, was second in the Group 3 6f Princess Margaret Stakes and is a half-sister to the useful sprinter Sheer Viking. The second dam, Schlefalora (by Mas Media), won at up to 1m in Sweden and is a half-sister to the 1,000 Guineas winner Las Meninas.
'A likeable colt, he's strong and there's no reason why he wouldn't race over six furlongs. There's a bit of speed on the dam's side and I like the horse.'

554. RIO CARNIVAL (USA) ★★★★★

b.f. Storm Cat – Zenda (Zamindar)
February 18. Half-sister to the unraced 2007 two year old Nile Cruise (by Danzig). The dam won the French 1,000 Guineas and is a half-sister to the July Cup and Nunthorpe Stakes winner Oasis Dream and the very useful dual listed 1m winner Hopeful Light. The second dam, Hope (by Dancing Brave), is an unraced sister to the very smart filly Wemyss Bight, a winner of five races from 9f (at two years) to 12f including the Group 1 Irish Oaks and the Group 2 Prix de Malleret. (Khalid Abdulla).
'A filly with a good attitude, she moves along nicely and does everything right. Like her mother, I wouldn't want to rush her and so August/ September time should be right for her. I'll probably start her over seven furlongs but she's a lovely, quality filly.'

555. RUN FOR THE HILLS ★★★★
b.c. Oasis Dream – Maid For The Hills
(Indian Ridge)
April 13. Eighth foal. Closely related to the quite useful two year old 6f winner Green Tambourine (by Green Desert) and half-brother to the useful 7f (at two years) and 10f winner Maid To Perfection (by Sadler's Wells), the useful two year old 7f winner Artistic Lad (by Peintre Celebre), the quite useful 8.6f winner King's Kama (by King's Best) and the fair 8.3f winner Maid To Believe (by Galileo). The dam was a useful two year old and won twice over 6f including the listed Empress Stakes. She is a half-sister to five winners including the Group 3 6f Princess Margaret Stakes second Maid For Walking. The second dam, Stinging Nettle (by Sharpen Up), a fairly useful two year old listed 6f winner, is a half-sister to four winners including the Group 2 1m Royal Lodge Stakes winner Gairloch.
'A nice colt and a good mover with some scope about him. He wouldn't want to be early but there's no reason why he wouldn't want to be coming out on the track in June. He goes well.'

556. SABI STAR ★★★★
b.c. Green Desert – Balisada (Kris)
May 5. Sixth foal. 140,000Y. Tattersalls October 1. Blandford Bloodstock. Brother to the quite useful 2007 7f placed two year old Green Diamond and half-brother to the quite useful 10f winner Galactic Star (by Galileo), the French two year old 1m winner Bradamante (by Sadler's Wells) and the minor US winner Watchtower (by Dubai Millennium). The dam won the Group 1 1m Coronation Stakes and is a half-sister to one winner. The second dam, Balnaha (by Lomond), a modest three year old 1m winner, is a sister to Inchmurrin (a very useful winner of the Child Stakes and herself dam of the very smart and tough colt Inchinor) and a half-sister to six winners including the Mill Reef Stakes winner Welney.
'He was a bit neat at the sales but fortunately he's grown, he has a good attitude and moves well. I'd be pleased with him and he's one for June time.'

557. SANCTUM ★★★
b.f. Medicean – Auspicious (Shirley Heights)
May 23. Fifth foal. Half-brother to the fairly useful two year old 7f and 1m winner Doctrine (by Barathea), to the quite useful two year old 1m winner Australian (by Danzero) and the quite 1m to 10f winner Prince Picasso (by Lomitas). The dam, a fairly useful 10.2f winner, is a sister to the smart Group 2 11.9f Great Voltigeur Stakes winner Sacrament and a half-sister to five winners and to the dam of the Group 1 winner Chorist. The second dam, Blessed Event (by Kings Lake), winner of the listed 10f Ballymacoll Stud Stakes and placed in the Yorkshire Oaks and the Champion Stakes, is a half-sister to four winners.
'A nice sort of filly, she's not going to be early and I had the half-siblings Doctrine and Australian who came out about around August time. Being a late foal I see this filly coming out in September.'

558. SEA OF LEAVES (USA) ★★
b.c. Stormy Atlantic – Dock Leaf (Woodman)
April 12. Third foal. Half-brother to Distinctive Image (by Mineshaft), unplaced in one start at two years in 2007. The dam, unplaced in one start, is a half-sister to the Grade 1 9f Hollywood Oaks winner Sleep Easy and to the dual US Grade 1 winner Aptitude. The second dam, Dokki (by Northern Dancer), is an unraced half-sister to the champion US colt Slew O'Gold and the Belmont Stakes winner Coastal. (Khalid Abdulla).
'A small, home-bred filly, she's a nice sort but I think I might have to move along a bit with her because she's lacking in scope.'

559. SEAWAY ★★★★
b.c. Dr Fong – Atlantic Destiny (Royal Academy)
February 18. Second foal. 160,000Y. Doncaster St Leger. John Ferguson. Half-brother to the fairly useful two year old 6f winner Atlantic Light (by Linamix). The dam, a useful winner of seven races from 5f to 7f including the listed Sirenia Stakes and a stakes event in the USA, is a half-sister to five winners including the Group 2 Royal Whip Stakes winner Make No Mistake.

The second dam, Respectfully (by The Minstrel), is an unplaced full or half-sister to six winners. *'He cost plenty for Doncaster, he's a nice horse and a good mover that goes well. He gives the riders a good feel but I don't intend giving him any work yet. He's probably going to wind up a seven furlong horse, but we'll see.'*

560. SEMINOLE (IRE) ★★★★
ch.c. Indian Ridge – Mystic Tempo (El Gran Senor)
April 29. Eighth foal. 140,000Y. Tattersalls October 1. John Gosden. Half-brother to the Group 1 1m Premio Vittorio di Capua, Group 2 Challenge Stakes and Group 2 Italian 2,000 Guineas winner Le Vie dei Colori (by Efisio), to the Italian listed-placed winner Stai Su (by Dr Fong), the fair 6f winner Mail Express (by Cape Cross) and a minor two year old winner in Italy by Alhijaz). The dam won over 6f at two years and two 6f sellers on the all-weather at three years and is a half-sister to three winners including the useful dual three year old 1m winner and Group 1 Moyglare Stud Stakes third Timely. The second dam, Doubling Time (by Timeless Moment), a smart winner at three years in France and second in the Group 3 10.5f Prix de Flore, is a full or half-sister to eight winners including Baillamont (Prix Ganay and Prix d'Ispahan).
'A solid little chestnut colt, he moves well and he's a tough little character. Like a lot of horses by Indian Ridge he'll probably appreciate a bit of cut in the ground.'

561. STAGE PERFORMANCE (IRE) ★★★
ch.f. Danehill Dancer – Stage Presence (Selkirk)
May 5. Fourth foal. 375,000Y. Tattersalls October 1. Hugo Lascelles. Sister to the Group 3 7f Sweet Solera Stakes winner and Group 1 Fillies' Mile third English Ballet and half-sister to the quite useful two year old 5f winner Spectacular Show (by Spectrum). The dam, a 7f and 1m three year old winner, is a half-sister to four winners including the 6f (at two years) and Group 3 7f Ballycorus Stakes winner Rum Charger. The second dam, Park Charger (by Tirol), a useful winner over 1m and 10f at three

years in Ireland, was listed-placed several times and is a half-sister to nine winners including the useful 6f (at two years) and 12f winner Indian Missile.
'A tall, elegant filly and light on her feet, she needs to fill that frame and is a filly for the July course over seven furlongs in mid-season onwards.'

562. STAR APPROVAL (IRE) ★★★
b.f. Hawk Wing – Mail Boat (Formidable)
March 26. Seventh foal. 95,000Y. Tattersalls October 2. Cheveley Park Stud. Half-sister to the Group 1 7f Moyglare Stud Stakes winner and Coronation Stakes third Mail The Desert (by Desert Prince), to the useful Irish 7f (at two years) and 9f winner and dual listed-placed Amarula Ridge (by Indian Ridge) and the Irish two year old 7f winner Email From Josh (by King's Best). The dam is an unraced half-sister to four winners including the Group 3 Chester Vase winner and St Leger third Dry Dock. The second dam, Boathouse (by Habitat), a smart winner of two races, was third in the Group 2 Sun Chariot Stakes and is a half-sister to eight winners including the Oaks winner Bireme and the Coronation Cup winner Buoy.
'A nice filly, she's got some scope about her and has a good stride on her. Very much a seven furlong type.'

563. STATE OF WAR (USA) ★★★
b.c. More Than Ready – You Again (Wild Again)
January 27. First foal. 210,000Y. Tattersalls October 2. J Gosden. The dam is an unraced half-sister to two winners including the US Grade 2 Peter Pan Stakes winner Best Of Luck. The second dam, Crowned (by Chief's Crown), won the Grade 2 Delaware Handicap in the USA and is a half-sister to three winners.
'He goes very nicely and is the kind of horse I'd like to run in June or July over seven furlongs. A nice, well-balanced colt.'

564. TAKE THE HINT ★★★
b.f. Montjeu – Insinuate (Mr Prospector)
March 6. Closely related to the fair 9.5f all-weather winner Indication (by Sadler's Wells)

and half-sister to the Group 3 7f Supreme Stakes winner Stronghold (by Danehill) and the quite useful 8.7f winner Imply (by Beat Hollow). The dam, a useful listed 1m winner, is a half-sister to numerous winners including the useful 6f and 7f winner and listed-placed Imroz. The second dam, All At Sea (by Riverman), was a high-class winner of five races from 1m to 10.4f including the Group 1 Prix du Moulin and was second in the Oaks, the Juddmonte International and the Nassau Stakes. (Khalid Abdulla).
'A very likeable filly, she's got a good shape to her and she's out of a decent mare. I'd be pleased with her at this stage but she's going to be wanting seven furlongs or a mile this year.'

565. TEJIME ★★★

b.c. Royal Applause – Pizzicato (Statoblest)
May 11. Sixth foal. 42,000Y. Tattersalls October 1. John Ferguson. Half-brother to the unraced 2007 two year old Astonish, to the two year old Group 2 5f Flying Childers Stakes and Group 3 5f Molecomb Stakes winner Wunders Dream (by Averti), the fairly useful 6f (at two years) and 7f winner Go Between (by Daggers Drawn), the quite useful 7f winner Plucky (by Kyllachy) and the Irish 7f winner and listed-placed Grecian Dancer (by Dansili). The dam, a modest 5f and 5.3f winner at three years, is a half-sister to five winners including the high-class Hong Kong horses Mensa and Firebolt. The second dam, Musianica (by Music Boy), was a fairly useful two year old dual 6f winner.
'A sharp little horse, he moves well but his knees are a bit immature, so I'll just have to wait. It's a pity because he's powerful and made for the job. I just have to be a bit patient.'

566. THE HAGUE ★★★

b.c. Xaar – Cox Orange (Trempolino)
February 1. Half-brother †o the useful 7f and 1m winner Vista Bella, to the fair 1m and 9f winner Ochre (both by Diktat) and to the minor French two year old winner Orlena (by Gone West). The dam won the Group 3 7f Prix du Calvados at two years and four US Grade 3 events and is a half-sister to six winners

including the Group 1 Prix Marcel Boussac winner Amonita. The second dam, Spectacular Joke (by Spectacular Bid). (Sheikh Mohammed).
'A nice horse, he has a good shape and a good stride. The riders like him, he's well-balanced and I'll move along with him and run him in May.'

567. TOWANDA (USA) ★★★★

f. Dynaformer – Desert Gold (Seeking The Gold)
The dam won six races including a stakes event in the USA and was Grade 3 placed. She is a half-sister to several winners out of the minor US four year old winner Desert Stormette (by Storm Cat), herself a sister to the Grade 1 Breeders Cup Sprint winner Desert Stormer.
'A nice filly and typical of the sire, we'd like to get her out around August time over seven furlongs. I'm pleased with her.'

568. TROOPINGTHECOLOUR ★★★

b.c. Nayef – Hyperspectra (Rainbow Quest)
March 3. Sixth foal. 230,000Y. Tattersalls October 1. John Ferguson. Half-brother to the modest 2007 6f placed two year old Southern Mistral, to the Group 3 7f Tetrarch Stakes winner and Irish 2,000 Guineas second France (both by Desert Prince) and the fair 11.8f winner Spectral Star (by Unfuwain). The dam, a fairly useful 10.2f winner, is a half-sister to three winners including the French winner and Group 3 Prix Eclipse second Hothaifah. The second dam, Hyabella (by Shirley Heights), a smart 1m winner of the listed Ben Marshall and the listed Atalanta Stakes, is a half-sister to six winners including the Group 2 10f Prince of Wales's Stakes winner Stagecraft.
'He's an elegant horse – you might say a shade effeminate. Nayef did well with his two-year-olds last year and you wouldn't have expected that. He goes well this horse but is very much one for seven furlongs and a mile in the autumn.'

569. TWISTED ★★★★

ch.c. Selkirk – Winding (Irish River)
January 14. Second foal. 155,000Y. Tattersalls October 1. Blandford Bloodstock. The dam is an unplaced half-sister to four winners including the Group 3 placed Silver Desert. The second dam, Silver Fling (by The Minstrel), won

the Group 1 Prix de l'Abbaye and the Group 3 King George Stakes and was placed in the William Hill Sprint Championship at York and the Vernons Sprint Cup (twice). She is a sister to the high-class filly Silverdip, winner of the Salisbury 1,000 Guineas Trial, the Strensall Stakes and the Montrose Handicap.
'A big, strong colt, he's done very well, he moves well and is a nice type of horse. The owner doesn't want early two year old's, he wants one that'll be a two year old, turning three.'

570. WAJAHA (IRE) ★★★
ch.f. Haafhd – Amanah (Mr Prospector)
April 22. Half-sister to the 1,000 Guineas and Group 2 7f Rockfel Stakes winner Lahan, to the quite useful 9f winner Borouj (both by Unfuwain) and the fairly useful 1m winner Tarbiyah (by Singspiel). The dam, a useful 1m winner, is a half-sister to the fairly useful two year old winners Alhufoof and Habub. The second dam, Cheval Volant (by Kris S), won five races from 5.5f to 8.5f in the USA including the Hollywood Starlet Stakes and the Las Virgines Stakes (both Grade 1 1m events) and is a half-sister to the dual US Grade 3 winner Chaldea. (Hamdan Al Maktoum).
'She was small when she came in but fortunately she's grown and has quite a bit of character about her. She's not the type to stand behind for too long because she'll have a crack at you! But she's a racey little thing and she has quite small feet so she'll want top of the ground.'

571. WARTIME ★★★★
ch.c. Bertolini – Follow Flanders (Pursuit Of Love)
April 7. Third foal. 85,000Y. Tattersalls October 2. Blandford Bloodstock. Brother to the unraced 2007 two year old Sir Billy Nick and half-brother to the quite useful dual 10f winner Fever (by Dr Fong). The dam, a fairly useful dual 5f winner, is a half-sister to nine winners including the top-class Group 1 5f Nunthorpe Stakes winner Kyllachy. The second dam, Pretty Poppy (by Song), a modest two year old 5f winner, stayed 7.6f and is a half-sister to four winners.
'A nice horse that moves well, he's a strong, quite

likeable colt and is very much going the right way.'

572. WRONG WAY ROUND (IRE) ★★★★
b.c. Barathea – Almansa (Dr Devious)
February 16. First foal. 30,000Y. Tattersalls October 1. Blandford Bloodstock. The dam, a minor winner at three years in France, is a half-sister to four winners including the listed winner and 1,000 Guineas third Alasha. The second dam, Alasana (by Darshaan), won twice at three years in France and is a half-sister to eight winners including the French dual Group 2 winner Altayan.
'A well-balanced colt, he's a nice type and didn't cost much. He moves well and is a grand sort with a very nice attitude.'

573. UNNAMED ★★★★
ch.c. Dr Fong – Carambola (Danehill)
March 3. Fifth foal. 110,000Y. Tattersalls October 1. Angie Sykes. Half-brother to Calistos Quest (by Rainbow Quest), a modest fourth over 7f at two years in 2007 and to the fairly useful three year old 1m winner and listed-placed Lady Stardust (by Spinning World). The dam, a useful listed Leopardstown 1,000 Guineas Trial winner and second in the Group 3 1m Matron Stakes, is a sister to the useful two year old 6f winner and South African Grade 1 second Toreador and a half-sister to seven winners including the Irish 1,000 Guineas winner Matiya. The second dam, Purchasepaperchase (by Young Generation), a useful winner of three races including the listed 1m Atalanta Stakes, was second in the Group 1 Prix Saint-Alary.
'A big, powerful horse that's going to be one for seven furlong maidens. I like the way he goes – I like everything about him. He looks tough.'

574. UNNAMED ★★★
b.f. Falbrav – First Exhibit (Machiavellian)
March 13. Third foal. 25,000Y. Tattersalls October 1. Blandford Bloodstock. Half-sister to the quite useful 2007 two year old 7f winner Prime Exhibit (by Selkirk). The dam is an unraced half-sister to two winners including the smart 12f and listed 14f winner Moments Of

Joy. The second dam, My Emma (by Marju), a smart winner of the Group 1 12f Prix Vermeille, is a half-sister to five winners including the Group 1 St Leger and Group 1 Ascot Gold Cup winner Classic Cliché.

'A nice type of filly, being by Falbrav she won't be early but she's goes nicely.' TRAINER'S BARGAIN BUY

575. UNNAMED ★★★

b.c. Indian Ridge – Flying Kiss (Sadler's Wells)
April 11. Fifth foal. 25,000Y. Tattersalls October 4. J Gosden. Half-brother to the fairly useful two year old 6f winner Sun Kissed (by Sunday Silence) and to a winner over jumps by Darshaan. The dam was placed once in two starts at three years in France and is a sister to the two year old Group 1 1m Racing Post Trophy winner Commander Collins and closely related to the Grade 1 Breeders Cup Sprint winner Lit de Justice and the very smart 7f Washington Singer Stakes winner and 2,000 Guineas, Derby and Irish Derby placed Colonel Collins. The second dam, Kanmary (by Kenmare), winner of the Group 3 6f Prix du Bois at two years, stayed 9f and is a half-sister to 11 winners including the Group 2 Prix de Royallieu winner Passionaria.

'A nice little colt and a good mover. I know the family and I'll be a bit patient with him because they get better with age.'

576. UNNAMED ★★

ch.f. Selkirk – Land Of Dreams (Cadeaux Genereux)
January 14. Fifth foal. 95,000Y. Tattersalls October 1. Rabbah Bloodstock. Sister to the Irish two year old 7f winner Only Make Believe and half-sister to the very smart listed 11f winner and Group 3 placed Into The Dark (by Rainbow Quest). The dam won the Group 2 5f Flying Childers Stakes and the Group 3 5f King George V Stakes and is a half-sister to four winners. The second dam, Sahara Star (by Green Desert), won the Group 3 5f Molecomb Stakes, was third in the Lowther Stakes and is a half-sister to six winners.

'A big, rangy filly, she's definitely going to take

some time and will start off at a minimum of a mile. She's big but you get that with Selkirk and there's nothing wrong with that.'

577. UNNAMED ★★★

b.c. Exceed And Excel – Strutting (Ela-Mana-Mou)
March 10. Eighth foal. 60,000Y. Tattersalls December. John Gosden. Half-sister to the Irish 7f and 10f winner and subsequent US Grade 3 winner Chiming (by Danehill) and to the quite useful 10f and 12f winner Hanella (by Galileo). The dam, a fairly useful 7f (at two years) and 10.2f winner, is a half-sister to four winners here and abroad. The second dam, Taking Steps (by Gay Fandango), won once at three years, was third in the Irish 1,000 Guineas and is a half-sister to three winners including the Gimcrack Stakes third Dee-Jay-Ess.

'A nice sort of horse, he was immature last year so he only made the December Sales. He's still a little bit 'up behind' but he has a nice bit of quality about him, he's a lovely mover and is not a horse I would rush. He goes nicely at this stage.'

578. UNNAMED ★★★

b.c. Seeking The Gold – Sunray Superstar (Nashwan)
Half-brother to the quite useful winner Northern Spy (by War Chant). The dam, a useful 12f winner, was third in the Cheshire Oaks and is a sister to the Group 1 10f Prix Saint-Alary winner and Group 1 Prix de Diane second Nadia. The second dam, Nazoo (by Nijinsky), was a very useful winner of all four of her two year old races in Ireland, from 6f to 7f and is a full or half-sister to numerous winners including the Group 1 6f Prix Morny placed Heeremandi and the US winner La Confidence (herself dam of the multiple US Grade 1 winner Flawlessly).

'A nice filly that moves well and has quality.'

579. UNNAMED ★★★

b.c. Pivotal – Tolyatti (Green Desert)
March 24. Fourth foal. 95,000Y. Tattersalls October 2. J Gosden. The dam, placed over 7f and 1m at two years in France, is a half-sister to two winners. The second dam, Xaymara (by

Xaar), won once at three years in France and is a half-sister to nine winners including the Grade 1 Washington Lassie Stakes winner Contredance and the dams of the 1,000 Guineas winner Wince and the Lanson Champagne Stakes winner Eltish.
'A strong colt, a good mover and a nice sort of horse, he's probably one for seven furlongs in mid-season – like most of mine.'

MICHAEL GRASSICK

580. CAPTAIN ALGREN (IRE) ★★
b.c. Cape Cross – Dame Alicia (Sadler's Wells)
April 14. Second foal. The dam, fourth in the Group 3 7f C L Weld Park Stakes at two years, won over 9f at three years and is a half-sister to the Irish Group 2 1m and US Grade 2 9f winner Century City. The second dam, Alywow (by Alysheba), a champion filly in Canada, won seven races including the Grade 3 8.5f Nijana Stakes and was second in the Grade 1 Rothmans International and the Grade 1 Flower Bowl Invitational. (Miss P F O'Kelly).
'A very attractive colt but he's backward and I haven't had him long. You'd be looking towards seven furlongs in August or September with him.'

581. ROCKFIELD LADY (IRE) ★★★★ ♠
b.f. Rock Of Gibraltar – Quiet Mouse (Quiet American)
March 30. Fourth foal. €270,000Y. Goffs Million. Brian Grassick. Sister to the quite useful 2007 Irish two year old 7f winner Houston Dynamo and half-sister to the Group 3 7f two year old C L Weld Park Stakes and three year old 6f listed winner and Group 1 7f Moyglare Stud Stakes second Ugo Fire (by Bluebird). The dam is an unraced half-sister to six winners including the fairly useful two year old 6f and 7f winner and smart broodmare Witch Of Fife. The second dam, Fife (by Lomond), a fairly useful 1m winner, is a half-sister to five winners including Piffle (dam of the Group 1 winners Frenchpark and Pearly Shells).
'This is the filly! She's absolutely gorgeous, she's just gone through a little stage of growing and has a lovely action and a very good attitude. You'd be looking at starting her off over six

furlongs in mid-summer and if you saw her in the string she stands out.'

582. UNNAMED ★★★
b.c. Soviet Star – Evictress (Sharp Victor)
May 5. Ninth foal. €65,000Y. Goffs Million. Brian Grassick. Half-brother to the Group 3 Brownstown Stakes winner Miss Sally (by Danetime), to the fairly useful Irish two year old 1m winner Majestic Eviction (by King's Theatre) and the smart jumper Quazar (by Inzar). The dam was placed three times from 6f (at two years) to 1m in Ireland and is a half-sister to seven minor winners. The second dam, Nurse Jo (by J O Tobin), ran twice unplaced in the USA and is a half-sister to the dual US Grade 1 winner Love Sign, the Irish and Italian Oaks winner Melodist and the US Grade 2 winner Fatih. (J Keeling).
'He's not over-big, but compact, we're happy with him and he'll be out mid-summer over six furlongs.'

583. UNNAMED ★★★
b.f. Montjeu – Gamra (Green Desert)
January 29. Second foal. 220,000foal. Tattersalls December. Brian Grassick. Half-sister to the two year old listed 5f winner and Group 3 Firth Of Clyde Stakes second Roxan (by Rock Of Gibraltar). The dam, a fair three year old 1m winner, is a full or half-sister to seven winners including the very smart Group 2 9.7f Prix Dollar winner Wiorno and the very smart Trusthouse Forte Mile, Gimcrack Stakes and Earl of Sefton Stakes winner Reprimand. The second dam, Just You Wait (by Nonoalco), is an unraced half-sister to the good broodmares Little Loch Broom and Kristana. (K Campbell).
'A lovely, big, backward filly, she's doing a lot of growing so I've only had her in light work. I like her a lot and she's a good, solid filly with a good temperament for a Montjeu. She's going to be quite a nice filly and although she's looking like one for the autumn I think she's a filly that could come to hand quite quickly – she's a quick learner and she could be my 'dark horse'.'

dam, a minor French middle-distance winner, is a half-sister to 5 other winners in France including the listed winner Barings (by Pistolet Bleu). The second dam, Sheba Dancer (by Fabulous Dancer), winner of the Group 3 Prix Vanteaux and second in the Group 1 Prix de Diane, is a half-sister to four winners. (Beadle, Booth, Davies & Jennings).

'She looks like being pretty early and the sire seems to have put plenty of speed into her even though the dam is by Bering. She's the earliest looking one we've got, but she's has a bit of a cough at the moment otherwise she'd be out in early May. She's doing everything nicely and is a good, sprinting-type filly.' TRAINER'S BARGAIN BUY

590. LASTROSEOFSUMMER ★★

ch.f. Haafhd – Broken Romance
(Ela-Mana-Mou)
February 25. Eighth foal. 50,000Y. Tattersalls October 1. Rae Guest. Half-sister to the smart 7f (at two years) to 2m winner and Group 2 placed Romantic Affair, to the useful 12f winner Gulf (both by Persian Bold), the Italian listed winner Little Italy (by Common Grounds), the quite useful 14f winner and listed-placed Zurbaran (by Alhaarth) and a winner over hurdles by Fairy King. The dam is an unraced half-sister to six winners including the Grade 1 9f Hollywood Derby winner Foscarini and the Group-placed Cobblers Cove and Guns Of Navarone. The second dam, Busted Flush (by Busted), won once at two years and is a half-sister to ten winners. (E P Duggan).

'She's bred to be a three year old really but she's going nicely and is a nice type. The sort we'd like to bring her out when the seven furlong races start. She's not a huge filly but she's well-made and the sort to do well towards the end of the year and better as a three year old.'

591. SERIOUS ATTITUDE (IRE) ★★★

b.f. Mtoto – Zameyla (Cape Cross)
March 23. First foal. 7,500Y. Tattersalls October 3. Five Star International Bloodstock. The dam, a quite useful 1m winner, is a half-sister to numerous winners including the smart 6f (at two

years) and listed 8.3f winner Army Of Angels, the useful two year old 6f winner and Group 2 Lowther Stakes second Seraphina and the fairly useful Irish 5f winner and listed-placed Alegranza. The second dam, Angelic Sounds (by The Noble Player), a minor two year old 5f winner, is a half-sister to six winners including the Group 1 Prix de la Foret winner Mount Abu. (Purple & Yellow Partnership and Mr Rae Guest).

'A nice filly, she's big and backward but we think a lot of her. She didn't look anything at the sales but in a few months she's changed and grown into a nice filly. One for later in the year.'

592. UNNAMED ★★★

ch.f. Rahy – Khazayin (Bahri)
February 11. Fourth foal. $47,000Y. Keeneland September. Rae Guest. Half-sister to the useful two year old 6f winner Jaish (by Seeking The Gold) and to the fair 11f winner Jawaaneb (by Kingmambo). The dam was placed over 10f and is a sister to the high-class Prix de l'Arc de Triomphe and Juddmonte International winner Sakhee and closely related to the useful 7f (at two years) and 10f winner Nasheed. The second dam, Thawakib (by Sadler's Wells), a useful dual 7f (at two years) and Group 2 12f Ribblesdale Stakes winner, is a half-sister to numerous winners including the top-class middle-distance colt Celestial Storm (winner of the Group 2 Princess of Wales's Stakes). (Mrs P Smith & Mr Rae Guest).

'A nice filly we bought in America, she's bred in the purple and was a bit small when we bought her but she's grown two inches since. We're very pleased with her, she's going the right way and she's stocky and well-made so being on the small side isn't going to be against her. She looks the type to be sharp but I haven't tried her yet. She'll be alright in the summer.'

593. UNNAMED ★★★★

b.f. Oasis Dream – Midnight Shift (Night Shift)
March 15. Sister to the unplaced 2007 two year old Midnight Oasis and half-sister to the Group 3 5f Ballyogan Stakes winner Miss Anabaa (by Anabaa), the smart 5f and 6f winner of six races (including the Portland Handicap) Out After

584. UNNAMED ★★★
b.f. Fasliyev. Grenouillere (by Alysheba),
April 8. Half-sister to the fair 2007 7f placed two
year old Prince Kalamoun (by Desert Prince)
and to six winners including the French listed
10f winner Ghost Dance (by Lure). The dam was
placed over 12f and is a half-sister to four
winners including the French Group 1 winners
Oczy Czarnie and Glaieul.
'She's fairly forward and would be ready to run
by the end of May. I like her and she has a good
temperament for a Fasliyev. Five or six furlongs
would suit her and she'll make a nice two year
old.'

585. UNNAMED ★★★★
gr.f. Verglas – La Tintoretta (Desert Prince)
March 9. First foal. €25,000Y. Goffs Sportsman's. Larry Stratton. The dam, an Irish 5f
winner, is a half-sister to the useful 2000 two
year old 6f winner Oreana. The second dam,
Lavinia Fontana (by Sharpo), a very smart
sprinter and winner of the Group 1 6f Haydock
Sprint Cup, the Group 2 6f Premio Umbria, the
Group 3 5f Prix du Petit-Couvert and the Group
3 7f Premio Chiusura, is a half-sister to three
winners. (Mrs S Grassick).
'A small, sharp filly, she could be running in May
and I like her. I trained the dam and if it wasn't
for training problems she'd have got some black
type. This filly will be a smart, sprinting type two
year old.'

586. UNNAMED ★★★★ ♠
ch.f. Pivotal – Lurina (Lure)
March 29. Fourth foal. €175,000Y. Goffs Million.
Not sold. Half-sister to the useful 2007 two year
old dual 1m winner and Group 3 1m Prix Thomas
Bryon second Centennial (by Dalakhani). The
dam, a smart 1m winner, was third in the Group
2 1m Prix de Sandringham and is a half-sister to
six winners including the dual Group 1 winner
Croco Rouge and the listed winner Alidiva
(herself dam of the Group 1 winners Sleepytime,
Ali Royal and Taipan). The second dam, Alligatrix
(by Alleged), a very useful two year old 7f winner,
was third in the Group 3 Hoover Fillies Mile and
is a half-sister to six winners.

'She's only just arrived and I thin
middle-distance filly next year. A ve
filly, she's done extremely well since th
has a good way of going. You'd like he
she's one for the second half of the sea

587. UNNAMED ★★★
b.f. Bertolini – Nirvana (Green Dancer)
March 15. Sixth foal. €75,000Y. Goffs N
John Flynn. Half-sister to four winners inc
the Italian Group 3 winner Il Cadetto (by Zi
the French Grade 1 hurdles winner Royal H
(by Highest Honor) and a minor winne
Germany by Hamas. The dam won at two ye
in Germany and is a half-sister to the Gro
winners Nasr Allah and Chato. The second da
Quick Blush (by Blushing Groom), won at fou
years in the USA and is a half-sister to si
winners.
'She's had a little setback so she hasn't arrived
yet but apparently she's a lovely filly and she
should be a two year old.'

RAE GUEST

588. FAT CHANCE ★★★
gr.f. Linamix – Hymenee (Chief's Crown)
February 10. Seventh foal. 32,000Y. Tattersalls
October 2. Dwayne Woods. Half-sister to the
French 10f and 11f winner and listed-placed
Harlem Dancer (by Dr Devious) and to a minor
winner in France by Robellino. The dam, a
minor French three year old winner, is a half-
sister to seven winners including the dam of
the Group 2 winner Housamix. The second
dam, Hippodamia (by Hail To Reason), won the
Group 1 Criterium des Pouliches. (Storm Again
Syndicate & Dwayne Woods).
'She's light framed and quite sharp, so despite
being by Linamix she ought to make the
racecourse from the middle of the season
onwards and she's going well.'

589. JEDABB ★★★
ch.f. Exceed And Excel – Sedna (Bering)
March 24. Fifth foal. 20,000Y. Tattersalls
October 2. Rae Guest. Half-sister to the fair 7f
and 8.2f winner Braddock (by Pivotal) and to a
four year old winner in Denmark by Bachir. The

Dark, the useful 5f and 6f winner of five races Move It (both Cadeaux Genereux), the modest 6f winner Mina (by Selkirk) and the moderate 5f winner Midnight Sky (by Desert Prince). The dam, a fair dual 6f winner at three years, is a half-sister to eight winners including the high-class Group 1 6f July Cup winner Owington. The second dam, Old Domesday Book (by High Top), a fairly useful three year old 10.4f winner, was third in the listed 10f Sir Charles Clore Memorial Stakes. (C J Mills).

'She came in late but she's done very well and she's very professional in that she's picked everything up very quickly. We've had a couple by Oasis Dream and this is probably the nicest one so far. The sire has done very well, so she should make up into a two year old, it's a fast family and we trained both the dam and Miss Anabaa. A very nice filly and she looks a typical sprinter.'

594. UNNAMED ★★★

b.c. Royal Applause – Millyant (Primo Dominie)
March 29. Eighth foal. Half-brother to the unraced 2007 two year old Fatal Attraction (by Oasis Dream), the useful 6f winner and listed 6f placed Millybaa (by Anabaa), the fairly useful two year old 5f winner Juantorena (by Miswaki) and the quite useful 5f winner of four races Millinsky (by Stravinsky). The dam, winner of the Group 2 5f Prix du Gros-Chene, is a half-sister to the Group 2 5f Flying Childers winner and very useful sire Prince Sabo and to the Irish listed winner Bold Jessie (herself dam of the Gimcrack Stakes winner Abou Zouz). The second dam, Jubilee Song (by Song), won once at three years and is a sister to the dual winner and Nell Gwyn Stakes second Shark Song and to the winner of 10 races and listed-placed Band On The Run. (C J Mills).

'He was quite small but he's done well and grown. He's picked everything up quickly so hopefully he'll be a two year old because the family is fast and the sire gets two year old's. He's bulked up now and is looking more like a sprinter.'

595. UNNAMED ★★★

b.f. Toccet – Vingt Et Une (Sadler's Wells)

April 30. Seventh foal. $95,000Y. Keeneland September. Rae Guest. Half-sister to four winners including the very useful 12f winner Year Two Thousand (by Darshaan) and the French three year old winner of three races Coconut Show (by Linamix). The dam, a minor French three year old winner, is a sister to the very useful Group 1 10.5f Prix Lupin and US Grade 2 1m winner Johann Quatz and to the smart French 10.5f to 13.5f listed winner Walter Willy and a half-sister to the top-class Group 1 Prix du Jockey Club and Group 1 Prix Lupin winner Hernando (by Niniski) and the dam of the 2007 two year old Group 2 Beresford Stakes winner Curtain Call. The second dam, Whakilyric (by Miswaki), won the Group 3 7f Prix du Calvados and was third in the Prix de la Salamandre and in the Prix de la Foret. (Mrs P Smith & Mr Rae Guest). The sire was a dual Grade 1 winner at two years in the USA.

'The sire was precocious and tough and the dam is very well-bred. She's a really nice filly, she won't be early and wasn't broken in until January but you'd be hoping that later in the season she could be special.'

WILLIAM HAGGAS

597. ADORING (IRE) ★★★★

b.f. One Cool Cat – Refined (Statoblest)
April 14. Sixth foal. 70,000Y. Tattersalls October 1. John Warren. Half-sister to the Group 2 6f Mill Reef Stakes winner and Group 1 placed Galeota, to the fairly useful dual 5f winner Vermilliann (both by Mujadil), the 11f and listed 13f winner Loulwa (by Montjeu), the fairly useful two year old 5f Weatherbys Supersprint winner Lady Livius (by Titus Livius) and the fair 2008 7f winner Savannah Poppy (by Statue Of Liberty). The dam, a fairly useful dual 5f winner, is a half-sister to six winners including the very smart Group 3 7f Criterion Stakes winner Pipe Major. The second dam, Annsfield Lady (by Red Sunset), a winner of three races in Ireland between 9f and 10f, is a half-sister to four winners including the high-class Prix Dollar winner and Champion Stakes second Insatiable. (Highclere Thoroughbred Racing (Gimcrack)).

'A tall filly, she's done well and moves well. The

seven furlong Tattersalls Sales race is her aim and she's got a bit of class about her. One for the mid-summer, she's had a bit of a break and has done well for it. A tall filly and a good mover. I'll hopefully be starting her off at six furlongs.'

598. A LITTLE TRICKY ★★
b.f. Tobougg – Composition (Wolfhound)
May 7. 9,500Y. Doncaster Festival. Not sold. Half-sister to the modest 2007 6f to 1m placed two year old Hellfire Bay (by Diktat), to the quite useful 7f to 10f winner of four races Ephesus (by Efisio), the fair three year old 1m winner Queen Jean (by Pivotal) and the modest 12f winner Atriffic Story (by Atraf). The dam, a quite useful two year old 6f winner, is a half-sister to three winners here and abroad. The second dam, Tricky Note (by Song), a fairly useful winner of three races including the listed National Stakes at Sandown, is a sister to the Group 3 Duke Of York Stakes winner Jester. (Tricky Bloke Partnership).
'Two of the partners in this filly were also partners in my first ever winner, Tricky Note, who happens to be the second dam. She's quite sweet and hopefully she'll pick up a race or two this year.'

599. AWFEYAA ★★★
ch.f. Haafhd – Aspen Leaves (Woodman)
January 26. Fifth foal. Half-sister to the fair 2007 6f and 7f placed maiden Deira Dubai (by Green Desert) and to the Irish 10f winner (on her only start) Agenda (by Sadler's Wells). The dam, a minor Irish 7f winner, is a sister to the champion American two year old colt Timber Country and a half-sister to the very smart Group 2 13.5f Prix de Pomone winner Colorado Dancer (herself the dam of Dubai Millennium), the Grade 1 Gamely Handicap winner Northern Aspen, the Group 1 July Cup winner Hamas, the Group 1 Grand Prix de Paris winner Fort Wood and the Prix d'Astarte winner Elle Seule (herself dam of the Group 1 winners Elnadim and Mehthaaf). The second dam, Fall Aspen (by Pretense). clearly one of the finest broodmares of recent times. won eight races notably the Grade 1 7f Matron Stakes. (Hamdan Al Maktoum).
'She's been quite backward and is out at the stud at the moment, but she's moves nicely and she's very straightforward. One for the mid-summer onwards.'

600. CAPE QUARTER ★★★★
b.c. Elusive Quality – June Moon (Sadler's Wells)
January 18. Eleventh reported foal. Closely related to the smart 6f, 7f (both at two years) and Group 2 1m German and Italian 2,000 Guineas winner Dupont, to the Japanese 7f and 1m stakes winner Zachariah, the German 2,000 Guineas winner Pacino (all by Zafonic) and the French three year old 1m winner Moon West (by Gone West) and half-brother to the useful 1m and UAE 9f winner Moon Dazzle (by Kingmambo), the two year old 7f all-weather winner Lunar Express (by Giant's Causeway), the all-weather 1m and UAE 10f winner Dawn Piper (by Desert Prince) and the 7f (at two years) to 12f winner Winsome George (by Marju) – the last 3 all quite useful. The dam is an unraced half-sister to five winners including the French 1,000 Guineas second Firth Of Lorne. The second dam, Kerrera (by Diesis), a smart winner of the Group 3 Cherry Hinton Stakes and second in the 1,000 Guineas, is a half-sister to the high-class two year old Rock City. (B Kantor).
'He's a half-brother to Dupont and it's a family I love. He's just had a small problem but he's a lovely, big horse and he could be anything. He'll be a July/August two year old and he's a nice horse that could go the 'Brunel' route and go for a race for unraced horses at Ascot, something like that.'

601. CHORAL SERVICE ★★
b.c. Pivotal – Choir Mistress (Chief Singer)
May 10. Half-brother to the Group 1 10f Curragh Pretty Polly Stakes and dual Group 3 winner Chorist (by Pivotal), to the very useful two year old 7f winner and Group 3 7f Prestige Stakes second Choirgirl (by Unfuwain), the fairly useful 1m winner Choir Leader (by Sadler's Wells), the fair 7f (at two years) and 14.8f all-weather winner Operatic (by Goofalik) and a winner in Turkey by Slip Anchor. The dam is an unraced half-sister to six winners including the

smart Group 2 11.9f Great Voltigeur Stakes winner Sacrament. The second dam, Blessed Event (by Kings Lake), a very useful winner of the listed 10f Ballymacoll Stud Stakes at three years, was second in the Yorkshire Oaks and fourth in the Champion Stakes. (Cheveley Park Stud).
'A nice horse but he's backward and one for much later in the year.'

602. COUNTENANCE ★★

ch.c. Medicean – Glamorous (Sanglamore)
January 27. Fifth foal. 90,000Y. Tattersalls October 2. John Warren. Half-brother to a winner in Spain by Groom Dancer. The dam is an unraced half-sister to two winners including the Group 3 Boland Stakes winner Polar Way. The second dam, Fetish (by Dancing Brave), won twice at three years and is a half-sister to eight winners including the Group 2 Lowther Stakes winner Kingscote. (Highclere Thoroughbred Racing (Ormonde)).
'He needs a bit of time, he was a big horse and has grown again, so he's just a juvenile at the moment and being a bit naughty but that's only because he's full of beans and doing well. He's cantering nicely and he's likely to be a seven furlong/ mile two year old at the back-end of the season.'

603. DAMANIYAT GIRL (USA) ★★

ch.f. Elusive Quality – Dabaweyaa (Shareef Dancer)
April 6. Closely related to the very useful two year old 6f winner and UAE Group 2 1m second Western Diplomat, the fairly useful 1m winner Blue Snake (both by Gone West) and half-sister to numerous winners including the fairly useful 5.7f (at two years) and 7f winner Ascot Cyclone, the quite useful two year old 7f winner Dubai Magic (both by Rahy), the two year old 6f winner and Group 1 7f Prix de la Salamandre second Bin Nashwan (by Nashwan), the US Grade 2 winner Magellan (by Hansel), the useful 7.6f to 1m winner Faithful Warrior and the quite useful two year old 6f winner Oman Gulf (both by Diesis). The dam, a smart winner of the 1m Atalanta Stakes and placed in the 1,000 Guineas, is a half-sister to the the smart Hoover

Fillies Mile and Nassau Stakes winner Acclimatise. The second dam, Habituee (by Habitat), won over 1m in France. (Mohammed Obaida).
'She's had terrible ringworm so I don't know much about her except that she's got a nice pedigree. I've hardly had her going at all and she'll only run this year if she's forward enough.'

604. DANEHILL DESTINY ★★★★★

b.f. Danehill Dancer – Comeraincomeshine (Night Shift)
February 25. First foal. 120,000Y. Tattersalls October 1. Cheveley Park Stud. The dam, a modest 5.5f winner, is a half-sister to five winners including the high-class Group 1 1m Queen Elizabeth II Stakes winner Where Or When and the smart 10f and 12f winner and Group 1 St Leger fourth All The Way. The second dam, Future Past (by Super Concorde), a winner of four races at up to 9f in the USA, is a half-sister to eight winners. (Cheveley Park Stud).
'This filly is sharp, she goes nicely and she might run at the Craven meeting. I loved her as a yearling and she's done well since then. There's a lot of the damsire Night Shift in her.' This filly duly won nicely on her debut at the Craven meeting!

605. DEMAND ★★★

b.f. Red Ransom – Coy (Danehill)
February 12. First foal. The dam won over 6f (at two years) and the listed 1m Valiant Stakes and is a sister to the fairly useful triple 7f winner Presumptive. The second dam, Demure (by Machiavellian), is an unraced half-sister to the very smart colt Diffident, winner of the Group 3 6f Diadem Stakes, the Group 3 6f Prix de Ris-Orangis and the listed 7f European Free Handicap. (Cheveley Park Stud).
'A small filly, she's a first foal and looks it. She'll be a two year old, her mother did OK as a two year old and she's one of those that will make it this year or not at all.'

606. DIDDUMS ★★★

b.c. Royal Applause – Sahara Shade (Shadeed)
April 15. Third foal. 8,000Y. Tattersalls October 3. W Haggas. Half-brother to the moderate

2007 6f and 7f placed Prunes (by Cadeaux Genereux) and to the fair 1m winner Getrah (by Barathea). The dam, a fair two year old 5f and 6f winner, is a half-sister to five winners including the Group 3 5f Queen Mary Stakes winner Nadwah. The second dam, Tadwin (by Never So Bold), was a very useful sprint winner of three races including the listed Hopeful Stakes and is a half-sister to four winners including the very smart sprinter Reesh and the dam of the smart sprinter Averti. (B Haggas).

'I think he's done OK this horse, he was a cheap yearling and recently he had a twisted testicle that had to be removed, but he'll make a sprinter around June time.'

607. DREAM DATE (IRE) ★★★★

b.f. Oasis Dream – Femme Fatale (Fairy King)
February 15. Fourth foal. 90,000Y. Tattersalls October 1. W Haggas. Half-sister to the fair two year old 7f winner Sadie Thompson (by King's Best). The dam, a useful dual 6f winner of two races (including a listed event at two years), was second in the Group 2 Sun Chariot Stakes and is a half-sister to the 6f (at two years) and smart dual listed 10f winner Foodbroker Fancy. The second dam, Red Rita (by Kefaah), a fairly useful four year old 6f winner, was second in the Group 3 6f Cherry Hinton Stakes and the Group 3 6f Princess Margaret Stakes at two years and is a half-sister to three minor winners. (F C T Wilson).

'A very nice filly, she's strong, sharp and keen to please. She'll be running in May and if she's good enough she'll run at Ascot. My fillies are much sharper then the colts this year and when I put this filly upsides for the first time she was the one that caught my eye.'

608. GASSAL ★★★★

b.f. Oasis Dream – Hasten (Lear Fan)
January 24. Third foal. Half-sister to the fair 2007 6f placed two year old Hasty Lady (by Dubai Destination). The dam was placed twice in the USA and is a half-sister to three winners including the two year old Group 3 Autumn Stakes winner and Group 1 Racing Post Trophy second Fantastic View. The second dam,

Promptly (by Lead On Time), a quite useful 6f winner here, subsequently won a minor stakes event over 1m in the USA and is a half-sister to five winners. (Hamdan Al Maktoum).

'She's nice, quite sharp and one of those that's been around and is barely noticeable because she's so straightforward. She'll be racing in May and she's got a chance of being a Royal Ascot filly if she's good enough.'

609. JARGELLE ★★★

b.f. Kheleyf – Winter Tern (Arctic Tern)
February 23. Eighth foal. 28,000Y. Tattersalls October 1. Gill Richardson. Closely related to the German three year old winner Serevi (by Cape Cross) and half-sister to the Irish 7f listed winner and Group 3 placed Orange Grouse (by Taufan) and the two year old 5f and 6f seller winner Little Blue (by Bluebird) and the two year old 7f seller winner Winter Dolphin (by Dolphin Street). The dam is an unraced half-sister to eight winners including the US stakes winner Boom And Bust. The second dam, Belle Gallante (by Gallant Man), won twice in the USA and is a half-sister to the champion US two year old Silent Screen. (B Smith, A Duke, J Netherthorpe, G Goddard).

'A small filly but she's quite sharp and she's not a bad filly without being a star. She'll be out by the end of April.'

610. LOVELY THOUGHT ★★★

b.f. Dubai Destination – Fairy Flight (Fairy King)
March 20. Seventh foal. 44,000Y. Tattersalls October 3. Jill Lamb. Half-sister to the 6f (at two years), Group 2 7f Challenge Stakes and Group 3 7f Jersey Stakes winner Just James (by Spectrum). The dam, a two year old 6f winner in Ireland, was listed-placed and is a sister to one winner and a half-sister to the French listed 10.5f winner Titled Ascent and the Irish listed winning sprinter Northern Tide. The second dam, Rising Tide (by Red Alert), was a useful two year old 5f winner and a half-sister to five winners including the Group 1 Phoenix Stakes winner King Persian.

'She came in late, she looks fine, is nice tempered and uncomplicated.'

611. MASTOORA ★★★★
b.f. Acclamation – Sacred Love (Barathea)
March 16. Second foal. 110,000Y. Tattersalls
October 2. Shadwell Estate Co. Half-sister to
Bona Fifelis (by Namid), unplaced in one start
at two years in 2007. The dam, placed fourth
once over 1m, is a half-sister to five winners. The
second dam, Abstraction (by Rainbow Quest), is
an unraced sister to two listed winners and a
half-sister to seven winners including the US
triple Grade 1 winner Wandesta. (Hamdan Al
Maktoum).
*'I like her a lot. She was one of my favourite
yearlings, she's grown a bit which won't do her
any harm but it might stop me from training her
early. She has a bit of quality.'*

612. MOOTRIBA ★★★
ch.f. Nayef – Tarbiyah (Singspiel)
March 19. Second foal. Half-sister to Mukhber
(by Anabaa), a quite useful 1m winner on his
only start at two years in 2007. The dam, fairly
useful 1m winner on her only start, is a half-
sister to the One Thousand Guineas and the
Group 2 7f Rockfel Stakes winner Lahan. The
second dam, Amanah (by Mr Prospector), a
useful 1m winner, is a sister to fair 1m winner
Alrayyih and a half-sister to the quite useful two
year old 6f winner Habub (by Danzig). (Hamdan
Al Maktoum).
*'She's a Nayef with a bit of a temperament but
she moves really well. I hope she'll make a two
year old, probably over seven furlongs later in
the year.'*

613. MUTAMAASHI ★★★
b.c. Sakhee – Almahab (Danzig)
February 11. The dam is an unraced half-sister
to the smart 6f (including at two years) and
listed 7f winner Munaddam. The second dam,
Etizaaz (by Diesis), a listed 1m winner and
second in the Group 1 12f Prix Vermeille, is a
half-sister to the listed 6f Sirenia Stakes winner
Santolina and the US Grade 3 7f Lafayette Stakes
winner Trafalgar. (Hamdan Al Maktoum).
*'A strong, colt, he goes very well and he's a nice
horse.'*

614. MUTAWARATH (IRE) ★★★
b.c. Marju – Castlerahan (Thatching)
March 9. 200,000foal. Tattersalls December.
Shadwell Estate Co. Brother to the Group 2 1m
Mehl-Mulhens Rennen and Group 3 7f Prix de
la Porte Maillot winner Brunel. The dam is an
unraced half-sister to three winners. The
second dam, Preening (by Persian Bold), won at
three years and is a half-sister to the triple
Group 3 winner Hadeer. (Hamdan Al Maktoum).
*'A lovely horse and a full-brother to Brunel. If he's
as good as that horse I'll be happy, but he's
backward and it'll be September before we see
him. Brunel was much more forward and so he
was ready in mid-summer. A nice horse.'*

615. NEMOROSA ★★★
b.f. Pivotal – Anthos (Big Shuffle)
March 5. First foal. The dam was a quite useful
two year old 6f winner. The second dam,
Anemone (by Motley), won two races in
Germany from 2-five years. (Cheveley Park Stud).
*'Yes, she's done well and she's a big, strong, rangy
filly. She'll be one for August and will make a nice
three year old as well. Bred the way she's is she'll
want soft ground.'*

616. PENITENT ★★★
b.c. Kyllachy – Pious (Bishop Of Cashel)
February 3. Third foal. Closely related to the
modest 2007 6f placed two year old Solemn
and to the fairly useful two year old 7f winner
Blithe (both by Pivotal). The dam, a fair dual 6f
winner (including at two years), is a half-sister
to three winners including the rare 6f, 8.5f and
hurdles winner Mister RM. The second dam, La
Cabrilla (by Carwhite), a fairly useful two year
old 5f and 6f winner, was third in the Group 3
Princess Margaret Stakes and is a half-sister to
six winners including the Group 1 Nunthorpe
Stakes winner Ya Malak. (Cheveley Park Stud).
*'I like him, he's a half-brother to Blithe who I had
and she was useful but went wrong. Penitent is a
really nice, straightforward, backward horse. He
might be ready by mid-season and I think he'll
be alright.'*

617. PROHIBITION (IRE) ★★★
b.c. Danehill Dancer – Crumpetsfortea (Henbit)
May 3. Sixth foal. 215,000Y. Tattersalls October
2. Charlie Gordon-Watson. Closely related to
the useful two year old 7f winner James Joyce
(by Danehill) and half-brother to the French
Group 3 7f Prix Miesque winner Contemporary
(by Alzao), the French dual 1m winner Yippee
(by Orpen) and the French 1m to 9.5f winner
Heinstein (by Night Shift). The dam is an
unraced half-sister to four winners. The second
dam, Butter Knife (by Sure Blade), is an unraced
half-sister to ten winners including the US
Grade 1 winner Danish. (Mrs Nicola Mahoney).
'He's quite a nice horse, he moves well and he's
uncomplicated so I'm quite hopeful for him. He
should be out around August time.'

618. PURE PERFECTION (IRE) ★★★★
b.f. Hawk Wing – Politesse (Barathea)
February 26. Second foal. Half-sister to the
fairly useful 6f and 7f winner of five races King's
Apostle (by King's Best). The dam is an unraced
half-sister to one winner out of the Group 1 6f
Cheveley Park Stakes and Group 3 6f Princess
Margaret Stakes winner Embassy (by Cadeaux
Genereux), herself a half-sister to four winners
including the Group 2 Pretty Polly Stakes winner
Tarfshi. (B Kantor).
'Everyone likes her, she's no problem at all and is
very straightforward. I would think she'll start off
at six furlongs and move up to seven. Her half-
brother King's Apostle did very well and he was
quite fast.'

619. QUASH ★★
b.g. Marju – Blue Crush (Entrepreneur)
February 22. First foal. 32,000Y. Doncaster St
Leger. W Haggas. The dam, a dual 5f winner at
two years in Ireland, was listed-placed and is a
half-sister to three winners. The second dam,
Prosaic Star (by Common Grounds), won once
over 1m at two years in Ireland and is a half-
sister to four winners. (Gibson, Goddard, Hamer
& Hawkes).
'He's had a problem and we've had to geld him
because he wasn't moving as well as he ought
to have done. He's quite small and he was

bought to be a sharp two year old so it's
disappointing that we've had to cut him now and
we're playing catch up a bit.'

620. RAINBOW SEEKER ★★★★
b.g. Dubai Destination – Zephirine Drouhin
(Desert Style)
February 15. First foal. 50,000Y. Tattersalls
October 1. Not sold. The dam is an unraced
half-sister to five winners including the dam of
Rock Of Gibraltar. The second dam, Push A
Button (by Bold Lad, Ire), won once at two years
and is a half-sister to six winners including the
French 2,000 Guineas winner and top-class
sire Riverman. (Mr Ricky Wong & Sentinel
Bloodstock).
'He's a strong, mature horse and the only slight
concern I have is that the sire doesn't tend to get
them early and yet he looks that way! I'll be
going for this horse and he'll start to work in
mid-April with a view to running him in May to
see if I can get him to Ascot.'

621. RAWAADAH ★★★
ch.f. Monsieur Bond – Amazed (Clantime)
January 29. Fourth foal. €240,000Y. Goffs
Million. Shadwell Estate Co. Half-brother to the
quite useful 2007 two year old 5f winner
Nawaaff (by Compton Place) and to the useful
two year old 5f and 6f and three year old listed
5f winner Dazed And Amazed (by Averti). The
dam, a modest 5f placed three year old, is a
sister to the Group 3 Prix du Petit Couvert
winner Bishops Court and a half-sister to five
winners including the listed winning sprinter
Astonished. The second dam, Indigo (by Primo
Dominie), a quite useful two year old 5f winner,
is a half-sister to five winners. (Hamdan Al
Maktoum).
'She's a lovely, scopey filly and she's having a
break at the moment but she'll be aimed at the
Goffs Million Fillies race. The only concern I have
is that it's a family where the colts do well and
the fillies don't, but we'll try and buck the trend.'

622. REJECT ★★★
b.c. Green Desert – Wardat Allayl (Mtoto)
March 8. Fourth foal. 78,000Y. Tattersalls

October 1. W Haggas. Brother to the quite useful 2007 two year old dual 6f winner Ramatni and to the fair 8.5f winner Shot Gun. The dam, a fairly useful two year old 7f winner, is a half-sister to five winners including the high-class two year old Group 2 6f Lowther Stakes winner Bint Allayl and the Group 3 7f Jersey Stakes winner Kheleyf (both by Green Desert). The second dam, Society Lady (by Mr Prospector), a fair 6f and 7f placed two year old, is a full or half-sister to nine winners. (J B Haggas).
'He's a nice horse but backward and he's much more of a three year old type. We'll try and get him onto the track in late summer to see what he's made of but he's a nice horse.'

623. RESPITE ★★★★
b.f. Pivotal – Truce (Nashwan)
May 11. Fourth foal. The dam is an unraced half-sister to four winners including the very smart Group 3 12f Prix la Force winner and French Derby second Nowhere To Exit and the useful listed 1m winner Embraced. The second dam, Tromond (by Lomond), a fairly useful 9f winner, was second in the listed 10f Ballymacoll Stud Stakes at Newbury and is a half-sister to four winners. (Cheveley Park Stud).
'A filly that's done very well. She was quite small when she came in but she's thriving at the moment and she also had a bit of a temperament which seems to be mellowing. I think she'll start off in July, there's something about her, and I like her more and more. I think she'll do well.'

624. RIMTHAH (IRE) ★★★★
b.f. Redback – Midnight Special (Danetime)
January 5. First foal. 52,000Y. Doncaster St Leger. Shadwell Estate Co. The dam, a fair dual 5f winner (including at two years), is a half-sister to one winner. The second dam, Daffodil Dale (by Cyrano de Bergerac), won over 5f at two years and is a half-sister to four winners. (Hamdan Al Maktoum).
'She can go a bit but we've backed off her for now, she's quite coarse looking but goes alright and she's got speed.'

625. RISAALA ★★★
b.f. Alhaarth – Perfect Plum (Darshaan)
February 23. Half-sister to the quite useful dual 12f winner Noble Plum (by King's Best). The dam won the Group 2 1m Prix Saint-Roman and the Group 3 1m Prix des Reservoirs (both at two years) and is a half-sister to two winners. The second dam, Damascene (by Scenic), is an unraced half-sister to the top-class sprinter and broodmare Marwell. (Hamdan Al Maktoum).
'She's a pretty filly, we've had a few problems with her steering but that's coming round now, she's moves well and I hope she'll be a nice filly – she looks it.'

626. SIR ISAAC ★★★
b.c. Key Of Luck – Rainbow Queen
(Rainbow Quest)
January 27. The dam, a fairly useful two year old 7f winner, is a half-sister to three winners. The second dam, Dazzle (by Gone West), a smart winner of the Group 3 6f Cherry Hinton Stakes and placed in both the Cheveley Park Stakes and the 1,000 Guineas, is a half-sister to the listed winners Fantasize and Hypnotize. (Mr & Mrs R Scott).
'I like him, he's a small horse with a nice temperament and he's straightforward.'

627. SOUTH EASTER (IRE) ★★★★
ch.c. Galileo – Dance Treat (Nureyev)
May 14. Seventh foal. 210,000Y. Tattersalls October 1. Anthony Stroud. Brother to the minor Italian four year old winner Jupiters Moon and half-brother to the 1m winner First Buddy (by Rock Of Gibraltar), the 7f winner River Treat (by Irish River), the 10f winner Jubilee Treat (by Seeking the Gold) – all three quite useful, and a minor winner in the USA by Woodman. The dam won the Group 3 10f La Coupe and the Group 3 10.5f Prix de Flore and is a half-sister to four winners. The second dam, Office Wife (by Secretariat), a stakes winner and Grade 3 placed in the USA, is a half-sister to the Derby winner Golden Fleece. (B Kantor).
'It's quite a backward family, they don't come good until they're 3 or 4, but that's the only thing

wrong with him. He was a beautiful yearling and he's got something about him. One for the back-end of the season and the plan is to go for the Tattersalls Million.'

628. TAGSEED (IRE) ★★★

b.c. Elusive City – Allegorica (Alzao)

February 8. Fourth foal. 100,000Y. Tattersalls October 1. Shadwell Estate Co. Half-brother to the fairly useful Irish dual 7f winner Miss Gorica (by Mull Of Kintyre) and to the fair 5f (at two years) to 1m winner Celtic Spa (by Celtic Swing). The dam won four races from 5f to 7f and from two to five years and is a half-sister to one winner. The second dam, Anne de Beaujeu (by Ahonoora), a listed-placed winner of five races in Ireland from 5f (at two years) to 7f, is a half-sister to five winners including the dual Group 3 winner Ahohoney. (Hamdan Al Maktoum).

'He had a problem with a testicle and he has to have it removed, but I like him. He's out of an Alzao mare and he's all Alzao. They're all tipping these Elusive City's like mad and this could be a really nice horse.'

629. THE MAGIC OF RIO ★★★

b.f. Captain Rio – Good Health (Magic Ring)

March 14. First foal. 18,000Y. Doncaster St Leger. W Haggas. The dam, a fair two year old 5f winner, is out of the three year old 5f winner Fiddling (by Music Boy), herself a half-sister to the smart sprinter Clantime. (Scotney, Asplin, Symonds Partnership).

'She's very sharp, her dam won twice as a two year old and this is a very fast family. For 18 Grand I think she was well-bought.' TRAINER'S BARGAIN BUY

630. WINGED HARRIET (IRE) ★★★★

b.br.f. Hawk Wing – Hawala (Warning)

February 27. Fifth foal. 115,000Y. Tattersalls October 1. W Haggas. Half-sister to the listed 6f (at two years) and listed 7f winner and Group 3 placed Misu Bond (by Danehill Dancer), to the dual sprint listed winner and Group 3 placed Slip Dance (by Celtic Swing), the fairly useful two year old 7f and 1m winner Numen (by Fath) and the minor French three year old winner Hawazi

(by Ashkalani). The dam, a useful 8.3f winner, is a half-sister to the French Group 3 winner Afaf. The second dam, the minor French three year old winner Halawa (by Dancing Brave), is a half-sister to five winners. (Mr F C T Wilson).

'She's lovely, a nice mover and very uncomplicated. I'm crossing my fingers that she'll be a good one. It's noticeable that she has a lot of the damsire, Warning, about her.'

631. UNNAMED ★★

b.f. Efisio – Council Rock (General Assembly)

May 8. Half-sister to the quite useful 2007 two year old 5f winner Rocking (by Oasis Dream), to the very smart Group 2 5f Flying Childers Stakes and Weatherbys Super Sprint winner Superstar Leo, the quite useful 5f and 6f winner Chiquita (both by College Chapel), the fairly useful 6f to 8.5f winner Royal Artist (by Royal Academy), the quite useful two year old 5f winner Horoscope (by Eagle Eyed), the fair 7f (at two years) to 8.3f winner Starship (by Galileo), the modest dual 1m winner Phi Phi (by Fasliyev) and minor winners abroad by Keen, Anshan and Royal Academy. The dam, a fair 9f and 10f placed three year old, is a half-sister to six winners including the Group 3 Prestige Stakes winner Glatisant and the listed Virginia Stakes winner Gai Bulga. The second dam, Dancing Rocks (by Green Dancer), was a very smart filly and winner of the Group 2 10f Nassau Stakes. (Mr A Hirschfeld & Partners).

'The dam's getting on a bit and this filly is quite small but she does move well, so I hope there's still a chance there. She had a very small Rock Of Gibraltar filly who never had any movement at all and this filly is small but she does move well, so hopefully she'll be alright.'

RICHARD HANNON

632. ACQUIESCED (IRE) ★★

b.f. Refuse To Bend – North East Bay (Prospect Bay)

January 23. Second foal. €150,000Y. Deauville August. Peter Doyle. Half-sister to the quite useful 2007 two year old 1m winner Strategic Mission (by Red Ransom). The dam was unplaced on her only start and is a half-sister to

five winners including the listed winner Hold To Ransom. The second dam, Wassifa (by Sure Blade), a fairly useful 11f winner here, subsequently won 3 minor races in the USA and was stakes-placed. (Mrs Julie Wood).
'She just ticking over and cantering at the moment. I haven't done anything with her yet, so apart from the fact that she cost quite a lot of money I can't tell you anything about her.'

633. ALWAYS THERE ★★★
b.f. Bachelor Duke – Ansariya (Shahrastani)
March 3. Tenth foal. €185,000Y. Deauville August. Peter Doyle. Half-sister to the quite useful dual 6f all-weather and subsequent US stakes winner Cummiskey (by Orpen), to the French 1m winner and listed-placed Answering (by King's Theatre) and the fair 6f and 7f winner Rubenstar (by Soviet Star). The dam, a winner over 1m in Ireland at two years, subsequently won in Switzerland and is a half-sister to eight winners including the high-class Prix Ganay and Prix d'Harcourt winner Astarabad. The second dam, Anaza (by Darshaan), only ran at two years when she was a useful listed 8.5f winner in France. (Mrs Julie Wood).
'A nice, strong filly, she won't be early but she'll probably start off at six furlongs in mid-season and she gets up the hill nicely.'

634. ANACAONA (IRE) ★★★
ch.f. Distant Music – Tarrara (Lammtarra)
January 24. Second living foal. 7,000Y. Tattersalls October 3. Peter Doyle. The dam is an unraced half-sister to five winners including the smart Group 2 10.5f Dante Stakes winner Torjoun and the very useful Group 2 10f Pretty Polly Stakes winner Takarouna. The second dam, Tarsila (by High Top), a winner over 1m and 9f, is a sister to Top Ville. (J A Lazzari).
'A sharp, early two year old and at the price she cost she was a bargain.' TRAINER'S BARGAIN BUY

635. APPRAISAL ★★★ ♠
ch.c. Mark Of Esteem – Anytime Baby (Bairn)
May 6. Seventh foal. 52,000Y. Tattersalls October 2. Will Edmeades. Half-brother to the

fair 2007 5f and 6f placed two year old Kalligal (by Kyllachy), to the fairly useful two year old 5.5f winner and listed placed Online Investor (by Puissance), the modest two year old dual 5f winner Acorn Catcher (by Emarati) and a minor winner abroad by Polar Falcon. The dam, a modest three year old 5f winner, is a half-sister to two winners. The second dam, Cindy's Gold (by Sonnen Gold), won once at three years and is a half-sister to seven winners including the listed winner Two Clubs (herself dam of the Group 1 Haydock Sprint Cup winner Red Clubs). (Waney Racing Group Inc).
'A lovely, good-moving horse but you wouldn't see him out until the six or seven furlong races. A fine, big, good-moving horse, his owner also owned Redback.'

636. ARUSHORE (IRE) ★★★★
b.c. Kyllachy – Cutting Reef (Kris)
February 7. Seventh foal. 66,000Y. Doncaster St Leger. A Smith. Half-brother to the quite useful 10.5f winner and listed-placed Bedara (by Barathea), to the German three year old 10f winner Sampa Coeur (by Caerleon) and a two year old winner in Japan by Polish Precedent. The dam, a staying winner of two races in France including a listed event at Maisons-Laffitte, is a half-sister to seven winners including the Irish listed winner Jazz Ballet. The second dam, Quiet Harbour (by Mill Reef), is an unplaced half-sister to ten winners including Quiet Fling (Coronation Cup), Peacetime (Guardian Classic Trial), Armistice Day (Prix Exbury). (A J Ilsley).
'This colt goes very well and he has a good pedigree too. He's a nice, strong, well-made colt and he'll be fairly early.'

637. AURORIAN (IRE) ★★
b.c. Fantastic Light – Aurelia (Rainbow Quest)
February 12. First foal. 27,000Y. Tattersalls October 3. Peter Doyle. The dam, a fair two year old 10f winner, is a half-sister to eight winners. The second dam, Fern (by Shirley Heights), a fairly useful 12f winner and third in the listed 10f Lupe Stakes, is a half-sister to six winners including the Group 1 Fillies Mile

winner and Oaks second Shamshir. (Mr M J Mitchell).

'A lovely, big colt, he'll make a two year old alright but it won't be until later in the year.'

638. BAILEYS CACAO (IRE) ★★★★
b.f. Invincible Spirit – Baileys Cream (Mister Baileys)
March 11. Fourth foal. €160,000Y. Goffs Million. Peter Doyle. Half-sister to the quite useful 2007 6f to 1m placed two year old Bailey (by Captain Rio) and to the minor Italian three year old winner Rich Of Promises (by Imperial Ballet). The dam, a fair two year old 7f winner, is a half-sister to five winners including the listed Chesham Stakes winner Fair Cop. The second dam, Exclusive Life (by Exclusive Native), won once in the USA and is a half-sister to eight winners including the US Grade 2 winner Special Warmth. (W Durkan).
'She has a bit of an issue with the stalls at the moment, so that'll decide how soon she hits the track but she goes well, she cost a lot of money but hopefully she'll be a very good filly and she might even make a Queen Mary filly – if she's good enough.'

639. BALLYALLA ★★★★
b.f. Mind Games – Molly Brown (Rudimentary)
April 2. Fifth foal. 65,000Y. Tattersalls October 2. Peter Doyle. Half-sister to the smart two year old dual 6f winner and Group 2 Mill Reef Stakes second Doctor Brown (by Dr Fong), to the quite useful two year old 5f and 6f winner Bright Moll (by Mind Games) and the modest 7f winner La Fanciulla (by Robellino). The dam, a fairly useful 5f (at two years) and 6f winner, is a half-sister to four winners including the listed 1m Premio Nearco winner Stato King. The second dam, Sinking (by Midyan), is an unraced half-sister to three winners. (D J Barry).
'A gorgeous filly, she could be a real nice one. She's big and she moves really well. I trained the dam and this filly won't be early but she's one to look forward to.'

640. BONNIE CHARLIE ★★★★ ♠
ch.c. Intikhab – Scottish Exile (Ashkalani)

February 18. First foal. 46,000Y. Doncaster St Leger. Will Edmeades. The dam, a fair triple 5f winner, is a sister to the fairly useful 6f winner of five races and listed-placed Million Percent and a half-sister to three winners. The second dam, Royal Jade (by Last Tycoon), a fairly useful 7f winner, is a half-sister to six winners including the Group 3 5f King George Stakes winner Averti. (Thurloe Thoroughbred XXII). This colt won first time out at Windsor in mid-April.

641. CAPITELLI (IRE) ★★★★
b.f. Cape Cross – Dear Girl (Fairy King)
March 14. Fourth foal. 60,000Y. Tattersalls October 1. John Warren. Half-sister to the fair dual 5f winner Musical Romance (by Mozart) and to the French two year old 9f winner Bucintoro (by Galileo). The dam won once over 9.5f at four years in France and is a half-sister to seven winners including the Sussex Stakes winner Ali Royal, the 1,000 Guineas winner Sleepytime and the Group 1 12f Europa Preis and Group 1 10f Premio Roma winner Taipan. The second dam, Alidiva (by Chief Singer), a useful listed winner of three races from 6f to 1m, is a half-sister to six winners including the dual Group 1 winner Croco Rouge. (Royal Ascot Racing Club).
'A very pretty, sweet filly, she's a good mover but a bit backward and she'll need a bit of time.'

642. CAPTAIN WALCOT ★★★★
b.c. Fantastic Light – Princess Minnie (Mistertopogigo)
April 6. Fourth foal. 40,000Y. Tattersalls October 2. Peter Doyle. Half-brother to the quite useful three year old 1m all-weather winner Palamoun (by Mtoto). The dam is an unraced half-sister to eight winners including the dual Group 3 winner, 2,000 Guineas third and Derby fourth Supreme Leader. The second dam, Princess Zena (by Habitat), a fairly useful two year old 5f winner, is a half-sister to four winners including the dam of Pebbles. (The Early Bath Partnership).
'A good-looking horse, I like him and he's been upsides and goes very well. We like him a lot.'

643. CARESSING ★★★

b.f. Kyllachy – Ella Lamees (Statoblest)
**May 12. Sixth foal. 14,000Y. Doncaster Festival.
Peter Doyle.** Sister to the fair 2008 three year old 6f winner Kingsgate Castle and half-sister to the quite useful 11f to 14f winner Broughton's Revival (by Pivotal) and the modest 6f and 7f winner of six races Mugeba (by Primo Dominie). The dam, a modest 6f winner, is a half-sister to six winners including the listed-placed Francesco Guardi and Dumnoni. The second dam, Lamees (by Lomond), is an unraced half-sister to six winners. (Mrs Julie Wood).
'She goes very well and she could be early. A nice filly, everything's all right with her, she's going well and she'll be suited by five or six furlongs.'

644. CAYMAN SKY ★★★

b.c. Fantastic Light – Comme Ca (Cyrano de Bergerac)
February 9. Fifth foal. 25,000Y. Doncaster St Leger. Peter Doyle. Half-brother to the 2007 6f placed two year old Alls Fair (by Bertolini), to the fair two year old 5f winner Grand Place (by Compton Place) and the modest two year old 6f winner Even Easier (by Petong). The dam is an unraced half-sister to five winners. The second dam, So It Goes (by Free State), won once at two years and is a sister to the Italian Group 2 winner Melbury Lad. (I.A.N Wight).
'This is a very good-looking horse and he was cheap at the price. A fine colt.'

645. CELTIC COMMITMENT ★★★★

gr.c. Mull Of Kintyre – Grey Again (Unfuwain)
March 18. Fifth foal. 37,000Y. Doncaster St Leger. Peter Doyle. Half-brother to the modest 1m to 11f and hurdles winner River Logic and to the modest French winner Yeva Winner (both by Fasliyev). The dam, a modest 7f (at two years) and 11f winner, is a half-sister to five winners. The second dam, Grey Goddess (by Godswalk), won the Group 3 Gladness Stakes and the Group 3 Matron Stakes and is a half-sister to two winners. (Joe Connolly).
'Goes well, he's a nice horse and he'll be fairly early.'

646. DAILY DOUBLE ★★

gr.c. Needwood Blade – Coffee To Go (Environment Friend)
February 11. Fourth foal. 36,000Y. Doncaster St Leger. R Doyle. Half-brother to Mr Tosi (by Wizard King), a winner of three races at two and three years in Italy. The dam is an unraced half-sister to eight winners here and abroad. The second dam, Piney Lake (by Sassafras), is a placed half-sister to ten winners including the Group 1 placed Beeshi and Chaumiere. (K T Ivory).
'He'll be a two year old alright and he's a nice big horse.'

647. DANE'S WORLD (IRE) ★★★★ ♠

b.f. Danehill Dancer – Khamseh (Thatching)
May 7. Seventh foal. 75,000Y. Tattersalls October 1. Peter Doyle. Sister to the quite useful 2007 1m placed Irish two year old Georgebernardshaw and half-sister to the smart Group 3 6f Phoenix Sprint Stakes winner of 10 races Bonus (by Cadeaux Genereux), the useful 7f and subsequent UAE listed 1m winner Third Set (by Royal Applause) and the quite useful 7f and 1m winner Corky (by Intikhab). The dam, a quite useful 7f winner at three years, is a half-sister to the high-class Group 2 12f Hardwicke Stakes and Group 2 12f Blandford Stakes winner Predappio. The second dam, Khalafiya (by Darshaan), won the Group 3 12f Meld Stakes and is a half-sister to four winners. (R C Tooth).
'A lovely filly and her pedigree has been updated since she was bought because one of them won a listed race in Dubai. We won't be in any hurry with her though.'

648. DOUGHNUT ★★★ ♠

b.f. Acclamation – Pure Speculation (Salse)
April 30. First foal. 16,000Y. Doncaster St Leger. Ross Doyle. The dam, a 7f winner at two years, is a half-sister to six minor winners here and abroad. The second dam, Just Speculation (by Ahonoora), won once at two years in Ireland and was third in the Group 3 Killavullan Stakes and is a half-sister to the Ascot Gold Cup second Tyrone Bridge. This filly was the first two-year-old winner for the yard, winning at Folkestone in early April.

649. ELIZA GRIFFITH (IRE) ★★★
b.f. King's Best – Raindancing (Tirol)
March 6. Seventh foal. 48,000Y. Tattersalls October 1. Peter Doyle. Half-brother to the fairly useful triple 5f winner and listed-placed Jack Spratt (by So Factual), to the fair three year old 7f winner Dash For Cover (by Sesaro), the fair 12f winner Yossi (by Montjeu) and the modest dual 1m winner Ballare (by Barathea). The dam, a fairly useful two year old 6f winner, was third in the Group 3 6f Princess Margaret Stakes and is a sister to the smart 7f (at two years) to 10f winner and Group 3 placed Mountain Song and a half-sister to four winners. The second dam, Persian Song (by Persian Bold), is an unplaced sister to the Kentucky Derby second Bold Arrangement. (Knockainey Stud Ltd).
'A lovely filly, she's goes nicely but she's only cantering at the moment. Seven furlongs or a mile should suit her.'

650. ELNAWIN ★★
b.c. Elnadim – Acicula (Night Shift)
April 13. Fifth foal. 28,000Y. Doncaster St Leger Festival. Peter Doyle. Brother to the quite useful 2007 two year old 6f and 7f winner Elna Bright and half-brother to the 5f and 6f seller winner Raphola (by Raphane) and the moderate 7f winner Alucica (by Celtic Swing). The dam, a useful two year old 5f and 6f winner, is a half-sister to two winners. The second dam, Crystal City (by Kris), was a minor 10f winner at three years in France and is out of the Fillies Mile and Yorkshire Oaks winner Untold. (Noodles Racing).
'He's had a bit of a setback so he's resting for a short while and we don't know much about him, but he's a very nice horse and he'll make a two year old later on.'

651. EVALUATION ★★
gr.f. El Prado – Day Of Reckoning (Daylami)
May 4. First foal. The dam, a quite useful 10f winner, is a half-sister to the smart Group 2 12f Ribblesdale Stakes and Group 2 13.3f Geoffrey Freer Stakes winner Phantom Gold (herself dam of the Oaks second Flight Of Fancy) and the useful 10f listed winner Fictitious. The second

dam, Trying For Gold (by Daylami), was a useful 12f and 12.5f winner at three years. (The Queen).
'A nice filly of the Queen's, she goes very well and she won't be too long. We're just waiting for her to come in her coat.'

652. FANDITHA (IRE) ★★★★
ch.f. Danehill Dancer – Splendid (Mujtahid)
May 6. Seventh foal. €140,000Y. Goffs Million. Peter Doyle. Sister to the unraced 2007 two year old Mildly Effective and half-sister to the quite useful two year old 6f winner Packing Hero (by Black Minnaloushe), to the US stakes-placed winner of four races Bohunk (by Polish Numbers) and a minor US four year old winner by Rahy. The dam is a placed half-sister to four winners including the very useful 1m (at two years) and 12f winner Peking Opera. The second dam, Braneakins (by Sallust), won three races over 12f in Ireland and is a half-sister to the Cheveley Park Stakes winners Park Appeal (the dam of Cape Cross) and Desirable (dam of the 1,000 Guineas winner Shadayid), the Irish Oaks winner Alydaress and the unraced dam of the 1,000 Guineas winner Russian Rhythm. (A P Patey).
'A lovely-moving filly with a lot of class, she'll make a two year old but not until the Newmarket July meeting. She's only cantering at present and she's out of a good family.'

653. FORMULA (USA) ★★★
b.br.c. Stormin Fever – Misty Gallop (Victory Gallop)
April 19. Second foal. 90,000Y. Tattersalls October 2. John Warren. The dam is an unraced half-sister to six winners including t he listed winner and triple Group 1 placed Blush Rambler. The second dam, Romanette (by Alleged), a stakes winner in the USA and Grade 2 placed, is a half-sister to six winners. (Highclere Thoroughbred Racing (Sun Chariot)).
'A well-made colt, with quality. He won't be an early sort, we'll look after him until the mid-season onwards.'

654. FULL TOSS ★★
b.c. Nayef – Spinning Top (Alzao)

February 8. Half-brother to the moderate dual 1m winner Life's A Whirl (by Machiavellian). The dam, a useful 10f winner, is a half-sister to two winners including the fairly useful three year old 7f and subsequent US dual 9f winner Daytime. The second dam, Zenith (by Shirley Heights), was a fairly useful two year old 8.5f winner. (The Queen).
'This colt goes very well, he's a really nice mover but he wouldn't be an early type.'

655. GRANSKI (IRE) ★★★★
b.c. Alhaarth – Purple Haze (Spectrum)
March 10. Second foal. €140,000Y. Goffs Million. John Warren. Half-brother to King Of Cadeaux (by Cadeaux Genereux), unplaced in two starts at two years in 2007. The dam, a useful 6f and 7f winner, is a half-sister to six winners including the Group 3 10f Sandown Classic Trial winner Chancellor. The second dam, Isticanna (by Far North), a useful two year old 5f and Italian 6f listed winner, is a half-sister to six winners. (Mrs A Williams).
'Very nice, well put together and strong. He could make an early two year old but I'd imagine he'd want six furlongs.'

656. HAWKSPUR (IRE) ★★
b.c. Hawk Wing – Lyric Fantasy (Tate Gallery)
January 17. Tenth foal. 50,000Y. Doncaster St Leger. J Warren. Half-brother to two winners in Japan by Woodman and Fusaichi Pegasus, and minor winners in Germany and Sweden by Thunder Gulch and Fusaichi Pegasus. The dam was the champion European two year old of 1992 and won six races including the Group 1 Keeneland Nunthorpe Stakes and the Group 3 Queen Mary Stakes. She is closely related to the Group 1 Dewhurst Stakes winner In Command and a half-sister to the Group 1 Middle Park Stakes and Group 1 Haydock Sprint Cup winner and sire Royal Applause. The second dam, Flying Melody (by Auction Ring), a sprint winner of two races in France, is a half-sister to the listed winners Pearl Star, Portese and Seadiver. (Royal Ascot Racing Club).
'We trained the mare, we worked this colt the other day and he surprised us because he

worked really well. He'll make a two year old alright.'

657. HEADS WILL TURN ★★
b.f. Royal Applause – Half Past Twelve (Cozzene)
January 24. Second foal. 90,000Y. Tattersalls October 1. Peter Doyle. The dam is an unraced half-sister to six winners including the Group 2 placed Political Fact and Major Inquiry. The second dam, Hire A Brain (by Seattle Slew), won once at three years and is a half-sister to eight winners including the US Grade 1 winner Twilight Agenda and the Group 3 placed Market Slide (herself dam of the 2,000 Guineas and Eclipse Stakes winner Refuse To Bend and the Melbourne Cup winner Media Puzzle). (R.H.W Morecombe).
'She'll wait for the seven furlong races later in the summer. A nice filly but she's growing like mad.'

658. HELIODOR (USA) ★★★★ ♠
b.c. Scrimshaw – Playing Footsie (Valiant Nature)
April 12. First foal. 35,000Y. Doncaster St Leger. Peter Doyle. The dam, a winner of five races in the USA from two to four years, is a half-sister to three other minor winners. The second dam, Put Your L'il Foot (by Explodent), won four minor races in the USA and is a half-sister to seven winners. (Mrs Julie Wood). The sire, a son of Gulch, won the Grade 2 8.5f Lexington Stakes and was third in the Grade 1 Preakness Stakes.
'A really fine horse. very broad. There's plenty of him and he's probably the only horse sired by Scrimshaw in the country. I'm very pleased with him.'

659. ICESOLATOR (IRE) ★★★
b.br.c. One Cool Cat – Zinnia (Zilzal)
March 10. Fifth foal. €65,000Y. Goffs Million. Peter Doyle. Half-brother to the modest 2007 6f placed two year old Don't Tell Anna (by Choisir), to the useful 5f (at two years) and 6f winner and Super Sprint second Don't Tell Mum (by Dansili) and the modest Irish 9f winner Fair Countenance (by Almutawakel). The dam ran once unplaced and is a half-sister to four

winners including the dam of the Group 3 Cornwallis Stakes winner Mubhij. The second dam, Ibtihaj (by Raja Baba), won at two years and is a half-sister to three winners including the outstanding sire Danzig. (Mr B Bull).
'A nice colt and he looks like he'll be a two year old. He's only cantering at the moment but he's doing alright.'

660. INDIAN ART (IRE) ★★★★
b.c. Choisir – Eastern Ember (Indian King)
March 4. Tenth foal. 85,000Y. Doncaster St Leger. Peter Doyle. Half-brother to the Group 2 5f Temple Stakes winner of 13 races Perryston View (by Primo Dominie), to the modest dual 6f (including at two years) and subsequent Italian winner Champagne Ateaster (by Hubby Bubbly) and the modest 7.6f winner Steal 'Em (by Efisio). The dam, a quite useful winner of five races at three and four years from 5f to 7f, is a full or half-sister to four winners. The second dam, Pithead (by High Top), won once on the flat and once over hurdles and is a sister to the Group 3 winner Miner's Lamp. (M R Green).
'A lovely colt and one of our nicest horses. He goes very well and we could send him out to the track very soon and it would take a good one to beat him I'd say.'

661. INSTALMENT ★★★
b.c. Cape Cross – New Assembly (Machiavellian)
March 18. Fourth foal. Closely related to the quite useful 10f winner Regent's Park (by Green Desert) and to the fair 1m winner Small Fortune (by Anabaa) and half-brother to Victoria Reel (by Danehill Dancer), unplaced in one start at two years in 2007. The dam, a useful 9f and 10f winner, is a sister to the 7f (at two years) and Group 1 9f Dubai Duty Free Stakes winner Right Approach and a half-sister to five winners. The second dam, Abbey Strand (by Shadeed), a fair Irish 10f winner, is a half-sister to numerous winners including the two year old Group three winners Grand Chelem and Splendid Moment. (The Queen).
'He looks quite sharp and so he should be a fairly

early two year old. A fine, big, strong horse. we have quite a few really nice horses for the Queen this year.'

662. JAZZ POLICE ★★★
b.c. Beat Hollow – Tease (Green Desert)
April 6. Second foal. 26,000Y. Tattersalls October 2. Ross Doyle. Half-brother to the unplaced 2007 two year old Illusionary (by Observatory). The dam, a fair three year old 7f winner, is a half-sister to the Irish listed winner Galistic. The second dam, Mockery (by Nashwan), won 2 minor races in France over 10.5f and 15f. (M Pescod).
'He'll be fairly early and certainly once the season gets under way properly he's one we'll be looking to run soon.'

663. LETHAL GLAZE (IRE) ★★★
gr.c. Verglas – Sticky Green (Lion Cavern)
April 24. Third foal. 30,000Y. Tattersalls October 3. Peter Doyle. Half-brother to the useful Irish two year old 6f winner Emerald Hill (by Piccolo). The dam, a fair 12f winner, is a half-sister to two winners including the useful sprint winner of eight races Piccled. The second dam, Creme de Menthe (by Green Desert), is an unraced half-sister to seven winners including the top class filly In the Groove, winner of the Champion Stakes, Juddmonte International Stakes, Irish 1,000 Guineas and the Coronation Cup. (N H Morris).
'A really nice horse and he looks quite sharp too but you wouldn't think he'd be going five furlongs. On pedigree he should need six to start with.'

664. LIKE FOR LIKE (IRE) ★★★★
ch.f. Kheleyf – Just Like Annie (Mujadil)
April 29. Seventh foal. 16,000Y. Tattersalls October 2. Peter Doyle. Half-sister to the 2007 Irish 6f placed two year old Lucy Honeychurch (by Acclamation), to the fairly useful two year old 5f and 6f winner Bella Chica (by Bigstone) and the fair Irish 1m winner Asanine (by Shinko Forest). The dam, a minor Irish three year old 5f winner, is a half-sister to six winners including the very smart Group 3 7f Criterion Stakes

winner Pipe Major and the dam of the Group 2 Mill Reef Stakes winner Galeota. The second dam, Annsfield Lady (by Red Sunset), a winner of three races in Ireland between 9f and 10f, is a half-sister to four winners including the Prix Dollar and the Brigadier Gerard Stakes winner Insatiable. (S French, R Morecombe, J Perryman). *'A nice filly, she's very sharp and she'll be running soon. She ought to be ideal for races like the Supersprint. Not there in her coat yet but she's the ideal size for a two year old.'*

665. LITTLE BLACKNUMBER ★★★

b.f. Superior Premium – The Synergist (Botanic) **February 1. Second foal. 57,000Y. Tattersalls October 2. Peter Doyle.** The dam is an unraced half-sister to seven winners including the listed Wokingham Stakes winner Baltic King. The second dam, Lindfield Belle (by Fairy King), won once at two years and is a half-sister to three winners. (Mrs S A F Brendish).
'She's quite heavy-topped so we'll go a bit steady with her but she's strong and she'll make a two year old. A nice filly and she looked really well at the sales.'

666. LUVMEDO (IRE) ★★★★

b.f. One Cool Cat – Dress Code (Barathea) **February 4. Third foal. €125,000Y. Goffs Million. Peter Doyle.** Half-brother to the quite useful 2007 Irish two year old 7f winner Slaney Rock (by Rock Of Gibraltar) and to the fair two year old 5f winner and listed 5f placed Dress To Impress (by Fasliyev). The dam, a quite useful two year old 5f winner, is a sister to the useful two year old Group 3 7f C L Weld Park Stakes winner Rag Top and a half-sister to several winners including the fairly useful 7.6f and subsequent US 1m winner Red Top. The second dam, Petite Epaulette (by Night Shift), a fair 5f winner at two years, is a half-sister to the Group 1 1m Gran Criterium second Line Dancer. (Mr M.G.J Dolan).
'She worked quite well this morning. Some of our two year old's by this sire showed a bit of temperament early on but they seem to be improving. This filly isn't very big but she'll make a two year old.'

667. LUXURIA (IRE) ★★★★

b.f. Kheleyf – Dust Flicker (Suave Dancer) **March 7. Second foal. 30,000foal. Tattersalls December. Catridge Farm Stud.** Half-sister to the 2007 two year old listed 5f winner and Group 3 6f Princess Margaret Stakes third Sweepstake (by Acclamation). The dam, placed fourth once over 10f, is a half-sister to six winners including the Group three winners Dust Dancer (dam of the US Grade 2 winner Spotlight) and Bulaxie (herself dam of the Group 2 winner Claxon). The second dam, Galaxie Dust (by Blushing Groom), a quite useful two year old 6f winner, is a half-sister to two minor winners. (Mrs Julie Wood).
'She hasn't stopped improving since she came in. A lovely filly and she looks like replacing her good half-sister Sweepstake.'

668. SOUL CITY ★★★★ ♠

b.c. Elusive City – Savage (Polish Patriot) **March 11. Seventh living foal. €88,000Y. Goffs Million. Peter Doyle.** Half-brother to the quite useful 2007 two year old 5f winner Chinese Temple (by Namid), the fair 11f and 12f winner Fascinating (by Desert King), the modest 7f and 1m winner Grande Terre (by Grand Lodge) and a minor winner in France by Cape Cross. The dam won two races at two and three years in Germany, was Group 2 placed over 6f at two years and is a half-sister to 2 other winners abroad. The second dam, Special Meeting (by Persian Bold), is an unraced half-sister to four minor winners.
'This is a lovely colt and he'll be racing in all the right places this year. We've got 3 Elusive City two year old's and we like them all.'

669. MIDNIGHT CRUISER (IRE) ★★

ch.c. Captain Rio – Kriva (Reference Point) **February 24. Sixth foal. 65,000Y. Tattersalls October 2. Peter Doyle.** Half-brother to the Scandinavia winner of 10 races and listed-placed Peruginos Flyer (by Perugino), to the fair 10f, 11f and hurdles winner Shrivar (by Sri Pekan), the fair all-weather 12f and 14f winner Rickety Bridge (by Elnadim) and a minor two year old winner abroad by Marju. The dam, a

fair 17.2f winner at three years, is a half-sister to three winners including the dam of the good Hong Kong horse Housemaster. The second dam, Kraemer (by Lyphard), won four races in France and the USA including the listed 8.5f Bay Meadows Oaks and is a half-sister to five winners including the high-class Prix du Rond-Point and Prix d'Astarte winner Shaanxi. (M Pescod).
'A fine, good-looking horse, not one for the five furlong races but he'll be along a bit later on.'

670. MINOR VAMP (IRE) ★★
b.f. Hawk Wing – Miss Champagne (Bering)
April 9. Third foal. €45,000Y. Goffs Million. Peter Doyle. Half-sister to the Irish two year old 6f winner (on her only start) Play Misty For Me (by Danehill Dancer. The dam is an unraced sister to the Group 3 Prix Eclipse winner Stella Berine and a half-sister to four winners. The second dam, Beaujolaise (by Thatching), won the Group 3 Prix Eclipse and is a half-sister to six winners. (Michael Pescod & Justin Dowley).
'She's only cantering away, so she's one for later in the year but she's a nice two year old alright.'

671. MISS FRITTON (IRE) ★★
b.f. Refuse To Bend – Golly Gosh (Danehill)
March 1. Second foal. 76,000Y. Doncaster St Leger. R Doyle. Half-sister to the modest 2007 1m placed two year old Tarbolton (by King's Best). The dam won three races over 12f and was listed-placed in Ireland and is a half-sister to the Irish listed-placed Misty Peak. The second dam, Miss Declared (by Alleged), is an unraced half-sister to nine winners in the USA. (Justin Dowley & Michael Pescod).
'A very nice filly, she's quite round and carries a bit of weight. She'll want six or seven furlongs later in the year as she's not ready yet.'

672. NOBLE JACK (IRE) ★★★★ ♠
b.c. Elusive City – Begine (Germany)
February 16. Fourth foal. 55,000Y. Doncaster St Leger. Peter Doyle. Half-brother to the modest 7f and 11f all-weather winner Tancredi (by Rossini). The dam is an unraced half-sister to six winners including the dam of the dual

Group 3 winning sprinter Eastern Purple. The second dam, Broadway Royal (by Royal Match), is an unraced half-sister to the Group 1 Kings Stand Stakes winner African Song. (M K George).
'One of our nicest colts. He goes well, had a touch of sore shins a few weeks ago so we slowed up with him. He moves really well, has a good attitude and is a really handsome colt. We're really pleased with him.'

673. ORATORY (IRE) ★★★ ♠
b.c. Danehill Dancer – Gentle Night (Zafonic)
February 22. Third living foal. €90,000Y. Goffs Million. John Warren. Half-sister to the four year old UAE 7f winner Knight Of Dance (by Singspiel). The dam ran once unplaced and is a half-sister to five winners including the Group 2 Flying Childers Stakes winner Land Of Dreams. The second dam, Sahara Star (by Green Desert), won the Group 3 Molecomb Stakes and is a half-sister to the Group 3 Greenham Stakes winner Yalaietainee. (Highclere Thoroughbred Racing (Munnings)).
'He moves well but he's very big and he'll want seven furlongs. A very nice, mature horse but he hasn't grown into his frame yet.'

674. OUR DAY WILL COME ★★★
b.f. Red Ransom – Dawnus (Night Shift)
January 10. Second foal. 23,000Y. Doncaster St Leger. A Walters Bloodstock. Half-sister to Cosenza (by Bahri), placed fourth once over 5f at two years in 2007. The dam, a useful listed 10f winner, is out of the French 1m winner Dame's Violet (by Groom Dancer), herself a full or half-sister to six winners including the Group 2 Princess Of Wales's Stakes winner Wagon Master. (Derek & Jean Clee).
'A nice filly, you can't help but like her and she's very sweet. She has a grey tail, which is always lucky for us. I have a lot of time for her.'

675. PARTY CAT (IRE) ★★★★
b.c. One Cool Cat – Congress (Dancing Brave)
April 14. Ninth foal. €90,000Y. Goffs Million. Peter Doyle. Half-brother to the quite useful

2007 two year old 7f winner Hawaana (by Bahri), to the Irish 7f (at two years) and listed 10f winner Royal Intrigue (by Royal Applause), the fairly useful 1m winner United Nations (by Halling), to the quite useful 7.7f winner Serra Negra (by Kris) and the fair 6f all-weather winner Promessa (by Reprimand). The dam, a quite useful two year old 1m winner, is a sister to the high-class Cherokee Rose, a winner of five races from 6f to 7f including the Group 1 6f Haydock Park Sprint Cup and the Group 1 Prix Maurice de Gheest and a half-sister to three winners. The second dam, Celtic Assembly (by Secretariat), a fairly useful 10.6f winner, was second in the Lupe Stakes and is a full or half-sister to 13 winners including the Group 1 Prix du Cadran winner Molesnes. (Thurloe Finsbury II).

'A lovely colt, he did have a bit of an attitude but he seems to have grown up over the last few weeks. Physically he'd be one of the nicest two year old's we've got.'

676. PENNY'S GIFT ★★★★
b.f. Tobougg – Happy Lady
(Cadeaux Genereux)
February 15. 10,000Y. Doncaster St Leger Festival. Ross Doyle. Half-sister to the unplaced 2007 two year old Scrap N'Dust (by Averti), to the modest 6f (at two years) and 7f winner Chorus Beauty and he moderate 1m winner Homme Dangereux (both by Royal Applause). The dam, a fair 1m placed maiden, is a half-sister to the smart middle-distance stayer and Group 2 Yorkshire Cup second Rainbow Ways. The second dam, Siwaayib (by Green Desert), a fairly useful winner of three races over 6f, is a half-sister to seven winners here and abroad. (Malcolm Brown).

'We worked her the other day and she surprised us. She's sharp and although she carries a lot of weight she goes quite well. When we get her fit I imagine she'll be quite nice and she'll be ideal for auction races.'

677. PRINCESS HANNAH ★★★
b.f. Royal Applause – Helloimustbegoing
(Red Ransom)

February 26. Third foal. 37,000Y. Doncaster St Leger. Peter Doyle. The dam, a fairly useful 1m winner, is a half-sister to seven winners. The second dam, Arsaan (by Nureyev), won over 7f at two years and a listed 1m event at three years and is a half-sister to the US Grade 1 winners Desert Wine and Menifee and the dam of the Phoenix Stakes and Prix Morny winner Fasliyev. (A P Patey).

'A lovely filly, he gave a bit of money for her and we won't be rushing her as she just needs to strengthen up a bit. She should be sharp enough for five furlongs though.'

678. PURE POETRY (IRE) ★★
b.c. Tagula – Express Logic (Air Express)
March 31. First foal. 40,000Y. Tattersalls December. Ross Doyle. The dam ran once unplaced and is a half-sister to one winner. The second dam, Hazarama (by Kahyasi), won over 13f and is a half-sister to five winners including the Group three winners Hazariya and Hazarista. The second dam, Hazaradjat (by Darshaan), won twice at two and three years and is a half-sister to ten winners including the Flying Childers and Middle Park Stakes winner Hittite Glory. (Mrs Julie Wood).

'A lovely, big colt. I can't imagine there being many two year old's bigger than him.'

679. REBECCA DE WINTER ★★★★
b.f. Kyllachy – Miss Adelaide (Alzao)
February 17. First foal. 20,000Y. Doncaster St Leger. Peter Doyle. The dam, a fair dual 5f winner at three years, is a half-sister to five minor winners. The second dam, Sweet Adelaide (by The Minstrel), a dual winner at two years and third in the Group 1 National Stakes, subsequently won in South Africa and is a half-sister to the listed winners Soiree and Solaboy. (Mrs Julie Wood).

'We worked her the other day and she goes very well. A likeable filly, very sweet, carries a lot of weight and she's going to want five furlongs. She was bought to win the Supersprint and normally the chances would be a million to one, but as she's owned by Julie Wood it'll probably come off!'

680. REDHEAD (IRE) ★★★ ♠
ch.f. Redback – Rinneen (Bien Bien)
**April 2. First foal. 80,000Y. Doncaster St Leger.
Peter Doyle.** The dam, a modest 6f (at two
years) and 12f placed maiden, is a half-sister to
five winners including the dual listed 6f winner
(including at two years) Lady Links (herself dam
of the dual listed winner Selinka). The second
dam, Sparky's Song (by Electric), a moderate
10.2f and 12f winner, is a half-sister to the very
smart Group 1 6.5f winner Bold Edge and to the
listed winner and Group 3 5f Temple Stakes
second Brave Edge. (Mrs Julie Wood).
*'This filly goes well, she hasn't come in her coat
yet but she'll be sharp.'*

681. RED ROSSINI (IRE) ★★★
b.c. Rossini – La Scala (Theatrical)
**February 17. First foal. 65,000Y. Doncaster St
Leger. Peter Doyle.** The dam, a quite useful
three year old 1m winner here, subsequently
won once in the USA and is a half-sister to three
winners. The second dam, Estala (by Be My
Guest), won over 1m at two years in France and
was listed-placed and is a half-sister to 4 stakes
winners. (Terry Neill).
*'He's been upsides, he goes very well and he's a
lovely colt. We're very pleased with him.'*

682. RETRO IRE) ★★
*b.c. Tagula – Cabcharge Princess
(Rambo Dancer)*
**May 5. Seventh foal. 68,000Y. Doncaster St
Leger. Peter Doyle.** Brother to the fair 5f and 6f
winner of 12 races Aahgowangowan, to the
Italian two year old 5f winner Super Genius and
the quite useful two year old 5f winner Stolt and
half-brother to the fair dual middle-distance
winner Luz Bay (by Tenby). The dam, a modest
two year old 5f winner, is a half-sister to one
winner abroad out of the unplaced Eiswave (by
Welsh Pageant). herself a daughter of a half-
sister to the 1,000 Guineas winner One In a
Million. (Mrs Julie Wood).
*'A very similar horse to the other Tagula we have
in that he's a big horse and we'll leave him alone
for now.'*

683. RIO DEL ORO (USA) ★★★★ ♠
b.c. Touch Gold – Diablo's Girl (Diablo)
**January 25. Second foal. 88,000Y. Tattersalls
October 2. Will Edmeades.** The dam won 5
minor races from 2 to five years in the USA and
is a half-sister to five winners including the US
Grade 3 winner B L's Appeal. The second dam,
B L's Girl (by Master Derby), a stakes-placed
winner of five races in the USA, is a sister to a
stakes winner and a half-sister to nine winners.
(Waney Racing Group Inc).
*'He cost a fair bit of money, he's a fine colt and
he'll make a two year old alright. It just depends
when we want to start him.'*

684. RIVER RYE (IRE) ★★★
*b.f. Acclamation – Rye
(Charnwood Forest)*
**February 1. First foal. 36,000Y. Doncaster St
Leger. Peter Doyle.** The dam, a fair three year
old 1m all-weather winner, is a sister to the
useful two year old 6f and 7f winner Forwood
and a half-sister to two winners. The second
dam, Silver Hut (by Silver Hawk), a quite useful
two year old 1m winner at York, is a half-sister to
six minor winners. (Bruce Coulthard).
*'A typical Acclamation, she's sharp and we'll soon
be stepping her work up.'*

685. ROLY BOY ★★★
b.c. Dansili – Night At Sea (Night Shift)
**March 25. Thirteenth foal. €38,000Y. Goffs
Sportsman's. 57,000 two year old. Kempton
Breeze-up. Peter Doyle.** Half-brother to the
fairly useful two year old 5f and 6f winner and
listed-placed Vikings Bay (by Intikhab), to the
fair two year old 7f winner Lost At Sea (by Exit To
Nowhere), the fair 7f winner Sea Drift, the fair 7f
and 1m winner of eight races Nautical Warning
(both by Warning), the modest 7f to 13f winner
Muhandis (by Persian Bold) and a winner abroad
by Brief Truce. The dam won three races including a listed event and is a half-sister to six
winners. The second dam, Into Harbour (by Right
Tack), is an unplaced half-sister to four winners.
*'We bought him at Kempton where he breezed
very well. He's been fairly relaxed since we
brought him here and he's a real nice horse.'*

686. RUASGRAYASME (USA) ★★★★
gr.f. Smoke Glacken – Newhall Road
(Dixieland Band)
March 17. Sixth foal. €50,000Y. Goffs Million.
Peter Doyle. Half-sister to the Argentinian dual
Grade 1 winner New Real Deal (by Roy) and to
2 minor US winners by Lord Carson, Prospect
Bay and Maria's Mon. The dam, a minor winner
at two years in the USA, is a half-sister to five
winners. The second dam, Maiden Road (by
Roberto), won 2 minor races in the USA and is a
half-sister to five winners. (F Jones).
'She's got a lot of class and I thought she was
very cheap when we bought her. She goes well,
we haven't done a whole lot with her but she's a
really lovely filly.'

687. SAUCY BROWN (IRE) ★★★
b.c. Fasliyev – Danseuse du Bois (Woodman)
April 17. Fourth foal. 25,000Y. Tattersalls
October 2. Peter Doyle. Half-brother to a three
year old winner in Italy by Danehill Dancer. The
dam is an unplaced half-sister to the minor
winner Zappeuse, herself dam of the French
Group 3 winner and US Grade 1 third Danzon.
The second dam, Danseuse du Nord (by
Kahyasi), won over 1m at two years in France
and was third in both the Group 2 Prix de
Malleret and the Group 3 Prix de Royaumont
and is a half-sister to ten winners including the
French 1,000 Guineas and Prix de la Foret
winner Danseuse du Soir. (Mr H R Heffer).
'A great, big, good-looking horse. I like him a lot.'

688. SAINTS BAY (IRE) ★★★
b.f. Redback – Alexander Eliott
(Night Shift)
January 15. Fourth foal. 28,000Y. Tattersalls
October 2. Peter Doyle. Half-sister to the fair
2007 two year old 5f winner Artistic License (by
Chevalier) and to the quite useful two year old
5f winner Brandywell Boy (by Danetime). The
dam, an Irish maiden, was placed at up to 10f.
The second dam, Olivia (by Ela-Mana-Mou),
won over 10f in Ireland and is a half-sister to
four winners. (N A Woodcock).
'A nice filly, she's very thick set and we haven't
done anything with her yet but we like her a lot.'

689. SECURITY JOAN (IRE) ★★★
ch.f. Dubai Destination – Divine Quest (Kris)
April 28. Eighth foal. 30,000Y. Tattersalls
December. Peter Doyle. Half-sister to the fairly
useful two year old 5f to 7f winner Grand Prix
(by Grand Lodge), to the fairly useful two year
old 7f winner Zabeel House, the quite useful
two year old 6f winner Celestia (both by
Anabaa), the quite useful two year old 6f winner
Ecstatic (by Nashwan) and a winner in Holland
by Zafonic. The dam, a quite useful 7f winner, is
a sister to the Prix du Gros Chene winner Divine
Danse and a half-sister to four winners including
the high-class Prix Maurice de Gheest winner
Pursuit of Love. The second dam, Dance Quest
(by Green Dancer), was a smart French two year
old sprinter and a half-sister to the Prix de la
Salamandre winner Noblequest. (Michael
Pescod & Justin Dowley).
'Quite a busy filly but quite likeable. She has a
high knee action but that's getting better as she
works along side other horses. She goes quite
well and she should be winning races by June I'd
say.'

690. SEQUILLO ★★★★
b.c. Lucky Story – Tranquillity (Night Shift)
May 2. Eighth foal. 33,000Y. Tattersalls October
2. Peter Doyle. Half-brother to the quite useful
two year old 5f winner Quiescent (by Primo
Dominie), to the quite useful all-weather 9f to
12f winner Tranquilizer (by Dr Fong), the quite
useful two year old 6f and 7f winner Tranquil Sky
(by Intikhab), the fair three year old 5f winner
Yellow Card (by Inchinor) and the fair two year
old 7f winner The Bull McCabe (by Efisio). The
dam, a fair winner of one race over 1m at three
years, is a half-sister to three winners here and
abroad. The second dam, Quiet Week-End (by
Town And Country), was a useful two year old 6f
and 7f winner and a half-sister to the Moyglare
Stud Stakes and Falmouth Stakes winner Lemon
Souffle and the Falmouth Stakes and Nassau
Stakes winner Caramba. (White Beech Farm).
'We've got a couple of Lucky Story's and they
both seem to go well. Physically he's a nice horse
but I've not done anything with him yet. I think
he should be out before June.'

691. SHARPENER (IRE) ★★★★

b.f. Invincible Spirit – Daily Double (Unfuwain)
March 27. Fourth foal. 75,000Y. Tattersalls
October 2. Peter Doyle. Half-sister to the fair 9f
and 10f winner of four races from three to five
years Princess Cocoa (by Desert Sun), to the fair
Irish four year old dual 6f winner Lady Power
(by Almutawakel) and the minor Italian two year
old winner Live To Run (by Intikhab). The dam is
an unraced half-sister to three minor winners in
France and Germany. The second dam, Double
Line (by What A Guest), is a placed half-sister to
five winners including the Group 3 winner and
good broodmare Perlee. (Mrs Julie Wood).
'A very well-made filly, we love the sire and she's
pleased us with the bit that she's done so far. I
wouldn't be surprised if she showed up at Royal
Ascot.'

692. SOHCAHTOA (IRE) ★★★

b.c. Val Royal – Stroke Of Six (Woodborough)
March 19. Second· living foal. 65,000Y.
Tattersalls October 1. Ross Doyle. The dam, a
quite useful 6f (at two years) and 1m winner, is
a full or half-sister to six winners including the
Group 2 10f Prix Eugene Adam winner
Revelation. The second dam, Angelus Chimes
(by Northfields), a quite useful Irish four year old
12f winner, is a half-sister to four winners. (Mrs
S.A.F Brendish).
'A nice horse, he's a big, cheeky begger but he's
going very well. One for the mid-summer.'

693. SUN SHIP (IRE) ★★★★

b.c. Xaar – Silky Dawn (Night Shift)
January 14. Third foal. 58,000Y. Doncaster St
Leger. Peter Doyle. Half-brother to the fair 7f
all-weather winner Catbang (by Zafonic). The
dam, a fairly useful 1m winner, is a half-sister to
two winners. The second dam, Bluffing (by
Darshaan), a two year old 1m winner at the
Curragh, was listed-placed over 9f (at two years)
and 12f and is a half-sister to six winners.
(Michael Pescod).
'A gorgeous colt. A good-looking, fine horse and
I like him a lot. He'll go six furlongs.'

694. SUPER FOURTEEN ★★★★

b.c. Lucky Story – Beechnut (Mujadil)
April 22. Second foal. 35,000Y. Doncaster St
Leger. Peter Doyle. The dam is an unraced sister
to the winner and Group 3 Molecomb Stakes
placed Connemara and to the listed-placed
winner Presentation and a half-sister to four
winners. The second dam, Beechwood (by
Blushing Groom), won over 10.8f in France and
is a half-sister to five winners. (Rory Donohue).
'A nice horse that goes well, he has a good
attitude and we like him a lot.'

695. TARQUA (IRE) ★★

b.f. King Charlemagne – Shining Creek
(Bering)
May 4. Seventh foal. €36,000Y. Goffs Million.
Peter Doyle. Half-sister to the unplaced 2007
two year old La Gazzetta (by Rossini) and to the
two year old Group 2 6f Mill Reef Stakes winner
Cool Creek (by Desert Style). The dam won
twice at around 7f at two and three years in Italy
and is a half-sister to six winners. The second
dam, High And Dry (by High Line), won once at
two years, was third in the Group 3 Waterford
Candelabra Stakes and is a half-sister to eight
winners. (Earl Of Carnarvon).
'A little bit backward but a nice filly with a good
pedigree. One for a bit later on.'

696. TARTAN TURBAN (IRE) ★★★★

b.c. Invincible Spirit – Tappen Zee
(Sandhurst Prince)
April 24. Ninth foal. €80,000Y. Goffs
Sportsman's. Peter Doyle. Half-brother to the
useful 2007 two year old dual 6f winner and
three year old listed 7f winner Paco Boy (by
Desert Style), to the quite useful 7f and 1m
winner Mawingo (by Taufan), the Irish three
year old dual 7f winner Zacholiv, the modest
1m and 10f winner Fuel Cell (both by Desert
Style) and a winner in Hong Kong by Mujadil.
The dam, a dual 7f winner at three years in
Ireland, is a half-sister to seven winners
including the dual listed winner and Irish Two
Thousand Guineas third Cape Town and the
listed 1m Easter Stakes winner Regiment. The
second dam, Rossaldene (by Mummy's Pet), a

quite useful two year old 5f winner, is a half-sister to six winners. (McKendrick, Mahal, Morecombe, Anderson).

'He's a nice horse that should make a two year old although we haven't done a lot with him yet. A likeable horse and he's not the biggest in the world so he should make a two year old.'

697. THE MINIVER ROSE (IRE) ★★★
b.f. High Chaparral – Bloemfontain (Cape Cross)
February 2. First foal. 100,000Y. Tattersalls October 1. Peter Doyle. The dam, a modest two year old 6f winner, is a half-sister to five winners including the listed-placed Ginger Tree. The second dam, Carotene (by Great Nephew), won 12 races including the Grade 1 Yellow Ribbon Invitational and Grade 1 Pan American Handicap and is a half-sister to five winners. (Mrs Julie Wood).

'A fine, big, good-looking filly. She's one for the middle-to-backend of the season over seven furlongs plus.'

698. TISHTAR ★★★
br.c. Kyllachy – Xtrasensory (Royal Applause)
March 27. Half-brother to the fair 2007 two year old 7f winner Redsensor (by Redback). The dam, a fairly useful two year old 6f winner, is a half-sister to numerous winners including the quite useful 5.2f (at two years) and 7f winner Song Of Skye. The second dam, Song Of Hope (by Chief Singer), a useful two year old 5f winner and second in the listed Firth of Clyde Stakes, is a half-sister to 10 minor winners. (Waney Racing Group Inc).

'A good-looking horse, he goes very well and he's out of a mare we trained for the same owner. A big, strong horse that's just cantering away at present.'

699. VERLEGEN (IRE) ★★★★ ♠
b.f. Royal Applause – Petite Epaulette (Night Shift)
March 13. Eleventh foal. 68,000Y. Tattersalls October 3. Ross Doyle. Half-sister to the useful two year old Group 3 7f C L Weld Park Stakes winner Rag Top, to the fair two year old 7f

winner Seamstress (herself dam of the two year old listed winner Elhamri), the quite useful two year old 5f winner Dress Code (all by Barathea), the fairly useful 7.6f and subsequent US 1m winner Red Top (by Fasliyev), the fairly useful two year old dual 5f winner Lady Sarka (by Lake Coniston), the quite useful two year old 5f winner Shalford's Honour (by Shalford), the fair two year old 6f all-weather winner Petite Spectre (by Spectrum) and the modest 7f winner One Giant Leap (by Pivotal). The dam, a fair 5f winner at two years, is a sister to the Sweet Solera Stakes second The Jotter and a half-sister to the Group 1 1m Gran Criterium second Line Dancer. The second dam, Note Book (by Mummy's Pet), a fairly useful 6f winner, is a sister to the Norfolk Stakes winner Colmore Row and a half-sister to the Horris Hill Stakes winner Long Row. (Mr J N Reus).

'This colt is very sharp. He'll be fairly early and he might have won by the time your book is published. He goes very quick and it's a good family.'

700. VERSAKI (IRE) ★★★★
gr.c. Verglas – Mythie (Octagonal)
March 17. First foal. €100,000Y. Deauville August. Peter Doyle. The dam, a minor French three year old winner, is a half-sister to four winners including the French listed winner Mytographie. The second dam, Mythologie (by Bering), won twice and is a half-sister to seven winners. (J A Lazzari).

'He goes very well and is definitely one for the notebook.'

701. WEALD PARK (USA) ★★★★
ch.c. Cozzene – Promptly (Lead On Time)
January 23. Seventh foal. 90,000Y. Tattersalls October 1. Peter Doyle. Brother to the quite useful two year old 6f and 7f winner To The Rescue and half-brother to three winners including the two year old Group 3 Autumn Stakes winner and Group 1 Racing Post Trophy second Fantastic View (by Distant View), the quite useful 8.5f winner Escape Clause (by Red Ransom), the fair 6f to 9f winner Dart Along (by Bahri) and the fair 1m winner Expedience (by

With Approval). The dam, a quite useful 6f winner here, subsequently won a minor stakes event over 1m in the USA and is a half-sister to six winners. The second dam, Ghariba (by Final Straw), won the Group 3 Nell Gwyn Stakes and is a half-sister to the Group 1 Prix Royal Oak winner Braashee. (Mr H R Heffer).

'A lovely, mature horse that moves very well. You'd think he was a three year old by the look of him and he's one for the nice races in mid-summer. We've trained a lot of the family as well.'

702. WILBURY STAR (IRE) ★★★

b.c. Trans Island – Gold Blended (Goldmark)
March 17. First foal. 25,000Y. Doncaster St Leger. R Doyle. The dam, a hurdles winner, is a half-sister to nine winners including the Group 3 Dubai Duty Free Arc Trial winner Compton Bolter. The second dam, Milk And Honey (by So Blessed), a useful sprint winner at two years, is a half-sister to nine winners including the Prix Foy winner Beeshi and the dams of the Cheveley Park Stakes winner Seazun and the Prix Dollar winner Insatiable. (Mr Raymond Keogh).

'He's got a bit of a wall-eye but he was a bit busy when he came in but he's settling in now. He goes OK and we're just waiting until he comes in his coat, then we'll pick our spot and see how he goes.'

703. UNNAMED ★★

ch.f. Namid – Dundel (Machiavellian)
March 5. Seventh foal. 110,000Y. Tattersalls October 2. Peter Doyle. Half-sister to the smart 2007 two year old 6f winner and Group 2 6f Coventry Stakes second Luck Money (by Indian Ridge), to the two year old Group 3 7f Prix du Calvados winner Charlotte O'Fraise (by Beat Hollow), the modest 2m 1f and hurdles winner Lodgician (by Grand Lodge), the Irish 1m and hurdles winner River Nurey (by Fasliyev) and the French three year old winner Wing And Wing (by Singspiel). The dam, a quite useful 7f winner, is a half-sister to six winners including the Group 3 6f Prix de Seine-et-Oise winner Seltitude. The second dam, Dunoof (by Shirley Heights), a fairly useful two year old 7f winner, is a sister to the Premio Roma, Park Hill Stakes and Ribblesdale

Stakes winner High Hawk (the dam of In the Wings) and to the winning dams of the Derby winner High-Rise and the Grade 1 Rothmans International winner Infamy. (P A Byrne).

'She was a lovely filly at the Sales and she's been bought as a longer term prospect. You won't be seeing her until the end of the summer.'

704. UNNAMED ★★★★ ♠

b.c. Marju – Night Owl (Night Shift)
February 23. Sixth foal. 65,000Y. Tattersalls October 1. Peter Doyle. Half-brother to the fair 2007 7f placed two year old Hamalka (by Alhaarth) and to the fairly useful 7f and 1m winner Distant Connection (by Cadeaux Genereux). The dam, a modest 6f placed maiden, is a half-sister to four winners including the Group 3 10.5f Prix de Flore winner Audacieuse and the Irish listed 14f winner Lord Jim. The second dam, Sarah Georgina (by Persian Bold), a quite useful two year old 6f winner, is a half-sister to nine winners including the French 1,000 Guineas winner Danseuse du Soir. (Mr A. T. J Russell).

'A lovely horse but he got a sore back for a bit and really put on a lot of weight – the way he looks after himself is abnormal! But he's a horse we like an awful lot.'

PATRICK HASLAM

705. ARES CHOIX ★★★

b.f. Choisir – Ares Vallis (Caerleon)
February 12. Third foal. 32,000Y. Doncaster St Leger. McKeever St Lawrence. The dam, a listed 10f winner in France, is a half-sister to two minor winners. The second dam, Hoedown Honey (by Country Light), won once in the USA and is a half-sister to four winners. (Mrs R J Jacobs).

'She's been showing a bit, she looks to have a bit of ability and I'd like to run her at Haydock at the end of April. In this cold spring you have to be a bit careful with fillies but I'm pleased with her so far. From what I can see of these Choisir horses they look quite big and rangy horses but they come to hand quite well, so I'd be disappointed if she doesn't win this year.'

706. ASIAN TALE (IRE) ★★★
b.f. Namid – Literary (Woodman)
February 8. Seventh foal. 8,000Y. Doncaster Festival. Bobby O'Ryan. Half-sister to the French triple three year old winner and listed-placed Valain (by Grand Lodge), to the Italian 6f (at two years) and 1m winner Bod Entrewood (by Entrepreneur) and the quite useful two year old 5f winner Binnion Bay (by Fasliyev). The dam, a fair three year old 1m winner, is a full or half-sister to five winners. The second dam, Book Collector (by Irish River), a stakes winner of four races, is closely related to the US Grade 2 Dixie Handicap winner Akabir and a half-sister to the Group 1 Middle Park Stakes winner Lycius. (Middleham Park Racing XXXIX).
'This is a nice filly and I'd be disappointed if she didn't run well on her debut which will be in April, probably at Pontefract. A big, scopey two year old, she goes well and looks like a two year old.' TRAINER'S BARGAIN BUY

707. BACHELOR DAYS (IRE) ★★★
b.g. Bachelor Duke – Anchorage (Slip Anchor)
April 21. Eleventh foal. 42,000Y. Tattersalls October 2. Ben Haslam. Half-brother to the fair 2007 1m placed two year old Little Miss Diva (by Diktat), to the quite useful 2m winner of four races Lord Alaska (by Sir Harry Lewis), the quite useful two year old 7f winner Red Leggings (by Shareef Dancer), the fair all-weather 10.5f and 11f winner Eagle's Landing (by Eagle Eyed) and two bumper winners by Hernando and Efisio. The dam, a quite useful dual 12.3f winner, is a half-sister to six winners including the Ormonde Stakes winner Brunico. The second dam, Cartridge (by Jim French), was a useful 6f and 7f winner and a half-sister to three winners. (Middleham Park Racing LI).
'I've gelded him because he was a bit heavy in front. He's a mid-season type, I might even start him at seven furlongs and in the autumn he'll be fine over seven furlongs or a mile. He's a nice, well-made gelding with a good temperament and my gut feeling is that he'll be alright.'

708. BLUE DAGGER (IRE) ★★★
ch.g. Daggers Drawn – Sports Post Lady (M Double M)
March 6. 20,000Y. Doncaster St Leger. Ben Haslam. Half-brother to the useful listed 5f winner of six races Our Little Secret (by Rossini), to the French 5f and 6f winner Sports Road (by Common Grounds) and the fair 5f winner of five races Jadan (by Imperial Ballet). The dam, a fair sprinter, is a half-sister to the useful sprinter Palacegate Episode (a winner of 11 races here and abroad including a Group 3 race in Italy and numerous listed events), to the fair sprinter Another Episode (a winner of 11 races and second in the Group 3 Molecomb Stakes) and the useful sprinter Palacegate Jack (also a winner of 11 races including listed events). The second dam, Pasadena Lady (by Captain James), is an unraced half-sister to five minor winners. (Blue Lion Racing).
'His pedigree suggests they all go better as three year old's, but he'll definitely make a two year old and I'll be campaigning him this year at a sensible level over six furlongs in June. I see no reason why he shouldn't be a potential winner.'

709. MONACO MISTRESS (IRE) ★★★★
b.f. Acclamation – Bendis (Danehill)
March 24. Third foal. 57,000Y. Doncaster St Leger. B Haslam. Brother to the quite useful 2007 two year old 6f winner Rubirosa. The dam, a 7f winner at three years in Germany, is a half-sister to three winners. The second dam, Berenice (by Groom Dancer), a fair 10f winner, was listed-placed and is a half-sister to three winners. (Team Fashion Rocks).
'Yes she's nice, I haven't rushed her and she's going to be ready in June and being by Acclamation you have to be optimistic about her winning at two. She has a bit of quality and there's nothing wrong with her.'

710. POUTY TURN ★★★★
b.f. Refuse To Bend – Total Aloof (Groom Dancer)
January 26. Eighth foal. 200,000Y. Tattersalls October 1. Blandford Bloodstock. Half-sister to the Tout Seul (by Ali-Royal), a winner of

six races including the Group 1 7f Dewhurst Stakes, to the quite useful two year old 6f winner Totally Yours (by Desert Sun) and the Irish two year old 6f winner Soaring Eagle (by Eagle Eyed). The dam, a fair dual 5f winner at three years, is a half-sister to two winners in Japan. The second dam, Bashkoosh (by Danzig), is a placed full or half-sister to six winners.
'A nice filly that's done nothing wrong at all and has a good temperament. A nice, well-balanced filly that has a bit of scope. A quality type, and although I'm guessing a bit I can see me running her at Ayr in late August or early September because it's a nice track and you usually get a bit of give in the ground at that time of the year. She has a lot of potential and is obviously one of those giving me a sporting chance of having a nice two year old.'

711. TITO GOBBI ★★★
ch.c. Lomitas – Nellie Melba (Hurricane Sky)
March 17. Sister to the quite useful 2007 two year old 5f winner Bosun Breese. The dam, a fair 7f and 1m winner of three races, is a half-sister to several winners out of the dual 10f and 12f winner Persuasion (by Batshoof). (Lady Lonsdale).
'This is a colt I quite like, he's nice and despite being by Lomitas he'll be a two year old. He's close-coupled, goes well and he isn't very big and has a very good temperament.'

712. UNNAMED ★★★
b.f. Bahamian Bounty – Marionetta (Nijinsky)
March 22. Half-sister to the fair two year old 6f winner Leonide (by Noverre) and to numerous winners in Italy. The dam, a minor middle-distance placed three year old, is a half-sister to seven winners. The second dam, Mariella (by Roberto), was a useful winner of 3 minor events over 12f (twice) and 13.8f and was second in the Princess Royal Stakes and is a half-sister to 11 winners including the dams of the US Grade 1 winner Too Chic and the Ascot Gold Cup winner Sadeem. (P D Player).
'She's been working well, she'll definitely want six furlongs and she's definitely alright.'

BARRY HILLS
It was a pleasure to speak to Charlie Hills, Barry's son and Assistant Trainer, about these two-year-olds. Hopefully between us we've managed to sort out plenty of winners!

713. ABOVE AVERAGE (IRE) ★★
b.c. High Chaparral – Crystal Valkyrie (Danehill)
March 31. Third foal. €70,000Y. Goffs Million. BBA (Ire). Half-brother to the modest two year old 6f winner Spinning Crystal (by Spinning World). The dam, a fair 10f winner, is a half-sister to three minor winners. The second dam, Crystal Cross (by Roberto), a quite useful winner of four races at up to 14f, is a half-sister to the Group 1 Haydock Park Sprint Cup winner Iktamal, the French Group 2 winner First Magnitude and the US Grade 2 winner Rockamundo.
'A well-made colt with a good temperament, but at the moment he's just growing and filling-out physically. He'll not be out until the mid-summer at the earliest.'

714. ALYARF (USA) ★★
b.c. Dixie Union – Tabheej (Mujtahid)
April 22. Fifth foal. Half-brother to the smart 2007 two year old 6f winner and Group 1 6f Middle Park Stakes third Tajdeef (by Aljabr) and to the fair 7f winner Tawaajud (by Dixieland Band). The dam, a useful two year old 5f and 6f winner, was third in the Lowther Stakes and is a sister to the Group 3 5f Cornwallis Stakes winner Mubhij. The second dam, Abhaaj (by Kris), a fairly useful two year old 5f winner, is a half-sister to two minor winners. (Hamdan Al Maktoum).
'Still in Dubai in early April.'

715. ART PRINCESS ★★★★
ch.f. Officer – Rhumb Line (Mr Greeley)
January 25. First foal. 62,000Y. Tattersalls October 1. BBA (Ire). The dam won three races at three years in the USA and is a half-sister to 4 other minor winners. The second dam, Rose Rhapsody (by Pleasant Colony), is a placed half-sister to three winners.

'She's done a couple of bits of work and the jockeys like her, so she should be out early doors.'

716. ASATEER (IRE) ★★★
b.c. Alhaarth – Catatonic (Zafonic)
February 21. Second foal. 220,000Y. Tattersalls October 1. Shadwell Estate Co. Half-brother to the fair all-weather 7f and 1m winner Hostage (by Dr Fong). The dam is an unraced half-sister to five winners including the two year old Group 3 Solario Stakes and multiple US Grade 2 winner Brave Act. The second dam, Circus Act (by Shirley Heights), is an unraced sister to the listed 10f Lupe Stakes winner Lady Shipley and a half-sister to six winners.
'A well-made colt and he'll make a two year old by the middle part of the year. He's well-balanced, has a nice temperament and is showing a bit of speed.'

717. BEST SHOT ★★★
b.f. Xaar – Xaymara (Sanglamore)
March 10. Half-sister to the unraced 2007 two year old Effortless (by Beat Hollow), to the useful triple 7f winner Dream Theme (by Distant View) and to the French two year old 5f winner and listed-placed Extinguisher (by Zamindar). The dam is a half-sister to the Grade 1 Washington Lassie Stakes winner Contredance, to the listed Roses Stakes winner Old Alliance, the Graded stakes winners Shotiche and Skimble (dam of the US Grade 1 winner Skimming), and to the dams of the 1,000 Guineas winner Wince and the Lanson Champagne Stakes winner Eltish. The second dam, Nimble Folly (by Cyane), is an unraced sister to the very useful two year old Group 3 winner and Group 1 third Misgivings. (Khalid Abdulla).
'She's a nice filly and a very similar model to Dream Theme in that she's a nice, big, lengthy filly. She shows some speed but she'll probably get a mile later on and we'll set her off at seven furlongs I should think.'

718. CAPTAIN DANCER (IRE) ★★★
ch.c. Danehill Dancer – Rain Flower (Indian Ridge)

April 12. Fifth foal. €175,000Y. Goffs Million. BBA (Ire). Half-brother to the two year old listed 5f St Hugh's Stakes winner Sumora, to the useful Irish 7f winner Fleeting Shadow (both by Danehill) and half-brother to the 2007 7f and 1m placed two year old Mikhail Fokine (by Sadler's Wells). The dam is an unraced three-parts sister to the top-class Epsom Derby, Irish Champion Stakes and Dewhurst Stakes winner Dr Devious and a half-sister to five winners including the Japanese listed winner Shinko King and the Group three winners Royal Court and Archway. The second dam, Rose Of Jericho (by Alleged), is an unraced half-sister to five winners.
'A strong colt with a rounded action at the moment, he's very straightforward and is a forward-going colt. He needs a bit of time yet, so we haven't asked many questions of him.'

719. CASTING COUCH ★★★
b.f. Royal Applause – McQueenie (Danehill)
January 2. First foal. 50,000Y. Tattersalls October 1. BBA (Ire). The dam, placed 7 times at up to 1m in Ireland, is a sister to the Group 3 Minstrel Stakes winner and Group 2 second Restructure and a half-sister to eight winners including the Dollar Stakes and Select Stakes winner Alderbrook. The second dam, Twine (by Thatching), is an unraced half-sister to the listed winners Academic and Tea House (dam of the Grade 1 winner Danish).
'A strongly made filly, she's just going through a growing phase so we haven't asked any questions yet but she has a good attitude and she'd have the speed for six furlongs.'

720. CHAPTER AND VERSE (IRE) ★★★★
b.c. One Cool Cat – Beautiful Hill (Danehill)
March 23. First foal. €140,000Y. Goffs Million. BBA (Ire). The dam, an Irish 9f winner, is a half-sister to six winners including the Irish Group 3 placed Beautiful Fire. The second dam, Beautiful France (by Sadler's Wells), an Irish 9f winner, is a half-sister to seven winners including the Irish listed 9f winner Rimpa and to the unraced dam of the St Leger winner Scorpion and the US Grade 2 winner Memories.
'He's going to make a two year old, he's forward-

going and has done a couple of bits of work upsides. He goes nicely he may be a horse we'll give a run before seeing if he's good enough for Royal Ascot.'

721. CHATEAUNEUF (IRE) ★★★
b.f. Marju – Night Eyes (Night Shift)
March 31. First foal. €100,000Y. Goffs Million. BBA (Ire). The dam was placed twice in France at three years and is a half-sister to the French listed winner and Group 2 placed Messoeurs. The second dam, Sweet Blue Eyes (by Seeking The Gold), is a placed half-sister to four winners. *'She's done a couple of fast bits of work and the lads say she has plenty of ability. Not at all backward and we should have her out in May.'*

722. CHERISH THE MOMENT (IRE) ★★
b.c. Galileo – Belleclaire (Bigstone)
March 20. Fourth foal. €150,000Y. Goffs Million. BBA (Ire). Half-brother to the fair Irish 1m winner Clonard (by Revoque). The dam is an unraced half-sister to four minor winners. The second dam, Bellissi (by Bluebird), is a sister to the Group 3 7f Concorde Stakes winner Wild Bluebell and a half-sister to six winners including the Group 1 Moyglare Stud Stakes winner Priory Belle. *'He was a bonny little horse that's done well and he's grown into a nice horse now. He's a good mover but the way he's bred he'll need a bit of time. I think he'll be out around June or July.'*

723. DABBERS CHIEF (USA) ★★★★
b.c. Broken Vow – Grey Matter (Housebuster)
February 13. Seventh foal. €120,000Y. Goffs Million. BBA (Ire). Half-brother to the 2007 two year old Wind Me Up (by Pleasant Tap), to the minor US stakes winner Chief What It Is (by Crafty Prospector), the US stakes-placed winner Lia's Luck (by Smoke Glacken) and 2 minor US winners by Souvenir Copy and Holy Bull. The dam, a minor US winner at two and four years, is a half-sister to eight winners. The second dam, Aubegris (by Green Forest), a minor winner of four races in the USA, is a half-sister to three stakes winners including the Italian 1,000 Guineas and Italian Oaks winner Miss Gris.

'The sire has been doing particularly well at the breeze-up sales in America. This is a nice horse that's shown plenty and we were actually thinking of running him in the Brocklesbury at Doncaster but we decided to wait a bit and aim him at the Craven meeting instead. He's a forward horse with a nice temperament and a strong individual. He settles well, so he should stay six furlongs OK.'

724. DAMIEN (IRE) ★★★
gr.c. Namid – Miss Shaan (Darshaan)
April 20. Seventh foal. 32,000Y. Doncaster St Leger. BBA (Ire). Half-brother to two minor two year old winners in France by Welkin and Homme de Roi. The dam is an unplaced half-sister to eight winners abroad. The second dam, Miss Mendez (by Bellypha), won twice at three years in France and is a sister to the Prix du Moulin winner Mendez. *'A nice, well-balanced colt, he's going to make a two year old and he's shown plenty of speed. Once he's got over a bout of sore shins he'll be the type for six or seven furlongs.'*

725. DESERT FEVER ★★★
b.c. Dubai Destination – Gaijin (Caerleon)
April 23. Thirteenth foal. 26,000Y. Tattersalls October 1. Highflyer Bloodstock. Half-brother to seven winners including the high-class 7f to 11f winner Hawksley Hill (by Rahy), winner of the Arcadia Handicap, El Rincon Handicap and San Francisco Mile (all US Grade 2 events), the US winner of four races Miss Natural (by Sir Harry Lewis), the fair 6f winner First Approval (by Royal Applause) and the Italian two year old winner Escape To Victory (by Salse and herself dam of the triple Group 3 winning sprinter Benbaun). The dam, a useful two year old 6f winner, is a full or half-sister to five winners including Thousla Rock, winner of the Group 3 Premio Umbria and third in the Diadem Stakes. The second dam, Resooka (by Godswalk), is an unraced half-sister to the Group 1 Nunthorpe Stakes winner So Factual and the Group 3 July Stakes winner Bold Fact. *'A nice, big colt with a lovely temperament. We haven't pressed any buttons with him and I*

would have thought we'd wait for the six furlong races. A good-looking colt with every-thing going for him at the moment.'

726. EQUININE (IRE) ★★★

ch.f. Namid – Goldilocks (Caerleon)
February 20. Seventh foal. €65,000Y. Goffs Million. BBA (Ire). Half-sister to the Irish 1m winner and listed-placed Dryandra (by Desert Prince) and to the quite useful 1m (at two years) to 14.5f winner Nessen Dorma (by Entrepreneur). The dam, a fair two year old 1m all-weather winner, is a half-sister to two winners. The second dam, Darayna (by Shernazar), a listed-placed winner of two races over 7f and 1m at three years, is a half-sister to three winners.
'A nice filly, very strongly made and typical of the sire. We'll start her off over six furlongs in May.'

727. FARAWAY FLOWER ★★★★

b.f. Distant View – Silver Star (Zafonic)
March 14. The dam won over 1m at two years in France, was listed placed over 1m at three years and is a sister to the champion European two year old Xaar (winner of the Group 1 Dewhurst Stakes and the Group 1 Prix de la Salamandre) and a half-sister to the Group 3 10.5f Prix Corrida winner Diese and the Group 3 1m Prix Quincey winner Masterclass. The second dam, Monroe (by Sir Ivor), a useful Irish 5f and 6f winner, is a sister to the good two year old Gielgud and to the very smart Malinowski and a half-sister to the dual Grade 1 winner Blush With Pride and to Sex Appeal. the dam of El Gran Senor and Try My Best. (Khalid Abdulla).
'She's a lovely, rangy filly, with a big stride. She's pretty forward going and you could get her ready whenever you wanted really but she'll benefit from a bit more time. A filly that stands out in the string.'

728. FEATHERWEIGHT (IRE) ★★★

ch.f. Fantastic Light – Dancing Feather (Suave Dancer)
April 9. Seventh foal. 27,000Y. Tattersalls October 2. Ed Dunlop. Half-sister to the fairly useful 1m (listed) and 9f winner of four races at four years Wagtail (by Cape Cross), to the fairly useful two year old 7f winner and listed placed Feathers Flying (by Royal Applause), the quite useful all-weather 1m (at two years) and 8.5f winner King's Empire (by Second Empire) and the quite useful two year old dual 6f winner Feather Boa (by Sri Pekan). The dam, a fair four year old 1m winner, stayed 12f and is a half-sister to eight winners including the Group 3 Prix Cleopatre winner Spring Oak and the 10f Lupe Stakes winner Fragrant Hill (herself dam of the French Group 1 winner Fragrant Mix). The second dam, English Spring (by Grey Dawn II), won seven races from 1m to 10f including the Group 2 Prince of Wales's Stakes and is a half-sister to the US Grade 1 winner Dance of Life.
'This filly is quite similar to her mother and all she wants to do is please. She's been sent home for a holiday but when she returns in mid-summer it won't take long to get her ready.'

729. FISADARA ★★★

b.f. Nayef – Success Story (Sharrood)
February 22. Ninth foal. Half-sister to the useful 10f and 12f listed winner Film Script (by Unfuwain), to the fairly useful 6f and 7f and subsequent US stakes winner National Park (by Common Grounds), the fair 7f all-weather winner Barney McGrew (by Mark Of Esteem) and the fair 8.5f and 10f winner Champagne (by Efisio). The dam, a modest 10f winner, is a half-sister to seven winners including the Group 2 13.5f Prix de Pomone winner Interlude. The second dam, Starlet, a smart 10f and 12f performer, won a Group 2 event in Germany and is a half-sister to eight winners including the US Grade 1 winner Unknown Quantity.
'A very scopey filly, she's done nothing wrong at all and everyone who rides her seems to like her. The way she's bred we'll probably wait for the seven furlong maidens. Nayef did really well with his first crop last year.'

730. FORTUNATE BID (IRE) ★★★★

ch.c. Modigliani – Mystery Bid (Auction Ring)
March 7. Fifteenth foal. 30,000Y. Doncaster St Leger. BBA (Ire). Half-brother to the quite useful

10f and hurdles winner Mystery Lot (by Revoque), to the quite useful two year old 7f winner Spy, the fair two year old 5f winner Keep Tapping (both by Mac's Imp), the fair 12f winner Secret Service (by Classic Secret), the modest 1m and 10f winner Contract Bridge (by Contract Law) and the moderate 1m winner Secret Tender (by Beckett). The dam was placed twice and stayed 12f and is a full or half-sister to five winners including the listed Ben Marshall Stakes winner Cresta Auction. The second dam, Baby Clair (by Gulf Pearl), won once at two years.

'He was a very nice yearling and pleased us over the winter. He just had a touch of sore shins, so he's just getting over that now and he's certain to make a two year old, probably over six or seven furlongs.'

731. GLEN MOLLY (IRE) ★★★★

b.f. Danetime – Sonorous (Ashkalani)
January 25. Second foal. €110,000Y. Goffs Million. BBA (Ire). The dam, an Irish 1m and 10f winner, was listed-placed and is a half-sister to four winners. The second dam, Nymphs Echo (by Mujtahid), is an unraced sister to the two year old winner and Group 3 Fred Darling Stakes second Glen Rosie and a half-sister to five winners including the Group 3 10f Derrinstown Stud Derby Trial and triple US stakes winner Artema.

'She's a lovely, attractive filly, not over-big but well-balanced and we'll start her off at six furlongs before stepping her up. An athletic type of filly, she's going to make a two year old and I think the Danetime fillies look particularly nice.'

732. GOLDEN ROSIE (IRE) ★★★★

ch.f. Exceed And Excel – Kelsey Rose (Most Welcome)
April 16. Third foal. 55,000Y. Tattersalls October 2. BBA (Ire). Half-sister to Distant Drummer (by Distant Music), unplaced in one start in Ireland at two years in 2007. The dam, a fairly useful two year old 5f winner of three races, was listed-placed three times and is a half-sister to three winners. The second dam, Duxyana (by Cyrano de Bergerac), is an

unraced half-sister to seven winners including the dam of the Group 2 Mill Reef Stakes winner Indian Rocket.

'She's a filly that improved an awful lot over the winter, we have a few Exceed And Excels and they're all nice. We like this filly very much, she ought to start off at six furlongs, she has a lovely action and is a well-balanced filly.'

733. HAIL PROMENADER (IRE) ★★★

b.c. Acclamation – Tribal Rite (Be My Native)
April 8. Sixteenth foal. €40,000Y. Goffs Million. BBA (Ire). Half-sister to the useful two year old 7f winner Arminius (by Shinko Forest), to the useful two year old 6f and 1m Italian listed winner Silent Tribute (by Lion Cavern), the fair 12.3f winner Danesrath (by Danehill), the fair Irish 6f and 7f winner Scalp (by Thatching) and the Italian two year old winner Back Tribal (by Mukaddamah). The dam, a fairly useful Italian two year old listed 6f and three year old 10f winner, is a half-sister to five winners including the Middle Park Stakes winner Balla Cove, the US stakes winner Burning Issue and the Irish listed winner Blasted Heath. The second dam, Coven (by Sassafras), won four races at three years in Ireland from 6f to 10f and is a half-sister to four winners.

'Just like our other Acclamation's, he's a very straightforward colt, very forward going and there's absolutely nothing wrong with him. Six furlongs in June should suit him well.'

734. HAPIPI ★★★★

ch.f. Bertolini – Arian Da (Superlative)
April 11. Sixth foal. 100,000Y. Doncaster St Leger. BBA (Ire). Sister to the smart 5f (at two years) and listed 6f and 7f winner Prime Defender and half-sister to the 2007 two year old Yattendon (by Compton Place). The dam, a fair two year old 5f winner, is a full or half-sister to seven winners including the minor US stakes placed Northern Cache. The second dam, Nell Of The North (by Canadian Gil), won five races in the USA and is a sister to the US Grade 2 winner Sprink.

'She's just taking a bit of time to mature and fill her frame. You could probably get on with her and run her now but she'll benefit if we're a bit more patient. She has a good temperament and hasn't done anything wrong. Improving every day and one to watch out for.'

735. HENRI CLEWS (IRE) ★★★
b.c. Sadler's Wells – Adjalisa (Darshaan)
April 22. Tenth foal. €55,000Y. Goffs Million. BBA (Ire). Half-brother to the listed Marble Hill Stakes and Group 1 Heinz 57 Phoenix Stakes second Access All Areas (by Approach The Bench), to the fair four year old 9f winner Golden Legend (by Last Tycoon), the Turkish winner of eight races Kurtaran (by Danehill) and a winner over hurdles by Desert Prince. The dam was placed once over 7f at four years and is a half-sister to five winners including the listed Leopardstown 2,000 Guineas Trial winner and Group 1 placed Adjareli. The second dam, Adjriyna (by Top Ville), won over 8.5f and is a half-sister to five winners.
'We thought we bought him quite well, particularly as the Sadler's Wells – Darshaan cross is about as good as you can get. If you saw him at the sales and again now you wouldn't recognise the horse. All he's done is thrive, he has a very good action and temperament and he's not going to be slow. We'll probably get on with him in mid-season.'

736. HIGH HEELED (IRE) ★★★
b.f. High Chaparral – Uncharted Haven (Turtle Island)
April 24. Third foal. €110,000Y. Goffs Million. BBA (Ire). The dam, a French two year old 1m and subsequent US Grade 2 San Clemente Handicap winner, is a half-sister to four winners including the useful two year old 7f winner Torinmoor. The second dam, Tochar Ban (by Assert), a quite useful 10f winner, is a half-sister to six winners.
'She's quite a character this filly, very light on her feet and well-balanced. She could be anything. We like the High Chaparral's we've had and this filly is just growing at the moment but she shows speed. She'll make a two year old in mid-summer.'

737. HIGH TWELVE (USA) ★★★
b.c. Giant's Causeway – Saree (Barathea)
January 13. First foal. 375,000Y. Tattersalls October 1. M H Goodbody. The dam, a fairly useful two year old 7f winner, subsequently won once at three years in the USA and was Grade 3 placed in Canada and is a sister to the two year old Group 1 6f Cheveley Park Stakes winner Magical Romance and a half-sister to the high-class 1m (at two years), Oaks, Irish Oaks And Yorkshire Oaks winner Alexandrova. The second dam, Shouk (by Shirley Heights), a quite useful 10.5f winner, is closely related to the listed winner and Group 3 Park Hill Stakes third Puce and a half-sister to seven winners.
'He's shown plenty of speed up to now, he just took a bit of time to mature over the winter. He cost plenty but he's a lovely, good-looking colt, well-balanced and we'll wait for the seven furlong races.'

738. INFIRAAD ★★★
ch.c. Haafhd – Razzle (Green Desert)
March 8. Second foal. 160,000Y. Tattersalls October 2. Shadwell Estate Co. The dam, a modest 10f placed two year old, is a sister to the very smart triple Group 3 6f and 7f winner and sire Desert Style and a half-sister to two winners. The second dam, Organza (by High Top), a useful three year old 10f winner, is a full or half-sister to seven winners including the Group 1 Prix de la Foret winner Brocade. herself the dam of Barathea and Gossamer.
'He's a very big horse, a bit gross at the moment but as the season goes on he'll improve and he has a good temperament and a good action. We like him.'

739. INTENSE ★★
b.f. Dansili – Modesta (Sadler's Wells).
March 9. First foal. The dam, a useful 11.5f and listed 14f winner, is closely related to the Oaks, Fillies Mile, Musidora Stakes and May Hill Stakes winner Reams of Verse (by Nureyev), the smart two year old 1m winner and Group-placed High Walden (by El Gran Senor) and the multiple 10f to 12f winner Modesto (by Al Nasr) and a half-sister to the high-class Group 1 10f Coral Eclipse

Stakes and Group 1 10f Phoenix Champion Stakes winner Elmaamul (by Diesis), the very useful 7f (at two years) and US Grade 3 8.5f winner Modernise (by Known Fact), the quite useful 11f winner and listed-placed Midsummer (by Kingmambo) and the quite useful two year old 7.5f winner Modern Day (by Dayjur). The second dam, Modena (by Roberto), is an unraced half-sister to the smart two year old 7f winner and Queen Elizabeth II Stakes third Zaizafon. herself the dam of Zafonic. (Khalid Abdulla).

'We haven't had her very long and she's also been growing so we don't know a lot about her. She's a little bit hot but she has a nice action and we'll just have to give her time to fill her frame.'

740. KEFALONIA (USA) ★★★★
gr.f. Mizzen Mast – Zante (Zafonic)
April 25. The dam, a very useful 1m and listed 10f winner, is a half-sister to the 11f winner and dual US Grade 1 second Requete. The second dam, Danthonia (by Northern Dancer), a quite useful two year old 5f winner, is closely related to the Group 3 1m Prix Quincey winner Masterclass and a half-sister to the Group 3 10.5f Prix Corrida winner Diese. (Khalid Abdulla).

'She's a lovely looking filly with plenty of size and scope and a great temperament. One for the back-end of the season but she's a lovely filly you could see winning an Oaks.'

741. KYLLORIEN ★★★
b.f. Kyllachy – L'Amour (Gone West)
January 26. Fourth foal. Half-sister to the Dubai 9f and 12f winner Lover Boy (by Alhaarth). The dam, a quite useful three year old 1m winner, is a half-sister to three winners including the Grade 2 Long Island Handicap, Group 3 May Hill Stakes and Group 3 Prestige Stakes winner Midnight Line. The second dam, Midnight Air (by Green Dancer), won the Group 3 1m May Hill Stakes at two years and is a half-sister to seven minor winners and to the placed dam of the Group 1 5f Prix de l'Abbaye winner Imperial Beauty.

'We've done a couple of bits of work with her and we won't be hanging around with her. Her conformation isn't the best but she's all heart and determination.'

742. LA DE TWO (IRE) ★★★
ch.c. Galileo – Firecrest (Darshaan)
May 9. Fifth foal. 115,000Y. Tattersalls December. Not sold. Half-brother to the fair 2007 two year old 7f all-weather winner Phoenix Flight (by Hawk Wing), to the quite useful 12.4f winner Grey Plover (by Alzao) and the fair 12f winner Lady Songbird (by Selkirk). The dam won five races at around 12f including the listed Galtres Stakes and is a half-sister to four minor winners. The second dam, Trefoil (by Blakeney), won three races in France and is a half-sister to six winners including the French Group 2 First Prayer, the US Grade 3 winner Water Lily (herself dam of the Grade 1 winner Talinum) and the dam of the Melbourne Cup winner Jeune.

'He's the most beautiful mover, so light on his feet and it's quite exciting to see a Galileo go up there as if he's got it all at the moment. His temperament is just a little hot and we're just trying to get him nice and settled at the moment.'

743. LA MARSEILLAISE (IRE) ★★★
ch.f. Medicean – Saturnalia
(Cadeaux Genereux)
March 25. Second foal. 50,000Y. Tattersalls October 1. BBA (Ire). Half-sister to the unplaced 2007 two year old Listed Art (by Night Shift). The dam is an unplaced sister to the German Group 3 6.5f winner Toylsome and a half-sister to two winners. The second dam, Treasure Trove (by The Minstrel), is a placed half-sister to the US Graded stakes winners Dance Parade and Ocean Queen.

'We really liked her at the Sales but she's just changed shape since we bought her. Just recently she's started to come to herself again and looks in better shape now. A bit backward at the moment, but when she's ready she isn't going to be slow.'

744. LASSARINA (IRE) ★★★
b.f. Sakhee – Kalanda (Desert King)

May 8. Third foal. 37,000Y. Tattersalls October 1. BBA (Ire). The dam is an unplaced half-sister to three winners including the Group 1 July Cup winner Continent. The second dam, Krisia (by Kris), won over 12f and is a half-sister to six winners including the French listed 10.5f and 12f winner Short Pause.

'She's a well-made filly with a nice action and although she's had one or two problems they were nothing major. She's certainly going to make a two year old and I would have thought six furlongs would be her starting point.'

745. LEGISLATE ★★★
b.c. Dansili – Shining Water (Kalaglow)

March 11. Closely related to the very useful two year old 7f winner and Group 1 Italian Oaks second Bright And Clear (by Danehill) and half-brother to the high-class Group 1 1m Ciga Grand Criterium and Group 2 10.4f Dante Stakes winner Tenby, to the very useful 1m (at two years) and 10f winner Bright Water, the useful two year old 7f and 1m winner River Usk, the fair 12.3f winner Bayswater (all by Caerleon), the very useful two year old 7f winner and Group 1 1m Racing Post Trophy second Bude (by Dancing Brave), the useful 12f winners Glistening (by Sadler's Wells) and Indian File (by Indian Ridge) and the quite useful 9f and 10f winner Reflecting (by Ahonoora). The dam was a very useful winner of the Group 3 7f Solario Stakes and was placed in the Group 2 Park Hill Stakes. The second dam, Idle Waters (by Mill Reef), was a smart winner of three races including the Park Hill Stakes. (Khalid Abdulla).

'A nice colt that's done nothing wrong. Very attractive with a very nice action, he's one for the late summer. He's shown enough to say he's quite forward and he'll just benefit with a bit more time.'

746. MAJESTIC LADY ★★★★
b.f. Royal Applause – Kiris World
(Distant Relative)

January 27. Second foal. 26,000Y. Doncaster St Leger. BBA (Ire). The dam won three races over 5f and 6f in Italy at three years including a Group 3 event and is a half-sister to the Italian

listed winner Solzah. The second dam, Solar Dawn (by Soviet Star), is a placed half-sister to three winners.

'She's grown recently and has done really well. We're delighted with her and it looks like she's going to be fast. We'll probably set her off at six furlongs in May or June.'

747. MAKHAALEB (IRE) ★★★★
b.c. Haafhd – Summerhill Parkes (Zafonic)

January 30. Second foal. Half-brother to the fair 2007 two year old 8.5f winner Seleet (by Sakhee). The dam, a useful three year old listed 6f winner, is a half-sister to numerous winners including the useful two year old 5f and 6f winner Ace Of Parkes, the useful dual 5f winner and Moyglare, Lowther and Queen Mary Stakes placed My Melody Parkes and the useful winner of 13 races over 5f Lucky Parkes. The dam was a fair winner of a 6f seller at three years. (Hamdan Al-Maktoum).

'This horse is so similar to his dad it's untrue. He has all the same characteristics – cheeky, but he looks like he's got ability! All the riders like him and he does everything easily. One to look out for hopefully. We're certainly not going to run him over five furlongs because he'll be better off if we give him a bit of time.'

748. MASSILAH ★★★
b.f. Namid – Loveleaves (Polar Falcon)

March 21. Third foal. 90,000Y. Doncaster St Leger. Shadwell Estate Co. Half-sister to the very smart Group 3 7f Supreme Stakes winner of five races Lovelace (by Royal Applause). The dam, a fairly useful 8.3f winner, is a half-sister to four winners. The second dam, Rash (by Pursuit Of Love), is an unraced half-sister to six winners including the useful two year old dual 6f winner Maid For The Hills and the useful two year old 5f and 6f winner Maid For Walking (herself dam of the US Grade 1 winner Stroll).

'A nice, big filly, she's quite well-balanced and although her joints are slightly immature we'll deal with them. A quality filly that wants a bit of time and we'll probably wait for seven furlongs.'

749. MASTER FONG (IRE) ★★★
b.c. Dr Fong – Last Cry (Peintre Celebre)
February 28. First foal. 35,000Y. Doncaster St Leger. BBA (Ire). The dam, a three year old 1m winner and listed-placed in France, is a half-sister to three winners. The second dam, Last Dream (by Alzao), won once at three years and is a half-sister to the French Group 1 winners Fijar Tango and Lost World.
'He looks like he'd make a fast two year old and yet he's out of a Peintre Celebre mare so we'll just take our time and introduce him in the middle of the year. He does show a bit of toe which is a good sign and he's a bonny little horse.'

750. MID WICKET (USA) ★★★★
b.c. Strong Hope – Sunday Bazaar (Nureyev)
May 17. Twelfth foal. Half-brother to the unraced 2007 two year old Promise Maker (by Empire Maker) and to several winners including the Group 3 11.5f Lingfield Derby Trial winner and Group 1 Grand Prix de Saint-Cloud second Perfect Sunday (by Quest For Fame), the smart US 10f winner Barter Town (by Cox's Ridge), the fair 8.6f to 10f winner Gala Sunday (by Lear Fan) and the fair 1m and hurdles winner Southern Bazaar (by Southern Halo). The won over 12f in France and is a half-sister to numerous winners including the US Grade 1 winners Bates Motel and Hatim and the Horris Hill Stakes winner Super Asset. (Khalid Abdulla). 'The nicest horse we've had out of this mare. A lovely looking colt, he has a good action and a good temperament but we haven't asked any questions of him yet. We'll start him off at seven furlongs.'

751. MISDAQEYA ★★★
br.f. Red Ransom – Crystal Power (Pleasant Colony)
March 21. Third foal. 65,000Y. Tattersalls October 2. Shadwell Estate Co. Half-sister to Bozeman Trail (by Averti), a modest fourth over 1m at two years in 2007. The dam won once at three years in the USA and is a half-sister to four winners including the US Grade 1 Flower Bowl Invitational Handicap winner Chelsey Flower. The second dam, Chelsey Dancer (by Affirmed), is an unplaced half-sister to ten winners. (Hamdan Al Maktoum).
'A nice, rangy filly, she's been growing but has a nice temperament and a good action. She'll make a two year old and she'll have a bit of quality.'

752. MISTER DEE BEE (IRE) ★★★★
b.c. Orpen – Acidanthera (Alzao)
February 24. Sixth foal. 32,000Y. Doncaster St Leger. BBA (Ire). Half-brother to the fairly useful dual 6f winner (including at two years) He's A Humbug and to the Spanish 1m and 10f winner Pacific Star (both by Tagula). The dam, a quite useful three year old 7.5f winner, is a half-sister to two winners. The second dam, Amaranthus (by Shirley Heights), is an unraced half-sister to six winners including the dam of the Group winners Wooton Rivers and Magellano.
'He was bought from Doncaster with the Sales race in mind. A lovely, big horse with plenty of scope and size. His action isn't too heavy and we'll probably run him over six furlongs in July.'

753. MR MELODIOUS ★★★
ch.c. Green Tune – Moly (Anabaa)
February 24. Third foal. 30,000Y. Tattersalls October 2. Highflyer Bloodstock. The dam, a French two year old 1m winner, is a half-sister to six winners. The second dam, Moon Review (by Irish River), won three races in France and is a half-sister to six winners.
'We ran him in the Brocklesbury because he'd been working great and he's a very straightforward horse. He'll improve a lot for that run, his temperament is such that he'll take it in and improve. He's come out of the race great and we might wait for the six furlong races now.'

754. MR PROLIFIC ★★★★
b.c. Haafhd – Rumpipumpy (Shirley Heights)
March 20. Fifth foal. 44,000Y. Tattersalls October 1. Highflyer Bloodstock. Half-brother to Ruby Light (by Fantastic Light), unplaced in two starts at two years in 2007, to the fairly useful 6f and 7f winner Banjo Patterson (by Green Desert) and the quite useful two year old 7f winner Persian Jasmine (by Dynaformer). The

dam won six races in the USA including the Grade 2 Diana Handicap and is a half-sister to ten winners including the Irish 1,000 Guineas winner Classic Park. The second dam, Wanton (by Kris), a useful two year old 5f winner and third in the Group 2 Flying Childers Stakes, is a half-sister to eight winners.

'A lovely model of a horse, he has a great brain and a good action. He looks very much like his dad and he'll certainly make a two year old over six furlongs but being out of a Shirley Heights mare he'll certainly stay further.'

755. MUSTAQER (IRE) ★★

b.c. Dalakhani – Al Ihtithar (Barathea)
February 16. Second foal. The dam, a very useful 10f and 10.3f listed winner, is a sister to the useful 7f to 11f winner Ihtiraz and a half-sister to numerous winners including the Group 3 Prix Berteux winner Samsaam, the 6f (at two years) to 11f winner Yarob and the 7f to 11f winner Ihtiraz (all 3 useful). The second dam, Azyaa (by Kris), a useful 7.5f winner, is a half-sister to five winners.

'This is the first Dalakhani we've had and he's a good-looking horse. He's been a little bit tricky training-wise but once we got him into a routine with plenty of work that hasn't been a problem. We'll wait until the autumn for him.'

756. MY SWEET GEORGIA (IRE) ★★★

b.f. Royal Applause – Harda Arda (Nureyev)
April 4. Fifth foal. 80,000Y. Tattersalls October 2. Peter Doyle. Half-sister to the minor US stakes winner Strike Rate (by Smart Strike), to the modest 10.5f winner Deccan Express (by Grand Lodge) and a minor US winner by A P Indy. The dam, a minor Irish three year old 9f winner, is a half-sister to eight winners including the Group 2 10f Derrinstown Stud Derby Trial and dual US Grade 2 winner Phantom Breeze. The second dam, Ask The Wind (by Run The Gantlet), was a useful winner of three races from 7f to 10f including the listed Hard Fought Stakes, was fourth in the Ribblesdale Stakes and is a half-sister to four minor winners.

'A very good-looking filly. We did a bit of work with her early on and then put her away to give her a

bit more time. A filly with a beautiful action and there's absolutely nothing wrong with her at all.'

757. OUQBA ★★★★ ♠

b.c. Red Ransom – Dancing Mirage (Machiavellian)
April 18. Fifth foal. 140,000Y. Doncaster St Leger. Shadwell Estate Co. Half-brother to the quite useful 2007 1m winner Robby Bobby (by Selkirk), to the very useful 7f (at two years) and 12f winner and listed-placed Foxhaven (by Unfuwain) and the quite useful 8.3f (at two years) and 12.5f winner Swiss Act (by Act One). The dam, a quite useful two year old 7f winner, is a half-sister to three winners including the dam of the good Hong Kong horse Housemaster. The second dam, Kraemer (by Lyphard), winner of the listed 8.5f Bay Meadows Oaks, is a half-sister to five winners including the Prix du Rond-Point and Prix d'Astarte winner Shaanxi.

'He's certainly going to make a two year old, he has a great temperament and you wouldn't know you had him in the yard. He's done one bit of work, he did it great and so he could well be out at the Craven meeting.' This colt did indeed start his career at The Craven meeting and looked very promising.

758. PARK LANE ★★

b.c. Royal Applause – Kazeem (Darshaan)
March 12. Fourth foal. 55,000Y. Tattersalls October 3. Charlie Gordon-Watson. Half-brother to King's Kazeem (by King's Best), placed fourth once over 7f at two years in 2007 and to the fair three year old 7f winner Azeema (by Averti). The dam is an unplaced sister to the winner and subsequent US Grade 2 winner Treasurer and a half-sister to six minor winners. The second dam, Kanz (by The Minstrel), won the Group 3 8.5f Princess Elizabeth Stakes and is a half-sister to nine winners including the dams of the Group 1 winners Ensconse, Diamond Shoal and Glint of Gold.

'He's a very big horse but he's got a good action and we just have to give him the time to fill into his big frame. But he hasn't shown any signs of being slow which is always a worry with a horse as big as he is.'

759. PHOTOGRAPHIC ★★★
b.f. Oasis Dream – Prophecy (Warning)
March 12. Half-sister to the 2007 two year old Group 3 7f Prix Miesque winner Modern Look (by Zamindar), to the useful listed 6f winner Arabesque, to the useful 5f and 6f winner Threat (both by Zafonic), the quite useful 7f and 9f winner Rule Of Life (by Dansili) and the quite useful three year old 7f winner Shoot (by Barathea). The dam was a very useful winner of the Group 1 6f Cheveley Park Stakes and was second in the Group 3 7f Nell Gwyn Stakes. The second dam, Andaleeb (by Lyphard), won the Group 3 12f Lancashire Oaks, was fourth in the Yorkshire Oaks and is out of the Kentucky Oaks winner Bag Of Tunes. (Khalid Abdulla).
'A filly with a very good temperament, she's a gem to deal with. A little bit light at the moment so we'll give her a bit of time to bulk up and grow. She has a good action and both the Oasis Dream's we have seem very nice.'

760. PURPLE SAGE (IRE) ★★★
b.f. Danehill Dancer – Kylemore (Sadler's Wells)
February 23. Fifth foal. €155,000Y. Goffs Million. BBA (Ire). Half-sister to the unraced 2007 two year old Annabelle's Charm (by Indian Ridge). The dam ran twice unplaced and is a sister to the Group 1 Criterium de Saint-Cloud and Grade 1 Canadian International Stakes winner Ballingarry and to the Group 1 1m Racing Post Trophy winner Aristotle and a half-sister to the Group 1 St James's Palace Stakes and Prix Jean Prat winner Starborough. The second dam, Flamenco Wave (by Desert Wine), won the Group 1 6f Moyglare Stud Stakes and is a half-sister to three winners.
'She's quite an angular, rangy filly with a good action. She has her own mind, so that's a good sign for a filly but we'll take our time with her and probably set her off around August time over seven furlongs.'

761. RULER OF ALL (IRE) ★★★★
b.c. Sadler's Wells – Shabby Chic (Red Ransom)
April 11. Sixth foal. 340,000Y. Tattersalls October 1. M H Goodbody. Half-sister to the 1m (at two years) and Group 2 Italian Oaks winner Fashion Statement (by Rainbow Quest) and to the fairly useful dual 12f winner Kerriemuir Lass (by Celtic Swing). The dam won the listed 10f Prix de Liancourt and was third in both the Grade 1 Yellow Ribbon Stakes and the Group 3 Prix Chloe. She is a sister to the Oaks winner Casual Look and a half-sister to three winners. The second dam, Style Setter (by Manila), a stakes-placed winner of three races in the USA, is a half-sister to two winners.
'We paid a lot of money for him as a yearling, he's a great looking colt and we haven't asked any questions of him as yet, but at the moment he looks to have it all. We'll start him off at seven furlongs and he appears to have plenty of speed.'

762. SAYYAAF ★★★
ch.c. Alhaarth – Almurooj (Zafonic)
April 26. Seventh foal. Brother to the useful listed 6f winner Judhoor and half-brother to the fairly useful 7f and 1m winner Muzher (by Indian Ridge) and the quite useful two year old 6f winner Al Sifaat (by Unfuwain). The dam, a moderate 5f and 6f placed maiden, is a half-sister to seven winners including the smart 6f (at two years), Group 2 7f Challenge Stakes and Group 3 7f Greenham Stakes winner Munir and the very useful Irish 1m listed stakes winner and Group 1 Coronation Stakes second Hasbah. The second dam, Al Bahathri (by Blushing Groom), was a high-class winner of six races from 6f to 1m, notably the Irish 1,000 Guineas and the Coronation Stakes. (Hamdan Al Maktoum).
'A bonny little horse, he's very straightforward and forward-going. We'll probably crack on with him and run him in June as he's not backward at all.'

763. SEEK N'DESTROY (IRE) ★★★★
b.c. Exceed And Excel – Very Nice (Daylami)
April 4. First foal. 60,000Y. Tattersalls October 2. BBA (Ire). The dam is an unraced half-sister to two winners. The second dam, All Time Great (by Night Shift), a fairly useful two year old 6f winner and fourth in the 7.3f Fred Darling Stakes, is closely related to the Dante Stakes and Craven Stakes winner Alnasr Alwasheek and a half-sister to the Juddmonte International Stakes winner

One So Wonderful and the Rockfel Stakes winner Relatively Special.

'He's a colt that's shown plenty, he has a good temperament and he's not going to be backward. We'll run him early on, he's a good-looking colt with size, scope and a good action.'

764. SENATORIAL ★★★★
b.c. Oasis Dream – Stormy Channel (Storm Cat)
March 24. The dam, a fairly useful 1m winner, is a half-sister to numerous winners including the very useful 7f winner Akimbo, the useful listed 1m winner Insinuate and the useful 6f and 7f winner and listed-placed Imroz. The second dam, All At Sea (by Riverman), a high-class winner of five races from 1m to 10.4f including the Group 1 Prix du Moulin, the Musidora Stakes and the Pretty Polly Stakes, was second in the Oaks, the Juddmonte International and the Nassau Stakes and is a half-sister to the Free Handicap winner Over the Ocean, the listed 10f winner Quandary and the US stakes winner Full Virtue. (Khalid Abdulla).

'One of those we'll race sooner rather than later. He's done nothing wrong at all, he's sharp and certainly looks like he'll warrant a place at Royal Ascot. A well-made, well-balanced colt.'

765. SERVOCA (CAN) ★★★★
gr.c. El Prado – Cinderellaslipper (Touch Gold)
March 8. First foal. €130,000Y. Goffs Million. BBA (Ire). The dam is an unplaced half-sister to two winners including the Peruvian Grade 1 winner and champion miler Eithan. The second dam, Double Slippers (by Thirty Eight Paces), won 2 minor races in the USA.

'A very straightforward colt, he has a very low action and will probably want fast ground. He looks to be speedy and six furlongs should be right up his street.'

766. TAQARUB ★★
b.f. Marju – Maraatib (Green Desert)
May 24. Half-sister to the very useful two year old listed 5f winner and subsequent French three year old 5f listed winner Khasayl, the quite useful 10f and hurdles winner of 10 races Mazeed (both by Lycius), the useful listed two

year old 7f winner Muklah (by Singspiel), the useful three year old dual 7f winner Al Aali (by Lahib), the fairly useful 6f winner Muwajaha (by Night Shift), the quite useful 7f winner Thabaat (by Pivotal), the quite useful 1m (at two years) and 10f winner Nebl (by Persian Bold) and the fair 6f winner Hewaraat (by Fasliyev). The dam, a quite useful 5f and 6f winner, is a half-sister to six winners. The second dam, Shurooq (by Affirmed), a fairly useful two year old 6f and 7f winner, stayed 12f at three years and is a half-sister to numerous winners including Smasher, winner of the Grade 2 San Felipe Handicap in the USA. (Hamdan Al Maktoum).

'Still in Dubai in early April.'

767. THREE STEPS TO HEAVEN ★★★
b.c. Haafhd – Bella Bianca (Barathea)
March 15. Third foal. 60,000Y. Tattersalls October 1. BBA (Ire). Half-brother to the unplaced 2007 two year old Sarah's Boy (by Nayef) and to the fair two year old 7f winner Bobbish (by Best Of The Bests). The dam, a quite useful two year old 6f winner, is a half-sister to one winner in Italy. The second dam, Alarme Belle (by Warning), a useful Irish dual 6f winner, was listed-placed and is a half-sister to four winners.

'He's a nice, bonny colt and he's just growing at the moment. One for the middle part of the year, he's done nothing wrong at all and he's very light on his feet.'

768. WABI SABI (IRE) ★★★
b.f. Xaar – Taroudannt (Danehill)
February 1. Second foal. €110,000Y. Goffs Million. BBA (Ire). Half-sister to the fair two year old 5f winner Durova (by Soviet Star). The dam is an unraced half-sister to three winners. The second dam, Taibhseach (by Secreto), winner of the listed 7f Blenheim Stakes in Ireland, is a half-sister to five winners including the US triple Grade 1 winner Mi Selecto and the US dual Grade 2 stakes winner Bar Dexter.

'A nice, big, strapping filly, she looks like she's got plenty of speed. She's had a few problems and is a funny shape at the moment but she has a good action and everyone like her. Six or seven furlongs around mid-summer should suit.'

769. WEST LEAKE (IRE) ★★★
b.c. Acclamation – Kilshanny (Groom Dancer)
April 19. Eighth foal. 42,000Y. Doncaster St Leger. BBA (Ire). Brother to the 2007 7f placed two year old Mega Watt and half-brother to the quite useful two year old 5f winner Leitrim Rock, the Italian two year old 7f winner Golden Gables (both by Barathea) and the modest dual 7f winner Shinko Femme (by Shinko Forest). The dam, a fair 11.8f winner, is a half-sister to three winners. The second dam, Kiliniski (by Niniski), a very smart winner of the Group 3 12f Lingfield Oaks Trial, was second in the Yorkshire Oaks and fourth in the Epsom Oaks and is a half-sister to five winners including the dam of the US triple Grade 1 winner Bienamado.
'He did a nice bit of work the other morning, Richard Hills rode him and liked him. We've liked all the Acclamations we've had as they're very professional and get on with their work. This colt would be just the same.'

770. UNNAMED ★★★
b.br.c. Elusive City – Arctic Flight (Polar Falcon)
March 25. Third foal. 46,000Y. Tattersalls December. BBA (Ire). The dam, a modest three year old 7f winner, is a half-sister to five winners including the Group-placed two year old's Lake Pleasant and Power Lake. The second dam, Laugharne (by Known Fact), ran once unplaced and is a half-sister to the Chester Vase winner Dry Dock and to the dams of the champion New Zealand two year old filly Good Faith, the South American Grade 1 winner Band Gypsy, the Group 1 Moyglare Stud Stakes winner Mail The Desert and the multiple Group 1 placed Norse Dancer.
'He's a colt that Dad bought and he really likes him. He's got a very easy action so he should be fast. He looks straightforward and we're still looking for an owner!'

771. UNNAMED ★★★
ch.f. Danehill Dancer – Crystal Curling (Peintre Celebre)
March 31. The dam, a fairly useful two year old 7f winner, is a half-sister to four winners including the 10f winner True Crystal and the 12f winner Time Crystal. The second dam, State Crystal (by High Estate), was a very useful winner of the Group 3 12f Lancashire Oaks and was placed in the Yorkshire Oaks and the Prix Vermeille. She is a half-sister to six winners including the Group 1 Fillies' Mile winner Crystal Music, the Group three winners Dubai Success and Solar Crystal and the Irish Derby third Tchaikovsky.
'She's not the biggest of fillies but she looks very tough and we'll probably wait until mid-season before we run her. She's done nothing wrong.'

772. UNNAMED ★★★
b.c. Noverre – Love In The Mist (Sliver Hawk)
April 15. First foal. €70,000Y. Goffs Million. BBA (Ire). The dam, a fair maiden, was placed fourth once over 6f at two years and is a six winners including the Irish Group 3 winner Raphane. The second dam, Fast Nellie (by Ack Ack), is an unraced sister to the US Grade 1 winner Caline.
'He's worked a few times and done great. He's shown all the signs of being promising and we're still looking for an owner for him.'

773. UNNAMED ★★★
b.c. Nayef – My Funny Valentine (Mukadammah)
February 28. Fifth foal. €110,000Y. Goffs Million. BBA (Ire). Half-brother to three minor winners in Italy by Nashwan, Mark Of Esteem and Singspiel. The dam, a winner of seven races at 2 to four years in Italy, was listed placed 10 times. The second dam, Imperfect Timing (by Coquelin), is an unraced half-sister to six winners.
'A very good-looking colt with a nice, big stride and a good temperament. He'll need a bit of time and will probably want seven furlongs but he's done nothing wrong and all the riders like him.'

JOHN HILLS

774. ASHRAM (IRE) ★★★
ch.c. Indian Haven – Tara's Girl (Fayruz)
March 25. Fifth foal. 70,000Y. Tattersalls October 2. Anthony Stroud. Half-brother to the

very useful 7f and 1m winner (including in the UAE) Blackat Blackitten (by Inchinor) and to the quite useful 6f and 7f winner (including at two years) Triple Two (by Pivotal). The dam, a fairly useful two year old dual 5f winner, was listed placed twice and fourth in the Queen Mary Stakes and is a full or half-sister to five winners. The second dam, Florissa (by Persepolis), a Belgian two year old 7f winner, is a half-sister to a winner over jumps in France. (Mountgrange Stud).

'A very nice horse that holds himself very well. I should imagine he'll make a two year old although his half-brother Blackat Blackitten apparently took a long time to come to hand. This colt will make a two year old by mid-summer and he seems to me to be the type to have the speed for six furlongs before moving up to seven.'

775. CABERNET SAUVIGNON ★★★★
b.c. Dansili – Halcyon Daze (Halling)
February 21. Half-brother to Sergeant Sharpe (by Cadeaux Genereux), a fair fourth once over 7f at two years in 2007. The dam, a quite useful 11.5f winner, is a half-sister to four winners including the very useful 14f winner and listed Lonsdale Stakes fourth Ashgar. The second dam, Ardisia (by Affirmed), a quite useful winner of three races at around 10f, is a half-sister to nine winners including the Oaks, Irish Oaks and Yorkshire Oaks winner Ramruma and the useful listed winners Royal Scimitar and Ausherra (herself the dam of 2 stakes winners). (C N Wright).

'He's a horse that will need some time but he does everything very easily. I think that, along with the Singspiel colt, he's pretty much as good a horse as I've got.'

776. FLAPPER (IRE) ★★
b.f. Selkirk – Pure Spin (Machiavellian)
March 16. Second foal. €135,000Y. Goffs Million. Not sold. Half-sister to the unraced 2007 two year old Emirates Ice (by Pivotal). The dam is an unraced half-sister to four winners including the smart 7f (at two years) and Group 3 10.5f Prix Fille de l'Air winner Goncharova. The

second dam, Pure Grain (by Polish Precedent), won five races including the Group 1 12f Irish Oaks and the Group 1 12f Yorkshire Oaks and is a half-sister to six winners.

'Only just arrived in the yard, she's a beautiful filly but being by Selkirk she's a big, scopey filly that could be anything one day but we're going to give her all the time she needs.'

777. JOHNNY JEWEL (USA) ★★
b.c. Diesis – Seeking The Jewel
(Seeking The Gold)
April 18. Third foal. $40,000Y. Keeneland September. James Delahooke. The dam, a minor winner at four years in the USA, is out of the minor US winner Seattle Drama (by Seattle Slew), herself a half-sister to four winners including the US Grade 1 Dramatic Gold. (Mountgrange Stud).

'A lovely, scopey horse but he does look very backward. He had a nasty cold when he arrived from America and so I don't know much about him yet.'

778. LAYER CAKE ★★
b.c. Monsieur Bond – Blue Indigo (Pistolet Bleu)
April 10. Fifth foal. 26,000Y. Doncaster St Leger. A Skiffington. Half-brother to the useful 1m (at two years) and subsequent US Grade 3 winner Genre (by Orpen). The dam was placed five times in France and is a half-sister to five winners. The second dam, Alcove (by Valdez), is an unplaced half-sister to eight winners including the Breeders Cup Classic winner Arcangues. (Gary & Linnet Woodward).

'I like him, he's always shown natural speed and been naturally balanced. He looks sure to make a two year old although at the moment he's going through a change period and it'll probably be June time before we see him. He does everything very easily and is a two year old that will probably want six furlongs.'

779. MILE HIGH LAD (USA) ★★★
b.c. Sky Mesa – Thunder Warmth
(Thunder Gulch)
March 2. Second foal. 30,000Y. Tattersalls October 2. Not sold. Half-brother to the 2007

US placed two year old Hotzy Thunder (by Touch Gold). The dam is an unplaced half-sister to seven winners including the US Grade 3 winner So Cozy and the dam of the US Grade 1 winner Marlin. The second dam, Special Warmth (by Lucky Mike), won the Grade 2 Arlington-Washington Lassie Stakes. (J Jamgotchian).

'I've started to do a little bit more with him and he's shown some speed. I don't know too much about the stallion except that he's had a nice horse in America. This colt is quite well put together so I'd flag him up as a two year old.'

780. MISS MOJITO (IRE) ★★★★
ch.f. Lucky Story – Lamanka Lass (Woodman)
March 21. 26,000Y. Tattersalls October. Not sold. Half-sister to the 7f (at two years), 1m and subsequent US Grade 2 9f Oak Tree Derby winner Dark Islander (by Singspiel), to the fair all-weather dual 12f winner Crocolat (by Croco Rouge) and a winner in Spain by Desert Prince. The dam, a fair three year old 1m winner, is a half-sister to four winners including the Group 3 Darley Stakes winner Far Lane. The second dam, Pattimech (by Nureyev), won at up to 7f in the USA and is a sister to Annoconnor, winner of the Santa Ana Handicap, the Vanity Handicap and the Ramona Handicap (all Grade 1 9f events) and a half-sister to the Group 1 16f Grand Prix de Paris and the Grade 1 Melbourne Cup winner At Talaq.

'She looks as though she'll be a natural two year old. The sire was a very good two year old himself and this filly is very taking. She's a bit highly strung, as soon as we get a bit of nice weather I'll start to bring her along. As things stand she looks promising, she does everything easily, looks like making a two year old and has natural speed.' TRAINER'S BARGAIN BUY

781. OMNIUM DUKE (IRE) ★★
*ch.c. Indian Haven – Please Be Good
(Prince Of Birds)*
March 15. First foal. €40,000Y. Tattersalls Ireland. A Skiffington. The dam won over 1m at two years in France and is a half-sister to the two year old listed 10f Zetland Stakes winner Forest Magic. The second dam, Adultress (by

Ela-Mana-Mou), is an unraced half-sister to six winners including the Group 3 Prix Chloe winner Adaiyka.

'He's a likeable horse but he looks as though he might take a bit of extra time over the other Indian Haven I have. A very smooth action, he looks more like one for seven furlongs and a mile.'

782. GOLDEN FLIGHT (IRE) ★★★★
*ch.c. Hawk Wing – Cassilis
(Persian Bold)*
February 16. Seventh foal. €40,000Y. Goffs Million. A Skiffington. Half-brother to the fairly useful 5.3f (at two years) and 9f winner and listed-placed Gold Guest (by Vettori) and the modest Irish 10f winner Lynott (by Pivotal). The dam is an unraced half-sister to seven winners including the German Group 3 1m winner Sinyar and to the unraced dam of the US Grade 2 winner Ventiquattrofogli. The second dam, Place Of Honour (by Be My Guest), won once at three years and is out of the Coronation Stakes winner Sutton Place.

'I like this horse, he came from Goffs and I'd say he's a six or seven furlong horse from June onwards. We'll just see how he progresses but he just ticks away and you wouldn't know he was there. A thoroughly likeable two year old and probably as nice as we've got.'

783. QUINSMAN ★★★★
b.c. Singspiel – Penny Cross (Efisio)
March 5. First foal. 50,000Y. Tattersalls October 1. Not sold. The dam, a useful 7f to 8.5f winner of three races including a listed event, is a half-sister to five winners including the smart listed 7f winner and Group 3 placed Priors Lodge. The second dam, Addaya (by Persian Bold), ran once unplaced and is a half-sister to eight winners abroad. (D M Kerr).

'He's got natural ability and is a very, very nice, promising two year old. You wouldn't imagine him being ready until July onwards and he'll be better next year, but if they're any good they tend to show you. I like him as much as anything in the yard.'

784. SWISS LAKE SWEETIE (USA) ★★★
ch.f. Action This Day – Almost Blue
(Mr Greeley)
**March 8. Second foal. 25,000Y. Tattersalls
December. Not sold.** The dam is an unplaced
half-sister to two winners including the dual
listed winner and Group 2 Flying Childers Stakes
second Swiss Lake. The second dam, Blue Iris (by
Petong), a useful winner of five races over 5f
and 6f including the Weatherbys Super Sprint
and the Redcar Two-Year-Old Trophy, is a half-
sister to nine winners. (J Jamgotchian).
*'It's a pretty fast family, she's rather light framed
but it looks like she's going to have some speed
and will make a two year old.'*

785. STREET OF HOPE (USA) ★★★
b.f. Street Cry – Cycle Of Life (Spinning World)
**January 26. First foal. 34,000Y. Tattersalls
October 1. Not sold.** The dam, a minor winner at
three years in the USA, is a half-sister to two
winners. The second dam, Autumn Moon (by Mr
Prospector), is an unraced sister to the Group 1
Middle Park Stakes winner Lycius and the Group
3 winner Tereshkova and a half-sister to the dual
Grade 2 winner Akabir. (J Jamgotchian).
*'This filly did a bit of work early on, she looks very
well-balanced, she's coming along quite well and
so far so good. It looks like she's going to make
a little two year old and she's got natural speed.'*

786. UNNAMED ★★★★
b.f. Royal Applause – Alyousufeya
(Kingmambo)
**March 10. First foal. 32,000Y. Tattersalls
December. BBA (Ire).** The dam, placed fourth
twice over 7f and 1m, is a half-sister to three
winners including the Group 2 Mill Reef Stakes
third Belasco. The second dam, Musicale (by
The Minstrel), won the Group 3 6f Cherry
Hinton Stakes, the Group 3 7f Rockfel Stakes,
the Group 3 Prestige Stakes (all at two years)
and the Group 3 7.3f Gainsborough Stud Fred
Darling Stakes and is a half-sister to six winners.
*'I really like this filly, she's not untypical of the sire
in that she isn't a big, burly filly and it looks as
though she's going to be quite fast. Sure to make
a two year old and I think she's very nice.'*

787. UNNAMED ★★★
br.f. Singspiel – Big Pink (Bigstone)
**March 21. Fifth foal. 32,000Y. Tattersalls
October 2. A Skiffington.** Half-sister to the fair
2007 10f placed two year old Flash Of Colour
and to the fair all-weather 7f winner Fuchsia
(both by Averti). The dam is an unraced half-
sister to eight winners including the triple
Group 3 winner Pink and the French listed
winners Ring Pink and Lypink. The second dam,
Pink Valley (by Never Bend), won the listed Prix
d'Aumale and is a half-sister to 12 winners
including the French 2,000 Guineas winner and
sire Green Dancer.
*'A beautiful filly, very attractive with lots of
quality and a very good mover. Definitely one for
later in the year and as a three year old however.'*

788. UNNAMED ★★
ch.c. Halling – Charlock (Nureyev)
**March 18. Fifth living foal. €50,000Y. Goffs
Million. A Skiffington.** Half-brother to the quite
useful Irish 1m winner Rain Lily (by Red
Ransom). The dam, an Irish three year old 7f
winner, was third in the Group 3 Matron Stakes
and is a half-sister to four winners. The second
dam, Charmante (by Alydar), won over 7f at two
years in Ireland and a minor 1m stakes event in
the USA and is a half-sister to the top-class miler
Zilzal. (R J Tufft).
*'A nice colt, he goes OK but on pedigree you've
got to expect him to need time. A good-looking
horse but he's on the back burner right now.'*

789. UNNAMED ★★
b.c. Dubai Destination – Possessive Artiste
(Shareef Dancer)
**February 23. Eighth foal. 21,000Y. Doncaster St
Leger. John Hills.** Half-brother to the Hong
Kong winner and listed-placed Blue Stitch (by
Selkirk) and to the modest 9.5f winner Velma
Kelly (by Vettori). The dam, a fair 11.5f winner, is
a sister to the very smart 1991 Irish Oaks and
Italian Oaks winner Possessive Dancer (herself
dam of the smart, though unreliable, middle-
distance colt Maylane). The second dam,
Possessive (by Posse), is an unraced half-sister to
ten winners including the smart miler Long Row

and the Norfolk Stakes winner Colmore Row. *'I think that the two Dubai Destination three year old's I have are as nice as I've got but they weren't precocious. This colt is also a very taking horse, he's quite tall and he's going to take some, particularly bearing in mind my limited experience of the sire.'*

790. UNNAMED ★★★
b.c. Invincible Spirit – Princess Caraboo (Alzao)
February 19. Third living foal. 28,000Y. Doncaster St Leger. J Hills. The dam is an unraced half-sister to nine winners including the Group 1 Fillies Mile winner Fairy Heights and the very useful Group 3 12f St Simon Stakes winner Persian Brave and the Irish Group 3 winner Puerto Rico. The second dam, Commanche Belle (by Shirley Heights), was placed four times from 10f to 2m and is a half-sister to 11 winners including the Yorkshire Cup winner Band and the Ormonde Stakes winner Zimbalon.
'He's going nicely and has done a bit of work. Not a natural five furlong horse, he looks like he'll want six and I would think we could have a late April/early May start.'

791. UNNAMED ★★
b.c. High Chaparral – Queens Wharf (Ela-Mana-Mou)
March 14. Second foal. €50,000Y. Goffs Million. A Skiffington. Half-brother to the 2007 8.5f and 10f placed two year old Synergistic (by In The Wings). The dam, a useful Irish listed 14f winner, is a half-sister to four winners. The second dam, Lady Bennington (by Hot Grove), is an unplaced half-sister to six winners including the dual Group 3 winner Ahohoney. (J W Hills).
'He goes well and he does everything easily. He's quite lively and so I might have to do something with him soon despite the pedigree telling me otherwise. I'd be relieved to see a few more winners by the stallion though.'

792. UNNAMED ★★★
ch.f. Refuse To Bend – Wondrous Joy (Machiavellian)
April 23. Second foal. €40,000Y. Goffs Million. A Skiffington. The dam, a useful 1m to 10f

winner, is a half-sister to three winners. The second dam, Girl From Ipanema (by Salse), a useful 7f (at two years) and listed 1m winner, was second in the Group 2 Falmouth Stakes and is a half-sister to eight winners.
'A very nice filly, it's quite hard to know how early these Refuse To Bend's are going to be, but this one's out of a Machiavellian mare and she does everything very easily and I think she's really nice.'

MICHAEL JARVIS
793. AAKEF (IRE) ★★★
b.c. Exceed And Excel – Bush Baby (Zamindar)
January 31. Second foal. 210,000Y. Tattersalls October 2. Shadwell Estate Co. The dam is an unplaced half-sister to nine winners including the very smart Group 2 12f Ribblesdale Stakes winner Gull Nook (herself dam of the top-class colt Pentire), the equally smart Group 3 12f Princess Royal Stakes winner Banket and the useful Group 3 Ormonde Stakes winner Mr Pintips. The second dam, Bempton (by Blakeney), was placed three times at up to 11f and is a half-sister to Shirley Heights. (Hamdan Al Maktoum).
'By the new sire Exceed And Excel, he's an early foal and he looks like a two year old although there's plenty of stamina on the dam's side. So combining the two I'd say we wouldn't see him out until mid-season. A nice colt and he's physically quite developed.'

794. AFRICA'S STAR (IRE) ★★★★★
b.f. Johannesburg – Grable (Sadler's Wells)
March 22. First foal. €230,000Y. Goffs Million. M Jarvis. The dam, placed six times at two and three years, is a sister to 2 listed-placed winners. The second dam, Movie Legend (by Affirmed), is an unraced sister to Group winners and good broodmares Trusted Partner and Easy To Copy. (Mrs C C Regalado-Gonzalez).
'A very nice, active filly and a good mover. She's quite forward and of course the sire can get two year old's so although there is some stamina on the dam's side I can see this filly making her two year old debut in the second half of May. Six furlongs will suit her and she's promising.'

795. ALAFOOR (FR) ★★★
gr.c. Linamix – Green Delight (Green Desert)
February 19. Fourth foal. €300,000Y. Deauville
August. Shadwell France. Half-brother to two
winners including the useful dual 1m winner
and Group 3 placed Balin's Sword (by
Spectrum). The dam is an unplaced half-sister
to five winners including Daawe, a useful dual 7f
winner here before proving a prolific winner of
minor events in the USA. The second dam, Capo
di Monte (by Final Straw), won over 6f at two
years, the 10f Pretty Polly Stakes and 10f
Virginia Stakes at three years and the Grade 3
11f Vineland Handicap in the USA. She is a half-
sister to the smart Group 1 12f Aral-Pokal
winner and Epsom Oaks second Wind In Her
Hair. (Hamdan Al Maktoum).
'An early foal, he's a lot stronger than the
previous ones I've had by Linamix – they've all
been angular and needed time. This horse looks
as if he could make a two year old, he's a nice,
strong horse and he's pretty precocious but he'd
need at least six furlongs to start with.'

796. ALAINMAR (FR) ★★★★
b.c. Johar – Lady Elgar (Sadler's Wells)
May 6. Seventh foal. €240,000Y. Deauville
August. Shadwell France. Half-brother to the
US Grade 1 12f Sword Dancer Handicap winner
Grand Couturier (by Grand Lodge), to the 7f
and listed 10f winner Yaqeen (by Green Desert)
and the quite useful 10f winner Sir Edward Elgar
(by King's Best). The dam, unplaced in one start
in France, is a sister to the Sha Tin Trophy winner
and Irish Derby third Desert Fox and a half-sister
to the US Grade three winners Poolesta and
Home Of The Free. The second dam, Radiant
(by Foolish Pleasure), won at three years and is
a half-sister to the Group 2 Royal Lodge Stakes
winner Gold And Ivory. (Hamdan Al Maktoum).
'By the Breeders Cup winner Johar, we had his
half-sister the listed winner Yaqeen last year but
this is a different type. He's 'on the leg', a May
foal, athletic and probably a horse than should
make a two year old by mid-summer.'

797. ALAZEYAB (USA) ★★
b.c. El Prado – Itnab (Green Desert)

March 2. The dam won the Group 3 12f
Princess Royal Stakes and is a sister to the very
useful 6f winner of four races Haafiz and the
useful 7f and 1m winner and Irish 1,000 Guineas
third Umniyatee and a half-sister to numerous
winners including the Group 1 Epsom Oaks
winner Eswarah. The second dam, Midway Lady
(by Alleged), won the Prix Marcel Boussac, the
1,000 Guineas and the Oaks and is a half-sister
to five winners including the very useful 11.8f.
listed winner Capias. (Hamdan Al Maktoum).
'Still in Dubai in early April. I did see him a few
weeks ago but he looked a bit immature.'

798. ALL GUNS FIRING (IRE) ★★
b.c. High Chaparral – Lili Cup
(Fabulous Dancer)
April 17. Ninth foal. €120,000Y. Goffs Million.
M Jarvis. Half-brother to the quite useful
2007 two year old 10f winner All The Aces
(by Spartacus), to the Italian Group 3 Premio
Umbria winner Uruk (by Efisio), the fair 5f and 6f
winner Grange Lili (by Daggers Drawn), the Irish
two year old 7f winner Marannatha (by Pursuit
Of Love), the fair dual two year old 7f winner
Sarraia (by Formidable) and the dual French four
year old winner Charming Lili (by Sharpo). The
dam is an unraced half-sister to nine winners
including the Group 3 Gallinule Stakes winner
and Irish Derby fourth Nysaean. The second
dam, Irish Arms (by Irish River), won in France
and is a half-sister to nine winners including the
US Grade 2 winner Morold. (A D Spence).
'We have his half-brother All The Aces. This is a
deep-bodied horse and we'd be looking at him
as an autumn two year old and more of a three
year old really.'

799. ALMIQDAAD ★★★★
b.c. Haafhd – Etizaaz (Diesis)
February 1. Fifth foal. Half-brother to the quite
useful 2007 6f placed two year old Alawaabel
(by Green Desert) and to the smart 6f (including
at two years) and listed 7f winner Munaddam
(by Aljabr). The dam, a listed 1m winner and
second in the Group 1 12f Prix Vermeille, is a
half-sister to the listed 6f Sirenia Stakes winner
Santolina and the US Grade 3 7f Lafayette Stakes

winner Trafalger. The second dam, Alamosa (by Alydar), is an unraced half-sister to the King George VI and Queen Elizabeth Diamond Stakes winner Swain out of the US Grade 1 winner Love Smitten. (Hamdan Al Maktoum).

'He's a nice colt and from what we've seen of him we like him. He's got a bit of quality and he'll make a two year old, probably around July time over six furlongs.'

800. AMSAAR ★★★

b.br.c. Kyllachy – Selkirk Rose (Selkirk)
February 5. Fourth foal. 150,000Y. Tattersalls October 1. Shadwell Estate Co. Closely related to the fairly useful two year old listed 5f and four year old 7f winner Miss Meggy (by Pivotal). The dam, a fair 5f (at two years) and 6f winner, is a half-sister to five minor winners. The second dam, Red Note (by Rusticaro), is an unplaced half-sister to four winners including the Belgian Group 2 winner Happy Reprieve. (Hamdan Al-Maktoum).

'Quite a well-developed, strong colt. His pedigree suggests he's a sprint type and he's actually grown quite a bit so he won't be as early as you might expect. One for the second half of the year.'

801. BENMALK (IRE) ★★

b.c. King's Best – Arhaaff (Danehill)
March 8. Third foal. 55,000Y. Tattersalls October 1. M Johnston. Closely related to Kayflaa (by Dubai Destination), unplaced in two starts at two years in 2007. The dam, a useful 1m winner, was listed-placed over 10f and is a half-sister to four winners including the US Grade 1 and Group 2 12f King Edward VII Stakes winner Subtle Power. The second dam, Mosaique Bleue (by Shirley Heights), is an unraced half-sister to the Prix Royal-Oak winner Mersey and the 10f Prix Saint-Alary winner Muncie. (Sheikh Ahmed Al Maktoum).

'A smallish yearling, he's actually grown quite a lot and he's now a well-developed colt. Hopefully he'll be out in August and his temperament is fine.'

802. CARTOON ★★★

br.f. Danehill Dancer – Elfin Laughter (Alzao)
March 27. Ninth foal. 110,000Y. Tattersalls October 1. John Warren. Half-sister to the UAE dual 6f winner Celtic King (by King's Best), to the smart listed winner of six races from 7f to 1m Smirk (by Selkirk), the very useful dual 6f winner (including at two years) Stetchworth Prince, the UAE three year old winner Joyous Gift (both by Cadeaux Genereux) and the Italian winner of eight races Sella del Diavolo (by Barathea). The dam, a fair two year old 7.5f and 1m winner, is a half-sister to 11 winners including the US Grade 2 winner Sign Of Hope. The second dam, Rainbow's End (by My Swallow) was a quite useful two year old 6f winner. (Highclere Thoroughbred Racing (Sun Chariot)).

'A well-grown filly out of a good, winner producing mare. She doesn't look particularly precocious and is probably one for the autumn.'

803. EBIAYN (IRE) ★★

b.c. Monsun – Drei (Lyphard)
February 16. 210,000foal. Tattersalls December. Shadwell Estate Co. Half-brother to the 5.3f (at two years) and US winner and Grade 2 placed Pina Colada (by Sabrehill), to the fairly useful two year old 6f winner and listed fourth Baltic Dip (by Benny The Dip), the quite useful 10f winner Triple Sharp (by Selkirk), the quite useful triple 9.4f all-weather winner Trois (by Efisio) and a winner in Holland by Darshaan. The dam, placed fourth over 1m at three years on her only outing, is a half-sister to the useful 1m winner Triode. The second dam, Triple Tipple (by Raise A Cup), won 10 races here and in the USA including the Grade 2 Wilshire Handicap, the Grade 3 Palomar Handicap and the listed Strensall Stakes and is a half-sister to six winners. (Hamdan Al Maktoum).

'A typical German type of horse in that as an individual he's quite plain and he's a big, raw-boned horse that will probably come out in the autumn and want some give in the ground.'

804. HAWDAJ ★★★

b.f. Nayef – Najayeb (Silver Hawk)
March 4. Second foal. Half-sister to the quite useful two year old 1m winner Mutadarrej (by Fantastic Light). The dam is an unraced half-

sister to the high-class Prix de l'Arc de Triomphe and Juddmonte International winner Sakhee and is closely related to the useful 7f (at two years) and 10f winner Nasheed. The second dam, Thawakib (by Sadler's Wells), a useful dual 7f (at two years) and Group 2 12f Ribblesdale Stakes winner, is a half-sister to numerous winners including the top-class middle-distance colt Celestial Storm (winner of the Group 2 Princess of Wales's Stakes). (Hamdan Al Maktoum).

'She's a bit on the small side but she's correct and looks as though she could come in the midsummer. A nice enough filly.'

805. HAZAYNA ★★★

b.f. Barathea – Hazaradjat (Darshaan)

March 27. Tenth foal. 280,000Y. Tattersalls October 1. Kern/Lillingston. Sister to the Group 3 Blue Wind Stakes winner Hazarista and half-sister to the Group 3 Athasi Stakes winner Hazariya (by Xaar) and 4 minor three year old winners by Alzao, Kahyasi, Perugino and Be My Guest). The dam won twice at two and three years and is a half-sister to ten winners including the Group 1 Flying Childers Stakes winner Hittite Glory. The second dam, Hazy Idea (by Hethersett), won five races including the March Stakes and is a half-sister to seven winners. (Lordship Stud).

'She's a lovely filly, well-grown and from a very good family. Her pedigree suggests she's more of a three year old type but she goes nicely and I would hope she'll be able to race in the autumn.'

806. JABROOT (IRE) ★★

ch.f. Alhaarth – Walesiana (Star Appeal)

May 26. Closely related to the Group 1 10f Nassau Stakes and Group 10.4f Musidora Stakes winner Zahrat Dubai and to the quite useful 9f winner Yaahomm (both by Unfuwain) and half-sister to the fairly useful two year old 7f all-weather winner Waiting Game (by Reprimand), the fair two year old 6f winner Samorra (by In The Wings) and the fair 12f all-weather winner Warluskee (by Dancing Brave). The dam won the German 1,000 Guineas and is a half-sister to six winners. The second dam, Wondrous Pearl

(by Prince Ippi) won a listed event over 9f. (Sheikh Ahmed Al Maktoum).

'A very late foal although physically she doesn't look it. She goes OK and hopefully she'll be running in the summer over six/seven furlongs.'

807. KALAHARI DANCER ★★★

b.f. Dalakhani – Bella Ballerina (Sadler's Wells)

May 4. Half-sister to the useful 10f winner and 10f listed placed Design Perfection (by Diesis) and to the fair 10f winner Ballet Ballon (by Rahy). The dam, a quite useful three year old 9f winner, is a sister to the high-class Group 2 10f Prince of Wales's Stakes and Group 3 10f Brigadier Gerard Stakes winner Stagecraft and to the useful listed 9f winner Balalaika and a half-sister to the very useful dual 1m listed stakes winner Hyabella. The second dam, Bella Colora (by Bellypha), won the Group 2, 9.2f Prix de l'Opera and the Group 3, 7f Waterford Candelabra Stakes and is a half-sister to the Irish Oaks winner Colorspin (herself dam of the Group 1 winners Zee Zee Top, Opera House and Kayf Tara) and to the Irish Champion Stakes winner Cezanne. (Meon Valley Stud).

'She hasn't been with us that long but she's a really easy-going filly. Obviously being a May foal by Dalakhani she won't be too early but she's one to look forward to later in the year.'

808. KAMMAAN ★★★

b.f. Diktat – Qasirah (Machiavellian)

February 6. First foal. The dam, a useful two year old 6f winner, was third in the Group 3 8.5f Princess Margaret Stakes is out of the useful 10.5f and 12f winner Altaweelah (by Fairy King), herself a half-sister to numerous winners including the useful 10f to 14f winner Lost Soldier Three. (Sheikh Ahmed Al Maktoum).

'She's out of a mare we trained called Qasirah who won first time out. She doesn't look like her mother who was tall whereas she's more of a Diktat – good-bodied with rather short cannon bones and she looks speedy. She's quite nice.'

809. KITE WOOD (IRE) ★★★★

b.c. Galileo – Kite Mark (Mark Of Esteem)

April 26. Fourth foal. 270,000Y. Tattersalls

October 1. M H Goodbody. Half-brother to the quite useful two year old 6f winner Legislation (by Oasis Dream) and to the fair 10f all-weather winner Daylami Dreams (by Daylami). The dam ran once unplaced and is a half-sister to the very smart Group 2 Park Hill Stakes and Group 2 Prix de Royallieu winner Madame Dubois (dam of the Group 1 winners Indian Haven and Count Dubois) and the two year old 1m winner Sun and Shade (dam of the Richmond Stakes winner Daggers Drawn). The second dam, Shadywood (by Habitat), a useful 10f winner, was second in the Lancashire Oaks and is a half-sister to eight winners. (T Barr).
'A quality colt, well-grown and a good mover. I suggest that going by his pedigree we'll be waiting for the seven furlong races but he should be racing by July hopefully.'

810. LAAHEB ★★

b.c. Cape Cross – Maskunah (Sadler's Wells)
February 245. Fifth foal. 200,000Y. Tattersalls October 1. Shadwell Estate Co. Half-brother to the fair 2007 7f placed two year old Skycruiser (by Dubai Destination) and to the fairly useful listed placed two year old and three year old 7f winner Guarantia (by Selkirk). The dam is an unraced half-sister to six winners including the high-class middle-distance horses and multiple Group 1 winners Warrsan and Luso, the Nell Gwyn Stakes winner Cloud Castle and the Group 2 Gallinule Stakes winner Needle Gun. The second dam, Lucayan Princess (by High Line), a very useful winner of the listed 6f Sweet Solera Stakes at two years, was third in the 12.3f Cheshire Oaks and is a half-sister to seven winners. (Hamdan Al Maktoum).
'He hasn't been here long but he's cantering away now. A well-grown, biggish horse with a nice way of going, we'll look to him as being an autumn two year old.'

811. LACROSSE ★★

b.c. Cape Cross – La Sky (Law Society)
March 31. Tenth living foal. 150,000Y. Tattersalls October 1. Not sold. Half-brother to the Group 1 12f Oaks winner Love Divine (herself dam of the St Leger winner Sixties Icon), to the quite

useful 11.5f winner Easy To Love (both by Diesis), the useful listed 12f winner Floreeda (by Linamix), the French 12f winner Laurentine and the US winner and Grade 1 fourth Security Code (both by Private Account). The dam, a useful 10f winner and second in the Lancashire Oaks, is closely related to the Champion Stakes winner Legal Case and a half-sister to four winners. The second dam, Maryinsky (by Northern Dancer), won twice at up to 9f in the USA and is a half-sister to the US Grade three winners Bold Place and Card Table. (Lordship Stud).
'A beautifully-bred colt, well-grown and very laid-back. As his pedigree suggests he'll hopefully make an autumn two year old with his three year old career in mind.'

812. LADY OF INTRIGUE (IRE) ★★

b.f. Sadler's Wells – Dedicated Lady (Pennine Walk)
January 8. Eleventh foal. 540,000Y. Tattersalls October 1. Charlie Gordon-Watson. Sister to the Irish 8.5f (at two years) and 10f winner and Prix de l'Arc de Triomphe fourth Acropolis and the fair Irish 12f winner De Laurentiis, closely related to the smart Group 2 12f Ribblesdale Stakes and Group 2 12.5f Prix de la Royallieu winner Fairy Queen (by Fairy King), the smart Group 2 1m Falmouth Stakes winner Tashawak and the fair 6f (at two years) and 1m winner Speedfit Free (both by Night Shift). The dam, a useful Irish two year old 5f and 6f winner, was listed-placed and is a half-sister to five winners including the German listed winner and Group 3 third Silk Petal (herself dam of the listed winner Star Tulip). The second dam, Salabella (by Sallust), is a placed half-sister to seven winners including the Irish St Leger and the Grosser Preis von Baden winner M-Lolshan. (Merry Fox Stud Ltd).
'An expensive purchase, she's very well-grown and is a laid back filly. Again, we'd look to introduce her in the autumn and then look towards her three year old career.'

813. MYSHKIN ★★★

b.c. Refuse To Bend – Marmaga (Shernazar)
February 14. Fifth foal. 62,000Y. Tattersalls

October 2. M Jarvis. Half-brother to the Italian winner of nine races Destination World (by Alzao) and to the modest Irish 8.5f winner Misima Sunrise (by Tagula). The dam is an unraced half-sister to seven winners including the Group 3 Prix des Reservoirs winner Masslama. The second dam, Marmana (by Blushing Groom), is a placed sister to the Group 3 Prix d'Hedouville winner Malakim. (D Spratt, M Rutherford & A Wilson).

'I quite like the Refuse To Bend's, we've got a couple and they're both nice horses. He's an athletic type, he goes well and it looks like he'll come to hand early enough to make a June two year old, probably over seven furlongs.'

814. MYSTERIA (IRE) ★★★

ch.f. Monsun – Calypso Grant (Danehill)
January 25. Fifth foal. €125,000Y. Deauville August. Peter Doyle. Half-sister to a minor French winner by Celtic Swing. The dam, winner of the listed 1m Masaka Stakes, is a sister to the listed 10f winner and Group 2 Sun Chariot Stakes third Poppy Carew and the Group 3 Winter Hill Stakes winner Leporello a half-sister to four winners. The second dam, Why So Silent (by Mill Reef), is an unraced half-sister to five winners including the US Grade 3 winner Supreme Sound. (Thurloe Thoroughbreds XXII).

'A nice, quality filly, she's not over-big but I like her, she's a pretty model and we like her. Being by Monsun we can't be in a hurry with her. Seven furlongs from August onwards will suit her.'

815. OSTAADI ★★★★★

b.c. Nayef – Blodwen (Mister Baileys)
February 17. Fourth foal. 280,000Y. Tattersalls October 2. Shadwell Estate Co. Half-brother to the unplaced 2007 two year old Black Heart (by Diktat) and to the German three year old winner and two year old Group 3 1m Premio Dormello third Carolines Secret (by Inchinor). The dam is an unplaced full or half-sister to six winners including the UAE listed winner Kassbaan. The second dam, Ma Biche (by Key To The Kingdom), was a top-class filly and winner of the 1,000 Guineas, the Prix de la Foret, the Cheveley Park Stakes and

the Prix Robert Papin. (Sheikh Ahmed Al Maktoum).

'He's a very attractive colt, tallish and with a lot of quality. He has a really nice way of going and I hope he'll make a decent two year old in the second half of the season. A very taking individual, seven furlongs should be his starting point.'

816. RUSSIAN JAR (IRE) ★★★★

b.c. Xaar – Lady Windermere (Lake Coniston)
February 22. Fifth foal. 80,000Y. Tattersalls October 1. Not sold. Half-brother to the useful Irish listed 6f winner and Group 3 placed Absolutelyfabulous (by Mozart). The dam is an unraced half-sister to four winners including the Group 1 7f Moyglare Stud Stakes winner and smart broodmare Sequoyah. The second dam, Brigid (by Irish River), a minor French three year old 1m winner, is a sister to the listed 7f Prix de l'Obelisque winner Or Vision (herself dam of the Group/Grade 1 winners Dolphin Street, Insight and Saffron Walden) and a half-sister to six winners. (J A R Partnership).

'He's a big colt from a very good family and he's a lovely horse. He could make a nice two year old and hopefully he'd have enough pace to go six furlongs. We'll see him on the racecourse in late May or early June I should think.'

817. SAIFAAN ★★

b.c. Needwood Blade – Gagajulu (Al Hareb)
May 14. Ninth foal. 85,000Y. Tattersalls October 2. Shadwell Estate Co. Half-brother to the useful Group 3 1m winner and Irish 1,000 Guineas second Ardbrae Lady (by Overbury), to the useful listed 5f (at two years) to 7f winner of six races Obe Gold (by Namaqualand), the quite useful 5f (at two years) and 6f winner Under My Spell, the modest 6f and 7f winner Obe Royal and the modest 7f and winner Beneking (all by Wizard King). The dam won five races over 5f at two years and is a half-sister to two winners. The second dam, Rion River (by Taufan), won once at three years and is a half-sister to four winners. (Sheikh Ahmed Al Maktoum).

'The sire was obviously a sprinter but this colt was a late foal and he's grown quite a bit

since he was purchased, so he doesn't look particularly early. A nice enough colt but we may have to be a bit patient with him.'

818. SANA ABEL (IRE) ★★
b.f. Alhaarth – Midway Lady (Alleged)
May 22. Closely related to the Oaks winner Eswarah (by Unfuwain) and half-sister to the Group 3 12f Princess Royal Stakes winner Itnab, the very useful 6f winner of four races Haafiz and the useful 7f and 1m winner and Irish 1,000 Guineas third Umniyatee (all by Green Desert), the useful triple 1m winner Shumookh (by Mujahid), the quite useful middle-distance winners Fatehalkhair and Alasad (both by Kris) and the 12f all-weather winner Abuljjood (by Marju). The dam won the Prix Marcel Boussac, the 1,000 Guineas and the Oaks and is a half-sister to five winners including the very useful 11.8f listed winner Capias. The second dam, Smooth Bore (by His Majesty), won 2 stakes races at around 1m in the USA at four years. (Hamdan Al Maktoum).
'She's gone home for a break as she's small and was a late foal, so she needs to grow and develop. Eswarah never ran as a two year old and neither did the dam's Cape Cross two year old of last year, so we'll have to wait and see if this filly makes it in time for the autumn.'

819. SHEMOLI ★★
ch.c. Singspiel – Felawnah (Mr Prospector).
February 22. Half-brother to the very smart listed 1m winner and Group 1 St James's Palace Stakes third Aramram (by Danzig), to the useful 9f and 10f winner Felona, the minor UAE 10f winner Inbhaar (both by Caerleon), the fairly useful two year old 7f winner Shelhom, the quite useful 13f winner Raffaas (both by Green Desert) and the quite useful 14f winner Follow Lammtarra (by Lammtarra). The dam, a very useful 10f winner, was fourth in the 1,000 Guineas and the Irish 1,000 Guineas and third in the Sun Chariot Stakes. She is closely related to the US Grade 3 1m winner Alydavid and a half-sister to the fairly useful two year old 6f winner Zakhir. The second dam, Ambassador Of Luck (by What Luck), was a champion older

mare in the USA and won 1four races including the Grade 1 Maskette Stakes. (Sheikh Ahmed Al Maktoum).
'He's a leggy type and a nice enough horse but very much one for the autumn.'

820. SILENT HERO ★★★
b.c. Oasis Dream – Royal Passion (Ahonoora)
April 7. Half-brother to the useful 7f (at two years) and 10.3f winner Attache (by Wolfhound), to the useful sprint winner of numerous races (including at two years) Tadeo (by Primo Dominie), the fairly useful two year old 7f winner Manchurian (by Singspiel), the modest dual 7f and 9f winner Midnight Lace (by Tomba) and the modest two year old 6f winner Chaska (by Reprimand). The dam, a fair triple 10f winner, is a half-sister to four winners. The second dam, Courtesy Call (by Northfields), is a placed half-sister to five winners. (Mrs P Good).
'Quite an early type, he's on the small side but he's quite solid and hopefully he'll be one of our earlier runners.'

821. SRI PUTRA ★★★★ ♠
b.c. Oasis Dream – Wendylina (In The Wings)
March 19. Fourth foal. 240,000Y. Tattersalls October 1. Charlie Gordon-Watson. Half-brother to the fairly useful 11f and hurdles winner Duty (by Rainbow Quest). The dam is an unraced half-sister to nine winners including the Group 1 10.5f Prix de Diane winner Caerlina. The second dam, Dinalina (by Top Ville), a French two year old 10f winner, is a half-sister to the Doncaster Cup winner Karadar and to the dams of the Group 1 winners Kartajana and Khariyda. (HRH Sultan Ahmad Shah).
'A nice-looking, deep-bodied horse and a good mover, he's by a sprinter but has a bit of stamina on the dam's side. He should make a summer two year old and we like him.'

822. WARDATI ★★
ch.f. Sulamani – Jathaabeh (Nashwan)
March 21. Third foal. Half-sister to the quite useful 2007 two year old 1m winner Yaddree (by Singspiel) and to the quite useful dual 1m winner Sky More (by Xaar). The dam, a useful

dual 1m winner, is a half-sister to several winners including the useful two year old Group 3 7f Prix du Calvados winner Kareymah. The second dam, Pastorale (by Nureyev), a fairly useful three year old 7f winner, is a half-sister to the Group 1 Lockinge Stakes winner and high-class sire Cape Cross out of the dual Group 1 winning two year old Park Appeal. (Sheikh Ahmed Al Maktoum).

'She's done quite well but she'll be given time to develop and we won't be in a hurry with her. We don't know about the sire but this is an active type and I think she'll make a two year old at the back-end of the season.'

823. TODAY'S THE DAY ★★★★
b.f. Alhaarth – Dayville (Dayjur)
February 25. Eighth foal. 42,000Y. Tattersalls October 2. Jill Lamb. Half-sister to the fairly useful 2007 listed 6f placed two year old Thought Is Free (by Cadeaux Genereux), to the quite useful 5f and 6f winner Day By Day (by Kyllachy), the quite useful two year old 1m all-weather winner Musical Day (by Singspiel), the quite useful 10f and 12f winner My Daisychain (by Hector Protector) and the Irish three year old 5f winner Alexander Ballet (by Mind Games). The dam, a quite useful triple 6f winner, is a half-sister to four winners including the Grade 1 Yellow Ribbon Handicap winner Spanish Fern. The second dam, Chain Fern (by Blushing Groom), is an unraced sister to the Irish 1,000 Guineas and Coronation Stakes winner Al Bahathri (herself dam of the 2,000 Guineas and Champion Stakes winner Haafhd). (M A Jarvis).

'She's from very much a sprinting family on the dam's side and she looks following that trait and have enough speed to start at five furlongs in late May and then progress to six furlongs.'

824. ZUZU ★★★
b.f. Acclamation – Green Life (Green Desert)
January 20. Tenth foal. 90,000Y. Tattersalls October 2. M Jarvis. Half-sister to the fair 2007 two year old 5f winner Bohobe (by Noverre), to the fairly useful two year old all-weather 7f and 1m winner Agilis (by Titus Livius), the Italian winner of four races at two and three years

including over 5f Green Band (by College Chapel) and the fair 6f (at two years) and 5.7f winner Tappit (by Mujadil). The dam, placed once at two years, is a half-sister to six winners including the Group 3 Molecomb Stakes winner Classic Ruler. The second dam, Viceroy Princess (by Godswalk), a modest two year old 7f seller winner, is a half-sister to seven winners. (S Dartnell).

'A nice-moving filly and an early foal. Being by Acclamation and out of a Green Desert mare you would have thought she'd make a two year old and although we haven't tried her yet hopefully she should be speedy. Six furlongs should suit her and she's a nice, correct, rangy filly with a bit of length to her.'

825. UNNAMED ★★★★
b.c. Refuse To Bend – Kardashina (Darshaan)
April 27. Seventh foal. €200,000Y. Goffs Million. M Jarvis. Closely related to the very useful two year old 10f listed Zetland Stakes winner Ayam Zaman (by Montjeu) and half-brother to Holly Hawk (by Dubai Destination), unplaced in one start at two years in 2007, the fairly useful 6f (at two years) and 12f winner John Terry (by Grand Lodge), the fairly useful 10f winner Rudood (by Theatrical) and the Irish 12f winner Russian Tsar (by King Of Kings). The dam won three races in France from 11f to 12.5f and is a half-sister to five winners including the listed winners Kart Star and Karmifira. The second dam, Karmiska (by Bikala), won the Group 3 10f Prix de la Nonette and is a full or half-sister to six winners. (A D Spence).

'The mare is a good winner-producer and this is a very leggy but active colt and a good mover. The family often produces light-framed, athletic types and this colt follows that pattern. We like him, he uses himself well and despite the fairly late foaling date he shouldn't be too backward.'

826. UNNAMED ★★★
b.c. Danehill Dancer – Veronica Cooper (Kahyasi)
May 7. Third foal. €210,000Y. Goffs Million. Charlie Gordon-Watson. The dam, a winner, is a half-sister to nine winners including the Japanese

Grade 1, German Group 2 11f and New Zealand Grade 2 winner Vialli, the champion Spanish filly and 6f to 11f winner La Strada (both by Niniski) and the French listed 1m winner Queenemara. The second dam, Vaison La Romaine (by Arctic Tern), a useful 7.5f winner, was fourth in the Group 3 Prix Cleopatre and is a half-sister to five winners. (HRH Sultan Ahmad Shah).

'He's went a bit weak on us after we broke him and being a May foal we'll give him some time. I don't think he'll be early but he's a nice enough horse.'

WILLIAM JARVIS

827. AGE OF COUTURE ★★★

ch.f. Hold That Tiger – Three Wishes (Sadler's Wells)
March 18. Fourth foal. 50,000Y. Tattersalls October 2. W Jarvis. Half-sister to the minor French two year old winner Todman Avenue (by Lear Fan) and to a minor Italian three year old winner by Diesis. The dam was placed third over 1m in Ireland and is a half-sister to four winners. The second dam, Valley Of Hope (by Riverman), is an unraced half-sister to five winners including the Group 1 Prix Jacques le Marois winner Vin de France and the Group 2 Mill Reef Stakes winner Vacarme. (Plantation Stud).

'She's quite sharp temperament-wise but maybe not so sharp as far as her athleticism is concerned, so she'll probably be a summer two year old. I would think she'd have enough toe for six furlongs and she's a good, strong filly.'

828. ARCHIE RICE (USA) ★★★★

b.c. Arch – Gold Bowl (Seeking The Gold)
March 8. First foal. $114,000Y. Keeneland September. J McCormack. The dam was placed at two years in the USA and is out of the US dual Grade 3 winner and Grade 1 second Shires Ende (by El Prado), herself a half-sister to three winners. (A Foster).

'Yes, I like him a lot, he's got a beautiful way of going, has a lovely temperament and is very well-balanced. He could be the one. He might not be an Ascot two year old but he could be a really nice horse and he'll be out around June time.'

829. CHURCHILLS VICTORY (IRE) ★★★

b.c. Danehill Dancer – Kingsridge (King's Theatre)
May 8. Fourth foal. 38,000Y. Tattersalls October 1. Blandford Bloodstock. Brother to the quite useful 7f and 1m winner Lap Of Honour (by Danehill Dancer). The dam won over 9f at three years in Ireland and is a half-sister to eight winners including the very useful two year old Group 1 5f Phoenix Stakes winner Pharaoh's Delight. The second dam, Ridge The Times (by Riva Ridge), a fair two year old 5f winner, is a half-sister to six winners in the USA.

'I like this colt. He just needs to fill out a bit because he's a bit narrow, but he has a very good way of going and he really points his toe. He's an enthusiastic worker, so he definitely has a chance and he should have enough speed for six furlongs.'

830. CLERK'S CHOICE (IRE) ★★★

b.c. Bachelor Duke – Credit Crunch (Caerleon)
March 19. Seventh foal. 18,000Y. Tattersalls December. Blandford Bloodstock. Half-brother to the Italian dual listed winner and Group 3 placed Clefairy (by Sri Pekan, to the Italian two year old winner and listed-placed Zemira, the modest 10f and 11f winner Crunchy, the modest two year old 6f winner Golden Charm (all by Common Grounds) and the minor Italian two and three year old winner Liberty City (by Lahib). The dam is an unplaced half-sister to one winner out of the Irish four year old 14f winner Ivory Thread (by Sir Ivor). (M C Banks).

'I like him, he's a well-balanced colt and has a great attitude. A tough, hard-knocking colt.'
TRAINER'S BARGAIN BUY

831. DANCE CLUB (IRE) ★★★

b.f. Fasliyev – Two Clubs (First Trump)
March 1. Fifth foal. 75,000Y. Tattersalls October 1. Barrie Olsen. Half-sister to the Group 1 Haydock Park Sprint Cup, Group 2 6f Coventry Stakes and Group 2 Diadem Stakes winner Red Clubs (by Red Ransom). The dam won five races over 6f including the listed Doncaster Stakes and the listed Prix Contessina and is a half-sister to seven winners including

the 5f Windsor Castle Stakes winner and Group 1 Phoenix Stakes third Gipsy Fiddler. The second dam, Miss Cindy (by Mansingh), a fairly useful 5f to 7f winner of six races, is a sister to the Vernons Sprint Cup winner and useful sire Petong. (Dr John Fike).
'A sharp little filly, not over-big but quite strong and she should be one for the first half of the season. She goes OK and she'll be alright.'

832. MONACO DREAM (IRE) ★★★★
b.f. Hawk Wing – Parvenue (Ezzoud)
February 1. First foal. €80,000Y. Goffs Million. Blandford Bloodstock. Half-sister to the 2007 Irish two year old 1m winner Vivaldi (by Montjeu), to the quite useful two year old 6f winner Three Decades (by Invincible Spirit) and a winner at two years in Italy by Fasliyev. The dam, a quite useful two year old 6f winner, is a half-sister to two winners including the useful 8.3f winner Pedrillo. The second dam, Patria (by Mr Prospector), a fair two year old 7.6f winner, is a sister to Lycius, winner of the Group 1 6f Middle Park Stakes and placed in numerous Group 1 events and to the Group 3 6f Prix de Cabourg winner Tereshkova and a half-sister to the US dual Grade 2 winner Akabir. (Monaco Dream Partnership).
'I like this filly, she's big and scopey, quite light on her feet and would have the Goffs Fillies Million as her main objective.'

833. PAPYRIAN ★★★
b.c. Oasis Dream – La Papagena (Habitat)
March 8. Half-brother to the champion two year old Grand Lodge, winner of the Group 1 7f Dewhurst Stakes and the Group 1 1m St James's Palace Stakes, to the useful 1m listed winner Papabile (both by Chief's Crown), the useful triple 10f winner and listed-placed La Persiana (by Daylami), the useful 10f winner Savannah, the Irish 1m (at two years) and 12f winner Sorcerous (both by Sadler's Wells), the fair 13.8f winner Red Opera (by Nashwan) and the minor 11.5f winner Rose Noble (by Vaguely Noble). The dam is an unraced half-sister to seven winners including the very useful 7f and 1m winner Pamina and the very useful 11f and 12.5f

winner Lost Chord. The second dam, Magic Flute (by Tudor Melody), won the Cheveley Park Stakes and the Coronation Stakes and is a half-sister to nine winners. (Lady Gillian de Walden).
'Interestingly Grand Lodge is the only two year old winner out of the dam, but Oasis Dream has made a good start to his stud career and we like this colt. He's a beautiful looking horse and he's got a bit of size and scope about him. Hopefully he'll buck the trend and be an August type two year old.'

834. PRIVATE EQUITY (IRE) ★★★
b.f. Haafhd – Profit Alert (Alzao)
April 28. Sixth foal. 30,000Y. Tattersalls October 2. Not sold. Half-sister to the quite useful 10f all-weather winner Pound Sign (by Singspiel). The dam, a useful Irish middle-distance winner of two races, is a sister to the Italian listed winner Raysiza and a half-sister to four winners and to the dam of the Group 2 May Hill Stakes winner Kinnaird. The second dam, Raysiya (by Cure The Blues), a fairly useful Irish 10f and 12f winner, is a half-sister to five winners including the Group 3 10f Royal Whip Stakes winner Rayseka. (Mrs S J Davis).
'A nice-looking filly, she's not over big but she's quite nice and has a good temperament. The family have threatened to have a good horse but they haven't quite achieved it yet, so hopefully this will be the one.'

835. ROYAL WILLY (IRE) ★★★
b.c. Val Royal – Neat Dish (Stalwart)
May 2. Twelfth foal. 50,000Y. Tattersalls October 1. Blandford Bloodstock. Brother to the fair 2006 two year old 6f winner Vitznau and half-brother to the smart 1m (at two years) to 14f and subsequent US Grade 3 winner and French Group 2 placed Riddlesdown, the minor Irish 9f winner Flags Up (both by Common Grounds), the Irish 7f (at two years) and 10f winner and Group 3 placed Fill The Bill (by Bob Back), the fair 11f and 12f winner Chater Knight (by Night Shift) and the Irish 10f winner For Starters (by In The Wings). The dam won once over 6f at two years in Ireland, was second in the Group 3 Railway Stakes and is a half-sister to

seven winners including the US stakes winner and Grade 1 placed Western Winter. The second dam, Chilly Hostess (by Vice Regent), won once in the USA and is a half-sister to seven winners. *'Yes, I like this colt. He's got a bit of scope and substance about him, he's one for the summer onwards and is in the Tattersalls Sales race. He'll get a mile in the end but he should be OK to start off at six furlongs.'*

836. SMOKEY STORM ★★★
b.br.c. One Cool Cat – Marisa (Desert Sun)
February 19. First foal. 22,000Y. Tattersalls October 3. Blandford Bloodstock. The dam is an unraced half-sister to five minor winners here and abroad. The second dam, Mithl Al Hawa (by Salse), a useful two year old 6f winner, was listed placed is a half-sister to eight winners including the dam of the Group 2 Cherry Hinton Stakes winner Jewel In The Sand. (The BK Partnership). *'He isn't very big and we need to be getting on with him. He should be my first two year old runner and hopefully he'll start his career in April. A sharp, neat colt.'*

837. WEST KIRK ★★
b.c. Alhaarth – Naughty Crown (Chief's Crown)
February 21. Fifth foal. 67,000Y. Tattersalls October 2. Blandford Bloodstock. Half-brother to the unraced 2007 two year old Love In The Park (by Pivotal), to the modest 7f all-weather winner Grand Lucre and the minor US three year old winner Behaving Naughty (both by Grand Slam). The dam, a quite useful 7.5f winner here, subsequently won once in the USA and is a sister to the winner and Australian Grade 2 placed Ihtiyati and a half-sister to the German Group 3 and listed Heron Stakes winner Tahreeb. The second dam, Native Twine (by Be My Native), a winner of four races including the listed 10f Ballymacoll Stud Stakes and a stakes race in the USA over 8.5f, is a half-sister to eight winners including the Group 2 Dollar Stakes winner and Group 1 placed Alderbrook. (Dr J Walker). *'He's just taking his time and is very much one for the second half of the season. Hopefully he'll be OK one day.'*

838. UNNAMED ★★
b.f. Hawk Wing – Grecian Glory (Zafonic)
February 23. Third foal. €50,000Y. Goffs Million. Blandford Bloodstock. The dam, a two year old 1m winner, is a half-sister to seven winners including the listed winners Grecian Dart and Dark Shell. The second dam, Grecian Urn (by Ela-Mana-Mou), won the Group 2 Criterium de Maisons-Laffitte and is a half-sister to two winners. (Mr Paul Shanahan). *'A backward filly, we haven't done a lot with her, but so far so good.'*

839. UNNAMED ★★★
b.f. Tiger Hill – Wellspring (Caerleon)
February 8. Sixth foal. 30,000Y. Tattersalls October 1. Blandford Bloodstock. Half-sister to the useful 7f (at two years) and 1m winner Almuraad (by Machiavellian), to the French 10f winner and listed-placed Quisisana (by Rainbow Quest) and a 7f winner in Hong Kong by Cadeaux Genereux. The dam, a quite useful 6f winner, is a sister to the good 5f to 1m colt Caerwent, a winner of four races and placed in the Prix de l'Abbaye, Irish 2,000 Guineas, St James's Palace Stakes and Vernons Sprint Cup and a half-sister to six winners including the Cheveley Park Stakes, Irish 1,000 Guineas, Coronation Stakes and Sussex Stakes winner Marling. The second dam, Marwell (by Habitat), was a champion sprinter and won 10 races, notably the July Cup, the Prix de l'Abbaye, the Kings Stand Stakes and the Cheveley Park Stakes. (Partnership). *'She's a neat filly with a very good pedigree and it looks like she has a bit about her. If we could get her into the winner's enclosure she'll be quite valuable as a broodmare.'*

EVE JOHNSON HOUGHTON
840. AUTUMN MORNING (IRE) ★★
b.f. Danetime – Soviet Maid (Soviet Star)
April 26. Eighth foal. 15,500Y. Tattersalls October 3. D Redvers. Half-sister to the fairly useful two year old dual 7f winner Ridgeway Dawn (by Mujtahid), to the modest 12f winner Cemgraft (by In The Wings), a winner in Turkey by Hamas and a 6f winner in Hong Kong by

Marju. The dam is an unraced half-sister to seven winners including the Group 2 12f Great Voltigeur winner Air Marshall and the Group 3 10f Prix La Force winner Break Bread. The second dam, Troyanna (by Troy), won at two years, was third in the listed 10f Lupe Stakes and is a half-sister to six minor winners. (Fighttheban Partnership).

'I don't know much about her because she seems to catch every bug that's going around. She's quite a nice filly though, she'll be quite sharp and I wouldn't rule her out.'

841. CHALK HILL BLUE ★★★

b.f. Reset – Golubitsa (Bluebird)
February 8. First foal. 6,000Y. Doncaster St Leger. Eve Johnson Houghton. The dam is an unplaced half-sister to the lightly raced Irish two year old 7f winner and Group 2 fourth Carnegie Hall. The second dam, Bolshaya (by Cadeaux Genereux), a modest winner of three races over 6f, is a half-sister to numerous winners including the very smart King's Stand Stakes and Temple Stakes winner Bolshoi and the useful sprinters Mariinsky, Great Chaddington and Tod. (Fyfield Racing).

'She's showing plenty of speed, she's just grown a bit and is getting her strength back now. I think she'll be ready by the end of April, she's just coming to herself now.'

842. DAVIDS MATADOR ★★★

b.c. Dansili – Mousseline (Barathea)
February 6. First foal. 50,000Y. Tattersalls October 2. Shefford Bloodstock. The dam is an unraced half-sister to five winners including the US stakes winner and Grade 2 placed Dover Dere. The second dam, Moss (by Woodman), is an unplaced half-sister to six winners including the dual Group 1 Prix de l'Abbaye winner Committed (herself dam of the US Grade 1 winner Pharma). (Mr D T Herbert).

'He's a lovely colt, he won't be early, he's got lots of bone and he's done everything asked of him so far but we're taking our time with him because he's one for July onwards, probably over seven furlongs.'

843. FRANK STREET ★★

ch.g. Fraam – Pudding Lane (College Chapel)
February 17. Third foal. 16,000Y. Tattersalls October 3. Not sold. Half-brother to the very useful listed 5f winner of six races Judd Street (by Compton Place). The dam, a modest maiden, ran only at two years and stayed 7f and is a half-sister to one winner. The second dam, Fire Of London (by Shirley Heights), was placed over 10f and is a full or half-sister to nine winners. (R.F Johnson Houghton).

'He's a half-brother to a horse we trained called Judd Street who didn't see a racecourse as a two year old until the end of the year. This family always takes time, we've gelded him and he'll be nice when he does come.'

844. GREEN POPPY ★★★

b.f. Green Desert – Vimy Ridge (Indian Ridge)
April 23. Second foal. 26,000Y. Tattersalls October 1. Eve Johnson Houghton. The dam is an unraced half-sister to nine winners including the very smart Group 1 7f Prix de la Foret winner Septieme Ciel, the Group 1 1m Prix Marcel Boussac winner Macoumba and the listed winner Manureva (herself dam of the US Grade 1 winner Riviera). The second dam, Maximova (by Green Dancer), won the Group 1 7f Prix de la Salamandre (in a dead-heat) and was placed in the French and Irish 1,000 Guineas. She is a half-sister to five winners including the Group winners Navratilovna and Vilikaia. (Mr J.R Hobby).

'She's a nice little filly, she's well-bred and she shouldn't be too far away from a run but she's really hanging onto her coat and is just waiting to thrive. She's done everything alright, nothing too exciting yet but everything that's been asked of her. TRAINER'S BARGAIN BUY.

845. HAY FEVER (IRE) ★★★

b.c. Namid – Allergy (Alzao)
January 22. Second foal. €18,000Y. Tattersalls Ireland. Eve Johnson Houghton. Half-brother to the modest f (At two years) and 1m winner Ten Spot (by Intikhab). The dam won over 1m at two years, was second in the listed 10f Zetland Stakes and is a half-sister to

two winners. The second dam, Rash Gift (by Cadeaux Genereux), is a placed half-sister to seven winners. (Eden Racing IV).

'He'll be ready to run by the end of April, he's been pleasing me on the gallops and although he went through a bit of a growing stage he's now pulling himself back together again.'

846. JEWELLED REEF (IRE) ★★★★
b.f. Marju – Aqaba (Lake Coniston)
March 9. Third foal. 30,000Y. Tattersalls October 1. R Frisby. The dam, a modest 6f placed two year old, is a half-sister to four winners including the smart Group 1 1m Prix Marcel Boussac and Group 2 1m Prix d'Astarte winner Lady Of Chad and the smart dual Group 3 Sagaro Stakes winner Alcazar. The second dam, Sahara Breeze (by Ela-Mana-Mou), a quite useful 7f and 1m placed maiden, is a half-sister to five winners including the Group 1 Fillies Mile winner Ivanka. (Wood Street Syndicate V).

'She's very nice, won't be too long in coming to hand but she could do with a bit of sun on her back. She'll hopefully be out at the beginning of May and I'll probably wait for six furlongs. She moves nicely.'

847. MR DEAL ★★★
b.c. King's Best – One Of the Family (Alzao)
May 5. Fifth foal. 35,000Y. Tattersalls October 1. Eve Johnson-Houghton. Half-brother to the fairly useful 14f to 18f winner Som Tala (by Fantastic Light) and to the quite useful 1m and 12f all-weather winner Pass The Port (by Docksider). The dam, a fair 1m placed four year old, is a sister to the Rockfel Stakes winner Relatively Special and a half-sister to seven winners including the Juddmonte International Stakes winner One So Wonderful and the Group 2 Dante Stakes winner Alnasr Alwasheek. The second dam, Someone Special (by Habitat), won over 7f, was third in the Coronation Stakes and is a half-sister to the Queen Elizabeth II Stakes winner Milligram. (Miss E.A Johnson Houghton).

'He'll be ready in mid-season, he's a nice colt and not overly-big but well put together. His temperament is nice and I'm pleased with him.'

848. SHARAV ★★★
b.c. Monsieur Bond – May Light (Midyan)
March 31. Tenth foal. 40,000Y. Doncaster St Leger. Eve Johnson Houghton. Half-brother to Well Informed (by Averti), a winner on his only start at two years in 2007, to the smart Group 3 6f Bentinck Stakes winner Bygone Days (by Desert King) and the fairly useful two year old 1m winner Trio (by Cyrano de Bergerac). The dam, a modest 7f placed maiden, is a half-sister to ten winners including the Group 3 Prix de Flore winner Lighted Glory (herself the dam of 3 Group winners), the Group 2 Prix Kergorlay winner King Luthier and the dam of the US Grade 1 winner Cool. The second dam, Lighted Lamp (by Sir Gaylord), was placed in the USA and is a half-sister to seven winners including the Middle Park Stakes winner Crocket. (Dr J A E Hobby).

'He's been entered up and he's ready to run. He's worked nicely and when he runs he'll be a good marker for our other two-year-olds. A sharp, early colt that's ready to go.'

849. UNNAMED ★★
b.c. Xaar – Veiled Beauty (Royal Academy)
March 2. Second foal. 58,000Y. Tattersalls October 1. Eve Johnson-Houghton. The dam is an unplaced half-sister to four winners including the French listed winner Arabride. The second dam, Model Bride (by Blushing Groom), is an unraced half-sister to six winners including the dam of Zafonic and Zamindar. (Anthony Pye-Jeary & Mel Smith).

'He's a big colt, but all there and well put together. One for the middle of the season over seven furlongs.'

MARK JOHNSTON
850. ALANBROOKE ★★★ ♠
gr.c. Hernando – Alouette (Darshaan)
April 18. Ninth foal. 380,000Y. Tattersalls October 1. M Johnston. Brother to the fairly useful dual middle-distance winner Alakananda and half-brother to the fair 2007 7f to 10f placed two year old Altitude (by Green Desert), the dual Champion Stakes winner Alborada, to the triple German Group 1

winner Albanova (both by Alzao), the very useful dual 12f winner and listed placed Albinus (by Selkirk), the fairly useful 12f and French listed 12.5f winner Alma Mater (by Sadler's Wells) and the fairly useful dual 12f winner Alba Stella (by Nashwan). The dam, a useful 1m (at two years) and listed 12f winner, is a sister to the listed winner and Irish Oaks third Arrikala and a half-sister to the Nassau Stakes and Sun Chariot Stakes winner Last Second (dam of the French 2,000 Guineas winner Aussie Rules) and the Doncaster Cup winner Alleluia. The second dam, Alruccaba (by Crystal Palace), was a quite useful two year old 6f winner. (Hamdan Al Maktoum).

851. ALAYALA ★★★
b.f. *Cape Cross – Lady's Secret (Alzao)*
January 24. Third foal. 100,000Y. Tattersalls October 1. Shadwell Estate Co. Half-sister to the unraced 2007 two year old Fosool (by Pivotal). The dam, a very useful 12f winner, was second in the Group 3 Lancashire Oaks and third in the Group 1 Irish Oaks. The second dam, Kaaba (by Darshaan), is an unraced half-sister to three winners. (Hamdan Al Maktoum)

852. AL MUGTAREB ★★★
b.c. *Acclamation – Billie Bailey (Mister Baileys)*
February 20. Second foal. €170,000Y. Goffs Million. Shadwell Estate Co. The dam is an unraced half-sister to four winners including the Irish triple listed winner Group 3 placed Lil's Boy. The second dam, Kentucky Lill (by Raise A Native), won in France and is a half-sister to three winners. (Hamdan Al Maktoum).

853. ATEEB ★★★
b.c. *Red Ransom – Design Perfection (Diesis)*
February 8. Second foal. 180,000Y. Tattersalls October 1. Shadwell Estate Co. The dam, a useful 10f winner, was listed-placed and is a half-sister to one winner. The second dam, Bella Ballerina (by Sadler's Wells), a quite useful three year old 9f winner, is a sister to the high-class Group 2 10f Prince of Wales's Stakes and Group 3 10f Brigadier Gerard Stakes winner Stagecraft and to the useful listed 9f winner

Balalaika and a half-sister to four winners. (Hamdan Al Maktoum).

854. BATTLE PLANNER (USA) ★★★
b.c. *War Chant – The Administrator (Afleet)*
April 20. Tenth foal. $50,000Y. Keeneland September. M Johnston. Half-brother to the US stakes winners and Graded stakes placed Sweet Lips (by Kris S) and Saint Marden (by Saint Ballado). The dam, a minor US stakes winner of four races, is a half-sister to nine winners including 2 stakes winners. The second dam, Shariza (by Cyane), was placed at two and three years. (Favourites Racing)

855. BECAUSEWECAN (USA) ★★★
b.c. *Giant's Causeway – Belle Sultane (Seattle Slew)*
May 8. Eighth foal. $90,000Y. Keeneland September. M Johnston. Half-brother to three winners including the listed Prix Joubert winner and US stakes-placed Shebane (by Alysheba). The dam is a placed sister to the US stakes winner Sleek Feet and a half-sister to three other stakes winners. The second dam, Sleek Belle (by Vaguely Noble), a minor US three year old winner, is a half-sister to several stakes winners. (Doug Livingstone).

856. BURNS NIGHT ★★★
ch.c. *Selkirk – Night Frolic (Night Shift)*
January 5. First foal. 210,000Y. Tattersalls October 2. M Johnston. The dam, a modest 1m winner, is a half-sister to four winners including the US Grade 3 Cardinal Handicap winner Miss Caerleona (by Caerleon and herself dam of the Group winners Karen's Caper and Miss Coronado) and the French listed-placed winners Mr Academy (by Royal Academy) and Mister Shoot (by Shining Steel). The second dam, Miss d'Ouilly (by Bikala), won a listed event over 9f in France and is a half-sister to the Prix Jacques le Marois winner Miss Satamixa and the dam of the Group/Graded stakes winners Mister Riv, Mister Sicy and Manninamix. (Hamdan Al Maktoum).

857. CHARLES DICKENS (IRE) ★★★
b.c. *Cape Cross – Carry On Katie (Fasliyev)*

February 1. First foal. The dam won three races at two years including the Group 1 6f Cheveley Park Stakes and the Group 2 6f Lowther Stakes. The second dam, Dinka Raja (by Woodman), a minor French three year old 1m winner, is a half-sister to three winners. (Hamdan Al Maktoum).

858. CRIMEA (IRE) ★★★
b.c. Kheleyf – Russian Countess (Nureyev)
February 26. Fourteenth foal. 120,000Y. Tattersalls October 2. M Johnston. Half-brother to the smart 7f (at two years) and 11.5f winner and Epsom Oaks third Crown Of Light (by Mtoto), the very useful two year old listed 1m Stardom Stakes winner and Group 1 Grand Criterium third Alboostan (by Sabrehill), the useful 7.5f and 8.5f winner Romanzof (by Kris), the Irish 6f winners Russian Empress (by Trans Island), Russian Waltz (by Spectrum) and Cossack Count (by Nashwan) and a winner in Belgium by Reference Point. The dam, a useful French two year old 1m winner and listed-placed, is a half-sister to five winners. The second dam, Countess Tully (by Hotfoot), won four races here and in the USA and was placed in the Brownstown Stakes and the Princess Royal Stakes. (Hamdan Al Maktoum).

859. DAMSELFLY ★★★
b.f. Dr Fong – Mazarine Bleu (Bellypha)
January 19. Tenth foal. 32,000Y. Tattersalls October 1. M Johnston. Half-sister to the smart dual two year old 6f winner and subsequent US Grade 2 9f stakes winner Sapphire Ring, to the Swedish winner of seven races Sufian, the modest 8.6f and jumps winner Blue Mariner (all by Marju), the smart 7f (at two years) to 9f winner of nine races including 2 listed events Putra Pekan (by Grand Lodge), the dual listed 6f winner (including at two years) Blue Echo (by Kyllachy), the modest 5f and 6f winner Ice Age (by Chilibang) and the modest two year old 5f winner Orange And Blue (by Prince Sabo). The dam, a modest sprint winner at three years, is a half-sister to seven winners including the Group 2 6f Richmond Stakes winner Rich Charlie. The second dam, Maiden Pool (by Sharpen Up), a quite useful 5f winner of three races, is a half-sister to three winners here and abroad. (Mr Hogarth).

860. DESERT SUNSET ★★★
ch.f. Dubai Destination – Racina (Bluebird)
February 21. Second foal. 50,000Y. Tattersalls October 1. M Johnston. Half-sister to the quite useful 2007 two year old 5f winner Wise Son (by Royal Applause). The dam, a useful two year old 5f winner, was third in the Group 3 Prix d'Arenburg and is a half-sister to three winners. The second dam, Swellegant (by Midyan), won once at two years and is a half-sister to five winners including the Group two winners Prince Sabo and Millyant. (Hamdan Al Maktoum).

861. DESIREE CLARY ★★★
b.f. Domedriver – Scandalette (Niniski)
March 14. Half-sister to the useful 2007 two year old 7f winner Lady Jane Rigby (by Oasis Dream), to the very smart Group 3 7f and 9f winner and Group 1 placed Gateman (by Owington), the fair two year old dual 6f winner Diablerette, the fair 8.6f winner Devil's Island (both by Green Desert), the smart 1m Royal Hunt Cup winner Surprise Encounter (by Cadeaux Genereux) and the fairly useful 7f (at two years) and dual 12f winner Night Flyer (by Midyan). The dam is an unraced half-sister to nine winners including the Group 1 July Cup winner Polish Patriot and the Italian listed winner Grand Cayman. The second dam, Maria Waleska (by Filiberto), won six races including the Group 1 Gran Premio d'Italia and the Group 1 Oaks d'Italia. (Miss K Rausing).

862. DIALOGUE ★★
b.c. Singspiel – Zonda (Fabulous Dancer)
January 27. Eleventh living foal. 90,000Y. Tattersalls October 2. M Johnston. Half-brother to the smart two year old 6f and 7f winner and 2,000 Guineas fourth Zoning (by Warning), to the fairly useful 7f and 1m winner Lady Zonda (by Lion Cavern), the fairly useful 7f winner Zibet (by Kris), the French 1m winner and listed-placed Zambezi (by Rahy), the quite useful 7f and hurdles winner Zero, the fair 9.7f winner Kristiansand (both by Halling) and a winner in

Spain by Groom Dancer. The dam, a useful 5f to 8.5f winner, was listed-placed and is out of the unraced Oh So Hot (by Habitat), herself a sister to the good fillies and broodmares Coronation Stakes winner Roussalka (dam of the Group winners Ristna and Shahid) and a half-sister to the Fillies Triple Crown winner Oh So Sharp (dam of the Group 1 winner Rosefinch). (Hamdan Al Maktoum).

863. GESSEEM (IRE) ★★
b.c. Indian Ridge – Castellane (Danehill)
April 7. Sixth foal. 200,000Y. Tattersalls October 2. Shadwell Estate Co. Half-brother to the quite useful 1m and 8.6f winner Tempsford Flyer (by Fasliyev). The dam, placed 10 times in France including over 10f, is a half-sister to eight winners. The second dam, Servia (by Le Marmot), won twice at three years in France and is a half-sister to seven winners including the Group 2 Prix de l'Opera winner Secret Form. (Sheikh Ahmed Al Maktoum).

864. GOING TIME (USA) ★★★
b.f. Forestry – Grub's Dancer (Grub)
April 5. Seventh foal. $60,000Y. Keeneland September. M Johnston. Half-sister to three winners including the US Grade 2 and Grade 3 winner Saratoga County (by Valid Expectations). The dam, a minor winner of two races at three years in the USA, is a half-sister to the stakes winner Dice Cup and to the dam of the US Grade 2 winner Ruby Surprise. The second dam, Rattling Fool (by Rattle Dancer), was a stakes winner of three races in the USA. (Jaber Abdullah).

865. GREEN AGENDA ★★★
b.c. Anabaa – Capistrano Day (Diesis)
April 28. Fourth foal. 62,000Y. Tattersalls October 1. M Johnston. Half-brother to the fairly useful 2007 two year old 6f winner Dream Day (by Oasis Dream) and to the useful 6f (at two years) to 1m winner and Group 3 Supreme Stakes third Sabbeeh (by Red Ransom). The dam, a smart listed 7f winner, was fourth in the 1,000 Guineas and is a half-sister to five winners. The second dam, Alcando (by Alzao), a smart 5f (at two years) to 10f winner, subsequently won

the Grade 1 9f Beverly Hills Handicap in the USA and is a half-sister to five winners. (Green Dot Partnership).

866. GREEN DYNASTY (IRE) ★★
ch.c. Giant's Causeway – Rose Gypsy (Green Desert)
February 10. Fourth foal. €110,000Y. Deauville August. M Johnston. Half-brother to the quite useful Irish 13f winner Chinese Mandarin (by Kingmambo). The dam won the French 1,000 Guineas and is a half-sister to five winners including the fairly useful 7f winners Egoli and Crystal Cavern. The second dam, Krisalya (by Kris), a fairly useful 10.4f winner, is a half-sister to 12 winners including the high-class Group 1 9.3f Prix d'Ispahan winner Sasuru and the high-class Challenge Stakes and Jersey Stakes winner Sally Rous.

867. JAN MAYEN ★★★
b.f. Halling – Simianna (Bluegrass Prince)
March 18. First foal. 55,000Y. Tattersalls October 2. M Johnston. The dam, a useful and tough listed sprint winner of five races, was Group 3 placed and is a half-sister to two winners. The second dam, Lowrianna (by Cyrano de Bergerac), a moderate two year old 5f winner, is a half-sister to the smart hurdler Grinkov. (Hamdan Al Maktoum).

868. JUKEBOX JURY ★★★
gr.c. Montjeu – Mare Aux Fees (Kenmare)
February 15. Thirteenth foal. €270,000Y. Deauville August. M Johnston. Half-brother to the French listed winner The Mask (by Saint Estephe), to the Italian listed winner Pierrot Solaire, the French two year old winner Albula (by Anabaa) and the minor Italian winner of five races Clair de Mer (both by Dancing Spree). The dam won once at three years in France and is a half-sister to eight winners. The second dam, Feerie Boreale (by Irish River), won once in France and was fourth in the Group 1 Prix Marcel Boussac and is a half-sister to six winners including the Grand Prix de Paris winner Soleil Noir. (Mr A Spence).

869. KIMBERLEY DOWNS (USA) ★★★
gr.c. Giant's Causeway – Fountain Lake (Vigors)
February 19. Ninth foal. $130,000Y. Keeneland
September. M Johnston. Brother to a minor US
three year old winner and half-brother to the
triple Grade 1 winner and Kentucky Derby,
Preakness Stakes and Belmont Stakes placed
Free House (by Smokester). The dam, a minor
US stakes winner, is a half-sister to one stakes
winner. The second dam, Hotsie Totsie (by
Icecapade), is an unplaced half-sister to five
winners. (Favourites Racing).

870. LOVE PEGASUS (USA) ★★★
b.br.c. Fusaichi Pegasus – Take Charge Lady
(Dehere)
January 27. Third foal. $85,000Y. Keeneland
September. M Johnston. The dam won 11 races
including the Ashland Stakes, Spinster Stakes
and Alcibiades Stakes – all Group 1 events, and
is a half-sister to 2 US stakes winners. The
second dam, Felicita (by Rubiano), is an unraced
half-sister to six winners. (M Doyle).

871. NUWAITH ★★★
ch.f. Efisio – Tourmalet (Night Shift)
February 6. Second foal. Half-sister to the fair
2007 7f and 1m placed two year old Stop On
(by Fraam). The dam, a quite useful two year old
5f winner, is a half-sister to the fairly useful two
year old 7f winner Fu Manchu. The second dam,
Robsart (by Robellino), a fairly useful 7f winner
at three years, is a half-sister to five minor
winners. (Jaber Abdullah).

872. MAKHAALEB (USA) ★★★
ch.c. Mr Greeley – Guerre Et Paix (Soviet Star)
March 2. Fifth foal. $450,000Y. Keeneland
September. Shadwell Estate Co. Half-brother to
the very useful listed 10f winner and Group 3
placed Zaham and to the quite useful Irish 10f
and hurdles winner Alqaab (both by Silver
Hawk). The dam, a 1m winner in France at two
years and listed placed, subsequently won once
in the USA and is a half-sister to 2 stakes-placed
winners. The second dam, Fire and Shade (by
Shadeed), was a fairly useful two year old 6f
winner. (Hamdan Al Maktoum).

873. PARTHENON ★★★
b.c. Dubai Destination – Grecian Slipper
(Sadler's Wells)
January 30. Half-brother to the 1m (at two
years) and Group 3 9f Prix de Conde winner
Graikos (by Rainbow Quest), to the Group 3
15.5f Prix de Barbeville winner Magna Graecia
(by Warning) and the Irish 9f winner Fustanella
(by Mtoto). The dam, a useful 8.3f to 11.6f
winner, is closely related to the quite useful two
year old 6f winner Mount Helena and a half-
sister to the French 1m and 12f winner and
listed-placed Sovetsky. The second dam, Helen
Street (by Troy), won three races including the
Irish Oaks. (Hamdan Al Maktoum).

874. PINOCCHIO ★★★
ch.c. Dr Fong – Party Doll (Be My Guest)
May 17. Fourteenth foal. 140,000Y. Tattersalls
October 2. M Johnston. Half-brother to the
2007 German two year old 7f winner Briseida (by
Pivotal), to the Group 2 6.5f Criterium des 2 Ans
and Group 2 5f Prix du Gros-Chene winner and
sire Titus Livius, the French and North American
winner of four races Bahama Dream, the UAE 5f
winner Zadalrakib (all by Machiavellian), the two
year old winner and listed-placed Party Zane (by
Zafonic), the fairly useful two year old 5f and
subsequent US winner Shegardi (by Primo
Dominie) and the minor French three year old
winner Doliouchka (by Saumarez). The dam, a
very useful winner of four races in France
including 3 listed events from 5f to 1m, was
Group 3 placed twice and is a half-sister to ten
winners. The second dam, Midnight Lady (by
Mill Reef), won once at two years and is a half-
sister to five winners including the US Grade 2
winner Regal Bearing. (Hamdan Al Maktoum).

875. ROMAN REPUBLIC (FR) ★★★
b.c. Cape Cross – Mare Nostrum (Caerleon)
February 4. Third foal. 200,000Y. Tattersalls
October 2. John Ferguson. Half-brother to the
minor French two year old 1m winner Hurricane
Mist (by Spinning World). The dam won the
Group 3 9.2f Prix Vanteaux and was placed in
both the Group 1 Prix Saint-Alary and Group 1
Prix Vermeille and is a half-sister to seven

winners including the US Grade 1 winner Aube Indienne. The second dam, Salvora (by Spectacular Bid), won once at three years in France and is a half-sister to seven winners and to the dam of the Australian triple Grade 1 winner Flying Spur. (Hamdan Al Maktoum).

876. ROYAL SOCIETY ★★★

b.c. King's Best – Nawaiet (Zilzal)
February 3. Half-brother to the very smart Group 2 Celebration Mile and Group 2 Queen Anne Stakes winner No Excuse Needed, to the useful two year old 5f winner and Group 3 Norfolk Stakes third Skywards and the quite useful 10f winner Nawadi (all by Machiavellian). The dam, a French 6f winner, is a half-sister to the high-class filly Fitnah, winner of the 10f Prix Saint-Alary, the Prix Vanteaux, the Prix de la Nonette and the Prix du Prince d'Orange. The second dam, Greenland Park (by Red God), was a high-class winner of the Queen Mary Stakes, the Molecomb Stakes and the Cornwallis Stakes, is a sister to the Coventry Stakes winner Red Sunset and a half-sister to the unraced Mary Martin, herself dam of the very useful filly Marina Park. (Hamdan Al Maktoum).

877. SAVE THE DAY ★★★

b.f. Dr Fong – Modelliste (Bering)
January 31. Half-sister to the fair 2007 two year old 8.7f winner Might Be Magic (by Fraam), to the quite useful two year old 1m winner Samara Middle East (by Marju) and the fair two year old 6f winner Moujoudh (by Mujadil). The dam, a 1m winner in the UAE, is a half-sister to the useful two year old 7f winner Velour and to the very useful listed 7f Oak Tree Stakes winner Beraysim. The second dam, Silk Braid (by Danzig), was a useful winner of a three year old 9f York maiden and a 12f Italian listed event and is a half-sister to the Belmont and Preakness Stakes winner and champion three year old colt Risen Star. (Jaber Abdullah).

878. SHAWEEL ★★★

b.c. Dansili – Cooden Beach (Peintre Celebre)
March 29. First foal. 120,000Y. Tattersalls October 2. Shadwell Estate Co. The dam, a

moderate 1m winner, is a half-sister to two minor winners. The second dam, Joyful (by Green Desert), a fair 7f all-weather winner at three years, is a half-sister to five winners including the top-class filly Golden Opinion, winner of the Group 1 1m Coronation Stakes and placed in the French 1,000 Guineas and the July Cup. (Sheikh Ahmed Al Maktoum).

879. STEP AT A TIME ★★★

ch.f. Danehill Dancer – Zing Ping (Thatching)
March 21. Ninth foal. 72,000Y. Tattersalls October 1. M Johnston. Half-sister to the Irish two year old 6f winner and Group 1 7f Moyglare Stud Stakes second Fear And Greed, to the two year old 6.5f Goffs Challenge and subsequent Hong Kong winner Serious Play and the quite useful 8.5f and 9.4f winner Fast And Furious (all by Brief Truce). The dam, a quite useful two year old 7f placed maiden, is a half-sister to four winners here and abroad. The second dam, Shebasis (by General Holme), is an unraced half-sister to six minor winners. (Stuart Counsell).

880. STEP FAST (USA) ★★★

ch.f. Giant's Causeway – Nannerl (Valid Appeal)
January 25. Seventh foal. $200,000Y. Keeneland September. M Johnston. Closely related to three winners including the US Grade 2 Schuylerville Stakes and Grade 2 Landaluce Stakes winner Magicalmysterycat and the Japanese stakes-placed winner Tsumujikaze (all by Storm Cat) and half-sister to two minor winners. The dam won 10 races including two Grade 2 events in the USA and is a half-sister to eight winners. The second dam, Allouette (by Proud Birdie), won 3 minor races in the USA and is a half-sister to the dual US Grade 1 winner Fact Finder. (Stuart Counsell).

881. TAAZUR ★★★ ♠

b.c. Needwood Blade – Mouchez Le Nez (Cyrano de Bergerac)
April 5. Eighth foal. 55,000Y. Tattersalls October 2. Shadwell Estate Co. Half-brother to the unraced 2007 two year old Springfield Lass (by Compton Place), to the fair 1m to 11f

winner of four races Kilmeny (by Royal Abjar), the fair two year old 5f winner Mouchoir (by Bahamian Bounty), the modest 5f winner Shaymee's Girl (by Wizard King) and two winners abroad by Nicolette and Case Law. The dam is an unplaced half-sister to two winners. The second dam, Gale Force Seven (by Strong Gale), is an unraced half-sister to the Group 2 Geoffrey Freer Stakes winner Swell Fellow. (Hamdan Al Maktoum).

882. TAKAATUF ★★★
b.c. Dubai Destination – Karlaka
(Barathea)
February 11. First foal. 100,000Y. Tattersalls October 2. Shadwell Estate Co. The dam is an unraced half-sister to four winners including the two year old Group 3 1m May Hill Stakes winner Karasta and the Group 2 2m 2f Doncaster Cup dead-heat winner Kasthari. The second dam, Karliyka (by Last Tycoon), a French winner of four races, was listed placed over 1m and 10f and is a half-sister to four winners. (Hamdan Al Maktoum).

883. TARTAN GUNNA ★★★
b.c. Anabaa – Embraced (Pursuit Of Love)
March 8. Fourth foal. 55,000Y. Tattersalls October 1. M Johnston. Half-brother to the quite useful 1m winner Fondled (by Selkirk) and to the quite useful 7.5f and 1m winner of three races Caressed (by Medicean). The dam, a useful listed 1m winner, is a half-sister to six winners including the Group 2 Summer Mile winner Cesare and the Group 3 12f Prix la Force winner and French Derby second Nowhere To Exit. The second dam, Tromond (by Lomond), a fairly useful 9f winner, was second in the listed 10f Ballymacoll Stud Stakes at Newbury and is a half-sister to six winners. (Mrs I Bird).

884. TARZAN (IRE) ★★★
ch.c. Spinning World – Run To Jane (Doyoun)
March 16. Fifth foal. 135,000Y. Tattersalls October 2. John Warren. Half-brother to the quite useful 2007 Irish 8.5f placed two year old Budapest (by Montjeu) and to the fair two year old 7f winner Emerald Penang (by Alzao). The dam is an unplaced half-sister to six winners including the Irish listed winner Broadway Rosie (herself dam of the dual Group 3 winner Eastern Purple). The second dam, Broadway Royal (by Royal Match), is an unraced half-sister to the Kings Stand Stakes winner African Song. (Highclere Thorough-bred Racing).

885. UNNAMED ★★★
b.c. Proud Citizen – Tom's Cat (Storm Cat)
April 12. Third foal. $200,000Y. Keeneland September. McKeever St Lawrence. Half-brother to the US Grade 2 and Grade 3 winner Cowtown Cat. The dam was a minor four year old winner in the USA. The second dam, Shouldn't Say Never (by Meadowlake), a stakes winner and Grade 3 placed in the USA, is a half-sister to three stakes winners. (Sheikh Hamdan bin Mohammed).

SYLVESTER KIRK
886. BARWELL BRIDGE ★★★★
b.c. Red Ransom – Sentimental Value (Diesis)
January 26. First foal. 35,000Y. Tattersalls October 2. Sylvester Kirk. The dam, a winner of 2 stakes events in the USA and Grade 3 placed, is a half-sister to two winners in Japan. The second dam, Stately Star (by Deputy Minister), a stakes winner of six races in the USA and is a half-sister to six winners. (N Pickett).
'A lovely horse, he's doing very well and has improved physically since we bought him. He's precocious enough for a big horse and I'll start him off at six furlongs early in the season. I'm very pleased with him.'

887. DR VALENTINE ★★★
ch.c. Dr Fong – Red Roses Story (Pink)
March 9. Fourth foal. 32,000foal. Tattersalls December. Littleton Stud. Half-brother to the quite useful two year old 6f winner In Full Cry (by Grand Lodge). The dam won the Group 1 Prix Royal-Oak and is a half-sister to two winners. The second dam, Roses For The Star (by Stage Door Johnny), a listed winner and second in the Oaks, is a half-sister to the Irish Derby winners Ribocco and Ribero. (J C Smith).

'A very, very nice colt but he's highly strung and if we can keep his mind right he'll be a really nice horse. He's grown and is tall and leggy and he also appears to be precocious but that's just his temperament because if we give him a bit of time he'll reap the rewards.'

888. EIGHTDAYSAWEEK ★★★

b.f. Montjeu – Figlette (Darshaan)
February 13. Second foal. 26,000Y. Tattersalls October 1. Not sold. Half-sister to the fair 2007 8.7f two year old winner Moment's Notice (by Beat Hollow). The dam is an unraced half-sister to three winners including the listed 1m and 10f winner Sublimity and the UAE Group 3 1m winner Marbush (by Linamix). The second dam, Fig Tree Drive (by Miswaki), a fairly useful two year old 6f winner on her only start, is a half-sister to four winners. (Mr C Wright).
'A lovely-moving filly but you won't see her until later in the year, although surprisingly for a Montjeu she's a short-coupled filly and looks more precocious than she really is. She goes along quite nicely and has a good attitude.'

889. FANTASTIC DAY ★★★

b.c. Fantastic Light – Seamstress (Barathea).
January 27. Third foal. 75,000Y. Tattersalls October 1. Sylvester Kirk. Half-brother to the moderate 2007 8.5f fourth placed two year old Lella Beya (by Diktat) and to the very useful two year old listed 5f Windsor Castle Stakes and 5.2f Weatherbys Super Sprint winner Elhamri (by Noverre). The dam, a fair two year old 7f winner, subsequently won over 1m in the USA and is a sister to two winners including the useful two year old Group 3 7f C L Weld Park Stakes winner Rag Top and a half-sister to four winners including the fairly useful 7.6f and subsequent US 1m winner Red Top and the fairly useful two year old dual 5f winner Lady Sarka. The second dam, Petite Epaulette (by Night Shift), a fair 5f winner at two years, is a full or half-sister to three winners. (Mr N Ormiston).
'Not as precocious as his half-brother Elhamri who was a pocket rocket. This fella has a lot more scope and hence we've given him more time. A nice horse.'

890. FISCAL LAD ★★★

ch.c. Efisio – Duty Paid (Barathea)
February 3. Second foal. Half-brother to the fair 2007 7f placed two year old Duty Doctor (by Dr Fong). The dam, a useful two year old listed 6f winner, is a sister to the useful 1m winner and listed-placed Lady Miletrian and a half-sister to three winners. The second dam, Local Custom (by Be My Native), was placed at up to 7f at two years and is a sister to the listed winner Tribal Rite and a half-sister to the Middle Park Stakes winner Balla Cove. (J C Smith).
'A nice horse, but dip-backed. He has a good attitude and he moves well but I won't be rushing him. He'll be setting off at six furlongs.'

891. FLEUR DE'LION (IRE) ★★★

ch.f. Lion Heart – Viburnum (El Gran Senor)
April 10. Fifth foal. 20,000Y. Doncaster St Leger. Sylvester Kirk. Half-sister to the Italian two year old winner Bod Stravinsky (by Stravinsky). The dam is an unraced sister to two winners including the Group 1 Middle Park Stakes third Cordoba and a half-sister to five winners. The second dam, Gay Senorita (by Raise A Native), won in the USA and is a full or half-sister to seven winners including the US Graded stakes winners Gulls Cry and Gala Regatta. (Mrs N F Lee).
'She's small but every week she improves and grows and she hasn't missed a day since we bought her. I could run her anytime but I think she'll benefit if we give her the chance to grow up. A fine filly and whatever trip we start her at I think she'll end up a seven furlong two year old.'

892. HARRY RAFFLE ★★★

b.br.c. Observatory – Encore My Love (Royal Applause)
March 2. Third foal. 22,000Y. Tattersalls October 3. Sylvester Kirk. Half-brother to the quite useful two year old 5f and 6f winner Prospect Place (by Compton Place). The dam, a modest 6f placed two year old, is a half-sister to six winners including the Group 1 Racing Post Trophy winner Be My Chief. The second dam, Lady Be Mine (by Sir Ivor), a minor three year old 1m winner at Yarmouth, is a half-sister to six

winners including Mixed Applause (dam of both the high-class miler Shavian and the Ascot Gold Cup winner Paean).
'I haven't done an awful lot with him because unfortunately he had an eye injury. I was looking forward to kicking on with him because he was a small, butty, sharp little horse. I'm going to have to wait with him now and he'll probably be a six furlong type in mid-season.'

893. HELLBENDER (IRE) ★★★★
ch.c. Exceed And Excel – Desert Rose (Green Desert)
January 30. Fifth foal. 65,000Y. Tattersalls October 2. Sylvester Kirk. Half-brother to the modest 12f winner Sir Sandicliffe (by Distant Music). The dam ran once unplaced and is a half-sister to the smart 6f winner Feet So Fast and the Group 2 Lowther Stakes winner Soar. The second dam, Splice (by Sharpo), a smart winner of seven races including the listed 6f Abernant Stakes, is a full or half-sister to seven winners. (Mr N Ormiston).
'A lovely horse, he's growing all the time, he's very laid back and I haven't worked him yet. I'm just hoping that when I do wind him up he'll be a really nice horse. Six furlongs should suit him and I was hoping that being by Exceed And Excel he'd be earlier. A really good-looking, strong colt.'

894. LENNY BRISCOE (IRE) ★★★★
b.c. Rock Of Gibraltar – Tammany Hall (Petorius)
April 10. Fifth foal. €90,000Y. Goffs Million. Sylvester Kirk. Half-brother to the unplaced 2007 two year old Carracove (by Key Of Luck) and to the Irish two year old 6f winner I Key (by Fasliyev). The dam is an unraced half-sister to three winners including the two year old Group 3 6f Coventry Stakes winner CD Europe. The second dam, Woodland Orchid (by Woodman), is an unplaced half-sister to the Group three winners D'Anjou and Truth Or Dare. (Mr N Ormiston).
'A lovely horse, he was very weak when we bought him at the sales but he's turned into a gorgeous horse that could be anything. He's

more of a three year old type and he'll start in the final quarter of the season, but he's not big and backward and is a horse that you could bring forward a couple of months. A nice horse and I really like him.'

895. LUCKIER (IRE) ★★★
gr.f. Key Of Luck – Ibiza (Linamix)
February 28. Fifth foal. €30,000Y. Goffs Million. Sylvester Kirk. Half-sister to the quite useful two year old 5f winner Spree (by Dansili). The dam won over 10.5f in Germany and is a half-sister to four winners including the German dual listed winner and Group 1 Italian Derby third Iberus. The second dam, Iberica (by Green Dancer), won a listed race in Germany and is a half-sister to three winners. (The Hon. Mrs J M Corbett & Mr C Wright).
'She had a minor setback but she'll be alright and she's a lovely filly, a good mover with a nice temperament. I like her a lot and although people tell me that Key Of Luck horses are temperamental I've had no issues with her. Seven furlongs should suit her.'

896. OUR WEE GIRL ★★★
b.br.f. Choisir – Zwadi (Docksider)
March 2. €24,000Y. Tattersalls Ireland. S A Kirk. The dam was placed 11 times from 6f to 1m at two and three years and is a half-sister to five winners including the listed winning two year old Duty Paid. The second dam, Local Custom (by Be My Native), was placed at up to 7f at two years and is a sister to the listed winner Tribal Rite and a half-sister to the Middle Park Stakes winner Balla Cove. (S A Kirk).
'A sharp, early filly that should be racing in late April or early May.' TRAINER'S BARGAIN BUY

897. SHORT CUT ★★★★
b.c. Compton Place – Rush Hour (Night Shift)
March 18. Fourth foal. 65,000Y. Doncaster St Leger. J Brummitt. Half-brother to the unplaced 2007 two year old Bouggler (by Tobougg) and to the quite useful 6f (at two years) and 7f winner of four races Lincolneurocruiser (by Spectrum). The dam is an unraced full or half-sister to five winners. The second dam, Hastening

(by Shirley Heights), is an unraced sister to the Group 2 10f Prince of Wales's Stakes winner Perpendicular and a half-sister to the very useful Group 3 1m Juddmonte Stakes winner Prismatic. (Brannon, Dennis, Dick, Holden).

'A colt with a wonderful temperament, he seems to have a bit of speed and he's a wonderful mover. He had a cough early on and I haven't done as much with him as I could have done. A real smart horse.'

898. SIENNA LAKE (IRE) ★★★★

b.f. Fasliyev – Lolita's Gold (Royal Academy)
February 15. Second foal. 18,000Y. Tattersalls October 1. S Kirk. The dam, placed at two and three years over 9f and 10f, is a half-sister to three winners including the Group 3 Jersey Stakes winner Membership. The second dam, Shamisen (by Diesis), a fairly useful two year old 7f winner and second in the Group 2 6f Lowther Stakes, is a sister to the Group 3 8.5f Diomed Stakes winner Enharmonic and a half-sister to nine winners including the listed 1m Atalanta Stakes winner Soprano. (S A Kirk).

'She's a lovely filly and she's more forward than most so she'll be one of the first of the fillies to run. She has the potential to be anything, she seems to be coming early and I'm pleased with her.'

899. TALKING HANDS ★★★

b.c. Mujahid – With Distinction (Zafonic)
February 26. Second foal. 16,000Y. Tattersalls October 3. Sylvester Kirk. Half-brother to the fair 2007 Irish two year old 7f winner Herbert Crescent (by Averti). The dam, placed once over 12f, is a half-sister to three winners. The second dam, Air Of Distinction (by Distinctly North), won three races including the Group 3 Anglesey Stakes and is a full or half-sister to nine winners. (Deauville Daze Partnership).

'A big horse, he had to be gelded because of his temperament – hardly surprising given he's by Mujahid and out of a Zafonic mare. He's a good mover, has a little bit of a high knee action and isn't an obvious five furlong type. I'm pleased with him and he's a good-looking horse that's doing everything nice.'

900. THEWAYTOSANJOSE (IRE) ★★

b.f. Fasliyev – Soltura (Sadler's Wells)
April 17. Ninth foal. €40,000Y. Tattersalls Ireland. John O'Byrne. Half-sister to the Italian two year old winner and listed placed Discover Roma (by Rock Of Gibraltar), to the fair Irish 7f winner Alcadia (by Thatching) and the minor Irish 10f and jumps winner Urban Hymn (by College Chapel). The dam is an unraced half-sister to nine winners including the US Grade 2 winner Sword Dance. The second dam, Rosa Mundi (by Secretariat), a listed-placed winner in Ireland, is a half-sister to five winners including the Group 1 National Stakes winner Fatherland. (S A Kirk).

'A nice, big, scopey filly, she's not an obvious two year old but she has a good attitude and she goes well. Six or seven furlongs should suit her this year.'

901. TRUE DECISION ★★

b.c. Reset – True Precision (Presidium)
April 21. Ninth foal. 8,000Y. Doncaster Festival Sales. S Kirk. Half-brother to the Group 2 Diadem Stakes and Group 3 Prix du Petit-Couvert winner Pivotal Point (by Pivotal), to the two year old 7f seller winner Madam Gaffer (by Tobougg), the fairly useful 6f and 7f winner Foreign Editor (by Magic Ring), the fair two year old 5f winner Uncle Exact (by Distant Relative) and the modest three year old all-weather 5f winner Hot Pants (by Rudimentary). The dam was a quite useful 5f to 7f winner of three races. The second dam, Madam Muffin (by Sparkler), is a placed half-sister to two minor winners.

'A smashing horse and a nice pedigree for a cheap one. He goes along quite nicely and he's a precocious horse with a great attitude. I haven't had him long but he's coming along really quickly.'

902. UNNAMED ★★★

b.f. Danehill Dancer – Windmill (Ezzoud)
May 4. Fourth living foal. 62,000Y. Tattersalls October 1. Sylvester Kirk. Closely related to the quite useful two year old 6f winner and subsequent US and Canadian winner Winds Of Time (by Danehill). The dam, a fair 13.8f winner,

is a half-sister to eight winners including the very smart Group 2 12f Ribblesdale Stakes winner Gull Nook (herself dam of the top-class colt Pentire), the equally smart Group 3 12f Princess Royal Stakes winner Banket and the useful Group 3 Ormonde Stakes winner Mr Pintips. The second dam, Bempton (by Blakeney), was placed three times at up to 11f and is a half-sister to Shirley Heights. (S A Kirk).

'She hasn't been in that long as she was having a break to grow up a bit. A small, short-coupled filly with an ambiguous pedigree being by a sprinter and out of a mare with plenty of stamina.'

WILLIAM KNIGHT

903. DALRADIAN (IRE) ★★★★
b.c. Dansili – Aethra (Trempolino)
May 3. 19,000Y. Tattersalls October 1. Not sold.
Half-brother to the French listed 1m winner Kane Ore (by Green Desert), to the useful 8.5f (at two years) and 10f winner Alphaeus (by Sillery), the fairly useful 12f and 14f winner Ogee (by Generous), the fair 5f and 7f winner Bob's Buzz (by Zilzal), the fair 9.5f winner View From The Top (by Mujahid), the fair 5f and 7f winner Bob's Buzz (by Zilzal) and the moderate 7f winner Barataria (by Barathea). The dam, a fairly useful 1m placed maiden, is a sister to the German listed winner Tamanna and a half-sister to three winners. The second dam, All For Hope (by Sensitive Prince), is an unraced half-sister to the 10.5f Prix de Diane winner Lacovia (herself dam of the champion two year old Tobougg). (Hesmonds Stud Ltd).

'He'll probably start off in a mile maiden around June/July time, he's a nice mover and looks like he's got plenty of ability. He didn't have the greatest of hocks and I think that's why he got overlooked at the sales. Fortunately they haven't been a problem and he's a strong-looking colt with a good attitude.'

904. DECEMBER DRAW (IRE) ★★★
br.c. Medicis – New York (Danzero)
April 14. First foal. 25,000Y. Tattersalls October 3. A Skiffington. The dam was placed 3 times over 7f at two and three years and is a half-sister

to 11 winners including the very smart Group 2 5f Flying Childers Stakes and Weatherbys Super Sprint winner Superstar Leo. The second dam, Council Rock (by General Assembly), a fair 9f and 10f placed three year old, is a half-sister to nine winners including the Group 3 Prestige Stakes winner Glatisant (herself dam of the 2,000 Guineas winner Footstepsinthesand). (Brook House).

'He's going to need more time than I thought and probably won't be out on the racecourse until September time. But he looks to be a nice colt, he's a nice size and a good-actioned horse. I think he'll have plenty of speed and might be a six/seven furlong horse.'

905. DESERT ICON (IRE) ★★★
b.c. Desert Style – Gilded Vanity (Indian Ridge)
March 6. Second foal. 36,000Y. Doncaster St Leger. L Norris. The dam, a minor Irish 5f winner, is a sister to two winners including the smart 1m winner and Irish 2,000 Guineas second Fa-Eq and a half-sister to the smart listed 7.3f and 1m winner Corinium and the useful dual 5f winner (including at two years) Ellway Star. The second dam, Searching Star (by Rainbow Quest), a modest 6f (at two years) to 11.3f placed maiden, is a half-sister to eight winners including the smart listed Blue Riband Trial winner Beldale Star. (Mr B & Mrs D Willis, Mr B & Mrs M Pullin).

'A neat, compact two year old that should be relatively early – around June time. A nice colt that should have a future over six or seven furlongs.'

906. EBONY EYES ★★★★
br.f. King's Best – Qui Liz (Benny The Dip)
February 4. Second foal. The dam is an unraced half-sister to ten winners including the Group 2 1m Lockinge Stakes winner Emperor Jones and the Group 1 1m William Hill Futurity Stakes winner Bakharoff. The second dam, Qui Royalty (by Native Royalty), a winner of five races at up to 1m in the USA, was second in the Grade 3 Boiling Springs Handicap and is a half-sister to eight winners. (D G Hardisty).

'She's very nice, a good size and a very nice mover with a bit of class. Probably an August type two year old and she'll make into a nice three year old. She should win this year.'

907. GIFT OF TIME ★★★

b.f. *Cadeaux Genereux – Watchkeeper (Rudimentary)*

March 28. Fourth foal. 32,000Y. Tattersalls October 2. Rabbah Bloodstock. Half-sister to the modest all-weather dual 10f winner Watchmaker (by Bering). The dam, a quite useful dual 10f winner at three years, is a half-sister to five winners. The second dam, Third Watch (by Slip Anchor), a 7f (at two years) and Group 2 12f Ribblesdale Stakes winner, is a half-sister to the Group winners Richard of York, Three Tails (herself dam of the high-class colts Tamure and Sea Wave) and Maysoon and to the dams of the Group winners Lend A Hand and Talented. (Hesmonds Stud).

'A neat, compact filly that got spun at the sales because of her wind but that doesn't seem to be a problem. I think she'll be out around July or August and probably over seven furlongs or a mile.'

908. MACKTEN ★★★

b.c. *Makbul – Tender (Zieten)*

April 10. First foal. The dam, a modest triple 5f winner (including at two years), is a half-sister to several winners. The second dam, is an unplaced half-sister to the very useful listed 7f winner Supercal. (Mrs F Ashfield).

'He's showing speed and he'll be an early two year old. A compact colt, he goes alright and is worth putting in the book.'

909. MISS SOPHISTICAT ★★

b.f. *Alhaarth – She's Classy (Boundary)*

March 5. Third foal. 75,000Y. Tattersalls October 2. Blandford Bloodstock. Half-sister to Royal Manor (by King's Best), unplaced in one start at two years in 2007 and to the minor US three year old winner Swanky (by Saint Ballado). The dam won two races at two years in the USA including a stakes event and was Grade 1 placed twice and is a half-sister to three minor winners. The second dam, Stately Dance (by Stately Don), won 2 minor races in the USA and is a half-sister to four winners including the Coronation Cup winner and sire Be My Native. (Mrs S M Mitchell).

'She's an attractive, scopey filly with a bit of a high knee action and she'll probably run a couple of times and then be put away for next year. Although she's scopey, she's also strong looking and looks to be a nice-enough filly.'

910. PENZINA ★★★★

ch.f. *Tobougg – Penmayne (Inchinor)*

February 6. Fifth foal. 45,000Y. Tattersalls October 2. Norris/Huntingdon. Half-sister to the fairly useful 2007 two year old 5f and 6f winner Kylayne (by Kyllachy) and to a four year old winner in Sweden by Dr Fong. The dam, a fairly useful two year old 7f winner, was listed-placed and is a half-sister to five winners including the useful 6f, 6.5f (both at two years) and listed 1m winner Salamanca. The second dam, Salanka (by Persian Heights), a fair three year old 10f winner, is a half-sister to one winner. (Spiers, Taylor, Taylor).

'A big, scopey filly, she'll be out around August time and will make up into a nice three year old. She's a lovely mover with a good attitude and I think she's a nice filly that looks as if she has a bit of class about her. She should be winning as a two year old but she's got plenty of size about her.'

911. ROYAL TOERAG ★★★

b.c. *Bertolini – Yesterday's Song (Shirley Heights)*

March 7. Sixth foal. 9,500Y. Tattersalls October 3. Not sold. Half-brother to the moderate 1m seller winner Audrey's Dilemma (by Piccolo) and to two minor winners abroad by Lujain and Piccolo. The dam is an unraced half-sister to five winners including the German Group 3 winner Miss Gazon. The second dam, Farewell Song (by The Minstrel), won twice at three years and is sister to the Italian St Leger winner Parting Moment. (Bryan Fry and the Toerags).

'He was cheap and is an attractive looking horse for five grand. I'm quite pleased with him and he's a nice mover. Quite heavy topped, he's not as

precocious as I'd hoped he'd be, so I'm thinking seven furlongs or a mile in July or August would be right for him.'

912. STRAIGHT LACED ★★★

b.f. Refuse To Bend – Gaelic Swan (Nashwan)
January 20. Third foal. Half-sister to Mardood (by Oasis Dream), a fair third over 7f from two starts at two years in 2007. The dam was placed over 12f and is a half-sister to five winners including the Group 2 Great Voltigeur winner Bonny Scot and the dam of the King George and 2,000 Guineas winner Golan. The second dam, Scots Lass (by Shirley Heights), won over 13f. (Mrs P A Cooke).
'A nice, attractive, big, scopey filly. She's a lovely mover with a good attitude and she'll hopefully run a couple of times and be put away to make up into a nice three year old. She's got a bit of class about her.'

913. TRANSFORMER (IRE) ★★★

b.c. Trans Island – Lady At War (Warning)
February 14. 20,000Y. Tattersalls October 2. Private Sale. Half-brother to the quite useful two year old 7f winner Sir Northerndancer (by Danehill Dancer), to the quite useful two year old 6f and subsequent US stakes winner Seeking Answers (by Shinko Forest), the modest 7f and 1m winner Lady Suesanne and the poor 7f winner Cape Sydney (both by Cape Cross). The dam is an unraced sister to four winners. The second dam, Naswara (by Al Nasr), won twice at three years and is a half-sister to six winners. (Miss S K Bowles).
'He hurt himself just being he was going to go into the sales ring and we bought him out of the ring. He looks to be a nice colt, he'll be out in June or July and is an attractive horse with a good attitude that could go and win a few races for us. Seven furlongs should suit him.'
TRAINER'S BARGAIN BUY

DAVID LANIGAN

914. CONVITEZZA ★★★

ch.c. Domedriver – Condoleezza (Cozzene)
February 13. Second foal. Sister to Indy Driver, unplaced in one start at two years in 2007. The

dam, a fair 14f winner, is out of the French 1m (at two years) to 11.5f listed winner Rosabella (by Niniski), herself a half-sister to six winners.
'She's a nice filly and she should be out by July time over six or seven furlongs. If she improves with the sun on her back as much as she has done over the past month she'll be a different filly. She goes very well and was quite small when she came in. She'll make a two year old.'

915. OTTOMAN EMPIRE (FR) ★★

ch.c. Pivotal – Chesnut Bird (Storm Bird)
May 7. Fourth foal. €360,000Y. Deauville August. Peter Doyle. The dam won three races, including 2 listed events, at three years in France and is a half-sister to the Group 3 winner Caesarion. The second dam, Carelaine (by Woodman), won once in the USA and is out of the triple Grade 1 winner Annoconnor.
'He's a big, strong horse that's going to take a bit of time. One for the back-end of the season over seven furlongs or a mile'

916. UNNAMED ★★★

b.f. Galileo – Desert Bluebell (Kalaglow)
April 16. Thirteenth foal. €80,000Y. Goffs Million. Not sold. Closely related to the minor US three year old winner Bluebird Day (by Sadler's Wells) and half-sister to six winners including the useful two year old 1m and subsequent US stakes winner Distant Mirage, the fairly useful two year old dual 7f winner Tayil (both by Caerleon), the useful 1m and subsequent US winner Roses In The Snow (by Be My Guest and herself dam of the triple US Grade 3 winner Snowdrop), the quite useful 9.5f and 10f winner Custodian (by Giant's Causeway) and the minor Italian winner of seven races Barbara Frietchie (by Try My Best). The dam was placed 3 times at three years and stayed 13.6f and is a sister to the Group 3 Solario Stakes winner Shining Water (herself dam of the Grand Criterium and Dante Stakes winner Tenby) and a half-sister to nine winners. The second dam, Idle Waters (by Mill Reef), won the Group 2 Park Hill Stakes.
'Owned by my father and John Magnier and she's actually for sale! She's a nice filly and sharp

enough t start off at for six or seven furlongs in July. He's very straightforward and I think the sales came too early for her because she's improving all the time.'

917. UNNAMED ★★★★
b.c. Rahy – Grand Ogygia (Ogygian)
March 25. Eleventh foal. $275,000Y. Keeneland September. Rabbah Bloodstock. Half-brother to three winners including the US stakes winner and Grade 3 placed Grand Deed (by Alydeed). The dam is an unplaced half-sister to the US Grade 1 winner Chain Bracelet. The second dam, Chain (by Herbager), won over 6f at two years, is a sister to the US Grade 1 winner Yamanin. (Saif Ali & Saeed H Altayer).
'He's a very strong horse and he'll do well as a two year old I think. I'll leave him until June time but I think he'll probably come to hand quickly. He's one of those horses that you'd probably start at six furlongs and then move up to seven. He has tons of scope but he's very laid-back and it'll take a race just to wake him up.'

918. UNNAMED ★★
b.c. Theatrical – Miasma (Lear Fan)
May 6. Seventh foal. $130,000Y. Keeneland September. Rabbah Bloodstock. Half-brother to three minor winners and to the dam of the 2008 Florida Derby winner Big Burn. The dam, a fairly useful two year old 6f winner, is out of the US two year old winner Syrian Circle (by Damascus), herself a half-sister to three stakes winners including the triple Grade 1 winner Hidden Lake. (Saif Ali & Saeed H Altayer).
'A lovely, big, tall horse, he's going through an ugly duckling stage at the moment but once he fills out his frame he'll be alright. If he makes a two year old it won't be until September time at the earliest and although the pedigree has a lot of speed in it you'd say by looking at him he'd want seven furlongs to start with.'

919. UNNAMED ★★
b.f. Galileo – Ninth Wonder (Forty Niner)
January 29. Sixth foal. 48,000foal. Tattersalls December. BBA (Ire). Half-brother to the fairly useful 10f winner Abbondanza (by Cape Cross)

and to the fair 7f winner Great Explorer (by Indian Danehill). The dam is an unraced half-sister to four winners including the UAE Group 3 winner Conroy. The second dam, Crystal Gazing (by El Gran Senor), won the Group 3 7f Nell Gwyn Stakes, was third in the 1,000 Guineas and is a half-sister to four winners. (John Magnier and Michael Tabor).
'She's improving all the time and although she's a nice filly I think she'll be better off first time out over seven furlongs.'

920. UNNAMED ★★★
b.f. Dubai Destination – Noble Lily (Vaguely Noble)
February 8. Thirteenth foal. 40,000Y. Tattersalls October 1. Rabbah Bloodstock. Half-sister to the Group 3 14.6f Park Hill Stakes winner Noble Rose (by Caerleon and herself the dam of the Group 2 winner Notability), to the Group 3 Classic Trial winner Simeon, the French listed winner Noctilucent (both by Lammtarra) and two minor winners by Caerleon and Belmez. The dam is a placed half-sister to eight winners including the US Grade 1 9f Flamingo Stakes winner Talinum. The second dam, Water Lily (by Riverman), was a very useful French two year old and subsequently winner of the Grade 3 Next Move Handicap in the USA. (Saif Ali & Saeed H Altayer).
'She'll make a two year old and she'll probably start off at six furlongs. A nice, compact filly, she has two year old written all over her.'

921. UNNAMED ★★★
ch.f. Dr Fong – Quiet Counsel (Law Society)
April 1. Eighth foal. 18,000Y. Tattersalls October. Rabbah Bloodstock. Half-sister to the Group 3 Park Hill Stakes winner Discreet Brief, to the minor French four year old winner Alithini (both by Darshaan) and a bumpers winner by Spectrum. The dam, a 12f winner in Ireland, is a half-sister to seven winners includ-ing the Yorkshire Oaks winner Key Change. The second dam, Kashka (by The Minstrel), won over 12f in France and is a half-sister to the Italian Group 3 winner Karkisiya and to the dam of the Derby winner Kahyasi. (Saif Ali & Saeed H Altayer).

'On pedigree she'd want seven furlongs but she's a small, compact filly and she has plenty of scope. I think she'll be alright over six furlongs in June or July.'

922. UNNAMED ★★★★
gr.f. El Prado – Sauterne (Rainbow Quest)
February 7. Third foal. 75,000Y. Tattersalls October 1. Charlie Gordon-Watson. Half-sister to the fair 2007 two year old 7f all-weather winner Determind Stand (by Elusive Quality). The dam, a listed winner of three races from 7f to 10f, is a half-sister to five winners including the smart two year old Group 2 6f Cherry Hinton Stakes winner Applaud. The second dam, Band (by Northern Dancer), is a placed half-sister to five winners including the US Grade 3 9f New Orleans Handicap winner Festive.
'A nice filly, I'll just sit on her until June or July time but I think she'll be alright over six furlongs and then get seven later on. She's a filly I like a lot, she's sharp, has a nice attitude and I think she's pretty useful.'

923. UNNAMED ★★★★
b.f. Refuse To Bend – Star Studded (Cadeaux Genereux)
March 24. Second foal. 90,000Y. Tattersalls October 1. Rabbah Bloodstock. Half-sister to Night Premiere (by Night Shift), unplaced in two starts at two years in 2007. The dam is an unraced sister to the Group 2 5f Flying Childers Stakes and Group 3 5f King George V Stakes winner Land Of Dreams (herself the dam of a listed winner) and a half-sister to four winners. The second dam, Sahara Star (by Green Desert), won the Group 3 5f Molecomb Stakes, was third in the Lowther Stakes and is a half-sister to six winners. (Saif Ali and Saeed H Altayer).
'A nice filly, she's big, strong and scopey and I'm sitting on her as long as I can because I don't think it's any use starting her at six furlongs, she'll be better when the seven furlong maidens start. She goes very well.'

924. UNNAMED ★★★★
b.c. King's Best – Wannabe Grand (Danehill)
April 11. Sixth foal. 75,000Y. Tattersalls

October 1. Charlie Gordon-Watson. Half-brother to the useful 7f to 10f winner King Of Argos (by Sadler's Wells), to the fairly useful triple 7f winner (including at two years) and subsequent Hong Kong winner Walkonthewildside (by Giant's Causeway), the fairly useful two year old 5f winner Bachelor Of Arts (by Stravinsky), the quite useful 10.2f winner King Of Argos (by Sadler's Wells) and a winner in Japan by Selkirk. The dam won the Group 1 6f Cheveley Park Stakes and the Group 3 6f Cherry Hinton Stakes and is a half-sister to three winners including the useful two year old dual 1m winner and Group 3 second. The second dam, Wannabe (by Shirley Heights), a quite useful 1m and 10f winner, is a half-sister to three winners including the Group 1 Cheveley Park Stakes second Tanami. (Saif Ali & Saeed H Altayer).
'I think he's a nice horse, he goes very well and he'll be sharp enough to run over six furlongs first time out. Some people have told me that King's Best horses can be temperamental, but the more he does the more sensible he's getting. I like to think he'll be a nice two year old.'

EDDIE LYNAM
925. CAPTAIN HENRY (IRE) ★★★
b.g. Captain Rio – Floralia (Auction Ring)
March 24. Tenth foal. 26,000Y. Doncaster St Leger. Eddie Lynam. Half-brother to the fairly useful 7f to 9f and hurdles winner Henry Afrika (by Mujadil), to the quite useful 6f winner of nine races My Gacho (by Shinko Forest), the fair dual 1m winner Dorissio (by Efisio), the minor French three year old winner Flavinia (by Cadeaux Genereux) and two minor winners abroad by Perugino and Alhaarth. The dam, a quite useful three year old 7f and 9f winner, is a half-sister to six winners including the listed 1m Easter Stakes winner Ultimo Imperatore and the smart dual Group 3 winner Sugarfoot. The second dam, Norpella (by Northfields), a fairly useful 10f and 12f winner, is a daughter of a half-sister to Teenoso.
'He's a gelding now and a half-brother to a nice horse I had called Henry Afrika. He has a nice way of going, he'll make a two year old and will

start over six furlongs. He'd like a little cut in the ground, which isn't unusual for the sire and he's a big, strong, burly horse that carries a lot of condition.'

926. CLODOVA (IRE) ★★★
gr.f. Clodovil – Zariyba (In The Wings)
February 2. Fourth foal. €125,000Y. Goffs Million. Ed Lynam. Half-sister to the modest two year old 6f all-weather winner She Whispers (by Royal Applause). The dam is an unraced half-sister to five winners including the smart Group 3 7f Greenham Stakes winner and Group 2 12f King Edward VII Stakes second Zayyani and the dam of the Australian Grade 2 winner Zerpour. The second dam, Zariya (by Blushing Groom), a quite useful winner of two races over 7f at two years, is a half-sister to four winners including the dam of the Group 1 Prix Saint-Alary winner Zainta. (Lady O'Reilly).
'A lovely filly, there's a lot to like about her and the idea would be to win the Fillies' Million race. She'll be suited by seven furlongs this year and she's a mid-season filly with a nice way of going and a bit of quality.'

927. CROWD PLEASER (IRE) ★★★
b.f. Royal Applause – Truly Yours (Barathea)
May 8. Third foal. €88,000Y. Goffs Million. Castlemartin Stud. Half-sister to the useful 10.5f listed winner and Group 3 1m third Truly Mine (by Rock Of Gibraltar), to the fairly useful 7f and 1m winner of four races Young Hero and to the quite useful 7f and 1m and subsequent Hong Kong winner Days Of My Life (both by Daylami). The dam, a two year old 1m winner in France, is a half-sister to three winners including the French 2,000 Guineas second Catcher In The Rye. The second dam, Truly A Dream (by Darshaan), won the Group 2 10f E P Taylor Stakes and the Group 3 12f Prix de Royaumont and is a half-sister to six winners including the dam of the Group 1 Prix Saint-Alary winner Cerulean Sky and the Group/Grade 1 placed L'Ancresse. (Lady O'Reilly).
'Her half-sister Truly Mine won a stakes race last week, so she's already gone up in value. A late foal, she's a nice filly for later in the year, she's pleasing us and we're happy with her.'

928. CROWN PRETENDER (IRE) ★★
b.c. Bachelor Duke – Rihla (Soviet Star)
March 6. First foal. 30,000Y. Tattersalls October 2. Eddie Lynam. The dam, an Irish 9f winner, is a half-sister to one winner. The second dam, Ridaiyma (by Kahyasi), a triple 12f winner, was Group 3 placed and is a half-sister to five winners.
'A nice colt, he canters well and he looks sharp and early but the way he's bred I think he's going to get a bit of a trip. One for the second half of the season.'

929. DECENT FELLA (IRE) ★★★
b.c. Marju – Mac Melody (Entrepreneur)
March 19. Second foal. €35,000Y. Tattersalls Ireland. Eddie Lynam. The dam, an Italian two year old listed 7.5f winner, is a half-sister to the very smart 11.6f to 14f winner of 12 races here and abroad and Grade 1 placed Scott's View. The second dam, Milly Of The Vally by Caerleon), a fairly useful 12f winner, is a half-sister to eight winners including the listed winner and Doncaster Cup third Bosham Mill.
'A well-made, very well-balanced colt but he's had a setback and won't be out for quite some time, which is a shame because he was looking like my best two year old.'

930. DENNY CRANE ★★
b.c. Red Ransom – Fleeting Rainbow (Rainbow Quest)
March 21. Tenth foal. 40,000Y. Tattersalls October 2. BBA (Ire). Half-brother to the high-class Group 1 10.5f Tattersalls Gold Cup and Group 2 10f Pretty Polly Stakes winner Rebelline, to the smart Irish colt Quws (both by Robellino), a winner of six races from 5f (at two years) to 11f including the Group 2 Blandford Stakes and the Group 3 Gallinule Stakes, the useful two year old 6f and 7f winner Moonlight Man (by Night Shift), the fair Irish 1m and 10f winner Danzelline (by Danzero) and the French 1m winner Partly Sunny (by Alhaarth). The dam, a modest 10f placed three year old, is a half-sister to three winners. The second dam, Taplow (by Tap On Wood), is an unraced half-sister to seven winners including the dams of

the Group winners Adam Smith, Braashee, Ghariba, Careafolie, Gouriev and Run And Gun. *'He's got a proper pedigree and I like him but I'll be taking my time with him this year I've named him after the eccentric character played by William Shatner in the TV series Boston Legal!'*

931. EMILY DICKINSON ★★★
b.f. Kheleyf – Dahlawise (Caerleon)
January 29. Eleventh foal. 13,000Y. Doncaster St Leger. Eddie Lynam. Half-sister to the two year old 7f nursery winner Alfayza (by Danehill), the modest three year old 6f winner Denton Lad (by Prince Sabo), the fair all-weather sprint winner of eight races Dahlidya (by Midyan), the moderate middle-distance winner Seraph (by Vettori) and two winners abroad by Slip Anchor and Robellino. The dam, a fair two year old 6f winner, is a half-sister to five winners. The second dam, Cornish Heroine (by Cornish Prince), won twice and was third in the Group 3 Oaks Trial.
'She won on her debut and the second has won since, so this is one to keep an eye on. A pocket rocket, she's a sharp filly and a typical Doncaster Sales type. The Sales race at Doncaster will be her Derby.' TRAINER'S BARGAIN BUY

932. KAMADO ★★★★
b.c. Kyllachy – Palacegate Episode (Drumalis)
March 8. Eighth foal. 130,000Y. Doncaster St Leger. Eddie Lynam. Half-brother to the promising 2007 Irish listed 6f placed two year old Longing To Dance (by Danehill Dancer), to the champion Swedish two year old 5f to 1m winner King Quantas (by Danehill), the fairly useful 6f winner Foreign Edition (by Anabaa), the fairly useful two year old 6f winner Gilded Edge (by Cadeaux Genereux) and the unplaced dam of the high-class sprinter Dutch Art. The dam, a useful sprinter and winner of 11 races here and abroad including a Group 3 race in Italy and numerous listed events, is a sister to the fair sprinter Another Episode and a half-sister to the useful sprinter Palacegate Jack. The second dam, Pasadena Lady (by Captain James), is an unraced half-sister to five minor winners.
'A real sharp, racey colt, he's growing a bit on me

at the moment. He was a small tank and now he's medium-sized and he's just got to strengthen back up again. He's doing his work very impressively, which is what you'd expect being bred the way he is, he'll be a sprinter and I expect it'll be a 'Goodbye starter – hello Judge' job!'*

933. OPTIMAL POWER (IRE) ★★★
gr.c. Verglas – Optimal (Green Desert)
March 9. First foal. 30,000Y. Doncaster St Leger. BBA (Ire). The dam, a fair 10f winner, is a sister to one winner and a half-sister to two winners including the useful 12f to 15.4f and subsequent US Grade 2 winner One Off. The second dam, On Call (by Alleged), a useful winner of seven races at up to 2m, is a half-sister to six winners.
'A nice, big, strong colt by Verglas, I've had luck with this family already and I like him a lot. He's getting his act together now, he should be out over six furlongs in May and he'll probably end up getting a mile. A very good-looking horse.'

934. PARABOLA ★★
ch.f. Galileo – Zietory (Zieten)
February 20. First foal. 125,000Y. Tattersalls October 1. BBA (Ire). The dam, a two year old 6f and three year old dual 1m listed winner, is a half-sister to two winners. The second dam, Fairy Story (by Persian Bold), won five races over 7f (including at two years) and is a half-sister to four winners.
'Out of a good racemare, she's had a few niggling issues so it's early days yet but she's done nothing wrong. It's very nice to have a Galileo – I thought she'd got on the wrong bus'!

935. SPRING HORIZON (IRE) ★★★
b.f. Namid – Bye Bold Aileen (Warning)
February 5. Sixth foal. 46,000Y. Doncaster St Leger. Eddie Lynam. Closely related to the two year old listed 6f winner Manston (by Indian Ridge) and half-sister to the quite useful 1m and 10f winner Best Be Going, the modest 7f winner Concubine (both by Danehill) and a winner abroad by Alzao. The dam was placed twice at up to 9f in Ireland and is closely related to the US stakes winner Sound Reasoning and a half-sister

to the Group 3 Waterford Candelabra Stakes winner Life At The Top and the listed Zetland Stakes winner Gentilhomme. The second dam, Bold Flawless (by Bold Bidder), a winner over 12f at three years, is a sister to the US Grade 2 winner John's Gold.

'Very quick, she'll probably want a bit of cut in the ground. She's not eating as well as I'd like – she wouldn't have a McCririck type appetite! A sharp, sprinting type of filly.'

936. SUGAR BABY LOVE (IRE) ★★★

gr.f. Verglas – No Sugar Baby (Crystal Glitters)
May 12. Eleventh foal. €50,000Y. Goffs Million. Castlemartin & Skymarc. Half-sister to the 2007 1m placed two year old Moville and to eight winners including the minor French winner Nampala (both by Alhaarth), the listed 15f winner of 10 races Sweetness Herself, the quite useful two year old 6f and subsequent US stakes winner Unrivalled, the US stakes-placed winner Karla June (all by Unfuwain) and the French winner of four races and listed 1m placed Texas Tornado (by Last Tycoon). The dam was placed 8 times at two and three years in France and is a half-sister to 11 winners including three French listed winners. The second dam, Nenana Road (by Kirkland Lake), is a placed half-sister to nine winners.

'A nice type, but she's had a break and has only just come back in. She's got a bit of boot so she might start off at six furlongs in the second half of the season.'

937. WARRIOR CHANT (USA) ★★

b.br.c. War Chant – Toocloseto Comfort (Mt Livermore)
April 4. First foal. 23,000Y. Tattersalls December. Eddie Lynam. The dam is an unplaced half-sister to five winners including the Group 3 Brigadier Gerard Stakes winner Husyan. The second dam, Close Comfort (by Far North), is an unraced half-sister to six winners including the champion French two year old filly Ancient Regime and the Group 2 6.5f Prix Maurice de Gheest winner Cricket Ball.

'A lovely horse, he's a bit backward and is one for the second half of the year.'

938. UNNAMED ★★★

b.c. Peintre Celebre – Across The Ice (General Holme)
May 2. Twelfth foal. 40,000Y. Tattersalls October 2. Eddie Lynam. Half-brother to the listed 5f Rockingham Handicap winner and Group 3 Flying Five second Timote (by Indian Ridge), to the quite useful Irish two year old 7f winner King Of Tory (by Giant's Causeway), the 5f (at two years), the fair Irish 7f (at two years) and 10f winner Georgia Peach (by Pennekamp), the Irish 7f winner Markova (by Marju), the Irish two year old 5f winner Savile's Delight (by Cadeaux Genereux) and a minor winner in France by In The Wings. The dam, a minor French three year old winner, is a half-sister to ten winners including Northern Premier (Group 3 1m Prix de la Grotte and Group 3 7f Prix de la Porte Maillot). The second dam, Madame Premier (by Raja Baba), won four races in the USA including a minor stakes and was fourth in the Grade 1 6f Spinaway Stakes.

'I like him a awful lot but obviously being by Peintre Celebre I'm taking my time with him. The dam's bred some fast horses and this one won't be slow. He's a very nice horse, it's hard to say what distance he'll want, but there's nothing wrong with him.'

939. UNNAMED ★★

gr.f. Marju – Legal Steps (Law Society)
April 7. Eleventh foal. €40,000Y. Tattersalls Ireland. Eddie Lynam. Sister to the smart Group 2 6f Goldene Peitsche winner Stormont and to the moderate 10f winner Lawyer To World and half-sister to the unplaced 2007 two year old Silky Steps (by Nayef), the Irish 5f and 6f winner Quinstars (by Thatching), the dual 1m winner Stilett (by Tirol) – both fairly useful – and two minor winners in Italy and Holland by Catrail. The dam, an Irish 12.5f winner, is a half-sister to six winners including the South African Grade 1 winner Super Sheila. The second dam, Keep In Step (by Dance In Time), won a French listed event at three years and is a half-sister to five winners including the US Grade 2 winner Regal Bearing.

'A sharp looking filly but still a bit on the weak

side, her mother's claim to fame was that she was the first winner for McCoy. I hope she'll come to hand by mid-summer.'

940. UNNAMED ★★★

b.f. Kyllachy – Rumuz (Marju)
April 11. Seventh foal. €37,000Y. Goffs Sportsman's. Eddie Lynam. Half-sister to the quite useful 5f winner Girl Power, to the fairly useful Irish two year old 6f winner and listed-placed Key Rose (both by Key Of Luck) and the fairly useful Irish 6f and 7f winner of five races Empirical Power (by Second Empire). The dam was placed 4 times at up to 10f and is a half-sister to seven winners. The second dam, Balqis (by Advocator), winner of the Group 3 6f Premio Primi Passi, is a half-sister to eight winners.
'Her knees are too open for fast work at the moment but we like really her and she's very impressive in her canters. We had two good winners out of the dam, Empirical Power and Key Rose, it's a fast family and she'll be fine but I have to take my time with her for now.'

941. UNNAMED ★★★

ch.c. Hawk Wing – Shoooz (Soviet Star)
March 26. First foal. €40,000Y. Tattersalls Ireland. R Williamson. The dam, a modest Irish four year old 9f winner, is a half-sister to the useful two year old dual 6f and subsequent US stakes winner Alinga. The second dam, Cheyenne Spirit (by Indian Ridge), a useful winner of seven races including a listed event over 6f, is a half-sister to five winners including the dam of the Group 3 winner Ashdown Express.
'A second half of the season type, the dam won over nine furlongs, but it's a fast family. He'll probably want seven furlongs and he's a nice colt that goes well.'

GER LYONS

942. CHIEF WILD CAT (IRE) ★★★

b.c. One Cool Cat – Soft (Lear Fan)
January 18. First foal. 38,000Y. Doncaster St Leger. G Lyons. The dam is an unraced sister to the listed Acomb Stakes winner Comfy. The second dam, Souplesse (by Majestic Light), a listed 10f winner in France, is a half-sister to

eight winners including the Group 2 Royal Lodge Stakes winner and Breeders Cup Juvenile second Eltish.
'He's had a run already, fourth at Tipperary. He was a horse that was doing everything nicely, I liked him a lot and he was fine temperamentwise. Then for some inexplicable reason he started to go backwards on me, but I thought I'd run him anyway and see. He behaved and ran like a gentleman and I expect him to win next time out.'

943. COOL STAR (IRE) ★★

b.c. One Cool Cat – Pack Ice (Wekiva Springs)
March 13. Second foal. 33,000Y. Doncaster St Leger. Not sold. Half-brother to the promising 2007 7f placed two year old Deo Valente (by Dubai Destination). The dam, placed over 10f in France, is a half-sister to six winners including the Group 3 Debutante Stakes winner Saranac Lake. The second dam, Lake Champlain (by Kings Lake), won 2 listed events in Ireland, was second in the Irish 1,000 Guineas and is a half-sister to nine winners including the dam of Theatrical.
'He's going to need plenty of time and he'll be very like his sire that he has a bit of an attitude problem. He has an engine but mentally he has to grow up and he'll run when all the pieces fit together.'

944. GLEAMING SILVER (IRE) ★★★★

b.f. Dalakhani – Green Lassy (Green Tune)
February 18. Second foal. €80,000Y. Goffs Million. Church Farm Bloodstock. Half-sister to the 2007 two year old Meiner Faunus (by High Chaparral). The dam won over 13f and 14f in Ireland and is a half-sister to three winners including the French dual Group 2 winner (over 15f and 2m) Cut Quartz. The second dam, Cutlass (by Sure Blade), is a placed half-sister to three stakes winners.
'I trained the dam to win the Ulster Derby and she would have got black type but she was in-foal and I had to stop with her. My concern when I went to see this filly was that the mare was a late developer and the sire is Dalakhani, so she probably wasn't going to make a two year old, but I'm pleasantly surprised and I think she's very

smart. *She's not gong to be rushed and is one for seven furlongs.'*

945. INITIATION (IRE) ★★★★
b.c. Rock Of Gibraltar – Alluring Park (Green Desert)
April 19. Third foal. 100,000Y. Tattersalls October 1. Ger Lyons. The dam, a 6f winner dual listed-placed at two years, is a sister to the Japanese stakes winner Shinko Forest and a half-sister to seven winners including the champion 2007 two year old New Approach and the Group 3 1m Matron Stakes winner and dual Group 1 placed Dazzling Park. The second dam, Park Express (by Ahonoora), won five races including the Group 1 10f Phoenix Champion Stakes and is a half-sister to six winners including the listed 6f Firth of Clyde Stakes winner Myra's Best.
'A lovely horse but he'll need time and won't be on the track before June or July. I'm delighted the owners have sent him to me. He'll run when I'm 100% happy with him and when he's physically grown up. He definitely has an engine and is a lovely horse.'

946. KINETIC QUEST ★★★
ch.g. Haafhd – Megdale (Waajib)
April 16. Eighth living foal. 42,000Y. Tattersalls October 1. Church Farm Bloodstock. Half-brother to the smart 7f (at two years) and triple listed middle-distance winner Frank Sonata (by Opening Verse), to the useful two year old listed 7f Sweet Solera Stakes winner Peaceful Paradise (by Turtle Island), the fairly useful dual 7f winner Coup d'Etat (by Diktat), the fair two year old 6f winner Castellano (by Mujahid), the French three year old winner Lunch Time (by Zamindar) and the German 10f and 11f winner Meg (by Be My Chief). The dam, a fair middle-distance placed maiden, is a sister to the useful 7f to 9f winner Wijara and a half-sister to ten winners including Alhijaz, a winner of four Group 1 events in Italy. The second dam, Nawara (by Welsh Pageant), was a fair 10.2f winner.
'He's been gelded but he's smart and is a definite maiden winner. He'd be a six/seven furlong two year old, I like him a lot and I'd been very keen on the sire.'

947. KITCHI (IRE) ★★★
b.f. Key Of Luck – Manuscript (Machiavellian)
March 1. First foal. €60,000Y. Goffs Million. Church Farm Bloodstock. The dam was placed at three years in France and is a half-sister to the Irish listed winner Dossier. The second dam, Papering (by Shaadi), won the Group 2 Premio Lydia Tesio and is a half-sister to two winners.
'I love the sire and I think I trained his first stakes winner. She's a nice filly, a bit on the fragile side mentally which would be typical of the sire, but she has ability and will make a two year old over six or seven furlongs.'

948. LAC A DANCER (IRE) ★★
b.f. Danehill Dancer – Lac Dessert (Lac Ouimet)
March 4. Fourth foal. €85,000Y. Goffs Million. Eire Thoroughbreds. Closely related to the unplaced 2007 two year old Govenor Eliott (by Rock Of Gibraltar) and half-sister to the fair 1m and 12f winner Exclusive Air (by Affirmed). The dam, a dual two year old 7f winner and subsequently a US stakes winner, is a half-sister to one winner. The second dam, Tiramisu (by Roberto), won at three years in France and is a half-sister to seven winners including the dam of the Group 1 winners Pas de Reponse and Green Tune.
'She's very small but has an engine. I can't change the shape of her but I have to give her as much time as I can. She's by the right sire but needs every inch she has.'

949. OHIYESA (IRE) ★★★★
b.f. Noverre – Crohal di San Jore (Saddlers' Hall)
January 25. Third foal. €45,000Y. Goffs Million. Church Farm Bloodstock. The dam, placed twice in France and Italy, is a half-sister to six winners. The second dam, Crodas (by Shirley Heights), won 3 listed races in Italy, was third in the Group 1 Oaks d'Italia and is a half-sister to seven winners.
'My wife's in the naming department and it's Red Indian year – so the name of this filly means speed! I looked at every Noverre at the Sales since the nice horse I trained by him called

Summit Surge but I didn't buy any of them until this one – and I love her. She's very speedy, could be anything, has a great attitude and she thinks she's a colt. I'd be disappointed if she's not a smart sprinter and she has her first run at Dundalk in mid-April.' This filly ran green and was reportedly in season on her debut in mid-April.

950. PALLAZONE (IRE) ★★★
b.c. Bertolini – Genny Lim (Barathea)
April 16. First foal. 40,000Y. Tattersalls October 3. R J & R Marley. The dam, a fairly useful Irish 1m winner, is a half-sister to four winners. The second dam, Atsuko (by Mtoto), placed once at two years over 1m at Leopardstown, is a half-sister to 4 stakes winners.
'A lovely colt, he's very straightforward and very typical of the ones I've been getting over the years. He comes into the yard and does his work and you'd hardly notice he was there. I'm happy with him, he's ready to run and he won't let me down.'

951. PASAR SILBANO (IRE) ★★★
b.f. Elnadim – Give A Whistle (Mujadil)
February 9. Third foal. €25,000Y. Goffs Sportsman's. D Redvers. Half-sister to the quite useful UAE three year old 6f winner Call For Liberty (by Statue Of Liberty). The dam, a dual 5f winner at three and four years, is out of Repique (by Sharpen Up), herself a winning half-sister to the Group winners Indian Lodge, Sarhoob and Sifting Gold.
'A nice, big, strapping filly, she's built like a colt. I like her a lot and she has a great temper-ament. Could be anything.' This filly won at Dundalk at the odds of 12-1 on her debut – two days after I'd spoken to Ger! TRAINER'S BARGAIN BUY

952. UNNAMED ★★★
b.c. Oasis Dream – Forever Phoenix
(Shareef Dancer)
March 21. First foal. €50,000Y. Tattersalls Ireland. BBA (Ire). The dam, a useful 5f and 6f winner of seven races, was listed-placed twice and is a half-sister to two winners. The second dam, With Care (by Warning), won at three

years and is a half-sister to four winners.
'He's a lovely colt, small and looks like an early type – but he's not. He's deceiving me and needs time, but he has a definite engine and will run when he grows up. Handy in size but has ability.'

GEORGE MARGARSON
953. PRICELESS SPEEDFIT ★★★
ch.c. Imperial Dancer – Princess Speedfit
(Desert Prince)
February 19. Second foal. 20,000Y. Tattersalls 3. Equine Services. Half-brother to the modest 2007 7f placed two year old Princess Speedfit (by Barathea Guest). The dam was a fair 8.3f winner at three years and is a half-sister to the French listed 12f Prix de la Porte de Madrid and Group 2 placed Sibling Rival. The second dam, Perfect Sister (by Perrault), a minor French winner, is a half-sister to the US Grade 1 winner Frankly Perfect and the French listed winner and US Grade 1 placed Franc Argument. (J D Guest).
'He's quite well-forward but on pedigree I wouldn't expect him to be any earlier than a six furlong horse. He's done some good sharp work already with the idea being to have him out before the end of May and he's showing a good level of ability. I think he'll be like his sire and improve as the season goes on. He's a big, strong horse and I expect him to be able to win his maiden quite early on.'

954. UNNAMED ★★★★
b.c. Noverre – Mandragore (Slew O'Gold)
February 21. Seventh foal. 45,000Y. Tattersalls October 2. Not sold. Half-brother to the French listed winner and Group 3 Prix de Flore second Marie de Bayeux (by Turgeon), subsequently Grade 3 placed in the USA. The dam is a placed half-sister to five winners including the French listed winner Martien. The second dam, Mersey (by Crystal Palace), won the Group 1 Prix Royal-Oak and is a half-sister to the Group 1 Prix Saint-Alary winner Muncie.
'He's lovely – the apple of my eye at the moment. I think he's a bit special – you find one every now and again and I have a lot of time for him. On pedigree you'd have to say he'd want a bit of time and a bit further and that's why I'm over the

moon with him. He has bags of pace and is a lovely horse to have around. He has a cracking temperament, he's worked with older horses already and he's shown that if I ran him now he'd hack up in a maiden. Quite a big horse, he'll start in May, he has enough toe to win over five and he'll go on to be a nice six/seven furlongs colt.'

955. UNNAMED ★★★
ch.c. Lomitas – Norcroft Joy (Rock Hopper)
February 7. Half-brother to the quite useful dual 12f winner Polish Red (by Polish Precedent) and to the fair 5f (at two years) and 6f winner of eight races Norcroft (by Fasliyev). The dam, a quite useful winner of eight races over middle-distances and from three to five years, is out of the fairly useful 10f and 12f winner Greenhills Joy (by Radetzky). (Norcroft Park Stud).
'This horse is quite forward and he shows enough to say he could start at the end of May. If he doesn't win his maiden he'll be put on the back burner until later on, but he looks a nice sort of horse, maybe for nurseries.'

956. UNNAMED ★★★
ch.f. Bertolini – Norcroft Lady (Mujtahid)
February 15. Third foal. Half-sister to Totoman (by Mtoto), unplaced in one start at two years in 2007. The dam, a quite useful two year old dual 6f winner, is a half-sister to two winners. The second dam, Polytess (by Polish Patriot), was second over 10f in France and is closely related to the smart French 9f to 11f winner Lichine. (Norcroft Park Stud).
'Very well-forward, I might run her over five furlongs but I like to see them over six really. She's showing plenty of pace and lots of promise. She hasn't come in her coat yet but she's a nice type and I'll be very surprised if she isn't good enough to win a maiden.'

957. UNNAMED ★★
b.f. Needwood Blade – Plentitude
(Ela-Mana-Mou)
April 27. 3,500Y. Tattersalls October 3. M Jenner. Half-sister to the modest 10.5f winner Plenty Cried Wolf (by Wolfhound). The dam is an unraced half-sister to four minor winners.

The second dam, Normanby Lass (by Bustino), won once at two years and is a half-sister to nine winners.
'She's got plenty of attitude (and if she'd been a chestnut I wouldn't have gone near her!), but she shows plenty of speed and she'll be out quite early. She was cheap because she was badly presented at the Sales. Being a bit backward in her coat I haven't pressed her yet but I'm hoping that when I do let her off the bridle she'll find a couple of gears. A nice sort of filly.' TRAINER'S BARGAIN BUY

ALAN McCABE
958. SIR GEOFFREY ★★★★
b.c. Captain Rio – Disarm (Bahamian Bounty)
March 7. Second foal. 7,000Y. Tattersalls December. Alan McCabe. Brother to the fair 2007 two year old 6f winner Caprio. The dam is an unraced half-sister to six winners including the useful lsted winner Nominator. The second dam, Najariya (by Northfields), is an unraced half-sister to the Cherry Hinton Stakes winner Nasseem. (Paul Dixon & Mr Brian Morton).
'A very nice horse and he's going really well at the moment. He'll start off at six furlongs.' TRAINER'S BARGAIN BUY

959. WELL OF ECHOES ★★
b.f. Diktat – Seeker (Rainbow Quest)
March 2. Fifth foal. Tattersalls October 3. Not sold. Half-sister to a bumpers winner by Generous. The dam, a fair 12f winner, is a half-sister to the listed winner Cybinka. The second dam, Sarmatia (by Danzig), is an unraced half-sister to Kris and Diesis.
'A very nice filly, she's showing all the right signs and she'll be ready to go soon.'

960. UNNAMED ★★★
gr.c. Verglas – Lake Nyasa (Lake Coniston)
April 9. Fifth foal. 12,000Y. Tattersalls October 3. Not sold. Half-brother to the fairly useful Irish two year old 6f winner Mrs Snaffles (by Indian Danehill) and to the fair 1m winner Angel Kate (by Invincible Spirit). The dam, a modest Irish maiden, stayed 10f and is a half-sister to six winners including the Gold Cup

winner Mr Dinos. The second dam, Spear Dance (by Gay Fandango), won over 7f and 1m and is a half-sister to the Group 3 7f Jersey Stakes winner Rasa Penang.
'A nice little horse that'll be racing by the end of April over five furlongs and he'll stay further later on.'

961. UNNAMED ★★★

ch.f. Tobougg – Marjurita (Marju)
April 22. Half-sister to the unplaced 2007 two year old Barbossa (by Bahamian Bounty). The dam, a quite useful 6f (at two years) to 9.4f winner of seven races, is a half-sister to three winners. The second dam, Unfuwaanah (by Unfuwain), a fair three year old 7f winner, is a half-sister to six winners including the Group 3 12f Gordon Stakes second Trebly. (P J Dixon).
'A nice little compact filly, she's going the right way and should be a six furlong horse, starting around mid-May.'

962. UNNAMED ★★★

ch.c. Haafhd – Trustthunder (Selkirk)
March 19. Third foal. Half-brother to the quite useful 2007 two year old 7f winner Thunderstruck (by Bertolini) and to the fair 7.5f winner Thunderousapplause (by Royal Applause). The dam, a fair 6f winner of three races (including at two years), is a half-sister to the German Group 2 6f winner Raffelberger and the German listed 6f winner Raptor. The second dam, Royal Cat (by Royal Academy), was unraced. (Mr P J Dixon).
'A beautiful, well-balanced colt we'll be aiming at the six/seven furlong races. A very exciting prospect.'

ED McMAHON

963. CASUAL STYLE ★★★

ch.f. Bahamian Bounty – Artistry (Night Shift)
January 26. First foal. 5,000Y. Doncaster Festival. J C Fretwell. The dam, a modest 7f all-weather winner, is a half-sister to the useful listed 7f winner of four races Attune. The second dam, Attune (by Most Welcome), was a useful 10f to 11.4f winner of three races including the listed Middleton Stakes and was second in the

Group 2 Sun Chariot Stakes. (J C Fretwell).
'She's had a little setback but she'll be fine and she's been doing very well. A scopey filly with a good action and for what she cost she was certainly a bargain. There's no doubt she'll win.'

964. DANEHILL'S PEARL (IRE) ★★★★

b.f. Danehill Dancer – Mother Of Pearl (Sadler's Wells)
April 9. 165,000foal. Tattersalls December. Paul Murphy. Half-sister to the useful 1m and 10f winner Pearly King and to the moderate 1m all-weather winner Pearl Island (both by Kingmambo). The dam won both her starts at two years including the Group 3 1m Prix Saint-Roman and was placed in the Group 3 Prix de la Nonette and the Group 3 Musidora Stakes. She is a closely related to the high-class colt Turtle Island, winner of the Group 1 6f Heinz '57' Phoenix Stakes, the Irish 2,000 Guineas and the Group 2 6f Gimcrack Stakes. The second dam, Sisania (by High Top), won two races in Italy at around 10f and is a half-sister to three winners. (P Murphy).
'She could be very nice. I'm not going to rev her up and I'll probably start her at six furlongs in mid-season. A nice, rangy filly, she's only doing strong canters at the moment but she eats the ground and I think when she comes out she'll make her presence known. The owner Mr Murphy has done well this year with his horses at Nicky Henderson's and it's about time he had a bit of luck.'

965. EVERY SECOND ★★

b.c. Kyllachy – Pendulum (Pursuit Of Love)
March 24. Fourth foal. 38,000Y. Doncaster St Leger. J Fretwell. Half-brother to the unplaced 2007 two year old Medici Time (by Medicean). The dam, a quite useful three year old 7f winner, is a half-sister to six winners. The second dam, Brilliant Timing (by The Minstrel), is a placed half-sister to the US Grade 1 winners Timely Writer and Timely Assertion. (J C Fretwell).
'A nice sort, he has a little bit of a round action and he'll be racing in late April/early May, he's pretty strong and he's doing nothing wrong at present.'

966. FLOOR SHOW ★★★★

ch.c. Bahamian Bounty – Dancing Spirit
(Ahonoora)
March 4. 10,000Y. Tattersalls October. J C Fretwell. Half-brother to four winners including the fairly useful two year old 5f winner and Group 3 Princess Margaret Stakes second Pastel (by Lion Cavern) and the quite useful two year old 6f winner Beware (by Warning). The dam, a fair 6f winner at three years, is a sister to the listed 10f Ballymacoll Stud Stakes winner and Group 2 Sun Chariot Stakes second Feminine Wiles and a half-sister to six winners. The second dam, Instinctive Move (by Nijinsky) won once at three years in the USA and is a half-sister to Law Society. (J C Fretwell).
'A nice sort, he won't be that early because he's a little bit immature mentally, but I intend entering him for the Racecall Gold Trophy because he's a strong type and at that time of the year he'll be absolutely spot on. He's pleasing me with what he's doing so far and hopefully he'll start off in mid-May.' TRAINER'S BARGAIN BUY

967. LIVELY BLADE ★★

ch.c. Needwood Blade – Breezy Day
(Day Is Done)
May 30. Ninth living foal. 40,000Y. Doncaster St Leger. R L Bedding. Half-brother to the quite useful three year old 6f winner Positive Air (by Puissance) and to the fair two year old 5f and subsequent UAE winner Divine Wind (by Clantime). The dam, a quite useful sprint winner of eight races from 3 to 6 years, is a half-sister to three winners. The second dam, Bedouin Dancer (by Lorenzaccio), won once at three years and is a full or half-sister to three minor winners. (R L Bedding).
'He's a late foal and I'm not getting him up to speed until he's nearly two. Whether he'll be as good as his Dad I'm not so sure – he's got a little bit of a rounded action and he's well-built. I'm hoping he's a nice horse for the owner's sake. He has Pivotal Flame and he's took it upon himself to buy this colt who we bred. He's set to be a five/six furlong horse and he probably wouldn't want extremes of ground.'

968. MAID FOR MUSIC (IRE) ★★★

b.f. Dubai Destination – Green Tambourine
(Green Desert)
March 2. Fourth foal. 25,000Y. Tattersalls October 2. J Fretwell. The dam, a quite useful two year old 6f winner, is a half-sister to four winners including the useful two year old 7f winner Artistic Lad and the useful 7f (at two years) and 10f winner Maid To Perfection. The second dam, Maid For The Hills (by Indian Ridge), was a useful two year old and won twice over 6f including the listed Empress Stakes. She is a half-sister to five winners including the dams of the US Grade 1 winner Stroll and the Group winners Lady In Waiting and Savannah Bay. (J C Fretwell).
'Quite professional about her job, she's not over-big and she'll be racing soon, probably over five before stepping her up to six. She'll probably go with a bit of cut in the ground and she's strong enough to start somewhere like Pontefract, where there's a stiff finish, in a fillies' race over five furlongs.'

969. NORWEGIAN DANCER (UAE) ★★★

b.c. Halling – Time Changes (Danzig)
March 8. Fifth foal. 15,000Y. Doncaster October. E McMahon. Brother to the fairly useful 1m (at two years) and 8.7f winner Age Of Reason and half-brother to the fair 9f winner Deadline (by Machiavellian). The dam won a 1m listed event in France at three years and is a half-sister to numerous winners including the dam of the US stakes winners and Grade 1 placed Andromeda's Hero and Superfly. The second dam, Make Change (by Roberto), a high-class US stakes winner and Grade 1 placed ten times, is a half-sister to six winners including the US Grade 3 9f winner Spur Wing. (Mr P A Wilkins).
'Sheikh Mohammed bought his full brother the three year old for 200,000 guineas – whereas I bought this fella from Doncaster for 15,000 – so I'm hoping I've got the value for money! He was the type of horse I was looking for but his brother hadn't run at that point so there was no form to go on.'

970. SNEAK PREVIEW ★★
ch.f. Monsieur Bond – Harryana (Efisio)
February 15. Fourth foal. 34,000Y. Doncaster St Leger. J Fretwell. Half-sister to the moderate French 10f winner Flaxby (by Mister Baileys). The dam, a fair two year old dual 5f winner, is out of the quite useful three year old 5f winner Allyanna (by Thatching), herself a half-sister to eight winners. (J C Fretwell).
'She'll probably be a bit later than some of my other fillies. She's not showing any sharpness yet and is a bit on the weak side but she's got quite a nice action and she's a nice filly.'

971. TO THE POINT ★★★
b.f. Refuse To Bend – Be Decisive (Diesis)
March 21. 17,000Y. Tattersalls October 2. J Fretwell. Half-sister to the quite useful 2007 Irish two year old 6f winner Be Fantastic (by Fantastic Light). The dam, a fair 1m winner, is a half-sister to five winners including the listed 7f winner Miss Ivanhoe. The second dam, Robellino Miss (by Robellino), won seven races at up to 9f in the USA, was stakes-placed and is a half-sister to the listed winners Grangeville and Palana.(J C Fretwell).
'A nice filly, not over-big but all there and she has a very nice action. She'll probably be one of our first runners and I'm quite hopeful for her.'

BRIAN MEEHAN
972. AFRICAN ART (USA) ★★
ch.c. Johannesburg – Perovskia (Stravinsky)
February 26. First foal. €160,000Y. Goffs Million. Blandford Bloodstock. The dam is an unraced half-sister to two minor winners. The second dam, Lignify (by Confidential Lady), won a Grade 1 event in Argentina and is a half-sister to the Argentine Grade 1 winner Litigado. (Sangster Family & Matthew Green).
'He's just a bit backward at present and we won't see him until August or September over seven furlongs.'

973. ALIMARR (IRE) ★★★
ch.f. Noverre – Tiger Desert (Desert King)
February 26. First foal. 58,000Y. Tattersalls October 1. Jane Allison. The dam, placed twice at three years in Germany, is closely related to the triple Group 1 winner Tiger Hill and a half-sister to four winners. The second dam, The Filly (by Appiani II), won four races in Germany and is a half-sister to three winners. (Mrs S M Roy).
'We've done a bit with her but she got a sore shin so we backed off her. A nice, strong filly, she'll probably be out in late May.'

974. ARABIAN MIRAGE ★★
b.f. Oasis Dream – Bathilde (Generous)
March 8. Fifth foal. 210,000Y. Tattersalls October 1. BBA (Ire). Half-sister to the smart two year old 7f winner and Group 2 Dante Stakes third Al Shemali (by Medicean), to the very useful listed 14f winner Tungsten Strike (by Smart Strike) and the quite useful two year old 7f winner Baillieston (by Indian Ridge). The dam, a useful 10.4f winner, was listed placed over 12f is a half-sister to six winners including the Group 2 Prix du Conseil de Paris winner Crimson Quest. The second dam, Bex (by Explodent), a smart winner of the Group 3 10.5f Prix de Flore, is a half-sister to 12 winners. (Mr D F O'Rourke).
'A nice filly for around July time over six furlongs. There's a bit of stamina in the pedigree but being by Oasis Dream I'd expect her to have speed.'

975. BLACK KAT (IRE) ★★★★
b.c. One Cool Cat – Dissidentia
(Dancing Dissident)
April 5. Sixth foal. 35,000Y. Doncaster St Leger. McKeever St Lawrence. Half-brother to the Group 3 6f Firth Of Clyde Stakes winner Golden Legacy (by Rossini) and to a sprint winner of eight races in Italy by Paris House. The dam, a minor French and Belgian winner over 5f, is a half-sister to 4 other winners abroad. The second dam, Ex-Imager (by Exhibitioner), is an unraced half-sister to two winners. (M C Denmark).
'A very nice colt, he'll be ready before the end of May and he's probably a six furlong two year old. Looks very sharp.'

976. BOLSHOI KING (IRE) ★★

b.c. Fasliyev – Nawaji (Trempolino)
January 23. Seventh foal. €50,000Y. Goffs Million. Favourites Racing. Half-brother to the useful two year old 7f winner Ahmedy (by Polish Precedent), to the quite useful 9.5f winner Noticeable (by Night Shift) and fair 7f (at two years) to 10f winner Press Express (by Entrepreneur). The dam, a poor placed maiden at up to 13f, is a sister to the Group 3 10f Select Stakes winner Triarius and a half-sister to the listed Fred Archer Stakes winner Sharp Noble and the unraced dam of the Group 3 Prix des Reservoirs winner Bint Alnasr. The second dam, Noble Decretum (by Noble Decree), is an unplaced half-sister to 12 winners. (Favourites Racing XV).
'He'll want plenty of time – probably until the back-end. and he's likely to be a five or six furlong type.'

977. BURNING FLUTE ★★★

ch.c. Piccolo – Fiamma Royale
(Fumo di Londra)
January 28. First foal. 58,000Y. Doncaster St Leger. McKeever St Lawrence. The dam, a modest winner of six races from 5f (at two years) to 7f, is a half-sister to seven winners including the listed-placed Another Fantasy. The second dam, Ariadne (by Bustino), a quite useful 2m winner at three years, is a sister to the Group 1 Premio Lydia Tesio winner Stufida. herself the grandam of Pivotal. (Clipper Group Holdings Ltd).
'He's nice and he's working well. I'd like to think he'll be running in early May over five or six furlongs and he looks very nice.'

978. CHEDDAR GEORGE ★★

ch.c. Pivotal – Grandalea (Grand Lodge)
February 2. First foal. 125,000Y. Tattersalls October 1. McKeever St Lawrence. The dam, a quite useful 7f all-weather winner, is a half-sister to two winners including the useful 7f (at two years) and 12f winner and Group 3 7f Prestige Stakes third Red Peony. The second dam, Red Azalea (by Shirley Heights), a fairly useful 7f (at two years) and 10f winner, is a half-sister to four winners including the Group 3 Prestige Stakes

winner and French 1,000 Guineas third Red Camellia (herself dam of the Fillies Mile winner Red Bloom). (Comic Strip Heroes).
'A mid-season colt, he's a nice horse but you never know whether Pivotal's need six or seven furlongs until you start working them.'

979. COURAGEOUS NATURE (IRE) ★★★★

b.g. Invincible Spirit – Special Park (Trempolino)
March 17. Fifth foal. 47,000Y. Doncaster St Leger. McKeever St Lawrence. Half-brother to the quite useful two year old 5f and 6f winner Bathwick Bill (by Stravinsky) and to the modest two year old 7f winner Colourful Lady (by Quest For Fame). The dam, a French 1m and 9f winner, is a half-sister to six winners including the US Grade 3 1m winner Wasatch. The second dam, Nureyev's Park (by Nureyev), won once in the USA and is a half-sister to five winners including the Canadian Grade 1 winner All For Victory.
'I'm cracking on with him and I expect to run him in May. He's doing plenty of work.'

980. DANCE AVENUE (IRE) ★★★

b.f. Sadler's Wells – Blanche Dubois (Nashwan)
February 18. Sixth foal. 75,000Y. Tattersalls October 1. Hugo Lascelles. Half-sister to the smart 7f and 1m winner and Group 3 Desmond Stakes third Middlemarch (by Grand Lodge), the useful two year old 6f and 7f winner and Group 2 6f Cherry Hinton Stakes second Lady High Havens (by Bluebird), the fairly useful two year old 7f winner Park Law (by Fasliyev), the quite useful 7f (at two years) and 10f winner Noble Gent (by Danehill) and the fair two year old 6f winner Apache Dream (by Indian Ridge). The dam is an unraced half-sister to six winners including the Irish 2,000 Guineas winner Indian Haven and the Group 1 Gran Criterium winner Count Dubois. The second dam, Madame Dubois (by Legend Of France), a winner of five races at three years from 9f to 14.6f including the Group 2 Park Hill Stakes and the Group 2 Prix de Royallieu, is a half-sister to the dam of the very smart two year old Daggers Drawn. (Sangster Family and Partners).
'A back-end type filly, she looks classy and is a very nice filly.'

981. DANGEROUS MIDGE (USA) ★★

b.c. Lion Heart – Adored Slew (Seattle Slew)
**March 4. $120,000Y. Keeneland September.
Angela Sykes.** Half-brother to three winners including the minor French 3 and four year old winner of five races Silver Traffic (by Carson City) and a minor US two year old winner by Royal Academy. The dam, a winner at three years in France and second in the Group 3 12f Prix de Minerve, is a half-sister to eight winners including the dams of the US Grade 1 winner Scorpion and the Prix du Bois winner Imperfect World. The second dam, Affirmatively (by Affirmed), a minor winner in the USA at three and four years, is a half-sister to three stakes winners including the US Grade 1 Santa Barbara Handicap winner Desiree (herself dam of the US Grade 1 winner Adored).
'A backward horse, he's one for the end of the season but he looks a quality colt.'

982. DREAM HUNTRESS ★★★

*ch.f. Dubai Destination – Dream Lady
(Benny The Dip)*
January 24. First foal. 40,000Y. Tattersalls October 1. Not sold. The dam is an unraced half-sister to the useful 12f, 13f and German listed winner Elusive Dream. The second dam, Dance A Dream (by Sadler's Wells), a smart winner of the Cheshire Oaks and second in the Epsom Oaks, is a sister to the 2,000 Guineas winner Entrepreneur and to the very useful middle-distance listed winner Sadler's Image and a half-sister to seven winners including the Coronation Stakes winner Exclusive. (Wyck Hall Stud).
'She's grand and has done a few bits of work so she'll be ready by the end of May. She looks to have a lot of speed and we'll start her at six furlongs but I'd expect her to get further in time.'

983. EXCELSIOR ACADEMY ★★★

b.c. Montjeu – Birthday Suit (Daylami)
March 6. 260,000Y. Tattersalls October 1. Charles Egerton. The dam, a useful two year old dual 5f winner and third in the Group 2 Cherry Hinton Stakes, is a half-sister to numerous winners including the Irish 1,000 Guineas winner Classic Park and the US Grade 2 winner Rumpipumpy. The second dam, Wanton (by Kris), a useful two year old 5f winner and third in the Group 2 Flying Childers Stakes, is a half-sister to eight winners including the listed 5f winner and Group 2 5f second Easy Option. (Lady M.C Laidlaw).
'A nice colt and very straightforward, he knows his job and won't take long but being by Montjeu we've got to be looking at seven furlongs in June or July for him. I suspect he'll get up to a mile by the end of the year.'

984. FANTASY LAND (IRE) ★★★★★

*ch.f. Danehill Dancer – Wondrous Story
(Royal Academy)*
February 19. First foal. €130,000Y. Goffs Million. BBA (Ire). The dam, a quite useful two year old 7f winner, is closely related to a winner in the USA by Caerleon and a half-sister to five winners including the very useful 6f Cherry Hinton Stakes, 7f Rockfel Stakes and 7.3f Fred Darling Stakes winner Musicale and the very useful two year old 1m winner and Group 2 12f King Edward VII Stakes third Theatre Script. The second dam, Gossiping (by Chati), a minor winner over 6f in the USA at three years, is a half-sister to the high-class sprinter Committed. (Sangster Family & Lady Bamford).
'A lovely, big, strong, good-looking filly, she's very forward mentally but we'll wait until June with her. She looks pretty smart.'

985. FIRST PASSAGE (USA) ★★★★

*b.br.f. Giant's Causeway – Win's Fair Lady
(Dehere)*
March 9. Second foal. $1,200,000Y. Keeneland September. Hugo Merry. The dam, a dual stakes winner in the USA, is a sister to the US triple Grade 2 winner Graeme Hall and a half-sister to the US Grade 1 winner Harmony Lodge. The second dam, Win Crafty Lady (by Crafty Prospector), a US stakes winner of eight races, is a half-sister to seven winners including the US Grade 2 winner Diligence. (Mr A Rosen).
'She looks a smart filly and went up the grass gallop yesterday and looked good. I'll be waiting for May or June with her but she does look a very nice filly.'

986. FLY BUTTERFLY ★★★
ch.f. Bahamian Bounty – Aconite
(Primo Dominie)
March 23. First foal. 37,000Y. Doncaster St Leger. McKeever St Lawrence. The dam is an unplaced half-sister to six winners including the Group-placed two year old's Lake Pleasant and Power Lake. The second dam, Laugharne (by Known Fact), ran once unplaced and is a half-sister to the Chester Vase winner Dry Dock and to the dams of the champion New Zealand two year old filly Good Faith, the South American Grade 1 winner Band Gypsy, the Group 1 Moyglare Stud Stakes winner Mail The Desert and the multiple Group 1 placed Norse Dancer. (Mrs J P E Cunningham).
'Very nice, she'll be racing in May and she's smart.'

987. FROGNAL (IRE) ★★★
b.c. Kheleyf – Shannon Dore (Turtle Island)
March 26. Fourth foal. 46,000Y. Doncaster St Leger. McKeever St Lawrence. Half-brother to the moderate 7f placed two year old maiden Transcendent (by Trans Island) and to the useful two year old 6f winner and listed placed Borthwick Girl (by Cape Cross). The dam, a quite useful two year old 6f winner, is a half-sister to one winner. The second dam, Solas Abu (by Red Sunset), a quite useful 9f and 10f winner in Ireland, is a half-sister to two winners. (R C Tooth).
'We're just getting on with him now, he's one for the middle of the season over six or seven furlongs. A nice horse.'

988. GALLAGHER ★★★★
ch.c. Bahamian Bounty – Roo (Rudimentary)
February 8. Fourth foal. 115,000Y. Tattersalls October 1. Charles Egerton. Half-brother to the quite useful 2006 two year old 7f winner Roodolph (by Primo Valentino) and to the useful 5f (a two years) and 7f winner and listed-placed Roodeye (by Inchinor). The dam, a quite useful two year old 5f and 6f winner, is a half-sister to four winners including the Group 2 6f Gimcrack Stakes winner Bannister (by Inchinor). The second dam, Shall We Run (by Hotfoot), placed once over 5f at two years, is a full or half-

sister to eight winners including the Group 1 6f Cheveley Park Stakes winner Dead Certain. (Manton Thoroughbred Racing).
'We've done quite a bit with him, he had a touch of sore shins so we give him a bit of a break. He'll be out in May and he looks a smart colt.'

989. GEORGE REX (USA) ★★★
b.br.c. Johannesburg – Royal Linkage (Linkage)
April 25. Tenth foal. €70,000Y. Goffs Million. McKeever St Lawrence. Half-brother to the US winner of four races and Grade 1 placed Royal Fact (by Known Fact) and to three minor winners in North America by Kris S (2) and Helmsman. The dam, a two year old stakes winner in the USA, is a sister to the US stakes winner Jump With Joy and a half-sister to five winners. The second dam, Leaping Lucy (by Restless Native), is a placed half-sister to six winners. (Tumbleweed Partnership).
'He looked like he was going to be early but we've given him a bit of a break. He has a lot of speed and is typical of the sire in that he improves all the time whatever you do with him. He'll probably start off at six furlongs at the end of May.'

990. GREENSWARD ★★★
b.c. Green Desert – Frizzante (Efisio)
March 12. The dam won seven races including the Group 1 July Cup and is a half-sister to four winners including the Stewards Cup winner Zidane and the dual 6f listed winner Firenze. The second dam, Juliet Bravo (by Glow), a modest two year old 5f winner, is a half-sister to the very smart filly Donna Viola, a winner of 11 races here and abroad including the Grade 1 Yellow Ribbon Handicap, the Grade 1 Gamely Handicap and the Group 2 Prix de l'Opera. (Lady Rothschild).
'He's very forward and we'll start him in late May or early June. We'll probably be looking at seven furlongs with him later on. A good-looking horse.'

991. HI FLING ★★★
b.c. Oasis Dream – Crafty Buzz
(Crafty Prospector)

April 12. 220,000Y. Tattersalls October 1. Charles Egerton Bloodstock. Half-brother to the fair 6f all-weather (at two years) and 1m winner Aesculus (by Horse Chestnut), to the modest 10f winner Blackwater Fever (by Irish River) and a minor US winner by St Jovite. The dam, a minor US two year old 6f stakes winner, is a half-sister to six winners including the US Grade 3 winner Gone for Real. The second dam, Intently (by Drone), a US stakes winner of eight races, is a half-sister to seven winners including the Grade 3 winner and Grade 1 placed Percipient. (Lady M C Laidlaw).
'He'll be racing in June and being by Oasis Dream I'll start him at six furlongs but I think he'll want seven in time.'

992. HIGHLAND LASSIE (IRE) ★★★★

b.f. Oasis Dream – Arlesiana (Woodman)
March 17. Fourth foal. 160,000Y. Tattersalls October 1. Charles Egerton. Half-sister to two minor winners in Italy and France by Hernando and Peintre Celebre. The dam is an unplaced half-sister to seven winners including the Group/Grade two winners El Angelo, Miswaki Tern and Via Borghese. The second dam, Angela Serra (by Arctic Tern), won the Group 2 12f Premio Legnano. (Lady M C Laidlaw).
'A lovely filly that's just done her first bit of work on the grass. I'm happy with her, hopefully she'll run at the end of May but she might be a bit later.'

993. HONESTLY (USA) ★★★★

b.f. Yes It's True – Sweetheart (Mr Prospector)
March 19. Fifth foal. $475,000Y. Keeneland September. Hugo Merry. Half-sister to the useful two year old 7f winner and Group 3 Craven Stakes third Sweet Band (by Dixieland Band). The dam, a French listed-placed winner, is a half-sister to several winners including the French listed winner and Group 2 placed Stunning. The second dam, Gorgeous (by Slew O'Gold), won two Grade 1 events in the USA, is closely related to the Kentucky Oaks winner Seaside Attraction (herself dam of the good winners Cape Town, Golden Attraction and Red Carnival) and a half-sister to the champion Canadian three year old Key To The Moon and

the dam of Fantastic Light. (A Rosen & R Clay).
'She's doing very well and she looked ready a little while back but she started to grow a little so we gave her a few weeks off. She looks fine again now, she'll be out in May and she looks talented.'

994. HOSANNA ★★★★★ ♠

b.f. Oasis Dream – Rada's Daughter (Robellino)
April 25. Fourth foal. 65,000Y. Tattersalls October 1. John Warren. The dam, a useful winner of five races at up to 12f, was second in the Group 3 Park Hill Stakes and is a half-sister to eight winners. The second dam, Drama School (by Young Generation), is an unplaced half-sister to three winners. (Highclere Thoroughbred Racing (St Simon)).
'She's working really well at the moment and seems a good, fast filly, so she'll be out in early May.'

995. IMPRESSIONIST ART (USA) ★★★

ch.f. Giant's Causeway – Chalamont (Kris)
April 8. Eighth foal. 55,000Y. Tattersalls October 1. Hugo Lascelles. Half-sister to the useful 2007 two year old 6f winner and Group 3 6f Sirenia Stakes third Lady Aquitaine (by El Prado), to the very useful 7f listed and 8.2f winner Secret Garden, the fairly useful two year old 7f all-weather and subsequent US winner Texas Hill (both by Danehill) and the minor US two and three year old winner Private Humor (by Distorted Humor). The dam, a quite useful two year old dual 6f winner, is a half-sister to five winners including the dual Ascot Gold Cup winner Gildoran. The second dam, Durtal (by Lyphard), won the Cheveley Park Stakes and the Fred Darling Stakes, was second in the French 1,000 Guineas and is a half-sister to the Prix de l'Arc de Triomphe winner Detroit (herself dam of the Arc winner Carnegie). (Sangster Family & Matthew Green).
'She looks very classy and I love the way she goes about her business – very professional. As soon as the six furlong races are out we'll run her. She's quite a character but the lads get on with her!'

996. IN HER SHOES ★★★

ch.f. Pivotal – Ebaraya (Sadler's Wells)

February 1. Third foal. 165,000Y. Tattersalls October 1. J McCalmont. The dam, a minor Irish 12f winner, is a sister to the Irish Oaks and Prix Royal-Oak winner Ebadiyla and a half-sister to the Group 1 7f Moyglare Stud Stakes winner Edabiya and the Ascot Gold Cup winner Enzeli. The second dam, Ebaziya (by Darshaan), a winner from 7f (at two years) to 12f including three listed races, was third in the Group 2 12f Blandford Stakes and is a half-sister to four winners. (S Dartnell).
'She's working and is a nice filly but she needs a bit more time. I'd expect her out by the end of May over six furlongs.'

997. KLYNCH ★★★
b.c. Kyllachy – Inchcoonan (Emperor Jones)
March 28. Second foal. 32,000Y. Doncaster St Leger. McKeever St Lawrence. Half-brother to the unraced 2007 two year old Heavenly Encounter (by Lujain). The dam, a modest winner of six races from 7f to 1m at three and four years, is a half-sister to four winners. The second dam, Miss Ivory Coast (by Sir Ivor), won twice in France and is a half-sister to three winners and to the dams of 5 stakes winners including the Italian Group 3 winner Don Raffael. (L P R Partnership).
'He shows a lot of speed but he's a bit green and will probably need his first race. A nice colt and he's very straightforward.'

998. LIGHT THE FIRE (IRE) ★★★★ ♠
b.c. Invincible Spirit – Rouge Noir
(Saint Ballado)
March 2. Second foal. 95,000Y. Tattersalls October 2. McKeever St Lawrence. The dam, a minor winner at three years in the USA, is a half-sister to a winner in Japan. The second dam, Ardana (by Danehill), won the Group 3 Premio Bagutta and is a half-sister to five winners. (J L Allbritton).
'He should be racing in May over six furlongs, he's working well and I like him a lot.'

999. MISTY GLADE ★★★
ch.f. Compton Place – Shifting Miss (Night Shift)
February 15. Ninth foal. 80,000Y. Doncaster St

Leger. McKeever St Lawrence. Sister to the Group 3 Premio Primi Passi winner Shifting Place and half-sister to the quite useful 6f winner of four races Our Sheila (by Bahamian Bounty) and the quite useful dual 1m and subsequent Swedish winner Cal Mac (by Botanic). The dam, a fair 10f to 14f winner, is a half-sister to seven winners including the dual Group 3 winner Needwood Blade. The second dam, Misty Halo (by High Top), won 20 races from 1m to 2m 2f and is a half-sister to four winners. (F C T Wilson).
'She's working at the moment, she's a nice, sharp filly and I expect she'll be racing in May.'

1000. MYSTIC PRINCE ★★★
b.g. Dubai Destination – Hazy Heights
(Shirley Heights)
March 14. Fourth foal. 9,000Y. Tattersalls October 2. Not sold. The dam, a moderate three year old 1m winner, is a half-sister to three winners including the fairly useful two year old 5f winner and Group 3 Princess Margaret Stakes second Pastel. The second dam, Dancing Spirit (by Ahonoora), a fair 6f winner at three years, is a sister to the listed 10f Ballymacoll Stud Stakes winner and Group 2 Sun Chariot Stakes second Feminine Wiles and a half-sister to six winners. (Wyck Hall Stud).
'He's just started growing again so I've sent him home for a while as he's a bit backward. But he does everything right and I'm very pleased with him.'

1001. PAGAN FLIGHT (IRE) ★★
b.c. Hawk Wing – Regal Darcey (Darshaan)
April 27. Third foal. 78,000Y. Tattersalls October 2. McKeever St Lawrence. The dam, placed fourth once over 13f in Ireland at four years, is a sister to the listed winner Talaash and a half-sister to two winners. The second dam, Royal Ballet (by Sadler's Wells), ran unplaced twice over 10f at three years and is a sister to King's Theatre, winner of the Group 1 Racing Post Trophy, the Group 1 King George VI and Queen Elizabeth Diamond Stakes and second in both the Epsom Derby and the Irish Derby and a half-sister to the champion two year old colt

High Estate. (GAP Partnership).

'A typical Hawk Wing in that he's big and strong and I wouldn't expect to see him until mid-June, but he's a nice colt and seven furlongs should be right for him.'

1002. PANSY POTTER ★★★

b.f. *Auction House – Ellway Queen (Bahri)*
February 14. Third foal. 60,000Y. Doncaster St Leger. McKeever St Lawrence. Sister to the quite useful 2007 two year old 7f winner Ghetto and to the fair two year old 6f winner Hythe Bay. The dam, a fair three year old 1m winner, is a half-sister to one winner. The second dam, Queen Linear (by Polish Navy), won once at three years and is a half-sister to six winners including the Group winners Castle Green and Hardgreen. (Comic Strip Heroes).
'I love the way she goes about her business, she's looks a nice type and six furlongs in mid to late May should be her starting point.'

1003. PARK MELODY (IRE) ★★★★

b.f. *Refuse To Bend – Park Charger (Tirol)*
April 26. Ninth foal. 250,000Y. Tattersalls October 1. McKeever St Lawrence. Half-sister to the unraced 2007 two year old Acclaimed (by Hawk Wing), to the 6f (at two years) and Group 3 7f Ballycorus Stakes winner Rum Charger (by Spectrum), the very useful two year old 6f winner and dual Group 3 placed Pakhoes (by College Chapel), the fairly useful two year old 6f winner Park Romance (by Dr Fong), the quite useful 7f winner Stage Presence (by Selkirk) and the quite useful two year old dual 6f winner Alpine Park (by Barathea). The dam, a useful winner over 1m and 10f at three years in Ireland, was listed-placed several times and is a half-sister to nine winners. The second dam, Haitienne (by Green Dancer), won once in France and is a half-sister to seven winners. (F C T Wilson)
'A very smart filly. She's done a lot of growing and we'll leave her until the back end of the season but she looks very nice.'

1004. PISTE ★★★

b.f. *Falbrav – Arctic Char (Polar Falcon)*

May 14. Third foal. Half-sister to the useful two year old 1m winner Alfathaa (by Nayef). The dam, a useful listed 7f winner, is a half-sister to six winners including the Group two winners Barrow Creek and Last Resort and the dam of the Group 2 winner Trans Island. The second dam, Breadcrumb (by Final Straw), a very useful 6f and 7f winner, is a half-sister to four winners including the Group 2 Prix Maurice de Gheest winner College Chapel. (Miss G J Abbey).
'She's working on the grass now and should be starting over five or six furlongs in mid to late May. She's skipping along now and enjoying herself.'

1005. ROAR OF APPLAUSE ★★

b.g. *Royal Applause – Les Hurlants (Barathea)*
February 21. Sixth foal. 50,000Y. Tattersalls October 3. McKeever St Lawrence. Half-sister to the useful 7f and 1m two year old winner and Group 3 1m Prix de Chenes third Happy Crusader (by Cape Cross) and to the quite useful 9f (at two years) and 12f winner Spear (by Almutawakel). The dam won once over 12f at three years in France and is a half-sister to three minor winners. The second dam, Howlin' (by Alleged), won once in France and is a half-sister to four winners. (R C Tooth).
'He'll want six or seven furlongs, we were just getting on with him but we've just gelded him so he won't be ready until June.'

1006. ROCKABOUT (IRE) ★★

b.f. *Rock Of Gibraltar – Capades Dancer (Gate Dancer)*
February 26. Half-sister to the Group 2 10f Prix d'Harcourt winner Vangelis, to the multiple French listed winner Marechal (both by Highest Honor) and the French 9f winner Great Gorge (by Gulch). (Lady Rothschild).
'A lovely, good-looking filly but she's going to want a bit of time as she's quite weak still. One for the back-end of the season.'

1007. ROCK ART (IRE) ★★★

ch.f. *Rock Of Gibraltar – Lindesburg (Doyoun)*
April 28. Sixth foal. €120,000Y. Goffs Million. BBA (Ire). Half-sister to the fairly useful two year

old Group 1 6f Phoenix Stakes second Amadeus Mozart (by Mozart), to the Irish 7f winner Dolce Voche (by Intikhab) and a winner in Japan by Grand Lodge. The dam was placed 3 times over 6f including at two years and is a half-sister to six winners including the very smart triple Group 2 1m winner Gothenburg. The second dam, Be Discreet (by Junius), won five races in France at up to 7f and is a half-sister to nine winners including three stakes winners. (Sangster Family and Matthew Green).

'A lovely, big, strong filly. I haven't done a lot with her and she'll make a two year old in the second half of the season, but she looks very nice.'

1008. SILK MEADOW (IRE) ★★★

b.f. Barathea – Perils Of Joy (Rainbow Quest)
March 22. Ninth foal. 180,000Y. Tattersalls October 1. McKeever St Lawrence. Sister to the Irish listed 1m winner Hymn Of Love and half-sister to the Irish 6f and subsequent US winner Still As Sweet (by Fairy King), the modest 12f and 14f winner Aura Of Calm (by Grand Lodge) and the minor US winner Epic Pursuit (by Salse). The dam, a three year old 1m winner in Ireland, is a half-sister to five winners including the Italian Group 3 winner Sweetened Offer. The second dam, Sweet Mint (by Meadow Mint), won the Group 3 Cork And Orrery Stakes. (F C T Wilson).

'We're just working her at the moment so she should be racing in May. These Barathea's can be anything, she looks nice and we'll what happens with her.'

1009. SISTER ROSE (FR) ★★★

b.f. One Cool Cat – Lady Of St Kilda (Mark Of Esteem)
January 30. First foal. 48,000Y. Tattersalls October 1. Not sold. The dam is an unraced half-sister to two winners including the UAE Group 2 winner Alkaadhem. The second dam, Balalaika (by Sadler's Wells), a four year old listed 9f winner, is a sister to the high-class Group 2 10f Prince of Wales's Stakes and dual US Grade 2 winner Stagecraft and a half-sister to five winners. (B J Meehan).

'A big, strong filly, she goes really well and she'll be ready in May or June.'

1010. SKANKY BISCUIT ★★★

ch.c. Peintre Celebre – Blushing Gleam (Caerleon)
April 13. Eighth foal. 30,000Y. Tattersalls October 1. Angie Sykes. Half-brother to two winners in France by Danehill and Gone West. The dam won the Group 3 Prix du Calvados and the listed Prix de Saint-Cyr and is a half-sister to seven winners including French Group winners Gold Away and Danzigaway. The second dam, Blushing Away (by Blushing Groom), won in France at three years and was listed-placed and is a half-sister to four winners. (I Parvizi).

'September or October should be the right time for him. He's got a great mind and you could run him now but it wouldn't be the right thing to do because his pedigree suggests he'll be better next year.'

1011. SUPER MIDGE ★★★

b.f. Royal Applause – Sabina (Prince Sabo)
April 27. Fifth living foal. 80,000Y. Tattersalls October 2. Angie Sykes. Sister to the smart two year old Group 3 6f Prix Eclipse winner Tremar and half-sister to the fair 2007 Irish two year old 5f winner Princess Zoe (by Kyllachy), the fairly useful two year old 6.5f winner Charlton (by Inchinor) and the two year old 5f seller winner Zafine (by Zafonic). The dam, a quite useful two year old 5.7f winner, is a half-sister to five winners including the Group 2 Sun Chariot Stakes winner Lady In Waiting. The second dam, High Savannah (by Rousillon), a middle-distance placed maiden, is a half-sister to six winners including the useful sprinters Maid For The Hills and Maid For Walking. (I Parvizi).

'She's taking her time to come in her coat but she looks a nice, sharp filly and it's a good family. I'm very pleased with her.'

1012. WAVE ASIDE ★★★

b.c. Reset – Crinkle (Distant Relative)
March 23. Second foal. 24,000Y. Doncaster St Leger. McKeever St Lawrence. Half-brother to the fairly useful dual 6f winner Mr Sandicliffe (by Mujahid) and the fair dual 1m winner Froissee (by Polish Precedent). The dam is an unraced half-sister to the useful two year old 6f winner

and Group 2 6f Richmond Stakes third Cedarberg. The second dam, Crinolette (by Sadler's Wells), unplaced over 8.2f on her only start at two years, is a half-sister to the very smart Group 3 7f Tetrarch Stakes and Group 3 7f Ballycorus Stakes winner Desert Style. (Mr N Attenborough, Mrs L Mann & Mrs L Way)
'I guess we're probably looking at the end of May with him, he's a nice horse and probably a nursery type over six/seven furlongs.'

1013. WHISPERING ANGEL ★★★★
b.c. Hawk Wing – Savignano (Polish Precedent)
February 16. Fifth foal. €95,000Y. Goffs Million. McKeever St Lawrence. Half-brother to the Italian listed winner Momix (by Selkirk). The dam, a French three year old winner, is a half-sister to five winners including the Group 1 Prix de la Foret winner Field Of Hope. The second dam, Fracci (by Raise A Cup), an Italian listed winner, was Group 3 placed. (Manton Thoroughbred Partnership).
'A mid-season type – maybe July or August, he's a big, strong horse and I like him a lot but I haven't done too much with him just yet.'

1014. UNNAMED ★★
ch.c. Dr Fong – Band (Northern Dancer)
April 26. 55,000Y. Tattersalls October 2. McKeever St Lawrence. Half-brother to the very useful Group 3 6f Cherry Hinton Stakes winner Applaud, to the useful two year old 7f winner Houston Time (both by Rahy), the useful listed 10.2f winner Sauterne (by Rainbow Quest), the useful 10f winner and Group 3 placed Glam Rock (by Nashwan), the fair 12f winner Abington Angel (by Machiavellian) and a minor winner in the USA by Seeking The Gold. The dam is a placed half-sister to five winners including the US Grade 3 9f New Orleans Handicap winner Festive. The second dam, Swingtime (by Buckpasser), a dual Group 3 winner here and a dual Grade 2 winner in the USA, is a half-sister to five winners including the Grade 2 Kentucky Oaks winner Bag Of Tunes. (J L Allbritton).
'A mid-season type, nursery horse, I'm not kicking on with him yet and he'll be a seven furlong two year old.'

1015. UNNAMED ★★★
b.f. Pivotal – Bolshaya (Cadeaux Genereux)
February 22. Fifth foal. 115,000Y. Tattersalls October 1. Hugo Merry. Half-sister to the Irish two year old 7f and subsequent Hong Kong winner Carnegie Hall (by Danehill). The dam, a fair triple 6f winner, is a half-sister to eight winners including the very smart King's Stand Stakes and Temple Stakes winner Bolshoi and the useful sprinters Mariinsky, Great Chaddington and Tod. The second dam, Mainly Dry (by The Brianstan), is an unraced half-sister to four winners. (A Rosen).
'She looked sharp but I pulled her back and decided to leave her debut until the end of May. She might be speedy enough for five furlongs.'

1016. UNNAMED ★★★
ch.c. Speightstown – Day Mate (Dayjur)
March 21. Sixth foal. $210,000Y. Keeneland September. Tony Nerses. Half-brother to the US Grade 2 winner and Grade 2 placed Tap Day (by Pleasant Tap) and to two minor winners in the USA by Silver Ghost and Honor And Glory. The dam, a winner at three years in the USA, is a half-sister to seven winners including the US Grade 2 winner Fairy Garden. The second dam, Possible Mate (by King's Bishop), won four Graded stakes events in the USA. (Saleh L Homaizi & Imad Al Sagar).
'A lovely colt and a very smart horse I'd say. He'll take a bit of time but I'd imagine he'll be ready by July.'

1017. UNNAMED ★★
b.f. Marju – Flatter (Barathea)
April 24. Second foal. 47,000Y. Tattersalls October 1. McKeever St Lawrence. The dam is an unraced half-sister to the listed winner and subsequent Hong Kong Grade 1 winner Comic Strip. The second dam, Comic (by Be My Chief), a quite useful 10f and 11.5f winner, is a half-sister to four winners including the two year old Group 3 Solario Stakes winner Brave Act. (M R Green).
'A backward filly, one for August or September but she's very nice.'

1018. UNNAMED ★★★★
b.c. Fasliyev – Graffiti Girl (Sadler's Wells)
February 23. Second foal. 36,000Y. Doncaster St Leger. McKeever St Lawrence. The dam, a poor middle-distance maiden, is a half-sister to five winners including the US Grade 1 placed Joe Bear. The second dam, Maharani (by Red Ransom), is a placed sister to the dual two year old Group 2 winner and sire Sri Pekan. (Mrs S Tucker).
'A quick, real sharp colt, he's Royal Ascot material and hopefully he'll start off at five furlongs in early May.'

1019. UNNAMED ★★
b.f. Halling – Hesperia (Slip Anchor)
March 6. Eighth foal. 50,000Y. Tattersalls October 1. McKeever St Lawrence. Sister to the fairly useful two year old 7f winner and listed-placed Lucky Date and half-sister to the fairly useful 1m winner Namroc (by Indian Ridge), the modest 11f and 12f winner Western Point (by Pivotal) and a minor three year old winner in Germany by Acatenango. The dam, a winner over 11f and 12f including a listed event in Italy, is a half-sister to the French listed winners Wavey and Rebuff . The second dam, Throw Away Line (by Assert), won once in the USA at four years and is a half-sister to nine winners including Go For Wand (a winner of seven Grade 1 events in the USA) and the US Grade two winners Dance Spell and Discorama. (M C Denmark).
'She'll be a mid-season filly over seven furlongs or a mile and she's a nice filly.'

1020. UNNAMED ★★★
b.c. Indian Haven – Kathy Desert
(Green Desert)
January 28. Fourth foal. 38,000Y. Doncaster St Leger. McKeever St Lawrence. Half-brother to a winner abroad by Tagula. The dam, a two year old 5f winner in Italy, is a half-sister to 2 other minor winners. The second dam, Alajyal (by Kris), is an unplaced half-sister to six winners.
'A nice, hardy colt, he'll start off at six furlongs in May. He looks nice.'

1021. UNNAMED ★★
b.br.c. Dixie Union – Miss Brickyard (A P Indy)
March 16. Third foal. $200,000two year old. Fasig-Tipton Calder two year old's-in-training. Newmarket/Merry/Meehan. The dam, a minor US four year old winner, is a half-sister to four winners including the Grade 1 Debutante Stakes winner Miss Houdini. The second dam, Magical Maiden (by Lord Avie), won the Grade 1 Hollywood Starlet Stakes and the Grade 1 Las Virgenes Stakes and is a half-sister to nine winners including the US Grade 2 winner Magical Mile.
'We're just about starting to get on with him, we bought him at Calder where he breezed well but I don't know an awful lot about him yet.'

1022. UNNAMED ★★★
b.c. Soviet Star – Putout (Dowsing)
March 24. Tenth living foal. €95,000Y. Goffs Million. McKeever St Lawrence. Half-brother to the two year old Group 3 Premio Primi Passi winner Palanca (by Inchinor), to the fairly useful two year old 6f winner Rajab (by Selkirk) and the fair triple 5f winner Bedevilled (by Beveled). The dam, a fair three year old 5f winner, is a half-sister to the Group 2 Sun Chariot Stakes winner Danceabout and to the Group 3 6f Prix de Meautry winner Pole Position. The second dam, Putupon (by Mummy's Pet), a fairly useful two year old 5f winner, is a half-sister to the good horses Jupiter Island (Japan Cup), Pushy (Queen Mary Stakes) and Precocious (Gimcrack Stakes).
'One for later on, maybe July, he's a nice colt that will want seven furlongs or a mile.'

1023. UNNAMED ★★★
ch.c. Hennessy – Reluctant Diva (Sadler's Wells)
March 23. Sixth foal. $280,000two year old. Fasig-Tipton Calder two year old's-in-training. Newmarket/Merry/Meehan. Half-brother to two winners including the dual US stakes winner After The Beep (by Phone Trick). The dam is an unplaced half-sister to eight winners including the minor US stakes winner and Cheveley Park Stakes fourth Royal Shyness. The second dam, Miss Demure (by Shy Groom), won the Group 2 6f Lowther Stakes.

'I don't know an awful lot about him as he's only just arrived from America and we're just about to get going with him.'

1024. UNNAMED ★★

ch.c. Mr Greeley – She's Enough (Exploit)
March 22. First foal. 88,000 two year old. Kempton Breeze-up. Merry/Meehan. The dam won 2 minor races in the USA and is closely related to the US Grade 1 winner D'Wildcat and a half-sister to a winner. The second dam, D'Enough (by D'Accord), was a stakes-placed winner of eight races in the USA.
'He looked very good at the breeze-ups but when he came here he got a bit sick, so we've given him a bit of time off and he'll be OK a bit later on.'

1025. UNNAMED ★★★

b.f. Street Cry – Something Mon (Maria's Mon)
April 9. Fourth foal. €260,000Y. Goffs Million. Eugo Montgomery Bloodstock. Half-sister to the useful 2007 two year old 5f and Group 3 7f Oh So Sharp Stakes winner Raymi Coya (by Van Nistelrooy), to the US two year old and four year old winner and stakes-placed Olympia Fields (by Alydeed) and the minor US two year old and four year old winner Cape Cod Gal (by Cape Town). The dam is an unraced half-sister to five winners including the champion German two year old and Group 2 winner Something-different. The second dam, Try Something New (by Hail The Pirates), won the Grade 1 Spinster Stakes in the USA and is a half-sister to five winners. (Mr A Rosen).
'You wouldn't expect anything by Street Cry to be early, but this filly should be alright in June over six or seven furlongs.'

1026. UNNAMED ★★★

b.br.f. Rock Of Gibraltar – Speak Softly To Me (Ogygian)
May 16. Eighth living foal. €165,000Y. Goffs Million. Hugo Merry. Closely related to the promising 2007 Irish two year old listed 7f placed Charlotte Bronte (by Danehill Dancer) and to the minor US stakes winner and Grade 3 placed High Maintenance (by Danehill). The

dam is an unraced half-sister to eight winners including Soundings (dam of the French Group 1 winners Green Tune and Pas de Reponse). The second dam, Ocean's Answer (by Northern Answer), a stakes winner of three races at two years in Canada, is a half-sister to Storm Bird and to the champion Canadian three year old Northernette. (Mr A Rosen).
'A big, strong filly, she'll probably be out around June time. She's very forward mentally but because she was a late foal and she's big we're giving her that bit more time.'

1027. UNNAMED ★★★

b.c. Kyllachy – Triple Sharp (Selkirk)
March 26. Fourth foal. 130,000Y. Tattersalls October 1. Tony Nerses. Half-brother to the useful 2007 two year old 6f all-weather winner and Group 2 7f Superlative Stakes third Ellmau (by Dr Fong), to the listed-placed Laureldean Express (by Inchinor) a winner in Spain by Vettori. The dam, a quite useful 10f and hurdles winner, is a half-sister to four winners including the US stakes winner and Grade 2 placed Pina Colada. The second dam, Drei (by Lyphard), placed fourth over 1m at three years on her only outing, is a half-sister to three winners. (Saleh Al Homaizi & Imad Al Sagar).
'A big, strong horse that only arrived in January but he caught on quickly and he'll be fairly early.'

1028. UNNAMED ★★★

gr.f. Hawk Wing – Waratah (Entrepreneur)
February 18. Second foal. €55,000Y. Goffs Million. McKeever St Lawrence. Half-sister to Singer Of Songs (by Spartacus), unplaced at two years in 2007. The dam won over 10f in Italy and is a half-sister to six winners including the very useful two year old 7f winner and Group 3 Musidora Stakes third Etoile. The second dam, La Luna (by Lyphard), a winner over 9f at three years in France, is a sister to the Group 3 Prix Daphnis and Group 3 Prix Thomas Bryon winner Bellypha and a half-sister to the Prix Eugene Adam winner Bellman and the Peruvian Grade 1 winner Run And Deliver.
'She's sharp and I've done a lot of work with her. She got sore shins last week so she's had a week

off, but she's one to crack on with and I should think she'll be out in May.'

1029. UNNAMED ★★★★
ch.c. Rainbow Quest – Wiener Wald (Woodman)
March 22. Tenth foal. 75,000Y. Tattersalls October 1. McKeever St Lawrence. Brother to the French listed 11f winner and Group 3 placed On Reflection and half-brother to the useful 12f winner Heron Bay (by Hernando), the fairly useful dual 6f winner (including at two years) Riotous Applause (by Royal Applause), the quite useful 7.5f winner Woodland River (by Irish River), the New Zealand winner Bering Island (by Bering) and to the placed dam of the US dual Grade 1 winner Ticker Tape. The dam is an unplaced half-sister to six minor winners abroad. The second dam, Chapel Of Dreams (by Northern Dancer), a dual Grade 2 winner in the USA, is a three-parts sister to the champion sire Storm Cat.
'He's working on the grass and I could run him now he's that forward, but with his pedigree I'll wait for June and start him off at six or seven furlongs. A nice horse.'

ROD MILLMAN
1030. BAHAMIAN CEILIDH ★★★
ch.f. Bahamian Bounty – Crofters Ceilidh (Scottish Reel)
March 12. Eighth foal. 17,000foal. Tattersalls December. Paul Murphy. Half-sister to the quite useful 2007 two year old 7f winner Clifton Dancer (by Fraam), to the useful two year old 5f and 6f winner Cop Hill Lad (by Atraf), the fair two year old 6f winner Okikoki (by Ishiguru) and the modest 5f winner of four races (including at two years) Making Music (by Makbul). The dam won three races over 5f including at two years and was listed placed. She is a half-sister to four winners including the useful 5f and 6f winner and Group 2 placed Lord Kintyre. The second dam, Highland Rowena (by Royben), a modest sprint winner of four races, is a half-sister to two minor winners. (P Murphy).
'She's a very nice filly and is showing up well on the gallops. She'll be out in May and I'd like to think she'll be as good as her half-brother Cop Hill Lad. Time will tell, but she's going the right

way. One of my better-bred horses, she has a nice character and should be well up to winning a maiden.'

1031. FYELEHK ★★★
b.c. Kheleyf – Opalescent (Polish Precedent)
February 21. First foal. 30,000Y. Doncaster St Leger. R Millman. The dam is an unraced half-sister to three winners including the Group 1 Phoenix Stakes third Polar Force. The second dam, Irish Light (by Irish River), won twice at three years and is a half-sister to five winners. (The Links Partnership).
'He's already had a run in what was quite a hot little race, but he didn't act on the soft ground. He'll come on for that, he's a good-looking individual and not over-big but strong. He'll win his maiden.'

1032. GEORGE THISBY ★★
b.c. Royal Applause – Warning Belle (Warning)
March 22. Seventh foal. 20,000Y. Tattersalls October 2. Rod Millman. Half-brother to the useful two year old 7f winner Desert Warning (by Mark Of Esteem), to the fair 6f winner Code Orange (by Green Desert) and the all-weather banded 7f and 1m winner Sierra (by Dr Fong). The dam is an unraced half-sister to seven winners including the high-class Group 2 10f Prince of Wales's Stakes and Group 3 10f Brigadier Gerard Stakes winner Stagecraft and the Group 3 Strensall Stakes winner Mullins Bay and the listed winners Balalaika and Hyabella. The second dam, Bella Colora (by Bellypha), won the Group 2 9.2f Prix de l'Opera, was third in the 1,000 Guineas and is a half-sister to the Irish Oaks winner Colorspin (herself dam of the Group 1 winners Zee Zee Top, Kayf Tara and Opera House) and the Irish Champion Stakes winner Cezanne.
'A well-bred horse, he's big and will probably want seven furlongs around August time. He was a bit backward when we bought him but he's just starting to come to himself now.'

1033. HI SHINKO ★★★
b.c. Shinko Forest – Up Front (Up And At 'em)
March 14. Second foal. 10,000Y. Tattersalls

October 3. **Rod Millman.** The dam, a dual 6f seller winner, is a half-sister to four winners including th Irish listed winner Karakorum. The second dam, Sable Lake (by Thatching), is a placed half-sister to 12 winners. (Always Hopeful).

'He's quite a nice horse but he's got a touch of sore shins so he'll be out at the end of May. He looks a sprinter and is nice and sharp.'

1034. MATTAMIA (IRE) ★★★★
b.c. Makbul – Lady Dominatrix (Danehill Dancer)
February 8. Second foal. 32,000Y. Doncaster St Leger. R Millman. Half-brother to the 2007 two year old listed 5f winner Janina (by Namid). The dam won four races including a Group 3 5f event, was second in the Group 2 Flying Five and is a half-sister to three winners. The second dam, Spout House (by Flash Of Steel), is a placed half-sister to three winners. (Mr C Roper).

'A big, strong horse, he's a bit backward just yet and he's very similar to a nice horse I had called Lord Kintyre. He's strong, good tempered and I'd expect him to be one of my nicer horses. He'll be out in mid-season over five or six furlongs.'

1035. MR CLEARVIEW ★★★
br.c. Makbul – Piccolo Cativo (Komaite)
February 28. Third foal. 11,000Y. Doncaster Festival Sales. R Millman. Brother to the modest 7f and 10f winner Pitbull. The dam, a modest 5f to 7f winner of seven races, is a full or half-sister to numerous winners including the two year old Group 3 5f Cornwallis Stakes winner Castelletto, the useful 6f winner (including at two years) Lake Garda and the useful 5f winner and listed-placed Final Dynasty. The second dam, Malcesine (by Auction Ring), a 1m seller winner at four years, is a half-sister to five winners including the Wokingham Handicap winner Red Rosein (herself dam of the listed winner Proud Boast).

'He's a full-brother to Pitbull who won early on but ended up staying longer trips, so although there's plenty of speed in the pedigree this colt might need a trip as well. He's already had a run and is quite a small, stocky horse and probably

just needed the race a bit. He'll win a nursery later in the season.'

1036. SHERMAN McCOY ★★
ch.c. Reset – Naomi Wildman (Kingmambo)
February 7. Second foal. 5,000Y. Doncaster Festival Sales. R Millman. The dam is an unplaced half-sister to four winners in France. The second dam, Divinite (by Alleged), won twice at three years in France and is a half-sister to five winners. (Mustajed Partnership).

'He's quite a big, scopey horse that needs six furlongs plus. I'd hope to have him out by the end of May or early June.'

1037. SOLDIER BAY ★★★
ch.c. Tobougg – Little Tramp (Trempolino)
March 8. 3,500Y. Tattersalls October 2. R Millman. Half-brother to the quite useful two year old 7f winner Toto Skyllachy (by Kyllachy), to the fair Irish 10f and 12f winner Not To Know (by Mujahid), the modest 5f winner Red China (by Inchinor) and the Italian winner at two and three years Fault Line (by Groom Dancer). The dam is an unraced half-sister to the fairly useful 12f winner Aymara. The second dam, Chipaya (by Northern Prospect), was a smart winner of six races including the Racecall Gold Trophy (at two years) and the listed 1m October Stakes and is a half-sister to four winners including the Group 3 Prestige Stakes second Fernanda. (Mrs L S Millman).

'A very strong individual but unfortunately he's thrown a splint so he's out until the middle of the season. An imposing individual, I think I got him so cheaply because everyone else was asleep!'

1038. SWIFT CHAP ★★★
b.c. Diktat – Regent's Folly (Touching Wood)
March 25. 18,000Y. Doncaster St Leger. R Millman. Half-brother to the quite useful 1m (at two years) to 12f and hurdles winner Spree Vision, the Japanese winner Maruichi Dancer (both by Suave Dancer), to the quite useful 1m (at two years) to 12f winner of six races Summer Charm (by Dansili), the modest 11.5f winner Our Emmy Lou (by Mark Of Esteem) and the modest 9f winner Falcon's Fire (by

Kalaglow). The dam won twice at two years and was third in the listed Pretty Polly Stakes and is a half-sister to four winners. The second dam, Regent's Fawn (by Vice Regent), a fair middle-distance placed maiden, is a sister to the top-class Canadian middle-distance filly Bounding Away and closely related to the Scottish Derby winner Ascot Knight. (M A Swift).
'He'd have been out early but he started coughing. Once that's cleared up he'll be out fairly soon, the dam stayed ten furlongs but this horse has the speed to win over five and yet he'll probably stay a mile.' TRAINER'S BARGAIN BUY

STAN MOORE

1039. GIVE US A SONG (USA) ★★
b.br.c. Songandaprayer – Mama G (Prospector's Bid)
February 7. Third foal. $25,000Y. Fasig-Tipton Kentucky. Not sold. Half-sister to two minor winners in the USA by Graeme Hall and Artax. The dam won 10 races in the USA from 2 to 7 years and is a half-sister to six winners. The second dam, Cherokee Mickey (by Cherokee Fellow), was unraced. (Mr J Wells & Mr J Wade)
'The horses I've bought at the Fasig-Tipton Kentucky sales have all done alright for me, so despite his modest purchase price you should put this colt in the book.'

1040. LOVE TO CHAT (USA) ★★★★
b.br.c. Officer – Luv To Stay n Chat (Candi's Gold)
April 20. $35,000Y. Fasig-Tipton Kentucky. Stan Moore. Half-brother to 2 minor US winners by Honour And Glory and Grindstone and to a winner in Mexico by Crowning Storm. The dam, a minor four year old winner in the USA, is a half-sister to six winners. The second dam, Kirt's Pride (by Kirtling), won at three years.
'He'll be one of my best horses and I see him being suited by six furlongs to start with but he'll get a mile. A real fine two year old, he's my favourite and he's got loads of gears.' TRAINER'S BARGAIN BUY

1041. TRIGGER McCANN ★★
b.c. Royal Applause – Roses Of Spring (Shareef Dancer)

March 23. Second foal. 12,000Y. Doncaster Festival Sales. Not sold. The dam, a quite useful 5f and 6f winner of 11 races, is a full or half-sister to four winners. The second dam, Couleur de Rose (by Kalaglow), is an unraced half-sister to three winners. (Bigwigs Bloodstock Ltd).
'He's just cantering at the moment, the dam was useful and he's a typical Royal Applause in that he's plain to look at but whatever he's done he's done it nicely.'

1042. UNNAMED ★★★★
b.c. Diktat – Ann's Annie (Alzao)
January 12. Fourth foal. 26,000Y. Tattersalls October 1. Stan Moore. Half-brother to the quite useful 12f all-weather winner of four races Sgt Schultz (by In The Wings), to the fair 12f winner Galianna (by Galileo) and the modest 14f all-weather winner Red River Rock (by Spectrum). The dam, a quite useful two year old 1m winner in Ireland, is a half-sister to six winners including the very smart Group 3 7f Criterion Stakes winner Pipe Major. The second dam, Annsfield Lady (by Red Sunset), a winner of three races in Ireland between 9f and 10f, is a half-sister to four winners including the Group 2 and dual Group 3 winner Insatiable.
'A fine, big horse that does everything easily – he just cruises and looking at him you could say he was a three year old that's won three or four races! I'd say he was a quality seven furlong two year old.'

1043. UNNAMED ★★
b.f. Officer – Inn Between (Quiet American)
March 19. First foal. €100,000Y. Goffs Million. Stan Moore. The dam, a winner of six races in the USA and listed placed twice, is a half-sister to six minor winners in the USA. The second dam, Dintel (by Bates Motel), a US stakes-placed winner of five races, is a half-sister to five winners.

1044. UNNAMED ★★★
b.br.f. Chapel Royal – Oldupai (Gulch)
March 4. fourth foal. $22,000Y. Fasig-Tipton Kentucky. Stan Moore. Half-sister to two minor winners in the USA and Mexico by Old Trieste.

The dam is an unraced half-sister to the US stakes winner Reflect The Music. The second dam, Light On Your Feet (by Nijinsky), was a minor four year old winner in the USA.

'She'll be a five/six furlong two year old and is a good, strong filly that shows good paces at home. The sire was a big speed horse in America.'

1045. UNNAMED ★★★
b.c. Pyrus – Spot In Time (Mtoto)
March 17. First foal. 17,000Y. Doncaster St Leger. Stan Moore. The dam, placed once in a bumper, is a half-sister to three winners including the listed winner Whitefoot. The second dam, Kelimutu (by Top Ville), won four races at four years and is a half-sister to six winners.

'A strong, good-looking horse with a lovely action. He does everything very easy and he'll be a smashing horse over seven furlongs plus.'

HUGHIE MORRISON
1046. BATTLE ★★★★
gr.c. Compton Place – Molly Moon
(Primo Dominie)
January 17. First foal. 75,000Y. Tattersalls October 1. Hugh Morrison. The dam, a useful two year old dual 5f winner, is a half-sister to the smart dual Group 3 sprint winner The Trader. The second dam, Snowing (by Tate Gallery), a quite useful dual 5f winner at three years, is a half-sister to two minor winners. (Mr & Mrs H Scott-Barrett & Partners).

'If I only have one two year old this will be the one. He's quite forward and sharp. The pedigree points to him being a two year old and I'll probably start him off at six furlongs before dropping him back to five – it's something I often do so they aren't too rushed off their feet first time out.'

1047. CAPE MELODY ★★★★
b.f. Piccolo – Cape Charlotte (Mon Tresor)
April 22. Second foal. 16,000Y. Tattersalls October 3. Norris/Huntingdon. Half-sister to the moderate unplaced 2007 two year old Sweet Mind (by Mind Games). The dam is an unraced half-sister to the dam of the Group 1 Golden Jubilee Stakes winner Cape Of Good

Hope. The second dam, Laena (by Roman Warrior), was placed once at two years and is a half-sister to one winner. (Mrs Anne Usher, Mrs Isabel Eavis & Partners).

'This is a nice filly. She's big but she's straightforward and will make a two year old. Everybody who rides her likes her.'

1048. FELDAY ★★★
b.c. Bahamian Bounty – Monaiya
(Shareef Dancer)
March 2. Ninth foal. 115,000Y. Tattersalls October 1. Hugh Morrison. Half-brother to the useful listed 10f Pretty Polly Stakes winner and Oaks fourth Musetta, to the fair 10f winner Simply Sensational (both by Cadeaux Genereux), the fairly useful 6f winner Fiametta (by Primo Dominie), the quite useful two year old 5f all-weather winner Awarding (by Mark Of Esteem), the fair Irish 9f winner Dictation (by Diktat), the modest two year old 5f winner Paradise News (by Sure Blade) and the French and Italian winner Captain Tim (by Lion Cavern). The dam, a French 7.5f and 1m winner, is a sister to a listed-placed winner in France and a half-sister to eight winners including the listed and subsequent Canadian Grade 2 winner Vanderlin. The second dam, Massorah (by Habitat), won the Group 3 5f Premio Omenoni and was second in the Group 3 Prix du Gros Chene. (Mrs R C A Hammond).

'A nice colt, he's very straightforward and he could potentially be a big horse so you wouldn't want to bash on with him. An early autumn two year old I'd say.'

1049. KING'S STARLET ★★★
b.f. King's Best – Brightest Star (Unfuwain)
March 12. Third foal. 48,000Y. Tattersalls October 1. Not sold. Half-sister to the Italian 1m to 10f winner of nine races from 3 to 6 years Strepadent (by Diesis) and to a hurdles winner by Giant's Causeway. The dam was placed over 10f and 11f is a half-sister to the Oaks winner Lady Carla. The second dam, Shirley Superstar (by Shirley Heights), a fairly useful two year old 7f winner, is a half-sister to two winners. (Helena Springfield Ltd).

'She hasn't been here that long but she looks quite nice and 'together.' She's quite keen, as King's Best horses can be, but I don't know too much about her yet. Physically you would think she'd run this year despite having stamina in the pedigree.'

1050. LABISA (IRE) ★★★

b.f. High Chaparral – Damiana (Thatching)
May 1. Fifth foal. 58,000Y. Tattersalls October 3. A Skiffington. Half-sister to the useful two year old 6f winner and Group 3 7f Horris Hill Stakes second Stimulation (by Choisir) and to the fairly useful 7f to 10f winner Desert Cristal (by Desert King). The dam was placed five times in France at two and three years and is a half-sister to four winners including the listed Prix Coronation winner and US Grade 2 placed Dirca. The second dam, Derena (by Crystal Palace), is an unraced half-sister to four winners. (M Kerr-Dineen & R P Tullett).
'A quality filly, she's athletic but being by High Chaparral we've had to back off her because we can't hurry her. She finds everything quite easy and messes about a lot, but hopefully by the end of the season I'd like to think I'd be winning a maiden with her.'

1051. MY KINGDOM ★★★

b.c. King's Best – Nebraas (Green Desert)
March 23. Second foal. €70,000Y. Goffs Million. Hugh Morrison. The dam is an unraced three-parts sister to the very useful 6f winner (including at two years) Mutaakkid and a half-sister to the Group 1 Golden Jubilee Stakes winner Malhub. The second dam, Arjuzah (by Ahonoora), a useful winner of the listed 7f Sceptre Stakes, is a half-sister to the Irish listed winner Ormsby. (Wood Street Syndicate).
'Quite a stuffy horse, he's going to need quite a bit of work and I suspect he'll be a late summer two year old. He could be quite nice and he's a pretty relaxed character.'

1052. NON DOM (IRE) ★★

b.c. Hawk Wing – Kafayez (Secreto)
March 30. Tenth foal. €50,000Y. Goffs Million. Hugh Morrison. Half-brother to the unplaced

(in two starts) 2007 two year old Blimey O'Riley (by Kalanisi), to the Italian winner at two and three years and listed-placed Persian Filly (by Persian Bold), the French two year old winner and listed placed Ascot Dream (by Pennekamp), the smart hurdles winner Warne's Way (by Spinning World), the fairly useful two year old 7f winner Almaviva (by Grand Lodge) and the modest 6f winner Gardrum (by Lycius). The dam is an unplaced half-sister to ten winners including three stakes winners. The second dam, Sham Street (by Sham), a minor winner of four races in the USA, is a half-sister to three listed winners including the smart broodmare Palace Street. (Mr R C Tooth).
'A nice, big, strong horse – just like his sire. You wouldn't want to be galloping him until later in the year. I was attracted to him at the sales partly because Palace Street is in the pedigree.'

1053. SCRABBLE ★★

b.f. Montjeu – Spry (Suave Dancer)
February 3. Half-sister to the fair dual 1m winner Bajan Pride (by Selkirk) and to the modest 11f to 2m winner Serramanna (by Grand Lodge). The dam, a quite useful 12f winner, is a half-sister to the smart triple 12f winner Sebastian (by Sadler's Wells) and to the very useful 10f Newmarket Pretty Polly Stakes winner Sardegna (by Pharly). The second dam, Sandy Island (by Mill Reef), was a very useful winner of the Group 3 12f Lancashire Oaks and the 10f Pretty Polly Stakes. She is closely related to Slip Anchor and a half-sister to the German 2,000 Guineas winner Swazi. (Lady Howard de Walden).
'A flighty, buzzy filly, like a lot of Montjeu's, I'm trying to get her to relax at the moment rather than do too much with her. She's quite sharp looking but I think she's starting to grow.'

1054. SKEEMEH ★★★

ch.c. Sakhee – Marah (Machiavellian)
February 13. Fourth foal. 48,000Y. Tattersalls October 1. Hugh Morrison. Half-brother to the fair 12f winner Remaal (by Unfuwain) and to the modest Irish 7.5f winner Mouseen (by Alhaarth). The dam, a fairly useful two year old 7f winner, is a half-sister to one winner. The second dam,

Samheh (by Private Account), a modest 7f placed two year old, stayed 10f and is a half-sister to five winners. (Thurloe Thoroughbreds). *'A lovely walker. He's a back-end two year old type but he's a sensible horse with a nice character and he could be alright.'*

1055. SOME SUNNY DAY ★★★
ch.f. *Where Or When – Palace Street (Secreto)*
March 29. Twelfth foal. Half-sister to the high-class Group 1 6f July Cup winner Sakhee's Secret (by Sakhee), to the smart listed winner of six races from 5f to 7f Palace Affair, the fairly useful 6f and 7f winner King's Caprice (both by Pursuit Of Love), the very useful 6f to 8.3f winner Duke Of Modena (by Salse), the useful dual 6f winner (including at two years) Marker (by Pivotal), the quite useful 6f winner Zacchera (by Zamindar) and the fair 7f winner Ca'd'Oro (by Cadeaux Genereux). The dam, a useful winner over 6f and 7f including the listed Cammidge Trophy, is a half-sister to the Extel Handicap winner Indian Trail and the Italian Group 3 winner Sfriss. The second dam, Majestic Street (by Majestic Prince), won twice in the USA at two years and is a half-sister to four US stakes winners. (Miss B E Swire).
'She's never stopped growing but I suspect we'll be running her around September time over seven furlongs. A nice filly and although the sire has yet to prove himself the mare has an excellent record with some sires that aren't particularly fashionable. She's the last foal of the dam.'

1056. SPRING GREEN ★★
b.f. *Bahamian Bounty – Star Tulip (Night Shift)*
January 29. Seventh living foal. Sister to the modest 2007 two year old 7f winner Kamal and half-sister to the smart and consistent sprint winner of 1four races Texas Gold (by Cadeaux Genereux), to the fair 6f (at two years) to 11f and hurdles winner Indian Sun (by Indian Ridge), the fair 6f winner Kansas Gold (by Alhaarth) and a four year old winner in Germany by Hector Protector. The dam was a useful winner of three races over 6f including the listed Sandy Lane Stakes and is a half-sister

to four minor winners. The second dam, Silk Petal (by Petorius), a useful winner of three races over 7f including a German listed event, was third in the Group 3 Prix de Flore and is a half-sister to five winners. (Nicholas Jones).
'She's built like an ox and she's very quirky so I have to have my best rider on her every day. Although she'll probably run as a two year old we'll have to wait and see how she goes.'

1057. SUAKIN DANCER (IRE) ★★
ch.f. *Danehill Dancer – Wedding Morn (Sadler's Wells)*
January 19. First foal. 75,000Y. Tattersalls October 1. Templeton Stud. The dam is an unplaced half-sister to two winners. The second dam, Wedding Bouquet (by Kings Lake), a useful 5f to 7f winner (including the Group 3 C L Park Stakes), was Group 1 placed in Ireland at two years and subsequently won the Grade 3 6.5f Monrovia Handicap in the USA and is closely related to the outstanding Derby, Irish Derby and King George winner Generous and a half-sister to the Oaks winner Imagine. (Dr Ornella Carlini Cozzi & J Bernstein).
'She's only just arrived but she's quite straight-forward and looks as if she'll make a two year old. I don't know anything about her yet though.'

1058. UNNAMED ★★★
b.f. *Dr Fong – Dead Certain (Absalom)*
April 13. Half-sister to the very useful two year old 5f and 6f winner and Cornwallis Stakes second Deadly Nightshade, to the fairly useful 6f to 1m winner True Night, the quite useful two year old 5f winner Night Speed (all by Night Shift), the useful Irish 7f and 10f winner Hamad, the quite useful 11.6f winner Dead Aim (both by Sadler's Wells), the fairly useful 6f winner Dodo (by Alzao), the quite useful two year old 7f winner Palatinate (by Desert Prince) and the French 1m winner Sinduda (by Anabaa). The dam, a very smart winner of the Group 1 6f Cheveley Park Stakes, the Queen Mary Stakes, the Lowther Stakes (all at two years) and the Group 2 6.5f Prix Maurice de Gheest, is a half-sister to seven winners including the fairly useful 10f handicapper Fire Top. The second dam, the

French 1m to 10f winner Sirnelta (by Sir Tor) is a daughter of a half-sister to the French Derby winner Sanctus II. (Crichel Racing).

'Not yet in training but I've seen her and she should make a two year old. A big, strong filly.'

1059. UNNAMED ★★

b.f. Danehill Dancer – Eurostorm (Storm Bird)
March 21. Half-sister to the smart 1m and 10f winner Man O'Mystery (by Diesis) and to the Irish two year old 6f winner Destorm (by Dehere). The dam won four races in Ireland and the USA including the listed 1m Brownstown Stud Stakes and the listed 10f Diamond Stakes at the Curragh. She is a half-sister to seven winners out of the smart Eurobird (by Ela-Mana-Mou), a winner of four races including the Irish St Leger and the Blandford Stakes and a half-sister to the French Derby winner Bikala and to the Irish Derby and French Derby winner Assert. (Stonethorn Stud Farms Ltd).

'A nice, big filly but she's not from an obvious two year old family so she's one for later in the year.'

1060. UNNAMED ★★

b.br.c. Fusaichi Pegasus – Gracie Lady (Generous)
January 29. Sixth foal. $230,000Y. Keeneland September. Liam Norris. Half-brother to the minor US winner Great Opinions (by Rahy). The dam was placed in France and is a half-sister to the French 2,000 Guineas winner No Pass No Sale and the Group 3 1m Prix de Sandringham winner Once In My Life. The second dam, No Disgrace (by Djakao), won once in France at two years over 7.5f and was fourth in three Group 3 events. (De la Warr Racing).

'A nice looking horse, he's a big baby and I'm told that if a Fusaichi Pegasus shows anything as a two year old you have to hang on with them. When the penny drops he might fly but at the moment he's very green!'

1061. UNNAMED ★★

b.c. Reset – Great Verdict (Christmas Tree)
March 19. Half-brother to the very smart South African Grade 1 13f and UAE Grade 3 12f winner Greys Inn (by Zabeel) and to the quite useful 10f winner Masterofthecourt (by Horse Chestnut). The dam is an unraced half-sister to the top-class Australian winner Zedative. (Mrs B Oppenheimer).

'He came straight from a field and he's very green and babyish but actually he goes alright. The family get better as they get older but this colt might make a two year old. He's growing so I'll look after him for a bit.'

WILLIE MUIR

1062. DEFECTOR (IRE) ★★

b.c. Fasliyev – Rich Dancer (Halling)
April 9. Second foal. 21,000Y. Doncaster St Leger. W Muir. Half-brother to the quite useful 2007 9f winner Stubbs Art (by Hawk Wing). The dam, a modest 10f placed maiden, is a half-sister to the Group 2 7f Challenge Stakes winner Just James. The second dam, Fairy Flight (by Fairy King), a two year old 6f winner in Ireland, is a full or half-sister to four winners including the listed winners Titled Ascent and Northern Tide. (Mr David Knox & Partners).

'Being by Fasliyev you'd think his best distance would be shorter than that of his half-brother Stubbs Art. He's a little bit keen and a strong, strapping horse. Fasliyev's usually like firm ground and there's every reason to hope this colt will make a two year old. I haven't worked him yet because I've been concentrating on keeping him relaxed.'

1063. DIKTALINA ★★★

b.f. Diktat – Oiselina (Linamix)
February 18. Seventh foal. 12,000Y. Tattersalls October 2. Not sold. Sister to a two year old winner in Japan and half-sister to the quite useful two year old 1m winner Salute The General (by Mark Of Esteem), to the modest 11f all-weather winner A Mother's Love (by Act One). The dam won once at three years in France, was listed-placed and is a half-sister to four winners including the Group 2 Prix de Royallieu winner Oiseau Rare. The second dam, Oiseau de Feu (by Nijinsky), won once at two years and is a half-sister to five winners including the US Grade 1 placed Casey Tibbs.

'She'll be one for the mid-summer and although

she didn't reach he reserve at the sales she now looks like a Rolls Royce when she works. A really nice filly and you'd be very pleased with her'

1064. ENTRANCER (IRE) ★★★
b.c. Key Of Luck – Corn Futures
(Nomination)
February 19. Eleventh foal. 30,000Y. Doncaster St Leger. W Muir. Brother to the useful two year old 5f Weatherbys Supersprint winner Siena Gold and half-brother to the very useful two year old Crazee Mental. a winner over 6f and placed in the Cheveley Park Stakes, the Queen Mary Stakes and the Cherry Hinton Stakes, the modest 7f all-weather winner Futuristic (both by Magic Ring), the fair 6f (at two years) and 7f winner Trading Aces (by Be My Chief), the fair all-weather 9.4f winner Reap (by Emperor Jones) and the fair 6f winner Three Days In May (by Cadeaux Genereux). The dam, a fair two year old 6f winner, is a half-sister to seven winners including the dam of the March Stakes and Glorious Stakes winner Midnight Legend. The second dam, Hay Reef (by Mill Reef), won once at three years and is a half-sister to the dam of the Irish 2,000 Guineas winner Wassl. (D G Clarke & C.L.A Edginton).
'He's quite a strong, sharp individual with a natural way about him and a great temperament. He does things well and he'll definitely be speedy.'

1065. HALLING GAL ★★
b.f. Halling – Saik (Riverman)
May 2. Sixth foal. 25,000Y. Tattersalls October 3. David Joseph. Sister to the promising 2007 two year old 7f winner Hallingdal and half-sister to the quite useful three year old 7f winner Wistman (by Woodman) and to two winners in Japan by Jade Robbery. The dam is an unraced half-sister to five winners including the smart Group 3 10f Brigadier Gerard Stakes and Group 3 10f Scottish Classic winner Husyan and the dam of the triple Group 2 winner Mubtaker. The second dam, Close Comfort (by Far North), is an unraced half-sister to the champion French two year old filly Ancient Regime (herself dam of 3 good winners in Crack Regiment, Rami and La

Grande Epoque) and to the Group 2 Prix Maurice de Gheest winner Cricket Ball. (David & Gwyn Joseph).
'A nice filly and since we bought her she's grown a lot. Like her full sister last year she wouldn't be out until late summer or into the autumn but I like her a lot and she moves well.'

1066. KING'S MASQUE ★★
b.c. Noverre – Top Flight Queen
(Mark Of Esteem)
March 31. Fourth foal. 14,000Y. Tattersalls October 2. W Muir. Half-brother to the fair 2007 7f placed two year old Anne Of Kiev (by Oasis Dream) and to the very useful 7f (at two years) and 10f winner Big Robert (by Medicean). The dam, a quite useful 10f winner, is a half-sister to six winners including the smart Group 2 11.9f Great Voltigeur Stakes winner Sacrament and to the unraced dam of the Group 1 Pretty Polly Stakes winner Chorist. The second dam, Blessed Event (by Kings Lake), winner of the listed 10f Ballymacoll Stud Stakes, was placed in 5 Group races including the Yorkshire Oaks and the Champion Stakes. (A Patrick, C Edginton & M Caddy).
'He's quite nice but backward although I recall that his half-brother Big Robert took a little time and yet I reckon he's going to win a Group race this year. This colt was quite cheap at the Sales because he's not got the best conform-ation in the world. A bit weak and immature at the moment, he'll take a bit of time and might start over seven furlongs around August time.'

1067. KING'S SABRE ★★★
ch.c. King's Best – Lightsabre (Polar Falcon)
March 25. Second foal. 21,000Y. Tattersalls October 1. W Muir. Half-brother to the 2007 two year old Light Box (by Medicean). The dam, a modest 6f placed three year old, is a placed half-sister to Megahertz, a 1m (at two years) to 10f winner of 1four races including three Grade 1 events in the USA. The second dam, Heavenly Ray (by Rahy), a fairly useful 7f and 1m winner, is a half-sister to three winners.
'I love this colt. He moves well, he won't be early but he does things nice. He was a cheap horse

because he has a proper pedigree and he's lengthened and grown since the sales. One for the middle of the season.'

1068. PETHER'S DANCER (IRE) ★★

b.c. Kyllachy – La Piaf (Fabulous Dancer)
April 25. Eleventh foal. 28,000Y. Doncaster St Leger. W Muir. Half-brother to Mick's Dancer (by Pivotal), placed fourth once from two starts at two years in 2007, to the fairly useful 5f and 6f winner Merlin's Dancer (by Magic Ring), the quite useful 7f and 1m winner Gilded Dancer (by Bishop Of Cashel), the fair two year old 8.6f winner Bridegroom, the fair 9f winner Show No Fear (both by Groom Dancer) and a winner of nine races in Turkey by Primo Dominie. The dam, a two year old French 7.5f winner, later won a minor stakes in the USA and is a half-sister to the Grade 1 Del Mar Oaks winner Golden Apples and the Group 3 Park Hill Stakes winner Alexander Three D. The second dam, Loon (by Kaldoun), was a French listed winner of four races. (Perspicacious Punters Racing Club).
'I've trained most of the family if not them all, including the three year old Mick's Dancer who I love. This colt will take time just as the others in the family did. He's a lovely colt but I'll take my time because I know if I press and kick he'll get injured. The family are slow-maturing, so I'm just looking to run him at the end of the season.'

1069. ROSY MANTLE ★★

b.f. Daylami – Dominion Rose (Spinning Rose)
March 20. Third foal. 10,000Y. Tattersalls October 3. Not sold. Half-sister to the fairly useful 2007 two year old 7.6f winner and listed-placed Al Muheer (by Diktat) and to the fair two year old 6f winner Suki Bear (by Xaar). The dam, a modest 7f all-weather winner at four years, is a half-sister to the Grade 1 Breeders Cup Mile and Grade 1 Santa Anita Derby winner Castledale. The second dam, Louju (by Silver Hawk), is an unraced half-sister to ten winners.
'She's one for later in the year but she's a nice filly. Her two half-siblings won as two year old's and although she went to the sales she's such a nice filly we didn't want to give her away so we bought her back.'

1070. SILVADOR ★★

gr.c. Selkirk – Dali's Grey (Linamix)
April 5. Fifth foal. 160,000Y. Tattersalls October 1. J Brummitt. Half-brother to the useful 10f to 14f winner Bauer (by Halling), to the fairly useful 10.2f to 12f winner Batik (by Peintre Celebre) and the fair 10f to 14f winner Boz (by Grand Lodge). The dam, a French 11f winner, is a sister to the French Group winners Diamilina and Diamonixa and a half-sister to the Group winner Diamond Green. The second dam, Diamonaka (by Akarad), a French 10.5f winner, was Group 2 placed and is a half-sister to the French Group winners Diamond Mix, Diasilixa and Diamond Dance. (C Edginton, K Jeffery & P Wheatley).
'The most expensive yearling I bought last year, he has a fantastic pedigree and everything in his family suggests he should take time. But he's got a fantastic action, he's a big, strong-looking animal and he doesn't look backward. Nevertheless we'll look after him and aim for his three year old career because I think such a lot of him.'

1071. TRIP SWITCH ★★

b.c. Reset – Caribbean Star (Soviet Star)
March 12. Seventh foal. 16,000foal. Tattersalls December. Emerald Bloodstock. Half-brother to the fairly useful 5f and 6f winner of eight races Caribbean Coral (by Brief Truce) and to the modest triple 1m winner Inquisitress (by Hernando). The dam, a fair 7f winner, is out of the Irish 7f winner Who The Blonde (by Cure The Blues). (Andrew and Jo Patrick).
'He'll be a nice horse but his half-brother Caribbean Coral wasn't early and I don't think this colt will be out until the autumn. He's a big, tall colt and I had to go easy on him because he wouldn't hold his condition but he's bulking up now and that's what I was waiting for. A great mover with a good temperament, he'll be a sprinter but not an early one.'

1072. TRUEBLUE WIZARD (IRE) ★★★

ch.c. Bachelor Duke – Truly Bewitched (Affirmed)
March 16. Fifth foal. 50,000Y. Doncaster St Leger. W Muir. Half-brother to the unplaced 2007 two year old Red Merlin, to the fair two

year old 5f winner Red Trance (both by Soviet Star), the fairly useful 7f and 1m winner Truly Enchanting (by Danehill Dancer) and the 1m winner and Group 3 Prix Miesque third Arabian Spell (by Desert Prince). The dam, a quite useful two year old 6f winner, is a half-sister to four winners including the US Grade 2 winner Chinese Dragon. The second dam, Fabulous Fairy (by Alydar), a fair three year old 10f winner, is a half-sister to five winners and to the dam of the top-class miler Desert Prince. (M J Caddy).
'We spent a few quid on him but they thought he'd make a lot more. He's a lovely individual, I like him and he'll be out in mid-season. He's a really nice colt and I think you'll hear a lot of him.'

1073. UNNAMED ★★
b.c. Mull Of Kintyre – Birthday (Singspiel)
January 6. Third foal. 14,500Y. Doncaster Festival. W Muir. Half-brother to the unplaced 2007 two year old Liberty Island (by Statue Of Liberty). The dam is an unraced daughter of the Group 3 Prix d'Aumale winner Kindergarten (by Trempolino), herself a half-sister to two minor winners.
'He was going well in training but he just got a touch of sore shins. I've laid off him for a bit, he'll be back in training soon and he looks quite sharp. He's still for sale.'

1074. UNNAMED ★★
b.c. Bachelor Duke – Gronchi Rosa (Nashwan)
March 15. First foal. 14,000Y. Tattersalls October 2. W Muir. The dam won two races at two and three years in Italy and is a half-sister to two winners including the Group 3 placed Euribor. The second dam, Anna Grassi (by Bound For Honour), won a listed event in Italy and is a half-sister to six winners.
'I still own him but he'll be one of our first runners. He's lengthened and grown since the sales and although he's out of a Nashwan mare she won as a two year old, so I think he'll be a six furlong type to start off with.'

DAVID MURRAY-SMITH
1075. AMERICAN CHAMP (IRE) ★★★
b.c. Pyrus – Sandy Fitzgerald (Last Tycoon)

April 28. Sixth foal. €35,000Y. Goffs Sportsman's. Bobby O'Ryan. Half-brother to the moderate 9.5f winner Lewis Lloyd (by Indian Lodge) and to the modest 14f and hurdles winner Corporate Express (by Sri Pekan). The dam is an unraced half-sister to one winner. The second dam, Sanndila (by Lashkari), a modest 12f, 2m and hurdles winner, is a half-sister to eight winners. (Mr & Mrs Washer).
'This is a very good-moving horse for the second half of the season. I haven't done much with him but I like what I've seen. I would have thought he'd be a seven furlong starter from mid-season onwards.'

1076. ANFIELD STAR (IRE) ★★★
b.c. Celtic Swing – Shenkara (Night Shift)
March 23. Third foal. €100,000Y. Goffs Million. Bobby O'Ryan. Half-brother to the fair 5f and 1m winner and listed placed Crocodile Bay (by Spectrum). The dam is a placed half-sister to two minor winners. The second dam, Sheriyna (by Darshaan), a listed winner in France, is a half-sister to the Prix de Diane winner Shemaka. (Mr Rob Lloyd).
'A very good-looking, strongly made colt, we're just starting to step up his work and he may start at five furlongs but he'd be better over further. We like what we've seen so far and he's a very nice horse.'

1077. BEST BIDDER (USA) ★★★
b.br.f. Mr Greeley – Party Stripes (Candy Stripes)
March 1. Second foal. €150,000Y. Goffs Million. Bobby O'Ryan. The dam is an unplaced half-sister to five minor winners. The second dam, Pudical (by Sassafras), a US stakes winner and Grade 3 placed, is a half-sister to four winners. (Rob Lloyd Racing Ltd).
'A very attractive, strongly made filly, she's a good, athletic mover. We haven't done anything with her yet but I'd have thought she'd be a mid-season filly, starting off at six furlongs. The sire has been very successful with his European runners.'

1078. DIAMOND JO (IRE) ★★
b.f. Johannesburg – Still As Sweet (Fairy King)
February 1. 32,000Y. Doncaster Festival Sales.

Bobby O'Ryan. The dam, an Irish 6f and subsequent US winner, is a half-sister to the Irish listed 1m winner Hymn Of Love. The second dam, Perils Of Joy (by Rainbow Quest), a three year old 1m winner in Ireland, is a half-sister to five winners including the Italian Group 3 winner Sweetened Offer. (Rob Lloyd Racing Ltd).
'A small filly and an early foal, she's been very backward of her coat and yet previously I thought she'd be one of our earliest runners but I haven't been able to do much with her yet. One to introduce in late May.'

1079. FIFER (IRE) ★★★
b.f. Soviet Star – Fife (Lomond)
May 10. €64,000Y. Tattersalls Ireland. Bobby O'Ryan. Half-sister to six winners including the listed-placed and smart broodmare Witch Of Fife (by Lear Fan), the quite useful 1m and 10f winner Hudood (by Gone West) and the French two year old 1m winner Delightful Lady (by Cozzene). The dam, a winner at three years and third in the listed Lupe Stakes, is a half-sister to five winners including the dam of the Prix Vermeille winner Pearly Shells. (Rob Lloyd Racing Ltd).
'A very nice filly, she was a mid-May foal so we haven't done much with her yet and I doubt her being out until August time. It's a pedigree that's being updated all the time and this is a good-moving, athletic filly and a good prospect. We like her very much.'

1080. GOODISON GLORY (IRE) ★★★
b.c. Tout Seul – Thorbella (Deploy)
April 26. Third foal. €40,000Y. Tattersalls Ireland. Bobby O'Ryan. Half-brother to the minor Italian two year old winner Sexy Baby (by Tobougg). The dam is a placed half-sister to five winners including a stakes winner in Malaysia. The second dam, Ever Genial (by Brigadier Gerard), won the Group 3 Hungerford Stakes and the Group 3 May Hill Stakes and is a half-sister to three winners. (Rob Lloyd Racing Ltd).
'The sire was a tough horse, running right through the season and winning the Dewhurst Stakes. We're very pleased with this horse, he's very nice and will start at six furlongs in May.'

1081. HIT THE SWITCH ★★★
b.c. Reset – Scenic Venture (Desert King)
March 3. Third foal. €80,000Y. Goffs Million. Bobby O'Ryan. The dam is an unraced half-sister to six winners including the dual Group 3 winner Lidanna. The second dam, Shapely Test (by Elocutionist), won at three years and is a half-sister to five winners. (Rob Lloyd Racing Ltd).
'A tall colt, he's grown a lot since we bought him, we like him very much and he'll be a seven furlong two year old from August onwards. His sire has just had a Group 3 winner in Australia from his first crop.'

1082. ICE ATTACK (IRE) ★★★
gr.f. Verglas – Little Whisper (Be My Guest)
March 18. First foal. €150,000Y. Goffs Million. Bobby O'Ryan. The dam, an Irish two year old 6f and 7f winner and listed-placed, is a half-sister to the Group 3 Killavullan Stakes winner Confuchias. The second dam, Schust Madame (by Second Set), won over 11f in Ireland and is a half-sister to four winners including the dual US Grade 2 winner Sweet Ludy and the Italian Group 3 winner Late Parade. (Rob Lloyd Racing Ltd).
'A very nice filly out of a fast family, she could be out in May over five furlongs but she'll definitely be better over six. She's a strongly made filly and I think the sire Verglas will have a good season as this is his first crop since he stood in Ireland. He did well in France from rather limited opportunities.'

1083. OCEANIC DANCER (IRE) ★★
b.f. Danetime – Almasa (Faustus)
April 5. Eighth foal. €60,000Y. Goffs Sportsman's. Bobby O'Ryan. Sister to the fair triple 7f winner (including at two years) Viva La Diva and half-sister to the fair 5f winner Mac's Express (by Mac's Imp) and to a winner in Spain by Indian Rocket. The dam, a fair dual 6f winner at two years, was second in the listed St Hugh's Stakes and is a half-sister to two winners. The second dam, Superfrost (by Tickled Pink), won at four years and is a half-sister to six winners. (Rob Lloyd Racing Ltd).
'A filly I haven't done much with, I thought she

might be early but we've just had to be patient with her. I can't tell you much about her but she's a strongly made filly and I like what I've seen so far.'

1084. SIMPLY SENSATIONAL (IRE) ★★★
ch.c. Tendulkar – Grange Clare (Bijou d'Inde)
April 19. Second foal. 3,100Y. Doncaster October. G Banner. Half-brother to the 2007 two year old 5f seller winner Drumalee Lass (by Quws). The dam, afaor two year old 5f winner, is a half-sister to eight winners including the listed winners Forget Me (in Italy) and Sao (in France). The second dam, Scarlet Slipper (by Gay Mecene), won once at three years in France. (Mr & Mrs Banner).
'He's a tough, hardy two year old and a tallish horse that's well put together and we're looking forward to running him from May onwards, probably over six furlongs. We certainly think he'll be value for money.' TRAINER'S BARGAIN BUY

1085. WATERSTOWN (IRE) ★★
ch.c. Noverre – Twany Angel (Double Form)
April 20. €18,000Y. Goffs Million. Bobby O'Ryan. Half-brother to seven winners including the Group 1 7f Prix de la Foret winner Mount Abu (by Foxhound), the Irish and US winner and Group 3 7f C L Weld Park Stakes second Melleray (by Danehill) and the Italian listed winner Chiquita Linda (by Mujadil). The dam is a placed half-sister to six minor winners in Scandinavia, France and the USA. The second dam, Athy Angel (by Three Dons), won the listed Birdcatcher Nursery in Ireland. (Lloyd Partnership).
'Quite a small horse but strong and well-made, he would have been early because he was a sharp sort but unfortunately he had a setback and is having box rest now. He'll resume training at the end of May and he'll now make a two year old in late summer. Nevertheless he's a horse that I like and I've always been keen on the sire.'

JEREMY NOSEDA

1086. ADORN ★★★
b.f. Kyllachy – Red Tiara (Mr Prospector)
April 22. Fifth foal. Half-sister to the modest

8.3f winner Argent (by Barathea). The dam, a moderate 7.6f fourth-placed maiden, is closely related to the Japanese sprint stakes winner Meiner Love and a half-sister to two winners. The second dam, Heart Of Joy (by Lypheor), won 10 races including the Grade 2 Palomar Handicap and the Group 3 Nell Gwyn Stakes, is a half-sister to eight winners.
'She's a small, racey filly and a good mover that will hopefully be out in the second half of May. A two year old type, she ought to win a race but I haven't done enough with her yet to be sure.'

1087. ALEXANDER LOYALTY ★★★
b.f. Invincible Spirit – Nassma (Sadler's Wells)
April 5. Eleventh foal. €300,000Y. Goffs Million. BBA (Ire). Sister to the two year old listed 5f Dragon Stakes winner and Group 2 5f Flying Childers Stakes second Bahama Mama and half-sister to the useful two year old 6f and 7f winner Calchas (by Warning), the quite useful 9f and 10f winner Traprain (by Mark Of Esteem), the quite useful 9f winner Dansker (by Darshaan), the UAE 6f and 7f winner Junction Line (by Indian Ridge) and a winner abroad by Marju. The dam, a listed middle-distance winner of two races, is a half-sister to five minor winners. The second dam, Pretoria (by Habitat), a useful 7f (at two years) and 10f winner, is a half-sister to four winners including the Group 1 Fillies' Mile winner Ivanka.
'She's just had a touch of sore shins so is having a bit of a break but this is a filly that I like and she's done well since the sales. I think she's got more size and substance than her sister Bahama Mama who I trained and although that doesn't necessarily mean she'll be a better racehorse, at the moment she's a nicer type.'

1088. APPLAUSE ★★★
b.f. Danehill Dancer – Sniffle (Shernazar)
April 2. Sixth foal. €90,000Y. Goffs Million. Demi O'Byrne. Closely related to the unraced 2007 two year old Lili St Cyr (by Rock Of Gibraltar) and to the Irish 7f, 1m (both at two years) and listed 12f winner Snippets (by Be My Guest). The dam is an unplaced half-sister to the Grade 1 12f Hollywood Turf Cup and Group 3

1m Beresford Stakes winner Frenchpark and the Group 1 Prix Vermeille winner Pearly Shells. The second dam, Piffle (by Shirley Heights), a quite useful 12f winner, is a sister to the useful stayer El Conquistador and a half-sister to four winners.
'The type of filly that's going to take a bit of time and would hopefully be out in late August. A good mover, there's something about her to like.'

1089. AUTHORITATIVE ★★
b.f. Diktat – Australian Dreams (Magic Ring)
February 2. Second foal. 65,000Y. Tattersalls October 1. Cheveley Park Stud. The dam, a listed winner of seven races at three and four years in Germany, is a half-sister to four winners including the smart Group 3 5f Palace House Stakes and subsequent US Grade 3 9f winner Needwood Blade and the US Grade 3 winner Islay Mist. The second dam, Finlaggan (by Be My Chief), a quite useful 11f to 2m winner, is a half-sister to seven winners.
'A filly that will take some time, she's a decent type but pretty backward at the moment.'

1090. AWINNERSGAME (IRE) ★★★★ ♠
b.c. Kyllachy – Polish Descent (Danehill)
March 6. Seventh foal. €260,000Y. Goffs Million. Charlie Gordon-Watson. Half-brother to the quite useful 2007 6f and 7f placed two year old Classic Descent, to the Irish 1,000 Guineas winner Saoire (both by Auction House), the quite useful 6f and 7f all-weather winner (including at two years) Foronlymo (by Forzando), the fair two year old 1m winner Whittle Warrior (by Averti) and the Italian dual 7f winner (including at two years) Naomi de Bergerac (by Cyrano de Bergerac). The dam is an unraced half-sister to four winners including the Group 3 Curragh Stakes third Wistful Tune. The second dam, Nolnocan (by Colum), won twice at four years and is a half-sister to eight winners including the Irish listed winner Lady Eileen. (Saeed Suhail).
'He's working at present, I'm happy with him and he's a six furlong horse that will hopefully be running in mid-May. I think he's a two year old that will win his races.'

1091. CALYPSO BAY ★★★★
b.c. Galileo – Poule de Luxe (Cadeaux Genereux)
May 10. First foal. 65,000Y. Tattersalls October 1. Demi O'Byrne. The dam, a modest 7f winner at three years, is a half-sister to two winners including the listed winner and Group 3 placed Squaw Dance. The second dam, Likely Story (by Night Shift), a dual 6f winner at two and three years including the listed Queensferry Stakes, is a half-sister to five winners.
'A backward type but a lovely mover, he's a horse I like a lot and he'll be fine in the autumn. I look at him each day and I wonder why he didn't cost a lot more. The pedigree isn't that great but he's a gorgeous horse with a good attitude.'

1092. DOUBLE ACT ★★
b.c. Where Or When – Secret Flame (Machiavellian)
February 15. First foal. 115,000Y. Tattersalls October 2. John Warren. The dam, a fair 9f winner, is a half-sister to seven winners including the useful two year old 6f winner and Group 3 third Obsessive (herself dam of the St James's Palace Stakes winner Excellent Art). The second dam, Secret Obsession (by Secretariat), a fairly useful 10f winner, is a half-sister to seven winners including the Group 2 12f King Edward VII Stakes winner Beyton.
'A good-looking horse and a good mover, he's going to be a seven furlong horse in the second half of the summer. He does everything right.'

1093. ERROL FLYNN (IRE) ★★★
b.br.c. Danehill Dancer – Warusha (Shareef Dancer)
April 28. Fifth foal. 180,000Y. Tattersalls October 1. Mountgrange Stud. Brother to the fair two year old 1m winner Economic and half-brother to two minor winners in Germany by Dashing Blade and Sternkonig. The dam, a triple sprint-mile winner in Germany at three and four years, is a half-sister to eight winners including the Group 2 German 1,000 Guineas winner Walesiana (herself dam of the Nassau Stakes winner Zahrat Dubai). The second dam, Wondrous Pearl (by Prince Ippi), a listed winner over 9f, was Group 3 placed and is a half-sister

to nine winners.

'He'll make a two year old but not this side of July. He's a big, scopey horse that moves well. I don't know enough about him yet but he's a good, physical specimen.'

1094. GLAMOROUS SPIRIT ★★★★★ ♠

b.f. Invincible Spirit – Glamorous Air (Air Express)

April 1. Third foal. 105,000 two year old. Kempton Breeze-up. Anthony Stroud. The dam won six races at two and three years in Italy and is a half-sister to three minor winners here and abroad. The second dam, Glamorous Bride (by Baillamont), is a placed half-sister to two winners.

'She's was bought to be sharp and early and I like the way she breezed at the Sales– she went very quickly. She's had a little break and I would hope she'd be a filly we could take to Royal Ascot.'

1095. HIGH ALERT ★★★

b.c. Kyllachy – Haste (Halling)

February 9. Third foal. 120,000Y. Tattersalls October 1. Jane Allison. The dam is an unraced half-sister to four winners including the Irish listed winner Royal Intrigue. The second dam, Congress (by Dancing Brave), a quite useful two year old 1m winner, is a sister to the high-class Cherokee Rose, a winner of five races from 6f to 7f including the Group 1 6f Haydock Park Sprint Cup and the Group 1 Prix Maurice de Gheest and a half-sister to three winners.

'A good, solid citizen, I would hope he'd be a June/July horse and he's a good, hardy workman.'

1096. HIGHTIME HEROINE (IRE) ★★★

b.f. Danetime – Esterlina (Highest Honor)

March 2. Third foal. 135,000Y. Tattersalls October 2. Cheveley Park Stud. Half-sister to the smart 2007 two year old 7f winner and Group 1 1m Criterium International third Redolent (by Redback). The dam won over 1m at three years in Ireland and is a half-sister to three minor winners in France. The second dam, Shaquick (by Shadeed), won in France and is a half-sister to eight winners including the dual

Group 3 winner Leap Lively (dam of the Irish 1,000 Guineas winner Forest Flower). (Cheveley Park Stud).

'We're just picking up the tempo with her, I think she's a two year old type and that she'll win her races although I haven't done enough with her yet to be sure what she's capable of.'

1097. HIMALYA ★★★★

b.c. Danehill Dancer – Lady Miletrian (Barathea)

February 6. Third living foal. 210,000Y. Tattersalls October 1. John Warren. Half-brother to the quite useful 6f all-weather winner Dama'a (by Green Desert). The dam, a useful 1m winner and fourth in the Group 3 Fred Darling Stakes, is a sister to the listed winning two year old Duty Paid and a half-sister to three winners. The second dam, Local Custom (by Be My Native), was placed at up to 7f at two years and is a sister to the listed winner Tribal Rite and a half-sister to the Middle Park Stakes winner Balla Cove.

'A nice horse, a good mover and an early July type two year old. He'd be a horse I like at this moment and he'll be suited by six/seven furlongs. One to follow.'

1098. ISN'T IT DELICIOUS ★★

b.f. Danehill Dancer – Moonavvara (Sadler's Wells)

January 8. Second foal. 150,000foal. Tattersalls December. Badgers Bloodstock. The dam is an unraced half-sister to the Group 1 Prix Marcel Boussac and Group 1 Moyglare Stud Stakes winner Rumpelstiltskin. The dam is a placed sister to the French 2,000 Guineas, the St James's Palace Stakes and Prix du Moulin winner Kingmambo and to the Group 3 6f Prix de Ris-Oranges winner Miesque's Son and a half-sister to the French 1,000 Guineas, Prix de Diane and Prix Jacques le Marois winner East of the Moon. The second dam, Miesque (by Nureyev), was a great filly and the winner of ten Group or Grade 1 events including the Breeders Cup Mile (twice).

'I've given her a break, she'll be back but I haven't got any firm opinions about her yet.'

1099. KAPSILIAT ★★★

b.f. Cape Cross – Kootenay (Selkirk)

April 20. Third foal. The dam, a useful two year old Italian listed 1m winner, is a half-sister to three winners including the fairly useful two year old dual 7f winner Jay Gee's Choice. The second dam, Llia (by Shirley Heights), a fairly useful two year old 7f winner, was third in the listed 10f Pretty Polly Stakes and is a half-sister to three winners including the useful 2m listed winner Lady Of The Lake.

'A backward type, the earliest you'd see her running would be at the end of July. A six/seven furlong type and a good mover, she's a nice filly and it's just how quickly she comes to hand.'

1100. KINGSHIP SPIRIT (IRE) ★★★★ ♠

b.c. Invincible Spirit – Jupiter Inlet
(Jupiter Island)

February 22. Ninth foal. 100,000Y. Tattersalls October 2. Charlie Gordon-Watson. Half-brother to the fair 2007 7f placed two year old Jonny Lesters Hair (by Danetime) and to three minor winners in Italy by Alhaarth, Ashkalani and Common Grounds. The dam, a listed winner of six races from 2 to five years in Italy, is a half-sister to five winners. The second dam, Anegada (by Shirley Heights), won once at four years in Italy and is a half-sister to four winners including three listed winners in Italy. (Saeed Suhail).

'He's working and could be running over five furlongs at the end of April or in early May. A racey horse, he'll definitely win his races at two.'

1101. KISSING THE CAMERA ★★★★

b.f. Galileo – Hoh Dear (Sri Pekan)

March 29. Fourth foal. 88,000Y. Tattersalls October 1. Not sold. Half-sister to the 2007 Irish two year old 7f all-weather winner Kalinka Malinka (by Pivotal), to the quite useful dual 6f two year old winner Musical Guest (by Mozart) and the fair two year old 7f winner Love And Laughter (by Theatrical). The dam won four races here and in North America including the 6f Empress Stakes (at two years) and the Grade 3 Natalma Stakes. The second dam, Miss Kristin (by Alzao), a listed-placed winner of two races in Ireland, is a half-sister to five winners.

'She has speed on the dam's side and has actually shown it. She's doing a little bit of work, I think she'll be running in May and I think she has talent. I like her and she's a nice, straightforward type.'

1102. LA BELLE DANE ★★

b.f. Danetime – Lindfield Belle (Fairy King)

April 26. Eleventh foal. 260,000Y. Tattersalls October 1. Charlie Gordon-Watson. Sister to the 2007 two year old Group 3 7f Prix Eclipse winner Domingues and to the smart listed 5f winner Baltic King and half-sister to the fair 9f winner Superior Star (by Superior Premium), to the fair two year old 6f winner Red Amazon (by Magic Ring), the Italian 7f (at two years) and 7.5f winner Whetly (by Dilum), the modest 5f winner of three races at five years Distant King (by Distant Relative) and a winner in Scandinavia by Kirkwall. The dam, a fair two year old 5f winner, is a half-sister to three minor winners here and abroad. The second dam, Tecmessa (by Home Guard), is an unraced sister to the Group 3 Prix du Petit Couvert winner Manjam. (Saeed Suhail).

'A backward filly, she's going to take a little time and is just having a break at the moment so I don't know an awful lot about her.'

1103. LEAHURST (IRE) ★★★★

gr.c. Verglas – Badee'a (Marju)

February 17. Third foal. 95,000Y. Tattersalls October 1. Jane Allison. Half-brother to the fair 2007 two year old 6f winner Writingonthewall (by Danetime) and to the smart 1m listed winner of four races (including at two years) Dunelight (by Desert Sun). The dam is an unraced sister to the Group 3 Prix Quincey winner Mahboob and a half-sister to four winners. The second dam, Miss Gris (by Hail The Pirates), won the Group 1 Italian 1,000 Guineas and the Group 1 Italian Oaks and is a half-sister to 2 US stakes winners.

'He's working and is a good, solid horse with a good temperament and attitude. I think he's more of a six furlong horse than five and he'll most probably get further. A hardy sort that could have a good, solid campaign as a two year old and run plenty of times. A nice, tough, honest performer.'

1104. MUZO USA) ★★★★

b.c. Gone West – Bowl Of Emeralds (A P Indy)
February 1. Fourth foal. $500,000Y. Keeneland September. John Warren. Half-brother to two winners including a minor US three year old winner by Monarchos. The dam, a stakes-placed winner of two races at three years in the USA, is a half-sister to one winner out of the US Grade 1 Flower Bowl Handicap winner Northern Emerald (by Green Dancer).
'A nice colt, he looks like a July type two year old and he's a big, scopey horse and a great mover. Physically, he's one of the nicest specimens I've got. Certainly a nice colt and to watch out for.'

1105. ROCKY'S PRIDE (IRE) ★★★

b.c. Rock Of Gibraltar – L'Animee (Green Tune)
March 28. Fifth foal. 135,000Y. Tattersalls October 2. Cheveley Park Stud. Half-brother to the minor French three year old 1m winner Miguel Do Brazil (by Spectrum). The dam, a minor French three year old 1m winner, is a half-sister to three winners including the Group 3 Grand Prix de Vichy winner Bailador. The second dam, Alymatrice (by Alysheba), won once at three years in France and is a full or half-sister to five winners including the Group 3 Prix de Royaumont winner Sadler's Flag.
'A good, solid horse that moves well, he looks like being a horse to run in the second half of the season and I think he'll win.'

1106. SECRET LIFE ★★★

b.c. Montjeu – Bright Halo (Bigstone)
January 24. Fifth foal. 200,000Y. Tattersalls October 1. Jane Allison. Half-brother to the fair 2007 two year old 1m winner Resplendent Light (by Fantastic Light) and to the useful 6f (at two years) and listed 1m winner and Group 2 6f Mill Reef Stakes third Nantyglo (by Mark Of Esteem). The dam, a minor French three year old 9f winner, is a half-sister to six winners including the Group 1 10f Prix Saint-Alary winner Cerulean Sky and the Breeders Cup second L'Ancresse. The second dam, Solo de Lune (by Law Society), a French 11f winner, is a half-sister to six winners including the Grade 2 E P Taylor Stakes winner Truly A Dream and the

French Group 2 winner Wareed.
'He's had a few setbacks during the winter so he's a bit behind where I want him to be, but he's a nice, well put together horse. Not a typical Montjeu and there's a lot of speed on the dam's side, so I would hope we'll see him around July time and I think he's a good, solid performer who would do a good job at two.'

1107. SECRET WITNESS ★★★★

ch.c. Pivotal – It's A Secret (Polish Precedent)
April 12. Fourth foal. Brother to the unraced 2006 two year old High Intrigue. The dam, a fairly useful 1m and 9f winner, is a half-sister to seven winners including the useful two year old 6f winner and Group 3 10.4f Musidora Stakes third Obsessive. The second dam, Secret Obsession (by Secretariat), a fairly useful 10f winner, is a half-sister to six winners including the Group 2 12f King Edward VII Stakes winner Beyton.
'A big horse and one for the late summer, he's a good mover and a horse with plenty of size and scope. I quite like him.'

1108. SLEEPY BLUE OCEAN ★★

b.c. Oasis Dream – Esteemed Lady
(Mark Of Esteem)
February 9. First foal. 40,000Y. Tattersalls December. Badgers Bloodstock. The dam, placed once over 6f at two years, is a half-sister to four winners including the two year old Group 2 6f Richmond Stakes winner Revenue. The second dam, Bareilly (by Lyphard), is an unraced three-parts sister to the Group 3 1m Prix de la Grotte winner Baya and the Italian Group 2 winner Narrative.
'You'd think he'd be an early type but when we bought him he had a few issues that meant we've had to give him some time, so he's one for the late summer or autumn, but he's still worthy of a mention.'

1109. STOIC ★★★★

b.c. Green Desert – Silver Bracelet
(Machiavellian)
March 27. Third foal. 65,000Y. Tattersalls October 1. John Warren. Half-brother to the

minor French 1m winner Dark Beauty (by Singspiel). The dam, a fairly useful 8.3f winner, was third in the listed Masaka Stakes and is a half-sister to one winner out of the very useful two year old Group 3 7f Prestige Stakes winner and Group 1 Prix Marcel Boussac third Love Of Silver (by Arctic Tern). herself a half-sister to six winners. (Highclere Thoroughbred Racing).
'A nice, scopey horse, he's one for the second half of the season and he's a good mover. I like him and he's much the nicest of the ones Highclere & the Royal Ascot Racing Club have sent me.'

1110. TARTARIA ★★★★

b.br.f. Oasis Dream – Habariya (Perugino)
February 25. Second foal. €280,000Y. Goffs Million. Not sold. Half-sister to the promising 2007 Irish two year old 1m winner and listed placed Maryellen's Spirit (by Invincible Spirit). The dam won once over 12f in Ireland and is a half-sister to five winners including the Group three winners Hazariya and Hazarista. The second dam, Hazaradjat (by Darshaan), won twice at two and three years and is a full or half-sister to ten winners including the Flying Childers and Middle Park Stakes winner Hittite Glory.
'A nice type of filly for the second half of the summer, she's a good, scopey type and a good mover. A nicely balanced filly. she's one that I like.'

1111. THOUSAND KNIGHTS (USA) ★★★

ch.f. Grand Slam – Our Josephina
(Tale Of The Cat)
January 31. First foal. $200,000Y. Keeneland September. Anthony Stroud. The dam, a stakes winner and Grade 3 placed in the USA, is a half-sister to one winner. The second dam, Ropa Usada (by Danzig), is an unraced half-sister to the US Grade 1 winner Mogambo.
'She's had a bit of an issue with sore shins and is having a break at the moment so she's one from July onwards. I was always hopeful she'd make a two year old type and she'll come back'

1112. WAFFLE ★★★★

ch.c. Kheleyf – Saphire (College Chapel)
April 13. Fourth foal. €180,000Y. Goffs Million.

Jane Allison. The dam, a fairly useful two year old 5f and 6f winner, was listed-placed twice and is a half-sister to four minor winners. The second dam, Emerald Eagle (by Sandy Creek), a fair 6f to 1m winner of five races, is a half-sister to four winners.
'A sharp colt, he looks like a five/six furlong horse and hopefully he'll be running in May.'

1113. WAR NATIVE ★★★★

b.c. Cape Cross – Walkamia (Linamix)
February 15. The dam won the Group 3 10.5f Prix Fille de l'Air and is a sister to the Group 2 11f Prix Noailles winner Walk On Mix. The second dam, Walk On Air (by Cure The Blues), is a placed half-sister to seven winners including the Group 1 Prix Vermeille winner Walensee.
'A good-moving horse, he's nice and scopey and is one for late August or early September. He'd be one of the nicest physical specimens among my two-year-olds and he looks like a racehorse.'

1114. WINNER'S CALL ★★

b.f. Indian Ridge – Damsel (Danzero)
February 9. First foal. 230,000Y. Tattersalls October 1. Charlie Gordon-Watson. The dam, a quite useful two year old 1m winner, is a half-sister to 13 winners including the US Grade 1 Oaklawn Handicap winner Jovial, the US Grade 3 winner Brave Note and the minor US stakes winner Never Force. The second dam, Rensaler (by Stop The Music), won at around 1m in the USA at four years and is a half-sister to ten winners including the US Grade 3 winner Rose Bouquet. (Saeed Suhail).
'A backward filly, she's a good-moving filly but she'll take lots of time and won't be running until around September time.'

1115. UNNAMED ★★★

b.f. Danehill Dancer – Bex (Explodent)
April 11. Twelfth foal. 360,000Y. Tattersalls October 1. Netherfield House Stud. Sister to the 2007 two year old Irish listed 1m winner Savethisdanceforme and half-sister to the Group 2 Prix de Conseil de Paris winner Crimson Quest (by Rainbow Quest), the French listed 15f winner Ballarat, the French listed 12f winner

Hijaz, the minor French winner Lady Bex (all by Sadler's Wells), the useful 10.4f winner Bathilde (by Generous and herself dam of the Group 2 winner Tungsten Strike) and a minor winner in France by Fairy King. The dam, a smart winner of the Group 3 10.5f Prix de Flore, is a half-sister to 4 stakes winners. The second dam, Bay Street (by Grundy), won the Group 3 Princess Elizabeth Stakes and is a half-sister to the listed winner Rose Of Montreaux.

'Quite a backward type, she'd be one to introduce around August time and is a lovely mover. At this stage you'd be very happy with her and everything is as it should be at this moment.'

1116. UNNAMED ★★★

b.c. Clodovil – Cafe Creme (Catrail)
February 8. Second foal. 135,000Y. Tattersalls October 2. Badgers Bloodstock. Half-brother to the fair 2007 5f placed two year old Red Expresso (by Intikhab). The dam is an unraced half-sister to four winners including the two year old Group 1 6f Cheveley Park Stakes winner Seazun and the two year old 7f winner and listed-placed Mahogany. The second dam, Sunset Cafe (by Red Sunset), a minor Irish 12f winner, is a sister to the Group 3 Prix Foy winner Beeshi and a half-sister to eight winners including the John Smiths Magnet Cup winner Chaumiere and the dam of the high-class 10f colt Insatiable.

'He'll be working in April and he's a good mover. A colt I quite like, he's a nice-moving horse and he's got a bit about him.'

1117. UNNAMED ★★★

b.f. Cape Cross – Dinka Raja (Woodman)
April 23. Sixth foal. 140,000Y. Tattersalls October 1. Hugo Merry. Half-sister to the Group 1 6f Cheveley Park Stakes and Group 2 6f Lowther Stakes winner Carry On Katie (by Fasliyev), to the two year old 6f all-weather winner Pinkabout (by Desert Style) and the minor US three year old winner Geebeekay (by Peintre Celebre). The dam, a minor French three year old 1m winner, is a half-sister to four winners. The second dam, Miss Profile (by Sadler's Wells), is an unraced half-sister to 4 stakes winners including the Group 1 Prix Saint-Alary winner Grise Mine and the triple US Grade 1 winner Kostroma.

'She's just had a little setback and we won't see her until August time at the earliest, but she's a good-moving filly with more size and scope than her half-sister Carry On Katie. I think she's alright but she's going to take time.'

1118. UNNAMED ★★★★

gr.f. Exchange Rate – Disperse A Star (Dispersal)
March 15. Fifth foal. $490,000 two year old. Ocala February. Half-sister to three winners including two minor winners in the USA by Appealing Skier and Wild Event. The dam, a minor US three year old winner, is a half-sister to six winners including the high-class Japanese stakes winner South Vigorous. The second dam, Darkest Star (by Star de Naskra), won four minor races in the USA at two and three years and is a half-sister to seven winners.

'I adored her at Calder where she breezed a furlong in 9.4 – she just flew. She should be a two year old and is a lovely looking filly. She's still in America where she'll do a few bits of work before coming over here. She doesn't have much of a pedigree but if anything ever looked like a racehorse it's her.'

1119. UNNAMED ★★★

b.f. One Cool Cat – Latest Chapter (Ahonoora)
February 6. Ninth foal. €230,000Y. Goffs Million. Demi O'Byrne. Half-sister to the very useful Irish Group 3 7f Boland Stakes winner Social Harmony (by Polish Precedent), to the fairly useful Irish 1m winner Artist's Tale (by Singspiel) and the Irish winners Lady Luck (over 1m by Kris), God Speed (over 6f by Be My Guest), Discreet Option (over 5f by Night Shift) and Bounce Back (over 7f by Alzao). The dam is an unraced half-sister to the Grade 1 Belmont Stakes winner Go And Go. The second dam, Irish Edition (by Alleged), won at three years and is a half-sister to the US Grade 1 winner Twilight Agenda and the dam of the Group 1 winners Refuse To Bend and Media Puzzle.

'I think she'll win at two, she's hasn't got a great deal of size and substance but she's be solid citizen'

1120. UNNAMED ★★★★
ch.c. Galileo – Llia (Shirley Heights)
April 6. Seventh foal. 450,000Y. Tattersalls October 1. John Warren. Half-brother to the very useful triple listed 1m winner (including at two years) and Group 2 Falmouth Stakes third Kootenay (by Selkirk), to the fairly useful two year old dual 7f winner Jay Gee's Choice (by Barathea), the fair 9.7f winner Gretna (by Groom Dancer) and the modest 14f winner Dilsaa (by Night Shift). The dam, a fairly useful two year old 7f winner, was third in the listed 10f Pretty Polly Stakes and is a half-sister to five winners including the Italian Group 3 winner Guest Connections and the useful 2m listed winner Lady Of The Lake. The second dam, Llyn Gwynant (by Persian Bold), was a very useful winner of five races including the Group 3 1m Desmond Stakes and the Group 3 1m Matron Stakes.
'A nice, big scopey horse and a good mover, he's done everything right since we've had him. He's a colt that I like and hopefully he'll be racing over seven furlongs in August.'

1121. UNNAMED ★★
gr.c. Johannesburg – Paiute Princess (Darshaan)
April 6. Fourth foal. €275,000Y. Goffs Million. Demi O'Byrne. Half-brother to a minor winner at three and four years in the USA by Marquetry. The dam is a placed half-sister to two minor winners. The second dam, Papago (by Sadler's Wells), won at two years in France and is a half-sister to seven winners.
'He's a horse that didn't really progress through the winter but he's going forward now and I think he's a good, solid citizen with a good attitude. A straightforward horse and I'm happier with him now than I was but it's too early to pass comment.'

1122. UNNAMED ★★★
b.f. Acclamation – Snap Crackle Pop (Statoblest)
February 6. Seventh foal. 350,000Y. Tattersalls October 1. Netherfield House Stud. Half-sister to the useful 2007 two year old 6f and listed 7f

Washington Singer Stakes winner Sharp Nephew (by Dr Fong), to the fairly useful triple 5f winner Handsome Cross (by Cape Cross) and the fair two year old 6f winner Snip Snap (by Revoque). The dam, a quite useful two year old 5f listed winner, is a half-sister to three minor winners. The second dam, Spinelle (by Great Nephew), a quite useful 11f winner, was second in the Group 3 Oaks Trial and is a half-sister to five winners.
'This filly has changed a lot since the sales. I was hopeful she'd be a sharp, early type and I can see now she isn't going to be that. Hopefully she'll be a June/July filly. A good-looking filly, very strong, racey and a good mover, but she didn't have a great winter and she's just on an upward curve now.'

1123. UNNAMED ★★★★
b.c. Lion Heart – V V S Flawless (Deputy Minister)
February 14. Third foal. $750,000 two year old. Fasig-Tipton Calder two year old's-in-training. Sir Robert Ogden. Half-brother to a minor US three year old winner by Smart Strike. The dam, a winner at two and three years, was stakes-placed and is out of the US stakes winner Singing Heart (by Palace Music), herself a half-sister to six winners. The sire, a son of Tale Of The Cat, won two Grade 1 stakes in the USA. His first crop are two year old's in 2008.
'This colt breezed well and looks the type to be a two year old but with the scope to go on at 3. Hopefully he'll be running in May and if all goes well he may be good enough to run in the Coventry Stakes at Royal Ascot.'

1124. UNNAMED ★★★★ ♠
b.c. Fasliyev – Ziffany (Taufan)
March 29. €310,000Y. Goffs. Half-brother to the very smart listed 7f winner of six races Major's Cast (by Victory Note) and to the very smart sprinter Jessica's Dream (by Desert Style), winner of the Group 3 Ballyogan Stakes and the Group 3 Premio Omenoni. The dam, a two year old 7f seller winner, is a half-sister to one winner abroad. The second dam, Bonnie Banks (by Lomond), is an unplaced half-sister to six

winners including the Group 3 Cornwallis Stakes winner Hanu.

'Clearly this mare can do it, just by looking at the sires of her two good foals, so the stallion might not be important. This is a lovely looking horse and a great mover. I'd hope he'd be running in June and he's much more precocious than his half-brother Major's Cast. A nice type of colt and I like him.'

AIDAN O'BRIEN

1125. AGE OF AQUARIUS (IRE) ★★★
b.c. Galileo – Clara Bow (Top Ville).
April 13. Tenth live foal. €1,400,000Y. Deauville August. Demi O'Byrne. Half-brother to six winners including the Group 1 Prix Jean Prat winner Turtle Bowl (by Dyhim Diamond), the Group 2 Prix d'Astarte winner Turtle Bow (by Turtle Island) and the French listed placed Whitton Court (by Cardoun). The dam is a half-sister to the French listed winner Houwayda. The second dam, Kamiya (by Kalamoun), won twice and is a half-sister to the Group three winners Karadar and Karamita.

1126. APT (IRE) ★★★
b.f. Danetime – Sheila Blige (Zamindar)
March 29. Third foal. €190,000Y. Goffs Million. Demi O'Byrne. Half-sister to the fairly useful two year old 5f and 6f winner and listed placed Lady Lily (by Desert Sun). The dam, a quite useful two year old 5f winner, is a half-sister to six winners including the very useful 1m (at two years) to 12f winner and Group 3 Gordon Richards Stakes third Naked Welcome. The second dam, Stripanoora (by Ahonoora), was placed once at three years and stayed 1m and is a full or half-sister to five minor winners.

1127. ARISTOCRAT ★★★
b.c. Galileo – Silver Colours (Silver Hawk)
February 13. Fourth foal. 75,000Y. Tattersalls October 1. Demi O'Byrne. Half-sister to the fairly useful listed 1m winner Silver Pivotal (by Pivotal) and to the quite useful two year old 7.5f winner Gold Queen (by Grand Lodge). The dam, a useful two year old listed 1m winner, is a half-sister to three winners including the Japanese

Grade 2 winner God Of Chance and the Royal Lodge Stakes third Desaru. The second dam, Team Colors (by Mr Prospector), is an unraced half-sister to four winners.

1128. BYZANTINE ★★
b.c. Sadler's Wells – Miss Satamixa (Linamix)
April 6. Ninth foal. 160,000Y. Tattersalls October 1. Demi O'Byrne. Brother to the minor French middle-distance winner of three races Mister Wells and half-brother to the minor French three year old 7f winner Man O Desert (by Green Desert). The dam, winner of the Group 1 1m Prix Jacques le Marois, is a half-sister to six winners including the dams of the Group/Graded stakes winners Miss Caerleona, Mister Riv, Mister Sicy and Manninamix. The second dam, Miss Satin (by Satingo), won the listed 7f Prix de l'Obelisque and is a half-sister to six winners including the Italian Group 2 winner Mister Ski.

1129. CANIS MAJOR (IRE) ★★
b.c. Montjeu – Crafty Example
(Crafty Prospector)
May 11. Eleventh foal. €450,000Y. Goffs Million. Demi O'Byrne. Half-brother to the high-class Group 2 Queen Anne Stakes and Group 3 Diomed Stakes winner Intikhab, to the minor French 10f winner Jadarah (both by Red Ransom) and a minor winner in the USA by Bates Motel. The dam ran once unplaced and is a half-sister to six winners abroad. The second dam, Zienelle (by Danzig), is an unraced sister to Polish Precedent.

1130. CARLITO BRIGANTE (IRE) ★★★
b.c. Haafhd – Desert Magic (Green Desert)
March 26. Fifth foal. €400,000Y. Deauville August. Demi O'Byrne. The dam, a winner of three races in Ireland over 7f including the listed Athasi Stakes, is a half-sister to five winners. The second dam, Gracieuse Majeste (by Saint Cyrien), won once at two years in France and is a half-sister to six winners including the French Group three winners Gay Minstrel and Greenway and the dam of the Prix de la Salamandre winner Oczy Czarnie.

1131. CHANGEOFTHEGUARD ★★
b.c. Montjeu – Miletrian (Marju)
February 19. Fourth foal. €200,000Y. Goffs Million. Demi O'Byrne. Half-brother to Millie's Rock (by Rock Of Gibraltar), unplaced in one start at two years in 2007. The dam, a smart 9f (at two years), Group 2 Ribblesdale Stakes and Group 3 Park Hill Stakes winner, is a sister to the useful two year old 6f winner Marksman and a half-sister to the Group 2 Geoffrey Freer Stakes winner Mr Combustible. The second dam, Warg (by Dancing Brave), is an unraced half-sister to five winners.

1132. CHINTZ ★★
b.f. Danehill Dancer – Gold Dodger
(Slew O'Gold)
March 25. Fifth foal. €250,000Y. Deauville August. Demi O'Byrne. Closely related to the minor French winner Artful (by Green Desert). The dam, a listed 10f winner of two races in France, is a half-sister to eight winners including the French dual Group 3 winner Prospect Park. The second dam, Brooklyn's Dance (by Shirley Heights), won the Group 3 Prix Cleopatre and is a half-sister to seven winners.

1133. COOL FOR CATS ★★★
ch.c. Storm Cat – Mythomania (Nureyev)
April 30. Ninth foal. $1,700,000Y. Keeneland September. Demi O'Byrne. Half-brother to five winners including the US dual Grade 3 winner Inexplicable (by Miswaki), the US stakes-placed Goldenbaum (by Halo) and minor winners in the USA by Woodman and Carson City. The dam was listed-placed in France prior to winning a minor event at four years in the USA and is a half-sister to eight winners including the Group 3 Nell Gwyn Stakes and subsequent US Grade 2 winner Heart Of Joy. The second dam, Mythographer (by Secretariat), is a placed half-sister to three stakes winners.

1134. CRIMSON SKY (IRE) ★★
b.c. Montjeu – Park Crystal (Danehill)
April 12. Third foal. €575,000Y. Goffs Million. Demi O'Byrne. Half-brother to the unraced 2007 two year old Pure Wonder (by Hernando).

The dam is an unraced half-sister to three winners including the French two year old 1m winner and Epsom Derby second Walk In The Park. The second dam, Classic Park (by Robellino), won three races including the Irish 1,000 Guineas and is a half-sister to ten winners including the US Grade 2 winner Rumpipumpy.

1135. CROWFOOT (IRE) ★★
b.c. Sadler's Wells – Grecian Bride
(Groom Dancer)
February 10. Sixth foal. 380,000Y. Tattersalls October 1. John Magnier. Closely related to the 7f, 1m (both at two years) and listed 10f and 12f winner Allexina and to the useful 1m winner and Group 3 12f second Athenian Way (both by Barathea) and half-brother to the modest dual 9f all-weather winner Champain Sands (by Green Desert). The dam is an unraced sister to the useful 7f (at two years) and listed 10f winner Athens Belle and a half-sister to the Group 1 Grand Prix de Saint-Cloud winner Gamut and the Group 2 13.3f Geoffrey Freer Stakes winner Multicolored. The second dam, the French 10f and 12f winner Greektown (by Ela-Mana-Mou) is a half-sister to the high-class stayer Sought Out (dam of the Derby winner North Light) and to Scots Lass (dam of the Group 2 Great Voltigeur Stakes winner Bonny Scot)

1136. DA VINCI CODE (IRE) ★★
b.c. Galileo – Onereuse (Sanglamore)
February 16. Fifth living foal. €650,000Y. Goffs Million. Demi O'Byrne. Closely related to the Group 1 10f Prix Saint-Alary winner and Group 1 Prix Vermeille third Fidelite (by In The Wings) and half-brother the French 10f and jumps winner Amour Multiple (by Poliglote). The dam was placed over 1m and 10f in France and is a half-sister to eight winners including the Irish Derby winner Winged Love. The second dam, J'ai Deux Amours (by Top Ville), winner of the listed 1m Prix de Lieurey at three years, dead-heated for third in the Group 2 9.2f Prix de l'Opera and is a half-sister to eight winners.

1137. DESERT EAGLE (IRE) ★★★
b.c. Hawk Wing – Announcing Peace (Danehill)

April 11. Sixth foal. €350,000Y. Goffs Million. Demi O'Byrne. Half-brother to the smart 6f (at two years), 7f and listed 12f winner Crosspeace, to the fairly useful two year old dual 7f winner So Sweet (both by Cape Cross) and the Italian 5f (at two years) and 7.5f winner Carburatore (by College Chapel). The dam is an unplaced full or half-sister to five minor winners. The second dam, Remoosh (by Glint Of Gold), is an unplaced half-sister to five winners including the Group 2 Richmond Stakes winner Nomination.

1138. DRUMBEAT ★★

b.c. Montjeu – Maskaya (Machiavellian)
April 5. Third foal. €650,000Y. Goffs Million. Demi O'Byrne. Half-brother to the fair 7.6f winner Red Blooded Woman (by Red Ransom). The dam, an Irish two year old 5f winner, is a half-sister to four winners including the dual Irish listed 7f winner and Group 2 placed Modeeroch and the Irish two year old 6f winner and Group 1 6f Cheveley Park Stakes third Danaskaya. The second dam, Majinskaya (by Marignan), winner of the listed 12f Prix des Tuileries, is a half-sister to six winners including the French two year old 7f winner Mabrova, herself dam of the Group 1 5f Prix de l'Abbaye winner Kistena.

1139. DUNKIRK ★★★

gr.c. Unbridled's Song – Secret Status (A P Indy)
January 23. Fourth foal. $3,700,000Y. Keeneland September. Demi O'Byrne. The dam won eight races including the Grade 1 Mother Goose Stakes and the Grade 1 Kentucky Oaks and is a sister to the US Grade 3 winner Alumni Hall. The second dam, Private Status (by Alydar), a minor US stakes winner, is a half-sister to two Grade 1 winners in Chile.

1140. EGYPT ★★★★

b.c. Dansili – Royal Flame (Royal Academy)
March 26. Fourth foal. 140,000Y. Tattersalls October 2. Blandford Bloodstock. Half-brother to the fair 2007 7f placed two year old Arabian Spirit (by Oasis Dream) and to a winner over hurdles by Germany. The dam, a modest 10f all-weather winner, is a half-sister to one winner. The second dam, Samnaun (by Stop The Music), is an unraced half-sister to eight winners including the Group 2 German 1,000 Guineas winner Quebrada.

1141. EL ROMO (IRE) ★★★

b.c. Montjeu – Check Bid (Grey Dawn II)
April 11. Twelfth foal. €150,000Y. Goffs Million. BBA (Ire). Half-brother to six winners including the listed 6f Blenheim Stakes winner and Group 3 5f Cornwallis Stakes second Check The Band (by Dixieland Band) and three minor US winners by Skip Away, Hennessy and Cox's Ridge. The dam ran twice unplaced in the USA and is a half-sister to five winners including the US stakes winner and Grade 2 placed Key Bid. The second dam, Delta Bid (by Delta Judge), a US stakes-placed winner of six races, is a half-sister to the US Grade 1 winner Adept.

1142. EUROPE (USA) ★★★

gr.c. Unbridled's Song – Zing (Storm Cat)
April 29. Fourth foal. $2,600,000Y. Keeneland September. Demi O'Byrne. Brother to the US Grade 2 winner Half Ours. The dam, a minor US winner at two and three years, is a sister to the US stakes winner Yankee Gentleman. The second dam, Key Phrase (by Flying Paster), won the Grade 1 Santa Monica Handicap.

1143. FAME AND GLORY ★★★ ♠

b.c. Montjeu – Gryada (Shirley Heights)
March 20. Half-brother to the smart 10.2f and 12f winner Grampian, to the fair two year old 1m all-weather winner Gryskirk (both by Selkirk), the useful 10f and 12.3f winner Guaranda and the quite useful 11f winner Graham Island (both by Acatenango). The dam, a fairly useful two year old 7f and 8.3f winner and third in the Group 3 1m Premio Dormello, is a full or half-sister to four middle-distance winners and to the useful stayer Gondolier. The second dam, Grimpola (by Windwurf), won over 6f and 1m in Germany including the Group 2 German 1,000 Guineas and stayed 12f.

1144. FOUR STAR GENERAL ★★★★
b.c. Danehill Dancer – Teslemi (Ogygian)
May 16. Closely related to the two year old Group 1 6f Phoenix Stakes and Group 1 1m Gran Criterium winner Spartacus, to the Group 2 10f Gallinule Stakes, Group 3 1m Beresford Stakes and Hong Kong Derby winner Johan Cruyff and the Irish three year old 6f winner Alstemeria (all by Danehill). The dam, a fair three year old 1m winner, is a half-sister to five minor winners. The second dam, Martha Queen (by Nijinsky), was placed twice in the USA and is a sister to the US Grade 1 Suburban Handicap winner Upper Nile and the Grade 1 Hollywood Derby winner De La Rose (herself the dam of the US Grade 1 winner Conquistarose)

1145. GLUTEUS MAXIMUS (IRE) ★★★
br.c. Statue Of Liberty – Skidmore Girl (Vaguely Noble)
February 23. Eighth foal. €42,000Y. Goffs Million. Margaret O'Toole. Half-brother to the smart 1m, listed 10f and hurdles winner and Group 2 Derby Trial second Mountain (by Montjeu) and to three winners in Italy by Danehill, Flying Spur and Bigstone. The dam is an unplaced half-sister to four winners. The second dam, Sanedtki (by Sallust), was a champion miler and won four Group/Grade 1 races.

1146. HELIUS ★★
b.c. Montjeu – Someone Special (Habitat)
April 3. Fourteenth foal. 200,000Y. Tattersalls October 1. Charlie Gordon-Watson. Closely related to the Group 2 10.4f Dante Stakes and Group 3 1m Craven Stakes winner Alnasr Alwasheek (by Sadler's Wells) and half-brother to the Group 1 10.4f Juddmonte International Stakes winner One So Wonderful, the quite useful 10f winner One So Marvellous (both by Nashwan), the very useful 7f Rockfel Stakes winner and Relatively Special (by Alzao), the French listed winner Raucous Lad (by Warning), the quite useful 1m winner You Are The One (by Unfuwain), the quite useful 6f winner All Time Great (by Night Shift) and the hurdles winner Someone Brave (by Commanche Run). The

dam, a useful 7f winner and third in the Group 1 1m Coronation Stakes, is a half-sister to the top-class miler Milligram. The second dam, One in a Million (by Rarity), won the 1,000 Guineas and the Coronation Stakes and is out of an unraced half-sister to Deep Run.

1147. INDIAN OCEAN (IRE) ★★
b.c. Montjeu – Dance Desire (Caerleon)
March 28. Fifth foal. €370,000Y. Goffs Million. Demi O'Byrne. Half-brother to the 2007 Irish 7f placed two year old Danse Aile (by Hawk Wing), to the fair two year old 5f winner Foxtrot Too (by Foxhound) and a three year old winner in Japan by Danehill. The dam is an unraced half-sister to nine winners including the Group 3 May Hill Stakes winner Intimate Guest. The second dam, As You Desire Me (by Kalamoun), won 2 listed events in France over 7.5f and 1m and is a half-sister to seven winners including the Group 2 King Edward VII Stakes winner Classic Example.

1148. JANE EYRE ★★★★ ♠
gr.f. Sadler's Wells – Albanova (Alzao)
April 2. First foal. €2,400,000Y. Goffs Million. Demi O'Byrne. The dam, a triple Group 1 12f winner in Germany, is a sister to the dual Group 1 10f Champion Stakes winner Alborada. The second dam, Alouette (by Darshaan), a 1m (at two years) and listed 12f winner, is a half-sister to the Nassau Stakes and Sun Chariot Stakes winner Last Second (dam of the Group 1 winner Aussie Rules) and the dams of the Group 1 winners Yesterday and Quarter Moon and the Group 2 winner Allegretto.

1149. JACQUES OFFENBACH (IRE) ★★★
ch.c. Galileo – Four Green (Green Tune)
February 14. Second foal. €210,000Y. Goffs Million. Demi O'Byrne. The dam won over 1m at three years in France and is a sister to the French listed winner Double Green. The second dam, Green Bend (by Riverman), is a placed half-sister to nine winners including the French Group 3 winner and smart broodmare Brooklyn's Dance.

1150. JOHANN ZOFFANY ★★★
b.f. Galileo – Belle Allemande (Royal Academy)
April 6. Third foal. 310,000Y. Tattersalls October 1. J Magnier. Half-sister to a minor winner abroad by Grand Lodge. The dam, a minor French 11f winner, is a half-sister to nine winners including the German Oaks winner Que Belle. The second dam, Qui Bid (by Spectacular Bid), is an unraced sister to the US Grade 3 winner Sum and a half-sister to nine winners including the Group 1 winner Bakharoff and the Group 2 winner Emperor Jones.

1151. LISZT (IRE) ★★★
ch.c. Galileo – Corrine (Spectrum)
March 4. First foal. €550,000Y. Goffs Million. Charlie Gordon-Watson. The dam won four races, including a listed event, in Norway and is a half-sister to six winners. The second dam, La Luna (by Lyphard), a winner over 9f at three years in France, is a sister to the Group 3 Prix Daphnis and Group 3 Prix Thomas Bryon winner Bellypha and a half-sister to the Prix Eugene Adam winner Bellman and the Peruvian Grade 1 winner Run And Deliver.

1152. MAN FRIDAY (IRE) ★★★
b.c. Sadler's Wells – Caladira (Darshaan)
May 5. Tenth foal. 140,000Y. Tattersalls December. Charlie Gordon-Watson. Brother to the Beresford Stakes (at two years), Dante Stakes, Doncaster Cup and Lonsdale Stakes (all Group 2 events) winner Septimus and half-brother to the 2007 Irish two year old 6.5f winner Hollow Hill (by Orpen) and the Italian winner Lady Poison (by Charnwood Forest). The dam won over 10f in Ireland at three years and is a half-sister to eight winners. The second dam, Cape Race (by Northern Dancer), won at three years and is a half-sister to the Group/Grade three winners Never Return and Legal Case and to the smart sire Lord Gayle.

1153. MR MISTOFFELEES (USA) ★★★★
b.br.c. Storm Cat – Country Romance (Saint Ballado)
February 10. Second foal. $1,500,000two year old. Fasig-Tipton Calder two year old's-in-training. Demi O'Byrne. The dam, a stakes winner of four races at three years in the USA, is a half-sister to the Grade 2 stakes winner Katz Me If You Can and to the unraced dam of two stakes winners. The second dam, Cuddles (by Mr Prospector), won seven races including the Grade 1 Hollywood Starlet Stakes and is a half-sister to four winners.

1154. MUNNINGS ★★★★
ch.c. Speightstown – La Comete (Holy Bull)
March 20. Fourth foal. $1,700,000two year old. Fasig-Tipton Calder two year old's-in-training. Demi O'Byrne. Half-brother to a minor winner in the USA by Distant View. The dam is an unraced half-sister to six winners including the US Grade 2 winner Lasting Approval. The second dam, La Gueriere (by Lord At War), a US Grade 1 winner, is a half-sister to 12 winners including the US Grade 1 winner Al Mamoon. The sire, a son of Gone West, won the Grade 1 Breeders Cup Sprint. His first foals are two year old's in 2008.

1155. NATION (IRE) ★★★
b.c. Sadler's Wells – Welsh Love (Ela-Mana-Mou)
May 25. Twelfth foal. €380,000Y. Goffs Million. Demi O'Byrne. Brother to the unraced 2007 two year old Queen Of Tara and to the minor Irish 10f winner Catalyst, closely related to the Irish 12f winner Galileo Galilei (by Galileo) and to the high-class two year old Group 1 1m Grand Criterium winner Second Empire (by Fairy King) and half-brother to the very useful 7f (at two years) to 10f winner Ihtiram, the minor Irish 9f winner Shi Ar (both by Royal Academy), the smart Group 3 10f Ballysax Stakes winner Balestrini (by Danehill), the very useful listed 10f winner Ajhiba (by Barathea) and the listed Acomb Stakes winner Hemingway (by Spectrum). The dam, a minor Irish three year old 12f winner, is a half-sister to the Coronation Stakes winner Flame of Tara (dam of the Group 1 winners Salsabil and Marju) and to the Lupe Stakes second Fruition (dam of the Breeders Cup Turf winner Northern Spur and the high-class stayer Kneller). The second dam, Welsh

Flame (by Welsh Pageant), was a useful three year old winner of four races at around 1m.

1156. PETER TCHAIKOVSKY ★★★★
b.c. Dansili – Abbatiale (Kaldoun)
March 8. Sixth foal. €950,000Y. Deauville August. Margaret O'Toole. Half-brother to two minor winners in France by Desert Prince and Barathea. The dam won the Group 3 Prix Penelope, was second in the Group 1 Prix de Diane and is a half-sister to the French listed winner and Group 2 placed Aubergade. The second dam, Anna Edes (by Fabulous Dancer), is a placed half-sister to eight winners. This colt won on his debut in April.

1157. PLUTO (USA) ★★★
b.c. A P Indy – House Party (French Deputy)
April 17. Second foal. $1,000,000Y. Keeneland September. Demi O'Byrne. The dam won seven races including the Grade 1 Prioress Stakes and is a half-sister to one winner. The second dam, Bill Back (by Relaunch), a US stakes-placed winner, is a half-sister to three winners.

1158. POEM (IRE) ★★★
b.f. Sadler's Wells – Spring Flight (Miswaki)
April 24. Ninth foal. 300,000Y. Tattersalls October 1. Demi O'Byrne. Half-sister to six winners including the Group 1 1m St James's Palace Stakes and Group 2 10f Prix Eugene Adam winner Dr Fong, the Group 2 Champagne Stakes and Group 2 Vintage Stakes winner Lucky Story (both by Kris S) and the minor US turf winner Stylized (by Sovereign Dancer). The dam, a stakes-placed winner of eight races in the USA, is a half-sister to two minor stakes winners. The second dam, Coco La Investment (by Coco La Terreur), won once at two years in the USA.

1159. PRIDE (USA) ★★★
ch.f. Lion Heart – Coffee Springs
(Crafty Prospector)
March 19. Tenth foal. $475,000 two year old. Ocala February. Demi O'Byrne. Half-sister to the US Grade 3 placed winner of four races Pine For Java (by Pine Bluff) and to a minor US

winner at three and four years by Storm Cat. The dam, a US stakes-placed winner of five races, is a half-sister to five winners. The second dam, Next Fall (by Alleged), was a minor two year old winner in the USA.

1160. ROCKHAMPTON (IRE) ★★
b.c. Galileo – Green Rosy
(Green Dancer)
February 10. Fourteenth foal. 375,000Y. Tattersalls October 1. John Magnier. Half-brother to eight winners including the French Group 2 12f winners America (by Arazi) and Majorien (by Machiavellian), the listed 6f Hopeful Stakes winner Rose Indien (by Crystal Glitters) and the 7f (at two years in France) and dual 9.5f winner Royal Racer (by Danehill). The dam, a French 10f winner and listed-placed, is a sister to the French listed winner Big Sink Hope and a half-sister to ten winners including the good broodmare Rensaler (dam of the US Grade 1 winner Jovial). The second dam, Round The Rosie (by Cornish Prince), won once at two years in the USA and is a half-sister to 2 stakes winners.

1161. SKATING (IRE) ★★★
b.f. Danetime – Dalal (Cadeaux Genereux)
January 5. Second foal. €160,000Y. Goffs Million. Demi O'Byrne. Half-sister to the fair Irish 1m winner Magnum Force (by Redback). The dam was placed fourth once over 1m and is a half-sister to five winners including the two year old listed 5.2f winner Head Over Heels. The second dam, Proudfoot (by Shareef Dancer), won over 14f in Ireland and is a full or half-sister to seven winners.

1162. SLUSAICHI PEGASUS (USA) ★★
b.br.c. Fusaichi Pegasus – Sluice
(Seeking The Gold)
February 7. Second foal. $450,000Y. Keeneland September. Demi O'Byrne. The dam, a minor US stakes winner of four races, is a half-sister to two winners. The second dam, Lakeway (by Seattle Slew), a winner of seven races including four Grade 1 events in the USA, is a half-sister to three winners.

1163. SOUTHAMPTON ★★
b.c. Sadler's Wells – Katiyfa (Auction Ring)
April 24. Thirteenth foal. €420,000Y. Goffs Million. Demi O'Byrne. Closely related to the fair 2007 1m placed two year old Katimont (by Montjeu) and to two winners including the fair 6f to 12f winner of 11 races Katiypour (by Be My Guest) and half-brother to the smart Irish listed 12f and 14f winner Katiykha (by Darshaan) and the fairly useful winners at up to 12f Kariniyd (by Blushing Groom), Katiniyd (by Kahyasi) and Katiymann (by Persian Bold). The dam won the listed 1m Prix de la Calonne and is a half-sister to three winners. The second dam, Kaloudiya (by Shantung), won at three years and is a half-sister to seven winners including the dual Group 2 winner Kamaraan.

1164. SWISS GUARD ★★★
b.c. Montjeu – Millennium Dash (Nashwan)
February 4. Fourth foal. 500,000Y. Tattersalls October 1. Demi O'Byrne. Brother to the very useful two year old 1m winner and Group 1 Fillies' Mile third Dash to The Top and half-brother to the listed 10.8f winner Dash To The Front (by Diktat). The dam, a fairly useful 10.2f winner, is a half-sister to three winners and to the unplaced dam of the Sun Chariot Stakes winner Kissogram. The second dam, Milligram (by Mill Reef), won the Group 1 Queen Elizabeth II Stakes and the Group 2 Coronation Stakes and is a half-sister to the Coronation Stakes second Someone Special (the dam of four stakes winners including the Group 1 winner One So Wonderful)

1165. TINSELTOWN ★★
b.c. Sadler's Wells – Peony (Lion Cavern)
May 4. Fifth foal. 380,000Y. Tattersalls October 1. Demi O'Byrne. Half-brother to the smart listed 11f winner and Group 3 placed Unfurled (by Unfuwain), to the fairly useful 10.5f winner Broomielaw (by Rock Of Gibraltar) and the modest 14f and 17f winner Synonymy (by Sinndar). The dam won four races in France over 7f and 1m including the listed Prix Imprudence, was second in the French 1,000 Guineas and is a half-sister to four winners. The second dam,

Persiandale (by Persian Bold), is an unraced half-sister to three winners including the Australian dual Grade 1 winner Raffindale.

1166. UNITED STATES (USA) ★★★
b.c. A P Indy – Blithe (Unbridled)
March 17. Second foal. $2,000,000Y. Keeneland September. Demi O'Byrne. The dam is an unraced half-sister to three winners including the Kentucky Derby winner Fusaichi Pegasus. The second dam, Angel Fever (by Danzig), a US stakes-placed winner, is a sister to the Grade 1 winner Pine Bluff and a half-sister to the Grade 1 winner Demons Begone.

1167. VICEROY OF INDIA ★★
ch.c. Galileo – Hishi Lover (Pleasant Colony)
May 13. Fifth foal. $350,000Y. Keeneland September. Demi O'Byrne. Half-brother to the US winner and dual Grade 3 placed Prince Rahy (by Rahy). The dam won twice at four years in Japan and is a sister to the Irish winner and listed-placed Fantasy Royale and a half-sister to four winners including the US Graded stakes winners Bashford Manor and Naninja. The second dam, Nijinsky's Lover (by Nijinsky), won four races in the USA including two minor stakes events and is a half-sister to seven winners including the listed 7f winner Or Vision (herself dam of the Group/Grade 1 winners Dolphin Street, Insight and Saffron Walden)

1168. VON JEWLENSKY (IRE) ★★
b.c. Montjeu – Zivania (Shernazar)
February 8. Eleventh foal. 600,000Y. Tattersalls October 1. Demi O'Byrne. Brother to Group 3 1m UAE Guineas winner Stagelight (by Montjeu) and half-brother to six winners including the 7f (at two years) and listed 1m Masaka Stakes winner Hathrah (by Linamix), to the smart Group 2 12f Premio Ellington and listed 12f Haydock Park July Trophy winner Ivan Luis (by Lycius), the German 9.5f listed winner and Group 2 10f Prix Guillaume d'Ornano third Zero Problemo (by Priolo) and the French listed 10f winner Amathia (by Darshaan). The dam, a useful Irish winner of four races from 1m to 9.5f, was listed-placed 3 times and is a half-sister to

the French Group 3 Prix Gontaut Biron winner Muroto and the French listed winners Vanya, Vellano and Mahalia. The second dam, Maresca (by Mill Reef), is a placed half-sister to the Champion Stakes winner Pevero and the Prix Ganay winner Romildo.

1169. YANKEE DOODLE ★★★
gr.c. Dalakhani – Bella Lambada (Lammtarra)
February 4. Fourth foal. 1,000,000Y. Tattersalls October 1. Charlie Gordon-Watson. Half-brother to the dual 6f winner (including at two years) and listed-placed Fontana Amorosa (by Cadeaux Genereux), to the fair 12f all-weather winner Bariloche (by Benny The Dip) and the modest 12f winner Bella Miranda (by Sinndar). The dam, a quite useful 10.4f winner, is a half-sister to six winners including the high-class Group 2 10f Prince of Wales's Stakes and dual US Grade 2 winner Stagecraft, the Group 3 Strensall Stakes winner Mullins Bay and the listed winners Hyabella and Balalaika. The second dam, Bella Colora (by Bellypha), won four races including the Group 2 9.2f Prix de l'Opera and the Group 3 7f Waterford Candelabra Stakes and was third in the 1,000 Guineas. She is a half-sister to the Irish Oaks winner Colorspin (herself dam of the Group 1 winners Zee Zee Top, Opera House and Kayf Tara) and to the Irish Champion Stakes winner Cezanne.

1170. UNNAMED ★★★
b.c. Danehill Dancer – Pay The Bank (High Top)
May 5. Eleventh foal. €280,000Y. Goffs Million. Demi O'Byrne. Half-brother to the listed 6f and listed 7f winner and 1,000 Guineas fourth My Branch (herself dam of the Group 1 Haydock Park Sprint Cup winner Tante Rose), to the smart 10f winner and Chester Vase third Celestial Halo (by Galileo), the quite useful 7f all-weather and 1m winner Guaranteed, a winner in Hong Kong (all by Distant Relative), the fairly useful 12f winner Banco Suivi (by Nashwan) and the 2m and hurdles winner High Prospect (by Lycius). The dam, a quite useful two year old 1m winner, stayed 10f and is a half-sister to four winners. The second dam, Zebra Grass (by Run The

Gantlet), was a quite useful two year old 6f and 7f winner and a half-sister to two minor winners.

1171. UNNAMED ★★★★
b.c. Storm Cat – Quarter Moon (Sadler's Wells)
February 19. The dam, winner of the Group 1 7f Moyglare Stud Stakes and the Irish 1,000 Guineas, is a half-sister to the Irish 1,000 Guineas winner Yesterday. The second dam, Jude (by Darshaan), a moderate 10f placed maiden, is a sister to the very useful Irish listed 14f winner and Irish Oaks third Arrikala and to the useful Irish 12f listed winner Alouette (herself dam of the Champion Stakes winner Alborada) and a half-sister to the very smart Group 2 10f Nassau Stakes and Sun Chariot Stakes winner Last Second (dam of the French 2,000 Guineas winner Aussie Rules)

JAMIE OSBORNE
1172. BLOWN IT ★★★★ ♠
b.br.c. More Than Ready – Short Shadow (Out Of Place)
February 14. First foal. 25,000Y. Doncaster St Leger. D Redvers. The dam, a stakes-placed winner of one race in the USA, is a half-sister to three winners. The second dam, Last Reflection (by Nostrum), a stakes-placed winner of eight races in the USA, is a half-sister to ten winners. *'I love this horse and mark my words you'll be hearing a lot more about him. He was a steal for 25 grand and I wouldn't sell him for a 100 grand now because I think he's a very smart colt. He's just got natural pace but on pedigree he shouldn't just be a five furlong horse and I pray he's not. He'll win his maiden at five furlongs and at this moment in time he has 'top hat and tails' written all over him and I'd be bitterly disappointed if he doesn't get there. I think he'll be the best of my early season types. I had two colts that ran very well in the Coventry Stakes last year and at the same stage they wouldn't live with him.'* TRAINER'S BARGAIN BUY

1173. CHEAP THRILLS ★★★★
ch.f. Bertolini – Licence To Thrill (Wolfhound)
April 19. Fourth foal. 150,000Y. Tattersalls October 2. Ross Doyle. Half-sister to the useful

2007 two year old dual 5f winner Group Therapy (by Choisir), to the dual 5f winner (including at two years) and Group 3 5f Norfolk Stakes third Classic Encounter (by Lujain) and the modest 6f all-weather winner Gimme Some Lovin (by Desert Style). The dam, a quite useful dual 5f all-weather winner, is a half-sister to four winners including the useful two year old 5f winner Master Of Passion. The second dam, Crime Of Passion (by Dragonara Palace), winner of the Group 3 Cherry Hinton Stakes and third in the Group 1 Prix Robert Papin, is a half-sister to four winners including the Ayr Gold Cup winner Primula Boy.
'Yes, she's a nice filly. Her half-brother Group Therapy was fairly fast last year and if anything she's a better model than him. I think she's pretty nice, she's fast and I'm going to have her running in April. One of the better fillies, I'd say.'

1174. GRAND PLAN (USA) ★★★
b.f. Grand Slam – Easabeau Fille (Capote)
February 13. $30,000Y. Keeneland September. Sister to the US two year old sprint winners Cherokee Wild and Don't Exploit Me. The dam, placed at two years in France, subsequently won in the USA and is a half-sister to the high-class US two year old Minister Eric.
'She's not an oil painting, but she's fast. She might just run a bit green first time out but she's quick and might have won before your book comes out.'

1175. KEY REGARD ★★★
b.c. Key Of Luck – Disregard That (Don't Forget Me)
April 28. Tenth foal. €75,000Y. Goffs Million. D Redvers. Brother to the Group 3 6f Greenlands Stakes winner Miss Emma, to the Irish two year old 5f winner and listed-placed Miss Serendipity and the quite useful two year old 7f winners Redesignation and Luck Wud Have It and half-brother to the fairly useful 5f and 5.7f two year old winner Eleventh Duke (by Imperial Frontier) and the Irish two year old 1m winner and Norwegian 2,000 Guineas third Crosskeys Lass (by Petorius). The dam is an unraced half-sister to five winners including the two year old

Group 3 Killavullen Stakes winner Sedulous and the listed Tyros Stakes winner Tapolite (herself the dam of three listed winners). The second dam, Pendulina (by Prince Tenderfoot), an Irish listed 1m winner, is a half-sister to the Moyglare Stud Stakes winner Gala Event.
'He's a nice horse with a proper pedigree, his sister was very fast and this horse is likely to be out in the mid-summer. He's done some work and now we'll back off him a bit, but he'll be OK.'

1176. LITTLE LOST ★★★
b.f. Tagula – Prima Marta (Primo Dominie)
March 8. Fourth foal. €5,000Y. Tattersalls Ireland. Not sold. Half-sister to the unplaced 2007 two year old Joint Agency (by Captain Rio). The dam is an unraced half-sister to two minor winners including the dam of the Australian Grade 3 winner Dama De Noche. The second dam, Martha Stevens (by Super Concorde), won the Group 3 Nell Gwyn Stakes and was third in the Coronation Stakes.
'A nice, big, strong filly and she's from a fast family. I've done well with the sire and this filly has shown a bit of speed but she's got some scope and she'll be racing by the beginning of May. A nice filly.'

1177. MANERO ★★★★
br.c. Millkom – Discoed (Distinctly North)
February 12. First foal. 28,000Y. Doncaster St Leger. D Redvers. The dam is an unplaced half-sister to the Group 1 Dewhurst Stakes and subsequent US Grade 1 winner Milk It Mick. The second dam, Lucky Candy (by Lucky Wednesday), is an unplaced half-sister to five winners.
'It's unusual really that we've had one very good Millkom (Milk It Mick) and I didn't think lightning would strike twice. I'm not saying this horse will win the Dewhurst but he's way above average. He's a very nice colt with a beautiful action and he has enough speed to go five furlongs but I'm hoping he'll go seven. He'll want fast ground and will be out in either late April or May.'

1178. MEAN MR MUSTARD ★★★
b.c. Invincible Spirit – White Lavender
(Mt Livermore)
April 14. Fourth foal. 50,000 two year old.
Kempton Breeze-Up. D Redvers. The dam,
placed once over 1m at two years in Ireland, is
a half-sister to three winners. The second dam,
Norfolk Lavender (by Ascot Knight), a modest
1m all-weather winner here, subsequently won
a stakes event in the USA and was Grade 3
placed. She is a half-sister to five winners
including the US stakes winner Concordene out
of the 1,000 Guineas winner Nocturnal Spree.
'He looks very nice and he's a solid two year old
type that I'd like to have out by the end of April
or early May. He's typical of the sire in that he's
good, solid and straightforward and we should
get loads of runs out of him.'

1179. MINUTE LIMIT ★★★★
b.f. Pivotal – Magic Cove (Kingmambo)
January 19. Third foal. 90,000Y. Tattersalls
October 1. D Redvers. Half-sister to the fairly
useful Irish dual 11f winner Davidii (by Act One)
and to the fair 8.5f winner Magic Peak (by
Danehill). The dam, a listed 1m Solonaway
Stakes winner at the Curragh at three years, is
a half-sister to ten winners including the
Group 2 5f Temple Stakes winner Tipsy Creek
and the Group 3 7f Ballycorus Stakes winner
Abunawwas. The second dam, Copper Creek
(by Habitat), a fair three year old 6f winner, is a
sister to the US Grade 3 winner Placer Queen
and a half-sister to ten winners including the
Group 3 Mulcahy Stakes winner My Sister.
'A very nice filly and obviously she has a proper
pedigree. I could see her running this side of
Royal Ascot, she's strong and just a very nice filly
– more correct than most Pivotal's as well.
Although she was expensive I think she was
pretty well bought especially as she has residual
value as a broodmare.'

1180. MOUNT ACCLAIM ★★★★
b.f. Acclamation – Final Trick (Primo Dominie)
March 17. Fourth foal. 50,000Y. Doncaster
Festival Sales. D Redvers. Half-sister to the fairly
useful two year old 6f winner Imperial Sound

(by Efisio). The dam, unplaced in two starts at
two years, is a half-sister to four winners
including the quite useful two year old 6f
winner Composition. The second dam, Tricky
Note (by Song), a fairly useful winner of three
races including the listed National Stakes at
Sandown, is a sister to the Group 3 Duke Of
York Stakes winner Jester and a half-sister to six
winners.
'A nice filly, she's been very backward in her coat
and looks a bit like an Afghan Hound! But she's
got speed. From what she's shown me so far I
wouldn't put her in the top three fillies but she
wouldn't be far behind them.'

1181. MOUNT ELLA ★★★★
b.f. Royal Applause – Hiraeth (Petong)
April 14. Fourth foal. 23,000Y. Doncaster
Festival Sales. D Redvers. Half-sister to the fair
dual 5f winner (including at two years)
Cocabana (by Captain Rio). The dam, a fair 6f
winner, is a half-sister to numerous winners
including the dual Group 3 5f winner Ringmoor
Down. The second dam, Floppie (by Law
Society), a minor three year old winner in
France, is a sister to a listed-placed winner there
and a half-sister to four winners including the
French listed winner Love Shack.
'She has a fast pedigree and she's a fast filly. I
would see her being out by the beginning of May
and physically she's done very well. She's got
speed and wouldn't be far behind my top three
fillies.'

1182. PASSAGE TO INDIA ★★★
ch.f. Indian Ridge – Kathy College
(College Chapel)
January 17. Second foal. 40,000Y. Tattersalls
October 1. D Redvers. The dam won eight races
including the Group 3 5f Premio Omenoni and
is a half-sister to two winners. The second dam,
Katy Guest (by Be My Guest), won at two and
three years in Italy and is a half-sister to three
winners.
'A nice filly, she's probably more of a second half
of the season type but I've done a bit with her
and she's got a bit of speed. She has a nice
pedigree and she's a good, solid filly.'

1183. PRECOCIOUS AIR ★★
b.f. Redback – Wee Merkin (Thatching)
February 19. Third foal. 42,000Y. Tattersalls
October 3. D Redvers. The dam is an unraced
half-sister to five winners including the listed
winners Clapham Common and Tempting Fate.
The second dam, West Of Eden (by Crofter), is
an unraced half-sister to nine winners.
*'She's more of a mid-summer filly, a very good
mover and she'll be OK.'*

1184. ROYAL ADELAIDE ★★★★
ch.f. Redback – Ball Cat (Cricket Ball)
March 2. Seventh foal. 30,000Y. Tattersalls
October 2. D Redvers. Half-sister to the two
year old listed 5f winner Drawnfromthepast, to
a minor winner in Greece (both by Tagula) and
the minor 12f French winner Aldiruos (by
Bigstone). The dam won once in Belgium and is
a half-sister to seven winners including the Irish
Group 3 winner Leading Time. The second dam,
Copy Cat (by King Of Macedon), a listed-placed
winner in France, is a half-sister to nine winners.
*'She's a very nice filly. Her half-brother last year
showed us at this stage that he was going to be
quite decent and this filly has done pretty much
the same. Obviously he went on to win at Royal
Ascot and the hope would be that this filly would
also go there to compete. With what she's shown
us so far that wouldn't be an impossible task.'*

1185. SHE WANTS IT ★★★
*b.f. Royal Applause – Clincher Club
(Polish Patriot)*
February 25. Seventh foal. 90,000Y. Tattersalls
October 2. Anthony Stroud. Half-sister to the
smart two year old 6f winner and Group 1 1m
Racing Post Trophy third Henrik (by Primo
Dominie) and to the quite useful two year old 6f
winners Bishop's Lake (by Lake Coniston) and
Spritzeria (by Bigstone). The dam, a fair 5f (at
two years) and 7.5f winner, is a half-sister to
seven winners. The second dam, Merry Rous (by
Rousillon), won once at two years and is a half-
sister to five winners including the dual Group 3
winning sprinter Tina's Pet.
*'She's a nice filly, although maybe a little bit
further behind than where I'd like her to be, but*

*she'll be racing in May. She's a speedy filly with
a speedy pedigree and physically she just needs
to build up a little bit. She's got some speed.'*

1186. SPIRITUAL HEALING ★★★ ♠
b.f. Invincible Spirit – Tarbela (Grand Lodge)
February 2. First foal. 68,000Y. Doncaster St
Leger. D Redvers. The dam, a moderate 7f
placed two year old in Ireland, is a half-sister to
two winners. The second dam, Tarwiya (by
Dominion), won the Group 3 7f C L Weld Park
Stakes, was third in the Irish 1,000 Guineas and
is a half-sister to five winners including the
Norfolk Stakes winner Blue Dakota.
*'A nice, solid filly, she's tough and is all two year
old. She's not slow and I could run her in April.
She's just outside of the top bracket of my two
year old's on work at the moment but I wouldn't
be surprised if in a week's time I was saying she's
on a par with them. She's just improving, she
takes her work very well, the sire has been a
phenomenal stallion and this filly will do his
record no harm.'*

1187. SUB PRIME ★★
*br.c. Danetime – Primo Supremo
(Primo Dominie)*
April 2. First foal. €28,000Y. Tattersalls Ireland.
Not sold. The dam is an unplaced half-sister to
one winner. The second dam, Anita At Dawn (by
Anita's Prince), a modest 6f (at two years) and 7f
winner, is a half-sister to eight winners including
the US Grade 3 winner Down Again and to the
dam of the Irish and French 2,000 Guineas
winner Bachir.
*'He'll be our first two year old runner and he's
sharp although probably the weakest link of our
early season horses. He's got a bit of speed but I'd
be surprised if he won first time out. He'll win a
maiden within the first two months of the year.'*

1188. THE DIAL HOUSE ★★★
b.c. Tagula – Marliana (Mtoto)
February 6. Fourth foal. 27,000Y. Doncaster
Festival. D Redvers. Half-brother to the 2007
two year old 7f seller winner Marmite (by
Vettori) and to the fair dual 6f winner Zambach
(by Namid). The dam, a French two year old 6f

winner, is out of the listed Prix Imprudence winner Mahalia (by Danehill), herself a half-sister to eight winners.

'A very nice horse. He's a big, scopey colt with bags of speed and strength. He'd have enough boot to win over five furlongs but he might even stay seven.'

1189. TRIBAL SQUAW ★★★
b.f. Royal Applause – Wild Woman (Polar Falcon)
April 30. Fifth foal. 42,000Y. Tattersalls October 1. D Redvers. Half-sister to the Italian winner of six races from 2 to four years Wild Daughter (by Bachir) and to the German triple three year old winner and listed-placed Wild Advice (by Desert Prince). The dam, a dual winner in Germany at two years and listed-placed, is a sister to the two year old listed 6f winner Resplendent Cee and a half-sister to five winners. The second dam, Western Friend (by Gone West), ran once unplaced and is a sister to the US triple Grade 3 winner Gold Land.

'She's probably not going to be seen in the first half of the year but she's a big, scopey filly that just needs to fill out. She's from a fast family and she's got bags of pace. I'd say of my second half of the season naps, she would come into it.'

1190. UNNAMED ★★★
b.c. Stroll – Afleet Summer (Afleet)
March 23. Fourth foal. €90,000Y. Goffs Million. D Redvers. Half-brother to the US stakes winner Carolina Sky (by Sky Classic) and to a minor US winner by Jump Start. The dam is an unplaced half-sister to four winners including the French listed winner Limelighting. The second dam, Steal The Thunder (by Lyphard), a listed-placed winner in Canada, is a sister to the dual US Grade 3 winner Storm On The Loose.

'A strong, forward colt, he's done some work and is going to be OK. He'll be out in May I should think and he's a nice, straightforward, strong colt with a bit of speed.'

1191. UNNAMED ★★★
b.f. Marju – Bel Sole (Spectrum)
April 26. Second foal. €16,500Y. Tattersalls Ireland. D Redvers. Half-sister to the fair 2007 two year old 6.5f winner Rivoletto (by Bahri). The dam won at three years in Italy and is out of the minor French winner Noble Conquest (by Vaguely Noble), herself a half-sister to the Group 1 Prix de la Salamandre winner Noblequest.

'A nice filly, she was a May foal and she has a real two year old look to her. She's shown us plenty of speed and Marju is a good sire of fillies. I need to back off her now but I can see her coming out in May and being OK.'

1192. UNNAMED ★★★
b.f. Royal Applause – Jezyah (Chief's Crown)
March 30. €21,000Y. Tattersalls Ireland. D Redvers. Half-sister to the French 6f to 9f and subsequent US winner Royal Guard (by Hector Protector), the moderate 12f and hurdles winner Plemont Bay (by Robellino) and a hurdles winner by Mark Of Esteem. The dam, a quite useful two year old 7f winner, is a half-sister to several winners including the listed winner Tajannub and the dam of the Flying Childers winner Chateau Istana. The second dam, Empress Jackie (by Mount Hagen), a US stakes winner of eight races, is a half-sister to the Grade three winners Star Of Gdansk and W D Jacks.

'She doesn't really have a five furlong pedigree but she shows a bit of speed. She reminds of the sire's best filly, Ticker Tape, who was here as a two year old as she's a very similar stamp of a filly and very laid back. A nice, strong filly, I'll wait until the six furlong races start but she's certainly not devoid of ability.'

1193. UNNAMED ★★★
b.f. Elusive City – King Of All (King Of Clubs)
March 25. Fourth foal. €41,000Y. Tattersalls Ireland. D Redvers. Half-sister to the quite useful 2007 two year old 5f winner Regal Rhythm (by Namid) and to the useful two year old 6f winner and listed 7f third Haunting Memories (by Barathea). The dam won 7 minor races at 2 to five years in Italy and is a half-sister to five winners and to the dam of the US Grade 2 winner Distinct Habit. The second dam, Amiel

(by Nonoalco), won once at four years in Italy and is a sister to the Sussex Stakes winner Noalcoholic and a half-sister to seven winners. *'She goes well although I was a little bit worried about her temperament initially. Her father as a bit quirky and she looked like she was the same but the more work I've done with her the better she's been. Not amongst the best of the fillies but she has ability and it wouldn't surprise me to see her doing well.'*

1194. UNNAMED ★★
ch.f. Captain Rio – Metisse (Indian Ridge)
January 2. First foal. €55,000Y. Goffs Million. D Redvers. The dam, a fair 5f and 6f placed maiden in Ireland, is a sister to the listed 5f Rockingham Handicap winner and Group 3 Flying Five second Timote and a half-sister to five winners. The second dam, Across The Ice (by General Holme), a listed-placed French three year old winner, is a half-sister to ten winners including Northern Premier (Group 3 1m Prix de la Grotte and Group 3 7f Prix de la Porte Maillot). *'A pretty nice filly. The sire had plenty of winners in his first crop, this filly is out of an Indian Ridge mare and there's a lot of Indian Ridge about her. I could see her running in May, she's doing plenty of work at the moment and doing it easily.'*

1195. UNNAMED ★★★
b.f. Elnadim – Vahine (Alysheba)
May 8. Ninth foal. €40,000Y. Goffs Million. D Redvers. Half-sister to the Group 2 1m 7f Prix Chaudenay winner Vendangeur (by Galileo), to the modest Irish 12f winner Posh Lady (by Peintre Celebre) and to 2 minor French winners by Sadler's Wells and Lure. The dam is an unraced half-sister to the Mill Reef Stakes and Richmond Stakes winner Vacarme and to the Prix Jacques le Marois winner Vin de France. The second dam, Virunga (by Sodium) won the Group 3 12f Prix de Malleret and is a half-sister to the Champion Stakes winner Vitiges. *'A lovely filly but she's just going to take a bit of time. Her pedigree is an odd mixture because it's all stamina on the dam's side and all speed on top. She's a May foal and a second half of the season filly but a nice one.'*

1196. UNNAMED ★★★★
ch.f. Danehill Dancer – Wadud (Nashwan)
January 29. Second foal. €70,000Y. Goffs Million. Stephen Hillen. Sister to Ice Queen, unplaced in two starts at two years in Ireland in 2007. The dam, placed fourth once over 12f, is a sister to three winners including the very smart 7f (at two years) and Group 3 12f Gordon Stakes winner Rabah and the useful two year old 6f winner and Group 1 Cheveley Park Stakes third Najiya and a half-sister to two winners. The second dam, The Perfect Life (by Try My Best), won the Group 3 5f Prix du Bois, was second in the Group 2 Prix Robert Papin and is a sister to the top-class colt Last Tycoon (winner of the Breeders Cup Mile, the Kings Stand Stakes and the William Hill Sprint Championship) and a half-sister to nine winners. *'She's not beautiful but she can go like the proverbial! She's a little bit light framed but seems to have a tremendous engine and she could be up to Royal Ascot. Very nice.'*

JOHN OXX
1197. ADJALIYA (IRE) ★★★
b.f. Sinndar – Adalya (Darshaan)
April 14. Closely related to the Irish two year old 1m winner Adalar and to the quite useful Irish two year old 1m winner Adalar (both by Grand Lodge) and half-sister to the useful Irish 7f and 1m winner Adajal (by Zilzal), the quite useful 7.5f winner Adawar (by Perugino), the fair Irish 8.5f winner Adarila (by Mujadil) and the minor 12f and 2m winner Adalpour (by Kahyasi). The dam is an unplaced sister to the high-class Group 3 12f Lingfield Oaks Trial winner and disqualified Epsom Oaks winner Aliysa and a half-sister to the minor French 9f winner Aleema (herself dam of the high-class middle-distance colt Altayan). The second dam, Alannya (by Relko), a smart 1m winner in France, is a half-sister to the dam of the French 2,000 Guineas winner Nishapour and the Rothmans International winner Nassipour. (H H Aga Khan). *'She's a nice filly and even though she's bred to need a bit of time she's precocious enough. She's cantering away and she's done a bit of work, so I hope she'll be ready to run when the early*

season races start in the early summer. The dam breeds winners, although they lack a bit of class I suppose and I think there's every chance this filly will win as a two year old.'

1198. ALAIYMA (IRE) ★★★
b.f. Refuse To Bend – Alasana (Darshaan)
March 23. Closely related to the useful 7f (at two years) and listed 1m winner Alasha (by Barathea) and half-sister to the 10f winner Alamouna (by Indian Ridge), the 1m and 10f winner Almiyan (by King's Best) and the 7f and 1m winner Alafzar (by Green Desert) – all 3 quite useful. The dam won twice in France over 1m and 9f and is a half-sister to the Prix Maurice de Nieuil winner Altayan and the Grand Prix de Vichy winner Altashar. The second dam, Aleema (by Red God), won over 9f in France and is a half-sister to the disqualified Oaks winner Aliysa. (HH Aga Khan).
'She's a particularly good-looking filly and a very fluent mover. Well put together, she's showing promise and has done a few bits of fast work. She isn't bred to be precocious but she should make a two year old by mid-summer.'

1199. ARAZAN (IRE) ★★★★★
b.c. Anabaa – Asmara (Lear Fan)
January 29. Half-brother to the Group 1 St James's Palace Stakes and Group 1 Irish Champion Stakes winner Azamour (by Night Shift), to the fairly useful Irish 7f winner Ardistan (by Selkirk), the Irish two year old 7f winners Ahsanabad and Surveyor (both by Muhtarram), the three year old 7f winner Arawan (by Entrepreneur), the Irish two year old dual 7f winner Arameen (by Halling) and the fair Irish 14f and hurdles winner Ardalan (by Sinndar). The dam, a useful winner in Ireland at up to 10f, is a half-sister to the high-class Prix Ganay and Prix d'Harcourt winner Astarabad. The second dam, Anaza (by Darshaan), only ran at two years when she was a useful 1m winner in France. (H H Aga Khan).
'He's a particularly nice colt, very mature, well-forward and he's a possible runner in late May. The dam bred Azamour along with a number of other colts that didn't do a lot. I'm hopeful that

this fellow will be better than the disappointing ones. At the moment he looks that way.'

1200. BIG GAME HUNTER (IRE) ★★
b.c. Sadler's Wells – Hill Of Snow
(Reference Point)
April 24. Brother to the Group 3 Lingfield Derby Trial winner Kong and to the useful listed 14f winner Kilimanjaro and half-brother to the smart two year old Group 1 7f Moyglare Stud Stakes winner Preseli, the fair 10f winner Valley Of Song (both by Caerleon) and the smart 7f winner and 1,000 Guineas second Snowfire (by Machiavellian). The dam, an Irish 10f winner, is a half-sister to the smart Group 2 Prix de Pomone winner Whitehaven. The second dam, White Star Line (by Northern Dancer), won 3 Grade 1 events in the USA and is a half-sister to the Prix Morny winner Filiberto and to the dam of the Group/Grade 1 winners Northern Trick and On The Sly. (Mr N L Jones).
'A lovely, big horse and a great mover, hopefully he'll have a couple of runs at the back-end and he's obviously more of a three year old type. But he's very athletic, he's had a good winter but both his size and his pedigree tells you he's not going racing for some time.'

1201. PALLAS ATHENA (IRE) ★★★★
b.f. Sadler's Wells – Ibtikar (Private Account)
March 22. Twelfth foal. $285,000Y. Keeneland September. BBA (Ire). Half-sister to six winners including the US stakes-placed Vegas Venture (by Gold Fever) and the South African stakes-placed Brown Linnet (by King Of Kings). The dam, a poor 6f (at two years) and 2m placed maiden, is closely related to the Grade 1 Hollywood Gold Cup, Charles H. Strub Stakes and Californian Stakes winner Desert Wine and a half-sister to five winners including the dual Grade 1 winner Menifee. The second dam, Anne Campbell (by Never Bend), won three races in the USA including a minor stakes event. (P McCarthy).
'A very good-looking filly, she's well grown and well put-together. I don't think she'll be too backward and she's a particularly nice filly. She's had a good winter and I like her.'

1202. PITTONI (IRE) ★★★

b.c. Peintre Celebre – Key Change (Darshaan)
March 3. Half-brother to the quite useful 12f winner Carenage (by Alzao), the quite useful Irish 1m winner and listed-placed Sandtime and the Irish 10f winner and listed-placed Calorando (both by Green Desert). The dam, a winner of four races including the Group 1 12f Yorkshire Oaks, is a full or half-sister to numerous minor winners. The second dam, Kashka (by The Minstrel), a winner over 12f at three years in France, is a half-sister to the Italian Group 3 winner Karkisiya and to the dams of the Derby winner Kahyasi and the Group three winners Kaliana and Kalajana and Kithanga. (Lady Clague).
'A very big colt, but he's particularly nice. He's rangy and a great mover and is one for later in the season.'

1203. QUIET LANE ★★★

ch.f. Cadeaux Genereux – Blue Sirocco (Bluebird)
February 23. Sixth foal. €85,000Y. Goffs Million. Not sold. Half-sister to the fairly useful 5f and 6f winner of five races Bluebok (by Indian Ridge), to the useful two year old 6f winner and listed-placed Johannes (by Mozart), the fair 11f winner Zamboozle (by Halling) and the modest 1m and 10f winner Blue Mistral (by Spinning World). The dam ran once unplaced and is a half-sister to eight winners including the listed 7f winner and Group 1 7f Moyglare Stud Stakes second Tamnia, the Group 2 13.3f Geoffrey Freer Stakes winner Azzilfi and the Group 3 15f Coppa d'Oro di Milano winner Khamaseen. The second dam, Tanouma (by Miswaki), a very useful 6f (at two years) and 7f winner, was third in the Group 3 7.3f Fred Darling Stakes and is a half-sister to seven winners. (H Spooner).
'She's a sharp looking filly and a good, strong, two year old type. She's starting fast work now so we'll see how she goes but she's certainly built for a two year old career. She should be out by early June, she's bred to be a two year old and looks it as well, so we'll just have to see if there's an engine there.'

1204. SAMOVAR ★★★

br.c. Dansili – Sahara Slew (Seattle Slew)
May 22. The dam won two races at three years including the Group 2 12f Ribblesdale Stakes and is a half-sister to two winners. The second dam, Sahara Sun (by Alysheba), won over 11f and was listed-placed in France and is a half-sister to the Great Voltigeur Stakes winner Zalazl. (Lady O'Reilly).
'A very nice horse and a fluent mover with a good temperament, but he's a late foal and he's at home having a break because he had a setback. I like him though and he'll be out later in the season and you should give him a mention.'

1205. SEA THE STARS (IRE) ★★★★★

b.c. Cape Cross – Urban Sea (Miswaki)
April 6. Closely related to the 2007 two year old Sea's Legacy (by Green Desert) and half-brother to the Derby, Irish Derby and King George VI and Queen Elizabeth Diamond Stakes winner Galileo, the Group 1 12f Gran Premio del Jockey Club and Group 1 10.5f Tattersalls Gold Cup winner Black Sam Bellamy, the Group 3 10.5f Middleton Stakes winner All Too Beautiful (all by Sadler's Wells), the US dual Grade 2 8.5f winner My Typhoon (by Giant's Causeway), the smart listed 10f Pretty Polly Stakes winner and Oaks third Melikah (by Lammtarra) and the smart 1m (at two years) and Group 2 10f Gallinule Stakes winner Urban Ocean (by Bering). The dam, a top-class winner of eight races from 1m (at two years) to 12f including the Group 1 Prix de l'Arc de Triomphe and the Group 2 Prix d'Harcourt, is closely related to the 2,000 Guineas winner King's Best and a half-sister to numerous winners. The second dam, Allegretta (by Lombard), a useful two year old 1m and 9f winner and second in the Lingfield Oaks Trial, is a sister to the German St Leger winner Anno. (C Tsui).
'A very nice horse, really good-looking and a very fluent mover. Despite the fact he's quite well grown he looks as if he'll show something as a two year old because he's not backward at all. Seven furlongs in early July should suit him to start with. You'd have to like him, he's a real good sort.'

1206. SECRETARIAT'S SOUL (IRE) ★★
b.f. Sadler's Wells – Ball Chairman (Secretariat)
March 22. Sister to the US Grade 1 Shadwell Mile and dual Grade 2 winner Perfect Soul and closely related to the US stakes-placed winner Dimontina (by Dixieland Band). The dam is a placed half-sister to several winners. The second dam, A Status Symbol (by Exclusive Native), was a stakes winner of seven races. (C Fipke).
'A backward filly that just needs to grow a bit and she's one for later in the year.'

1207. TAKASIMA (IRE) ★★★
b.f. Daylami – Takariya (Arazi)
January 19. Half-sister to the quite useful Irish 7.5f winner Takestan (by Selkirk). The dam, an Irish two year old 6f winner, is a half-sister to the smart 2000 Irish 10f and 12f winner Takali and to the Group 3 12f Meld Stakes winner Takarian, subsequently winner of the Bay Meadows Derby in the USA. The second dam, Takarouna (by Green Dancer), a very useful winner of the Group 2 12f Pretty Polly Stakes at the Curragh, is a sister to the smart Group 2 Dante Stakes winner Torjoun and a half-sister to the quite useful 2m Northumberland Plate winner Tamarpour (by Sir Ivor). (H H Aga Khan).
'She's quite nice, a good mover and she's started some fast work and goes OK. We'll be able to get her out before June perhaps because she's precocious enough and well-developed.'

1208. TANOURA (IRE) ★★★★
b.f. Dalakhani – Takarouna (Green Dancer)
March 27. Half-sister to the Group 3 12f Meld Stakes winner Takarian (by Doyoun), subsequently winner of the Bay Meadows Derby in the USA, to the smart Irish 10f and 12f winner Takali (by Kris), the Irish two year old 6f winner Takariya (by Arazi) and the fair French 10.5f winner Takaniya (by Rainbow Quest). The dam, a very useful winner of the Group 2 12f Pretty Polly Stakes at the Curragh, is a sister to the smart Group 2 Dante Stakes winner Torjoun and a half-sister to the quite useful 2m Northumberland Plate winner Tamarpour (by Sir Ivor). The second dam, Tarsila (by High Top), won over 1m and 9f and is a sister to Top Ville. (H H Aga Khan).

'A very nice filly, very well put together and sharp-looking. She's seems a quick learner and she goes well so I expect her to show us plenty as a two year old. The dam was quite speedy, so even though she's by Dalakhani I wouldn't be surprised if this filly had the speed for six furlongs.'

1209. THEATRIKOS (IRE) ★★★
b.f. Theatrical – Amanda Louise (Perugino)
February 26. Second foal. €50,000Y. Goffs Million. Frances Cleary. The dam, a 5f all-weather seller winner, subsequently won and was stakes-placed in the USA and is a half-sister to five winners. The second dam, Duly Elected (by Persian Bold), was fourth twice over 1m and 9f in Ireland, is a sister to the Group 1 Heinz 57 Phoenix Stakes winner King Persian and a half-sister to the dam of two listed winners. (H O'Neill).
'She's a nice filly, might need a bit of time but she's had a good winter and she's quite forward at the moment. I wouldn't be running her until July but she's a good moving filly, very athletic and a good-looker, so she could well be alright.'

1210. WHATAGOODCATCH (IRE) ★★
b.f. Bachelor Duke – Truly Generous (Generous)
April 3. Ninth foal. 82,000Y. Tattersalls October 2. BBA (Ire). Half-sister to the French listed 1m winner and Group 3 Prix de Psyche third Antique (by Dubai Millennium) and to 2 minor three year old winners in France by Darshaan and Fantastic Light. The dam won the listed Prix Petite Etoile, is closely related to the very smart Truly Special (winner of the Group 3 10.5f Prix de Royaumont and herself dam of the E.P. Taylor Stakes winner Truly A Dream) and a half-sister to seven winners including the Group 2 13.5f Grand Prix de Deauville winner Modhish and the Group 2 12.5f Prix de Royallieu winner Russian Snows. The second dam, Arctique Royale (by Royal and Regal), won the Irish 1,000 Guineas and the Moyglare Stud Stakes and is a half-sister to the dam of Ardross. (Byerley Racing).
'She was nice as a yearling but she didn't grow in the winter and the others left her behind. Now she's beginning to sprout a bit so she just needs a bit of time to develop. We'll take our time with her.'

1211. UNNAMED ★★★

b.c. Alhaarth – Alasha (Barathea)

March 7. The dam, a useful 7f (at two years) and listed 1m winner, is a half-sister to several winners. The second dam, Alasana (by Darshaan), won twice in France over 1m and 9f and is a half-sister to the Prix Maurice de Nieuil winner Altayan and the Grand Prix de Vichy winner Altashar. (HH Aga Khan).

'A good-looking horse, the dam was smart and this is a well put-together colt that looks reasonably precocious. He hasn't done any fast work yet but he's not far off it. A nice colt and hopefully he'll be out in mid-summer.'

1212. UNNAMED ★★★★

b.f. Dalakhani – Balanka (Alzao)

January 22. Eighth foal. Closely related to the French 11f winner Balankiya (by Darshaan) and half-sister to the very smart Group 2 10f King Edward VII Stakes winner Balakheri (by Theatrical) and the fair 12f winner Belanak (by Sinndar) and Balakan (by Selkirk). The dam, a French listed winner and second in the Group 2 9.2f Prix de l'Opera, is a half-sister to several winners. The second dam, Banana Peel (by Green Dancer), won two races in the USA at four years and is a half-sister to ten winners including the Group 3 Grand Prix de Vichy winner Bulington and the French listed winners Catman and Beaune (herself the dam of Bering). (H H Aga Khan).

'She's quite nice, she's goes well and is bred to need a bit of time and distance but she shows promise and is an athletic filly. We like her and she's a January foal so she should be running in mid-summer.'

1213. UNNAMED ★★★★

b.f. Oasis Dream – Catch The Blues (Bluebird)

May 5. Half-sister to the fairly useful two year old 7f winner Blue Mirage (by King's Best) and to the quite useful all-weather 7f winner Beacon Wood (by Woodman). The dam, a smart 5f to 7f winner of three races including the Group 3 5f Ballyogan Stakes, was third in the Group 1 Haydock Park Sprint Cup and is a half-sister to six winners. The second dam, Dear Lorraine (by Nonoalco), won over 10f in France and is a half-sister to four winners. (Mrs H Keaveney).

'A good-looking filly, she's well-made and is just as you'd expect from the pedigree – nice and sharp. Being a May foal she does need a bit of time and she's growing a bit now. A very nice filly, she's one for the second half of the season and she'll be a sprinter.'

1214. UNNAMED ★★★★

b.c. King's Best – Ebadiyla (Sadler's Wells)

April 9. Half-brother to the useful 1m winner and Group 1 National Stakes third Eyshal (by Green Desert), to the useful Irish 10f winner Ehsan (by Sinndar) and the dual 12f and very smart hurdles winner Ebaziyan (by Daylami). The dam won the Group 1 Irish Oaks and the Group 1 Prix Royal-Oak and is a half-sister to the smart Group 1 7f Moyglare Stud Stakes winner Edabiya and the high-class Ascot Gold Cup winner Enzeli. The second dam, Ebaziya (by Darshaan), won from 7f (at two years) to 12f including three listed races and was third in the Group 2 12f Blandford Stakes. (H H Aga Khan).

'A very nice horse and quite precocious-looking even though he's by an Oaks winner that didn't run at two. He does look a sharp, particularly good-looking horse, very athletic and a quick learner. so he could be racing in early June. The dam also won the French St Leger over a mile and seven, so this colt would need seven furlongs to begin with.'

1215. UNNAMED ★★★★

ch.f. Dubai Destination – Ebaziya (Darshaan)

April 19. Half-sister to the Group 1 7f Moyglare Stud Stakes winner Edabiya, to the two year old 7f winner and 12f listed-placed Elasouna (by Rainbow Quest), to the Irish Oaks and Prix Royal-Oak winner Ebadiyla, the minor Irish 12f winner Ebariya (both by Sadler's Wells) and the Ascot Gold Cup winner Enzeli (by Kahyasi). The dam won from 7f (at two years) to 12f including three listed races and was third in the Group 2 12f Blandford Stakes. The second dam, Ezana (by Ela-Mana-Mou), won over an extended 11f in France and is a half-sister to the French dual Group 3 winner Demia. (H H Aga Khan).

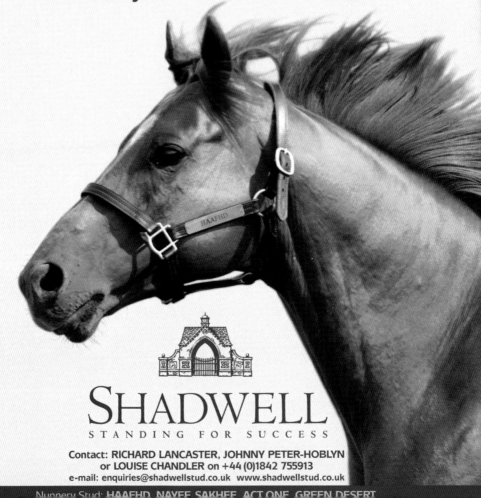

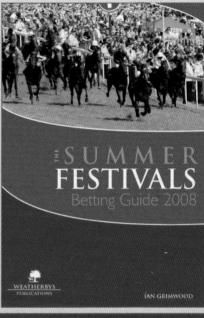

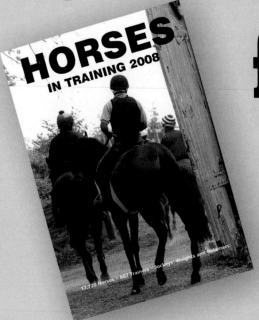

'A particularly good-looking filly, big but well put-together. I'd hope she'd make a two year old a bit later on, in the second half of the year. She's a very nice filly and a half-sister to three Group 1 winners, so she's a good sort. I like her, she's done a couple of bits of work already and she looks nice.'

1216. UNNAMED ★★★

b.f. Montjeu – Ingozi (Warning)

April 19. Eleventh foal. 60,000Y. Tattersalls October 1. Not sold. Half-sister to the useful 2007 two year old 7f winner and Group 2 1m May Hill Stakes second Kotsi (by Nayef), to the useful Tattersalls Houghton Sales Stakes winner and German Group 1 fourth Sir George Turner (both by Nashwan), the 7f (at two years) and Thirsk Classic Trial winner Tissifer, the quite useful two year old 5f and 6f winner Abunai (by Pivotal), the minor French two year old 9f winner Icknield (both by Polish Precedent), the fair 9f winner Oshiponga (by Barathea) and a winner in Hong Kong by Cadeaux Genereux. The dam, a fairly useful winner over 7f and 1m at three years including a listed event at Sandown Park, is a half-sister to numerous winners including the very smart and tough triple Group 3 7f winner Inchinor. The second dam, Inchmurrin (by Lomond), a very useful winner of six races from 5f to 1m including the Group 2 Child Stakes, is a half-sister to seven winners including the Mill Reef Stakes winner Welney. (Mrs C McStay).

'She's a good-moving filly, very fluent, not very big and she goes well. Like a lot of Montjeu fillies she isn't without a bit of temperament but I quite like her and I can see her out in July.'

1217. UNNAMED ★★★★

b.c. Dalakhani – Josh's Pearl (Sadler's Wells)

March 31. Third foal. Half-brother to the quite useful Irish two year old 7f winner Lifetime Romance (by Mozart) and to the quite useful Irish 1m winner Joshua's Princess (by Danehill). The dam, a minor Irish 13f winner, is a half-sister to two winners. The second dam, the top-class Ridgewood Pearl (by Indian Ridge), won the Coronation Stakes, the Irish 1,000 Guineas, the Prix du Moulin and the Breeders Cup Mile (all Group/Grade 1 events over 1m) and is a sister to the Group 3 7f Gladness Stakes winner and Irish 2,000 Guineas third Ridgewood Ben. (Mrs A M Coughlan).

'A particularly nice colt, he goes well and looks promising. He's one for July onwards and he's a nice colt you'd expect would need seven furlongs.'

1218. UNNAMED ★★★

b.c. Alhaarth – Mouramara (Kahyasi)

March 22. Half-brother to the useful 9f to 12f winner Mourilyan (by Desert Prince). The dam, winner of the Group 2 12.5f Prix de Royallieu, is a half-sister to several winners in France and Germany. The second dam, Mamoura (by Lomond), won over 10f and 12f in Ireland and is a half-sister to five winners including the Group 3 12f Meld Stakes third Mirana (herself dam of the Group 3 Prix de Flore winner Miliana). (H H Aga Khan).

'A good-looking horse out of a good racemare, he's very nice, big and rangy. He goes well and will hopefully be out in late June or July.'

1219. UNNAMED ★★★

b.f. Danetime – Rose Vibert (Caerleon)

March 2. Seventh foal. 31,000Y. Doncaster St Leger. Peter Doyle. Half-sister to the quite useful 10f and 11f winner of six races Sky Quest, the fair 12f to 17f and hurdles winner Serbelloni (both by Spectrum) and the modest 11f and 12f winner Aimee Vibert (by Zilzal). The dam is an unraced full or half-sister to six winners. The second dam, Premier Rose (by Sharp Edge), won four races including the listed Strensall Stakes and is a sister to the Group 3 Fred Darling Stakes winner Shapina. (Byerley Racing Ltd).

'A nice, sharp-looking filly, she threw a splint in February which held us up but she goes well and has a good temperament. You'd expect to see something fairly early from a Danetime, so I'm looking forward to getting her into some fast work shortly. Hopefully she'll be able to make up for the month she lost in February.'

1220. UNNAMED ★★★★

b.br.f. Speightstown – Sapphire n'Silk (Pleasant Tap)

April 23. Sixth foal. $360,000Y. Keeneland September. BBA (Ire). Half-sister to the US Grade 2 Kentucky Cup Classic Stakes winner Shaniko (by A P Indy) and to the minor US stakes winner Silky Smooth (by Mr Greeley). The dam won the Grade 2 Prioress Stakes and the Grade 3 La Troienne Stakes and is a out of the minor US two year old winner Golden Tiy (by Dixieland Band), herself a half-sister to nine winners including the US Grade 2 winner Pok Ta Pok. (T Jones).

'A nice filly that came from Keeneland, she's started to grow a bit now so I can't push her at the minute but she is a smart looking filly and a good mover with a good temperament. I like her and she looks racey.'

1221. UNNAMED ★★★★

ch.c. Selkirk – Tarakala (Dr Fong)

January 25. First foal. The dam, a useful listed 11.9f Galtres Stakes winner, is a half-sister to several winners. The second dam, Tarakana (by Shahrastani), won 9f in Ireland at three years, was placed in four listed events from 7f to 12f and is a half-sister to six winners. (H H Aga Khan).

'A very nice colt, he's big but quite a powerful horse. A good galloper, I'd be disappointed if he doesn't have ability and he's done everything right so far. Even though he's big he isn't backward and I'd hope to get him out in July. He's an early foal and he looks it because he's well-developed.'

1222. UNNAMED ★★★

gr.f. Linamix – Timarida (Kalaglow)

May 1. Half-sister to the Irish Group 3 9.5f winner Timarwa (by Daylami) and to the Irish four year old 1m and 12f winner Timawari (by Sadler's Wells). The dam, a high-class 10f filly, won the Group 1 Irish Champion Stakes, the Group 1 Dallymayr-Preis and the Grade 1 Beverly D Stakes and is a half-sister to numerous winners and to the dam of the listed winners Miss Sacha and Pinta. The second dam, Triumphant (by Track Spare), a fairly useful 7.6f

winner, is a half-sister to the Group 1 Benson and Hedges Gold Cup winner Relkino. (H H Aga Khan).

'She's at home at the moment having had a bit of a setback, but she's a very nice filly and very athletic. She'll run this year alright and I'd say she's a quick learner. I like her but I haven't seen her for a while.'

1223. UNNAMED ★★

ch.f. Danehill Dancer – Zarannda (Last Tycoon)

February 16. Half-sister to numerous winners including the useful Irish 1m winner and dual Group 3 placed Zarad (by Selkirk) and the fair dual 7f winner Zarabad (by King's Best). The dam, a dual French listed winner over 7f and 1m, is a half-sister to the dam of the Group 3 Prix de Sandringham winner Zarkiya. The second dam, Zarna (by Shernazar), won once at three years and is a half-sister to four winners including the dam of the French Oaks and Prix Saint-Alary winner Zainta. (H H Aga Khan).

'She had a little setback and had to go home but previously she looked like a precocious type and I liked her. She's been away for a few months now and is one for later in the year, but you should give her a mention because she's nice and if she comes back and stays sound you could hear from her alright.'

AMANDA PERRETT

1224. ADMIRAL SANDHOE (USA) ★★★

ch.c. Diesis – Dancing Sea (Storm Cat)

April 24. Fifth foal. $65,000Y. Keeneland September. James Delahooke. Half-brother to a winner in Germany by Daylami. The dam is a placed sister to the Irish 2,000 Guineas winner Black Minnaloushe and a half-sister to the 2,000 Guineas winner Pennekamp and the US multiple Grade 1 winner Nasr El Arab. The second dam, Coral Dance (by Green Dancer), was a very useful winner at up to 1m in France and the USA and was second in the Group 1 Prix Marcel Boussac. (D M Slade).

'A nice, forward-going type of horse, I think he'll be running over six furlongs before step him up to seven. A horse with a good pedigree and he's not going to take a long time to come to hand.'

1225. BLUE DYNASTY (USA) ★★

*b.br.c. Dynaformer – Saudia
(Gone West)*

January 29. Third foal. $170,000Y. Keeneland September. James Delahooke. Half-brother to the US stakes-placed winner The West's Awake (by Theatrical). The dam is an unraced half-sister to the listed winner and Italian Group 3 winner Revere. The second dam, Bint Pasha (by Affirmed), won the Prix Vermeille, the Yorkshire Oaks and the Group 2 Pretty Polly Stakes. (The Green Dot Partnership).

'Quite a big, strapping sort of horse and although he was an early foal I don't think we're going to see him much before the seven furlong races. He'll probably be a ten furlong horse next year.'

1226. CHASCA (IRE) ★★★

b.f. Namid – Daganya (Danehill Dancer)

March 23. The dam won two races including a listed 6f event in Ireland and was second in the Group 2 5f Flying Five. She is a sister to the listed 5f winner Snaefell and a half-sister to three winners including the quite useful 5f winner of 10 races Henry Hall. The second dam, Sovereign Grace (by Standaan), won over 5f in Ireland and is a half-sister several winners. (Lady Clague).

'A sharp filly, she's not over-big (about 15 hands) and her dam was a listed winner at Leopardstown. It would be nice if she was a Queen Mary filly!'

1227. CLASSIC VINTAGE (USA) ★★

b.c. El Prado – Cellars Shiraz (Kissin Kris)

March 20. First foal. $350,000Y. Keeneland September. J Delahooke. The dam, a winner of 10 races in the USA including a Grade 3 event, is a half-sister to four winners. The second dam, Cellar's Best (by Band Practice), was a stakes winner of 10 races. (R & P Scott and A & J Powell Gallagher Stud).

'A colt with a lovely pedigree, he'll need some time. Seven or eight furlongs at the end of the year should suit and he has a bit of class about him but he'll be on the back burner for a little while yet.'

1228. COILED SPRING ★★★★

b.c. Observatory – Balmy (Zafonic)

February 28. The dam, a fairly useful 1m winner, is a sister to winner in Greece and a half-sister to the very useful French 6f (at two years) and 1m listed winner Barricade and the useful 14f winner War Cabinet. The second dam, Balleta (by Lyphard), a quite useful three year old 10f winner, also won three races in the USA, is a sister to the great 'Arc', 'King George' and 2,000 Guineas winner Dancing Brave and to Jolypha (winner of the Group 1 12f Prix Vermeille and Group 1 10.5f Prix de Diane). (Khalid Abdulla).

'A lovely, well-balanced horse and the second dam is a sister to Dancing Brave. There's a lot to like about him, we'll start him off at seven furlongs and he's one to note.'

1229. COUNT OF TUSCANY (USA) ★★★

b.c. Arch – Corsini (Machiavellian)

March 19. Half-brother to the useful 10f winner Corsican Native and to the quite useful two year old 7f winner Corcoran (both by Lear Fan). The dam, a quite useful two year old 7f winner, is a half-sister to the French listed 6f two year old winner Danzari. The second dam, Dangora (by Sovereign Dancer), a very useful two year old, won twice over 6f and was second in the Group 2 Lowther Stakes. She is closely related to the smart filly Zaizafon (the dam of Zafonic) and a half-sister to the unraced Modena (the dam of Elmaamul). (Khalid Abdulla).

'He hasn't arrived here yet but I'm told he's very nice. He's from a good family and we've trained two nice horses out of the dam. I'm very much looking forward to getting this strong horse who stands about 16 hands. Being a March foal by Arch he might be a touch quicker than Corsican Native and Corcoran.'

1230. CRY FOR THE MOON (USA) ★★

b.br.c. Street Cry – Kafaf (Zilzal)

May 1. Sixth foal. $190,000Y. Keeneland September. James Delahooke. Half-brother to four winners in the USA including the Grade 2 and Grade 3 placed Littlebitofzip (by Littlebitlively). The dam, a quite useful 7f winner, is a half-sister to the US dual Grade 2 winner

Intidab. The second dam, Alqwani (by Mr Prospector), won over 6f at two years. (Mr A Christodoulou & Mr J H Richmond-Watson).
'A nice colt and a May foal that will need a bit of time, he's very much a three year old type but there's a lot to like about him.'

1231. DIMANDER (IRE) ★★★
b.c. Namid – Red Liason (Selkirk)
January 21. Second foal. Half-brother to the 2007 Irish 7f and 1m placed two year old Thoroughly Red (by King's Best). The dam, a useful dual 6f (at two years) and listed 7f winner, is a half-sister to two winners including the fairly useful Irish 1m (at two years) and 7f winner Redstone Dancer. The second dam, Red Affair (by Generous), an Irish listed 10f winner, is a half-sister to the smart 7.6f to 10f winner Brilliant Red and to the useful 12f to 14f winner and Group 3 2m Queens Vase third Kassab (by Caerleon). (Lady Clague).
'A big, strong colt, he's built like a sprinter and he's a January foal but I don't think we'll see him out until the middle of the season due to his size. He's done nothing wrong and the dam was a listed winner.'

1232. DIMENSIONAL ★★★
b.f. Dansili – Nashmeel (Blushing Groom)
February 2. Sister to the quite useful 6f all-weather winner Chervil, closely related to the US Grade 1 0f Yellow Ribbon Stakes winner Light Jig (by Danehill) and half-sister to the very useful French two year old listed 1m winner Battle Dore (by Sanglamore), to the useful French 7.5f and 1m winner Light Music (by Nijinsky) and the fairly useful 10f winner Light Programme (by El Gran Senor), the French two year old 1m winner Shrewdness (by Selkirk) and the minor French middle-distance winner of three races Garonne (by Zafonic). The dam was a very smart winner of three races over 1m including the Group 2 Prix d'Astarte and was second in the Prix Jacques le Marois (to Miesque), the Yellow Ribbon Invitational and the Matriarch Stakes. The second dam, Donut's Bunnie (by Donut King), won four races in the USA and was stakes-placed at up to 1m. (Khalid Abdulla).

'She's not over-big and in that respect she has more of the sire in her than the dam. A full sister to Chervil who won for me as a two year old over six furlongs, I would think this filly will be a six/seven furlong two year old.'

1233. DUBAI CREST ★★★
b.c. Dubai Destination – On The Brink (Mind Games)
March 17. Second foal. 120,000Y. Tattersalls October 1. A Perrett. Half-brother to the quite useful 2007 Irish 5f to 7f placed two year old Precipice (by Observatory). The dam, a quite useful two year old listed 5f winner, is a half-sister to three winners including the useful two year old triple 6f winner and listed-placed Blue Tomato. The second dam, Ocean Grove (by Fairy King), a quite useful two year old 6f winner, is a half-sister to five winners here and abroad. (A D Spence).
'The dam was quite quick (she was a listed winning two year old) and I hope this horse will start over six furlongs.'

1234. INSIDE KNOWLEDGE (USA) ★★★
gr.c. Mizzen Mast – Kithira (Danehill)
April 4. Third foal. Half-brother to the unraced 2007 two year old Malta (by Gone West). The dam, a French 6f (at two years) and listed 1m Prix de la Calonne winner, was Group 3 placed twice at two years and is a half-sister to the Group 3 Prix de Psyche winner Tenuous. The second dam, Atropa (by Vaguely Noble), was placed over 12f and is a half-sister to four winners. (Khalid Abdulla).
'A sharp colt, he's coming to hand now and he'll have a run over five furlongs but will want six. He looks a typical two year old and I should think he'll start off in May.'

1235. JAZACOSTA (USA) ★★★★ ♠
ch.c. Dixieland Band – Dance With Del (Sword Dance)
February 14. Sixth foal. $165,000Y. Keeneland September. James Delahooke. Half-brother to five winners including the minor US stakes-placed Dyna Del (by Dynaformer) and two minor winners by Conquistador Cielo and

Devil's Bag. The dam is a placed half-sister to eight winners including two minor US stakes winners. The second dam, Sugar Del (by Crozier), was a US stakes-placed winner of six races. (J P Connolly).

'He'll have a run over five furlongs in early May before I step him up to six. A big, strong, robust type of two year old, he was my Dad's pick at the Keeneland Sales. I like him a lot'

1236. KYLLACHY KING ★★

b.c. Kyllachy – Baileys Dancer (Groom Dancer)
February 21. First foal. 34,000Y. Doncaster St Leger. J Delahooke. The dam, a fairly useful 1m and 8.3f (at two years) and 12f winner, is a half-sister to four winners including the useful 1m (at two years) and 10f winner and listed-placed Deal Fair. The second dam, Darshay (by Darshaan), a quite useful maiden here, later won over 9f in Belgium and is a half-sister to eight winners. (Cotton, James, Slade and Tracey).

'They all say that Kyllachy's take a while to come and they're not much good until the soft ground comes along. Despite being a first foal he's a big horse that won't be ready until mid-season and he'll start off at six furlongs.'

1237. LOCATION ★★★★

b.f. Dansili – Well Away (Sadler's Wells)
February 10. Half-sister to the fairly useful 6f (at two years) to 1m winner of four races Free Trip (by Cadeaux Genereux) and the quite useful 5f and 6f winner Endless Summer (by Zafonic). The dam, a minor winner over 1m in France at two years, is a sister to the very smart colt Scenic, winner of the Group 1 7f Dewhurst Stakes (in a dead-heat) and the Group 3 10f William Hill Classic at Ayr and a half-sister to the Group 3 9f Prix Daphnis winner Silent Warrior. The second dam, Idyllic (by Foolish Pleasure), is an unraced half-sister to the Oaks second Slightly Dangerous (herself the dam of Commander in Chief, Warning, Deploy, Dushyantor and Yashmak) and I Will Follow (the dam of Rainbow Quest). (Khalid Abdulla).

'A nice filly, she's fairly sharp and will hopefully start off at six furlongs in late May. She goes well and is one to follow.'

1238. PAGAN FORCE (IRE) ★★★

b.c. Green Desert – Brigitta (Sadler's Wells)
March 21. Fourth foal. 68,000Y. Tattersalls October 1. James Delahooke. Brother to the fair 2007 two year old 7f winner Albaraari. The dam won over 1m and 10f at three years in France and is a sister to the two year old Group 1 1m Racing Post Trophy winner Commander Collins and closely related to the Grade 1 Breeders Cup Sprint winner Lit de Justice and the very smart 7f Washington Singer Stakes winner and 2,000 Guineas, Derby and Irish Derby placed Colonel Collins. The second dam, Kanmary (by Kenmare), a smart French two year old Group 3 5f Prix du Bois winner, stayed 9f and is a half-sister to 11 winners including the Prix de Royallieu winner Passionaria. (The Gap Partnership).

'He has a beautiful pedigree and is quite a forward horse that'll be suited by six furlongs in the middle of May. He wouldn't want it too soft, he isn't that big and it looks like he'll be able to shift.'

1239. ROCOPPELIA (USA) ★★★★

ch.c. Hennessy – Eternally
(Timeless Moment)
February 6. Eighth foal. $150,000Y. Keeneland September. James Delahooke. Brother the French winner and listed-placed Etenia and half-brother to four winners including the US stakes winner Spark Of Dubai (by E Dubai) and the US two year old winner and Grade 1 Matron Stakes third Carrielle (by Carr de Naskra). The dam is an unraced half-sister to six winners including the Group 1 Premio Roma winner Fire Of Life. The second dam, Spark Of Life (by Key To The Mint), won the Grade 1 Ladies Handicap and is a half-sister to the US Grade 1 winner Musical Lark. (J P Connolly).

'He's pretty sharp, he goes well and could be an Ascot colt over five furlongs.'

1240. SABORIDO (USA) ★★★

gr.c. Dixie Union – Alexine (Runaway Groom)
May 2. Second foal. $125,000Y. Keeneland September. James Delahooke. Half-brother to the quite useful 2007 two year old 7f winner

Silver Regent (by Silver Touch). The dam, a Grade 1 winner in Argentina and Grade 1 placed in the USA, is a half-sister to three minor winners. The second dam, Sentimental Gift (by Green Dancer), is an unraced half-sister to 2 stakes winners. (Cotton, James, Slade, Tracey). *'A May foal, so he'll want a bit of time, he'll be a seven furlong/mile horse at the end of the season. His half-brother Silver Regent won for us last year and I can see this horse doing the same thing.'*

1241. SHOW STOPPING ★★★★
br.f. Observatory – Sing For Fame (Quest For Fame)
January 17. Third foal. Half-sister to the quite useful 2007 two year old 7f winner Autocue (by Dansili) and to the fairly useful 10f and 12f winner and Group 3 2m Queens Vase third Secret Tune (by Generous). The dam, a quite useful 9f winner, is a half-sister to two winners. The second dam, Singing (by The Minstrel), won over 7f and is a half-sister to the Group 2 Prince Of Wales's Stakes winner Two Timing. (Khalid Abdulla).
'We trained the dam who won for us at Lingfield and the first two foals have both won. This is a nice, active filly that's very like Mum, she's 15.2 hands and a January foal so she'll be rocking and rolling by June over six furlongs to start with.'

1242. SILENT ACT (USA) ★★★
b.f. Theatrical – Vinista (Jade Hunter)
May 2. Sixth foal. $300,000Y. Keeneland September. James Delahooke. Sister to the US Grade 3 winner Roman Dynasty and to the minor US winner Candace In Paris. The dam, a US stakes winner, was Graded stakes placed 6 times and is a half-sister to five winners. The second dam, Sky Niniski (by Nijinsky), won twice at three years in Ireland and was second in the Group 3 C L Weld Park Stakes. (Mr & Mrs R Scott).
'A nice filly, she's a May foal that stands 16 hands but she does everything easily and will be a seven/eight furlong filly from Goodwood time onwards.'

1243. SPANISH CYGNET (USA) ★★★
b.f. El Corredor – Dixie Dos (Dixieland Band)

March 11. First foal. $100,000Y. Keeneland September. James Delahooke. The dam, a minor four year old winner in the USA, is a half-sister to 3 other minor winners. The second dam, Capote's Way (by Capote), was a US stakes-placed winner of three races. (Cotton, James, Slade, Tracey).
'A sharp, speedy filly. I should think we'll be seeing her over six furlongs towards the end of May.'

1244. TUDOR KEY (IRE) ★★
b.c. Key Of Luck – Anne Boleyn (Rainbow Quest)
April 18. Third foal. 21,000Y. Doncaster St Leger. James Delahooke. Half-brother to the fair two year old 7f winner Abbotts Ann (by Marju). The dam is an unraced half-sister to five winners Annus Mirabilis, winner of the Group 3 Winter Hill Stakes three times. The second dam, Anna Petrovna (by Wassl), won twice at three years and is a half-sister to five winners. (Coombelands Racing Syndicate).
'He goes alright, he'll run over six furlongs and step up to seven. A nice colt, he stands at about 15.3 and he'll get further next year.'

1245. WILFRED PICKLES (IRE) ★★★
ch.c. Cadeaux Genereux – Living Daylights (Night Shift)
March 23. Third foal. 30,000Y. Doncaster St Leger. J Delahooke. The dam, a fair dual middle-distance winner at four years, is a half-sister to six winners including the Group 3 Classic Trial winner Shield. The second dam, Shesadelight (by Shirley Heights), was placed at up to 2m and is a sister to the Grade 1 Rothmans International winner Infamy (herself the dam of four stakes winners). (Mrs A J Perrett).
'This is Jim Crowley's pick – he likes him so much. A big horse, he's done his work well so far and I should think we'll see him out towards the end of May over six furlongs.'

1246. UNNAMED ★★
b.c. Captain Rio – Lady Nasrana (Al Nasr)
February 26. Fourth foal. 40,000Y. Tattersalls

October 2. James Delahooke. Half-brother to Arhar (by Traditionally), placed third over 7f at two years on his only start. The dam won once over 5f at two years in Belgium and is a half-sister to seven winners including the US dual Grade 1 winner Janet. The second dam, Bid Dancer (by Spectacular Bid), won one at three years in France and is a half-sister to seven winners. (Mrs A J Perrett).

'He's not named yet because I still own him but he's almost ready to run and I'm looking for an owner. He goes well, he'll start at five furlongs and then he'll step up to six. If he'd been at the breeze-ups he'd have made a few quid!'

JONATHAN PORTMAN

1247. ABBEY BELLE ★★★

gr.f. Verglas – Abbey Park (Known Fact)
April 24. Third foal. 40,000Y. Tattersalls October 2. T & J Parrott. Half-sister to the quite useful 2007 Irish 7f and 1m placed two year old Invincible Joe (by Invincible Spirit) and to the modest 7f all-weather winner Nashharry (by Ishiguru). The dam, placed over 7f at two years, is a half-sister to eight winners including the US stakes winner Foxy Ferdie. The second dam, Taylor Park (by Sir Gaylord), a stakes winner of five races in the USA, is a half-sister to three winners including the Group 3 Greenlands Stakes winner Drama. (T J Parrott).

'She's been doing a lot of growing so I haven't asked her any questions at the moment but she's a filly with a nice action and temperament and she's very straightforward. Hopefully she'll be out by the end of May or beginning of June, she doesn't have the look of a sprinter so we'll start her at six furlongs and see what happens.'

1248. ACCEDE ★★★

b.f. Acclamation – Here To Me (Muhtarram)
March 10. First foal. 24,000Y. Doncaster October. G Howson. The dam, a fair three year old 6f winner, is a half-sister to one winner out of the unraced Away To Me (by Exit To Nowhere), herself a half-sister to five winners. (Mrs D. O. Joly).

'Not over-big but growing all the time, a month ago I thought she'd take some time but she's

coming to hand pretty quickly now. She's about to do some fast work with a view to running from the end of April onwards. She'll start at five furlongs, will probably get six and she's quite nice.'

1249. BAYCAT (IRE) ★★★★

b.c. One Cool Cat – Greta d'Argent (Great Commotion)
March 3. 21,000Y. Doncaster October. Sophie Portman. The dam, a fairly useful 1m (at two years) to 12f winner of four races, is a half-sister to four winners including the listed winner and Group 2 placed Winged d'Argent. The second dam, Petite-D-Argent (by Noalto), won over 6f (at two years) and 7f. (A.S.B Portman).

'I call him Jaws at home because he's quite a tidy biter! I've never known a horse quite like him. But he's OK and a very neat little horse that finds life very easy at the moment. I'm surprised he's come to hand so quickly because he's bred to get closer to a mile. He'll start his career at Newbury in April.' This colt won on his debut at Newbury and did it very nicely indeed!

1250. LILY OF THE NILE (UAE) ★★★

ch.f. Halling – Covet (Polish Precedent)
April 29. First foal. 11,000Y. Tattersalls October 3. Prof. C D Green. The dam won once at three years in France and is a half-sister to three winners including the Group 3 Prix du Lys winner and Group 1 Grand Prix de Paris second Desideratum. The second dam, Desired (by Rainbow Quest), is an unraced half-sister to the Group 1 Racing Post Trophy winner Medaaly and the dual Group 2 winner Charnwood Forest. (Prof. C D Green).

'She's nice and will hopefully go in one of the first six furlong races at the end of May. I thought when we bought her that she'd take time but she does everything easily and she'd run tomorrow if there was a suitable race.' TRAINER'S BARGAIN BUY

1251. RUSSIAN RAVE ★★★

ch.f. Danehill Dancer – Russian Ruby (Vettori)
February 16. First foal. 45,000Y. Tattersalls October 2. J Portman. The dam, a quite useful

two year old 6f and 7f winner, is a half-sister to three winners. The second dam, Pink Sovietstaia (by Soviet Star), was awarded a 9f event at four years in France and is a half-sister to nine winners including the listed winner Pinaflore (herself dam of the Group/Graded stakes winners Pinakaral, Pinfloron and Pinmix). (The Traditionalists).

'A big, backward type, she'll hopefully run in June over six furlongs. She finds life easy at the moment and maybe isn't quite as backward as her physique would suggest.'

1252. UNNAMED ★★★
b.c. Mind Games – Exotic Forest (Dominion)
March 5. Tenth foal. 22,000Y. Tattersalls October 4. Sophie Portman. Brother to the fairly useful 2007 two year old 5f and 6f winner Mesmerize Me and half-brother to the fairly useful 5f (at two years) to 1m winner of five races Threezedzz, to the fair two year old 6f all-weather winner Blue Charm (by Averti), the modest all-weather 5f and 6f winner Zoena (both by Emarati), the fair 1m winner Smoothly Does It (by Efisio) and a winner over hurdles by Tragic Role. The dam, a modest three year old 1m winner, is a half-sister to five winners including the listed October Stakes winner Toffee Nosed. The second dam, Ever Welcome (by Be My Guest), won over 10f at four years and is a half-sister to five winners including the Group 3 1m Matron Stakes winner Chanzi. (J G B Portman).

'He's a big horse that's not done any fast work yet but he's just starting to do a bit more now. We'll take a view as to whether or not he'll be able to run in June. He's nice but just a bit bigger than the others and so he's bound to take a bit more time, but there's nothing wrong with him, he goes very well and I'd be surprised if he didn't go a bit. We've trained most of his relations and they're not just two year old's, they train on, so we're not rushing him.'

KEVIN PRENDERGAST
1253. AJSAAM (IRE) ★★★★
ch.c. Pivotal – Ulfah (Danzig)
January 30. First foal. The dam, an Irish dual

listed 6f winner, is a sister to the listed 6f (at two years) and Group 3 7f Athasi Stakes winner Waleyef and to the Group 2 6f Diadem Stakes winner Haatef. The second dam, Sayedat Alhadh (by Mr Prospector), a US 7f winner, is a sister to the US Grade 2 7f winner Kayrawan and a half-sister to the useful winners Amaniy, Elsaamri and Mathkurh. (Hamdan Al Maktoum).

'A nice horse out of a mare we trained, he goes nicely and he'll want six furlongs plus from mid-summer onwards. We like him. Being by Pivotal he'll probably want a bit of cut in the ground.'

1254. ALHABAN (IRE) ★★★★
gr.c. Verglas – Anne Tudor (Anabaa)
February 5. First foal. €100,000Y. Goffs Million. Shadwell Estate Co. The dam, a quite useful three year old 7f winner, is a half-sister to two winners including the fairly useful triple 7f winner (including at two years) Silk Fan. The second dam, Alikhlas (by Lahib), a fair three year old 1m winner, is a half-sister to three winners including the listed winner and Group 2 Lancashire Oaks second Sahool and to the dam of the dual Group 2 winner Maraahel. (Hamdan Al Maktoum).

'He's had one start and won, he'll appreciate better ground and six or seven furlongs or even a mile wouldn't be a problem for him. A February foal, he's very well developed and after his next start we'll be able to assess him better.'

1255. ALYAZWA ★★★
b.c. Selkirk – Rose Croix (Chief's Crown)
March 7. Fourth foal. 160,000Y. Tattersalls October 1. Shadwell Estate Co. Half-brother to a winner in New Zealand by Kingfisher Mill. The dam, placed once at two years, is a sister to the champion two year old Grand Lodge, winner of the Group 1 7f Dewhurst Stakes and half-sister to the listed winners Papabile and La Persiana. The second dam, La Papagena (by Habitat), is an unraced half-sister to seven winners including the listed winners Pamina and Lost Chord. (Hamdan Al Maktoum).

'A big horse, he's going to take a bit of time but we like him and he'll be a nice horse at the back-end over seven furlongs plus.'

1256. ARFAJAH (IRE) ★★★

b.f. Invincible Spirit – Banadiyka (Darshaan)
**January 17. Second foal. 64,000Y. Doncaster St
Leger. Shadwell Estate Co.** The dam is an
unraced half-sister to four winners. The second
dam, Banaja (by Sadler's Wells), is an unraced
half-sister to the Group 1 Prix Saint-Alary winner
Behera. (Hamdan Al Maktoum).
*'She goes well and I expect her to win. We'll
probably start her at five furlongs but she'd be
better at six.'*

1257. BEA BEA THREE (IRE) ★★★

b.f. Montjeu – Miss Beabea (Catrail)
January 31. Half-sister to the two year old
Group 1 7f Moyglare Stud Stakes winner Miss
Beatrix (by Danehill Dancer). The dam, an Irish
two year old 6f winner and second in the Group
1 6f Phoenix Stakes, is a half-sister to three
winners including the very useful 5f winner
Ellen's Lad. The second dam, Lady Ellen (by
Horage), a modest 5f placed two year old, is a
half-sister to three winners including Indian
Ridge. (Bill Durkan).
*'A nice filly, most Montjeu's need time and she's
the same. One for the back-end over seven
furlongs, but we like her a lot.'*

1258. BRAZILIAN SPIRIT (IRE) ★★★★

b.f. Invincible Spirit – Braziliz (Kingmambo)
February 20. Half-sister to the very useful 2007
two year old 7.5f winner and Group 3 7f second
Brazilian Star (by Galileo), to the two year old
Group 3 6f Swordlestown Stud Sprint Stakes
winner Brazilian Bride (by Pivotal) and the Irish
three year old 6f winner Brazilian Sun (by
Barathea). The dam is an unplaced half-sister to
the two year old winner Or Vision (dam of the
Irish 2,000 Guineas winner Saffron Walden, the
Grade 1 E P Taylor Stakes winner Insight and the
Group 1 7f Prix de la Foret winner Dolphin
Street. The second dam, Luv Luvin' (by Raise a
Native), won two races in the USA. (Lady
O'Reilly).
*'She goes nicely and we like her a lot. She's
typical of the other two out of the dam we
trained. She isn't a big filly, but she's very
muscular and six furlongs should suit her.'*

1259. CARRIGFERGUS (IRE) ★★★

b.c. Rock Of Gibraltar – Zvezda (Nureyev)
**April 29. Third foal. €35,000Y. Goffs Million.
Frank Barry.** Half-brother to the fairly useful
Irish two year old Group 3 7f C L Weld Park
Stakes third Silk Dress (by Gulch). The dam is an
unplaced full or half-sister to five winners
including the 7f (at two years) and subsequent
US stakes winner and Group 1 Dewhurst Stakes
and US Grade 1 third Zentsov Street. The
second dam, Storm Fear (by Coastal), is a US
placed half-sister to nine winners including the
dam of Bakharoff and Emperor Jones.
*'A nice horse I own in partnership with 3 friends,
he was immature but he's developing into a nice
horse. One for the middle of the season.'*

1260. CATALPA (IRE) ★★★

ch.c. Verglas – Blueberry Walk (Green Desert)
**April 23. Tenth foal. €50,000Y. Goffs Million.
Not sold.** Half-brother to the 1m winner
Basserah (by Unfuwain), to the French 1m (at
two years) and 10f winner Jungle Rumbler (by
Charnwood Forest), the two year old 7f all-
weather winner Buona Sera (by Marju), the
three year old 9.4f all-weather winner Joondey
(by Pursuit Of Love) – all 4 quite useful – and
the Italian winner Armenian Heritage (by
Bluebird). The dam is an unraced sister to the
listed 2m George Stubbs Stakes winner Hawait
Al Barr and a half-sister to three winners. The
second dam, Allegedly Blue (by Alleged), won
once at three years, was placed in the Park Hill
Stakes and is a full or half-sister to four winners
including the dams of the Kentucky Derby and
Preakness Stakes winner Real Quiet and the
Queen Anne Stakes winner Allied Forces. (Trevor
Reily).
*'He'll be running soon and we expect a good
show from him. He's a nice horse with a good
temperament and we like him. Although we'll
run him over five furlongs to start him off, he'll
get further later on.'*

1261. DACTIK (IRE) ★★★

b.c. Diktat – Septembers Hawk (Machiavellian)
**February 22. Second foal. €27,000Y. Tattersalls
Ireland. Frank Barry.** Half-brother to the

modest 2007 7f placed two year old Georgie the Fourth (by Cadeaux Genereux). The dam is an unraced half-sister to two winners. The second dam, Reunion (by Be My Guest), won the Group 3 Nell Gwyn Stakes and is a half-sister to seven winners. (Lady O'Reilly).

'He was cheap but we like him a lot. He's as strong as a bull – a lovely, big horse, a two year old type and Machiavellian is a good broodmare sire. He'll do well over seven furlongs.' TRAINER'S BARGAIN BUY

1262. DRIVING SNOW ★★★

gr.c. Verglas – Dazzling Dancer (Nashwan)
March 11. First foal. 42,000Y. Doncaster St Leger. BBA (Ire). The dam, a quite useful Irish 12f winner, is a half-sister to one winner. The second dam, Danse Classique (by Night Shift), a listed-placed winner in Ireland, is a half-sister to the triple Group 1 winner Petrushka. (Lady O'Reilly).

'We like him a lot, he's out of a mare that I trained and it's a good family but he'd want seven furlongs now. He has a much better temperament than the dam – she was a bit of a girl!'

1263. EXCELLENT GIRL ★★★

b.f. Exceed And Excel – Dame Blanche
(Be My Guest)
February 22. Second foal. 140,000Y. Tattersalls October 1. BBA (Ire). Half-sister to the fairly useful 2007 6f and 7f placed 2-yo Major Willy (by Xaar). The dam, a modest 1m placed three year old, is a half-sister to the US Grade 1 winner and Irish 1,000 Guineas third Luas Line. The second dam, Streetcar (by In The Wings), is a placed half-sister to nine winners. (Lady O'Reilly).

'I like her well, she won't be ready until mid-season but the sire seems to be doing well.'

1264. FINAL APPROACH ★★★

b.c. Pivotal – College Fund Girl (Kahyasi)
May 14. Second foal. €180,000Y. Goffs Million. McKeever St Lawrence. The dam, a fair 12f winner, is a half-sister to four winners including the high-class dual Group 2 7f winner Naayir

and the very smart UAE Group 3 12f winner and Group 1 Coronation Cup second Highest. The second dam, Pearl Kite (by Silver Hawk), a useful two year old 1m winner and third in the Group 2 12f Ribblesdale Stakes, is a half-sister to three winners. (Douglas Taylor).

'An immature colt but we like him a lot. The owner wants to have a crack at the Goffs Million in September if possible so we'll aim him for that time of the year.'

1265. GLEBE QUEEN (IRE) ★★★

b.f. Hawkeye – Burnin' Memories (Lit de Justice)
February 10. First foal. €60,000Y. Tattersalls Ireland. Frank Barry. The dam won five races at 2 to five years in the USA including a minor stakes event and is a half-sister to four winners. The second dam, Adorable Vice (by Vice Regent), a US stakes-placed winner of three races, is a half-sister to four winners including the Italian Group 1 winner Looking For and the Italian Group 2 winner Life On Mars. (N Ormiston).

'She'll definitely make a two year old, we like her a lot and six furlongs should suit her.'

1266. HEART OF FIRE (IRE) ★★★

b.c. Mujadil – Heart's Desire (Royal Applause)
February 1. First foal. €70,000Y. Tattersalls Ireland. Frank Barry. The dam, a fair 7f and 1m placed maiden, is a half-sister to five winners including the French listed winner and Group 3 placed Bashful. The second dam, Touch And Love (by Green Desert), a two year old winner in France, was second in the Group 2 Prix du Gros-Chene and is a half-sister to eight winners. (Geordie McGrath).

'He'll have his first race before the end of April, over five furlongs. That'll be a bit short for him but I expect him to run well.'

1267. LISTA LIGHTNING (IRE) ★★

b.c. Intikhab – Alassio (Akarad)
April 26. Fourth foal. Half-brother to the unplaced 2007 two year old Piverina (by Pivotal). The dam, a quite useful 9f winner in Ireland at three years, is a half-sister to a winner in Japan. The second dam, Royal Ballerina (by

Sadler's Wells), won six races including the Group 2 Blandford Stakes, was second in the Oaks and the Irish Oaks and is a half-sister to seven winners including the Nassau Stakes and Sun Chariot Stakes winner Free Guest. (M Berger).

'A nice, good-sized horse belonging to a long-standing owner of ours, we like him but he wouldn't want the ground too firm so we'll try and get him out before too long.'

1268. MARK OF AN ANGEL (IRE) ★★★

ch.f. Mark Of Esteem – Dream Time (Rainbow Quest)

February 1. Third foal. €120,000Y. Goffs Million. Frank Barry. The dam, placed once over 12f at three years, is a half-sister to three winners. The second dam, Grey Angel (by Kenmare), won eight races at around 1m including a Group 3 event in South Africa and was Group 1 placed.

'We like her a lot, she's a big filly and seven furlongs will be ideal for her.'

1269. NAFAATH (IRE) ★★★

ch.c. Nayef – Alshakr (Bahri)

March 6. Fourth foal. Half-brother to the quite useful Irish 2007 7f placed two year old Sufad (by Alhaarth). The dam, a very useful winner of the Group 2 1m Falmouth Stakes, is a half-sister to the dam of the 1,000 Guineas winner Harayir. The second dam, Give Thanks (by Relko), won the Irish Oaks, the Lancashire Oaks and the Musidora Stakes. (Hamdan Al Maktoum).

'A very promising horse. He looks like one for the back-end of the season but he's a nice colt.'

1270. QUIET OCEAN (IRE) ★★

b.c. Alhaarth – Asfurah (Dayjur)

March 11. Half-brother to the quite useful 10.2f winner Ijtihad (by Darshaan), to the fair UAE 1m winner Africanus (by Dubai Millennium) and a minor 1m winner abroad by Machiavellian. The dam, a very useful winner of the Group 3 6f Cherry Hinton Stakes and the listed 5f Windsor Castle Stakes, is closely related to the fairly useful 5.3f (at two years) and 6f winner Alumisiyah and a half-sister to the US dual

Grade 3 winner Istintaj. The second dam, Mathkurh (by Riverman), a useful 5f (at two years) and 6f winner, is a half-sister to the Group 3 6f Princess Margaret Stakes winner Muhbubh. (Hadi Al Tajir).

'A nice horse that goes well, he's one for the middle of the season onwards and over seven furlongs.'

1271. QUILCA (USA) ★★★

b.c. Van Nistelrooy – Fabulist (Devil's Bag)

February 27. Sixth foal. €150,000Y. Goffs Million. Frank Barry. Closely related to the fairly useful Irish two year old 1m winner Border Cat (by Storm Cat) and to a minor winner in the USA by Deputy Commander. The dam, a minor US three year old winner, is a half-sister to four winners including the Middle Park Stakes and Phoenix Stakes winner Minardi, the US Grade 2 King's Bishop Stakes winner Tale Of The Cat and the dam of the champion two year old Johannesburg. The second dam, Yarn (by Mr Prospector), won at three years in the USA and is a sister to the Grade 1 Frizette Stakes winner Preach (herself dam of the US Grade 2 winner Pulpit). (N Ormiston).

'We like him a lot and six furlongs will be no problem for him. He's very strong, not over-tall but very muscular and well-made.'

1272. RANTAVAN WOOD (IRE) ★★

b.c. One Cool Cat – Dream Valley (Sadler's Wells)

January 16. First foal. €58,000Y. Goffs Million. Frank Barry. The dam is an unplaced half-sister to three winners including the Group 1 1m Coronation Stakes and Group 2 7f Rockfel Stakes winner Maid's Causeway. The second dam, Vallee des Reves (by Kingmambo), is an unraced half-sister to the Group 2 Prix du Muguet winner Vetheuil, the Group 3 Prix de l'Opera winner Verveine (herself dam of the Grade 1 winners Vallee Enchantee and Volga) and the dam of the Group 1 Grand Prix de Paris winner Vespone. (N Ormiston).

'He'll make a two year old later on but he's just had a little setback so we won't see him out for a while.'

1273. SAMBA SCHOOL (IRE) ★★★
b.f. Sahm – Lulua (Bahri)
February 19. First foal. €120,000Y. Goffs Million. Frank Barry. The dam, a minor winner of two races at three years in the USA, is a half-sister to five winners. The second dam, Sajjaya (by Blushing Groom), a useful two year old 7f and three year old 1m winner, is a half-sister to eight winners including the top-class Group 1 1m Queen Elizabeth II Stakes and Group 2 1m Queen Anne Stakes winner Lahib. (Lady O'Reilly).
'A nice filly, she'll run in May and will appreciate dry ground. We like her.'

1274. SHAKALAKA (IRE) ★★
b.c. Montjeu – Sweet Times (Riverman)
May 7. Eighth foal. Half-brother to the Group 3 Killavullan Stakes winner Stonemason (by Nureyev), to the fair 6f (at two years) and 9f winner Pelham Crescent (by Giant's Causeway) and the French 2m and jumps winner Saddler's Times (by Sadler's Wells). The dam, a moderate 6f placed three year old, is a sister to the Group 3 7f Jersey Stakes winner and US Grade 2 placed River Deep and a half-sister to four winners including the US stakes winner Dreamer. The second dam, Affection Affirmed (by Affirmed), won four races in the USA and is a half-sister to six winners including the dam of the dual Group 1 winner Zoman. (Exors of the late C Ryan).
'A big, backward sort, he'll be OK towards the end of the season though.'

1275. SHIMAH (USA) ★★★★★
ch.f. Storm Cat – Sayedat Alhadh
(Mr Prospector)
February 26. Half-sister to the Group 2 6f Diadem Stakes winner Haatef, to the listed 6f (at two years) and Group 3 7f Athasi Stakes winner Walayef and the Irish dual listed 6f winner Ulfah (all by Danzig). The dam, a US 7f winner, is a sister to the US Grade 2 7f winner Kayrawan and a half-sister to the useful winners Amaniy, Elsaamri and Mathkurh. The second dam, Muhbubh (by Blushing Groom), a winner of the Group 3 6f Princess Margaret Stakes at two years, is a half-sister to the quite useful 6f and

10f winner Mathaayl. (Hamdan Al-Maktoum).
'We've had all the family, they've all done us proud and in particular Haatef. She moves nicely, we like her a lot, she's smaller and sharper than the rest of the family and looks more of a two year old than they did.'

1276. VILASOL (IRE) ★★★
gr.c. Verglas – Pitrizza (Machiavellian)
March 24. Fourth foal. 47,000Y. Tattersalls October 2. F Barry. Half-brother to the fair 6f and 7f winner Perfect Treasure (by Night Shift). The dam won once over 12f in France and is a half-sister to 3 other minor winners. The second dam, Unopposed (by Sadler's Wells), is an unraced half-sister to 11 winners including the dam of the dual Group 2 winner and sire Titus Livius.
'He's had one run at the Curragh where he finished fourth. I was happy enough with him and he may turn out at Leopardstown over six furlongs next. He's a very good, strong, ball of a horse – like his father.'

SIR MARK PRESCOTT
1277. AESTIVAL ★★ ♠
b.c. Falbrav – Summer Night (Nashwan)
April 29. Sixth foal. 100,000Y. Tattersalls October 1. Charlie Gordon-Watson. Half-brother to the quite useful 2007 two year old dual 7f winner Sourire (by Domedriver), to the two year old Group 3 1m Prix des Reservoirs winner Songerie, the fairly useful two year old 7.2f winner and Group 3 1m Prix des Reservoirs third Souvenance (both by Hernando), the useful listed 9.5f winner of three races Soft Morning (by Pivotal) and a minor winner of six races in Italy by Selkirk. The dam, a fairly useful three year old 6f winner, is a half-sister to four winners including the useful listed 6f winner Sea Dane. The second dam, Shimmering Sea (by Slip Anchor), a fairly useful Irish two year old 5f and 7f winner and third in the Group 3 Silken Glider Stakes, is a half-sister to five winners including the King George VI and Queen Elizabeth Stakes winner Petoski. (Lady K M Watts).
'I've had all the family, they're jolly good but this colt is turned out and he won't run until the back-end.'

1278. AIR MAZE ★★★
b.f. Dansili – Begueule (Bering)
January 16. Third foal. €600,000Y. Deauville August. Peter Doyle. Half-sister to the fair 10f winner Pivotal Answer (by Pivotal). The dam, a quite useful 7f-1m winner at two and three years in France, was listed-placed several times and is a half-sister to ten winners. The second dam, Bathyale (by Green Dancer), won twice at three years and is a half-sister to five winners. (Plantation Stud).
'She'll be a 7f staying filly from August onwards and is a tall, leggy filly.'

1279. ALICANTE ★★★
gr.f. Pivotal – Alba Stella (Nashwan)
April 17. Second foal. Half-sister to the unplaced 2007 two year old Aleatricis (by Kingmambo). The dam, a fairly useful dual 12f winner, is a half-sister to four winners including the high-class dual Champion Stakes winner Alborada and the triple German Group 1 winner Albanova. The dam, a useful 1m (at two years) and listed 12f winner, is a sister to the listed winner and Irish Oaks third Arrikala and a half-sister to the Nassau Stakes and Sun Chariot Stakes winner Last Second (dam of the French 2,000 Guineas winner Aussie Rules) and the Doncaster Cup winner Alleluia. (Miss K Rausing).
'A lengthy filly and she'll want seven furlongs in mid-summer.'

1280. ASCENDANT ★★★
ch.c. Medicean – Ascendancy (Sadler's Wells)
April 23. Fifth foal. 50,000foal. Tattersalls December. Not sold. Half-brother to the Irish 11f winner Enamoured (by Groom Dancer). The dam is an unraced full or half-sister to six winners including the listed winner and Group 2 placed Polar Bear and the Group 1 Fillies' Mile second Dance To The Top. The second dam, Aim For The Top (by Irish River), a very useful filly and winner of the Group 3 7f Premio Chiusura, is a half-sister to six winners including the Gimcrack Stakes winner Splendent. (Cheveley Park Stud).
'I haven't had one from this family before, but people tell me they usually come around mid-

season and he looks that way too. He's done plenty of growing and he's now quite a tall horse.'

1281. BRAVEHEART MOVE (IRE) ★★
b.c. Cape Cross – Token Gesture (Alzao)
April 24. Eighth foal. €160,000Y. Goffs Million. Half-brother to the unraced 2007 two year old Central Station, to the Irish two year old 7f winner and Group 2 1m Beresford Stakes second Relaxed Gesture (both by Indian Ridge), the Irish 1m and subsequent US Grade 2 9.5f American Derby winner Evolving Tactics (by Machiavellian) and the Irish 1m, 12f and hurdles winner Turn Of Phrase (by Cadeaux Genereux). The dam, a smart winner of the Group 3 7f C L Weld Park Stakes, is a half-sister to the US Grade 2 9f winner Wait Till Monday, to the useful Irish 10f to 12.3f winner Blazing Spectacle and the useful Irish middle-distance stayer and Triumph Hurdle winner Rare Holiday. The second dam, Temporary Lull (by Super Concorde), is an unraced sister to the Nell Gwyn Stakes winner Martha Stevens. (Moyglare Stud Farms Ltd).
'A colt for September onwards, he's the first one I've had for Moyglare Stud Farm.'

1282. BRETT VALE (IRE) ★★★
b.c. Sinndar – Pinta (Ahonoora)
April 13. Ninth foal. €55,000Y. Goffs Million. G Waters. Half-brother to the fairly useful two year old 6f winner Teodora (by Fairy King), to the fair two year old 6f winner Stiletto (by Danehill), the quite useful 7f to 9f winner of six races Rain Stops Play and the modest 7f and 1m winner Koukalova (both by Desert Prince) and the modest 8.5f winner Prince Dimitri (by Desert King). The dam won over 5f in Ireland and a listed event in Italy over 7.5f and is a half-sister to six winners including the Irish listed winner Miss Sacha (herself the dam of 2 stakes winners). The second dam, Heaven High (by High Line), is a placed half-sister to the Group 1 10f Irish Champion Stakes, Grade 1 Beverly D Stakes and German Group 1 winner Timarida.
'He'll be starting work in May, so he should be running in June. He's not over-big and is out of a speedy mare but despite that, being by Sinndar he's not likely to be a six furlong two year old.'

1283. BY REQUEST ★★★
b.f. Giant's Causeway – Approach (Darshaan)
February 16. The dam, a 7.5f (at two years) and listed 10f winner, was second in a US Grade 2 9.5f event and is a sister to the very useful two year old 8.5f winner and Group 1 Prix Marcel Boussac fourth Intrigued and a half-sister to the French 2,000 Guineas and US Grade 1 winner Aussie Rules. The second dam, Last Second (by Alzao), winner of the 10f Nassau Stakes and the 10f Sun Chariot Stakes, is a half-sister to seven winners including the Moyglare Stud Stakes third Alouette (herself dam of the Group 1 winners Albanova and Alborada) and to the placed dam of the Group 1 winners Yesterday and Quarter Moon. (Faisal Salman).
'From an excellent family, she'll be a September/ October filly and is mainly a three year old type. A big filly, she'll be suited by seven furlongs and a mile as a two year old.'

1284. CASTLE HEIGHTS ★★
b.c. Selkirk – Cheviot Hills (Gulch)
April 22. Fifth foal. Half-brother to the unplaced 2007 two year old's Cheviot Red (by Red Ransom) and to the quite useful three year old 7f winner Enrapture (by Lear Fan). The dam, a French 10f winner, is a half-sister to five winners including the listed Prix Djebel and subsequent dual US Grade 3 winner Fantastic Fellow (by Lear Fan). The second dam, Chateaubaby (by Nureyev), a modest 5f and 7f placed two year old, is a half-sister to the Derby winner Henbit and to the dam of the US Grade 1 winners Mr Purple and Queens Court Queen. (Cheveley Park Stud).
'She's turned out at the moment but will come back in with a view to getting her ready for an autumn campaign.'

1285. CECILY ★★★★
b.f. Oasis Dream – Odette (Pursuit Of Love)
February 22. Sixth foal. Half-sister to the Group 3 6f Firth Of Clyde Stakes winner and Group 2 Rockfel Stakes second Violette (by Observatory), to the listed 6f (at two years) and Group 3 7f Nell Gwyn Stakes winner Silca's Gift (by Cadeaux Genereux) and the fair three year old 5f all-weather winner On Point (by Kris). The dam, a fair three year old 5f and 5.7f winner, is a half-sister to four winners including the useful 6f (at two years) and 7f winner and Group 2 5f Flying Childers Stakes fourth Caballero. The second dam, On Tiptoes (by Shareef Dancer), a useful winner of five races at around 5f including the Group 3 Queen Mary Stakes, is a half-sister to two winners. (C G Rowles Nicholson).
'She's bred to go early but she's had a few niggling health issues and she's only just perking up now. But the dam, grandam, great-grandam and her half-sister Violette all came to hand early. The family are all quick and if she's any good she will be too!'

1286. CHORAL FESTIVAL ★★★
b.f. Pivotal – Choirgirl (Unfuwain)
January 31. Fourth foal. Sister to the quite useful dual 12f winner Chord (by Pivotal). The dam, a very useful two year old 7f winner and second in the Group 3 7f Prestige Stakes, was listed-placed twice over 10f and is a half-sister to numerous winners including the Group 1 10f Curragh Pretty Polly Stakes winner Chorist. The second dam, Choir Mistress (by Chief Singer), is an unraced half-sister to six winners including the smart Group 2 11.9f Great Voltigeur Stakes winner Sacrament. (Cheveley Park Stud).
'A mid-season, seven furlong filly, she's grown a lot recently and is tall and leggy.'

1287. FLORENTIA ★★★★
ch.f. Medicean – Area Girl (Jareer)
April 8. Tenth foal. 45,000Y. Tattersalls October 1. G Howson. Half-sister to the 2007 two year old 6f all-weather winner High Tribute (by Mark Of Esteem), to the useful 6f and 7f (all-weather) winner of four races Flying Officer, the fair all-weather 6f and 7f winner Fission (both by Efisio), the fairly useful two year old 5f and 6f winner of five races Clarion (by First Trump), the quite useful 6f (at two years) to 9f winner of six races Outlook (by Observatory), the quite useful 5f and 6f winner of five races Dominant Air, the modest 5f winner Birdwatching (both by Primo Dominie) and the modest 7f and 1m (all-

weather) winner Critical Air (by Reprimand). The dam, a fair two year old 5f winner, is a half-sister to three minor winners. The second dam, Shannon Lady (by Monsanto), was an unplaced half-sister to eight winners. (W N Greig).

'The family all run at two, we've had them all and they've won 27 races for us – nearly all as two year old's. So hopefully she'll follow suit despite having grown a bit lately. I can't say she's a nice mover because she isn't! But her mother wasn't either and I don't think it'll stop her.'

1288. FORTUNI (IRE) ★★

b.c. Montjeu – Desert Ease (Green Desert)
April 13. Eighth foal. €300,000Y. Goffs Million.
Closely related to the Irish 6f (at two years) and 10f winner and listed-placed Unique Pose, to the Irish three year old 7f winner and two year old Group 3 7f C L Weld Park Stakes third Easy Sunshine (both by Sadler's Wells) and half-brother to the Irish 12f and hurdles winner Ease The Way (by Nashwan) and the hurdles winner Outside Investor (by Cadeaux Genereux). The dam, an Irish two year old listed 6f winner, is a half-sister to several winners including the Group 3 Tetrarch Stakes and Group 3 7f Concorde Stakes winner Two-Twenty-Two. The second dam, Easy To Copy (by Affirmed), won five races from 5f up to 12f here including the Group 2 Premio Legnano and subsequently performed well in America and is a sister to the Irish 1,000 Guineas winner Trusted Partner (dam of the Grade 1 winner Dress To Thrill). (Pacific International Management).

'A nice horse in the making, one hopes, but he's very big and turned out at the moment. Needs plenty of time.'

1289. GLIMMER ★★★

b.f. Royal Applause – Mythic (Zafonic)
March 17. Half-sister to the 2008 7f winner Underworld (by Cadeaux Genereux). The dam, a listed-placed 8.2f winner, is a half-sister to six winners including the two year old 7f and subsequent US winner and Group 3 Solario Stakes second Staffin and to the two year old winner and Group 3 Horris Hill Stakes third Mindful. The second dam, Fetlar (by Pharly), is

an unraced half-sister to eight winners including the Jersey Stakes winner Ardkinglass. (Dr C Wills).

'Likely to appear in the latter part of September I should think. She's from a good family, she's not over-big and she might make a two year old if she comes to hand in time.'

1290. GOOD HUMOURED ★★★

b.c. Rock Of Gibraltar – Humouresque (Pivotal)
May 4. Second foal. 62,000Y. Tattersalls October 1. Half-brother to Solid Air (by Lomitas), unplaced in two starts in Ireland at two years in 2007. The dam, a smart Group 3 10.5f Prix Penelope winner, is a half-sister to the very smart sprinter Danehurst, winner of the Cornwallis Stakes (at two years), the Curragh Flying Five, the Prix de Seine-et-Oise and the Premio Umbria (all Group 3 events). The second dam, Miswaki Belle (by Miswaki), second over 7f on her only start, is a half-sister to eight winners including the smart Group 3 6f Cherry Hinton Stakes winner and 1,000 Guineas third Dazzle. (Charles C Walker – Osborne House II).

'Much more of a three year old than a two year old, but he might be mature enough to shape up at two. He's quite a chunky colt and not a huge thing like most of mine!'

1291. HAVEN'T A CLUE ★★★★

b.f. Red Ransom – Cool Question (Polar Falcon)
April 9. Second foal. Half-sister to the quite useful two year old 5f winner Fairfield Princess (by Inchinor). The dam, a useful two year old 5f and listed 6f winner, is a half-sister to two winners. The second dam, Quiz Time (Efisio), a fairly useful two year old 5f winner, was second in the listed St Hugh's Stakes and is a half-sister to six winners including the Group 3 Premio Dormello winner Brockette. (Lady Fairhaven).

'She'll make a two year old – they all do from this family. I trained the mother who was good and the grandam was quick too – she stayed four and a half furlongs! This filly has more scope than either of them and I see her being out in June or July.'

1292. INFLAMMABLE ★★★★
b.f. Pivotal – Flame Valley (Gulch)
May 5. Seventh foal. Half-sister to the fairly useful two year old 1m winner and listed 1m fourth Aglow (by Spinning World). The dam, a smart 10f listed winner, was placed in the Group 2 10f Sun Chariot Stakes and in the Grade 1 10f E P Taylor Stakes and is a half-sister to three winners including the US Grade 2 winner Beyrouth. The second dam, Lightning (by Kris), won the listed Prix Imprudence, and is a sister to the Prix de la Salamandre winner and very useful sire Common Grounds and a half-sister to the Prix de Psyche winner Angel In My Heart. (Cheveley Park Stud).
'Interestingly bred in that both the sire and the dam are influences for ability and also for temperament – hence the name! We all knew what she'd be like and sure enough she was difficult when breaking-in, but she's become very solid now. The breeding suggests ability and temperament and I suspect she'll have plenty of both. Much will depend upon how she copes with the stresses of galloping and the racecourse, but she's jolly good and jolly well behaved now. She'll run in mid-season, the mare has had a lot of chances and hasn't really produced the goods – but this is a change of mixture for her.'

1293. INGENUE ★★
b.f. Hernando – I Do (Selkirk)
March 15. The dam, a quite useful two year old dual 7f winner, is a half-sister to two winners including the useful two year old dual 7f winner and listed-placed Oblige. The second dam, Acquiesce (by Generous), is an unraced half-sister to two winners. (Miss K Rausing).
'Very much a three year old and unlikely to do much at two years – although Hernando's sometimes do!'

1294. KIND HEART ★★
b.f. Red Ransom – Portorosa (Irish River)
March 6. Fourth foal. Half-sister to the fair two year old 1m all-weather winner Mardi (by Montjeu). The dam, a French 9.5f winner, is out of the Group 3 10.f Prix Cleopatre winner Garendare (by Vacarme). (B Haggas).

'A big, strong, solid filly with a good nature, she might come at two but you'd expect her to be a three year old really.'

1295. NIGHT OF FORTUNE ★★★
b.c. Key Of Luck – La Nuit Rose (Rainbow Quest)
April 16. Fifth foal. €55,000Y. Goffs Million. Half-brother to the Group 3 10f Winter Hill Stakes winner Tam Lin, to the quite useful 6f and 7f winner Finders Keepers (both by Selkirk) and the quite useful two year old 7f winner Finger Of Fate (by Machiavellian). The dam won over 7f at two years and was placed in both the French and Irish 1,000 Guineas. The second dam, Caerlina (by Caerleon), won the Group 1 10.5f Prix de Diane. (P J McSwiney – Osborne House).
'More precocious than his pedigree would indicate and he'll be running in June or July over six furlongs minimum.'

1296. PAMPERED KING USA) ★★★
b.c. Kingmambo – Last Second (Alzao)
March 21. Eighth foal. $325,000Y. Keeneland September. Blandford Bloodstock. Half-brother to the French 2,000 Guineas and US Grade 1 winner Aussie Rules (by Danehill), to the useful 7.5f (at two years) and listed 10f winner and US Grade 2 second Approach and the very useful two year old 8.5f winner and Group 1 Prix Marcel Boussac fourth Intrigued (both by Darshaan). The dam, winner of the 10f Nassau Stakes and the 10f Sun Chariot Stakes, is a half-sister to seven winners including the Moyglare Stud Stakes third Alouette (herself dam of the Group 1 winners Albanova and Alborada) and to the placed dam of the Group 1 winners Yesterday and Quarter Moon. The second dam, Alruccaba (by Crystal Palace), a quite useful two year old 6f winner, is out of a half-sister to the dams of Aliysa and Nishapour. (Faisal Salman).
'A small, solid colt he was retained by his breeder at the Sales. He comes from a family that could be anything, so he could surprise me and do well. He'll make a two year old, but being small we'll have to get on with him.'

1297. PASSKEY ★★
b.f. Medicean – Revival (Sadler's Wells)
March 15. Fourth foal. Half-sister to the quite useful Irish 8.5f winner Uva Fragola (by Nashwan) and to the 10f seller winner Danalova (by Groom Dancer). The dam, a quite useful 10f winner, is a half-sister to three winners including the Group 1 6f Nunthorpe Stakes winner and sire Pivotal. The second dam, Fearless Revival (by Cozzene), was a useful two year old 6f and 7f winner and was listed-placed over 10f at three years. (Cheveley Park Stud).
'*This filly will need a bit of time, she had a setback in the very early spring but she's back now. As a result she's a bit behind the others but I think she'll run in mid-season over seven furlongs and then a mile.*'

1298. PATRONNE ★★★ ♠
b.f. Domedriver – Pat Or Else (Alzao)
May 7. Eighth foal. Half-sister to the smart 2007 Irish two year old listed 7f winner Triskel (by Hawk Wing), to the fairly useful 7f and 1m winner Trafalgar Square (by King's Best), the quite useful two year old 10f winner Dumfries (by Selkirk), the quite useful 12f winner Saluem (by Salse) and the two year old 6f and 7f seller winner Run Lucy Run (by Risk Me). The dam is a placed half-sister to six winners including the Group 1 12f Prix Vermeille winner My Emma and the Group 1 St Leger and Group 1 Ascot Gold Cup winner Classic Cliché. The second dam, Pato (by High Top), a fairly useful two year old 7f and triple four year old 10f winner, is a sister to the very smart sprinter Crews Hill. (Miss K Rausing).
'*A small filly and a May foal but naturally quite precocious and she should be out in June. One would think she'd get better as she went on.*'

1299. POINT OF LIGHT ★★★
b.c. Pivotal – Lighthouse (Warning)
March 3. Fifth foal. 90,000Y. Tattersalls October 1. Highflyer Bloodstock. Half-brother to the very useful 7f and 1m winner Kehaar and to the fairly useful two year old 5f winner and listed placed All For Laura (both by Cadeaux Genereux). The dam, a fairly useful three year

old 8.3f winner, is a half-sister to four winners including the Group 1 Middle Park Stakes, Group 3 July Stakes and Group 3 Richmond Stakes winner First Trump. The second dam, Valika (by Valiyar), was placed three times from 1m to 12f at three years and is a half-sister to six winners including the high-class sprinter Mr Brooks. (Syndicate 2007).
'*He'd be a June/July type and he's a good-looking horse. With Pivotal's it depends on the individual – not the pedigree – as to how far they'll stay.*'

1300. RAPID RELEASE (CAN) ★★★
ch.c. Action This Day – Bail Money (St Jovite)
March 7. Second foal. €75,000Y. Goffs Million. The dam, a stakes-placed winner of six races in the USA, is a half-sister to seven winners. The second dam, Bailrullah (by Bailjumper), won the Grade 2 Diana Handicap and the Grade 3 Columbiana Handicap and is a half-sister to seven winners. (W E Sturt – Osborne House III).
'*An all-American pedigree, but there's plenty of turf form in there. He's quite a nice horse and he'll make a two year old at some point.*'

1301. ROCK RELIEF (IRE) ★★★
gr.c. Daylami – Sheer Bliss (Sadler's Wells)
February 17. Second foal. €200,000Y. Goffs Million. Half-brother to the unplaced 2007 two year old Sheer Bluff (by Indian Ridge). The dam, a fair two year old 1m winner, is a half-sister to nine winners including the Derby winner Oath and the triple Group 1 winner Pelder. The second dam, Sheer Audacity (by Troy), was placed twice in Italy and is closely related to the Ribblesdale Stakes winner and good broodmare Miss Petard. (S E Munir).
'*He's from a decent family, we trained the dam and she was decent as a two year old but didn't train on. This horse looks to be more scopey and so needs more time, so he won't run until September time but he might come to hand enough to make a show as a two year old over seven furlongs or so.*'

1302. ROYAL DIAMOND (IRE) ★★★
b.c. King's Best – Irresistible Jewel (Danehill)
February 9. Second foal. €70,000Y. Goffs

Million. Half-brother to the Irish two year old 7f winner and dual Group 1 placed Mad About You (by Indian Ridge). The dam won the Group 2 12f Ribblesdale Stakes and the Group 3 10f Blandford Stakes and is a half-sister to numerous winners including the listed 12f winner Diamond Trim and the useful Irish 1m winner Legal Jousting. The second dam, In Anticipation (by Sadler's Wells), won over 12f and 14f in Ireland. (E B Rimmer – Osborne House).

'He'll run earlier than you'd expect from his pedigree, simply because he was a difficult horse to break-in. He's much more together and behaves well now but I'll keep on top of him and I'll run him early. A normal horse of his type would have benefited from being trained more as a three year old prospect.'

1303. SPECIAL CUVEE ★★★
b.c. Diktat – Iris May
(Brief Truce)
February 23. Sixth foal. Half-brother to the useful dual 5f (at two years) and 1m winner and listed placed Joseph Henry (by Mujadil), to the quite useful two year old 5f winner Royal Engineer (by Royal Applause) and the fair two year old 7f all-weather winner Leonard Charles (by Best Of The Bests). The dam, a dual 5f winner, including at two years, is a half-sister to four winners including the very useful listed sprint winner Cathedral. The second dam, Choire Mhor (by Dominion), a useful winner of three races over 6f at two years, is a half-sister to six winners including the Group 3 Prix de la Jonchere winner Soft Currency and the listed winner Fawzi. both useful. (John Brown and Megan Dennis).

'I've only trained one out of the mare and he won a couple, called Leonard Charles. This is a big, strong horse with slackish pasterns and he may require some cut in the ground – or the all-weather. You'd think that the all-weather races, instead of being held predominantly during the wintertime, would be during the summer when racecourses can be too firm for some animals. But the 'powers that be' know as much about horses as I do about crèches for unmarried mothers!'

1304. STARRY SKY ★★★★
b.f. Oasis Dream – Succinct (Hector Protector)
April 10. The dam, a useful three year old listed 10f winner, is a half-sister to the fairly useful 7f and 1m winner Succession. The second dam, Pitcroy (by Unfuwain), a useful 10f winner, is a half-sister to eight winners including the very useful Group 3 7f Jersey Stakes winner Ardkinglass. (Dr C Wills).

'She's dip-backed and I've never had much luck with horses like that, but she moves nicely and comes from a tough family. We had the dam's half-sister Succession who won three races as a two year old. This filly isn't a beauty to look at but it's a family that does well.'

1305. VALID POINT (IRE) ★★
b.g. Val Royal – Ricadonna (Kris)
February 25. Third foal. 68,000Y. Tattersalls October 1. Half-brother to the French two year old listed 7.5f winner Iron Fist (by Desert Style) and to the Italian 1m winner of four races from 2 to four years Pavoncella (by Bachir). The dam is an unraced half-sister to four winners including the Group 2 Prix Robert Papin winner Greenlander. The second dam, Pripet (by Alleged), a quite useful 2m winner, is a sister to the 1,000 Guineas and Oaks winner Midway Lady and to the very useful 11.8f listed winner Capias. (W E Sturt – Osborne House).

'Basically a three year old type, he's been gelded and turned out, but he might mature enough to show something at two.'

1306. VEILED ★★★
b.f. Sadler's Wells – Evasive Quality
(Highest Honor)
May 17. First foal. The dam is an unraced half-sister to the Group 2 6f Cherry Hinton Stakes winner Spinola and the Group 3 1m winner Shot To Fame. The second dam, Exocet (by Deposit Ticket), a minor sprint winner in the USA, is a half-sister to five winners. (Cheveley Park Stud).

'A nicely-bred filly, it's a family I haven't had before now. She a jolly nice, attractive filly but a late foal and she'll want seven furlongs in August.'

1307. WATERGATE (IRE) ★★★★

gr.c. Verglas – Moy Water (Tirol)

April 26. Eighth foal. €60,000Y. Goffs Million.
Half-sister to the French listed sprint winner
Mona Em (by Catrail), to the three year old 7f
winner and Irish 2,000 Guineas fourth Maumee
(by Indian Ridge), the quite useful two year old
1m winner Kharish (by Desert Prince) and the
Irish three year old 8.5f winner Mandhoor (by
Flying Spur). The dam, an Irish 1m (at two years)
and 9f winner, is a half-sister to eight winners
including the very useful listed sprint winners
Bufalino and Maledetto. The second dam,
Croglin Water (by Monsanto), is an unplaced
half-sister to the smart sprinter Governor
General. (Charles C Walker – Osborne House III).
*'More precocious than you would have thought
with the pedigree and the look of him. He'll run
around July time over six furlongs plus.'*

MICHAEL QUINLAN

1308. GEMINI JIVE ★★★ ♠

ch.f. Namid – Pearl Bright (Kaldoun)

**March 30. Third foal. 28,000Y. Tattersalls
October 3. Not sold.** Half-sister to the useful
2007 two year old 6f winner and Group 2 6f Mill
Reef Stakes third Berbice (by Acclamation). The
dam, a quite useful two year old 7f winner, is a
half-sister to four winners. The second dam,
Coastal Jewel (by Kris), is an unraced half-sister
to five winners. (W P Flynn).
*'She should be ready for when the six furlong
races start and might then move up to seven.
She's done everything asked of her and her half-
brother Berbice was a good horse last year.'*

1309. SORREL RIDGE (IRE) ★★★★

ch.c. Namid – She Legged It (Cape Cross)

**March 31. First foal. €10,000Y (private sale).
Tattersalls Ireland.** The dam, placed once over
10f in Ireland. The second dam, Mrs Siddons
(by Royal Academy), was placed once over 7f at
two years and is a half-sister to five winners
including the Italian Group 3 winner Lear White.
*'He's done plenty of work, he's a nice, strong colt
and will suited by five and six furlongs. He'll be
racing in April, he's a nice, straightforward colt
and he'll win.'*

1310. VERY DISTINGUISHED ★★★

b.f. Diktat – Dignify (Rainbow Quest)

**May 8. Fourth foal. 26,000Y. Tattersalls
October 2. BBA (Ir.e)** Half-sister to the quite
useful 6f (at two years) and 1m winner of three
races Personify (by Zafonic). The dam won the
Group 3 1m Prix d'Aumale at two years and is a
half-sister to five winners. The second dam, Her
Ladyship (by Polish Precedent), a French listed
10.5f winner, was second in the Group 1 10.5f
Prix de Diane and is a half-sister to the Group 1
7f Prix de la Salamandre winner Lord of Men.
*'We like her a lot, we had the half-sister last year
but she had bad joints but this filly is totally
different. She's going to be very easy to train and
came from the Darley consignment.'*

1311. UNNAMED ★★

*b.f. One Cool Cat – Exultate Jubilate
(With Approval)*

**March 21. Third foal. 24,000Y. Tattersalls
October 2. Not sold.** The dam ran twice
unplaced in the USA and is a half-sister to eight
winners including the Group 3 Prix Quincey
winner Heraldiste and two French listed
winners. The second dam, Heiress (by Habitat),
is an unraced half-sister to the Group 1 Prix
Saint-Alary winner Saraca. (Mr R J Turner).
*'We like her a lot but she's not the best of movers.
If we can keep her sound she'll be alright.'*

1312. UNNAMED ★★★

b.f. Namid – Inspiring (Anabaa)

**March 10. Third foal. 32,000Y. Tattersalls
October 2. David McGreavy.** Half-sister to the
Group 3 5f and listed 6f winner Dixie Belle (by
Diktat) and to the fair 6f all-weather winner
Moon Bound (by Observatory). The dam is an
unraced half-sister to three minor winners. The
second dam, Mareha (by Cadeaux Genereux), a
fairly useful three year old 7f and 1m winner,
was listed-placed and is a half-sister to two
winners. (Burns Farm Racing).
*'Not dissimilar to her half-sister Dixie Belle in
many ways but just a touch narrower and
leggier. Not an early type but no buttons have
been pressed yet. A lovely filly.'*

1313. UNNAMED ★★★ ♠
ch.f. Bachelor Duke – Isadora Duncan
(Sadler's Wells)
May 2. Fifth foal. €6,500Y. Tattersalls Ireland.
D McGreavy Bloodstock. The dam is an
unraced half-sister to three minor winners. The
second dam, Leopardess (by Ela-Mana-Mou), is
a sister to a listed winner and a half-sister to the
Group 2 Queen Anne Stakes winner Alflora.
'Just losing her winter coat, she's coming along
and is a very nice filly. The dam is by Sadler's
Wells but she hasn't produced a winner yet. She's
not a five furlong horse but she'll hopefully start
at six furlongs before progressing to seven. She
hasn't put a foot wrong so far and she has a
lovely temperament.'

1314. UNNAMED ★★
b.c. Lemon Drop Kid – Tolltally Light
(Majestic Light)
May 7. Eighth foal. 29,000Y. Tattersalls October
2. David McGreavy. Half-brother to the fair 12f
winner Crimson Monarch (by Red Ransom) and
to three minor winners in the USA by Dixie Brass
(2) and Pay The Toll. The dam is a placed half-
sister to five winners including the dam of the
US Grade 1 winner Riskaverse. The second dam,
Toll Fee (by Topsider), a US stakes winner and
Grade 2 placed, is a half-sister to ten winners
including the US Grade 1 winners Christiecat
and Plugged Nickle. (P C Ashmore).
'He'll be ready for the mid-summer, he's done
well and he has the right attitude. A seven
furlong type two year old, he hasn't come to
himself yet.'

KEVIN RYAN
1315. AFRICAN SKIES ★★★
b.f. Johannesburg – Rababah (Woodman)
February 4. Third foal. 52,000Y. Tattersalls
October 1. Stephen Hillen. The dam is an
unraced half-sister to two winners including the
very useful two year old listed 1m winner
Nakheel. The second dam, Matiya (by Alzao), a
smart winner of the Irish 1,000 Guineas winner
and second in the 1,000 Guineas, is a half-sister
to eight winners.

1316. APACHE RIDGE (IRE) ★★★
ch.c. Indian Ridge – Seraphina (Pips Pride)
March 10. 90,000Y. Milan. Anthony Stroud.
The dam, a useful two year old 6f winner, was
second in the Group 2 Lowther Stakes and is a
sister to one winner and a half-sister to the
smart 6f (at two years) and listed 8.3f winner
Army Of Angels, the fairly useful two year old
6f winner Alovera and the fairly useful Irish 5f
winner Alegranza. The second dam, Angelic
Sounds (by The Noble Player), a minor two year
old 5f winner, is a half-sister to six winners
including the Group 1 Prix de la Foret winner
Mount Abu.

**1317. CARNABY
HAGGERSTON (IRE)** ★★★ ♠
gr.c. Invincible Spirit – Romanylei
(Blues Traveller)
February 6. Third foal. €260,000foal. Goffs Foal
Sales. Rathmore Stud. Half-brother to the quite
useful 2007 7f and 1m winner Den's Gift (by City
On A Hill) and to the fair Irish 12f winner
Certainlei (by Definite Article). The dam, an Irish
5f (at two years) and 6f winner, is a half-sister to
three winners here and abroad. The second
dam, Krayyalei (by Krayyan), a fairly useful Irish
6f and 6.5f winner, is a half-sister to four
winners. (Mr & Mrs Duncan Davidson)

1318. DOUGIE PEEL ★★★
b.c. Diktat – Omission (Green Desert)
February 28. First foal. 36,000Y. Doncaster St
Leger. McKeever St Lawrence. The dam is an
unraced half-sister to the two year old Group 3
1m Prix Thomas Bryon winner and Group 2 10f
UAE Derby second Songlark, to the Dubai
Group 3 and Irish 1m listed winner Blatant, the
useful 7f and 1m winner Nabonassar, the useful
7f (at two years) and 1m winner Asad and the
useful two year old 7f winner Shawanni. The
second dam, Negligent (by Ahonoora), a
champion two year old filly, won the 7f Rockfel
Stakes at two years and was third in the 1,000
Guineas. She is a sister to the dual two year old
6f winner Ala Mahlik and a half-sister to the
Queen Alexandra Stakes winner Ala Hounak. (R
Peel).

1319. DRACHENFELS ★★★
b.c. Mind Games – Its Another Gift
(Primo Dominie)
April 13. Fifth foal. 52,000Y. Tattersalls October 2. Axel Donnerstag. Brother to the two year old listed-placed 5f winner Gifted Gamble and half-brother to the 2007 two year old 6f winner and Group 3 Princess Margaret Stakes second Reel Gift (by Reel Buddy) and the two year old listed-placed 5f winner Scented Present (by Foxhound) – all fairly useful. The dam, a modest sprint placed maiden, is a half-sister to two winners. The second dam, Margaret's Gift (by Beveled), won four races from 2 to four years, was listed placed and is a half-sister to four winners.

1320. EL GUEVARA (IRE) ★★
b.c. Spartacus – Reddish Creek (Mt Livermore)
February 23. Second foal. 24,000Y. Tattersalls October 2. Stephen Hillen. The dam, a minor two year old winner in Italy, is a half-sister to seven winners including the US stakes winner Nurse Goodbody. The second dam, Nonesuch Bay (by Mill Reef), was second in the Group 3 Hoover Fillies Mile and is a half-sister to six winners. (S J Carr).

1321. ESPRIT DE MIDAS ★★★
b.c. Namid – Spritzeria (Bigstone)
February 19. Second live foal. 100,000Y. Tattersalls October 1. Stephen Hillen. The dam, a quite useful two year old 6f winner, is a half-sister to two winners including the smart two year old 6f winner and Group 1 1m Racing Post Trophy third Henrik. The second dam, Clincher Club (by Polish Patriot), a fair 5f (at two years) and 7.5f winner, is a half-sister to seven winners. (Joseph Ogden, J Hanson, John Ogden).

1322. MAGGIE LOU (IRE) ★★★
b.f. Red Ransom – Triomphale (Nureyev)
March 19. Fifth foal. 77,000Y. Tattersalls October 1. Stephen Hillen. Half-sister to the very useful 6f listed winner of four races (including at two years) One Putra (by Indian Ridge), to the quite useful 10f winner Rondelet (by Bering) and the moderate 6f winner

Lambency (by Daylami). The dam, a French two year old 6f winner, is a half-sister to three winners including the dual US stakes winner and Grade 2 placed Tresoriere. The second dam, Time Deposit (by Halo), is an unraced half-sister to four winners including the Group 2 Richmond Stakes winner Gallant Special. (Highbank Syndicate).

1323. MAJUBA (USA) ★★★
b.c. Johannesburg – Rumored
(Royal Academy)
April 25. Third foal. $110,000Y. Keeneland September. Stephen Hillen. Half-brother to the US stakes-placed winner Preferred Yield (by High Yield). The dam is a placed daughter of the Italian Oaks winner and Group 1 Moyglare Stud Stakes second Bright Generation (by Rainbow Quest). (Hambleton Racing Ltd V).

1324. MISS SCARLET ★★★
b.f. Red Ransom – Give Warning (Warning)
April 9. Seventh foal. €31,000Y. Tattersalls Ireland. Stephen Hillen. Half-sister to the quite useful 9f all-weather winner of seven races Just Bond (by Namid), to the Italian two year old winner Grass King and a winner in Germany (both by Temporal). The dam, a two year old winner in Germany, is a sister to the very smart Group 2 1m Prix du Rond-Point, Group 2 7f Challenge Stakes and Group 3 7f Hungerford Stakes winner Decorated Hero and a half-sister to four winners. The second dam, Bequeath (by Lyphard), a minor French three year old 9f winner, is a half-sister to three winners.

1325. RIEVAULX WORLD ★★
b.c. Compton Place – Adhaaba (Dayjur)
March 4. Second foal. 32,000Y. Doncaster St Leger. Stephen Hillen. Half-brother to the fair 2007 two year old 7f placed Advertisement (by Averti). The dam, placed once at two years, is a half-sister to three winners. The second dam, Girchoop (by Storm Cat), is an unraced sister to the useful 5f and 6f listed winner and Group 3 Criterion Stakes second Elrafa Ah (herself dam of the Group 1 Dewhurst Stakes winner Mujahid).

1326. SHIFTING GOLD (IRE) ★★★
b.c. Night Shift – Gold Bust (Nashwan)
March 23. Fifth foal. 26,000Y. Doncaster St Leger. Stephen Hillen. Half-brother to the French 10f winner Machinale (by Kingmambo). The dam, a 10f winner in France, is a half-sister to two winners including the Group 1 Coronation Stakes and Group 1 Prix Marcel Boussac winner Gold Splash. The second dam, Riviere d'Or (by Lyphard), won the Group 1 10f Prix Saint-Alary, is closely related to the Group 3 winner Chercheur d'Or and the French 2,000 Guineas second Goldneyev.

1327. SWEET SMILE (IRE) ★★★
b.c. Catcher In The Rye – Quivala
(Thunder Gulch)
March 9. Second foal. Brother to the quite useful 2007 two year old 5f winner Kersaint. The dam won over 1m in France at three years on her only start and is out of the smart French Group 2 placed Leonila (by Caerleon), herself a sister to the Prix de Diane winner Caerlina.

1328. TITUS ANDRONICUS (IRE) ★★★
b.c. Danetime – Scarlet Empress
(Second Empire)
January 27. First foal. €50,000Y. Tattersalls Ireland. Stephen Hillen. The dam, a fair two year old 6f winner, is out of the unraced Daltak (by Night Shift), herself a half-sister to seven winners including the Group 1 Nunthorpe Stakes winner Ya Malak.

1329. UNDAUNTED AFFAIR (IRE) ★★★
ch.f. Spartacus – Party Bag
(Cadeaux Genereux)
February 16. First foal. 47,000Y. Doncaster St Leger. Stephen Hillen. The dam is an unraced half-sister to two winners including the French listed winner Winter Fashion. The second dam, Ontherebound (by Dayjur), won once at two years and is a half-sister to seven winners including the US Grade 1 winners Thirty Six Red and Corrazona.

1330. UNION ISLAND (IRE) ★★
b.c. Rock Of Gibraltar – Daftiyna (Darshaan)
May 7. Tenth foal. €70,000Y. Goffs Million. Hugo Merry. Half-brother to the useful 1m, 10.3f and subsequent German listed winner Golden Island (by Selkirk), to the fairly useful 9f winner Gandor (by Cape Cross), the quite useful dual 10f winner Golden Grimshaw (by Grand Lodge) and the fair two year old 8.3f winner Oakley Heffert (by Titus Livius). The dam was placed twice at up to 9f in Ireland and is a half-sister to three winners. The second dam, Dafayna (by Habitat), was a smart winner of the Group 3 Cork and Orrery Stakes and was placed in the July Cup and the Vernons Sprint Cup. She is a half-sister to the 2,000 Guineas winner Doyoun.

1331. WEE GIANT ★★★
ch.c. Giant's Causeway – Christmas In Aiken
(Affirmed)
May 9. Ninth foal. $140,000Y. Keeneland September. Stephen Hillen. Closely related to a minor winner in Japan by Storm Cat and half-sister to five winners including the triple Grade 1 winner Harlan's Holiday. The dam, a minor dual three year old winner in the USA, is a half-sister to five winners including the stakes-placed Dr Holiday (by Kayrawan) and Boxcar Cat (by Railway Cat). The second dam, Dowager (by Honest Pleasure), is an unplaced half-sister to the Group 2 Blandford Stakes winner Lords. (Errigal Racing).

1332. UNNAMED ★★
b.f. Montjeu – Almond Mousse
(Exit To Nowhere)
January 22. First foal. €110,000Y. Tattersalls Ireland. Stephen Hillen. The dam, a French 1m listed and 11f winner, was third in the Group 2 Sun Chariot Stakes and is a half-sister to two winners. The second dam, Missy Dancer (by Shareef Dancer), won at three years in Switzerland and is a half-sister to seven winners.

1334. UNNAMED ★★★
b.c. Johannesburg – Bello Cielo
(Conquistador Cielo)
February 18. Fifth foal. $410,000Y. Keeneland September. Stephen Hillen. Half-brother to three winners including the minor US stakes

winner Ayla Bella (by Touch Gold) and a minor winner by Thunder Gulch. The dam, a US Grade 1 winner of three races, is a half-sister to 3 minor winners. The second dam, Double Advantage (by Nodouble), a minor winner and stakes-placed in the USA, is a half-sister to nine winners.

1335. UNNAMED ★★★
ch.f. Spinning World – High Spot (Shirley Heights)
January 26. Fourth foal. €90,000Y. Goffs Million. Stephen Hillen. Half-sister to the very useful 2007 two year old 6f winner and Group 2 7f Rockfel Stakes second Missit (by Orpen) and to the quite useful Irish two year old 7f winner Night Sphere (by Night Shift). The dam was placed over middle-distances and is a half-sister to three winners including the listed-placed Allergy. The second dam, Rash Gift (by Cadeaux Genereux), is a placed half-sister to seven winners. (Highbank Syndicate)

1336. UNNAMED ★★★
b.g. Fraam – Medina de Rioseco (Puissance)
May 11. Fifth foal. 25,000Y. Doncaster St Leger. Stephen Hillen. Brother to the modest three year old 6f all-weather winner Crown Of Medina and half-brother to the useful two year old 6f winner and Group 3 Sirenia Stakes third We'll Confer (by Piccolo). The dam, placed 3 times at two years, is a half-sister to five winners including the quite useful two year old dual 5f winner Bond Domingo. The second dam, Antonia's Folly (by Music Boy), a modest two year old 5f winner, stayed 6f and is a half-sister to two minor winners. (K Shannon)

1337. UNNAMED ★★
ch.f. Lemon Drop Kid – Radu Cool (Carnivalay)
January 25. Seventh foal. $80,000Y. Keeneland September. Stephen Hillen. Half-sister to three winners including minor winners in Japan and the USA by Gone West and Charismatic. The dam, a winner of nine races including the Grade 2 Chula Vista Handicap in the USA, is a half-sister to two winners. The second dam, Purify (by Fappiano), a minor US winner at three and

four years, is a half-sister to four winners including the high-class broodmare Morning Devotion. (K Lee & L M Rutherford)

1338. UNNAMED ★★★
br.f. Hawk Wing – Ruby Affair (Night Shift)
March 13. Sixth foal. 55,000Y. Tattersalls October 2. Stephen Hillen. Half-sister to the useful 2007 two year old 6f winner Hammadi (by Red Ransom), to the very useful 6f (including at two years) and 6.5f winner Khabfair (by Intikhab) and the quite useful two year old 6f all-weather winner Frances Cadell (by Cadeaux Genereux). The dam, a modest 7f placed three year old, is a half-sister to the 2,000 Guineas winner Island Sands. The second dam, Tiavanita (by J O Tobin), is a half-sister to eight winners including the Group 2 Great Voltigeur Stakes winner Corrupt. (Malih L Al Basti)

DAVID SIMCOCK
1339. BRENIN TARAN ★★★
gr.c. Lujain – Silver Chime (Robellino)
April 26. First foal. 800gns two year old. Tattersalls February Horses in Training. Not sold. The dam, a modest dual 6f winner at three and four years, is a half-sister to one winner. The second dam, Silver Charm (by Dashing Blade) is an unraced full or half-sister to six winners.
'A sharp colt, he'll be running from mid-April onwards and he goes nicely. He's a very natural horse and I'm very pleased with him. I trained the mare and she was my first winner.'
TRAINER'S BARGAIN BUY

1340. CRUSH ★★★
b.c. Kheleyf – Premier Amour (Salmon Leap)
April 7. Fourteenth foal. 18,000Y. Tattersalls October 3. Blandford Bloodstock. Half-brother to six winners in Germany by Surumu, Kendor, Lando, Kings Lake, Master Willie and Polar Falcon. The dam, a German Group 3 winner, is a half-sister to nine winners including the French listed winner Fleur d'Oranger and the dam of the Grade 1 Hollywood Gold Cup winner Running Flame. The second dam, Flamme d'Amour (by Gift Card), won over the jumps in France and is a half-sister to four winners

including the Group 3 Prix du Calvados winner and good broodmare Zolinana.

'A nice horse and he was a bargain. He's sharp, has a lovely action and a good brain. He's got a touch of a sore shin at the moment, which surprised me slightly for what I'd done with him. But he's done everything well and he'll be racing over six furlongs in mid-May.'

1341. DOWNSTREAM ★★★

b.f. Marju – Sister Moonshine (Piccolo).
January 21. First foal. The dam won over 5f and 6f in France and was third in the Group 3 5f Prix du Bois (all at two years). The second dam, Cootamindra (by Double Bed), won over 1m.

'A home-bred by Major Wyatt, she's a nice filly and the dam actually won in March as a two year old in France. A very likeable, attractive filly that should be out by the beginning of June.'

1342. DUBAI LEGEND ★★★

ch.f. Cadeaux Genereux – Royal Future (Royal Academy)
May 2. Ninth foal. 34,000Y. Tattersalls October 1. Rabbah Bloodstock. Half-sister to the modest 9f to 12f winner They All Laughed (by Zafonic), to the German winner of four races and listed-placed Royal Fire (by Bin Ajwaad), the German winners Royal Hero (by Slip Anchor) and Royal Flower (at two years, by Pursuit Of Love) and a two year old winner in Slovakia by Dashing Blade. The dam is an unraced half-sister to six winners including the high-class Group 1 1m Queen Elizabeth II Stakes winner Where Or When and the smart 10f and 12f winner and Group 1 St Leger fourth All The Way. The second dam, Future Past (by Super Concorde), a winner of four races at up to 9f in the USA, is a half-sister to eight winners. (Ahmad Al Shaikh).

'She looks very nice, she's done plenty and we'd like to think she'll be a six/seven furlong horse. She's done everything right and shows a fair amount of natural speed. I'm very happy with her and she's just starting to look very well.'

1343. SPIRIT OF DUBAI (IRE) ★★★

b.f. Cape Cross – Questina (Rainbow Quest)
April 5. Seventh foal. 85,000Y. Tattersalls

October 1. Rabbah Bloodstock. Half-sister to the Group 3 10f Prix Corrida and Group 3 10.5f Prix de Flore winner Trumbaka (by In The Wings) and to the French listed winner Arctic Hunt (by Bering). The dam won twice at three years in France and is a half-sister to five winners. The second dam, Soviet Squaw (by Nureyev), won once at three years in France and is a full or half-sister to eight winners including the Italian Group 1 winner Antheus. (Ahmad Al Shaikh).

'A very classy filly, but she's very much one for the future. We haven't done a lot with her but she has a massive amount of quality about her and the mare's produced a couple of decent horses. We like her a lot and she'd be a horse for August onwards over seven furlongs.'

1344. UNNAMED ★★

b.c. Oasis Dream – Egoli (Seeking The Gold)
February 27. Fifth foal. 35,000Y. Tattersalls October 3. Rabbah Bloodstock. Half-brother to the fairly useful 1m (at two years) to 10f winner of five races Luis Melendez (by Horse Chestnut). The dam, a fairly useful 7f winner here, later won over 9f in the USA and is a half-sister to five winners including the French 1,000 Guineas winner Rose Gypsy. The second dam, Krisalya (by Kris), a fairly useful 10.4f winner, is a half-sister to 12 winners including the high-class Group 1 9.3f Prix d'Ispahan winner Sasuru and the high-class Challenge Stakes and Jersey Stakes winner Sally Rous. (Saif Misfer).

'A nice colt, he's done enough work but he's gone slightly weak in the last month, he shows a very natural action and for a relatively inexpensive horse he could be quite nice in the second half of the season.'

1345. UNNAMED ★★★

b.br.f. Harlan's Holiday – Henderson Band (Chimes Band)
March 22. Fifth foal. $120,000Y. Keeneland September. Rabbah Bloodstock. Half-sister to the US Grade 1 Oak Leaf Breeders Cup Stakes winner Cash Included (by Include). The dam is an unraced half-sister to four winners including the French dual Group 2 winner and French

Derby second Lord Flasheart. The second dam, Miss Henderson Co (by Silver Hawk), a minor winner of two races in the USA, is a sister to the Delaware Oaks winner Like A Hawk and a half-sister to six winners including the US dual Grade 1 winner By Land By Sea (herself dam of the Group 3 Rose Of Lancaster Stakes winner Fahal). (Saeed Misleh).

'Probably one of my sharpest two year old's, she didn't come in until December because she'd been given a kick in America and was recuperating. A five/six furlong filly, she's very tough and genuine and is a filly that shows plenty. I quite like her.'

1346. UNNAMED ★★★

br.f. Dubai Destination – In Full Cry
(Seattle Slew)
May 1. Twelfth foal. 55,000Y. Tattersalls October 1. Rabbah Bloodstock. Half-sister to the fairly useful 6f (at two years) and 7f winner Saville Row (by Mozart), to the US stakes-placed winner of three races Private Seductress (by Private Account and herself dam of the Italian Oaks winner Menhoubah) and to two minor winners by Lammtarra and Easy Goer. The dam, a winner of two races in the USA and second in the Grade 2 6f Adirondack Stakes, is a half-sister to six winners including the top-class miler Posse and the Group/Grade three winners Late As Usual and Hot Rodder. The second dam, In Hot Pursuit (by Bold Ruler), a top two year old filly in the USA, is a half-sister to nine winners including the top-class broodmare Bold Example. (Sultan Ali).

'Potentially my nicest two year old filly. She's got a lovely action and a lot of natural speed. She's ready to kick on with now and she should be racing in May in one of the first six furlong maidens. A smart filly.'

1347. UNNAMED ★★

b.c. Dubai Destination – Lady Bankes (Alzao)
March 6. Eighth foal. 52,000Y. Tattersalls October 1. Rabbah Bloodstock. Half-brother to the fairly useful 5f (at two years) and 6f winner Danzili Bay (by Dansili) and to the quite useful 6f (at two years) to 1m winner of three races

Moten Swing (by Kris). The dam, a fair three year old 10f winner, is a half-sister to five winners including the Group 3 Prestige Stakes winner Circle Of Gold and to the listed Rose Bowl Stakes winner Crystal Crossing. The second dam, Never So Fair (by Never So Bold), is an unplaced half-sister to nine winners including the Queen Mary Stakes winner Amaranda and the Nell Gwyn Stakes winner Favoridge. (Saif Ali & Saeed H Altayer).

'A horse that's just grown and grown. He's very natural and has shown enough speed but he's gone slightly weak and I'll give him all the time he needs.'

1348. UNNAMED ★★★

ch.c. Singspiel – Lady Zonda (Lion Cavern)
March 29. Third foal. 70,000Y. Tattersalls October 1. E Vaughan. Half-brother to the 2007 two year old 6f winner and listed 6f second May Meeting (by Diktat). The dam, a fairly useful 7f and 1m winner, is a half-sister to six winners. The second dam, Zonda (by Fabulous Dancer), was a useful 5f to 8.5f winner. (Mohammed Al Nabouda).

'A very attractive colt. He was slightly headstrong when he was broken but he's very natural and the whole family seem to be seven furlong/milers. He's a colt I like and although on pedigree he'd be one for the back-end he actually shows natural speed now.'

1349. UNNAMED ★★★

b.br.f. Gone West – Magicalmysterycat
(Storm Cat)
March 7. Fifth foal. $140,000Y. Keeneland September. Rabbah Bloodstock. Half-brother to the minor US three year old winners I'm A Caution and Codasco (both by A P Indy). The dam won the Grade 2 Landaluce Stakes and the Grade 2 Schuylerville Stakes and is a half-sister to three winners. The second dam, Nannerl (by Valid Appeal), won the Grade 2 Distaff Handicap and the Grade 2 Bed O'Roses Handicap and was Grade 1 placed. (Dr Ali Ridha).

'An attractive filly, she hasn't done a great deal and isn't particularly precocious, but she shows all the right signs. Quite a nice filly.'

1350. UNNAMED ★★★
ch.c. King's Best – Needles And Pins (Fasliyev)
**May 2. First foal. 37,000Y. Doncaster St Leger.
M Abdullah.** The dam, a useful two year old
listed 5.2f winner and second in the Group 3
5.5f Prix d'Arenburg, is a half-sister to one
winner. The second dam, Fairy Contessa (by
Fairy King), is a 6f placed half-sister to five
winners including River Falls, a winner of three
races including the Group 2 6f Gimcrack Stakes
and third in the Group 1 Middle Park Stakes.
*'A precocious colt, he'll be one of my first two-
year-old runners and he shows natural speed.
The mare was quick herself and I don't think she
really got beyond six furlongs. He's due to work
soon and he's a very likeable horse. Considering
that some King's Best horses can be a bit
temperamental and the mare was an absolute
cow this colt is actually well behaved!'*

1351. UNNAMED ★★★★
*ch.f. Refuse To Bend – Oulianovsk
(Peintre Celebre)*
**January 14. First foal. 45,000Y. Tattersalls
October 1. Rabbah Bloodstock.** The dam, a
minor three year old winner in France, is a half-
sister to three winners including the French
listed winner Otaiti (herself dam of the Group 2
winner Ostankino. The second dam, Ode (by
Lord Avie), winner of the Group 2 Grand Prix
d'Evry and Grade 1 placed 3 times in France and
the USA, is a half-sister to six winners. (Dr Ali
Ridha).
*'A filly I like a lot, she has a lot of quality and
shows a lot of natural speed. Potentially a seven
furlong filly, she's very mature and I have a lot of
time for her.'*

1352. UNNAMED ★★★
*b.f. Oasis Dream – Royal Alchemist
(Royal Academy)*
**April 6. Second foal. 60,000Y. Tattersalls
October 1. Rabbah Bloodstock.** Half-sister to
Prevailing Wind (by Gone West), placed fourth
over 6f on his only start at two years in 2007.
The dam, placed once at three years in the USA,
is a half-sister to four winners including the
Grade 1 9.5f Beverly D Stakes and the Grade 2

Wilshire Handicap winner Fire The Groom (herself dam of the dual Group 1 winner Stravinsky)
and the Group 1 6f Vernons Sprint Cup winner
Dowsing. The second dam, Prospector's Fire (by
Mr Prospector), is a placed half-sister to 11
winners including the Grade 1 winner Royal
And Regal. (Dr Ali Ridha).
*'A filly with lot of quality, she threw a splint early
on so we didn't do a lot with her but she's
starting to catch up now. She has a good action
and is a good size. She's a filly I like.'*

1353. UNNAMED ★★
b.c. Tiger Hill – Sagamartha (Rainbow Quest)
**April 13. Third foal. €140,000Y. Goffs Million.
Blandford Bloodstock.** Half-brother to the
minor French 10f (at two years) and 12f winner
Sahara Lady (by Lomitas). The dam, a minor
French three year old winner, is a half-sister to
four winners including the Group 2 Lowther
Stakes and Group 2 Queen Mary Stakes winner
Flashy Wings. The second dam, Lovealoch (by
Lomond), a very useful 7f (at two years) and 9f
winner here and placed in the Group 2
Falmouth Stakes and the Group 2 Premio Lydia
Tesio, subsequently won once in the USA and is
a half-sister to seven winners. (Abduallah Saeed
Belhab).
*'He's not over-big, he has a middle-distance
pedigree but he's done enough work already
considering. I'm easing off him, he's our only
Derby entry and I think he'll make up into a nice
middle-distance horse next year.'*

1354. UNNAMED ★★★
b.br.f. Singspiel – Shepherd's Moon (Silver Hawk)
**January 30. Seventh foal. $85,000Y. Keeneland
September. Rabbah Bloodstock.** Half-sister to
the US winner and Grade 2 placed Deed I Do
(by Alydeed) and to minor US winners by
Carson City, Maria's Mon and Golden Gear. The
dam is an unplaced half-sister to the US dual
Grade 3 winner Raja's Revenge. The second
dam, Look North (by Northern Dancer), is a
placed half-sister to the US Grade 1 winner
Trumpet's Blare. (Dr Ali Ridha).
*'A very natural filly and she shows far more
speed than the pedigree would suggest. Despite*

that I'll take my time with her and I think she'll be a nice filly from August onwards over seven furlongs.'

1355. UNNAMED ★★★★
b.c. King's Best – Tegwen (Nijinsky)
April 15. Ninth living foal. 90,000Y. Tattersalls October 1. Mohammed Moubarak. Half-brother to the Group 1 Fillies Mile and Group 3 May Hill Stakes winner Teggiano (by Mujtahid), to the fairly useful 9.4f all-weather winner Halawellfin Hala (by Kris), the fairly useful 9f to 15f winner Bronwen (by King's Best), the quite useful 10f winner Rio de Jumeirah (by Seeking The Gold), the fair 14f winner Tegyra (by Trempolino) and the French three year old winner Welsh Motto (by Mtoto). The dam, a quite useful 10f winner, is a half-sister to four winners including two US stakes-placed winners. The second dam, Beautiful Aly (by Alydar), is an unraced half-sister to five winners including the US Grade 1 winner Jeanne Jones. (Abdullah Saeed Belhab).
'The nicest colt I've got, he's got an awful lot of quality about him, he's very, very natural and does everything right. He shows a tremendous amount of speed and is from a very good family. A very likeable, mature, attractive horse.'

BRYAN SMART
1356. LOCK 'N' LOAD (IRE) ★★★
b.f. Johannesburg – Margay
(Irish River)
February 22. Third foal. €85,000Y. Tattersalls Ireland. Paul Mason. Half-sister to the 2007 French 5f placed two year old Pull The Plug (by Pulpit) and to a minor three year old winner in the USA by Hennessy. The dam, an Irish two year old 7f winner, was second in the Group 2 German 1,000 Guineas and is a half-sister to three winners. The second dam, Almarai (by Vaguely Noble), is a placed half-sister to five winners including the US Grade 1 winner Buckhar.

1357. MYTHICISM ★★★
b.f. Oasis Dream – Romantic Myth
(Mind Games)
March 23. Fourth foal. 40,000Y. Doncaster St Leger. McKeever St Lawrence. Half-sister to two placed two year old's by Primo Valentino and Observatory. The dam won three races at two years including the Group 3 5f Queen Mary Stakes and is a half-sister to 5 sprint winners including Romantic Liason – also winner of the Queen Mary. The second dam, My First Romance (by Danehill), ran twice unplaced and is a full or half-sister to six minor winners here and abroad.

1358. PRIME CLASSIQUE (USA) ★★
b.f. Elusive Quality – Via Borghese
(Seattle Dancer)
February 6. Tenth foal. €80,000Y. Goffs Million. Prime Equestrian. Closely related to the fairly useful two year old 6f winner Venetian Pride and the quite useful 7f winner Pietro Siena (both by Gone West) and to two minor two year old winners in Japan and the USA (both by Seeking The Gold). The dam, a winner of 11 races in Ireland and the USA including the Grade 2 9f Diana Handicap and the Group 3 1m Desmond Stakes, is a half-sister to the Grade 2 American Handicap winner El Angelo, the Group 2 Premio Ribot winner Miswaki Tern and the Group 3 Prix du Bois winner Porto Varas. The second dam, Angela Serra (by Arctic Tern), won the Group 2 12f Premio Legnano.

1359. PRIME ELUSE (USA) ★★★
b.f. Tale Of The Cat – Out Of Sync
(Out Of Place)
April 9. Third foal. €105,000Y. Goffs Million. Prime Equestrian. Half-sister to the minor US winner at two and three years Ballacolla (by Street Cry). The dam, a US winner and second in the Group 1 Frizette Stakes, is a half-sister to four winners. The second dam, Demodee (by El Asesor), won in Argentina and was Grade 3 placed and is a half-sister to three winners.

1360. PRIME MOOD (IRE) ★★★
ch.c. Choisir – There With Me (Distant View)
March 27. Second foal. €115,000Y. Goffs Million. Prime Equestrian. Half-brother to the fairly useful two year old triple 5f winner and

listed placed Give Me The Night (by Night Shift). The dam, a 6f winner at four years, is a half-sister to seven winners. The second dam, Breeze Lass (by It's Freezing), a minor winner in the USA, is a half-sister to seven winners.

1361. QUATERMAIN ★★★
ch.c. Peintre Celebre – Fancy Lady
(Cadeaux Genereux)
March 8. Second foal. €100,000Y. Goffs Million. Prime Equestrian. Half-brother to the quite useful 2007 two year old 6f winner Sam's Cross (by Cape Cross). The dam, a useful two year old dual 6f winner, is a half-sister to two winners including the useful two year old 5f and 7f winner Asia Winds. The second dam, Ascot Cyclone (by Rahy), a fairly useful 5.7f (at two years) and 7f winner, is a half-sister to 11 winners including the two year old 6f winner and Group 1 7f Prix de la Salamandre second Bin Nashwan and the US Grade 2 winner Magellan.

1362. VERINCO ★★★
b.c. Bahamian Bounty – Dark Eyed Lady
(Exhibitioner)
March 5. Eighth foal. €50,000Y. Tattersalls Ireland. Prime Equestrian. Half-brother to the fair 8.5f winner Leptis Magna (by Danehill Dancer), to the fair two year old dual 5f and subsequent minor US stakes winner Green Eyed Lady (by Greensmith), the quite useful two year old 5f winner Oh So Dusty, the modest dual 6f winner Piccleyes (both by Piccolo), the quite useful two year old 7.5f winner Bridge Place (by Polar Falcon) and the two year old 6f all-weather winner Vision Of Dreams (by Efisio). The dam, a quite useful two year old 5f and 6f winner, is out of the minor 6f winner of six races Tribal Eye (by Tribal Chief)

1363. VOVEEN (IRE) ★★★
ch.f. Exceed And Excel – Princess Nutley
(Mujtahid)
April 5. Third foal. €50,000Y. Goffs Million. Prime Equestrian. The dam, an Irish two year old 6f winner, was listed-placed 3 times and is a half-sister to the Irish listed 7f winner and Group

3 7f Athasi Stakes third Bon Expresso. The second dam, Queen Leonor (by Caerleon), won three races at four years in France and was listed-placed and is a half-sister to three minor winners.

1364. UNNAMED ★★★
b.c. Haafhd – Annapurna (Brief Truce)
January 27. Fourth foal. 100,000Y. Tattersalls October 1. Anthony Stroud. Half-brother to the quite useful dual 10f and subsequent minor US stakes winner Solva (by Singspiel) and to the fair 6f (at two years) and 1m winner Aberdovey (by Mister Baileys). The dam, a useful 7f winner (at two years) and 9f listed placed, is a half-sister to three winners including the very useful two year old Group 3 7f Rockfel Stakes and listed 7f winner Name Of Love. The second dam, National Ballet (by Shareef Dancer), is an unraced half-sister to seven winners including the listed winners Broken Wave, Guarde Royale, Clifton Chapel and Saxon Maid.

1365. UNNAMED ★★★
b.c. Refuse To Bend – Bush Cat (Kingmambo)
March 30. Second foal. 50,000Y. Tattersalls October 2. McKeever St Lawrence. Half-brother to the quite useful 2007 two year old 1m winner Meer Kat (by Red Ransom). The dam, a quite useful two year old 7f winner, is a half-sister to two winners. The second dam, Arbusha (by Danzig), won the listed 1m Schwarzgold Rennen and is a sister to the Group 2 6f Goldene Peitsche winner Nicholas and a half-sister to nine winners.

1366. UNNAMED ★★★
b.f. Exceed And Excel – Cefira (Distant View)
February 16. First foal. 50,000Y. Tattersalls October 3. McKeever St Lawrence. The dam, a modest three year old 6f winner, is a half-sister to four winners including Abou Zouz (Group 2 Gimcrack Stakes). The second dam, Bold Jessie (by Never So Bold), an Irish two year old listed winner, is a half-sister to the Group two winners Prince Sabo and Millyant.

1367. UNNAMED ★★
b.f. Red Ransom – String Quartet
(Sadler's Wells)
March 20. Fifth foal. 110,000Y. Tattersalls
October 1. Anthony Stroud. Half-sister to the
smart 1m winner (at two years) and Group 2 12f
Princess Of Wales's Stakes second Shahin (by
Kingmambo). The dam, a 12.5f listed winner in
France and third in the Group 3 Lancashire
Oaks, is a sister to the Irish listed 10f winner
Casey Tibbs and a half-sister to five winners. The
second dam, Fleur Royale (by Mill Reef), won
the Group 2 Pretty Polly Stakes, was second in
the Irish Oaks and is a half-sister to four winners.

1368. UNNAMED ★★★
b.c. Dr Fong – Trick (Shirley Heights)
March 13. Eighth foal. 70,000Y. Tattersalls
October 2. Anthony Stroud. Half-brother to the
fairly useful two year old 6f winner and 1m
listed-placed White Rabbit (by Zilzal), to the
quite useful 6f (at two years) to 11.8f winner
Cap Ferrat (by Robellino), the fair 14f winner
Onyergo (by Polish Precedent) and the modest
two year old 6f winner Shinner (by Charnwood
Forest). The dam, a fair 10f winner, is a half-sister
to six winners. The second dam, Hocus (by High
Top), a quite useful three year old 7f winner, is a
half-sister to ten winners including the Group 1
5f Flying Childers and Group 1 6f Middle Park
Stakes winner Hittite Glory.

TOMMY STACK
1369. ALEXANDER FAMILY (IRE) ★★★
b.f. Danetime – Villa Nova (Petardia)
March 13. Sixth foal. 160,000Y. Tattersalls
October 1. BBA (Ire). Sister to the fairly useful 5f
(at two years) to 9f winner and listed-placed
Prince Of Denmark and half-sister to the fairly
useful triple 10f winner Six Of Diamonds (by
Redback) and the fair dual 11f and hurdles
winner Star Of Canterbury (by Beckett). The
dam is an unplaced half-sister to six winners
including the Group 3 winner and Group 1
Dewhurst Stakes third Impressionist. The second
dam, Yashville (by Top Ville), is an unraced half-sister
to eight winners.
'A fine, big, very good-looking filly, she's a good

mover and you couldn't be happier with her at
the moment. She doesn't have the complete look
of a sprinter.'

1370. BEYOND OUR REACH (IRE) ★★★★
ch.f. Danehill Dancer – Bluebell Wood
(Bluebird)
February 10. Third foal. 50,000Y. J O'Byrne.
Doncaster St Leger. The dam, a quite useful
triple 10f winner, is a half-sister to five winners
including the useful two year old 5.7f and 6f
winner and Group 3 7f Criterion Stakes third
Lady Lindsay. The second dam, Jungle Jezebel
(by Thatching), a very useful two year old 7f
winner, was listed-placed twice.
'She might have run before the end of April, she
goes nicely and probably wouldn't want it too
soft. We'll set her off at five furlongs maybe but
she'll definitely get seven in time.'

1371. BRIDAL DANCE (IRE) ★★★
b.f. Danehill Dancer – Feather Bride
(Groom Dancer)
April 20. Ninth living foal. €195,000Y. Goffs
Million. Halcyon Bloodstock. Half-sister to Soxy
Doxy (by Hawk Wing), unplaced in one start at
two years in 2007, to the listed 7f King Charles
II Stakes and subsequent US Grade 3 winner
Millennium Dragon (by Mark Of Esteem), the
fair 10.2f winner Bless The Bride (by Darshaan),
the minor Italian three year old winner of three
races Enduring Freedom (by In The Wings) and
a winner in Greece by Bluebird. The dam, a
minor 10.5f winner at three years in France, is a
half-sister to five winners. The second dam,
Bubbling Danseuse (by Arctic Tern), won once
and was second in the Group 3 1m Prix de
Sandringham and is a half-sister to six winners.
'She's going to be early and it seems she'll want
quickish ground. We'll set her out over five or six
furlongs. Not over-big but a good-looking filly,
she's strong and mature.'

1372. DOUBLE EX ★★★
b.c. Exceed And Excel – Mikara (Midyan)
February 24. First foal. €65,000Y. Goffs Million.
C McCormack. The dam won four races at 2 to
four years in Belgium and France and is a half-

sister to 3 other minor winners. The second dam, Karaferya (by Green Dancer), a listed winner in Ireland, is a half-sister to the dam of Kalanisi.
'Probably more of a seven furlong type as he's from an Aga Khan family there's some stamina influence there. He's a good model, he'll want fast ground and he seems to go quite nicely.'

1373. IZAGONAWIN (IRE) ★★★
ch.f. Choisir – No Reservations (Commanche Run)
February 6. Eighth foal. €40,000Y. Goffs Million. Fozzy Stack. Half-sister to the Irish 2007 7f and 1m placed two year old Zorija Rose (by Oasis Dream) and to Hot Tin Roof (by Thatching), a winner of five races including 3 listed events over 6f and 7f. The dam, a quite useful 6f (at two years) and 7f winner, was listed placed over 7.3f and is a half-sister to the very useful sprinters Hanu (winner of the Cornwallis Stakes) and Sanu. The second dam, Light Link (by Tudor Music), was a useful two year old 5f and 6f winner and a half-sister to three winners.
'She's a bit like her sire in that she's a big, heavy filly, but she's very mature to go with it. We'll probably set her off in May over six furlongs and she'll be OK.'

1374. LADY BONES (IRE) ★★★★
b.f. Royal Applause – Leukippids (Sadler's Wells)
March 1. First foal. €185,000Y. Goffs Million. Newtown Anner Stud. The dam is an unraced half-sister to the Group 1 1m Gran Criterium winner Spartacus and to the Group 2 10f Gallinule Stakes and Hong Kong Derby winner Johan Cruyff. The second dam, Teslemi (by Ogygian), a fair three year old 1m winner, is a half-sister to five minor winners.
'We did a few bits of work with her and she seemed to go quite nicely but she started to grow. She'll definitely make a two year old by early summer and we'd be hopeful for her future.'

1375. LEKHANI (IRE) ★★★
b.f. Imperial Ballet – Dulceata (Rousillon)
April 23. Eleventh foal. 38,000Y. Tattersalls December. C McCormack. Half-sister to the high-class 2007 two year old Group 1 6f Prix

Morny winner and Group 1 7f National Stakes third Myboycharlie (by Danetime), to the quite useful 1m and 10f winner of four races Byzantium (by Shirley Heights), the minor Irish 6f winner Book Binder, the Italian winner of four races Don Chisciotte (both by Perugino) and two minor winners in France and Germany by Brief Truce and Dolphin Street. The dam once unplaced and is a half-sister to seven winners. The second dam, Snowtop (by Thatching), an Irish sprint winner of three races including a listed event, is a half-sister to nine winners including the Group 1 1m William Hill Futurity Stakes winner Al Hareb.
'She wouldn't be as physically imposing as her half-brother Myboycharlie, she's probably a handier type but she's quite strong and she'll definitely make a two year old. Six furlongs should suit.'

1376. MALLOREY ★★
ch.c. Medicean – In Luck (In The Wings)
March 28. 34,000Y. Doncaster Festival. Irish Racing Shares. Brother to Murcar, unplaced in his first start at three years in 2008. The dam, placed 8 times from three to five years, is a half-sister to two minor winners. The second dam, Lucca (by Sure Blade), is an unplaced sister to the Group 2 Gallinule Stakes winner Needle Gun and a half-sister to the Group 1 winners Luso and Warrsan.
'A nice horse from Clive Brittain's family, he's a good mover, we haven't done a lot with him yet but I would imagine he'd be a seven furlong/mile type. He'll definitely want quickish ground and he'll racing in the summer.'

1377. MY BOY JACK (IRE) ★★★
b.c. Exceed And Excel – Angel Alydar (Alysheba)
March 8. Fifth foal. 46,000Y. Doncaster St Leger. Irish Racing Stables. Half-brother to a minor US five year old winner by Hennessy. The dam is an unraced half-sister to 11 winners including the French listed winners L'Orangerie and Liska's Dance. The second dam, Liska (by Lyphard), a French listed winner, is a half-sister to the multiple Group 1 winner and sire Irish River.

'Quite a nice horse, he's grown a bit lately, he seems to go nicely and I'd say six or seven furlongs on goodish ground should be ideal for him.'

1378. MYSTIKA (IRE) ★★★★★
b.f. Sadler's Wells – Tarascon (Tirol)
April 28. Fifth foal. €300,000Y. Goffs Million. John Magnier. Closely related to the Irish dual 9f Beucaire (by Entrepreneur) and half-sister to the French dual 7f winner (including at two years) Mayano Sophia (by Rock Of Gibraltar) and the Irish 12f winner Perfecto (by Peintre Celebre). The dam, winner of the 7f Moyglare Stud Stakes and the Irish 1,000 Guineas, is a half-sister to the Group 2 Prix Guillaume d'Ornano winner Mister Monet and to the very useful 5f winner and Moyglare Stud Stakes and Cheveley Park Stakes placed Mala Mala. The second dam, Breyani (by Commanche Run), a useful winner at up to 2m, is a half-sister to four winners.
'She seems to be a very nice filly and is very mature for a Sadler's Wells, so she probably takes after her mother. You'd think she'd want seven furlongs but her mother wasn't slow. A very good mover, she could be quite exciting.'

1379. NUBAR LADY (IRE) ★★★
b.f. Danetime – Sarah Stokes (Brief Truce)
March 7. Fourth foal. €78,000Y. Goffs Million. Irish Racing Shares. The dam, a fair three year old 6f winner, is a half-sister to four winners including the very useful Group 3 5f Curragh Stakes and Group 3 5f Molecomb Stakes winner Almaty. The second dam, Almaaseh (by Dancing Brave), placed once over 6f at three years, is a half-sister to seven winners including the 2,000 Guineas and Champion Stakes winner Haafhd and the Group 2 Challenge Stakes winner Munir.
'She probably wants good ground and we'll start her at five furlongs – whether she'll get further I don't know. She seems to be quick and she'll be racing in late April/early May.'

1380. OUI SAY OUI (IRE) ★★★
b.f. Royal Applause – Mohican Princess
(Shirley Heights)
April 7. Fifth foal. €130,000Y. Goffs Million. C

McCormack. Half-sister to the smart two year old Group 3 6f Sirenia Stakes and Group 3 1m Joel Stakes winner Satchem (by Inchinor). The dam ran once when fourth over 10f at three years and is a half-sister to two winners including the fairly useful three year old 1m winner The Prince. The second dam, Mohican Girl (by Dancing Brave), a dual listed 10f winner, is a half-sister to the good fillies Untold, Sally Brown (both winners of the Yorkshire Oaks) and Shoot Clear (Waterford Candelabra Stakes winner).
'Quite a nice filly, hopefully she'll be out around June time, maybe over six furlongs.'

1381. PROGRESSOR (IRE) ★★★
ch.c. Danehill Dancer – Castilian Queen (Diesis)
May 7. Ninth foal. €80,000Y. Goffs Million. Independent Traders. Closely related to the fairly useful three year old 7f winner and listed-placed Three Secrets (by Danehill) and half-brother to the useful 2007 two year old 5f and 6f winner Major Eazy (by Fasliyev), the high-class Group 1 5f Prix de l'Abbaye winner Carmine Lake (by Royal Academy) and the fair two year old 7f winner Star Of Grosvenor (by Last Tycoon). The dam, a fair two year old 6f winner, is a half-sister to four winners including the useful 6f and 7f winner and Diomed Stakes third Regal Sabre. The second dam, Royal Heroine (by Lypheor), won 10 races including the 6f Princess Margaret Stakes (at two years) and the 9f Hollywood Derby, the 9f Matriarch Stakes and the Breeders Cup Mile (all Grade 1 events).
'He's not over-big, but he's all there and seems to have plenty of pace as you'd expect the way he's bred. He might start his career at Naas in mid-April, he goes nicely and he'll probably get six furlongs but not much more.'

1382. RYEHILL DREAMER (IRE) ★★★
b.c. Catcher In The Rye – No Way
(Rainbows For Life)
February 5. Fourth foal. 41,000Y. Doncaster St Leger. Irish Racing Shares. Half-brother to the French three year old and hurdles winner Fair Attitude (by King's Theatre). The dam, a French three year old 9f winner, is a sister to the French

listed winner No Lies and a half-sister to seven winners including the French 2,000 Guineas winner No Pass No Sale. The second dam, No Disgrace (by Djakao), won at two years in France and was Group 3 placed.

'He might start his career at Leopardstown in April. He's a good-bodied colt with a good action and he'll probably want fastish ground. We'll set him at six furlongs but he'll definitely get seven.'

1383. SOCIETY GAL (IRE) ★★★

b.f. Galileo – Pillars Of Society (Caerleon)
April 9. Fourth foal. 150,000Y. Tattersalls October 1. Margaret O'Toole. Half-brother to the French two year old and subsequent US Grade 3 9f Regret Stakes winner Good Mood (by Danehill Dancer). The dam an Irish three year old 10f winner, was Group 3 placed and is a half-sister to five winners. The second dam, Grise Mine (by Crystal Palace), won the Group 1 10f Prix Saint-Alary and the Group 3 Prix Vanteaux and is a half-sister to three winners including the triple US Grade 1 winner Kostroma.

'She's bred to get ten furlongs or more, she's a good mover and a very straightforward filly. She should definitely run this year because she's very mature for a Galileo.'

1384. SUGAR FREE (IRE) ★★★

b.f. Oasis Dream – Much Faster (Fasliyev)
February 20. First foal. The dam won four races including the Group 2 6f Prix Robert Papin and the Group 3 5f Prix du Bois. The second dam, Interruption (by Zafonic), is an unraced half-sister to the Grade 2 La Prevoyante Handicap winner Interim and the Group 2 Prix Maurice de Gheest winner Interval.

'Quite strong and a good looker, she should be quite sharp and although she's grown a bit lately she should definitely be out sometime in May. She'll be a sprinter which isn't surprising given her pedigree!'

1385. THECREDITCRUNCHIE (IRE) ★★★

b.c. Danetime – Defined Feature (Nabeel Dancer)
April 1. Sixth foal. 34,000Y. Tattersalls October 3. C McCormack. Half-brother to the moderate

1m winners Ranny (by Emperor Jones) and Tacid (by Diktat). The dam, a fairly useful two year old 5f and 6f winner, was listed-placed and is a half-sister to six winners. The second dam, Meissarah (by Silver Hawk), is an unraced half-sister to six winners.

'He took a little while to come to hand but he's really thrived in the last month and he looks he should be racing by the end of May or early June. He's definitely going the right way.'

1386. TIME AND TIDE (IRE) ★★★

b.f. Danetime – Unfortunate (Komaite)
April 9. Fourth foal. €58,000Y. Goffs Sportsman's. Castlemartin & Skymarc. Sister to the fairly useful 2007 two year old dual 5f winner and listed-placed Look Busy and to the modest 6f to 9f all-weather winner of six races The City Kid and half-sister to a winner in Greece by Raise A Grand. The dam, a 6f winner at two and three years, is out of the unplaced Honour And Glory (by Hotfoot), herself a half-sister to six winners including the dual Group 3 winning sprinter Singing Steven.

'She was quite a nervous type but she's settled down lately. I couldn't imagine her getting much further than five or six furlongs, she's not very big but she's all there and I expect she'll be out early.'

1387. WANNA (IRE) ★★★★

b.f. Danehill Dancer – Wannabe (Shirley Heights)
April 26. Ninth foal. 240,000Y. Tattersalls October 1. Bobby O'Ryan. Closely related to the Group 1 6f Cheveley Park Stakes and Group 2 6f Cherry Hinton Stakes winner Wannabe Grand (by Danehill) and half-sister to the useful two year old dual 1m winner and listed placed Assaaf (by Night Shift), the fairly useful 11.5f and 12f winner and Group 3 second Wannabe Posh (by Grand Lodge) and the minor French three year old winner Masseera (by Alzao). The dam, a quite useful 1m and 10f winner, is a half-sister to three winners including the very useful 5f and 6f winner and Group 1 Cheveley Park Stakes second Tanami (herself dam of the Group 2 Rockfel Stakes winner Cairns). The second

dam, Propensity (by Habitat), a fairly useful two year old 5f winner, was second in the Queen Mary Stakes and is a half-sister to two winners. 'A fine, big, scopey filly, she's very good-bodied and is one for the second half of the season. A filly with a good action, she looks quite exciting.'

1388. WICKLOWS CALL (IRE) ★★★
b.c. Exceed And Excel – Miss Tardy (Lammtarra)
February 27. Fourth foal. €32,000Y. Goffs Million. Irish Racing Shares. Half-brother to a minor three year old winner by Kalanisi. The dam was placed in France and is a half-sister to five winners including the Group 2 Dante Stakes winner Torjoun and the Group 2 Pretty Polly Stakes winner Takarouna. The second dam, Tarsila (by High Top), a winner over 1m and 9f, is a sister to Top Ville.
'One for six or seven furlongs from mid-summer onwards, he's a good looker that just needs a bit of time. For what he cost I think he was well bought.' TRAINER'S BARGAIN BUY

1389. UNNAMED ★★
b.f. Danehill Dancer – An Mosey (Royal Academy)
March 27. Third foal. €110,000Y. Goffs Million. Irish Racing Shares. Sister to the unraced 2007 two year old Spanish Eyes. The dam is an unraced half-sister to three winners including the dam of the Kentucky Derby and Belmont Stakes winner Thunder Gulch. The second dam, Shoot a Line (by High Line), won six races from 7.5f to 14.5f including the Irish Oaks and the Yorkshire Oaks and is a half-sister to six winners including the Gordon Stakes winner More Light.
'Goes quite nicely and is quite a big filly that we'll probably bring out sometime in July. She's likely to want a bit of ease in the ground and seven furlongs.'

1390. UNNAMED ★★★ ♠
b.f. Smarty Jones – Djebel Amour (Mt Livermore)
March 10. Third foal. $340,000Y. Keeneland September. Brian Grassick. Half-sister to the useful two year old 6f winner Dodge City (by Gone West). The dam, a 1m winner in the USA,

is a half-sister to the smart two year old Group 2 7f Champagne Stakes winner Almushahar. The second dam, Sayyedati (by Shadeed), won the Group 1 7f Moyglare Stud Stakes and the Group 1 6f Cheveley Park Stakes at two years, the 1,000 Guineas and Prix Jacques le Marois at three years and the Sussex Stakes at five years. She is a full or half-sister to numerous winners including the multiple Group 1 winner Golden Snake.
'She came to us about six weeks ago, she seems a nice filly with a good action and she's a good looker.'

SIR MICHAEL STOUTE

1391. ALBAASHA (IRE) ★★★
ch.c. Lemon Drop Kid – Cozy Maria (Cozzene)
January 27. Second foal. 220,000Y. Tattersalls October 1. Shadwell Estate Co. The dam, a useful 10f winner, was listed-placed twice and is a half-sister to five winners in the USA. The second dam, Mariamme (by Verbatim), won twice at three years in the USA and is a half-sister to seven winners including the Grade 1 Breeders Cup Turf winner Miss Alleged. (Hamdan Al Maktoum)

1392. ALMUKTAHEM ★★★
b.c. Green Desert – Nasanice (Nashwan)
March 18. Brother to the fair 1m winner Safwa and half-brother to the high-class Group 2 12f Hardwicke Stakes winner Maraahel, the useful two year old 7f winner and Group 1 Fillies Mile fourth Huja (both by Alzao) and the smart 7f and 1m Britannia Handicap winner Mostashaar (by Intikhab). The dam, a fairly useful Irish three year old 9f winner, is a half-sister to the listed 12f winner Sahool. The second dam, Mathaayl (by Shadeed), a quite useful 6f and 10f winner, is a half-sister to the Group 3 Princess Margaret Stakes winner Muhbubh (herself dam of the US Grade 2 winner Kayrawan) and to the dam of the Group/Graded stakes winners Asfurah and Istintaj. (Hamdan Al-Maktoum)

1393. BARYNA ★★★★
ch.f. Pivotal – Russian Rhythm (Kingmambo)
February 9. First foal. The dam won the 1,000

Guineas, Coronation Stakes, Nassau Stakes and Lockinge Stakes and is a half-sister to the two year old Group 2 1m Royal Lodge Stakes winner Perfectperformance. The second dam, Balistroika (Nijinsky), is an unraced half-sister to numerous winners including Park Appeal (winner of the Cheveley Park Stakes and the Moyglare Stud Stakes and the dam of Cape Cross), Alydaress (Irish Oaks) and Desirable (winner of the Cheveley Park Stakes and the dam of Shadayid). (Cheveley Park Stud)

1394. BATTLE HERO ★★★
b.c. Red Ransom – Appointed One
(Danzig)
April 9. Half-brother to the smart 7f and 1m winner (at two years) and Group 3 10f Select Stakes second Battle Chant (by Coronado's Quest), to the fairly useful 7f winner Matoaka (by A P Indy), the quite useful 1m winner Constitute (by Gone West) and the fair triple 1m winner Officer (by Medicean). The dam, a minor US stakes winner, is a sister to the Group 2 1m Lockinge Stakes winner Emperor Jones and the listed 6f Sirenia Stakes winner and Group 1 Middle Park Stakes third Majlood and a half-sister to the Group 1 1m William Hill Futurity Stakes winner Bakharoff. The second dam, Qui Royalty (by Native Royalty), a winner of five races at up to 1m in the USA, was second in the Grade 3 Boiling Springs Handicap and is a half-sister to eight winners including the US Grade 3 winner Qui Native. (Cheveley Park Stud)

1395. BEST START ★★★
ch.c. Medicean – Preference (Efisio)
February 25. Fourth foal. 190,000Y. Tattersalls October 1. Charlie Gordon-Watson. Half-brother to the fairly useful 5f and 6f winner of four races Ice Planet (by Polar Falcon) and to the modest dual 6f winner Maia (by Observatory). The dam is an unraced sister to the Group 3 Beeswing Stakes winner Casteddu and to the listed winner Barbaroja. The second dam, Bias (by Royal Prerogative), won six races at two and three years. (Saeed Suhail)

1396. BRIANDA'S GIRL (USA) ★★★
b.f. Mr Greeley – Brianda (Alzao)
March 20. Fourth foal. $350,000Y. Keeneland September. C Gordon-Watson. Closely related to the minor US three year old winner Gone Irish (by Gone West) and half-sister to the minor French three year old winner Anoush (by Giant's Causeway). The dam, a French and US winner, was Grade 2 placed twice and is a half-sister to several winners including the stakes Aliena. The second dam, Gracious Line (by Fabulous Dancer), a minor French three year old winner, is a half-sister to the Group three winners Gay Minstrel and Greenway. (Mr Peter Watson).

1397. COLLABORATOR ★★★
b.c. Medicean – Confidante (Dayjur)
May 1. Seventh foal. Half-brother to the Group 3 7f (at two years) and Group 1 10.5f Prix de Diane winner Confidential Lady (by Singspiel), to the fairly useful three year old 7f winner Crown Counsel and the fair 7f winner Registrar (both by Machiavellian). The dam, a fairly useful three year old dual 7f winner, is a half-sister to six winners including the two year old 6f winner Wind Cheetah, the Group 3 7f Solario Stakes winner White Crown and the 11.8f winner Zuboon. all useful. The second dam, Won't She Tell (by Banner Sport), a minor stakes winner of nine races in the USA at up to 9f, is a half-sister to the American Triple Crown winner Affirmed. (Cheveley Park Stud).

1398. CORDOBA ★★★
b.f. Dansili – Spanish Sun (El Prado)
January 15. The dam, a 7f (at two years) and Group 2 12f Ribblesdale Stakes winner, is a half-sister to four winners including the fairly useful middle-distance winners Eagle's Cross and Galvanise. The second dam, Shining Bright (by Rainbow Quest), a French 10f winner, is a half-sister to the Group 2 12f Grand Prix de Chantilly winner Daring Miss and the Group 3 12f Prix de Royaumont winner Apogee. (Khalid Abdulla).

1399. CUSTODY (IRE) ★★★
b.c. Fusaichi Pegasus – Shahtoush (Alzao)
January 21. Fourth foal. 65,000Y. Tattersalls

October 1. John Warren. Half-brother to the minor Irish two year old 7.5f winner Satine (by Danehill). The dam won the Oaks and was second in the 1,000 Guineas and is a half-sister to ten winners including the Group 2 10f Pretty Polly Stakes winner and Epsom Oaks second Game Plan. The second dam, Formulate (by Reform), was a very smart filly and winner of four races including the Group 3 Hoover Fillies Mile. (Highclere Thoroughbred Racing).

1400. DANCOURT (IRE) ★★

b.c. Cadeaux Genereux – Stage Struck
(Sadler's Wells)
April 5. Ninth foal. Brother to the very smart Group 2 10.3f York Stakes, Group 3 10f La Coupe and Group 3 9f Darley Stakes winner Stage Gift and half-brother to the useful 10.2f winner Drama Class (by Caerleon and herself dam of the Irish Oaks second Scottish Stage) and a hurdles winner by Soviet Star. The dam, a quite useful 12f winner, is a sister to the high-class Group 1 7f Dewhurst Stakes dead-heater Prince of Dance and to the useful middle-distance winners Ballet Prince and Golden Ball. The second dam, Sun Princess (by English Prince), a top-class winner of the Oaks, the St Leger and the Yorkshire Oaks, is a half-sister to the high-class middle-distance colt Saddlers Hall.

1401. DREAM WIN ★★★★

b.c. Oasis Dream – Wince (Selkirk)
January 21. Half-sister to the Group 1 Yorkshire Oaks winner Quiff and to the useful 10f winner and Group 3 Chester Vase second Arabian Gulf (both by Sadler's Wells). The dam won the 1,000 Guineas and the Group 3 Fred Darling Stakes and is a half-sister to three winners including the very smart middle-distance winner Ulundi. The second dam, Flit (by Lyphard), is a half-sister to the Grade 1 Washington Lassie Stakes winner Contredance, the listed Roses Stakes winner Old Alliance and the Graded stakes winners Shotiche and Skimble (herself dam of the US Grade 1 winner Skimming). (Khalid Abdulla).

1402. DUBAI CHALLENGE (USA) ★★★

b.br.c. Dynaformer – Surf N Sand
(Boston Harbor)
March 19. First foal. $450,000Y. Keeneland September. Charlie Gordon-Watson. The dam, a stakes winner of seven races in the USA, is a half-sister to five winners including 2 US stakes winners. The second dam, Affordable Prince (by Drouilly), was a Grade 2 placed listed winner in the USA. (Saeed Suhail).

1403. DUBAI ECHO (USA) ★★★★ ♠

b.br.c. Mr Greeley – Entendu (Edgy Diplomat)
May 9. First foal. $300,000Y. Keeneland September. Charlie Gordon-Watson. The dam won 13 races in Chile and the USA including the Grade 2 Princess Rooney Handicap. The second dam, Coceta (by Dimineau), was an unraced half-sister to the champion sprinter in Chile, Danes. (Saeed Suhail).

1404. ENTICEMENT ★★

b.f. Montjeu – Ecoutila (Rahy)
February 13. Second foal. 310,000Y. Tattersalls October 1. John Warren. The dam is an unraced half-sister to the US winner and Grade 2 placed Listen Indy. The second dam, Ecoute (by Manila), a winner of 2 listed events in France and the USA and third in the Group 1 Prix Saint-Alary, is a half-sister to five winners including the Group 1 winners Pas de Reponse and Green Tune. (The Queen).

1405. EXPRESSIVE ★★★★

b.f. Falbrav – Exclusive (Polar Falcon)
April 25. Half-sister to the Group 1 1m Matron Stakes winner Echelon (by Danehill) and to the dual Group 2 1m winner Chic (by Machiavellian). The dam, winner of the Group 1 1m Coronation Stakes, is a half-sister to the 2,000 Guineas winner and Derby fourth Entrepreneur, the smart Cheshire Oaks winner and Epsom Oaks second Dance a Dream, the very useful middle-distance listed winner Sadler's Image and the useful French two year old listed 7f winner Irish Order. The second dam, Exclusive Order (by Exclusive Native), won four races in France including the Group 2 6.5f Prix

Maurice de Gheest and the Group 3 7f Prix de la Porte Maillot. (Cheveley Park Stud)

1406. FASCINATING RHYTHM ★ ★
b.f. Galileo – Fascinating Rhythm (Slip Anchor)
February 14. Fifth foal. 320,000Y. Tattersalls October 1. M V Magnier. Half-sister to the fairly useful 10f and 12f winner Pentatonic (by Giant's Causeway). The dam, a useful two year old 8.2f winner, is a half-sister to three winners including the useful 10f to 11f winner of five races (including on the all-weather) Migwar. The second dam, Pick Of The Pops (by High Top), a very useful two year old 7f winner, was second in the Group 2 Hoover Fillies Mile and is a half-sister to six winners. (Smith, Magnier, Tabor)

1407. GOLDEN STREAM (IRE) ★★★
b.f. Sadler's Wells – Phantom Gold (Machiavellian)
April 25. Seventh foal. Sister to the smart two year old 6f winner and Group 1 12f Oaks second Flight Of Fancy, to the quite useful 12f winners Hypoteneuse and Well Hidden and half-sister to the useful two year old 7f winner Desert Star (by Green Desert) and the fairly useful 12f winner Daring Aim (by Daylami). The dam, a very useful filly, won from 1m (at two years) to 12f including the Group 2 Ribblesdale Stakes and the Group 3 St Simon Stakes. The second dam, Trying For Gold (by Northern Baby), was a useful 12f winner out of the Ribblesdale Stakes winner Expansive (by Exbury). (The Queen).

1408. HARBINGER ★★★ ♠
b.c. Dansili – Penang Pearl (Bering)
March 12. Fifth foal. 180,000Y. Tattersalls October 1. John Warren. Half-brother to the fair 7f to 12f winner Penang Cinta (by Halling) and to the modest two year old 5f winner Penang Sapphire (by Spectrum). The dam was a very useful three year old 1m listed winner of three races. The second dam, Guapa (by Shareef Dancer), won twice over 1m and is a half-sister to seven winners including the Group two winners Dusty Dollar and Kind Of Hush. (Highclere Thoroughbred Racing).

1409. HIGHLAND GLEN ★★★
b.c. Montjeu – Daring Aim (Daylami)
January 25. First foal. The dam, a fairly useful 12f winner, is a half-sister to four winners including the smart two year old 6f winner and Group 1 12f Oaks second Flight Of Fancy. The second dam, Phantom Gold (by Sadler's Wells), a very useful filly, won from 1m (at two years) to 12f including the Group 2 Ribblesdale Stakes and the Group 3 St Simon Stakes. (The Queen).

1410. HARVEST SONG (IRE) ★★
b.c. Sadler's Wells – La Mouline (Nashwan)
April 5. Second foal. 290,000Y. Tattersalls October 1. John Warren. The dam, a useful dual 10.5f winner including at two years, was listed-placed over 7f at two years. The second dam, Lamarque (by Nureyev), was unraced and is closely related to the Prix de l'Arc de Triomphe winner Carnegie and to the Group 2 10f Prix Guillaume d'Ornano winner Antisaar and a half-sister to Group 3 St Simon Stakes winner Lake Erie. (The Queen).

1411. HUNTING HORN ★★★
b.c. Pivotal – Princess Athena (Ahonoora)
April 19. Thirteenth foal. 320,000Y. Tattersalls October 1. Charlie Gordon-Watson. Half-brother to the Group 2 6f Diadem Stakes winner of six races and good sire Acclamation (by Royal Applause), to the fairly useful 6f and 7f winner Waypoint (by Cadeaux Genereux and herself dam of the Group 2 Prix Robert Papin winner Never A Doubt), the quite useful 5f winner of five races (including at two years) Kissing Time, the quite useful three year old 6f winner Conjuror, the modest 5f winner Amira (both by Efisio) and a winner in Germany (both by Lugana Beach). The dam, a very smart winner of the Group 3 5f Queen Mary Stakes and placed in numerous Group events over sprint distances, is a half-sister to four winners. The second dam, Shopping Wise (by Floribunda), won once at three years and is a half-sister to seven winners. (Smith, Magnier, Tabor).

1412. IMPOSING ★★
b.c. Danehill Dancer – On Fair Stage
(Sadler's Wells)
**February 21. Seventh foal. 170,000Y. Tattersalls
October 1. Demi O'Byrne.** Half-brother to the
French listed 12f winner Gale Force (by Sinndar),
to the minor French three year old 1m winner
Power Of Love (by Zafonic) and a winner over
hurdles by Bering. The dam, an Irish four year
old listed 1m winner, is a half-sister to six
winners including the Group 3 1m Prix Quincey
winner Perfect Vintage and the very useful
listed 1m Sceptre Stakes winner and 1,000
Guineas fourth Perfect Circle. The second dam,
Fair Salinia (by Petingo), won the Epsom Oaks,
the Irish Oaks (awarded race) and the Yorkshire
Oaks and is a half-sister to the US Grade 2
winner Rambo Dancer.

1413. ITHINKBEST ★★★
b.c. King's Best – Monturani (Indian Ridge)
**February 15. First foal. 200,000Y. Tattersalls
October 2. Charlie Gordon-Watson.** The dam,
winner of the Group 2 Blandford Stakes, is a
half-sister to the smart 6f and 7f listed winner
Monnavanna and to the very useful two year
old 7f winner Mezuzah. The second dam,
Mezzogiorno (by Unfuwain), a very useful 7f (at
two years) and 10f listed winner and third in the
Oaks, is a half-sister to three winners. (Saeed
Suhail).

1414. MOHALHAL (IRE) ★★★
b.c. Cape Cross – Madame Dubois
(Legend Of France)
**March 5. Twelfth foal. 210,000Y. Tattersalls
October 2. Shadwell Estate Co.** Half-brother to
the Irish 2,000 Guineas winner Indian Haven (by
Indian Ridge), to the smart Group 1 Gran
Criterium winner Count Dubois (by Zafonic), the
useful dual 12f winners Massif Centrale (by
Selkirk) and Place de l'Opera (by Sadler's Wells
and herself the dam of three stakes winners),
the fairly useful 10f all-weather winner Paragon
Of Virtue (by Cadeaux Genereux), the fairly
useful 12f winner Galette (by Caerleon) and the
quite useful 12f winner Richelieu (by Kris). The
dam, a very smart filly, won five races from 9f

to 14.6f including the Group 2 Park Hill Stakes
and the Group 2 Prix de Royallieu and is a half-
sister to four winners including the dam of the
very smart two year old Daggers Drawn. The
second dam, Shadywood (by Habitat), a useful
10f winner, was second in the Lancashire Oaks
and is a half-sister to eight winners. (Hamdan Al
Maktoum).

1415. NEWSFORYOU ★★★
b.c. Dansili – Rowan Flower (Ashkalani)
**March 20. Third foal. 120,000Y. Tattersalls
October 2. Charlie Gordon-Watson.** Half-
brother to the quite useful 2007 two year old 7f
winner Boy Blue (by Observatory). The dam, a
fair Irish three year old 7f winner, is a half-sister
to ten winners including the smart Group 3 10f
Meld Stakes winner Muakaad. The second dam,
Forest Lair (by Habitat), won over 1m at two
years in Ireland and is a half-sister to the US
Grade 2 winner Great Sound and the French
triple Group 3 winner Pampabird. (Saeed
Suhail). (Saeed Suhail).

1416. PICTORIAL (USA) ★★
b.c. Pivotal – Red Tulle (A P Indy)
**February 20. Fifth foal. 165,000Y. Doncaster St
Leger. John Warren.** Half-brother to the fair 7f
winner Danger Zone (by Danzero) and to a
minor winner abroad by Polish Precedent. The
dam was placed once over 10f and is a half-sister
to six winners including the French two year old
and US three year old Grade 3 8.5f Lamplighter
Handicap winner Namaqualand. The second
dam, Namaqua (by Storm Bird), a minor winner
at three years in the USA, is a half-sister to the
champion US two year old filly Althea (herself
dam of the champion Japanese two year old filly
Yamanin Paradise), to the Grade 1 winners Ali
Oop and Ketoh and the dam of Green Desert.
(Highclere Thoroughbred Racing).

1417. PIED PIPER ★★★
b.c. Pivotal – Flight Of Fancy (Sadler's Wells)
March 2. Fourth foal. Half-sister to the quite
useful 10.2f winner Fleeting Memory (by
Danehill). The dam, a smart two year old 6f
winner and second in the Oaks, is a half-sister

to several winners including the useful two year old 7f winner Desert Star. The second dam, Phantom Gold (by Machiavellian), won from 1m (at two years) to 12f including the Group 2 Ribblesdale Stakes and the Group 3 St Simon Stakes. (The Queen).

1418. POLE POSITION ★★★★
b.f Pivotal – Danehurst (Danehill)
January 22. Second foal. The dam, winner of the Cornwallis Stakes (at two years), the Curragh Flying Five, the Prix de Seine-et-Oise and the Premio Umbria, is a half-sister to the Group 3 10.5f Prix Penelope winner Humouresque (by Pivotal). The second dam, Miswaki Belle (by Miswaki), second over 7f on her only start, is a half-sister to six winners including the smart Group 3 6f Cherry Hinton Stakes winner and 1,000 Guineas third Dazzle. (Cheveley Park Stud).

1419. PUMPKIN ★★★
b.f. Pivotal – Gallivant (Danehill)
January 5. Second foal. The dam, a quite useful two year old 6f winner, is a closely related to the smart two year old Group 2 6f Mill Reef Stakes winner Byron and a half-sister to three winners including the useful 1m and 10.3f winner Gallant Hero. The second dam, Gay Gallanta (by Woodman), a very smart winner of the Group 1 6f Cheveley Park Stakes and the Group 3 5f Queen Mary Stakes, was second in the 1m Falmouth Stakes and is a half-sister to ten winners including the Group 2 10f Gallinule Stakes winner Sportsworld. (Cheveley Park Stud).

1420. RESORT ★★★
b.f. Oasis Dream – Gay Gallanta (Woodman)
May 15. Seventh foal. Closely related to the smart two year old Group 2 6f Mill Reef Stakes winner Byron and to the fairly useful 7f and 1m winner Gallantry (both by Green Desert) and half-sister to the useful 1m and 10.3f winner Gallant Hero, the fairly useful 9f winner Gallant (both by Rainbow Quest), the useful 10.4f listed-placed maiden Gay Heroine (by Caerleon) and the quite useful two year old 6f winner Gallivant (by Danehill). The dam, a very smart winner of the Group 1 6f Cheveley Park Stakes and the

Group 3 5f Queen Mary Stakes, was second in the 1m Falmouth Stakes and is a half-sister to the smart Group 2 10f Gallinule Stakes winner Sportsworld. The second dam, Gallanta (by Nureyev), a useful winner of three races from 5.5f to 1m including the Prix de Coburg, was second in the Group 1 Prix Morny and is a half-sister to the top-class French middle-distance colt Gay Mecene and to the dam of Wolfhound. (Cheveley Park Stud).

1421. STANDPOINT ★★★
b.c. Oasis Dream – Waki Music (Miswaki)
April 18. Third foal. Half-brother to the fair Irish 1m winner Hum The Tune (by Beat Hollow). The dam, a fairly useful two year old 7f winner and third in the Group 3 7f Prestige Stakes, subsequently won over 1m in the USA. The second dam, the useful French 7.5f and 1m winner Light Music (by Nijinsky), is a half-sister to numerous winners including the very useful French two year old listed 1m winner Battle Dore. (Khalid Abdulla).

1422. STRAWBERRYDAIQUIRI ★★★
gr.f. Dansili – Strawberry Morn
(Travelling Victor)
January 15. Fifth foal. 105,000Y. Tattersalls October 1. Hugo Merry. Half-sister to the quite useful 9f and 10f winner Strawberry Lolly (by Lomitas) and to the modest 6f and 7f winner Strabinios King (by King's Best). The dam, a dual Canadian stakes winner of 1five races, is a half-sister to six winners. The second dam, Strawberry's Charm (by Strawberry Road), a minor winner at three years in the USA, is a half-sister to five winners. (Mrs R J Jacobs).

1423. THE FONZ ★★★
b.c. Red Ransom – Crystal Cavern (Be My Guest)
April 17. Half-brother to the useful two year old listed 7f Radley Stakes winner and Group 3 Fred Darling Stakes second Crystal Star, to the fair two year old 1m winner True Dream (both by Mark Of Esteem), the Irish four year old 7f to 8.5f winner of four races Christavelli (by Machiavellian) and the French 10f winner Vracca (by Vettori). The dam, a fairly useful two

year old 7f winner here and subsequently a dual winner in Canada, is a half-sister to four winners including the French 1,000 Guineas winner Rose Gypsy. The second dam, Krisalya (by Kris), a fairly useful 10.4f winner, is a half-sister to 12 winners including the high-class 9.3f Prix d'Ispahan winner Sasuru and the high-class Challenge Stakes and Jersey Stakes winner Sally Rous. (Anthony & David de Rothschild).

1424. TOWERING HABAB (IRE) ★★★
b.f. Red Ransom – Dance Parade (Gone West)
May 1. Third foal. 170,000Y. Tattersalls October 1. Charlie Gordon-Watson. Half-sister to the fair 2007 6f placed two year old Castles In The Air (by Oasis Dream) and to the minor US three year old winner Special Jig (by Theatrical). The dam won seven races in England and the USA including the Grade 2 Buena Vista Handicap, the Group 3 Queen Mary Stakes, the Group 3 Fred Darling Stakes and two other Grade 3 events in the USA. She is a half-sister to three winners including the Grade 3 9f Bay Meadows Derby winner Ocean Queen. The second dam, River Jig (by Irish River), a useful two year old 9f winner here, later won over 12f in Italy and is a half-sister to six winners including the dam of the Prix Gladiateur and Australian Grade 1 winner Always Aloof. (Saeed Suhail).

1425. WAY TO FINISH ★★★
b.c. Oasis Dream – Suedoise (Kris)
February 8. Seventh foal. €230,000Y. Deauville August. Charlie Gordon-Watson. Closely related to the Group 3 Tropical Turf Handicap winner Ballast (by Desert Prince) and half-brother to the useful 5f and 1m winner and listed-placed Blue Spinnaker (by Bluebird) and a minor French winner by Fasliyev. The dam, a two year old 1m winner in France on her only start, is a half-sister to six winners including the Group 2 12f Princess Of Wales's Stakes winner Wagon Master. The second dam, Sunny Flower (by Dom Racine), was placed twice in France and is a half-sister to the dam of the good miler Then Again and to the top-class broodmare Sunny Valley (the dam of Sun Princess and Saddlers Hall). (Saeed Suhail).

1426. ZACINTO ★★★
b.c. Dansili – Ithaca (Distant View)
March 6. First foal. The dam, a useful two year old 7f winner and second in the Group 3 7f Prestige Stakes, is a half-sister to several winners including the useful dual 10f winner Many Volumes. The second dam, Reams Of Verse (by Nureyev), won the Oaks, the Fillies Mile, the Musidora Stakes and the May Hill Stakes and is a half-sister to numerous winners including the high-class Group 1 10f Coral Eclipse Stakes and Group 1 10f Phoenix Champion Stakes winner Elmaamul. (Khalid Abdulla).

SAEED BIN SUROOR (GODOLPHIN)
Many thanks to Diana Cooper for speaking to me at length about these beautifully-bred horses.

1427. ANMAR (USA) ★★★★
ch.c. Rahy – Ranin (Unfuwain)
February 28. Third foal. The dam, a smart Group 2 14.6f Park Hill Stakes winner, is a half-sister to six winners including the very useful 7f and 1m winner Ghalib, the useful two year old 1m and listed 9f placed Wahchi and the useful 6.5f (at two years) to 7f winner Qhazeenah. The second dam, Nafhaat (by Roberto), a fairly useful 12f winner, stayed 15f.
'One of our nicest colts, he's attractive and a good mover. He's not bred to be very early but he's athletic and should come to hand some time in mid-to-late summer over seven furlongs.'

1428. ASSABIYYA (IRE) ★★★
b.f. Cape Cross – Coretta (Caerleon)
February 5. Fifth foal. Half-sister to the fairly useful 10f winner and listed placed Shared Dreams (by Seeking The Gold) and to the modest 14f winner Call Me George (by Rainbow Quest). The dam, won the Grade 2 Long Island Handicap and the Grade 2 La Prevoyante Handicap and is a half-sister to the very useful 10f winner and listed-placed Trumpet Sound, the very useful 10.5f winner and listed placed Rosa Parks and the two year old 9f listed winner Mikado. The second dam, Free At Last (by

Shirley Heights), won three 7f events at two years including the listed Somerville Tattersall Stakes, was fourth in the 1,000 Guineas and won the Grade 3 8.5f Countess Fager Handicap in the USA. She is a half-sister to the high-class milers Barathea and Gossamer.
'She's a big filly and is still growing. A filly with a lovely outlook, she's very pretty but is one for the autumn.'

1429. BAB AL SHAMS ★★
b.c. Halling – Polska (Danzig)
March 15. Brother to the very useful two year old listed 7f winner and Group 2 1m May Hill Stakes second Queen Of Poland and the modest 12.5f winner Hill Billy Rock and half-brother to the useful two year old dual 7f winner White Hawk (by Silver Hawk), the fair 10f winner Abydos (by King's Best) and the fair 5f and 6f all-weather winner Grizel (by Lion Cavern). The dam, a useful winner of the two year old listed 6f Blue Seal Stakes, was listed-placed over 7f at three years and is closely related to the useful filly Millstream, a winner of five races over 5f including the Group 3 Ballyogan Stakes and the Group 3 Cornwallis Stakes. The second dam, Aquaba (by Damascus), a Grade 3 stakes winner of seven races in the USA, won from 7f to 9f and is a half-sister to six winners.
'He's beginning to sharpen up but he's still only cantering and we'll see how he comes on in the next month or so.'

1430. BLACK EAGLE (IRE) ★★★
b.c. Cape Cross – Shimna (Mr Prospector)
February 21. Fifth foal. 200,000Y. Tattersalls October 1. John Ferguson. Half-brother to the useful 1m (at two years) and 10f winner and Group 3 Derby Trial second Hazeymm (by Marju) and to the useful two year old 7f winner Santa Fe (by Green Desert) and the fairly useful 1m (at two years) and dual 10f winner Sahrati (by In The Wings). The dam, placed fourth over 10f in Ireland on her only outing, is a half-sister to the St Leger and Gran Premio del Jockey Club winner Shantou. The second dam, Shaima (by Shareef Dancer), a very useful 7.3f (at two

years) and 9f listed winner here, later won the Grade 2 12f Long Island Handicap and is a half-sister to six winners including the Prix Saint Alary winner Rosefinch.
'A big, powerful horse, we're in no rush with him and we'll aim for August/September time for his debut.'

1431. BURJ DUBAI (USA) ★★★★★
ch.c. Distorted Humor – Alchemist (A P Indy)
February 22. First foal. $1,000,000Y. Keeneland September. John Ferguson. The dam, a winner and Grade 3 placed in the USA, is a sister to the stakes-placed winner Altesse. The second dam, Aldiza (by Storm Cat), won six races including the Grade 1 Go For Wand Stakes and is a half-sister to the US Grade 2 winner Atelier.
'A colt with a lot of class and quality, he has a good action and is a horse we look forward to racing in the summer over seven furlongs.'

1432. DUBAI CREEK (IRE) ★★
b.c. Cape Cross – Humilis (Sadler's Wells)
April 2. First foal. 290,000Y. Tattersalls October 1. John Ferguson. The dam, a winner of three races including the listed Blue Wind Stakes, is a sister to the Irish two year old 1m winner, Group 3 7f Futurity Stakes third and subsequent US stakes winner Stage Call and to the three year old winner and listed-placed Blue Oasis. The second dam, Humble Eight (by Seattle Battle), winner of the Grade 3 8.5f Honeybee Handicap in the USA, is a half-sister to the listed winners April Starlight, Royal Devotion and Thady Quill.
'A big, imposing type, he'll need a bit of time.'

1433. EMERGING ARTIST (FR) ★★★★
b.c. Dubai Destination – Picture Princess (Sadler's Wells)
April 4. Half-brother to the fair 1m winner Perfect Blend (by Linamix). The dam ran once unplaced and is a half-sister to several winners including the Irish 2004 two year old 7f winner and Group 1 7f Moyglare Stud Stakes second Pictavia and the US two year old 6.5f and UAE dual 1m winner Janadel. The second dam, Insijaam (by Secretariat), a dual listed 10f winner at three years in France, is a half-sister to the

1,000 Guineas and Prix de l'Opera winner Hatoof and the 1m (at two years) and 12f listed winner Fasateen.

'Very nice and professional, he's well balanced and is coming together well, he should be quite early and could have enough speed for six furlongs before stepping up to seven.'

1434. EMIRATES AVIATION ★★★

b.c. Dalakhani – Time Honoured (Sadler's Wells)
January 28. Second foal. 480,000Y. Tattersalls October 1. John Ferguson. The dam, a quite useful two year old 1m winner, is a sister to the very useful Group 3 12f Princess Royal Stakes winner Time Allowed and a half-sister to Group 3 12f Jockey Club Stakes winner Zinaad and the dams of the Group winners Anton Chekhov, First Charter, Plea Bargain and Time Away. The second dam, Time Charter (by Saritamer), was an exceptionally talented filly and winner of the Oaks, the King George VI and Queen Elizabeth Diamond Stakes, the Champion Stakes, the Coronation Cup, the Prix Foy and the Sun Chariot Stakes.

'Bound to be a horse for next year really, but he has plenty of class and is a nice horse for the future.'

1435. EMIRATES CHALLENGE (IRE) ★★

b.c. Cape Cross – Evil Empire (Acatenango)
March 29. Half-brother to the 1m (at 2years) and listed 10f winner Empire Day (by Lomitas) and to the useful 11f and 12f winner Counterpunch (by Halling). The dam, a Group 3 12f winner in Germany, is a sister to the German triple listed winner El Tango and a half-sister to the German listed winner El Tiger.

'He'll take a bit more time and is bred to enjoy a bit of a trip. One for later on in the year.'

1436. EMIRATES CHAMPION ★★★★

b.c. Haafhd – Janaat (Kris)
March 7. Half-brother to the quite useful 2007 two year old 5f winner Grand Fleet (by Green Desert), to the very smart Group 1 1m Gran Criterium winner and 2,000 Guineas second Lend A Hand (by Great Commotion), the quite

useful 10f and 12f winner Soldiers Quest (by Rainbow Quest) and the quite useful 10f to 14f winner Double Deputy (by Sadler's Wells). The dam, a fair 12f winner, is a sister to the French three year old listed 10.5f winner Trefoil and a half-sister to numerous winners including the smart middle-distance winners Maysoon, Richard of York, Three Tails (dam of the high-class middle-distance colt Tamure) and Third Watch. The second dam, Triple First (by High Top), won seven races including the Group 2 10f Nassau Stakes and the Group 2 10f Sun Chariot Stakes.

'A very nice, attractive horse, he's a very easy mover with a good temperament and we'd like to see him out around June/July time.'

1437. EMIRATES ROADSHOW (USA) ★★★★

ch.c. Distorted Humor – Just A Bird (Storm Bird)
February 6. Fifth foal. $800,000Y. Saratoga August. John Ferguson. Half-brother to two minor winners in the USA by Conquistador Cielo and Dynaformer. The dam is an unraced half-sister to five winners including the US Grade 3 winner Recording. The second dam, Ratings (by Caveat), won eight races in the USA including the Grade 2 Diana Handicap and is a half-sister to seven winners.

'He's filling out his frame nicely and is an easy-actioned horse who will be a nice seven furlong type in August.'

1438. EMIRATES SPORTS ★★★★

b.c. King's Best – Time Saved (Green Desert)
March 27. Fourth foal. 150,000Y. Tattersalls October 1. John Ferguson. Half-brother to the useful 2007 two year old 7f winner and Group 3 1m Prix des Chenes second Dubai Time (by Dubai Destination), to the smart 7f (at 2years) and Group 2 12f King Edward VII Stakes winner Plea Bargain (by Machiavellian) and the modest 1m winner Tipsy Me (by Selkirk). The dam, a fairly useful 10f winner, is a sister to the useful 1m winner Illusion and a half-sister to five winners including Zinaad and Time Allowed, both winners of the Group 2 12f Jockey Club Stakes and the dams of the Group winners

Anton Chekhov, First Charter, Plea Bargain and Time Away. The second dam, Time Charter (by Saritamer), was an exceptional filly and winner of the Oaks, the King George VI and Queen Elizabeth Diamond Stakes, the Champion Stakes, Coronation Cup, Prix Foy and Sun Chariot Stakes.

'A very pleasing colt, he's one of the most forward, seems to find life easy and should be one of our first runners. Hopefully he'll be running in May and we'll take it from there. A bonny horse.'

1439. EMIRATES WORLD (IRE) ★★★
b.c. Exceed And Excel – Enrich (Dynaformer)
May 5. Fifth foal. Half-brother to the quite useful two year old 7f winner Princeton and to the quite useful two year old 7f all-weather winner Blue Grouse (both by Maria's Mon). The dam, a fairly useful two year old 6f winner and third in the Group 3 7f C L Weld Park Stakes, is a half-sister to three winners including the 6f (at two years) and UAE 1,000 Guineas winner Infinite Spirit (by Maria's Mon). The second dam, Eternal Reve (by Diesis), a smart French 6f (at two years) to 1m winner, is a half-sister to the US Grade 1 9f winner Eternity Star.

'He's a May foal and still quite babyish but he doesn't know it himself as he's loving the routine. We'll just see how quickly he comes together but hopefully he'll be a six furlong horse.'

1440. ENTISARAT ★★★
b.c. Dansili – Morning Queen (Konigsstuhl)
February 12. Half-brother to the fair 10f (at two years) to 2m 2f winner Love Brothers (by Lomitas) and to the French and Swiss winner of four races Moonrise (by Grand Lodge). The dam won once at three years in Germany and is a sister to the German Group 1 winner and champion sire Monsun. The second dam, Mosella (by Surumu), won a listed race at three years in Germany and is a half-sister to five winners.

'A big horse that's doing everything right and will probably want a trip later in the year.'

1441. FURSAN AL FAHRA (USA) ★★★★
ch.c. Rahy – Forty Marinesca (Roar)
March 24. Second foal. $350,000Y. Keeneland September. John Ferguson. The dam, a winner and Grade 1 placed in Argentina, is a half-sister to 2 Graded stakes winners in Argentina. The second dam, Ma Sirene (by Mountdrago), is an unplaced half-sister to 2 Graded stakes winners in Argentina.

'The name means Desert Horseman. He's a nice, athletic type and one for seven furlongs in August.'

1442. HAJOUM (IRE) ★★
b.c. Exceed And Excel – Blue Iris (Petong)
February 23. Half-brother to the dual listed 5f winner (including at two years) Swiss Lake (by Indian Ridge). The dam, a useful winner of five races over 5f and 6f including the Weatherbys Super Sprint and the Redcar Two-Year-Old Trophy, is a half-sister to numerous winners including the quite useful triple 6f winner Abbajabba. The second dam, Bo' Babbity (by Strong Gale), a fair two year old 5f winner, is a half-sister to the high-class Group 3 5f King George Stakes winner Anita's Prince.

'He's quite a big horse but he's shaping up OK and could be one of our earlier types.'

1443. HAWSA (USA) ★★★
ch.f. Rahy – Jood (Nijinsky)
Sister to the top-class colt Fantastic Light, a winner of six Group/Grade 1 events including the Breeders Cup Turf, the Prince Of Wales's Stakes and the Irish Champion Stakes and to the listed 10f Pretty Polly Stakes winner and dual Group 1 placed Hi Dubai and half-sister to the fairly useful all-weather 10f winner Westbound Road (by Gone West) and the 7f UAE winner Madraar (by Mr Prospector). The dam was placed over 7f (at two years) and 10f (both her starts) and is a half-sister to the Grade 1 Ashland Stakes and Grade 1 Hollywood Oaks winner Gorgeous and to the Grade 1 Kentucky Oaks winner Seaside Attraction (herself dam of the Cherry Hinton Stakes winner Red Carnival. The second dam, Kamar (by Key to the Mint), a champion Canadian three year old filly, is a

sister to the Grade 1 winner Love Smitten (dam of the top-class middle-distance colt Swain).
'She's a big filly and will need a bit of time but she's doing everything right. One to start off at seven furlongs around autumn time, this filly is from a lovely family and Jood has done us proud'!

1444. HYPNOTIST (UAE) ★★
b.c. Halling – Poised (Rahy)
March 23. Third known foal. Brother to the very useful 2007 two year old 6f and 7f winner Gothenburg. The dam was second over 9f at Chantilly at three years and is closely related to the outstanding 1991 two year old Arazi, winner of the Breeders Cup Juvenile, the Prix Robert Papin, the Prix Morny, the Prix de la Salamandre and the Ciga 1m 1m Grand Criterium (all Group 1 events between 5f and 8.5f). The second dam, Danseur Fabuleux (by Northern Dancer), was placed in the Group 3 12f Prix de Minerve and is closely related to the US Grade 1 winner Joyeux Danseur and the very useful 12f winner Fabulous Dancer.
'He's just doing steady canters at the moment and doesn't look as if he has the speed for six furlongs.'

1445. IBN AL NAFIS (USA) ★★★★
ch.c. Distorted Humor – Stormy Bear (Storm Cat)
January 25. Third foal. $1,900,000Y. Keeneland September. John Ferguson. The dam is an unraced half-sister to the US Grade 1 winners Chief Bearhart (Breeders Cup Turf, Canadian International, Manhattan Handicap) and Explosive Red (Hollywood Derby). The second dam, Amelia Bearhart (by Bold Hour), was a stakes-placed winner in the USA.
'An athletic colt, he's a middle-distance type for next year and should be out around September time.'

1446. KARTA (IRE) ★★★
br.f. Diktat – Echo River (Irish River)
January 10. Second foal. Half-sister to the quite useful two year old 7f winner Ravi River (by Barathea). The dam was a useful two year old

6f and listed 7f winner. The second dam, Monaassabaat (by Zilzal), a very useful 6f (at two years) and listed 10f Virginia Stakes winner, is a half-sister to the US 1m stakes winner Air Dancer and to the Group 2 Criterium de Maisons-Laffitte winner Bitooh.
'Probably not as sharp as her dam, but she's shaping up nicely and we hope she'll be ready to run in July. She should have the speed for six furlongs.'

1447. KNIGHT'S VICTORY (IRE) ★★
b.c. Cape Cross – Diminuendo (Diesis)
March 11. Half-brother to the smart two year old Group 3 1m May Hill Stakes winner and French 1,000 Guineas third Calando (by Storm Cat), to Carpathian (by Danzig), a winner of five races at around 12f including on the all-weather and to the minor French winner Dimity (by Soviet Star). The dam won all four of her juvenile races from 6f to 1m including the Hoover Fillies Mile and the Cherry Hinton Stakes and at three years she won the Epsom Oaks, the Irish Oaks (in a dead-heat) and the Yorkshire Oaks. The second dam, Cacti (by Tom Rolfe), won at around 1m in the USA at three years and is out of the 8.5f Vanity Handicap winner Desert Love.
'Just going through the motions at present, he's a nice enough colt but he'll take a bit of time and will be running in the summer.'

1448. KULAIB ★★★
b.c. Invincible Spirit – Nofa's Magic (Rainbow Quest)
February 7. First foal. 200,000Y. Tattersalls October 1. John Ferguson. The dam, placed over 10f and 12f, is a half-sister to five winners including the Group 1 9f Prix Jean Prat winner Olden Times. The second dam, Garah (by Ajdal), a very useful winner of four races over 6f, was second in the Group 3 5f Duke Of York Stakes and is a half-sister to six winners.
'The dam is by Rainbow Quest but he's coming together quickly and will be one of our earlier types.'

1449. MAHYOUB ★★★
b.c. Elusive Quality – Mysterial (Alleged)
February 22. Half-brother to the Group 1 1m Queen Anne Stakes and Group 2 7f Champagne Stakes winner Dubai Destination, to the useful 10f and 10.5f winner Destination Dubai (both by Kingmambo) and the very useful dual 7f winner Librettist (by Danzig). The dam ran unplaced twice and is a half-sister to the top-class Prix de l'Abbaye and July Cup winner Agnes World (by Danzig), to the champion Japanese sprinter/miler Hishi Akebono and the US stakes winner My Sea Castles. The second dam, Mysteries (by Seattle Slew), was third in the Group 3 Musidora Stakes and is out of the Group 3 Prix Quincey winner Phydilla.
'From a fabulous family, this horse appears to have lots of class but he's a big colt and won't be rushed. He'll want seven furlongs or a mile later in the year.'

1450. MANAAQEB ★★★
b.f. Cape Cross – Al Sifaat (Unfuwain)
February 18. First foal. The dam, a quite useful two year old 6f winner, is a half-sister to the useful listed 6f winner Judhoor (by Alhaarth). The second dam, Almurooj (by Zafonic), a moderate 5f and 6f placed maiden, is a half-sister to seven winners including the smart 6f (at two years), Group 2 7f Challenge Stakes and Group 3 7f Greenham Stakes winner Munir and the very useful Irish 1m listed stakes winner and Group 1 Coronation Stakes second Hasbah. (Hamdan Al Maktoum).
'A smart filly and a very easy mover, she's quite forward and pleasing. She could be out in mid-summer over six furlongs.'

1451. MARMOOM FLOWER (IRE) ★★★
b.f. Cape Cross – Requesting (Rainbow Quest)
January 27. Closely related to the fair two year old 6f all-weather winner Desert Flora (by Green Desert) and half-sister to the fairly useful 2007 two year old 1m winner Dr Faustus (by Sadler's Wells). The dam is an unraced half-sister to the very useful Irish listed 14f winner and Irish Oaks third Arrikala, to the useful Irish 12f listed winner Alouette (herself dam of the dual Champion Stakes winner Alborada and the triple German Group 1 winner Albanova), the Doncaster Cup winner Alleluia, the very smart Group 2 10f Nassau Stakes and Sun Chariot Stakes winner Last Second (dam of the French 2,000 Guineas winner Aussie Rules) and the placed dam of the Group 1 winners Yesterday and Quarter Moon. The second dam, Alruccaba (by Crystal Palace), a quite useful two year old 6f winner, is a half-sister to three minor winners.
'She's backward at present and will take a bit of time to strengthen up but she's a very attractive filly and is a nice prospect for later in the year.'

1452. MY VISION (USA) ★★★★
b.br.c. Dynaformer – Preach
(Mr Prospector)
May 17. Tenth foal. $2,900,000Y. Keeneland September. John Ferguson. Half-brother to the dual US Grade 2 winner Pulpit, to the minor US two year old winners Orate and Convent (all by A P Indy) and the minor US stakes-placed winner Tell It (by Storm Cat). The dam won the two year old Grade 1 1m Frizette Stakes and was Grade 1 placed twice and is a half-sister to 3 stakes-placed winners. The second dam, Narrate (by Honest Pleasure), won eight races including the Grade 3 8.5f Falls City Handicap and is a half-sister to the US Graded stakes winners Announce, Double Feint and Region.
'A May foal and a big horse, he has quite a lot of strengthening to do but he's very promising and going the right way.'

1453. NASEEHAH (USA) ★★★
ch.c. Rahy – Helwa (Silver Hawk)
January 23. Fourth foal. 175,000Y. Doncaster St Leger. R O'Gorman. Half-brother to the US winner of three races at three and four years Whimsical Day (by Spinning World). The dam is an unraced sister to the two year old listed 1m winner Silver Colours and a half-sister to three winners including the Japanese Grade 2 winner God Of Chance. The second dam, Team Colors (by Mr Prospector), is an unraced half-sister to four winners.
'A useful, willing colt and a nice prospect for the mid-summer.'

1454. SILK TRAIL ★★★
b.f. Dubai Destination – Satin Flower (Shadeed)
February 24. Half-sister to the very smart two year old Group 1 6f Middle Park Stakes winner Lujain, to the useful two year old 6f winner and Group 3 6f Coventry Stakes second Botanical (both by Seeking The Gold), the very useful listed 7f (at two years) and listed 12f winner Lilium (by Nashwan) and the fairly useful two year old 5f winner Deceptor (by Machiavellian). The dam, a smart winner of the Group 3 7f Jersey Stakes and second in the Grade 1 9f Queen Elizabeth II Challenge Cup, is a half-sister to seven winners including the US Grade 1 10f Santa Anita Handicap winner Martial Law. The second dam, Sateen (by Round Table), won two 6f stakes events in the USA.
'This is a lovely filly. Tough and strong, she should be able to show us plenty of speed and we hope she'll be out by early July.'

1455. SPIRIT OF EMIRATES (USA) ★★★★
b.c. Gone West – Myth To Reality
(Sadler's Wells)
March 30. Twelfth foal. 1,000,000Y. Tattersalls October 1. John Ferguson. Closely related to three winners by Kingmambo including the French Oaks, French 1,000 Guineas, Prix Marcel Boussac and Prix Morny winner Divine Proportions and half-brother to numerous winners including the Prix Jacques Le Marois winner Whipper (by Miesque's Son), the French listed winner Assos (by Alleged) and the useful 7f winner and Group 3 placed Mythical Kid (by Lemon Drop Kid). The dam, a listed winner of four races at three years in France, was second in the Group 3 Prix de Minerve and is a half-sister to six winners. The second dam, Millieme (by Mill Reef), a useful French Group 3 1m placed maiden, is a sister to Shirley Heights and to the dam of the Ribblesdale Stakes winner and high-class broodmare Gull Nook.
'He's a lovely type and is thriving at the moment. We hope he'll have the speed to start off at six furlongs in mid-summer.'

1456. SUBA (USA) ★★★
b.f. Seeking The Gold – Zomaradah (Deploy)
April 13. Half-sister to the high-class miler Dubawi (by Dubai Millennium) and to the listed 10f winner Princess Nada (by Barathea). The dam, a winner of six races including the Group 1 Italian Oaks, the Group 2 Royal Whip Stakes and the Group 2 Premio Lydia Tesio, is a half-sister to several winners. The second dam, Jawaher (by Dancing Brave), was placed over 1m and 9f and is a half-sister to the Derby winner High Rise.
'A very pretty filly with a lot to like about her, she's from a family that has served us well. A nice filly, she should have the speed for six furlongs and we'd like to see her racing in mid-summer.'

1457. TAARAB ★★★★
ch.c. Refuse To Bend – Tanzania (Darshaan)
April 8. Half-brother to the fairly useful 9f and 10f winner Serengeti (by Singspiel), to the French two year old and subsequent high-class US winner Amorama and the quite useful triple 12f winner Milwaukee. The dam, a dual 12f and 13f winner, is a half-sister to the very useful listed 10f Predominate Stakes winner Roscius. The second dam, Rosefinch (by Blushing Groom), a smart filly, ran seven times at three years and won twice over 10f including the Group 1 Prix Saint-Alary. She is a half-sister to the very useful 7.3f and 9f English winner and subsequent Grade 2 Long Island Handicap winner Shaima.
'This colt has an excellent temperament and is loving everything he does. He has class and should be one for seven furlongs in mid-summer.'

1458. YIRGA ★★★
b.c. Cape Cross – Auratum (Carson City)
March 5. The dam won over 6f at two years at Deauville and was a fairly useful fourth in the listed 6f Cecil Frail Stakes at three years. She is a half-sister to numerous winners in the USA, notably the Breeders Cup Juvenile winner Gilded Time. The second dam, Gilded Lilly (by What A Pleasure), won four races in the USA and is a half-sister to the Belmont Stakes winner High Echelon.
'The dam raced for Godolphin when we were at Evry. This colt is a forward type, very willing and appears to have speed.'

ALAN SWINBANK

1459. ACCLABEN (IRE) ★★★
b.c. Acclamation – Jour de Grace (Steve's Friend)
April 29. Fourth foal. €40,000Y. Tattersalls Ireland. J Glover. Half-brother to two winners in Norway by In The Wings and Turtle Island. The dam won four races in Scandinavia and is a half-sister to three winners. The second dam, Annee de Grace (by Chief Singer), won at three years in France and is a half-sister to seven winners. (Mr A Butler).
'He's very forward and looks very much like his sire. Like a lot of our two year old's he needs a bit of sun on his back but he'll win and he'll probably be better over six furlongs than five.'

1460. HONIMIERE (IRE) ★★★★
b.f. Fasliyev – Sugar (Hernando)
April 1. Fifth foal. €8,500Y. Tattersalls Ireland. R Lappin. Half-sister to a minor winer abroad by Daggers Drawn. The dam is an unraced half-sister to seven winners including the French listed winner Amato. The second dam, Ahohoney (by Ahonoora), won the Group 3 Prix Fille del'Air (twice) and is a half-sister to five winners.
'She's a lovely filly – a superstar! She'll win first time out and was a cheap horse bought in Ireland. The owner nicked her off me one morning over breakfast! Probably one of the best fillies we've ever had, she's very straightforward and learned very quickly, the first time we tried her in the stalls it was as if she'd been doing it all her life. We'll start her at five and see where we go from there but she's got scope and we'll probably have a nice filly on our hands next year.'
TRAINER'S BARGAIN BUY

1461. IVOR NOVELLO (IRE) ★★★★ ♠
b.c. Noverre – Pearly Brooks (Efisio)
April 14. Third foal. 43,000Y. Doncaster St The dam, a fair three year old 6f winner, is a sister to four winners including the Group 1 Phoenix Stakes winner Pips Pride and a half-sister to four winners. The second dam, Elkie Brooks (by Relkino), is a placed half-sister to one winner. (Duncan Davidson).
'A lovely horse and he's probably going to be our first runner. He will win, he wasn't very big when

we bought him but he's grown into a nice individual now. I think he'd be the sort we should just have as a two year old because I don't think he'll train on and his future next year might be as a dirt horse in America. He'll be fine over five furlongs because he's a very sharp horse.'

1462. RISING KHELEYF (IRE) ★★
ch.c. Kheleyf – Rising Spirits (Cure The Blues)
March 7. Eleventh living foal. 18,000Y. Doncaster St Leger. Not sold. Half-brother to five winners including the listed winner and Group 2 10f Sun Chariot Stakes second Gino's Spirits (by Perugino) and the 12f winner Nine Barrow Down (by Danehill). The dam, a fair two year old 7f winner, later won in the USA and is a half-sister to six winners including the dual Group 3 winner Citidancer. The second dam, Mrs McArdy (by Tribal Chief), won the 1,000 Guineas. (Mr D Bamlett).
'He's a bit on the lean side and he's got sore shins at the minute but he's alright and he's shown enough. He'll probably win over five or six furlongs and I think he'll go on fast ground judging by his action.'

1463. UNNAMED ★★★★
b.br.g. One Cool Cat – Amizette (Forty Niner)
April 17. Ninth foal. €42,000Y. Goffs Million. J Glover. Half-brother to the fairly useful 2007 Irish two year old 7.5f winner King Of Rome (by Montjeu), to the minor US winner of five races Trident House (by A P Indy), the minor US two year old winner Dancingintheaisles (by Giant's Causeway) and a minor winner at four years in Dubai by Storm Cat. The dam is a placed sister to the Grade 2 Peter Pan Stakes and Grade 2 Withers Stakes winner Twining and a half-sister to 1four winners including the US Grade 1 winners Althea, Ali Oop and Ketoh and to the unraced dam of Green Desert. The second dam, Courtly Dee (by Never Bend), won four races at up to 6f. (Mrs J Porter).
'Probably a mid-summer horse over six or seven furlongs. He's another one that will win, he did have a bit of a temperament but we got him cut. That sorted him out and he's never looked back since. A big, strapping horse.'

1464. UNNAMED ★★★
b.g. Danehill Dancer – Band Of Angels (Alzao)
May 7. Sixth foal. €37,000Y. Goffs Million. J J O'Leary. Half-brother to the Hawkstar Express (by Hawk Wing), unplaced in two starts at two years in 2007, to the quite useful 11f winner Mont Saint Michel (by Montjeu) and the quite useful Irish two year old 7f winner Dance On The Moon (by Fasliyev). The dam is an unraced half-sister to five winners including the top-class Epsom Derby, Irish Champion Stakes and Dewhurst Stakes winner Dr Devious, the Japanese listed winner Shinko King, the smart Group 3 13.4f Ormonde Stakes winner Royal Court and the very useful 6f Greenlands Stakes winner Archway. The second dam, Rose Of Jericho (by Alleged), is an unraced half-sister to five winners. (Mrs J Peat).
'This is a very interesting colt, he's coming along nicely, he's very sharp and he'll be running in May I should think. Five and six furlongs will suit him. He's a lovely individual with scope and I'm very pleased with him.'

1465. UNNAMED ★★★
b.g. Val Royal – Boley Lass (Archway)
April 4. Second living foal. €36,000Y. Goffs Sportsman's. R Haggas. The dam, a quite useful 6f (at two years) and 7f winner of six races in Ireland, is a half-sister to two winners. The second dam, Indian Sand (by Indian King), is an unplaced half-sister to eight winners.
'He has a bit of a temperament so we're having him cut. I love these Val Royal's – they're very good horses. I had the first good winner Val Royal had, he was called Val Benny and he won a maiden for me at Ayr before we sold him on to America where he won a Grade 2. This colt will be racing in June or July I should think and he'll make a three year old as well. He's a big, scopey horse and we love him.'

1466. UNNAMED ★★
b.c. Bernstein – Lady Carson (Carson City)
April 4. Fifth foal. $25,000Y. Keeneland September. D McKeown. Half-brother to the very useful Irish 5f winner Followmyfootsteps

(by Giant's Causeway), to the US turf winner of nine races Jacqui's Promise (by Loup Sauvage) and the minor US sprint winner of three races Quiet Style (by Real Quiet). The dam, a sprint stakes winner of four races in the USA, is out of the unplaced Heathers Surprise (by Best Turn), herself a half-sister to the top-class broodmare Ballade.
'A lovely horse but we ha problems with breaking him so he's a bit behind the others. He could do with putting a bit of weight on actually but he's a horse for the future and if he's half as good as his half-brother Followmyfootsteps he'll be alright. He'll probably be a six or seven furlong horse next year.'

TOM TATE

1467. BOB'S SMITHY ★★★
ch.c. Compton Place – Marie La Rose (Night Shift)
January 18. Ninth foal. 27,000Y. Doncaster St Leger. Tom Tate. Half-brother to the fair two year old 8.5f winner Prime Meridian (by Observatory), to the French two year old 1m and subsequent hurdles winner Contemporary Art (by Blushing Flame) and the French winner of six races from 2 to 6 years Danni La Rose (by Lycius). The dam, a French 10f winner, is a half-sister to six winners. The second dam, Rose Bonbon (by High Top), a winner over 13f in France, is a half-sister to the French Group 1 winners Le Nain Jaune, Indian Rose and Vert Amande and to the dam of Groom Dancer.
'He's a very strong, sprinting type two year old. He's nice and should be a mid-season runner.'

1468. KNOW BY NOW ★★★
b.c. Piccolo – Addicted To Love (Touching Wood)
February 14. Ninth reported foal. 52,000Y. Doncaster St Leger. Tom Tate. Half-brother to the fair triple 5f winner Daddy Cool (by Kyllachy), to the 5.7f winner Go Go Girl (by Pivotal), the 7f and 1m winner of five races Unchain My Heart (by Pursuit Of Love), the Irish 1m and 10f winner Can't Buy Me Love (by Bijou d'Inde) and a bumpers winner by Danzero – all only modest. The dam, a fair 10f to 14f winner,

is a half-sister to seven winners including the smart Group 1 6f Middle Park Stakes second Red Carpet. The second dam, Fleur Rouge (by Pharly), a fair two year old 6f winner, is a half-sister to five winners including the US Grade 2 winner Colway Rally. (Mrs Sylvia Clegg & Louise Worthington).

'A nice, big, strong colt that won't be particularly early but he should be out before mid-summer. He's a sprinting type two year old.'

1469. REGAL LYRIC (IRE) ★★
b.c. Royal Applause – Alignment (Alzao)
February 26. Sixth foal. Half-brother to a winner over hurdles by Sadler's Wells. The dam was placed 3 times including when second in the Group 3 Prestige Stakes and is a half-sister to four winners including the Group 2 Great Voltigeur winner Bonny Scot and the dam of the King George and 2,000 Guineas winner Golan. The second dam, Scots Lass (by Shirley Heights), won over 13f.

'Going nicely but much more of a three year old type and he'll only make a two year old towards the back-end of the season.'

MARK TOMPKINS
1470. ASTRABRAVA ★★★
ch.f. Falbrav – Nutmeg (Lake Coniston)
February 28. Third foal. Half-sister to the fair 2007 6f placed two year old Spice Trade (by Medicean). The dam, a fair 7f winner at five years, is a half-sister to nine winners here and abroad. The second dam, Overdue Reaction (by Be My Guest), is an unplaced half-sister to seven winners including the US Grade 2 winner Wait Till Monday. (Mystic Meg Ltd).

'She's definitely alright. She goes well and she's a nice, strong filly. I'm very happy with her and she's be fine from the middle of the season onwards.'

1471. ASTRALEO ★★★
ch.c. Groom Dancer – Astrolove (Bigstone)
March 1. Second foal. 9,000Y. Tattersalls October 4. Not sold. The dam is an unplaced half-sister to five minor winners here and abroad. The second dam, Pizzazz (by Unfuwain),

is an unplaced half-sister to four winners including the Group 3 Nell Gwyn Stakes winner Thrilling Day (by Groom Dancer). (Mystic Meg Ltd).

'He definitely goes alright. He's a very strong, attractive colt and built like a brick outhouse. He'll be one of our early runners, probably from late April onwards.'

1472. BERTIE SMALLS ★★★
b.c. Xaar – Largo (Selkirk)
January 29. Second foal. 12,000Y. Tattersalls October 3. M Tompkins. Half-brother to Mashrai (by Dubai Destination), unplaced in two starts at two years in 2007. The dam, a fairly useful dual 12f winner, is a half-sister to the useful 1m (at two years) and 2m winner Coventina. The second dam, Lady Of The Lake (by Caerleon), a useful 2m listed winner of four races, is a half-sister to five winners including the Italian Group 3 winner Guest Connections. (The Grass Partnership).

'A lovely, strong, scopey horse. He's doing everything right at present and although he won't be early he should be out in May or June and is sure to win a race. More of a nursery type horse over six or seven furlongs and he'll improve as the season goes on.'

1473. CALL IT ON ★★
ch.c. Raise A Grand – Birthday Present (Cadeaux Genereux)
April 11. Third foal. €36,000Y. Goffs Sportsman's. Mark Tompkins. Half-brother to the quite useful 2007 two year old 6f winner and Group 3 6f third May Day Queen (by Danetime). The dam is an unraced half-sister to three winners including the Group 1 Moyglare Stud Stakes third Supposition. The second dam, Topicality (by Topsider), won once at three years and is a sister to the Cherry Hinton and Fred Darling Stakes winner Top Socialite and a half-sister to the US Grade 1 winners Expelled and Exbourne. (GPD Investments UK Ltd).

'I like him, he's done nothing but grow and he's a big, strong, scopey horse – typical of those I buy. One for the mid-to-backend of the year and he's a decent horse. He looks the part.'

1474. CORNISH ROSE ★★★★
b.f. Kheleyf – Kiva (Indian Ridge)
May 3. €41,000Y. Tattersalls Ireland. M Tompkins. Half-sister to the modest 6f winner Simpsons Gamble (by Tagula). The dam is an unraced half-sister to three winners. The second dam, Hagwah (by Dancing Brave), a very useful dual listed winner from 1m to 12f, is a half-sister to the very useful two year old listed 1m winner and subsequent US Grade 1 winner Sarafan. (M A W Winter).
'I think Kheleyf could turn out to be a good sire. This filly is a natural and has looked that way from day one. We're getting on with her and hopefully she'll be out in May. She goes well, has plenty of scope and she should mature as the year goes on.' TRAINER'S BARGAIN BUY

1475. DAZINSKI ★★★
ch.c. Sulamani – Shuheb (Nashwan)
February 13. First foal. 20,000Y. Tattersalls October 3. M Tompkins. The dam, placed fourth once over 10f from two starts, is a half-sister to three winners including the Group 3 Derby Trial third Hazeymm. The second dam, Shimna (by Mr Prospector), is a placed half-sister to the St Leger winner Shantou.
'This is a very easy moving horse, he's strong and does everything right and we like him a lot. He's going to be a very nice horse, he has a good temperament and we love him. He'll run from the mid-season onwards and he'll win a race this year without a doubt.'

1476. INTIKAMA (IRE) ★★★
ch.f. Intikhab – Really Gifted (Cadeaux Genereux)
March 2. Fifth foal. €18,500Y. Tattersalls Ireland. Mark Tompkins. Half-brother to the quite useful 12f all-weather winner Actodos (by Act One). The dam is an unraced half-sister to five winners including the listed 6f (at two years) and Group 3 7f Nell Gwyn Stakes winner Misterah. The second dam, Jasarah (by Green Desert), was a fair 7f placed maiden. (Vallance, John & Kelly).
'She's a very strong, two year old type. A great mover, a great goer and she's doing everything right. I got her going early but then I had to back

off her because she started growing. She'll be a nice filly, starting around June time and I think the sire is good too. I've never had an Intikhab before because although I've liked them I haven't been able to buy.'

1477. KHAYAR (IRE) ★★★
b.c. Refuse To Bend – Khatela (Shernazar)
April 11. Fifth living foal. 26,000Y. Tattersalls December. Not sold. Half-brother to the useful two year old 7.2f winner and Group 3 9f Prix de Conde second Massive (by Marju), to the French 11f winner Jimbeck and a winner over jumps in France (both by Night Shift). The dam won over 1m and 9f in Ireland and is a half-sister to four minor winners. The second dam, Khatima (by Relko), won at three years and is a half-sister to two winners.
'A lovely, great big, strong horse. He's a scopey horse that'll make a start in late summer and he'll be a proper horse in time. We like him a lot.'

1478. MT KINTYRE (IRE) ★★★★
b.c. Mull Of Kintyre – Nihonpillow Mirai (Zamindar)
March 16. First foal. €70,000Y. Goffs Million. M Tompkins. The dam is an unplaced half-sister to five winners. The second dam, Ala Mahlik (by Ahonoora), won twice over 6f at two years, was fourth in the 1,000 Guineas and is a sister to the Rockfel Stakes winner Negligent. (Mrs G A E Smith).
'He belongs to the same owners as Bob's Return and this is a really nice horse. If he hadn't been by Mull Of Kintyre he'd have made 300,000. A big, strong, scopey horse that'll be out in mid-summer. He goes very well, he's sure to win a race this year and then go on and be quite a nice horse.'

1479. MY GIRL JODE ★★
ch.f. Haafhd – Brush Strokes (Cadeaux Genereux)
March 27. Half-sister to the quite useful 12f winner Kassiopeia (by Galileo), to the moderate 6f winner Tenancy (by Rock Of Gibraltar) and the minor French three year old 10.5f winner

Craft Fair (by Danehill). The dam is an unraced sister to the Japanese two year old winner Christian Name and a half-sister to four winners including the very useful two year old dual 7f winner and Group 1 Racing Post Trophy second Mudeer. The second dam, Colorvista (by Shirley Heights), is an unraced half-sister to nine winners including Colorspin (winner of the Irish Oaks and dam of the Group 1 winners Zee Zee Top, Opera House and Kayf Tara), Bella Colora (winner of the Prix de l'Opera and dam of the very smart colt Stagecraft) and the Irish Champion Stakes winner Cezanne. (Mrs G A E Smith).

'A very backward filly, but she's a good walker, she's strong with a good temperament and she canters well. Will be alright in time but should stay well next year.'

1480. OLAUDAH EQUIANO ★★★

ch.c. Dubai Destination – Magongo
(Be My Chief)
May 6. Eighth foal. 22,000Y. Tattersalls October 2. John Hassett. The dam won over 5f at two years and was second in the Group 3 Prix de Cabourg and is a half-sister to eight winners including the Irish 1,000 Guineas winner Classic Park, the US Grade 2 winner Rumpipumpy and the Group 3 July Stakes third Wilde Rufo. The second dam, Wanton (by Kris), a useful two year old 5f winner and third in the Group 2 Flying Childers Stakes, is a half-sister to the listed 5f St Hugh's Stakes winner and Group 2 5f Prix du Gros-Chene second Easy Option (herself dam of the Group 1 Prix de la Foret winner Court Masterpiece). (Countess of Halifax).

'I like the sire and this is a strong, real two year old type. He's quite quick so he should be running in early May I should think, but we think he can go alright – he isn't useless! He's a May foal so he'll improve as the year goes on.'

1481. ORTHOLOGY (IRE) ★★

b.c. Kalanisi – Al Shakoor (Barathea)
April 5. Second foal. 13,000Y. Tattersalls October 3. M Tompkins. The dam is an unraced half-sister to one winner. The second dam, Gold Dodge (by Slew O'Gold), a listed 10f winner of

two races in France, is a half-sister to eight winners including the French dual Group 3 winner Prospect Park.

'A strong horse that's going to need time. I've been quite lucky with the sire and this colt is a great walker but he's one for later on.'

1482. PREMIER SUPERSTAR ★★★

ch.f. Bertolini – Absolve (Diesis)
January 18. Third foal. €14,000Y. Tattersalls Ireland. M Tompkins. Half-sister to the fair dual 5f winner Windjammer (by Kyllachy). The dam is an unraced half-sister to four winners including the listed winners Aljhaarif and Wunderwood. The second dam, Jasoorah (by Sadler's Wells), won three races at two and three years and is a half-sister to five winners. (Mr R M Jones).

'She's strong and scopey and we're just starting to kick on with her a little bit so she should be running from May onwards I should think. She looks like being a two year old and she was cheap too. She goes alright and will be a five/six furlong filly.'

1483. ROYAL ACCLAIM ★★★

b.f. Royal Applause – Movie Queen
(Danehill)
January 28. First foal. The dam is an unraced half-sister to numerous winners including the Irish two year old listed 6f winner Desert Ease and the Group 3 7f Concorde Stakes and Group 3 7f Tetrarch Stakes winner Two-Twenty-Two. The second dam, Easy To Copy (by Affirmed), was a useful winner of five races from 1m to 12f including the Group 2 Premio Legnano, is a sister to the Irish 1,000 Guineas winner Trusted Partner (dam of the Grade 1 winner Dress To Thrill). (J H Ellis).

'She's a strong filly out of a lovely mare, she looks the part and is cantering. She's grown a bit but she'll be out when she gets a bit of sun on her back. from May or June onwards I should think. She could be anything and she's from a lovely family.'

1484. TOP TINKER ★★

b.c. Vettori – Topatori (Topanoora)
April 29. Half-brother to the Group 3 10.3f

winner Topatoo (by Bahamian Bounty), to the quite useful 1m to 14f winner Toparudi (by Rudimentary), the fair dual 1m winner Top Shot (by College Chapel) and the fair 1m winner Top Tiger (by Mtoto). The dam was a quite useful 7f to 11f winner of four races. The second dam, Partygoer (by Cadeaux Genereux), was unplaced. *'It's a marvellous family and this colt goes well, he's got a great attitude and he'll be racing from June or July onwards. None of the family have really been two year old's and they all get better in time.'*

1485. UNNAMED ★★

b.c. Tagula – Allurah (Goldmark)
April 12. Fourth foal. €20,000Y. Tattersalls Ireland. M Tompkins. Half-sister to a winner in Macau by Titus Livius and to the modest Irish three year old 1m winner Roy's Delight (by Indian Lodge). The dam is an unraced half-sister to three winners. The second dam, Genetta (by Green Desert), is a placed half-sister to ten winners. *'She's a nice little filly and I haven't sold her yet. I like her, she has a very good attitude, she's genuine and a good mover. I think she'll always give her best.'*

1486. UNNAMED ★★

b.f. Hernando – Dulcinea (Selkirk)
March 2. Sister to the useful 7f winner and listed-placed Hideaway Heroine (by Hernando) and half-sister to the modest triple 1m winner Emily's Place (by Mujadil) and the modest 12f all-weather winner Two Of A Kind (by Ashkalani). The dam, a fair 7f and 1m winner, is a half-sister to five winners including the French listed winner Amato. The second dam, Ahohoney (by Ahonoora), won the Group 3 10.5f Prix Fille de l'Air (twice) and is a half-sister to five winners. (Dullingham Park Stud). *'She's alright but backward and won't be running until the autumn when she'll give us a bit of fun and go on from there.'*

1487. UNNAMED ★★★

br.c. Indian Haven – Lady Cinders (Dance Of Life)
March 14. Fourth foal. €54,000Y. Tattersalls

Ireland. M Tompkins. The dam, a quite useful 7f and 1m winner of three races at four years, is a half-sister to seven winners including the Irish 2,000 Guineas winner Flash Of Steel. The second dam, Spark Of Fire (by Run The Gantlet), is an unplaced half-sister to the US Grade 1 winners Spark of Life (herself dam of the Premio Roma winner Fire Of Life) and Musical Lark and to the French Group 3 Prix de la Grotte winner Hartebeest. *'This is a lovely colt. I think Indian Haven might make a good sire as we have two of them and they're both alright. I bought this lovely, big, black horse from Fairyhouse and I'd have bought him whatever the price. He moves well and he'll be out from the middle of the season onwards. He'll be a proper horse later on.'*

1488. UNNAMED ★★★

ch.f. Medicean – Sosumi (Be My Chief)
January 17. Second foal. Half-sister to the fair 1m winner Tevez (by Sakhee) and to the two year old 1m seller winner Benayoun (by Inchinor). The dam, a useful two year old dual 5f winner, was fourth in the Group 3 Prix du Calvados. The second dam, Princess Deya (by Be My Guest), ran twice unplaced and is a half-sister to the Eclipse Stakes winner Compton Admiral and the Group 1 1m Queen Elizabeth II Stakes winner Summoner. (Sakal Family). *'She's grown a bit on me so that's stopped me from getting on with her, but she's strong and active. I've trained all the family and she'll be one for the middle of the season. Six or seven furlongs will suit her and she'll be fine.'*

MARCUS TREGONING

1489. ALBASEET (IRE) ★★★

b.g. Desert Style – Double Eight (Common Grounds)
February 15. Seventh foal. 52,000Y. Doncaster St Leger. Shadwell Estate Co. Brother to the useful two year old 6f winner and listed-placed Destinate and half-brother to the fair 11.6f winner Fiza (by Revoque) and the fair all-weather 13f winner Principal Witness (by Definite Article). The dam, a fair dual 12f winner, is a sister to three winners including the useful

two year old listed 6f Doncaster Stakes winner Proper Madam and a half-sister to two winners. The second dam, Boldabsa (by Persian Bold), won over 9f and 10f in Ireland and is a half-sister to five winners. (Hamdan Al Maktoum).
'We gelded him because he wasn't quite sound but having had a month off he's been fine and he'll definitely make a two year old. I haven't done much with him but he moves well and he's a set little two year old type.'

1490. ALMUTAWAAZIN ★★★
b.c. Nayef – Crown Water (Chief's Crown)
April 20. Eleventh foal. 120,000Y. Tattersalls October 1. Shadwell Estate Co. Half-brother to the Italian two year old winner Rabarama (by Xaar), to four minor winners in the USA by Cherokee Run, Holy Bull, Tammany and Virginia Rapids and a winner in Greece by Cherokee Run. The dam, a minor US two year old 1m winner, is a half-sister to four winners including the minor stakes winner Track Gossip (herself dam of the US dual Grade 3 winner Crash Course). The second dam, Water Crystals (by Crystal Water), a winner of eight races in the USA including a stakes event and Grade 1 placed, is a half-sister to seven winners. (Hamdan Al Maktoum).
'Yes, he's a very nice horse bred by Harry Ormesher who also bred Sir Percy. He's a good mover and the thing I particularly like about Nqyef's is that they're particularly good doers and they tend to be sound like he was. This colt is actually quite like Nayef as he's got a very similar hind leg and he's a similarly topped horse. I think he's particularly nice.'

1491. ARWAAH (IRE) ★★★★
b.f. Dalakhani – Sahool (Unfuwain)
February 18. First foal. The dam, a 1m (at two years) and listed 12f winner, was second in the Group 2 Lancashire Oaks and is a half-sister to two winners. The second dam, Mathaayl (by Shadeed), a quite useful 6f and 10f winner, is a half-sister to three winners including the dams of the Group/Graded stakes winners Kayrawan, Asfurah and Istintaj. (Hamdan Al Maktoum).
'I trained the dam who was useful if not top-

class. Like a lot of Dalakhani's this filly is quite leggy and extremely athletic and I like her a lot. I think she's very, very nice. A look at her pedigree shows she's obviously one for later in the year but she's done a few sharp canters, she moves well and has a good attitude. A nice filly for the autumn I would have thought.'

1492. BEDAYAAT ★★★
ch.f. Alhaarth – Elhida (Muktahid)
May 16. Sixth foal. Half-sister to the quite useful 2007 two year old dual 5f winner Hadaf (by Fasliyev) and to the fair three year old 6f winner Katheer (by Anabaa). The dam, a useful two year old 6f winner, is a sister to the useful two year old 6f winner and Group 3 July Stakes second Juwwi. The second dam, Nouvelle Star (by Luskin Star), won from 5f to 8.2f in Australia including a Grade 2 event and was the champion older filly at four years. (Hamdan Al Maktoum).
'This filly has natural speed, she's done quite a bit already and she's one of my earlier types. Despite her late foaling date she's got plenty of speed and she looks strong enough. I think she'll be a six furlong filly.'

1493. COLORADO DAWN ★★
ch.f. Fantastic Light – Colorspin (High Top)
April 15. Half-sister to the top-class King George VI and Queen Elizabeth Diamond Stakes winner Opera House, to the Ascot Gold Cup and Irish St Leger winner Kayf Tara (both by Sadler's Wells), the Group 1 10f Prix de l'Opera winner Zee Zee Top (by Zafonic), the very useful 10f and 11.7f winner and Brigadier Gerard Stakes and Hardwicke Stakes placed Highland Dress (by Lomond) and the quite useful 12f winner Turn Of A Century (by Halling). The dam won three races, notably the Irish Oaks and is a half-sister to the Irish Champion Stakes winner Cezanne and the Group 2 Prix de l'Opera winner Bella Colora (herself dam of the high class colt Stagecraft). The second dam, Reprocolor (by Jimmy Reppin), won three races including the Group 3 Lingfield Oaks Trial and the Group 3 Lancashire Oaks. (Meon Valley Stud).
'It's very nice to have one owned by the Meon

Valley Stud. She's only just arrived but she's very active, holds herself well and I like her.'

1494. DIAMOND HEIST ★★★
ch.c. Domedriver – Carenage (Alzao)
January 2. Second foal. 11,000Y. Tattersalls October 3. M Tregoning. Half-brother to the fair 2008 three year old 9.5f winner Caribana (by Hernando). The dam, a quite useful 12f winner, is a half-sister to two winners. The second dam, Key Change (by Darshaan), won the Yorkshire Oaks and is a half-sister to seven winners.
'We bought him very cheaply at Newmarket because he turned his off-fore out but as he's got wider through his chest the conformation has improved dramatically. I'd say it's pretty good, he's done lots of sharp canters and you wouldn't expect him to be particularly early but he's improving and will probably be one for a seven furlong start.'

1495. DREAM CITY (IRE) ★★★
b.f. Elusive City – On View (Distant View)
March 20. Second foal. €21,000Y. Goffs Sportsman's. M Tregoning. The dam is an unplaced half-sister to two minor winners. The second dam, Wandesta (by Nashwan), won three Grade 1 events in the USA and is a half-sister to eight winners.
'She's got bags of pace and I just hope she's going to get a trip but she's pretty quick. She looks like she really wants to go and if I get one of these two year old's out fairly quickly this will be the one. A sharp filly that knows her job.'

1496. FINJAAN ★★★★ ♠
b.c. Royal Applause – Alhufoof (Dayjur)
March 12. Fifth foal. Brother to the modest three year old 7f winner Fustaan . The dam, a fairly useful two year old 6f winner, was fourth in the Group 3 7f Nell Gwyn Stakes and is closely related to the quite useful two year old 6f winner Habub and a half-sister to the useful 1m winner Amanah. The second dam, Cheval Volant (by Kris S), won five races from 5.5f to 8.5f in the USA including the Hollywood Starlet Stakes and the Las Virgines Stakes (both Grade 1 1m events). (Hamdan Al Maktoum).

'He'll be an early two year old and he shows bags of promise, I'm quite excited by him and I like him a lot. If we're going to have a little team that might make it to Ascot he'll be one of them. Hopefully he'll make the grade but he'll have to win a couple of times first. He could easily do that though. He has a much better temperament than his older full-brother.'

1497. GHAAYER ★★
ch.c. Nayef – Valthea (Antheus)
March 5. Tenth foal. 220,000Y. Tattersalls October 2. Shadwell Estate Co. Half-brother to the listed 7f Prix du Pin winner Vert Val (by Septieme Ciel and herself dam of the Group 3 Norfolk Stakes winner Russian Valour) and to the minor French and US winner Prospectheus (by Gone West). The dam won once at three years in France and is a half-sister to 12 winners including the Observer Gold Cup, French 2,000 Guineas and 10.5f Prix Lupin winner and good sire Green Dancer, the US Grade 3 winner Ercolano and the US Graded stakes winner Val Danseur. The second dam, Green Valley (by Val de Loir), was an unraced daughter of the Prix de l'Abbaye and Prix Robert Papin winner Sly Pola.
'A nice, straightforward horse, the type to start over seven furlongs. He's done a lot of sharp canters, he's held his condition well and of course I like the Nayef's.'

1498. HASEILA (USA) ★★
b.f. Forestry – Unify (Farma Way)
April 21. Seventh foal. $500,000Y. Keeneland September. Shadwell Estate Co. Closely related to the quite useful Irish 7.5f Arcadius (by Giant's Causeway) and half-sister to the minor US winner of four races Coherent (by Danzig). The dam, a winner and Grade 3 placed in the USA, is a half-sister to the Graded stakes winners Caress, Country Cat, Della Francesca and Bernstein. The second dam, La Affirmed (by Affirmed), a winner at three years, is a half-sister to the champion filly Outstandingly. (Hamdan Al Maktoum).
'An expensive yearling but she's out in Dubai and I haven't seen her yet.'

1499. HAZY DANCER ★★

b.f. *Oasis Dream – Shadow Dancing (Unfuwain)*
April 28. Second foal. 90,000Y. Tattersalls October 1. Not sold. Closely related to the moderate 2007 6f placed two year old Dirty Dancing (by Green Desert). The dam, winner of the listed Cheshire Oaks, was third in the Oaks and second in the Group 2 Ribblesdale Stakes and in the Group 2 Prix de Pomone and is a half-sister to six winners. The second dam, Salchow (by Niniski), won the Cheshire Oaks and is a half-sister to seven winners. (Minster Stud & Mrs Hugh Dalgety).
'She wasn't particularly well at the sales and she came in rather late but she's nice and correct and a good tempered filly. She's moving well now but I haven't done enough with her to say how soon it'll be before she's ready. I trained the dam and I wouldn't expect her to be that early. The pedigree suggests she'll take a bit longer.'

1500. HEKAAYA (IRE) ★★★★

b.f. *Kheleyf – Victoria Regia (Lomond)*
February 20. Fifth foal. 180,000Y. Tattersalls October 2. M Tregoning. Half-sister to the useful 5f (at two years) and 6f listed winner and triple Group 3 placed Topkamp (by Pennekamp) and to the useful 5f winner of four races and listed-placed Morinqua (by Cadeaux Genereux). The dam, a stakes winner of three races from 6f to 1m here and in the USA, is a half-sister to nine winners including the listed winners Fight To The Last and Seattle Victory. The second dam, Will Of Victory (by Dancer's Image), won once at two years and is a half-sister to six winners including the Prix Vermeille winner and smart broodmare Walensee. (Sheikh Ahmed Al Maktoum).
'I'm very pleased with her. It's a reasonably good, solid family and one that can produce good horses. She's scopey and history relates that she's probably not going to be that early. One for mid-summer perhaps and she'd have more scope than most of the sharper types I have. A filly that's improving and I'm pleased with her.'

1501. ISTISHARRY ★★★

b.f. *Haafhd – Eshaadeh (Storm Cat)*
January 28. First foal. The dam, unplaced in two starts, is a half-sister to the once-raced quite useful 10f winner Sundus (by Sadler's Wells), to the fair 1m winner Itqaan (by Danzig) and the fair 12f winner Atayeb (by Rahy). The second dam, Sarayir (by Mr Prospector), winner of a 1m listed event, is closely related to the top-class Champion Stakes winner Nayef and a half-sister to numerous winners including the Two Thousand Guineas, Eclipse, Derby and King George winner Nashwan and the high-class middle distance colt Unfuwain. (Hamdan Al Maktoum).
'She's pretty small but she's an early foal and I shall be pressing on with her because you'd hope she'd be a two year old. A good mover, she should be quite busy this year I would have thought.'

1502. JANADIL ★★★★

b.c. *Green Desert – Amenixa (Linamix)*
May 2. Sixth foal. 78,000Y. Tattersalls October 2. Shadwell Estate Co. Brother to the quite useful 2007 two year old 7f and 1m winner Palm Court and half-brother to the two year old Group 2 6f Criterium de Maisons-Laffitte and Group 3 Prix Eclipse winner Zinziberene (by Zieten). The dam, a four year old 10f winner, is a sister to the dual Group 1 Prix Royal-Oak winner Amilynx and the listed winner Amie De Mix and a half-sister to the Group 2 Criterium de Maisons-Laffitte winner Amiwain. The second dam, Amen (by Alydar), was a Grade 3 placed winner of five races in the USA and a half-sister to four winners. (Hamdan Al Maktoum).
'He's a nice colt, I do like him and he's a good-moving horse. A nice sort, he's up to speed with the other early sorts of mine so he's a definite two year old.'

1503. KHAN TENGRI (IRE) ★★

gr.c. *Sadler's Wells – Ela Athena (Ezzoud)*
May 1. Fourth foal. 190,000Y. Tattersalls October 1. M Tregoning. The dam, a winner of three races including the Group 3 Lancashire Oaks, was placed in 7 Group/Grade 1 events and is a half-sister to four winners. The second dam, Crodelle (by Formidable), a French three

year old 9.5f winner, is a half-sister to seven winners. (N Bizakov).

'He's a nice horse but very much a three year old type. He's only been cantering steadily up to now but he has a nice attitude and as his purchase price would suggest he's a good-looking horse. One for the backend of the season however.'

1504. MAKAAM (USA) ★★
ch.c. Giant's Causeway – Elaflaak (Gulch)
April 28. First foal. The dam, a useful listed 5f winner, is out of the US 12f winner Catnip (by Flying Paster), herself a half-sister to the Belmont Stakes winner Editor's Note. (Hamdan Al Maktoum).

'Still in Dubai but I trained the dam and she was mightily quick, so hopefully this colt will be the same.'

1505. MARSOOL ★★★
br.c. Key Of Luck – Chatifa (Titus Livius)
February 9. Second foal. The dam, a quite useful 1m winner, is a half-sister to the champion two year old filly and Group 1 6f Cheveley Park Stakes winner Queen's Logic and to the top-class multiple Group 1 winner Dylan Thomas. The second dam, Lagrion (by Diesis), was placed five times in Ireland and stayed 12f and is a full or half-sister to three winners. (Hamdan Al Maktoum).

'I like him, although I've had no luck with either the dam or the first foal because they both had pelvis problems. But this colt is fine, he's quite short-coupled and I'm very pleased with him. As far as we can see he's showing quite a bit of pace and he could easily make a two year old.'

1506. MOBAGHIT (USA) ★★
ch.c. Dixieland Band – Hazimah (Gone West)
April 26. Third foal. The dam, a fair 7f and 1m placed maiden, is a half-sister to the high-class two year old Mujahid, winner of the Group 1 7f Dewhurst Stakes and subsequently third in the 2,000 Guineas. The second dam, Elrafa Ah (by Storm Cat), was a useful winner of three races over 5f and 6f including the listed Bentinck Stakes. The second dam, Bubbles Darlene (by Fappiano), won twice at up to 1m. (Hamdan

Al Maktoum).
'Still in Dubai by early April.'

1507. MOJEERR ★★★
b.c. Royal Applause – Princess Miletrian (Danehill)
March 25. Third foal. 80,000Y. Tattersalls October 2. Shadwell Estate Co. Half-brother to the unraced 2007 two year old Heaven Bound (by Medicean). The dam, a fair three year old 8.2f winner, is a half-sister to six winners including the German Group 3 1m winner Sinyar and to the unraced dam of the US Grade 2 winner Ventiquattrofogli. The second dam, Place Of Honour (by Be My Guest), won once at three years and is a half-sister to two winners. (Sheikh Ahmed Al Maktoum).

'I've always liked him ever since I saw him at the Sales. I would think he'd be a relatively precocious type and he's done a few sharp canters. He's shown a good attitude since he's been in training after having tried to kick a few people at the Sales.'

1508. MUTARAAMI ★★
b.c. Cape Cross – Esloob (Diesis)
March 6. The dam, a 7f (at two years) and listed Pretty Polly Stakes winner, was third in the Fillies' Mile and is a half-sister to the Pretty Polly Stakes winner Siyadah. The second dam, Roseate Tern (by Blakeney), a very smart winner of the Group 1 12f Yorkshire Oaks and the Group 2 12f Jockey Club Stakes was second in the Epsom Oaks and third in the St Leger and is a half-sister to the high-class middle-distance stayer Ibn Bey. (Hamdan Al Maktoum).

'Still in Dubai in early April.'

1509. OASIS KNIGHT (IRE) ★★★★
b.c. Oasis Dream – Generous Lady (Generous)
February 21. Seventh foal. 100,000Y. Tattersalls October 1. Peter Doyle. Half-brother to the very smart 7f (at two years), Group 2 12f King Edward VII Stakes and dual Group 3 12f Cumberland Lodge Stakes winner High Accolade (by Mark Of Esteem), to the quite useful 12f to 2m winner Highland Legacy (by Selkirk) and the quite useful 12f all-weather

winner Summer Wine (by Desert King). The dam, a middle-distance winner of four races in Ireland including a listed event, is a half-sister to six winners including the Group 2 Premio Guido Beradelli and Group 3 St Leger Italiano winner Jape. The second dam, Northern Blossom (by Snow Knight), was a champion three year old filly in Canada and won two Graded stakes events. (Lady Tennent).

'I particularly like this colt, he's really nice and is a half-brother to High Accolade (who I trained) and that's really why we bought him for Lady Tennent. He was nicely proportioned but hadn't developed much at the Sales and I think he rather slipped through the sale really. He's done particularly well since and although he's a little bit behind the early ones as you'd expect, he's catching up now and I do like him. A lovely-moving horse and although you might look at the pedigree and think that Oasis Dream and Generous are two opposites this is the nicest foal the mare has had since High Accolade.'

1510. SAHAAL (USA) ★★
b.c. Rahy – Thaminah (Danzig)
February 18. First foal. The dam, a quite useful two year old 6f winner, is a half-sister to four winners including the fairly useful dual 1m winner Mosayter. The second dam, Bashayer (by Mr Prospector), a useful dual 1m winner, is a sister to the useful 1m and 10.4f winner Wijdan and the useful 10f listed winner Sarayir and a half-sister to several winners including Nashwan and Unfuwain. (Hamdan Al Maktoum).

'Still in Dubai in early April.'

1511. STERLING SOUND (USA) ★★★★
b.f. Street Cry – Lady In Silver (Silver Hawk)
April 24. Eleventh foal. $120,000Y. Keeneland September. Blandford Bloodstock. Half-sister to four minor winners including the US winner of 11 races Solid Silver Star (by Silver Deputy) and to the unraced dam of the US Grade 2 winner Quintons Gold Rush. The dam, winner of the Group 1 Prix de Diane and second in the Grade 1 Arlington Million, is a half-sister to eight winners. The second dam, Lorn Lady (by Lorenzaccio), won once at three years and is a

half-sister to the Prix de Royallieu winner Riverside. herself dam of the Grand Prix de Saint-Cloud, French 1,000 Guineas and Prix Saint-Alary winner Riverqueen. (Miss K Rausing).

'This filly was bought in America and I can't understand why she wasn't more expensive. She's a very nice filly and I really do like her. She's a very nice mover, she's come together well and done plenty of sharp canters. It's very exciting to have one for Kirsten Rausing and I do hope I can start off with a winner for her'

1512. SUMBE (USA) ★★★★
br.c. Giant's Causeway – Sumoto (Mtoto)
April 16. Eleventh foal. 290,000Y. Tattersalls October 1. M Tregoning. Half-brother to the Group 1 10f Coral Eclipse Stakes, Group 3 1m Craven Stakes and Group 3 7f Solario Stakes winner Compton Admiral (by Suave Dancer), to the Group 1 1m Queen Elizabeth II Stakes winner Summoner, the Irish two year old 7f and 1m winner Anchor (both by Inchinor), the useful 9f winner and Group 2 12f Ribblesdale Stakes second Twyla Tharp (by Sadler's Wells) and the quite useful four year old 12f all-weather winner So Vital (by Pivotal). The dam, a useful 6f (at two years) and 7f winner, is a half-sister to five winners including the good mare Lalindi (dam of the US Grade 2 winner Arvada and the Group 3 Craven Stakes winner Adagio). The second dam, Soemba (by General Assembly), a quite useful 9f winner, is a half-sister to four minor winners here and abroad. (N Bizakov).

'He's nice and is a half-brother to two Group 1 winners so you'd have to be hopeful. He's doing well and has done plenty of sharp canters. Depending on how he takes his training once it gets a bit tougher we might see him out around June time. A nice type that's developed well since the sale and he's the best moving Giant's Causeway we've had.'

1513. TA ALEEM ★★★
ch.f. Galileo – Tadris (Red Ransom)
April 22. Second foal. The dam, a dual listed 1m winner, is a half-sister to the US dual Grade 3 winner Mustanfar. The second dam, Manwah (by Lyphard), was placed four times at three

years and is a three-parts sister to Unfuwain and a half-sister to Nashwan and Nayef. (Hamdan Al Maktoum).
'She's just started sharp cantering and I was very pleased with her this morning. She's very deep through the chest and quite short of the neck but a good mover and I think she might well come to hand nicely. A two year old type.'

1514. TAAMEER ★★
b.c. Beat Hollow – Vayavaig (Damister)
March 10. Eleventh foal. 150,000Y. Tattersalls October 1. Shadwell Estate Co. Half-brother to the useful 6f and 6.5f (at two years) and dual listed 1m winner Expensive (by Royal Applause), to the useful 6f (at two years) and 8.5f winner and US Grade 3 placed Sweet Prospect (by Shareef Dancer), the fairly useful dual 6f all-weather winner Wolfhunt (by Wolfhound) – subsequently a minor winner in the USA, the quite useful 11.6f to 14f winner Dr Cool (by Ezzoud), the Irish three year old 6f winner Green Pursuit (by Green Desert) and the Italian winner of seven races Zaigon (by Zilzal). The dam, a fair two year old 6f winner, is a half-sister to six winners including the Group 3 Palace House Stakes winner Vaigly Great and July Cup second Vaigly Star (herself dam of the Group three winners Sahara Star and Yalaietanee). The second dam, Dervaig (by Derring-Do), won over 5f at two years and is a half-sister to the dam of the Group 1 Premio Presidente Della Repubblica winner Hoche. (Hamdan Al Maktoum).
'One for the back-end of the year because he's a late developing colt.'

1515. TEST MATCH ★★★
b.c. Exceed And Excel – Reunion (Be My Guest)
February 24. Sixth foal. €22,000Y. Goffs Sportsman's. M Tregoning. Half-brother to the quite useful four year old 6f and 7f winner Gunfighter (by Machiavellian) and to a four year old winner in Japan by Giant's Causeway. The dam, a very useful 6f (at two years) and Group 3 7f Nell Gwyn Stakes winner, is a half-sister to seven winners. The second dam, Phylella (by Persian Bold), won in France (over 10f) and in the USA, is a sister to the US stakes winner

Karman Girl and a half-sister to four winners.
'This is a lovely horse, he really reminds me of all the Australian two year old's that you see and after all he is by Exceed And Excel. The interesting thing about the sire is that apart from the Danehill influence the dam's side of his pedigree is all New Zealand and it'll be interesting to see if he makes it over here. I'm very keen on New Zealand breeding, they get very sound stock and it's a fantastic ground for rearing horses. This colt is quite solid and chunky and I feel he'll take a bit more time but he's well made. A lovely moving horse and the lads tell me he's got plenty of speed.

1516. UNCLE KEEF (IRE) ★★
b.c. Sadler's Wells – Love For Ever (Darshaan)
April 20. Seventh foal. 100,000Y. Tattersalls October 1. M Tregoning. Brother to the 7f (at two years) and Group 3 Dee Stakes winner Gypsy King, to the useful 12f winner Albanov, the French 10f winner Salila and the Irish 10f winner Napoleon. The dam, a dual three year old winner in France, is a half-sister to six winners including French listed winner and US Grade 2 placed Wedding Ring. The second dam, Fleur d'Oranger (by Northfields), won the listed 12f Prix de la Ville Trouville, was placed in three Group 3 events in France and is a half-sister to nine winners including the German Group 3 winner and French Oaks third Premier Amour.
'We bought this horse he's a full brother to a colt that had potential for the Derby. He'll probably run a couple of times in the autumn and he's quite striking looking.'

1517. WOODLARK ISLAND (IRE) ★★★
b.c. Tagula – Be My Lover (Pursuit Of Love)
February 27. 50,000Y. Doncaster St Leger. Peter Doyle. Brother to the modest 2007 two year old 7f and 1m winner Tuanku and half-brother to a minor flat and hurdles winner in France by Revoque. The dam won one race over jumps in France and is a half-sister to 3 other minor winners. The second dam, Shamwari (by Shahrastani), is a placed half-sister to the Derby winner Golden Fleece. (Lady Tennant).

'A colt that's done nothing wrong, he's done a number of sharp canters and he's quite mature. The pedigree is a funny mixture but he's a nice type and a solid colt. He shouldn't take that long to get ready.'

ED VAUGHAN
1518. BICKSTA ★★★
b.f. Haafhd – Premiere Dance (Loup Solitaire)
January 27. Fourth foal. 35,000Y. Tattersalls October 1. Blandford Bloodstock. Half-sister to the quite useful 6f (including at two years) and 5f winner Prince Tamino (by Mozart). The dam won once over 1m at three years in France and is a half-sister to four winners including the Group 1 7f Prix de la Foret winner Poplar Bluff. The second dam, Plume Bleu Pale (by El Gran Senor), a listed-placed three year old winner in France, is a half-sister to five winners including the multiple US Grade 3 winner Premier Ministre. (M.J.C Hawkes).
'I like her a lot, she looks to me to be more of a seven furlong filly.'

1519. DOCTOR PARKES ★★★
b.c. Diktat – Lucky Parkes (Full Extent)
February 21. Seventh foal. 29,000Y. Tattersalls December. Not sold. Half-brother to Senorita Parkes (by Medicean), unplaced in one start at two years in 2007, to the fairly useful 5f winner Charlie Parkes (by Pursuit Of Love), the quite useful two year old 5f and 6f winner Robinia Parkes (by Robellino) and the fair two year old 5f winner Johnny Parkes (by Wolfhound). The dam, a useful winner of 13 races, is a half-sister to six winners including the useful dual 5f winner and Moyglare, Lowther and Queen Mary Stakes placed My Melody Parkes. The second dam, Summerhill Spruce (by Windjammer), was a fair winner of a 6f seller at three years and a half-sister to six winners. (J Heler).
'I'm just keeping on with him, he's quite big but he looks quite well-grown. It's a very fast family, he's done everything asked of him and he's close to his first piece of work. He looks OK and he's very much a two year old type for five or six furlongs.'

1520. GREY GHOST ★★
gr.c. Linamix – Isla Azul (Machiavellian)
February 22. Second foal. 48,000Y. Tattersalls October 1. Not sold. The dam is a placed sister to the high-class Group 1 1m Coronation Stakes winner Rebecca Sharp and a half-sister to eight winners including the smart Group 3 11.5f Lingfield Derby Trial winner Mystic Knight, the useful listed 11.4f Cheshire Oaks winner Hidden Hope, the useful dual 7f winner Rosse and the useful 10f winner Mayo. The second dam, Nuryana (by Nureyev), was a useful winner of the listed 1m Grand Metropolitan Stakes and is a half-sister to five winners. (A E Oppenheimer).
'This is a horse that's going to need seven furlongs, he's a good-moving horse and he's not over-big so he should make a two year old by mid-season.'

1521. KONKA (USA) ★★★★
ch.f. Johannesburg – Defining Style
(Out Of Place)
March 25. Fourth foal. $120,000Y. Keeneland September. Blandford Bloodstock. The dam, a minor US stakes winner, is a half-sister to two stakes winners in the USA including the Grade 3 winner Sister Swank. The second dam, Max Donnell (by Critique), was a stakes-placed winner of three races. (M.J.C Hawkins).
'I like this filly a lot. The dam won a stakes race at 2, this filly looks very sharp, she's quite well-grown and there's a lot to like about her.'

1522. MISS TIKITIBOO
b.f. Elusive City – Sabindra (Magic Ring)
March 15. First foal. 10,000Y. Tattersalls October 3. Ed Vaughan. The dam, a winner at three years in France, is a half-sister to five winners including the very smart two year old filly Hoh Magic, winner of the Group 1 Prix Morny and the Group 3 Molecomb Stakes. The second dam, Gunners Belle (by Gunner B), a modest 7f and 10f winner, is a half-sister to the very smart Prince Of Wales's Stakes winner Crimson Beau.
'The pedigree is all about speed, I like her a lot, she'll make a two year old and she'll be a bargain alright!' TRAINER'S BARGAIN BUY

1523. NOBLE DICTATOR ★★★

b.c. Diktat – Noble Desert (Green Desert)
February 11. First foal. 10,000Y. Tattersalls October 2. Not sold. The dam is an unplaced half sister to five winners. The second dam, Sporades (by Vaguely Noble), won the Group 3 Prix de Flore and is a half-sister to nine winners including Mill Native (Arlington Million).
'He's quite a big horse but he seems to be mature enough and quick enough for six furlongs. He's one we could see running by the end of May. He goes very well.'

1524. PACHAKUTEK (USA) ★★★★

ch.c. Giant's Causeway – Charlotte Corday (Kris)
April 14. Sixth foal. 90,000Y. Tattersalls October 1. Blandford Bloodstock. Half-brother to the fair two year old 7f winner Sainte Just (by Polish Precedent). The dam, a quite useful 1m winner, was listed-placed 3 times and is a half-sister to eight winners including the very useful two year old Group 3 7f Prestige Stakes winner Glatisant (herself dam of the 2,000 Guineas winner Footstepsinthesand by Giant's Causeway, and the placed dam of the good two year old Superstar Leo. The second dam, Dancing Rocks (by Green Dancer), won over 5f and 6f at two years and the Group 2 10f Nassau Stakes at three years and is a half-sister to the very useful 7f winner Cragador. (El Caforce).
'I like this colt a lot, the dam hasn't produced a lot yet but this fellow looks the business and the cross has obviously worked before (with Footstepsinthesand). I'd like to start him at six furlongs but if he gets a bit above himself I might even start him at sooner than expected. He loves his work and finds it so easy. He's owned by the Chelsea footballer Claudio Pizarro who is Peruvian and the name Pachakutek is an Aztec king.'

1525. PELINNORE ★★★

b.br.f. Giant's Causeway – Glatisant (Rainbow Quest)
February 20. Seventh foal. 100,000Y. Tattersalls October 1. Not sold. Sister to the 2,000 Guineas winner Footstepsinthesand and half-sister to the fairly useful two year old 6f winner Frappe (by Inchinor and herself dam of the Ribblesdale Stakes winner Thakafaat) and the Irish 12f to 2m and bumpers winner Theme Song (by Singspiel). The dam, a very useful winner of the Group 3 7f Prestige Stakes at two years, is a half-sister to eight winners including the very useful triple 10f winner Gai Bulga and to the placed dam of the very smart two year old Superstar Leo. The second dam, Dancing Rocks (by Green Dancer), won over 5f and 6f at two years and the Group 2 10f Nassau Stakes at three years and is a half-sister to four winners.
'She'll definitely make a two year old, she could be quick enough for six furlongs, maybe seven, on fast ground in mid-season.'

1526. PRINCESS REBECCA ★★

ch.f. Compton Place – Sunley Stars (Sallust)
March 21. Thirteenth foal. 14,000Y. Doncaster St Leger. McKeever St Lawrence. Sister to the useful listed 5f and Weatherbys Supersprint winner If Paradise, closely related to the fairly useful 1m in UAE and 9.4f winner Don Sebastian (by Indian Ridge) and half-sister to the two year old 5f winner All She Surveys (by Mazilier). The dam is an unplaced half-sister to five winners. The second dam, Russeting (by Mummy's Pet), won once at two years and is a sister to the Group 2 Vernons Sprint Cup winner Runnett.
'From a very sharp family, she'll make a two year old alright and although she wasn't expensive she's worth putting in the book.'

1527. SCRAPPER SMITH ★★★

b.c. Choisir – Lady Ounavarra (Simply Great)
March 30. Eighth foal. 38,000Y. Doncaster St Leger. Blandford Bloodstock. Half-brother to a winner in Hong Kong by Danehill, to the quite useful 5f (including at two years) and 6f winner Dellagio (by Fasliyev) and two winners in Italy by King's Theatre and Night Shift. The dam won over 1m in Ireland and up to 12f in Italy and was third in the Group 3 C L Weld Park Stakes. She is a half-sister to six winners out of the two year old winner Hostess (by Be My Guest). (Comic Strip Heroes).
'An out-and-out two year old and the sooner I get him out the better. A nice horse, he's all there

and he'll probably be running in May over five furlongs. He has a nice, relaxed way of going so he might stay six.'

1528. SINCHIROKA (FR) ★★★

b.c. Della Francesca – Great Care
(El Gran Senor)
March 10. Sixth foal. 30,000Y. Doncaster St Leger. McKeever St Lawrence. Half-brother to four minor winners in France by Enrique (2), Saumarez and Sabrehill. The dam is a placed half-sister to the French listed winner Casual Fame. The second dam, Never A Care (by Roberto), won once at two years and is a half-sister to ten winners including the Canadian Grade 2 winner Cool Northerner. (El Caforce).
'A very nice mover, he'll need a bit of a trip I think and he's done very well physically since he came in. We might try him over six furlongs but he looks a seven furlong horse to me.'

1529. UNNAMED ★★

b.c. Royal Applause – Caldy Dancer
(Soviet Star)
April 19. First foal. The dam, a useful two year old dual 5f winner and second in the Group 3 7f Debutante Stakes, is a half-sister to one winner. The second dam, Smile Awhile (by Woodman), ran once unplaced and is a full or half-sister to three winners. (Mohammed Rashid).
'He's OK, he should make a two year old although he's had a couple of minor setbacks. It took a long time for the penny to drop and he's got a bit of a knee action.'

1530. UNNAMED ★★

b.br.f. Cape Cross – Demure (Machiavellian)
March 16. Seventh foal. $475,000Y. Keeneland September. Not sold. Half-sister to the fairly useful two year old 7f winner Il Waard (by Pivotal), to the smart 6f (at two years) and listed 1m winner Coy, the fairly useful 7f winner Presumptive (both by Danehill) and the 8.6f all-weather placed two year old Sinnomore (by Sinndar). The dam is an unraced half-sister to eight winners including the very smart Group 3 6f Diadem Stakes and Group 3 6f Prix de Ris-Orangis winner Diffident. The second dam, Shy

Princess (by Irish River), a smart French two year old 7f winner and second in the Group 1 Prix Morny, is a half-sister to seven winners including the Breeders Cup Mile winner Opening Verse.
'More of a three year old type perhaps, but she might just come to hand from mid-season onwards. A nice moving filly, very relaxed with a laid-back attitude, she'll probably want seven furlongs this year.'

1531. UNNAMED ★★★

b.f. Barathea – Ludynosa
(Cadeaux Genereux)
February 26. Third foal. 62,000Y. Tattersalls October 1. Rabbah Bloodstock. Half-sister to Psitta (by Grand Lodge), a winner of four races at two and three years in Italy. The dam, a fairly useful 6f and 7f winner, is a half-sister to seven winners including the Group 2 1m Prix d'Astarte winner Daneskaya and the French dual Group 3 middle-distance winner Silverskaya. The second dam, Boubskaia (by Niniski), a listed-placed winner in France, is a half-sister to seven winners including the Group 1 1m Gran Criterium winner Will Dancer and the Group 2 6f Premio Umbria winner Dancing Eagle. (Saif Ali & Saeed H Altayer).
'She doesn't look a two year old but she goes quite well. I like her a lot, she'll probably prefer soft ground and I'd be looking to introduce her in the second half of the season. For a big filly she's taking her work very well.'

NICKY VAUGHAN

1532. JONNY MUDBALL ★★

b.c. Oasis Dream – Waypoint
(Cadeaux Genereux)
April 20. Seventh foal. 50,000Y. Doncaster St Leger. N Vaughan. Half-sister to the two year old Group 2 5.5f Prix Robert Papin winner Never A Doubt (by Night Shift), to the fairly useful 6f and 7f winner Primo Way (by Primo Dominie) and the modest 7f all-weather winner Fabine (by Danehill Dancer). The dam, a fairly useful 6f and 7f winner (including on the all-weather), is a half-sister to five winners including the Group 2 6f Diadem Stakes winner and sire Acclamation. The second dam, Princess Athena

(by Ahonoora), a very smart winner of the Group 3 5f Queen Mary Stakes, was placed in numerous Group events over sprint distances and is a half-sister to four winners. (Woodgate Family).

'A nice individual but he won't be early and is one for the middle of the season. He's doing everything right, he has a good pedigree and he'll be a sprinter. He's done a lot of growing and he's filled out really well and is just starting to mature into a nice-looking horse.'

1533. MIDNIGHT STRIDER ★★★★
br.c. Golan – Danish Gem (Danehill)
March 20. Third foal. 21,000Y. Doncaster October. N Vaughan. Half-brother to the modest 2007 6f placed two year old Papillio (by Marju) and to the fairly useful 5f and 6f (at two years) and listed 1m winner Ponty Rossa (by Distant Music). The dam, a 1m winner at three years in France, is a half-sister to four winners. The second dam, Gemaasheh (by Habitat), is an unraced half-sister to five winners.
'I like him a lot, he'll be a seven furlong horse and is one of those horses that catches your eye. He has a nice, low action, he's very professional and I do like him.'

1534. UNNAMED ★★★
b.c. Domedriver – Lavinia's Grace (Green Desert)
February 18. First foal. 40,000Y. Tattersalls October 2. M Hofer. The dam, a minor two year old winner in France, is a half-sister to one winner. The second dam, Lesgor (by Irish River), won over 10f in France, was third in the Group 3 10f Prix de Psyche and is a half-sister to two winners.
'He'll be racing in May over six furlongs but he'll be better over seven. He has quite a high action, he's a nice type of horse and I don't think he'll do much more growing. I'm very happy with what he's done at the moment.'

1535. UNNAMED ★★
b.c. Pivotal – Treble Heights (Unfuwain)
March 9. Second foal. The dam, a listed winner, is a half-sister to numerous winners including

the very useful winner of five races and Group 1 Ascot Gold Cup third Warm Feeling and the useful 7.6f (at two years) and 10f (all-weather) winner Rainbow Heights. The second dam, Height Of Passion (by Shirley Heights), is an unplaced half-sister to eight winners. (Owen Promotions Ltd).

'He's a close-coupled horse and quite 'butty' with a high action. A colt with a nice way of going, I'm not going to rush him and he's one for the mid-season onwards.

MARK WALLACE
1536. ANGEL SONG ★★★
b.f. Dansili – Something Blue (Petong)
April 28. Seventh foal. 75,000Y. Tattersalls October 1. BBA (Ire). Half-sister to the useful 5f and 6f winner (including a listed event in Germany) Mood Music (by Kyllachy), to the fairly useful 5f (at two years) and 6f winner of eight races Steel Blue, the fair 6f and 7f winner of 12 races Yorkshire Blue (both by Atraf) and the quite useful 5f and 6f winner of six races (including at two years) Memphis Man (by Bertolini). The dam is an unplaced sister to one winner and a half-sister to five winners including the Group 3 5f Palace House Stakes second Blues Indigo and the two year old winner Indigo (herself dam of the smart sprinters Astonished and Bishops Court). The second dam, Blueit (by Bold Lad, Ire), was a useful two year old 5f winner and a full or half-sister to three winners.
'She's a lovely filly but she's not an early sort and is one for the second half of the season. She gets up the gallop nicely and I'm just going to take my time with her and give her a chance.'

1537. CHANTILLY DANCER (IRE) ★★
b.f. Danehill Dancer – Antiguan Jane (Shirley Heights)
February 6. Sixth foal. 15,000Y. Doncaster St Leger. Stephen Hillen. Half-sister to the minor US winner of three races from 5 to 7 years Crafty Captain (by Crafty Prospector). The dam is a placed sister to the US Grade 3 winner and Grade 2 placed Party Season and a half-sister to three winners. The second dam, Dabbiana (by Fappiano), won once at three years in Canada

and is a half-sister to the US Graded stakes winners Madame Adolphe and Gem Master.
'She should be running in April, she's not over-big but she looks sharp and has a grand attitude. Although she isn't a star she'll win.'

1538. DARK RANGER ★★★
b.c. Where Or When – Dark Raider (Definite Article)
March 22. First foal. €12,000Y. Goffs Sportsman's. Bobby O'Ryan. The dam, a modest 9f winner at three years, is a half-sister to a two year old winner. The second dam, Lady Shikari (by Kala Shikari), is an unraced half-sister to two minor winners.
'He's not particularly well-bred but he's a grand little horse. He'll be winning over six furlongs and he's tough.'

1539. EXTRACURRICULAR (USA) ★★★
ch.f. Thunder Gulch – Frans Lass (Shanekite)
April 5. Eleventh foal. 30,000Y. Tattersalls October 2. BBA Shipping. Sister to the minor US winner Amerikaner and half-sister to the US stakes-placed winner French Lass (by French Deputy) and three minor winners in the USA by Candi's Gold, Deputy Commander and Gilded Time. The dam won 2 stakes events in the USA and is a full or half-sister to 3 other US stakes winners. The second dam, Metropo's Lass (by The Irish Lord), won 2 minor races in the USA and is a half-sister to four winners.
'A very nice filly, she'll be running in May. Not over-big, but very sharp and she definitely looks capable of winning over five or six furlongs.'

1540. KATE THE GREAT ★★★
b.f. Xaar – Ros The Boss (Danehill)
February 11. Second foal. €56,000foal. Goffs Foal Sales. Airlie Stud. The dam, a quite useful 7f and 1m winner, is a half-sister to three winners including the Irish two year old 1m and listed 9f winner Yehudi. The second dam, Bella Vitessa (by Thatching), is an unplaced half-sister to six winners including the German Group 1 12f Aral-Pokal winner Wind In Her Hair and the Grade 3 Vineland Handicap and Pretty Polly Stakes winner Capo di Monte.

'If she doesn't win first time out she'll win her second race. She's very sharp and speedy, a grand little filly with a good attitude and I'll be very surprised if she doesn't win races.' Mark was correct. she won on her debut in early April.

1541. MISTER GREEN (FR) ★★★
b.c. Green Desert – Summertime Legacy (Darshaan)
February 3. Third foal. 16,000Y. Doncaster St Leger. Stephen Hillen. Half-brother to Lavender And Lace (by Barathea), unplaced in two starts at two years in 2007. The dam won the Group 3 1m Prix des Reservoirs at two years, was third in the Group 1 Prix Saint-Alary and is a half-sister to four winners. The second dam, Zawaahy (by El Gran Senor), a fairly useful 1m winner, was placed at up to 11.5f and is closely related to the Derby winner Golden Fleece.
'A lovely horse, he'll want six furlongs but he was very cheap. He didn't look great at the Sales but he's really gone the right way recently and he'll be running in the middle of May.'

1542. PIVOTAL EXPRESS (IRE) ★★
ch.c. Pivotal – Forest Express (Kaaptive Edition)
February 28. Fifth foal. 12,000Y. Tattersalls October. Stephen Hillen. Half-sister to the unraced 2005 two year old Silky Oak (by Green Desert). The dam, a Grade 3 winner and Grade 2 placed in Australia, is a half-sister to four winners including the German listed winner Waky Na (dam of the Italian Group 1 winner Waky Nao). The second dam, Myra's Best (by Pampapaul), won the listed 5f Firth Of Clyde Stakes and is a half-sister to six winners including the Irish Champion Stakes winner Park Express.
'A well-bred colt, he needs time and he wasn't expensive because he was backward. One for the back-end of the season and I'd be surprised if he couldn't do something but he's more of a three year old type.'

1543. SPARTA REBEL (IRE) ★★
b.f. Spartacus – Safkana (Doyoun)
February 1. Sixth living foal. €11,000Y. Goffs Sportsman's. Not sold. Half-brother to two

minor winners in Italy by Second Empire and Catrail and one in Spain by Barathea. The dam, a three year old 1m winner in Ireland, is a half-sister to seven winners including the very useful listed 1m Heron Stakes winner and Group 1 7f Prix de la Salamandre third Speedfit Too. The second dam, Safka (by Irish River), a useful two year old 5f winner, was third in the Group 3 5f Cornwallis Stakes and is a half-sister to nine winners including the Group 2 7f Lockinge Stakes winner Safawan.

'She looks very sharp, she's tough and hardy and I'd say you could run her all year. She gets up the gallop alright and I'd say she'll win races.' TRAINER'S BARGAIN BUY

1544. SPRING TALE (USA) ★★★★
b.f. Stravinsky – Sadler's Profile (Royal Academy) **February 7. Third foal. €34,000Y. Goffs Sportsman's. Stephen Hillen.** The dam is an unraced half-sister to five winners. The second dam, Miss Profile (by Sadler's Wells), is an unraced half-sister to the triple Grade 1 winner Kostroma.

'She'll be winning in April or early May, she's sharp and looks like she's got ability. A nice filly.'

1545. UNNAMED ★★★
b.c. Invincible Spirit – Aravonian (Night Shift) **March 17. Third foal. 24,000Y. Doncaster St Leger. Stephen Hillen.** Brother to the fairly useful 2007 Irish two year old dual 5f winner Age Of Chivalry. The dam, a 1m winner at three years, is out of the placed Age Of Reality (by Alleged), herself a sister to the Italian listed winner Whatcombe and a half-sister to the Group 2 Royal Whip winner Chancellor.

'He'll be running in April, he's very sharp and worked at Lingfield the other day. He'd be the type that could win on his debut. A grand little horse, he'll have a few runs before June and I'll be surprised if he doesn't win early.'

1546. UNNAMED ★★★
b.f. Kheleyf – Boudica (Alhaarth) **March 20. Third foal. 25,000Y. Doncaster St Leger. Stephen Hillen.** Half-sister to the quite useful dual 6f winner (including at two years)

Sandrey (by Noverre). The dam is an unplaced half-sister to six winners including the useful 5f and 6f winner and Group 3 Cornwallis Stakes third Grand Lad. The second dam, Supportive (by Nashamaa), won four races over 5f at two and three years in Ireland and is a half-sister to three winners.

'A lovely filly, she needs a bit of time and would be one for June or July. She looks like she's got ability, but she's big and powerful and just needs time.'

1547. UNNAMED ★★★★
b.c. Dubai Destination – Craigmill (Slip Anchor) **April 3. Tenth foal. 55,000Y. Tattersalls October 2. Stephen Hillen.** Half-brother to the fair 2007 7f fourth placed two year old Craigstown, to the smart 1m winner and listed-placed Castleton (both by Cape Cross), the German listed winner and Group 3 placed Fleurie Domaine (by Unfuwain), the fairly useful 12f and 2m winner Astyanax (by Hector Protector), the quite useful 10.5f winner Heather Mix (by Linamix), the quite useful 9.5f all-weather winner Oscillator (by Pivotal) and the German two year old winner Global Champion (by Elnadim). The dam, a fair two year old 7f winner, is a half-sister to the Group 3 Park Hill Stakes winner Coigach, to the listed Cheshire Oaks winner Kyle Rhea and the Park Hill Stakes second Applecross. The second dam, Rynechra (by Blakeney), was a useful 12f winner and a half-sister to six winners.

'A lovely horse that probably wants seven furlongs. I really like him and he could be a proper horse. He's not working yet but he gets up the gallop real easy.'

1548. UNNAMED ★★★★
b.f. Oasis Dream – Grail (Quest For Fame) **March 23. Fifth foal. 60,000Y. Tattersalls October 1. Stephen Hillen.** Sister to King Of The Nile, unplaced in one start at two years in 2007 and half-sister to the fairly useful two year old 6f winner Divine Right (by Observatory) and the quite useful four year old 7f winner Aliceinwonderland (by Danehill). The dam won once over 12f in France and is a half-sister to five winners including the Group 3 Coventry Stakes

winner and subsequent US Grade 2 winner Three Valleys. The second dam, Skiable (by Niniski), won four times at up to 9f in France and the USA and is a half-sister to the outstanding broodmare Hasili (dam of the Group/Grade 1 winners Banks Hill, Intercontinental and Heat Haze and the Group two winners Cacique and Dansili).

'She's doing her first piece of work this week and I'm aiming to run her at Haydock at the end of April. She looks the part, she looks fast and she's a lovely filly that's bred to be nice. An early type, strong and sharp, but she's got scope and won't just be an early two year old.'

1549. UNNAMED ★★★

b.f. *Exceed And Excel – Karayb*
(Last Tycoon)
March 9. Ninth foal. 120,000Y. Tattersalls October 1. Stephen Hillen. Half-sister to the listed 10f Prix de la Seine winner Ghyraan (by Cadeaux Genereux), to the fairly useful triple 1m winner Plum Pudding (by Elnadim), the fair two year old 1m winner Red Chief (by Lahib) and the modest 8.5f winner Aqribaa (by Pennekamp). The dam, a fairly useful 6f (at two years) and 7f winner, was listed placed and is a half-sister to two minor winners abroad. The second dam, Deira (by Sir Tristram), won the Grade 3 Dalgety Stakes in Australia.

'One for the middle of the season, she's a lovely, big filly and the stallion started his career well in Australia last year. I really like her, she cost plenty of money and I'd be very surprised if she wasn't any good. A big, powerful filly that'll want six of seven furlongs to start with.'

1550. UNNAMED ★★★

b.c. *Danetime – Muckross Park*
(Nomination)
April 17. Ninth foal. 115,000Y. Doncaster St Leger. Stephen Hillen. Brother to the useful listed 5f Field Marshal Stakes winner No Time and half-brother to two winners abroad by Petardia and Mac's Imp. The dam, a moderate sprint maiden, is a sister to the useful Nominator, a winner of six races including the listed 7f Somerville Tattersall Stakes and a half-

sister to four winners. The second dam, Najariya (by Northfields), is an unraced half-sister to the Cherry Hinton Stakes winner Nasseem.

'An early two year old, he'll be ready around May time, he's done his first bit of work and I'm very happy with him. He looks like he's got ability and he should win races over five or six furlongs.'

DERMOT WELD

1551. AADAAT (USA) ★★

b.f. *Dixie Union – Aljawza (Riverman)*
January 1. Half-brother to six winners including the smart two year old Group 2 1m Royal Lodge Stakes winner Al Jadeed (by Coronado's Quest), the fairly useful 1m winner Elsundus (by Gone West), the fairly useful two year old 6f winner Ishtihar (by Woodman) and the quite useful 10f winner Mezya (by Gulch). The dam, an Irish two year old 6f winner, is a half-sister to the smart Group 2 10f Gallinule Stakes winner Sportsworld, the smart Group 1 6f Cheveley Park Stakes winner Gay Gallanta, the useful 10.4f John Smiths Cup winner Porto Foricos and the useful 6f (at two years) and 7f winner Sundance Kid. The second dam, Gallanta (by Nureyev), a useful 5.5f to 1m winner, was second in the Group 1 Prix Morny and is a half-sister to the top-class French middle-distance colt Gay Mecene and to the US Grade 3 winner Lassie Dear (dam of the high-class sprinter Wolfhound). (Hamdan Al-Maktoum).
'She's yet to arrive here from Dubai.'

1552. AKRISRUN (IRE) ★★★★★

b.c. *Danehill Dancer – Labrusca (Grand Lodge)*
February 19. Third foal. €240,000Y. Goffs Million. D K Weld. The dam was third over 10f on her only start and is a half-sister to seven winners including the high-class Group 1 12f Yorkshire Oaks and Group 3 12f Lancashire Oaks winner Catchascatchcan (herself dam of the very smart miler Antonius Pius) and the listed 10f winner Licorne. The second dam, Catawba (by Mill Reef), a useful 10.5f winner, is a half-sister to seven winners including the Ribblesdale Stakes winner Strigida. (Newtown Anner Stud).
'He's a very nice horse, he's well-forward and will be running in May. Despite the stamina on the

dam's side he's an early foal that's just pushed himself forward. He'll be a six/seven furlong type and is a very forward horse that's showing potential.'

1553. APRIL (IRE) ★★★★
ch.f. Rock Of Gibraltar – Agnetha (Big Shuffle)
April 29. Half-sister to the fair UAE 7f winner Pure Bluff (by Indian Ridge). The dam was a smart winner of the listed Silver Flash Stakes (at two years) and the Group 3 5f King George 200th Anniversary Stakes at three years. She is a sister to the smart German Group 2 sprint winner Areion and to the Irish listed winner Anna Frid and a half-sister to four winners. The second dam, Aerleona (by Caerleon), a German two year old 6f winner, is a half-sister to five winners including the Fillies' Mile winner Nepula. (Mrs C L Weld).
'She's a very nice filly of my mother's and I see her as a six furlong type and running towards the end of May.'

1554. AZORELLA (USA) ★★★★
b.f. Empire Maker – Phantom Wind (Storm Cat)
March 10. First foal. The dam, a very useful 6f (at two years) and Group 3 7f Oak Tree Stakes winner, was third in the Group 1 1m Matron Stakes. The second dam, Ryafan (by Lear Fan), was a high-class winner of the Group 1 Prix Marcel Boussac, the Grade 1 Queen Elizabeth II Challenge Cup, the Grade 1 Yellow Ribbon Stakes, the Grade 1 Flower Bowl Invitational and the Group 2 Nassau Stakes. (Khalid Abdulla).
'She's a nice filly and one for the second half of the year. A quality filly.'

1555. BARREL OF FUN (IRE) ★★
b.c. Sadler's Wells – Mabrova (Prince Mab)
May 8. Eleventh foal. 200,000Y. Tattersalls October 1. D K Weld. Half-brother to the high-class filly Kistena (by Miswaki), a winner of six races including the Group 1 5f Prix de l'Abbaye, the Group 3 6f Prix de Meautry and the Group 3 5f Prix de Seine-et-Oise, to the French two year old 7.5f winner and listed-placed Sallivera (by Sillery), the French two year old 1m winner and listed-placed Welimena (by Sadler's Wells)

and to Spend a Rubble (by Spend A Buck), a minor winner of four races over 10f at three years in France. The dam, a winner over 7f at two years in France, was fourth in the Group 3 Prix des Reservoirs. The second dam, Makarova (by Nijinsky), was a middle-distance winner of three races in France. (Mr Donald Keough).
'He's a big colt and nice but he's very like Sadler's Wells and won't be out until October.'

1556. BLACKANGELHEART (IRE) ★★★
b.f. Danehill Dancer – Magical Cliché (Affirmed)
April 26. Half-sister to the Irish three year old 6f winner Clever Myth (by Green Desert) and to the Irish 9f to 12f winner Legend Has It (by Sadler's Wells). The dam was placed 4 times at up to 1m and is a sister to several good winners including the Group 2 Premio Legnano winner Easy To Copy and the Irish 1,000 Guineas winner Trusted Partner (dam of the high-class filly Dress To Thrill). The second dam, Talking Picture (by Speak John), the champion American filly of 1973, won at up to 7f. (Moyglare Stud Farm).
'A medium-sized filly, slightly more backward than some but she'll make a two year old in July or August.'

1557. BLUE RIDGE LANE (IRE) ★★★
ch.c. Indian Ridge – Upperville (Selkirk)
January 24. First foal. €220,000Y. Goffs Million. D K Weld. The dam, a fair Irish 12f winner, is a half-sister to six winners including the useful Irish listed 12f and jumps winner Mutakarrim and the very useful Irish listed 10f winner Nafisah. The second dam, Alyakkh (by Sadler's Wells), a fair three year old 1m winner, is a half-sister to the Champion Stakes and 2,000 Guineas winner Haafhd and to the 1m listed stakes winner and Group 1 Coronation Stakes second Hasbah. (Mr B R Firestone).
'He's another colt that will take a bit of time and I see him wanting seven furlongs or a mile in the second half of the season.'

1558. BROAD MEETING ★★★★
b.c. Oasis Dream – Avoidance (Cryptoclearance)
May 7. Second foal. Half-brother to Foresight (by Observatory), third over 1m on only start at

two years in 2007. The dam, a fairly useful 7f and 1m winner at two years, is a half-sister to several winners including the useful 1m and 10f winner Averted View. The second dam, Averti (by Known Fact), a fairly useful 7f (at two years) and 6f winner, is a half-sister to the US Grade 1 winner Defensive Play. (Khalid Abdulla).

'He's a nice colt and one of the nicer ones I have from Prince Khalid. He strikes me as having a bit of stamina, so I see him being out in late summer over seven furlongs.'

1559. CAREFREE SMILE (IRE) ★★★

b.f. Invincible Spirit – Frippet (Ela-Mana-Mou)
March 1. Third foal. €200,000Y. Goffs Million. D K Weld. Half-sister to the fair all-weather dual 12f winner Pagano (by Night Shift). The dam, a quite useful 11f winner, is a half-sister to four winners including two year old listed 10f Zetland Stakes winner Trigger Happy. The second dam, Happy Tidings (by Hello Gorgeous), is a half-sister to the triple Group 1 winner Snurge. (Dr Ronan Lambe).

'There's stamina on the dam's side and I see her as a nice filly but one for seven furlongs in the second half of the year.'

1560. CHARIYA (IRE) ★★★★

b.f. Cape Cross – Indaba (Indian Ridge)
April 1. Third foal. €115,000Y. Goffs Million. Bobby O'Ryan. Half-sister to the unraced 2007 two year old Lady Soughton (by Daylami). The dam, a useful 6f and 7f winner, is a half-sister to eight winners including the useful dual 1m winner So Sedulous (herself dam of the German Derby and Breeders Cup Turf winner Shirocco). The second dam, Sedulous (by Tap On Wood), a very useful winner from 5f to 1m at two years in Ireland including the Group 3 Killavullen Stakes, subsequently won in the USA and is a sister to the listed Tyros Stakes winner Tapolite. (Mr Hassen Adams).

'A sharp filly I could see running towards the end of May over six furlongs. She's by Cape Cross but you can see speed coming through from the dam's side.'

1561. DARK HUMOUR (IRE) ★★★

b.c. Bahri – Idilic Calm (Indian Ridge)
May 16. Fifth foal. 70,000Y. Tattersalls October 1. D K Weld. Half-brother to the very promising 2007 two year old 6f winner Calming Influence (by King's Best), to the Irish listed and subsequent Canadian Grade 2 Nearctic Handicap winner Steel Light (by Stravinsky) and the fair 6f winner Marajel (by Marju). The dam, a fair Irish 7f winner, is a half-sister to two winners. The second dam, Miracle Drug (by Seattle Slew), ran unplaced twice and is a half-sister to nine winners including the US Grade 1 winner Twilight Agenda and the dams of the Group 1 winners Go And Go, Refuse To Bend and Media Puzzle. (Newtown Anner Stud).

'He's a very good mover and a typical top of the ground horse. He'll be suited by seven furlongs in June or July.'

1562. DISCREET AFFAIR (IRE) ★★★

b.f. Invincible Spirit – Lady Elysees (Royal Academy)
March 15. First foal. €270,000Y. Goffs Million. D K Weld. The dam is an unraced half-sister to eight winners including the US Grade 3 winner Gone For Real and the dam of the US Grade 2 winner Josh's Madelyn. The second dam, Intently (by Drone), a US stakes winner of eight races and Grade 3 placed, is a half-sister to seven winners. (Dr Ronan Lambe).

'She seems a sharp sort of filly and should be running over six furlongs in mid-summer.'

1563. DREAMS FOR EVER (IRE) ★★★★

b.c. Bachelor Duke – Lidanna (Nicholas)
February 13. Fifth foal. 100,000Y. Tattersalls October 1. D K Weld. Half-brother to the quite useful 2007 Irish 7f placed two year old Capall An Ibre (by Traditionally), to the Irish two year old 5f and subsequent Hong Kong listed winner Prince Monalulu (by Intikhab) and the fairly useful Irish 7f winner and listed-placed Lidanski (by Soviet Star). The dam, a very useful winner of the Group 3 6f Greenlands Stakes, is a half-sister to five winners including the Czech 1,000 Guineas winner Shapely Star. The second dam, Shapely Test (by Elocutionist), won over 1m in Ireland and is a half-sister to a listed winner in

Australia and to four minor winners in the USA. (Mr Donald Keough).

'He'll have had a race over five furlongs before your book is published. He'll get six furlongs in time and is a sharp horse with a lot of pace.'

1564. DUC DE SAVOIE (USA) ★★★★

b.c. Harlan's Holiday – Tea For Three (Lil E. Tee)
March 31. Sixth foal. $300,000Y. Saratoga August. Blandford Bloodstock. Half-brother to two winners including the US stakes-placed East Bay (by Stormin' Fever). The dam, a minor US three year old winner, is a half-sister to the winner and Group 3 placed Robbama. The second dam, Table The Rumor (by Round Table), a stakes winner of 11 races, as Grade 1 placed. (Sir M W J Smurfit).

'He's a strong, powerful colt and he'll run in May or June. The sire was the leading first season sire in America last year. This colt should be suited by six or seven furlongs.'

1565. GALILEO'S CHOICE (IRE) ★★★★

b.c. Galileo – Sevi's Choice (Sir Ivor)
April 18. Sixth foal. 155,000Y. Tattersalls October 1. Bobby O'Ryan. Half-brother to the fair 2007 7f placed Tharawaat (by Alhaarth), to the fairly useful listed 10f placed Almendrados (by Desert Prince) and the fair two year old 5f winner Dontstopthemusic (by Night Shift). The dam, a minor 10f winner at three years in Germany, is a sister to the Canadian stakes-placed winner Ivory Dance and a half-sister to five winners. The second dam, Dance Call (by Nijinsky), a minor winner in the USA, is a half-sister to eight winners including the US Grade 1 winner Miss Toshiba and the dam of the champion sprinter Committed. (Sir M W J Smurfit).

'A particularly nice colt and one for August or September over a mile. These Galileo's are bloody good horses!'

1566. GRACE O'MALLEY (IRE) ★★★

b.f. Refuse To Bend – Lionne (Darshaan)
March 21. Sixth foal. 140,000Y. Tattersalls October 1. Bobby O'Ryan. Half-sister to the unraced 2007 two year old Hall Hee, to the

fairly useful 11f and 12f winner Coeur de Lionne (both by Invincible Spirit), the listed 14f March Stakes winner Jadalee (by Desert Prince), the useful dual 7f winner Alexander Duchess, the fairly useful 10.2f two year old winner Jadalee (both by Desert Prince) and the quite useful Irish two year old 7f winner Great Idea (by Lion Cavern). The dam is an unraced half-sister to five winners including the Derby and Dewhurst Stakes winner Sir Percy. The second dam, Percy's Lass (by Blakeney), a very useful winner from 6f (at two years) to 11.5f including the Group 3 September Stakes, is a half-sister to six winners including the Grade 1 10f E P Taylor Stakes winner Braiswick. (Mrs C L Weld).

'A lovely filly, she's full of quality and will be racing in late summer/early autumn.'

1567. GRANDIFLORA (IRE) ★★

b.f. Oasis Dream – Zathonia (Zafonic)
February 10. First foal. The dam, placed over 1m on all three of her starts, is a half-sister to the US dual Grade 1 placed Requete and to the very useful 1m and listed 10f winner Zante. The second dam, Danthonia (by Northern Dancer), a quite useful two year old 5f winner, is closely related to the Group 3 1m Prix Quincey winner Masterclass and to the useful triple 6f winner Didicoy and a half-sister to the Group 3 10.5f Prix Corrida winner Diese. (Khalid Abdulla).

'An active filly, but there must be a touch of stamina in there because this filly strikes me as one that will be better as a three year old and is possibly a seven furlong horse in the second part of this year.'

1568. HASEILA ★★★

b.f. Oasis Dream – Miss Anabaa (Anabaa)
February 8. Second foal. The dam, a winner of three races including the Group 3 5f Ballyogan Stakes, is a half-sister to two winners including Out After Dark, a smart 5f and 6f winner of six races, including the Portland Handicap. The second dam, Midnight Shift (by Night Shift), a fair dual 6f winner at three years, is a half-sister to eight winners including the high-class Group 1 6f July Cup winner Owington. (Hamdan Al Maktoum).

'A sweet filly that goes nicely, she's one for the mid-summer and she's likely to be a six furlong type.'

1569. HAUNTING MELODY (IRE) ★★★
b.c. Danetime – Optional (Prince Sabo)
May 16. Fourth foal. €240,000Y. Goffs Sportsman's. Bobby O'Ryan. The dam, a modest 6f winner, is a half-sister to four winners. The second dam, My Polished Corner (by Tate Gallery), is a placed half-sister to seven winners including two listed winners. (Dr Ronan Lambe).
'He's a nice horse and although he looks sharp I think he's going to take a bit more time, so he'll make a two year old from August onwards over six/seven furlongs.'

1570. HIDDEN UNIVERSE (IRE) ★★★
gr.c. Linamix – Hint Of Humour (Woodman)
May 9. Sixth foal. €150,000Y. Goffs Million. D K Weld. Half-brother to the unraced 2007 two year old Matter At Hand (by Red Ransom), to the smart Irish 1m (at two years) and 10f winner and US Grade 2 placed Jazz Beat (by Darshaan), the Irish 7f and 1m winner National Honour (by Nashwan) and the Irish 10f and smart hurdles winner Jubilant Note (by Sadler's Wells). The dam a dual Irish 7f winner (including at two years), is a half-sister to five winners out of the Italian Group 3 10f winner High Competence (by The Minstrel). (Dr Ronan Lambe).
'He's a nice colt but he's going to want seven furlongs plus in September/October.'

1571. HILDOR (IRE) ★★★★
ch.f. Pivotal – My Giddy Aunt (Danehill)
February 3. Second foal. €260,000Y. Goffs Million. Newtown Anner Stud. Half-sister to the unraced 2007 two year old Vasu (by Hold That Tiger). The dam was placed twice at three years in the USA and is a half-sister to four winners. The second dam, Regal Portrait (by Royal Academy), is a placed half-sister to the Group 1 King George winner King's Theatre and the champion two year old High Estate. (Newtown Anner Stud).
'She's a sharp filly that should be racing in May. Goes well.'

1572. INTIMATE SECRET (IRE) ★★★
b.f. Invincible Spirit – Habaza (Shernazar)
April 8. Sixth foal. 100,000Y. Tattersalls October 1. D K Weld. Half-sister to the quite useful 1m and 10f winner of five races Killena Boy (by Imperial Boy), to the fair 8.6f (at two years) and 12f winner Aypeeyes (by King Charlemagne) and the modest 12f all-weather winner Gentle Peace (by Orpen). The dam is an unplaced half-sister to six winners including the Group three winners Hazariya and Hazarista. The second dam, Hazaradjat (by Darshaan), won twice at two and three years and is a half-sister to ten winners including the Flying Childers and Middle Park Stakes winner Hittite Glory. (Dr Ronan Lambe).
'There's a bit of stamina on the dam's side and she'll want seven furlongs in September or October.'

1573. LEGEND OF GREECE (IRE) ★★★★
b.c. Danetime – Lodema (Lycius)
April 17. Fifth foal. €80,000Y. Goffs Million. D K Weld. Half-brother to the modest 5f to 7f winner Monashee Prince (by Monashee Mountain) and to a winner in Italy by Orpen. The dam is an unraced half-sister to two minor winners. The second dam, Lancea (by Generous), is an unraced half-sister to five winners including the dual Group 3 winner Riyadian. (Dr Ronan Lambe).
'He's a nice colt and he's pretty forward. I see him running in May and he goes well.'

1574. LUMINOUS EYES (IRE) ★★★★
ch.f. Bachelor Duke – Mood Indigo (Indian Ridge)
April 9. Fourth foal. €160,000Y. Goffs Million. D K Weld. Half-sister to the unraced 2007 two year old Katoom (by Soviet Star) and to the Irish 1m winner Michikabu (by Grand Lodge). The dam, an Irish three year old 7f winner, is a half-sister to two winners including the minor US stakes winner Got A Crush. The second dam, Glowing Ardour (by Dancing Brave), won the Group 3 1m Silken Glider Stakes in Ireland and is a half-sister to seven winners including the top-class Breeders Cup Turf, Japan Cup,

Champion Stakes and Eclipse Stakes winner Pilsudski and the Japanese £2.5 million earner Fine Earner. (Dr Ronan Lambe).
'She's very forward and could be running in late April. She goes well and might find herself running over six furlongs at Leopardstown.'

1575. LUXURY BRAND (USA) ★★★
b.f. Dynaformer – Light Jig (Danehill)
April 4. The dam, a US Grade 1 10f Yellow Ribbon Stakes winner, is a half-sister to numerous winners including the very useful French two year old listed 1m winner Battle Dore. The second dam, Nashmeel (by Blushing Groom), was a very smart winner of three races over 1m including the Group 2 Prix d'Astarte and was second in the Prix Jacques le Marois (to Miesque), the Yellow Ribbon Invitational and the Matriarch Stakes. (Khalid Abdulla).
'She's a slightly more backward filly and one for September or October over seven furlongs to a mile.'

1576. MAQSOOD (USA) ★★
ch.c. Forestry – La Riviera (Affirmed)
March 14. Sixth foal. $340,000Y. Keeneland September. Shadwell Estate Co. Brother to the US stakes winner and Grade 2 placed Frenchglen and half-brother to the 2007 two year old winner Dr Nick (by Authenticate). The dam, a minor US three year old winner, is a half-sister to seven winners including the Graded stakes placed May Night and Sangam. The second dam, Colophon (by Nijinsky), was a minor US three year old winner. (Hamdan Al Maktoum).
'Still in Dubai in early April.'

1577. MAZIONA ★★★★
b.f. Dansili – Polygueza (Be My Guest)
January 18. Eighth foal. 250,000Y. Tattersalls October 1. Shadwell Estate Co. Half-sister to the very smart Group 3 Gordon Stakes winner and Group 1 St Leger, Group 2 Great Voltigeur and Group 2 Dante Stakes second The Geezer (by Halling), to the Italian winner of five races from 2 to 5 years and listed-placed Big Sinisa (by Barathea), the quite useful 1m to 10f winner of five races Doctored (by Dr Devious) and the quite

useful two year old 7f winner Flight Captain (by In The Wings). The dam, a minor three year old 7f winner in Ireland, is a half-sister to four winners including the Irish listed winner Lepoushka. The second dam, Polifontaine (by Bold Lad, Ire), won twice at two years in France and is a half-sister to the Irish 1,000 Guineas and Coronation Stakes winner Katies. (Hamdan Al-Maktoum).
'She's a nice filly and for a Dansili she's a forward type, so she could well be running in mid-summer over seven furlongs.'

1578. MEDICIO (FR) ★★★
b.c. Medicean – Cospicua (High Estate)
April 18. Sixth foal. €200,000Y. Goffs Million. Shadwell Estate Co. Half-brother to the French winner of six races (including over 1m at two years) Ashbourne (by Ashkalani) and to 2 minor French winners by Groom Dancer and Kaldounevees. The dam, a French 10f winner, is a half-sister to four winners including the French Derby third Sestino. The second dam, Stellina (by Caerleon), won at two years in France and is a sister to the Group 3 Prix d'Aumale winner Mackla out of the Group 1 Premio Roma winner Mariella. (Hamdan Al Maktoum).
'He's quite a nice horse, he looks like a two year old and seven furlongs should suit him in mid-summer.'

1579. MIDDLE PERSIA ★★★★
gr.f. Dalakhani – Massarra (Danehill)
February 23. Second foal. 150,000Y. Tattersalls October 1. BBA (Ire). The dam, a useful listed 6f winner and second in the Group 2 Prix Robert Papin at two years, is a sister to one winner, closely related to the Group 1 6f Haydock Park Sprint Cup winner Invincible Spirit and a half-sister to four winners including the Group three winners Acts Of Grace and Sadian. The second dam, Rafha (by Kris), a very smart winner over 6f (at two years) and the Group 1 10.5f Prix de Diane, the Group 3 Lingfield Oaks Trial and the Group 3 May Hill Stakes, is a half-sister to nine winners. (Lady O'Reilly).
'A very quality filly and although there's speed on the dam's side she seems to take after the sire and is one for the second part of the year.'

1580. MOVING HEART (IRE) ★★★
b.f. Anabaa – Lady Luck (Kris)
May 1. Half-sister to the promising 2007 Irish two year old 7f winner Casual Conquest (by Hernando), to the Irish two year old listed 7f winner Elusive Double (by Grand Lodge) and the quite useful Irish 9f winner Media Asset (by Polish Precedent). The dam won over 1m in Ireland and is a half-sister to several winners including the Irish Group 3 Boland Stakes winner Social Harmony. The second dam, Latest Chapter (by Ahonoora), is an unraced half-sister to the Grade 1 Belmont Stakes winner Go And Go. (Moyglare Stud Farm).
'She's a biggish filly and will take time, so September/October should be the right time for her to start her career.'

1581. MY TOPAZ (IRE) ★★★★
*b.c. Celtic Swing – Magical Peace
(Magical Wonder)*
April 16. Sixth foal. 140,000Y. Tattersalls October 1. D K Weld. Half-brother to the fair 2007 5f placed two year old Magical Speedfit, to the useful two year old 5f and 6f winner and listed-placed Dario Gee Gee (both by Bold Fact), the smart Group 3 winning sprinter and two year old Group 2 placed Hoh Mike (by Intikhab) and the quite useful two year old 6f winner Hogmaneigh (by Namid). The dam, a quite useful Irish 6f winner, is a half-sister to one winner. The second dam, Peace In The Woods (by Tap On Wood), is an unraced half-sister to two winners including the dam of the multiple staying Group 1 winner Vinnie Roe (Sir M W J Smurfit).
'A sharp colt, he goes well and he'll be a six furlong horse beginning in May. A nice horse and one to note.'

1582. NAIAZEK ★★★
ch.c. Refuse To Bend – Elshamms (Zafonic)
May 2. Fifth foal. Half-brother to the useful triple 6f (including at two years) and subsequent UAE listed 5f winner Taqseem (by Fantastic Light) and to the fairly useful Irish 7f and 10f winner Aqraan (by In The Wings). The dam, a fairly useful two year old 7f winner and third in the Group 3 Prestige Stakes, is a half-sister to numerous winners including the very useful 10f winner Shaya. The second dam, Gharam (by Green Dancer), a very useful two year old 6f winner, was third in the French 1,000 Guineas and is a half-sister to the US Grade 1 9f winner Talinum. (Hamdan Al Maktoum).
'He's the most forward of the two year old's by Refuse To Bend that I have and I would hope to run him in June or July.'

1583. NETHAAM (IRE) ★★★★
gr.c. Dalakhani – Balaabel (Sadler's Wells)
April 15. Half-brother to the very useful Group 2 7f Rockfel Stakes winner Sayedah (by Darshaan), to the French dual 1m winner Maksad, the modest 7f winner Alsharq (both by Machiavellian) and the quite useful three year old 7f winner Marasem (by Cadeaux Genereux) and the French 1m winner Ghareer (by Sinndar). The dam, a quite useful 1m winner, is a half-sister to three winners including the US Grade 2 7f winner Kayrawan. The second dam, Muhbubh (by Blushing Groom), won the Group 3 6f Princess Margaret Stakes and was second in the Group 2 6f Lowther Stakes. (Hamdan Al Maktoum).
'He's a nice horse, very active for a Dalakhani and I see him running over seven furlongs or a mile in July or August.'

1584. POPSPEED (IRE) ★★★★
*ch.c. Rock Of Gibraltar – Claxton's Slew
(Seattle Slew)*
May 16. Twelfth foal. €255,000Y. Goffs Million. D K Weld. Closely related to the Group 2 12f Blandford Stakes winner Humbel, to the US Grade 3 winner Showlady and the minor US winners of Kazan and Krato (all by Theatrical) and half-brother to the US multiple Grade 1 winner $2.9 million earner Escena (by Strawberry Road). The dam won three races in Ireland including the 1,000 Guineas Trial, was third in the Group 2 Pretty Polly Stakes and is a half-sister to the US stakes winner Motee. The second dam, Nutmeg Native (by Raise A Native), is an unraced half-sister to 2 stakes winners. (Newtown Anner Stud).

'A very powerful colt and I trained the dam who was good. I can see him being a very nice horse over seven furlongs in mid-summer.'

1585. POWERFUL PRESENCE (IRE) ★★★
ch.c. *Refuse To Bend – Miss A Note (Miswaki)*
March 24. Second foal. €170,000Y. Goffs Million. Bobby O'Ryan. Half-brother to the unraced 2007 two year old Montelago (by High Chaparral). The dam, a minor winner at three years in the USA, is a half-sister to six winners including the US Grade 3 winner Skip Away. The second dam, Heavenly Note (by Sunny's Halo), a minor US stakes winner of seven races, is a half-sister to four winners. (Dr Ronan Lambe).
'He's a very nice horse and typical of the sire so I'd expect him out in late summer/early autumn.'

1586. PRECIOUS GEM (IRE) ★★★★
b.f. *Sadler's Wells – Ruby (Danehill)*
April 3. First foal. €230,000Y. Goffs Million. D K Weld. The dam is an unraced sister to the top-class miler Rock Of Gibraltar and he Group 3 placed Nell Gwyn and a half-sister to six winners. The second dam, Offshore Boom (by Be My Guest), an Irish two year old 6f winner, was listed-placed and is a half-sister to four winners. (Mrs C L Weld).
'She's a lovely filly that I see running in August or September. She goes well and is a grand filly.'

1587. RAMLA (IRE) ★★★
b.f. *Rock Of Gibraltar – March Hare*
(Groom Dancer)
April 10. Sixth foal. €125,000Y. Goffs Million. D K Weld. Closely related to the quite useful triple 10f winner (including at two years) Toy Show (by Danehill) and to the minor Italian three year old winner Krone (by Danehill Dancer) and half-brother to the quite useful 11.6f winner Kappelmeister (by Mozart) and the quite useful 12f winner Boxhall (by Grand Lodge). The dam, a modest middle-distance placed maiden, is a half-sister to five winners including the smart 1m and 10f listed winner Inglenook. The second dam, Spring (by Sadler's Wells), a very useful winner of three races from 12f to 14f including a Group 3 event in Italy, was placed in several

other Group races and is a half-sister to seven winners including Pentire, winner of the King George VI and Queen Elizabeth Diamond Stakes. (Mr Ananda Krishnan).
'She's a quality filly and I see her making a two year old in July or August over seven furlongs.'

1588. REFLECTED IMAGE (IRE) ★★★★
b.f. *Refuse To Bend – Angelic Sounds*
(The Noble Player)
February 12. Ninth foal. 150,000Y. Tattersalls October 1. Anthony Stroud. Half-sister to the smart 6f (at two years) and listed 8.3f winner Army Of Angels, to the fairly useful two year old 6f winner Alovera (both by King's Best), the useful two year old 6f winner and Group 2 Lowther Stakes second Seraphina, the moderate 10.8f winner Harp Player (both by Pips Pride), the fairly useful Irish 5f winner Alegranza, the quite useful two year old 5f winner Brantwood (both by Lake Coniston) and the quite useful 1m winner Zameyla (by Cape Cross). The dam, a minor two year old 5f winner, is a half-sister to six winners including the Group 1 Prix de la Foret winner Mount Abu. The second dam, Twany Angel (by Double Form), is a placed half-sister to six minor winners. (Lady O'Reilly).
'She's a very nice filly, one we won't see out until the autumn over seven furlongs, but a quality filly.'

1589. SHEENA'S PALACE (IRE) ★★★
b.f. *Exceed And Excel – Pacific Grove*
(Persian Bold)
January 21. Eighth foal. €155,000Y. Goffs Million. D L Weld. Half-sister to the fair 2007 6f placed two year old Privet, to the useful two year old triple 6f winner Mokabra (both by Cape Cross), the fairly useful two year old 6f winner Caroline Island (by Catrail), the quite useful two year old 6f all-weather winner Major Speculation (by Spectrum) and the Irish three year old 6f winner John Doran's Melody (by Bluebird). The dam, a fairly useful winner of three races from 7f to 1m, is a half-sister to five winners including the listed Oak Tree Stakes winner Mauri Moon. The second dam, Dazzling Heights (by Shirley Heights), a useful winner of

four races from 7f (at two years) to 11f including a listed event at Toulouse, is a full or half-sister to six winners. (Mr Hassen Adams).
'She's a sweet filly, there's a little bit of stamina coming through the dam's side so I see her running over six or seven furlongs in mid-summer.'

1590. SILVER SHOON (IRE) ★★★★★
gr.f. Fasliyev – Limpopo (Green Desert)
March 18. Thirteenth foal. 165,000Y. Tattersalls October 1. D K Weld. Sister to the useful two year old 5f winner and Group 2 5f Flying Childers Stakes second China Eyes and half-sister to the Group 1 6f Haydock Park Sprint Cup and Group 3 5f Palace House Stakes winner Pipalong (by Pips Pride), the quite useful 2007 Irish two year old 6f winner Raja (by Pivotal), the fairly useful two year old 6f listed winner Out Of Africa, the minor US winner of two races Henry Kitchener (both by Common Grounds), the quite useful two year old 7f winner Corton, the quite useful 7f to 12f winner Smoothie (both by Definite Article). The dam, a poor 5f placed two year old, is a half-sister to six winners here and abroad. The second dam, Grey Goddess (by Godswalk), was a smart winner of five races in Ireland from 7f to 8.5f including the Group 3 Gladness Stakes and the Group 3 Matron Stakes. (Mrs C L Weld).
'A sharp filly, I could see her starting over five furlongs in May. It's a fast family, she goes well and shows a lot of potential.'

1591. SPIRIT WATCH (IRE) ★★★★
b.f. Invincible Spirit – Watch The Clock (Mtoto)
March 7. Seventh foal. €440,000Y. Goffs Million. Newtown Anner Stud. Half-sister to Mille Feuille (by Choisir), third over 6f on her only start at two years in 2006, to the quite useful triple 7f winner (including at two years) Go Padero (by Night Shift), the quite useful 12f and all-weather 14f winner E Minor (by Blushing Flame) and the modest 12f winner of five races Feed The Meter (by Desert King). The dam won twice and was third in the listed Sweet Solera Stakes and is a half-sister to six winners. The second dam, Brilliant Timing (by The Minstrel), is a placed half-sister to the US Grade 1 winners

Timely Roman and Timely Assertion. (Newtown Anner Stud).
'Full of quality, but she's out of a mare by Mtoto so I see her as wanting seven furlongs or a mile in September/October. She's a super looking filly.'

1592. SPORTING ICON (IRE) ★★★★
b.c. Sadler's Wells – Dress To Thrill (Danehill)
January 18. Second foal. The dam won Grade 1 9f Matriarch Stakes and Group 2 1m Sun Chariot Stakes and is a sister to one winner and a half-sister to six winners. The second dam, Trusted Partner (by Affirmed), winner of the Group 3 7f C.L. Weld Park Stakes (at two years) and the Irish 1,000 Guineas, is a sister to the useful middle distance performers Easy to Copy and Epicure's Garden. (Moyglare Stud Farm).
'He's a very nice colt, very likeable and I would hope to see him running in August or September. A lovely horse.'

1593. TELESCOPIC VISION (IRE) ★★★
b.c. Galileo – Silly Game (Bigstone)
February 6. Second foal. €190,000Y. Goffs Million. D K Weld. Closely related to the fairly useful 2007 two year old 7f winner Better Hand (by Montjeu). The dam, a winner in Italy over 7.5f at two years and over hurdles, is a half-sister to five winners. The second dam, Scarduza (by High Top), won over jumps in Italy and is a half-sister to seven winners including the Group 3 winner Midnight Air (dam of the Group 2 Long Island Handicap winner Midnight Line) and to the dam of the Group 1 Prix de l'Abbaye winner Imperial Beauty. (Dr Ronan Lambe).
'He's a quality colt that should be racing in August or September over seven furlongs.'

1594. UNNAMED ★★★
b.f. Galileo – Beautiful Note (Red Ransom)
February 22. First foal. €130,000Y. Goffs Million. Robert Blacoe. The dam is an unraced half-sister to the US Grade 3 and German listed winner Society Hostess. The second dam, Touch Of Truth (by Storm Cat), a minor US winner of four races, is a half-sister to the US Grade 1 winner Twilight Agenda and the dams of the Group/Grade 1 winners Refuse To Bend, Media

Puzzle and Go And Go. (Mr R Blacoe).
'She's a nice filly and typical of the sire, so she'll take a bit of time and is one for September or October.'

1595. UNNAMED ★★
b.br.f. Elusive Quality – Committed Actress (Theatrical)
May 11. Second foal. $150,000Y. Keeneland September. Newmarket International. The dam is an unraced sister to the US Grade 1 winner Pharma and the US Grade 2 winner Hap and a half-sister to the unraced dam of the multiple Grade 1 winner English Channel. The second dam, Committed (by Hagley), won the Group 1 Prix de l'Abbaye (twice) and the Group 1 William Hill Sprint Championship. (Mrs C L Weld).
'She's a very nice filly but very much one for October and as a three year old.'

1596. UNNAMED ★★★
b.c. Fasliyev – Savieres (Sadler's Wells)
March 19. Second foal. 50,000Y. Doncaster St Leger. Bobby O'Ryan. Half-brother to the unraced 2007 two year old Abbaleen (by Traditionally). The dam, a minor Irish 11f winner, is a sister to five winners including the Irish 9f winner and Group 1 National Stakes second Coliseum. The second dam, Gravieres (by Saint Estephe), won the Grade 1 Santa Ana Handicap and the Grade 3 California Jockey Club Handicap and is a half-sister to nine winners. (M R Green).
'He probably has a fair bit of the damsire Sadler's Wells about him, he's a quality colt but he won't see the racecourse until the autumn.'

PETER WINKWORTH

1597. DEAL CLINCHER ★★★
b.f. Reset – Princess Of Garda (Komaite)
April 21. Third foal. 15,000Y. Doncaster St Leger. Highflyer Bloodstock. Half-sister to the fair triple 6f winner (including at two years) Tipsy Prince (by Tipsy Creek). The dam, a fair two year old dual 5f winner, is a sister to the two year old Group 3 5f Cornwallis Stakes winner Castelletto, to the useful 6f winner (including at two years) Lake Garda, the useful 5f winner and

listed-placed Final Dynasty and the quite useful 5f (at two years) and 6f winner of eight races Baby Barry. The second dam, Malcesine (by Auction Ring), a 1m seller winner at four years, is a half-sister to five winners including the Wokingham Handicap winner Red Rosein (herself dam of the listed winner Proud Boast). (Badger's Second Set). Peter's assistant, Anton Pearson, discussed the two-year-olds with me.
'She's small and neat and like a lot of our two-year-olds she's hanging on to her coat because the winter seems to have dragged on. As regards the sire, I love these Australian sprinters. I think they've got the best sprinters in the world and they've proved the point by coming over here and running at Ascot the way they have. My only criticism of this filly is that she's quite small, but she is quite sharp. She's very difficult to get into the starting gates and I would think she'll have to be hooded every time. She'll be racing in May over five furlongs.'

1598. FOXTROT ALPHA (IRE) ★★★
b.f. Desert Prince – Imelda (Manila)
April 27. Seventh foal. €37,000Y. Goffs Million. D Redvers. Sister to the fair 1m and 9f winner of four races Todlea and half-sister to the fair 5f winner Haajes (by Indian Ridge) and the quite useful two year old 6f all-weather winner Rapadash (by Boundary), subsequently a winner and Grade 3 placed in the USA. The dam ran once unplaced at two years and is a half-sister to six winners including the high-class Group 2 Prix du Rond-Point and Group 2 Prix d'Astarte winner Shaanxi. The second dam, Rich And Riotous (by Empery), won once over 1m in France and is a half-sister to six winners. (Foxtrot Racing Partnership).
'I like her but she's a late April foal so won't be early. She has a nice temperament for a Desert Prince, I like her and she'll certainly make a two year old – probably in early summer. She'll be fast enough for six furlongs.'

1599. THE SAUCY SNIPE ★★
b.c. Josr Algarhoud – The Dark Eider (Superlative)
February 18. Third foal. 6,000Y. Ascot Sales.

Not sold. Sister to the modest 2007 1m placed two year old The Willowy Widgeon. The dam is an unraced half-sister to the smart dual Group 3 middle-distance winner The Whistling Teal. The second dam, Lonely Shore (by Blakeney), won over 13.5f abroad. (Mrs F A Veasey).

'She's nice, she's coming to hand well and mentally she's a proper racehorse. She'll be one of our first runners.' TRAINER'S BARGAIN BUY

1600. TROPICAL PARADISE (IRE) ★★★★ ♠
gr.f. Verglas – Ladylishandra (Mujadil)
January 28. Third foal. €42,000Y. Tattersalls Ireland. D Redvers. Half-sister to the fair all-weather 9f and 10f winner Nicomedia (by Key Of Luck). The dam, an Irish two year old 6f winner, is a half-sister to six winners including the fairly useful two year old 6f winner Pigeon Point. The second dam, Mevlana (by Red Sunset), a French 11f and 12f winner, is a sister to the Group 3 10f Royal Whip Stakes winner Dancing Sunset. (Team Safari).

'A stunning filly and as soon as she come in her coat she's be racing. She's tall and quite sparsely made and I'll run her over five but I think she'll actually want beyond that. I've worked her with two three year old's at Lingfield and she crucified them, which might not mean anything but I really like her and she's a very nice sort.'

STALLION REFERENCE

This section deals with those sires represented by at least four two-year-olds in the book. Amongst the stallions listed in this section are most of the best sires of America and Europe, horses like the US-based sires Distorted Humor, Dynaformer, Giant's Causeway, Gone West, Seeking The Gold and Storm Cat. The top European sires include Cape Cross, Danehill Dancer, Dansili, Galileo, Green Desert, Indian Ridge, Invincible Spirit, Montjeu, Pivotal, Sadler's Wells and Selkirk.

ACCLAMATION *2000 Royal Applause – Princess Athena (Ahonoora)* Racing record: won six times, including Diadem Stakes. Also placed in King's Stand and Nunthorpe. Stud record: first crop now three-year-olds, he was an instant hit with his first crop in 2007, notably with his Group 1 winner Dark Angel, so much so his fee as more than trebled. Standing at Rathbarry Stud, Ireland. 2008 fee: €30,000.

ALHAARTH *1993 Unfuwain – Irish Valley (Irish River)* Racing record: champion two year old of 1995 when winner of four group races, notably Dewhurst Stakes. Showed very smart form up to 10f at three to four years, winning three Group 2 events. Stud record: first runners in 2001. Sire of high-class Haafhd (2000 Guineas and Champion Stakes), very smart performers Bandari and Phoenix Reach (Canadian International, Hong Kong Vase and Dubai Sheema Classic), and smart performers Dominica, Hoh Buzzard and Maharib. Standing at Derrinstown Stud, Ireland. 2008 fee: €12,500.

ANABAA *1992 Danzig – Balbonella (Gay Mecene)* Racing record: won eight races including the July Cup and the Prix Maurice de Gheest. Stud record: first runners in 2000. Sire of Anabaa Blue (Prix du Jockey Club), Martillo, and Precision (Hong Kong Cup), all three very smart, and of smart performers Amonita, Ana Marie, Celtic Slipper, Blue Ksar, Loup Breton, Marshall, Miss Anabaa, Rouvres, Shaard, Tarzan City and Victorieux. Standing at Haras du Quesnay in France. 2008 fee: €27,000.

ARCH *1995 Kris S – Aurora (Danzig)* Racing record: won five races including the Grade 1 Super Derby at Louisiana Downs. Stud record: sire of the July Cup and Golden Jubilee Stakes winner Les Arcs, the US Grade 1 winners Arravale, Pine Island and Prince Arch and the South African Grade 1 winner Overarching. Standing at Claiborne Farm, Kentucky. 2008 fee: $25,000.

BACHELOR DUKE *2001 Miswaki – Gossamer (Seattle Slew)* Racing record: won Irish 2,000 Guineas. Stud record: first crop now two-year-olds. Standing at Ballylynch Stud, Ireland. 2008 fee: €8,000.

BAHAMIAN BOUNTY *1994 Cadeaux Genereux – Clarentia (Ballad Rock)* Racing record: Winner of three races at two years, notably Prix Morny and Middle Park. Also fourth in July Cup at three years. Stud record: first runners in 2001. Sire of high-class performer Pastoral Pursuits (July Cup), very smart Goodricke (Sprint Cup) and smart performers Babadona, Dubaian Gift, Naahy, Paradise Isle and Topatoo. Standing at National Stud, Newmarket. 2008 fee: £9,000.

BAHRI *1992 Riverman – Wasnah (Nijinsky)* Racing record: won three races, including St James's Palace Stakes and Queen Elizabeth II Stakes. Stud record: sire of top-class Sakhee (Juddmonte International, Prix de l'Arc de Triomphe), smart performer Louveteau and several very useful performers. Standing at Derrinstown Stud, Ireland. 2008 fee: €7,000.

BARATHEA *1990 Sadler's Wells – Brocade (Habitat)* Racing record: five wins, notably Breeders Cup Mile and Irish 2000 Guineas. Stud record: first runners in 1998. Sire of high-class Tobougg (Prix de la Salamandre/Dewhurst) and Tante Rose (Sprint Cup), and numerous smart performers including Alasha, Cornelius, Hazarista, Jumbajukiba, One Off, Opera Cape, Pongee, Port Vila and Shield. Standing at Rathbarry Stud, Ireland. 2008 fee: €25,000.

BEAT HOLLOW *1997 Sadler's Wells – Wemyss Bight (Dancing Brave)* Racing record: winner in Europe/USA including Grand Prix de Paris and 3 US Grade 1 events including Arlington Million. Stud record: first runners in 2006. Sire of useful performers Charlotte O Fraise, Donoma, Riario and Streets Ahead. Standing at Banstead Manor Stud, Newmarket. 2008 fee: £8,000.

BERTOLINI *1996 Danzig – Aquilega (Alydar)* Racing record: won two races, including July Stakes at two years, and placed in July Cup, Sprint Cup and Nunthorpe Stakes. Stud record: first runners in 2005. Sire of useful performers Blades Girl, Come Out Fighting, Donna Blini (Cheveley Park), Moorhouse Lad, Prime Defender, Rochdale and Signor Peltro. Standing at Dalham Hall Stud, Newmarket. 2008 fee: €10,000.

CADEAUX GENEREUX *1985 Young Generation – Smarten Up (Sharpen Up)* Racing record: seven wins notably July Cup and William Hill Sprint Championship. Stud record: best winners include high-class Bijou d'Inde (St James's Palace Stakes) and Touch of The Blues (Atto Mile in Canada), very smart Gift Horse and numer-ous smart performers including Bahamian Bounty (Middle Park Stakes),

Embassy (Cheveley Park Stakes), Hoh Magic (Prix Morny) and Toylsome (Group 1). Standing at Whitsbury Manor Stud, Hampshire. 2008 fee: £15,000.

CAPE CROSS *1994 Green Desert – Park Appeal (Ahonoora)* Racing record: won four races, including Lockinge Stakes, Queen Anne Stakes and Celebration Mile. Stud record: first runners in 2003. Sire of top-class Ouija Board (seven Group 1 wins including the Oaks and the Breeders' Cup Filly and Mare Turf), very smart Hazyview, and numerous smart performers including Borthwick Girl, Cape Fear, Castleton, Charlie Farnsbarns, Crossing The Line, Crosspeace, Halicarnassus, Hatta Fort, Mac Love, Madid, Mazuna, Musicanna and Privy Seal. Standing at Kildangan Stud, Ireland. 2008 fee: €50,000.

CAPTAIN RIO *2000 Pivotal – Beloved Visitor (Miswaki)* Racing record: won four times, including Criterium de Maisons-Laffitte at two years. Stud record: first crop included the New Zealand Grade 1 winner Il Quello Veloce and the Group 3 Sirenia Stakes winner Philario. Standing at Ballyhane Stud, Ireland. 2008 fee: €6,000.

CHOISIR *2000 Danehill Dancer – Great Selection (Lunchtime)* Racing record: Group 1 winner in both Australia and Britain, including King's Stand Stakes and Golden Jubilee Stakes. Stud record: first crop were two-year-olds in 2007 and included the listed winners Fat Boy, Luna Nel Pozzo and Porto Marmay. Standing at Coolmore Stud, Ireland. 2008 fee: £12,500.

CLODOVIL *2001 Danehill – Clodora (Linamix)* Racing record: won five races, including Poule d'Essai des Poulains. Stud record: first crop were two-year-olds in 2007 and included the Group winners Nahoodh and Beacon Lodge. Standing at Rathasker Stud, Ireland. 2008 fee: €12,000.

COMPTON PLACE *1994 Indian Ridge – Nosey (Nebbiolo)* Racing record: won three races, notably July Cup. Stud record: first runners in 2002. Sire of very smart Borderlescott, smart Boogie Street and Intrepid Jack, US Grade 2 winner Passified, the Group 2 winner Godfrey Street and numerous useful performers, including Judd Street and Hunter Street. Standing at Whitsbury Manor Stud, Hampshire. 2008 fee: £7,500.

DALAKHANI *2001 Darshaan – Daltawa (Miswaki)* Racing record: won eight of nine starts, including Prix du Jockey Club and Arc. Stud record: first crop were two-year-olds in 2007. Standing at Gilltown Stud, Ireland. 2008 fee: €40,000.

DANEHILL DANCER *1993 Danehill – Mira Adonde (Sharpen Up)* Racing record: winner of four races,

including Heinz 57 Phoenix Stakes and National Stakes at two years and Greenham at three. Stud record: first runners in 2001. Sire of high-class performer Choisir (Golden Jubilee Stakes), very smart Alexander Tango (US Grade 1 Garden City Stakes winner) Indesatchel and Where Or When (Queen Elizabeth II Stakes) and numerous smart performers including Anna Pavlova, Blue Sky Thinking, Fast Company, Jeremy, Lady Dominatrix, Lizard Island, Miss Beatrix (Moyglare Stud Stakes), Monsieur Bond and Speciosa (1000 Guineas). Standing at Coolmore Stud, Ireland. 2008 fee: €115,000.

DANETIME *1994 Danehill – Allegheny River (Lear Fan)* Racing record: won three races, including Stewards Cup. Stud record: first runners in 2002. Sire of Group 1 winning two year old Myboycharlie, the smart winners Baltic King, Miss Sally, The Kiddykid and Vital Equine and of numerous useful performers. Died in 2005.

DANSILI *1996 Danehill – Hasili (Kahyasi)* Racing record: won five races in France, and placed in six Group/Grade 1 events including Sussex Stakes and Breeders' Cup Mile. Stud record: first runners in 2004. Sire of top-class Rail Link (Arc, Grand Prix de Paris, Prix Niel), Zambezi Sun (Group 1 Grand Prix de Paris) and several smart performers including Home Affairs, Passage Of Time, Price Tag (US Grade 1 winner and first past post in Poule d'Essai des Pouliches), Proviso, Sense Of Joy, Silver Touch and Strategic Prince. Standing at Banstead Manor Stud, Newmarket. 2008 fee: £75,000.

DAYLAMI *1994 Doyoun – Daltawa (Miswaki)* Racing record: won seven Group 1 races, including Poule d'Essai des Poulains, Eclipse Stakes, King George and Queen Elizabeth Diamond Stakes, and Breeders' Cup Turf. Stud record: first runners in 2003. Sire of high-class Grey Swallow (Irish Derby), and of smart performers Bull Run, Centaurus, Cougar Bay, Hidden Hope, La Persiana, Remaadd and Timarwa. Exported to South Africa in 2006.

DESERT STYLE *1992 Green Desert – Organza (High Top)* Racing record: won Tetrarch Stakes, Ballycorus Stakes and Phoenix Sprint Stakes (all Group 3). Stud record: first runners in 1999. Sire of very smart Caradak (Prix de la Foret), Mandesha (Prix Vermeille, Prix de l'Opera) and Next Desert (Deutsches Derby), and of smart performers Albuhera, Bachir (Poule d'Essai des Poulains/ Irish 2000 Guineas), Cape Town, Captain Hurricane and Jessica's Dream. Standing at Morristown Lattin Stud, Ireland. 2008 fee: €12,000.

DIESIS *1980 Sharpen Up – Doubly Sure (Reliance II)* Racing record: winner of three races, notably Dewhurst Stakes and the Middle Park Stakes. Stud record: best winners include Love Divine (Oaks), Diminuendo (Oaks, Irish Oaks, Yorkshire Oaks), Elmaamul (Coral-Eclipse Stakes, Phoenix Champion Stakes), Halling (Coral-Eclipse Stakes (twice), International Stakes (twice), Prix d'Ispahan), Husband (Rothmans International), Keen Hunter (Prix de l'Abbaye), Knifebox (Premio Roma), Magistretti (Man O'War Stakes), Docksider (Hong Kong Mile), Rootentootenwooten (Demoiselle Stakes), Ramruma (Oaks, Irish Oaks and Yorkshire Oaks) and Three Valleys (first past post in Middle Park Stakes). Standing at Mill Ridge Farm, Lexington, Kentucky. Has been retired from stud.

DIKTAT *1995 Warning – Arvola (Sadler's Wells)* Racing record: Seven wins, including Prix Maurice de Gheest and Sprint Cup. Stud record: first runners in 2004. Sire of smart performers Dixie Bell, Formal Decree, Rajeem and Short Skirt, and of several very useful performers. Now standing in Japan.

DISTORTED HUMOR *1993 Forty Niner – Danzig's Beauty (Danzig)* Racing record: won 11 races in the USA including the Champagne Stakes, Futurity Stakes, Haskell Invitational and Travers Stakes (all Grade 1). Champion two year old. Stud record: sire of six Grade 1 winners (Coronado's Quest, Ecton Park, Editor's Note, Gold Fever, Marley Vale and Nine Keys). Standing at Win Star Farm, Kentucky. 2008 fee $300,000.

DIXIELAND BAND *1980 Northern Dancer – Mississippi Mud (Delta Judge)* Racing record: US dual Grade 2 winner. Stud record: sire of over 100 stakes winners including the Group/Grade 1 winners Drum Taps, Dixie Union, Dixie Brass, Spinnin Round, Menhoubah and Roaring Twenties. Standing at Lane's End Farm, Kentucky. 2008 fee: $50,000.

DIXIE UNION *1997 Dixieland Band – She's Tops (Capote)* Racing record: won seven races including the Haskell Invitational and the Malibu Stakes (both Grade 1 events in the USA). Stud record: sire of the US Grade 1 winner Dixie Chatter, the Group 2 Cherry Hinton Stakes winner Sander Camillo and the US Grade 2 winners Most Distinguished and Nothing But Fun. Standing at Standing at Lane's End Farm, Kentucky. 2008 fee: $50,000.

DOMEDRIVER *Indian Ridge – Napoli (Baillamont)* Racing record: won six races, including Breeders' Cup Mile. Stud record: first crop now two-year-olds. Standing at Fresnay-le-Buffard. 2008 fee: €7,000.

DR FONG *1995 Kris S – Spring Flight (Miswaki)* Racing record: won five races, including St James's Palace Stakes. Stud record: first runners in 2003. Sire of the US Grade 1 winner Shamdinan, the smart performers Andronikos, Ask For The Moon, Doctor Brown, Fong's

Thong, Forward Move and Spotlight, and of several very useful performers. Standing at Highclere Stud, Berkshire. 2008 fee: £9,000.

DUBAI DESTINATION *Kingmambo – Mysterial (Alleged)* Racing record: won four times, including Champagne Stakes and Queen Anne Stakes. Stud record: first crop were two year olds in 2007 and included the Group 1 winner Ibn Khaldun. Standing at Dalham Hall Stud, Newmarket. 2008 fee: £15,000.

DYNAFORMER *1985 Roberto – Andover Way (His Majesty)* Racing record: seven wins in USA including Grade 2 Florida Derby and Grade 2 Discovery Handicap. Stud record: best winners include the Group 1 winner Lucarno, the very smart Beat All and (in USA) Grade 1 winners Barbaro, Film Maker and Perfect Drift, and numerous smart performers including Ocean Silk, Sharp Susan and Spanish John. Standing at Three Chimneys Farm, Kentucky. 2008 fee: $150,000.

EFISIO *1982 Formidable – Eldoret (High Top)* Racing record: eight wins from 6f to 1m including Group 1 Premio Emilio Turati and Group 3 Challenge Stakes. Stud record: best winners include Group 1 winners Attraction (five, including 1000 Guineas), Frizzante (July Cup), Hever Golf Rose (Prix de l'Abbaye), Le Vie Dei Colori (Premio Vittorio di Capua), Pearly Shells (Prix Vermeille), Pips Pride (Phoenix Stakes) and Tomba (Prix de la Foret). Died in 2006.

ELNADIM *1994 Danzig – Elle Seule (Exclusive Native)* Racing record: won five races, notably Diadem Stakes and July Cup. Stud record: first runners in 2004, first European runners in 2005. Sire of smart performers Caldra, Elletelle and Al Qasi. Standing at Derrinstown Stud, Ireland. 2008 fee: €6,000.

EL PRADO *1989 Sadler's Wells – Lady Capulet (Sir Ivor)* Racing record: won Group 1 National Stakes and Group 2 Beresford Stakes. Stud record: sire of five Grade 1 winners (Artie Schiller, Asi Siempre, Borrego, Kitten's Joy and Medaglia d'Oro). Standing at Adena Springs, Kentucky. 2008 fee: $75,000.

ELUSIVE CITY *2000 Elusive Quality – Star of Paris (Dayjur)* Racing record: won Group 1 Prix Morny and Group 2 Richmond Stakes. Also placed in Middle Park. Stud record: first crop are two year olds in 2008. Standing at Irish National Stud. 2008 fee: €8,000.

ELUSIVE QUALITY *1993 Gone West – Touch of Greatness (Hero's Honor)* Racing record: won nine races in USA, including Grade 3 events at 7f/1m. Stud record: sire of top-class Kentucky Derby/Preakness Stakes winner Smarty Jones, Prix Morny winner Elusive City and several US graded stakes winners, including Chimichurri, Elusive Diva, Girl Warrior, Maryfield and Omega Code. Standing at Darley,

Kentucky. 2008 fee: $75,000.

EXCEED AND EXCEL *2000 Danehill – Patrona (Lomond)* Racing record: champion sprinter in Australia, won seven races including the Grade 1 Newmarket Handicap, the Grade 1 Dubai Racing Club Cup and the Grade 2 Todman Stakes. Stud record: first northern hemisphere runners in 2008. His 2007 Australasian two-year-old winners include the Group 3 winners Exceedingly Good, Believe 'n' Succeed and Wilander. Standing at Dalham Hall Stud, Newmarket. 2008 fee: £10,000.

FALBRAV *1998 Fairy King – Gift Of The Night (Slewpy)* Racing record: won eight Group 1 events including the Prix d'Ispahan, Queen Elizabeth II Stakes, Eclipse Stakes, Juddmonte International and Japan Cup. Stud record: sire of the two-year-old winners of 1nine races in Japan in 2007. Now standing in Australia.

FANTASTIC LIGHT *1996 Rahy – Jood (Nijinsky)* Racing record: won 12 races, including Prince of Wales's Stakes, Irish Champion Stakes and Breeders' Cup Turf. Stud record: first runners in 2005. Sire of Group 1 winner Scintillo, smart performers New Guinea and Prince of Light, and of useful performers Imperial Star, Roshani and Som Tala. Standing at Dalham Hall Stud, Newmarket. Now standing in Australia/Japan.

FASLIYEV *1997 Nureyev – Mr P'S Princess (Mr Prospector)* Racing record: Unbeaten in five starts at two years (only season to race), including Coventry Stakes, Heinz 57 Phoenix Stakes and Prix Morny. Stud record: first runners in 2003. Sire of Carry On Katie (Cheveley Park Stakes), very smart performer Chineur, smart performers Fyodor, City Leader, Kings Point, Much Faster, Russian Valour and Steppe Dancer and of several useful performers. Now standing in Japan.

FRAAM *1989 Lead On Time – Majestic Kahala (Majestic Prince)* Racing record: won five races including a listed event and Group 3 placed twice. Stud record: sire of the US Grade 2 winners Marble Maiden and Shir Dar and the Group 3 winners Cool Jazz and Leading Time. Standing at Tweenhills Stud. 2008 fee: £2,750.

FUSAICHI PEGASUS *1997 Mr Prospector – Angel Fever (Danzig)* Racing record: won six races in the USA including the Kentucky Derby. Stud record: first runners in 2004. Sire of very smart US performers Bandini (Blue Grass Stakes) and Roman Ruler (Haskell Invitational), of smart winners Excusez Moi, Ravel and Race For The Stars, and of several useful winners. Standing at Ashford Stud, Kentucky. 2008 fee: $45,000.

GALILEO *1998 Sadler's Wells – Urban Sea (Miswaki)* Racing record: won six races, including Derby, Irish Derby and King George And Queen Elizabeth Diamond Stakes. Stud record: first runners in 2005. Sire of champion two year olds New Approach (Dewhurst Stakes and National Stakes) and Teofilo (National Stakes, Dewhurst Stakes), Sixties Icon (St Leger), Red Rocks (Breeders' Cup Turf), Allegretto (Prix Royal-Oak), Soldier Of Fortune (Irish Derby) and Nightime (Irish 1000 Guineas). Standing at Coolmore Stud, Ireland. 2008 fee: €150,000.

GIANT'S CAUSEWAY *1997 Storm Cat – Mariah's Storm (Rahy)* Racing record: won nine races, six of them Group 1 events, including Prix de la Salamandre, Juddmonte International and Sussex Stakes. Stud record: first runners in 2004. Sire of high-class Shamardal (Dewhurst Stakes, St James's Palace Stakes and Prix du Jockey Club), very smart Footstepsinthesand (2000 Guineas) and several smart performers including Maids Causeway (Coronation Stakes), My Typhoon (US Grade 1 winner) and First Samurai (US two year old Grade 1 winner). Standing at Ashford Stud, Kentucky. 2008 fee: $125,000.

GOLAN *1998 Spectrum – Highland Gift (Generous)* Racing record: won four races, including 2000 Guineas and King George VI and Queen Elizabeth Diamond Stakes, latter at four years. Stud record: first runners in 2006. Sire of Group 3 winner Regime. Standing at Coolmore Stud, Ireland. 2008 fee: €5,000.

GONE WEST *1984 Mr Prospector – Secrettame (Secretariat)* Racing record: six wins including Grade 1 Dwyer Stakes. Stud record: best winners include US performers Commendable (Belmont Stakes), Da Hoss (Breeders' Cup Mile), Johar (Breeders' Cup Turf), Link River (John A. Morris Handicap) and West By West (Nassau County Handicap), and in Europe Zafonic (four Group 1 wins including Dewhurst Stakes and 2000 Guineas). Standing at Mill Ridge Farm, Kentucky. 2008 fee: $85,000.

GREEN DESERT *1983 Danzig – Foreign Courier (Sir Ivor)* Racing record: five wins including July Cup, Vernons Sprint Cup and Flying Childers Stakes. Stud record: best winners (all very smart or better) include Alkaadhem, Cape Cross (Lockinge Stakes), Desert Lord (Prix de l'Abbaye), Desert Prince (Irish 2000 Guineas, Prix du Moulin, Queen Elizabeth Stakes), Desert Style, Desert Sun, Gabr, Invincible Spirit (Haydock Sprint Cup), Oasis Dream (Middle Park, July Cup, Nunthorpe Stakes), Owington (July Cup), Sheikh Albadou (Nunthorpe Stakes/Haydock Sprint Cup), Tamarisk (Haydock Sprint Cup) and Tropical. Standing at Nunnery Stud, Norfolk. 2008 fee: £40,000.

HAAFHD *2001 Alhaarth – Al Bahathri (Blushing Groom)* Racing record: won five races, notably 2,000 Guineas and Champion Stakes. Stud record: first crop now two year olds. Standing at Shadwell Stud, Norfolk. 2008 fee: £12,000.

HALLING *1991 Diesis – Dance Machine (Green Dancer)* Racing record: won 12 races including Coral-Eclipse Stakes (twice), Juddmonte International (twice) and Prix d'Ispahan. Stud record: first runners in 2000. Sire of high-class Norse Dancer, very smart Hala Bek and The Geezer, and of numerous smart performers including Chancellor, Dandoun, Foodbroker Fancy, Hero's Journey, Mkuzi, Parasol and Vanderlin. Standing at Dalham Hall Stud, Newmarket. 2008 fee: £12,000.

HAWK WING *2000 Woodman – La Lorgnette (Val de l'Orne)* Racing record: won five times, including National Stakes, Eclipse and Lockinge. Stud record: first crop were two year olds in 2007 and included listed winner Triskel. Standing at Coolmore Stud, Ireland. 2008 fee: €15,000.

HERNANDO *1990 Niniski – Whakilyric (Miswaki)* Racing record: won seven races including Prix Lupin and Prix du Jockey Club. Stud record: first runners in 1999. Sire of high-class Holding Court (Prix du Jockey Club) and Sulamani (Prix du Jockey Club, Arlington Million, Turf Classic Invitational, Juddmonte International), very smart performers Asian Heights and Mr Combustible, and numerous smart performers. Standing at Lanwades Stud, Newmarket. 2008 fee: £12,000.

HIGH CHAPARRAL *2000 Sadler's Wells – Kasora (Darshaan)* Racing record: won ten races, including Derby, Irish Champion Stakes and Breeders' Cup Turf (last event twice). Stud record: first crop were two year olds in 2007. Standing at Coolmore Stud, Ireland. 2008 fee: €15,000.

INDIAN DANEHILL *1996 Danehill – Danse Indienne (Green Dancer)* Racing record: four wins including Prix Ganay. Stud record: first runners in 2004. Sire of useful performers Indian Pipe Dream and Premier Dane. Standing at Glenview Stud, Ireland (also shuttling to New Zealand).

INDIAN HAVEN *2000 Indian Ridge – Madame Dubois (Legend Of France)* Racing record: won three races including the Group 1 Irish 2,000 Guineas. Stud record: first crop are two year olds in 2008. Standing at the Irish National Stud. 2008 fee: €6,000.

INDIAN RIDGE *1985 Ahonoora – Hillbrow (Swing Easy)* Racing record: won five races including Kings Stand Stakes, Duke of York Stakes and Jersey Stakes. Stud record: best winners include Compton Place (July Cup), Domedriver (Breeders' Cup Mile), Indian Haven (Irish 2000 Guineas), Indian Ink (Coronation Stakes), Linngari (Premio Vittorio di Capua), Relaxed Gesture (Canadian International), Ridgewood Pearl (Irish 1,000 Guineas, Coronation Stakes, Prix du Moulin, Breeders Cup Mile) and Namid (Prix de l'Abbaye), high-class Imperial Stride and Nayyir, and very smart Definite Article and Handsome Ridge. Died in 2006.

INTIKHAB *1994 Red Ransom – Crafty Example (Crafty Prospector)* Racing record: eight wins including Diomed and Queen Anne Stakes. Stud record: first runners in 2003. Sire of Red Evie (Lockinge Stakes and Matron Stakes), smart Hoh Mike, Khabfair, Moon Unit and Motashaar, and of several useful performers including Anousa, Ascertain, Fine Silver, Leg Spinner and Mudawin. Standing at Derrinstown Stud, Ireland. 2008 fee: €8,000.

INVINCIBLE SPIRIT *1997 Green Desert – Rafha (Kris)* Racing record: seven wins, notably Sprint Cup at five years. Stud record: first runners in 2006. Sire of dual Group 1 winner Lawman (French Derby and Prix Jean Prat), Fleeting Spirit (Flying Childers Stakes and Molecomb Stakes), smart performers Captain Marvellous and Conquest, and of useful performers Bahama Mama, Invincible Force and Stevie Gee. Standing at Irish National Stud. 2008 fee: €35,000.

JOHANNESBURG *1999 Hennessy – Myth (Ogygian)* Racing record: unbeaten at two years, when seven wins included Phoenix Stakes, Prix Morny, Middle Park and Breeders' Cup Juvenile. Below form at three years. Stud record: first runners in 2006. Sire of useful performers Hammody and Rabatash, and to US Grade 1 winner Scat Daddy. Standing at Ashford Stud, Kentucky. 2008 fee: $65,000.

KEY OF LUCK *1991 Chief's Crown – Balbonella (Gay Mecene)* Racing record: winner of Prix d'Arenberg at two years and Dubai Duty Free at five years, when also runner-up in US Grade 1 9.5f event. Stud record: first runners in 2001. Sire of top-class Alamshar (Irish Derby, King George VI and Queen Elizabeth Diamond Stakes), smart Irish performers Miss Emma and Right Key, and of several useful performers. Standing at Tara Stud, Ireland. 2008 fee: €9,000.

KHELEYF *2001 Green Desert – Society Lady (Mr Prospector)* Racing record: won three races including the Group 3 Jersey Stakes. Stud record: first crop now two-year-olds. Standing at Dalham Hall Stud, Newmarket. 2008 fee: £5,000.

KING'S BEST *1997 Kingmambo – Allegretta (Lombard)* Racing record: won three races, including 2000 Guineas. Stud record: first runners in 2004. Sire of high-class Proclamation (Sussex Stakes), very smart Best Name and smart performers Best Alibi, Creachadoir, Dubai Surprise, Elliots World and Oiseau Rare. Standing at Kildangan Stud, Ireland. 2008 fee: €15,000.

KYLLACHY *1998 Pivotal – Pretty Poppy (Song)* Racing record: Winner of six races, including Nunthorpe Stakes at four years. Stud record: first runners in 2006. Sire of Group 2 winners Arabian Gleam and Tariq and numerous other smart performers. Standing at Cheveley Park Stud, Newmarket. 2008 fee: £12,000.

LEMON DROP KID *1996 Kingmambo – Charming Lassie (Seattle Slew)* Racing record: won seven US Grade 1 events, including Belmont Stakes. Stud record: first runners in 2004. Sire of US Grade 1 winners Christmas Kid, Citronnade and Lemons Forever and numerous smart performers. Standing at Lane's End Farm, Kentucky. 2008 fee: $35,000.

LINAMIX *1987 Mendez – Lunadix (Breton)* Racing record: won four races, notably Poule d'Essai des Pouliches. Stud record: best winners include Amilynx (dual Prix Royal-Oak winner), Carlotamix (Criterium International), Cherry Mix (three Group 1 wins), Fair Mix (Prix Ganay), Fragrant Mix (Grand Prix de Saint-Cloud), Reefscape (Prix du Cadran), Goldamix (Criterium de Saint-Cloud), Miss Satamix (Prix du Haras de Fresnay le Buffard), Sagamix (Prix de l'Arc de Triomphe), Slickly (four Group 1s including Grand Prix de Paris and Prix du Moulin) and Vahorimix (two Group 1 wins). Standing at Haras du Val Henry, France.

LION HEART *2001 Tale Of The Cat – Satin Sunrise (Mr Leader)* Racing record: won the Hollywood Futurity and the Haskell Invitational (both Grade 1 events). Stud record: first crop are two year olds of 2008. Standing at Ashford Stud, Kentucky. 2008 fee: $20,000.

LOMITAS *1988 Niniski – La Colorada (Surumu)* Racing record: won ten races, including three Group 1 events in Germany at three years. Stud record: sire of Arlington Million winner Silvano, German Derby winner Belenus, Italian Oaks winner Meridiana, German St Leger winner Liquido, US graded stakes winners Blue Moon and Sumitas and Group 3 winner Trick Or Treat. Standing at Fahrhof Stud, Germany. 2008 fee: €12,000.

LUCKY STORY *2001 Kris S – Spring Flight (Miswaki)*. Racing record: won four races including the Group 2 Champagne Stakes and Group 2 Vintage Stakes. Stud record: first crop (bred in Japan) were two year olds in 2007. Standing at Tweenhills Stud. 2008 fee: £4,000.

MARJU *1988 Last Tycoon – Flame of Tara (Artaius)* Racing record: three wins including St James's Palace Stakes and runner-up in Derby. Stud record: first runners in 1993. Sire of high-class Soviet Song (five Group 1 events, including Sussex Stakes), very smart performer Indigenous in Hong Kong (formerly known as Qualtron when in Ireland), and of numerous smart

performers including My Emma (Prix Vermeille) and Sil Sila (Prix de Diane). Standing at Derrinstown Stud, Ireland. 2008 fee: €20,000.

MEDICEAN *1997 Machiavellian – Mystic Goddess (Storm Bird)* Racing record: six wins included Lockinge Stakes and Eclipse. Stud record: first runners in 2005. Sire of very smart Dutch Art (Prix Morny, Middle Park), smart performer Nannina (Fillies' Mile, Coronation Stakes), German Group 3 winner Love Academy and useful Abigail Pett, Big Robert and Duke of Tuscany. Standing at Cheveley Park Stud. 2008 fee: £30,000.

MIND GAMES *1992 Puissance – Aryaf (Vice Regent)* Racing record: won seven sprint races including the Group 2 Temple Stakes (twice), the Group 3 Norfolk Stakes and the Group 3 Palace House Stakes. Stud record: sires plenty of precocious two-year-old winners. Standing at Yorton Farm Stud. 2008 fee: £1,500.

MONSIEUR BOND *2000 Danehill Dancer – Musical Essence (Song)* Racing record: won six races including the Group 2 6f Duke Of York Stakes and Group 3 7f Gladness Stakes. Stud record: first crop now two year olds. Standing at Whitsbury Manor, Hampshire. 2008 fee: £3,500.

MONTJEU *1996 Sadler's Wells – Floripedes (Top Ville)* Racing record: won 11 races, including Prix de l'Arc de Triomphe and King George VI and Queen Elizabeth Diamond Stakes. Stud record: first runners in 2004. Sire of top-class Hurricane Run (Irish Derby, Prix de l'Arc de Triomphe, Tattersalls Gold Cup and King George), Authorized (Racing Post Trophy, Derby and Juddmonte International) and Motivator (Racing Post Trophy and Derby), high-class Scorpion (Grand Prix de Paris and St Leger), very smart Corre Caminos (Prix Ganay), Papal Bull and Walk In The Park, and numerous smart performers. Standing at Coolmore Stud, Ireland. 2008 fee: €125,000.

MR GREELEY *1992 Gone West – Long Legend (Reviewer)* Racing record: Triple Grade 3 winner in USA, and runner-up in Breeders' Cup Sprint. Stud record: first runners in 1999. Sire of Finsceal Beo (English and Irish 1,000 Guineas), Saoirse Abu (Phoenix Stakes, Moyglare Stud Stakes), very smart El Corredor (Cigar Mile Handicap) and several smart performers including Reel Buddy (Sussex Stakes). Standing at Gainesway Farm, Kentucky. 2008 fee: €125,000.

MUJADIL *1988 Storm Bird – Vallee Secrete (Secretariat)* Racing record: three wins (at two years) including Group 3 Cornwallis Stakes. Stud record: best winners include Kingsgate Native (Nunthorpe Stakes), Bouncing Bowdler (Group 2 Mill Reef Stakes), Galeota (Group 2 Mill Reef Stakes), the Group 3 winners

Daunting Lady, Leggy Lou, Master Plasta, Satri and Show Me The Money and numerous useful performers. Standing at Rathasker Stud, Ireland. 2008 fee: €10,000.

MULL OF KINTYRE *1997 Danzig – Retrospective (Easy Goer)* Racing record: won two races at two years, including Gimcrack Stakes. Stud record: first runners in 2005. Sire of high-class Arafaa (Irish 2000 Guineas, St James' Palace Stakes), Group 3 winner La Dancia and useful performers Mullaad and Not for Me. Now standing in Australia/USA.

NAMID *1996 Indian Ridge – Dawnsio (Tate Gallery)* Racing record: won five races, including Prix de l'Abbaye. Stud record: first runners in 2004. Sire of smart performer Resplendent Glory and several useful performers including Blue Dakota, Buachaill Dona, Burning Incense, Hogmaneigh, Pike Bishop and Redstone Dancer. Standing at Rathbarry Stud, Ireland. 2008 fee: €10,000.

NAYEF *1999 Gulch – Height of Fashion (Bustino)* Racing record: won nine races, including Champion Stakes and Juddmonte International Stakes. Stud record: first crop were two year olds in 2007 and included the Group 2 May Hill Stakes winner Spacious. Standing at Nunnery Stud, Norfolk. 2008 fee: £10,000.

NEEDWOOD BLADE *1998 Pivotal – Finlaggan (Be My Chief)* Racing record: won nine races here and in the USA including the Group 3 5f Palace House Stakes and the Grade 3 9f Bay Meadows Breeders Cup Handicap. Stud record: first crop are two year olds in 2008. Standing at Mickley Stud. 2008 fee: £3,000.

NOVERRE *1998 Rahy – Danseur Fabuleux (Northern Dancer)* Racing record: won four races at two years, including Champagne Stakes, and Sussex Stakes at three years. Placed in seven Group 1 events afterwards. Stud record: first runners in 2006. Sire of the Group 2 Challenge Stakes winner Miss Lucifer, the Group 3 Albany Stakes winner Nijoom Dubai and the useful performer Elhamri. Standing at Kildangan Stud, Ireland. 2008 fee: €10,000.

OASIS DREAM *2001 Green Desert – Hop (Dancing Brave)* Racing record: won four races, including Middle Park Stakes, July Cup and Nunthorpe Stakes. Stud record: first crop were two-year-olds in 2007 and included the Group 3 winners Captain Gerrard, Starlit Sands, Visit and Young Pretender. Standing at Banstead Manor Stud, Newmarket. 2008 fee: £30,000.

OBSERVATORY *1997 Distant View – Stellaria (Roberto)* Racing record: six wins included Queen Elizabeth II Stakes and Prix d'Ispahan. Stud record: first runners in 2005. Sire of useful performers Nidhaal, Star Cluster and Violette. Standing at

Banstead Manor Stud, Newmarket. 2008 fee: £10,000.

OFFICER *1999 Bertrando – St Helens Shadow (Septieme Ciel)* Racing record: won the Grade 1 Champagne Stakes, the Grade 2 Del Mar Futurity and the Grade 3 Del Mar Best Pal Stakes. Stud record: sire of the US Grade 3 winners Officer Cherrie and Officer Rocket and numerous other minor stakes winners. Standing at Taylor Made Farm, Kentucky. 2008 fee: $35,000.

ONE COOL CAT *2001 Storm Cat – Tacha (Mr Prospector)* Racing record: at two in Ireland won Group 1 6f Phoenix Stakes and Group 1 7f National Stakes. Stud record: first crop now two year olds. Standing at Coolmore Stud, Ireland. 2008 fee: €12,500.

PEINTRE CELEBRE *1994 Nureyev – Peintre Bleue (Alydar)* Racing record: won five races, including Prix du Jockey Club, Grand Prix de Paris and Prix de l'Arc de Triomphe. Stud record: first runners in 2002. Sire of high-class Pride (Grand Prix de Saint-Cloud, Champion Stakes and Hong Kong Cup), multiple Australian Grade 1 winner Bentley Biscuit, very smart performers Castledale (dual US Grade 1 winner), Daijin (German Derby), Helene Mascot (Grade 1 Hong Kong Classic Mile), Pearl of Love (Gran Criterium), Salford Mill (Hong Kong Classic Mile), Sudan (Group 1 Gran Premio de Milano) and Vallee Enchantee (Hong Kong Vase), Australasian Grade 1 winners Mr Sandgroper and Mr Celebrity, and the Group 3 winners Hearthstead Maison and Peppertree Lane. Standing at Coolmore Stud, Ireland. 2008 fee: €25,000.

PICCOLO *1991 Warning – Woodwind (Whistling Wind)* Racing record: four wins including Nunthorpe Stakes and Kings Stand Stakes. Stud record: first runners in 1999. Sire of smart performers Hunting Lion, La Cucaracha (Nunthorpe Stakes) and Pan Jammer, and of several useful performers, including Steward's Cup winner Bond Boy. Standing at Lavington Stud, West Sussex. 2008 fee: £4,000.

PIVOTAL *1993 Polar Falcon – Fearless Revival (Cozzene)* Racing record: four wins including the Nunthorpe Stakes and King's Stand Stakes. Stud record: first runners in 2000. Best winners include high-class Excellent Art (St James's Palace Stakes), Kyllachy (Nunthorpe Stakes) and Somnus (Sprint Cup, Prix de la Foret, Prix Maurice de Gheest), and very smart Beauty Is Truth (Group 2 Prix du Gros-Chene), Captain Rio (Group 2 Criterium des Maisons-Laffitte), Chorist (Pretty Polly Stakes), Golden Apples (triple US Grade 1 winner), Leo (Group 2 Royal Lodge Stakes), Peeress (Lockinge Stakes, Sun Chariot Stakes) and Pivotal Point (Group 2 Diadem Stakes) and numerous smart performers including Megahertz (2 US Grade 1 events), Silvester Lady (German Oaks) and Saoire (Irish 1000 Guineas). Standing at Cheveley Park Stud, Newmarket. 2008 fee: £85,000.

PROUD CITIZEN *1999 Gone West –Drums Of Freedom (Green Forest)*. Racing record: won three races including the Grade 3 Lexington Stakes and second the Kentucky Derby. Stud record: retired to stud in 2004. First crop were two year olds in 2007. Sire of the US Grade 2 Matron Stakes winner Proud Spell and the Group 3 Somerville Tattersall Stakes winner River Proud. Standing at Airdrie Stud, Kentucky. 2008 fee: $25,000.

PYRUS *2000 Mr Prospector –Most Precious (Nureyev)*. Racing record: won Group 2 6f Richmond Stakes and Grade 3 9f Fort Marcy Handicap. Stud record: first crop now two-year-olds. Standing at Ballyhane Stud, Ireland. 2008 fee: €4,000.

RAHY *1985 Blushing Groom – Glorious Song (Halo)* Racing record: won three races in Britain, two at two years when second in Middle Park Stakes. Later Grade 2 1m winner in US. Half-brother to Singspiel. Stud record: best winners include top-class Fantastic Light (7 Group/Grade 1 successes, including Irish Champion Stakes and Breeders' Cup Turf), and high-class Hawksley Hill, Noverre (Sussex Stakes, also first past post in French 2000 Guineas), Rio de la Plata (Prix Jean-Luc Lagardere) and Serena's Song (won 11 US Grade 1 events). Standing at Three Chimneys Farm, Kentucky. 2008 fee: $60,000.

REDBACK *1999 Mark of Esteem – Patsy Western (Precocious)* Racing record: won Solario Stakes and Greenham Stakes. Stud record: winners include the Group 2 Queen Mary Stakes winner Gilded, listed winner Sonny Red and Group 1 placed Redolent. Standing at Tally-Ho Stud, Ireland. 2008 fee: €6,500.

RED RANSOM *1987 Roberto – Arabia (Damascus)* Racing record: two wins in US, at 5f and 6f, from three outings. Stud record: best performers include outstanding miler Intikhab, high-class Ekraar and Electrocutionist (Dubai World Cup, Juddmonte International), very smart performers Casual Look (Oaks), China Visit (Group 2 Prix du Rond-Point), Bail Out Becky (Del Mar Oaks), Perfect Sting (Queen Elizabeth II Challenge Cup and BC Filly and Mare Turf), Red Clubs (Haydock Park Sprint Cup), Australian Grade 1 winners Red Dazzler and Charge Forward and the German Group 1 winner Ransom O'War. Standing at Dalham Hall Stud, Newmarket. 2008 fee: £25,000.

REFUSE TO BEND *2000 Sadler's Wells – Market Slide (Gulch)* Racing record: won seven races including National Stakes, 2,000 Guineas, Eclipse Stakes and

Queen Anne Stakes. Stud record: first crop now two-year-olds. Standing at Kildangan Stud, Ireland. 2008 fee: €20,000.

RESET *2000 Zabeel – Assertive Lass (Zeditave)*. Racing record: won five races in Australia at three years including the Grade 1 7f Futurity Stakes and the Grade 1 1m Australian Guineas. Stud record: first crop now two-year-olds. Standing in Australia.

ROCK OF GIBRALTAR *1999 Danehill – Offshore Boom (Be My Guest)* Racing record: won seven Group 1 races, including Dewhurst Stakes, 2000 Guineas and Sussex Stakes. Stud record: first runners in 2006. Sire of smart Eagle Mountain (dual Group 2 winner), Mount Nelson (Group 1 Criterium International), South African Grade 1 winner Seventh Rock and Group 2 Rockfel Stakes winner Kitty Matcham. Standing at Coolmore Stud, Ireland. 2008 fee: €35,000.

ROYAL APPLAUSE *1993 Waajib – Flying Melody (Auction Ring)* Racing record: winner of nine races, including Middle Park at two years and Haydock Park Sprint Cup at 4. Stud record: first runners in 2001. Sire of the US dual Grade 1 winner Ticker Tape, Grade 2 winners Acclamation, Mister Cosmi and Nevisian Lad, and numerous smart performers including Auditorium, Majestic Missile and Peak To Creek. Standing at The Royal Studs, Norfolk. 2008 fee: £9,000.

SADLER'S WELLS *1981 Northern Dancer – Fairy Bridge (Bold Reason)* Racing record: winner of Irish 2,000 Guineas, Phoenix Champion Stakes and Coral-Eclipse Stakes. Stud record: outstanding sire of numerous Group/Grade 1 winners, including top-class performers Doyen, Galileo, High Chaparral, Kayf Tara, Montjeu, Northern Spur, Old Vic and Salsabil, and the 2007 Group 1 winners Listen, Saddex and Yeats. Standing at Coolmore Stud, Ireland. 2008 fee: private.

SAKHEE *1997 Bahri – Thawakib (Sadler's Wells)* Racing record: won eight races, including Juddmonte International and Prix de l'Arc de Triomphe, and runner-up in Derby. Stud record: first runners in 2006. Sire of the Group 1 July Cup winner Sakhee's Secret and the Group-placed Darsha and Sakhee's Song. Standing at Nunnery Stud, Norfolk. 2008 fee: £10,000.

SEEKING THE GOLD *1985 Mr Prospector – Con Game (Buckpasser)* Racing record: eight wins in USA, notably Grade 1 events Dwyer Stakes and Super Derby. Stud record: first runners in 1993. Best winners include outstanding Dubai Millennium (Dubai World Cup, Prix Jacques le Marois, Queen Elizabeth II Stakes), high-class Cape Town, Heavenly Prize and

Pleasant Home (Breeders' Cup Distaff),Japanese Grade 1 winner Gold Tiara and very smart Dream Supreme, Flanders, Meiner Love and Seeking The Pearl (Prix Maurice de Gheest and Japanese Group 1 event). Standing at Claiborne Farm, Kentucky. 2008 fee: $125,000.

SELKIRK *1988 Sharpen Up – Annie Edge (Nebbiolo)* Racing record: six wins including Queen Elizabeth II Stakes, Lockinge Stakes, Beefeater Gin Celebration Mile and Challenge Stakes. Stud record: sire of high-class Leadership, very smart Altieri (Premio Presidente Repubblica twice), Border Arrow, Etlaala, Highest, Prince Kirk (Prix d'Ispahan), Kastoria (Irish St Leger), Scott's View, Squeak, Tam Lin and The Trader, and of numerous smart performers including Field of Hope (Prix de la Foret), Red Bloom (Fillies' Mile), Sulk (Prix Marcel Boussac), Wince (1000 Guineas) and Wordly (Grade 2 La Jolla Handicap). Standing at Lanwades Stud in Newmarket. 2008 fee: £35,000.

SINGSPIEL *1992 In The Wings – Glorious Song (Halo)* Racing record: winner of nine races, notably Canadian International and Japan Cup at four years and Dubai World Cup, Coronation Cup and Juddmonte International at five. Stud record: first runners in 2001. Sire of top-class performer Moon Ballad, US dual Grade 1 winner Lahudood, high-class Lohengrin (in Japan), very smart Asakusa Den'en (Japanese Group 1 winner), Confidential Lady (Prix de Diane), Lateral (Gran Criterium), Papineau (Gold Cup), Silkwood (Ribblesdale Stakes), Singhalese (Grade 1 Del Mar Oaks) and of numerous smart performers. Standing at Dalham Hall Stud, Newmarket. 2008 fee: £15,000.

SINNDAR *1997 Grand Lodge – Sinntara (Lashkari)* Racing record: won seven races, including Derby and Prix de l'Arc de Triomphe. Stud record: first runners in 2004. Sire of very smart performer Shawanda (Irish Oaks and Prix Vermeille) and Youmzain (Preis Von Europa), Four Sins (Blandford Stakes), smart Albahja, Pictavia and Visindar (Prix Greffulhe) and useful Casual Glance, Ensan and Kerashan. Standing at Haras du Bonneval, France. 2008 fee: €20,000.

SOVIET STAR *1984 Nureyev – Veruschka (Venture VII)* Racing record: won Poule d'Essai des Poulains, Sussex Stakes and Prix de la Foret at three years and July Cup and Prix du Moulin at four years. Stud record: best winners include top-class French performer Freedom Cry, high-class Ashkalani (Poule d'Essai des Poulains, Prix du Moulin), Starborough (St James's Palace Stakes) and Starcraft (Prix du Moulin, Queen Elizabeth II Stakes), and very smart Boris de Deauville (Prix d'Harcourt), Pressing (Premio Roma), Soviet Line (Lockinge Stakes) and Volochine. Standing at Ballylinch Stud, Ireland. 2008 fee: €10,000.

SPARTACUS *2001 Danehill – Teslemi (Ogygian)* Racing record: won three times at two years, including Phoenix Stakes and Gran Criterium. Stud record: first crop were two-year-olds in 2007 and included the Italian listed winner Rastignano. Now standing in New Zealand.

SPEIGHTSTOWN *1998 Gone West – Silken Cat (Storm Cat)* Racing record: won ten races including the Grade 1 Breeders Cup Sprint and four Grade 2 events. Stud record: first crop two year olds in 2008. Standing at Winstar Farm, Kentucky. 2008 fee: $40,000.

STORM CAT *1983 Storm Bird – Terlingua (Secretariat)* Racing record: four wins from 6f to 8.5f notably Grade 1 Young America Stakes. Stud record: best winners include Group/Grade 1 winners After Market, Aljabr, Black Minnaloushe, Cat Thief, Catinca, Desert Stormer, Forestry, Giant's Causeway, Good Reward, Hennessy, High Yield, Nebraska, One Cool Cat, Seeking The Dia, Sharp Cat, Storm Flag Flying, Sweet Catomine, Tabasco Cat, Tornado and Vision And Verse, all at least very smart. Standing at Overbrook Farm, Kentucky. 2008 fee: $300,000.

STREET CRY *1998 Machiavellian – Helen Street (Troy)* Racing record: five wins including Dubai World Cup. Stud record: first runners in 2006. Sire of the Group/Grade 1 winners Street Sense (Breeders' Cup Juvenile, Kentucky Derby, Travers Stakes), Cry And Catch Me (Oak Leaf Stakes) and Majestic Roi (Sun Chariot Stakes). Standing at Jonabell Stud Farm, Kentucky (also shuttling to Australia). 2008 fee: $100,000.

TAGULA *1993 Taufan – Twin Island (Standaan)* Racing record: won four races including the Group 1 6f Prix Morny (at two years) and the Group 3 7f Supreme Stakes. Stud record: sires plenty of winners which in 2000 included the Group 3 winner Tax Free and the listed winners Drawnfromthepast and King Orchisios. Standing at the Rathbarry Stud. 2008 fee: €6,000.

TOBOUGG *1998 Barathea – Lacovia (Majestic Light)* Racing record: won three times at two years, including Dewhurst Stakes, and subsequently placed in four other Group 1 events, including Derby and Eclipse. Stud record: first runners in 2006 when he was the leading British-based first season sire. Sire of the Grade 1 New Zealand 1,000 Guineas winner The Pooka, listed winners Biz Bar, Market Day and Sweet Lilly and the useful performers Dubai Builder and Tobosa. Standing at Dalham Hall Stud, Newmarket. 2008 fee: £5,000.

VAL ROYAL *1996 Royal Academy – Vadlava (Bikala)* Racing record: won 7 of 11 starts, including Breeders'

Cup Mile. Stud record: first runners in 2006. Sire of the dual Guineas winner Cockney Rebel and of the US Grade 2 and Grade 3 winner Valbenny. Standing at the National Stud, Newmarket. 2008 fee: €10,000.

VERGLAS *1994 Highest Honor – Rahaam (Secreto)* Racing record: won three races including the Group 3 6f Coventry Stakes. Stud record: sire of the Group 1 Prix Jean Prat winner Stormy River and of the US dual Grade 2 winner Blackdoun. Standing at the Irish National Stud. 2008 fee: €15,000.

WAR CHANT *1997 Danzig – Hollywood Wildcat (Kris S)* Racing record: won five races including the Grade 1 Breeders Cup Mile. Stud record: sire of the US Graded stakes winners Brilliant, Karen's Caper and En Roblar and the French Group 3 winner Asperity. Standing at Three Chimneys Farm, Kentucky. 2008 fee: $20,000.

XAAR *1995 Zafonic – Monroe (Sir Ivor)* Racing record: champion two year old of 1997, when his four wins included Prix de la Salamandre and Dewhurst Stakes. Won only once after but placed in Group 1 events at 10f. Stud record: first runners in 2004. Sire of smart Balthazaar's Gift (Group 2 Criterium de Maisons-Laffitte), Royal Power (Group 2 German 2,000 Guineas) and Tony James (Group 2 Gimcrack Stakes), the Australian Grade 2 winner No Questions, Group 3 winners Hazariya, Overclock and Wake Up Maggie and the useful winners Coeur Courageux, Dickensian, Mystical Land, Qadar and Sir Xaar. Now standing in Japan.

RACING TRENDS

The tables in this section focus on particular two-year-old races that seem to have the knack of producing winners that improve the following year as three-year-olds. Some of these races have long been important races on the two-year-old calendar (the Dewhurst Stakes for example), but some others will come as a surprise. This type of analysis can enable us to select some of the best of this year's classic generation.

In last year's book the selected races highlighted the Group 1 winners Authorized (Derby), Finsceal Beo (English & Irish 1,000 Guineas), Indian Ink (Coronation Stakes) and Simply Perfect (Falmouth Stakes). Previously, selections have included the classic winners George Washington, Haafhd, King Of Kings, Pennekamp, Mister Baileys, Refuse To Bend, Rock Of Gibraltar, Rodrigo de Triano and Zafonic (all 2,000 Guineas), Bosra Sham, Cape Verdi, Harayir, Russian Rhythm, Sayyedati (1,000 Guineas), Gossamer and Marling (Irish 1,000 Guineas), Dubawi (Irish 2,000

Guineas), Culture Vulture (French 1,000 Guineas), American Post (French 2,000 Guineas), Shamardal (French 2,000 Guineas and French Derby), Sir Percy, High Chaparral, Motivator and Dr Devious (Derby), Lammtarra, Sinndar (Derby and 'Arc'), Alamshar (Irish Derby and the 'Arc'), Desert King, (Irish 2,000 Guineas and Irish Derby), Reams Of Verse (Oaks), Celtic Swing (French Derby), Rule Of Law, Brian Boru, Silver Patriarch and Bob's Return (St Leger), Aussie Rules (French 2,000 Guineas) along with the Prix de l'Arc de Triomphe winner Sakhee and a multitude of other top-class winners.

In the tables, the figure in the third column indicates the number of wins recorded as a three-year-old, with GW signifying a Group race winner at that age.

The horses listed below are the winners of the featured races in 2007. Anyone looking for horses to follow in the Group and Classic events of this season might well want to bear them in mind. I feel that those in bold text are particularly worthy of close scrutiny.

Almajd	Kitty Matcham	**Rio De La Plata**
Centennial	Listen	River Proud
Fast Company	McCartney	Rosa Grace
Fireside	Nahoodh	Sharp Nephew
Ibn Khaldun	**Natagora**	**Twice Over**
Jupiter Pluvius	**New Approach**	You'resothrilling

LOWTHER STAKES York, 6 furlongs, August

1991	Culture Vulture	2 GW
1992	Niche	2 GW
1993	Velvet Moon	1
1994	Harayir	4 GW
1995	Dance Sequence	0
1996	Bianca Nera	0
1997	Cape Verdi	1 GW
1998	Bint Allayl	NR
1999	Jemima	0
2000	Enthused	0
2001	Queen's Logic	1 GW
2002	Russian Rhythm	3 GW
2003	Carry On Katie	0
2004	Soar	0
2005	Flashy Wings	0
2006	Silk Blossom	0
2007	Nahoodh	

Despite a few disappointing years, this race usually has a big say in the following season's 1,000 Guineas. For example Harayir, Cape Verdi and Russian Rhythm won the English 1,000 and Culture Vulture and Al Bahathri took the respective French and Irish versions. Add on the top-class sprinters Habibti and Polonia (both winners prior to 1991) and clearly this race is an important pointer. Mick Channon has won this race 4 times in the last 10 years, including the 2007 renewal, but he's yet to get one in the first three in the 1,000 Guineas. Nahoodh should stay the trip alright but she was disappointing on her 3-y-o debut at Newbury, partly because reportedly she was backward.

DEWHURST STAKES
Newmarket, 7 furlongs, October

1991	Dr Devious	2 GW
1992	Zafonic	1 GW
1993	Grand Lodge	1 GW
1994	Pennekamp	2 GW
1995	Alhaarth	1 GW
1996	In Command	0
1997	Xaar	1 GW
1998	Mujahid	0
1999	Distant Music	1 GW
2000	Tobougg	0
2001	Rock Of Gibraltar	5 GW
2002	Tout Seul	0
2003	Milk It Mick	0
2004	Shamardal	3 GW
2005	Sir Percy	1 GW
2006	Teofilo	NR
2007	New Approach	

The Dewhurst Stakes remains our premier race for two-year-old colts. Rock of Gibraltar was a star of course, but other outstanding colts in this line up include Shamardal, Zafonic, Dr Devious, Grand Lodge and Sir Percy. Sadly Teofilo didn't make it to the races again and was retired. His paternal half-brother New Approach carries on where he left off, having given Jim Bolger and the sire Galileo a remarkable Dewhurst double. He can surely win more Group 1 races this season.

ZETLAND STAKES
Newmarket, 10 furlongs, October/November

1991	Bonny Scot	2 GW
1992	Bob's Return	3 GW
1993	Double Trigger	1 GW
1994	Double Eclipse	1
1995	Gentilhomme	0
1996	Silver Patriarch	2 GW
1997	Trigger Happy	0
1998	Adnaan	1
1999	Monte Carlo	0
2000	Worthily	0
2001	Alexandra Three D	2 GW
2002	Forest Magic	NR
2003	Fun And Games	NR
2004	Ayam Zaman	0
2005	Under The Rainbow	0
2006	Empire Day	NR
2007	Twice Over	

Previous winners of this race include the St Leger and Coronation Cup winner Silver Patriarch, the good four-year-olds Double Eclipse and Rock Hopper, Bob's Return (St Leger) and the Ascot Gold Cup winner Double Trigger - surely the most notable of them all. The Cecil trained Twice Over returned to Newmarket this year to win the Craven Stakes in a tenacious battle with Raven's Pass and prove himself a genuine classic contender, although I would expect him to relish a longer trip than Guineas mile. His sire Observatory was a miler but the dam won an Oaks Trial, so maybe Henry Cecil has another Derby horse on his hands.

CHAMPAGNE STAKES
(formerly the Laurent Perrier Champagne Stakes) Doncaster, 7 furlongs, September

1991	Rodrigo de Triano	4 GW
1992	Petardia	1
1993	Unblest	1 GW
1994	Sri Pekan	NR
1995	Alhaarth	1 GW
1996	Bahhare	0
1997	Daggers Drawn	0
1998	Auction House	0
1999	Distant Music	1 GW
2000	Noverre	1 GW
2001	Dubai Destination	0
2002	Almushahar	0
2003	Lucky Story	0
2004	Etlaala	0
2005	Close To You	1
	Silent Times (dead-heat)	0
2006	Vital Equine	0
2007	McCartney	

The bare figures don't look good, but Dubai Destination came good as a 4-y-o and both Lucky Story and Etlaala were high-class colts, so this race continues to be important as far as the following season's big 3-y-o races are concerned. Rodrigo de Triano and Don't Forget Me both won the English 2,000 and the Irish 2,000 Guineas and Noverre was unlucky not to end the season with two Group 1 victories to his name. McCartney, being by In The Wings, should improve as a 3-y-o and I expect him to win another Group race, probably over ten furlongs or more.

CHEVELEY PARK STAKES
Newmarket, 6 furlongs, October

1991	Marling	3 GW
1992	Sayyedati	2 GW
1993	Prophecy	0
1994	Gay Gallanta	0
1995	Blue Duster	1
1996	Pas de Reponse	2 GW
1997	Embassy	NR
1998	Wannabe Grand	1
1999	Seazun	0
2000	Regal Rose	NR
2001	Queen's Logic	1 GW
2002	Airwave	1 GW

2003	Carry On Katie	0
2004	Magical Romance	0
2005	Donna Blini	1
2006	Indian Ink	1 GW
2007	Natagora	

A number of these fillies have gone on to further Group race success, although it is some years now since a classic winner emerged. Indian Ink, saved her best day for Royal Ascot having previously been fifth in the 1,000 Guineas. Natagora, who is by the Japanese raced sire Divine Light, surely has another good race at her mercy and she is one of several fillies who have a good chance in the 1,000 Guineas.

WASHINGTON SINGER STAKES
Newbury, 7 furlongs, August

1991	Rodrigo de Triano	4 GW
1992	Tenby	2 GW
1993	Colonel Collins	0
1994	Lammtarra	3 GW
1995	Mons	0
1996	State Fair	0
1997	Bahr	2 GW
1998	Valentine Girl	0
1999	Mana-Mou-Bay	0
2000	Prizeman	0
2001	Funfair Wane	1
2002	Muqbil	1 GW
2003	Haafhd	3 GW
2004	Kings Quay	0
2005	Innocent Air	1
2006	Dubai's Touch	2
2007	Sharp Nephew	

As can be seen from the table, this race can provide us with Group or Classic pointers and in that regard Lammtarra, Rodrigo de Triano and Haafhd were outstanding. Sharp Nephew ran in the Royal Lodge Stakes over a mile after winning at Newbury, but he was unplaced. Nevertheless he's a smart prospect and should stay a mile, although his dam was a five furlong winner by Statoblest.

VEUVE CLICQUOT VINTAGE STAKES
Goodwood, 7 furlongs, July

1991	Dr Devious	2 GW
1992	Maroof	1
1993	Mister Baileys	1 GW
1994	Eltish	0
1995	Alhaarth	1 GW
1996	Putra	0
1997	Central Park	2 GW
1998	Aljabr	1 GW
1999	Ekraar	3 GW
2000	No Excuse Needed	1 GW
2001	Naheef	1 GW
2002	Dublin	1
2003	Lucky Story	0
2004	Shamardal	3 GW
2005	Sir Percy	1 GW
2006	Strategic Prince	0
2007	Rio De La Plata	

All in all, this race is very informative in terms of sorting out future stars, with the classic winners Sir Percy, Shamardal, Don't Forget Me, Dr Devious and Mister Baileys and the King George winner Petoski standing out. Aljabr, Central Park, Ekraar and No Excuse Needed were all high-class colts too. Bought at the breeze-ups for 170,000 guineas, Rio de la Plata went on from winning this race to snatch first prize in the Prix Jean-Luc Lagardere at Longchamp. He is one of several colts Sheikh Mohammed is likely to aim at the 2,000 Guineas. However he fares in that classic he certainly seems capable of winning another important race or two this year.

NATIONAL STAKES Curragh, 7f, September

1991	El Prado	0
1992	Fatherland	0
1993	Manntari	1
1994	Definite Article	1
1995	Danehill Dancer	1 GW
1996	Desert King	3 GW
1997	King Of Kings	1 GW
1998	Mus-If	0
1999	Sinndar	5 GW
2000	Beckett	1
2001	Hawk Wing	1 GW
2002	Refuse To Bend	3 GW
2003	One Cool Cat	1 GW
2004	Dubawi	2 GW
2005	George Washington	2 GW
2006	Teofilo	NR
2007	New Approach	

As one can see by the list of recent winners, this race is as important as any for figuring out the following year's top performers. George Washington continued the trend by winning two Group 1 events, including the 2,000 Guineas. New Approach copied Teofilo's record of winning this race before going on to score in the Dewhurst Stakes. Further Group race glory can be expected.

RACING POST TROPHY
Doncaster, 8 furlongs, October

1991	Seattle Rhyme	0
1992	Armiger	1 GW
1993	King's Theatre	2 GW
1994	Celtic Swing	2 GW
1995	Beauchamp King	1 GW
1996	Medaaly	0
1997	Saratoga Springs	1 GW
1998	Commander Collins	0
1999	Aristotle	0
2000	Dilshaan	1 GW
2001	High Chapparal	5 GW
2002	Brian Boru	1 GW
2003	American Post	3 GW
2004	Motivator	2 GW
2005	Palace Episode	0
2006	Authorized	3 GW
2007	Ibn Khaldun	

Some notable performers have won this race, including one of my own favourites the French Derby winner Celtic Swing, the outstanding colt High Chaparral and the Derby heroes Motivator and Authorized. Last year's winner, Ibn Khaldun is by Dubai Destination out of Gossamer – both of them high-class milers. We can expect this colt to win another important event, but I doubt him continuing the trend of this race by becoming a Derby winner.

FILLIES CONDITIONS RACE
Newbury, 7 furlongs, September

1991	Freewheel	1
1992	Sueboog	1 GW
1993	Balanchine	2 GW
1994	Musetta	1
1995	Wild Rumour	0
1996	Etoile	0
1997	Amabel	NR
1998	Fragrant Oasis	1
1999	Veil Of Avalon	1
2000	Palatial	1
2001	Fraulein	2 GW
2002	L'Ancresse	1
2003	Silk Fan	1
2004	Shanghai Lily	0
2005	Mostaqeleh	0
2006	Darrfonah	1
2007	Rosa Grace	

The brilliant fillies Balanchine and Milligram stand out in this group and although the race has thrown up a few disappointments of late, both Fraulein and L'Ancresse came up with excellent performances over the Atlantic, with the former taking Canada's Grade 1 E P Taylor Stakes and Ballydoyle's L'Ancresse only just getting touched off in the Breeders Cup Filly & Mare Turf. Rae Guest's filly, Rosa Grace, should stay a mile alright and being by Lomitas you'd expect her to train on and win again this year.

HAYNES, HANSON AND CLARK STAKES
Newbury, 8 furlongs, September

1991	Zinaad	1
1992	Pembroke	1
1993	King's Theatre	2 GW
1994	Munwar	2 GW
1995	Mick's Love	1
1996	King Sound	1
1997	Duck Row	0
1998	Boatman	0
1999	Ethmaar	0
2000	Nayef	4 GW
2001	Fight Your Corner	1 GW
2002	Saturn	0
2003	Elshadi	0
2004	Merchant	NR
2005	Winged Cupid	NR
2006	Teslin	2
2007	Centennial	

The high-class horses Rainbow Quest, Unfuwain, King's Theatre and Nayef have all won this race and indeed Shergar won it in 1980, but it's been a while since those glory days. The John Gosden trained Centennial, a son of Dalakhani, finished his season in second place in the one mile Prix Thomas Bryon. He should stay at least ten furlongs this year and win more races.

MEON VALLEY STUD FILLIES' MILE
Ascot, 8 furlongs, September

1991	Midnight Air	0
1992	Ivanka	0
1993	Fairy Heights	0
1994	Aqaarid	1 GW
1995	Bosra Sham	3 GW
1996	Reams of Verse	2 GW
1997	Glorosia	0
1998	Sunspangled	0
1999	Teggiano	0
2000	Crystal Music	0
2001	Gossamer	1 GW
2002	Soviet Song	0
2003	Red Bloom	1 GW
2004	Playful Act	1 GW
2005	Nannina	1 GW
2006	Simply Perfect	1 GW
2007	Listen	

Diminuendo (in 1987), Bosra Sham, Reams of Verse, Gossamer and Soviet Song stand out amongst recent winners of this race, although the latter had to wait until after her 3-y-o career before reaching her full potential. Listen suffered a setback in the spring, keeping her out of the classic and Group events of the first half of the season. If she comes back she'll be a major force in the top fillies races up to a mile and a half.

SOMERVILLE TATTERSALL STAKES
Newmarket, 7 furlongs, September/October

1991	Tertian	0
1992	Nominator	0
1993	Grand Lodge	1 GW
1994	Annus Mirabilis	1
1995	Even Top	1 GW
1996	Grapeshot	1
1997	Haami	1
1998	Enrique	1 GW
1999	Scarteen Fox	0
2000	King Charlemagne	3 GW
2001	Where Or When	2 GW
2002	Governor Brown	NR
2003	Milk It Mick	0
2004	Diktatorial	0
2005	Aussie Rules	2 GW
2006	Thousand Words	0
2007	River Proud	

The bare figures in this table don't really tell the whole story, for there are some very good horses here. The Group winners speak for themselves but Milk It Mick, Opening Verse and Annus Mirabilis all went on to win good races abroad and Haami was certainly a smart colt too. Last year Aussie Rules won the French Guineas and then a Grade 1 event in the USA. River Proud is a smart colt but was put in his place in the Group races he contested, his short head second in the July Stakes being his best effort.

NGK SPARK PLUGS MAIDEN
(formerly the Westley Maiden Stakes)
Newmarket, 7 furlongs, September/October

1991	DIV 1 Modernise	0
	DIV 2 Pursuit of Love	3 GW
1992	DIV 1 Placerville	2 GW
	DIV 2 Barathea	1 GW
1993	Darnay	0
1994	DIV 1 Painter's Row	1 GW
	DIV 2 Smart Alec	Non-runner
1995	Astor Place	1
1996	Mashhaer	0
1997	Quiet Assurance	0
1998	Easaar	0
1999	DIV 1 Zentsov Street	NR
	DIV 2 Qamoos	0
2000	DIV 1 Demophilos	0
	DIV 2 Malhub	0
2001	Millennium Dragon	2
2002	Desert Star	NR

2003	Secret Charm	1
2004	Rob Roy	1
2005	Arm Candy	1
2006	DIV 1 Desert Dew	1
	DIV 2 Supersonic Dave	0
2007	DIV 1 Fireside	
	DIV 2 Almajd	

The stand-outs amongst recent winners are the 1988 2,000 Guineas winner Doyoun, Prince of Wales's Stakes winner Placerville, the July Cup second Pursuit of Love and, best of all, the Breeders Cup Mile winner Barathea. Connections of Fireside expect him to make up into a smart colt and he certainly ought to win more races. The same ought to be said about Almajd, a half-brother to Alhaarth. I expect both of them to be suited by a mile.

ACOMB STAKES York, 7 furlongs, August

1991	Torrey Canyon	1
1992	Woodchat	0
1993	Concordial	0
1994	Options Open	0
1995	Bijou d'Inde	1 GW
1996	Revoque	1
1997	Saratoga Springs	1 GW
1998	Auction House	0
1999	King's Best	1 GW
2000	Hemingway	NR
2001	Comfy	NR
2002	Bourbonnais	0
2003	Rule Of Law	2 GW
2004	Elliots World	1
2005	Palace Episode	0
2006	Big Timer	0
2007	Fast Company	

There have been a few disappointing seasons since the victories of such as King's Best (2,000 Guineas) and Bijou d'Inde (St James's Palace Stakes), but Rule Of Law turned things around in 2004 with his St Leger victory. Fast Company went very close to winning the Dewhurst Stakes, showing his Group 1 potential over a mile.

KILLAVULLAN STAKES
Leopardstown, 7 furlongs October

1991	Misako-Togo	3
1992	Asema	3 GW
1993	Broadmara	0
1994	Kill The Crab	2 GW
1995	Aylesbury	0
1996	Shell Ginger	0
1997	Kincara Palace	1
1998	Athlumney Lady	0
1999	Monashee Mountain	2 GW
2000	Perigee Moon	0
2001	Stonemason	0
2002	New South Wales	1
2003	Grey Swallow	2 GW
2004	Footstepsinthesand	1 GW
2005	Frost Giant	1 GW
2006	Confuchias	1 GW
2007	Jupiter Pluvius	

During the period researched, seven of the winners subsequently went on to Group success as three-year-olds, most notably the Irish Derby winner Grey Swallow and the English 2,000 Guineas winner Footstepsinthesand. Last year's winner Jupiter Pluvius has a fast pedigree and will surely be aimed at good races at up to a mile.

CHERRY HINTON STAKES
Newmarket, 6 furlongs, July

1991	Musicale	1 GW
1992	Sayyedati	2 GW
1993	Lemon Souffle	1 GW
1994	Red Carnival	0
1995	Applaud	0
1996	Dazzle	1
1997	Asfurah	0
1998	Wannabe Grand	1
1999	Torgau	0
2000	Dora Carrington	0
2001	Silent Honor	NR
2002	Spinola	0
2003	Attraction	4 GW
2004	Jewel In The Sand	0
2005	Donna Blini	1
2006	Sander Camillo	0
2007	You'resothrilling	

The remarkable filly Attraction brought to an end a slump in fortunes for this race and but the 3 winners since have been largely disappointing. The O'Brien trained You'resothrilling ran twice more after winning this but had no luck in running. She should win more races at up to a mile.

ROCKFEL STAKES
Newmarket, 7 furlongs, October

1991	Musicale	1 GW
1992	Yawl	0
1993	Relatively Special	0
1994	Germane	0
1995	Bint Salsabil	1
1996	Moonlight Paradise	0
1997	Name Of Love	NR
1998	Hula Angel	1 GW
1999	Lahan	1 GW
2000	Sayedah	0
2001	Distant Valley	0
2002	Luvah Girl	1 in USA
2003	Cairns	0
2004	Maids Causeway	1 GW
2005	Speciosa	1 GW
2006	Finsceal Beo	2 GW
2007	Kitty Matcham	

Three Newmarket 1,000 Guineas winners have hailed from the winners of this race in the last 10 years – Lahan, Speciosa and Finsceal Beo. For good measure Maids Causeway won the Coronation Stakes and Hula Angel won the Irish 1,000 Guineas (a race Finsceal Beo also added to her tally). So Kitty Matchem has a lot to live up to, but she might well improve further as a three-year-old.

Charles Dickens (IRE) 857
Chasca (IRE) 1226
Chateauneuf (IRE) 721
Cheap Thrills 1173
Cheddar George 978
Cherish The Moment (IRE) 722
Chiberta King 19
Chic Retreat (USA) 82
Chief Wild Cat (IRE) 942
Chintz 1132
Choral Festival 1286
Choral Service 601
Churchills Victory (IRE) 829
Citizenship 465
Classically 325
Classic Vintage (USA) 1227
Clerk's Choice (IRE) 830
Clockmaker (IRE) 524
Clodoline 342
Clodova (IRE) 926
Close Alliance 525
Cloudy Start 214
Coiled Spring 1228
Collaborator 1397
Colorado Dawn 1493
Come On Toby 405
Commendation 526
Compton Ford 381
Conakry 241
Conciousness 215
Conclusive 51
Congregation 527
Convitezza 914
Cool Art (IRE) 184
Cool For Cats 1133
Cool Star (IRE) 943
Cordoba 1398
Cornish Rose 1474
Countenance ·602
Countess Zara (IRE) 20
Count Of Tuscany (USA) 1229
Countrywide City 290
Courageous Nature (IRE) 979
Crimea (IRE) 858
Crimson Sky (IRE) 1134
Crowd Pleaser (IRE) 927
Crowfoot (IRE) 1135
Crown Pretender (IRE) 928
Crush 1340
Cry For The Moon (USA) 1230
Crystal Moments 406
Custody (IRE) 1399
Cutting Comments 382
Cyflymder (IRE) 504
Cygnet 361

Daanaat (IRE) 242
Dabbers Chief (USA) 723
Dactik (IRE) 1261
Daily Double 646
Dalradian (IRE) 903
Damaniyat Girl (USA) 603
Damien (IRE) 724
Damselfly 859
Dance Avenue (IRE) 980
Dance Club (IRE) 831
Dancing Bandit (USA) 129
Dancourt (IRE) 1400
Danehill Destiny 604
Danehill's Pearl (IRE) 964
Dane's World (IRE) 647
Dangerous Midge (USA) 981
Danidh Dubai (IRE) 243
Dante Deo (USA) 41
Dark Humour (IRE) 1561
Dark Lane 42
Dark Mischief 207
Dark Ranger 1538
Davids Matador 842
Da Vinci Code (IRE) 1136
Day Of The Eagle (IRE) 362
Dazinski 1475
Deal Clincher 1597
Debussy (IRE) 528
December Draw (IRE) 904
Decent Fella (IRE) 929
Defector (IRE) 1062
Demand 605
Demeanour (USA) 407
Denices Desert 149
Denny Crane 930
Derbaas (USA) 408
Der Rosenkavalier (IRE) 21
Desert Eagle (IRE) 1137
Desert Fever 725
Desert Icon (IRE) 905
Desert Sunset 860
Desiree Clary 861
Desire To Excel (IRE) 343
Deya's Dream 22
Dialogue 862
Diamond Gift (USA) 291
Diamond Heist 1494
Diamond Jo (IRE) 1078
Diamond Twister (USA) 107
Diddums 606
Diktalina 1063
Dimander (IRE) 1231
Dimensional 1232
Discreet Affair (IRE) 1562
Doctor Parkes 1519
Doggerbank (IRE) 216
Donavitum 529
Double Act 1092
Double Ex 1372

Doughnut 648
Dougie Peel 1318
Dove Mews 83
Downstream 1341
Drachenfels 1319
Dream City (IRE) 1495
Dreamcoat 530
Dream Date (IRE) 607
Dream Huntress 982
Dream In Waiting 344
Dream Runner 326
Dreams For Ever (IRE) 1563
Dreamwalk (IRE) 52
Dream Win 1401
Driving Snow 1262
Dr Speed 505
Drumbeat 1138
Dr Valentine 887
Dubai Challenge (USA) 1402
Dubai Creek (IRE) 1432
Dubai Crest 1233
Dubai Echo (USA) 1403
Dubai Gem 244
Dubai Legend 1342
Dubai's Gazal 245
Duc De Savoie (USA) 1564
Dunes Queen (USA) 246
Dunkirk 1139

Eagles Call (USA) 292
Earthshine (IRE) 84
Easily Forgiven 208
Ebiayn (IRE) 803
Ebony Eyes 906
Echo Dancer 185
Eddie Boy 85
Egypt 1140
Eightdaysaweek 888
Electric Flight (USA) 345
Eleganta (IRE) 506
El Guevara (IRE) 1320
Eliza Griffith (IRE) 649
Elnawin 650
El Romo (IRE) 1141
Elusive Ronnie (IRE) 186
Embracing The King 383
Emerging Artist (FR) 1433
Emily Dickinson 931
Emirates Aviation 1434
Emirates Challenge (IRE) 1435
Emirates Champion 1436
Emirates Roadshow (USA) 1437
Emirates Sports 1438
Emirates World (IRE) 1439
Enticement 1404
Entisarat 1440
Entrancer (IRE) 1064

Equinine (IRE) 726
Errol Flynn (IRE) 1093
Esprit De Midas 1321
Europe (USA) 1142
Euston Square 531
Evaluation 651
Every Second 965
Excellent Girl 1263
Excelsior Academy 983
Exceptional Art 293
Expressive 1405
Extracurricular (USA) 1539

Failte Isteach (IRE) 130
Falbrina 175
Fallen In Love 445
Fame And Glory 1143
Fanditha (IRE) 652
Fantasia 363
Fantastic Day 889
Fantastic Dubai (USA) 247
Fantasy Land (IRE) 984
Faraway Flower 727
Fareer 409
Fascinating Rhythm 1406
Fast Flow 473
Fat Chance 588
Father Time 217
Fault 327
Favours Brave 532
Featherweight (IRE) 728
Felday 1048
Fenomen 364
Fiancee (IRE) 328
Fifer (IRE) 1079
Final Approach 1264
Finjaan 1496
Finnegan McCool 53
First Passage (USA) 985
Fisadora 729
Fiscal Lad 890
Flapper (IRE) 776
Flash Mans Papers 108
Fleur De'Lion 891
Fleuron 474
Flintlock (IRE) 533
Floodlit 534
Floor Show 966
Florentia 1287
Fly Butterfly 986
Fondant Fancy 436
Forgotten Dreams (IRE) 437
Formula (USA) 653
Fortunate Bid (IRE) 730
Fortuni (IRE) 1288
Four Star General 1144
Foxtrot Alpha (IRE) 1598
Frank Street 843
Free Falling 365
Frognal (IRE) 987

La Tizona (IRE) 330
Layer Cake 778
Leahurst (IRE) 1103
Legend Of Greece (IRE) 1573
Legislate 745
Lekhani (IRE) 1375
Lenny Briscoe (IRE) 894
Lethal Glaze (IRE) 663
Lhashan (GB) 257
Liffey Dancer (IRE) 368
Light Sleeper 296
Light The Fire (IRE) 998
Like For Like (IRE) 664
Lily Of The Nile (UAE) 1250
Lista Lightning (IRE) 1267
Liszt (IRE) 1151
Little Blacknumber 665
Little Calla (IRE) 413
Little Conker 331
Little Lost 1176
Lively Blade 967
Location 1237
Lochan Mor 89
Lock 'N' Load (IRE) 1356
London Bridge 541
Lookafternumberone (IRE) 508
Lost In The Desert 154
Lovely Thought 610
Love Pegasus (USA) 870
Love To Chat (USA) 1040
Luckier (IRE) 895
Luminous Eyes (IRE) 1574
Luvmedo (IRE) 666
Luxuria (IRE) 667
Luxury Brand (USA) 1575

Mabait 369
Mackten 908
Mafaaz 542
Magaling (IRE) 370
Maggie Lou (IRE) 1322
Mahyoub 1449
Maid For Music (IRE) 968
Maid Of Stone 477
Majestic Lady 746
Major Phil 371
Majuba (USA) 1323
Makaam (USA) 1504
Makhaaleb (IRE) 747
Makhaaleb (USA) 872
Mallorey 1376
Manaaqeb 1450
Managua 258
Manero 1177
Man Friday (IRE) 1152
Maqsood (USA) 1576
Marjury Daw (IRE) 509
Mark Of An Angel (IRE)

1268
Marmoom Flower (IRE) 1451
Marsool 1505
Masamah (IRE) 414
Massilah 748
Master Fong (IRE) 749
Mastoora 611
Maswerte (IRE) 372
Mattamia (IRE) 1034
Maxwell Hawke 297
Mayaalah 543
Mayolynn (USA) 221
Maziona 1577
Mean Mr Mustard 1178
Medicean Man 495
Medicio (FR) 1578
Mejala (IRE) 456
Merdaam 457
Mesyaal 259
Meydan 349
Midday 222
Middle Persia (GB) 1579
Midnight Cruiser (IRE) 669
Midnight Strider 1533
Mid Wicket (USA) 750
Mile Highland (USA) 779
Miliemil 350
Millway Beach 466
Minor Vamp (IRE) 670
Minute Limit 1179
Misdaqeya 751
Miss Fritton (IRE) 671
Miss Scarlet 1324
Miss Sophisticat 909
Miss Tikitiboo 1522
Mister Bombastic (IRE) 386
Mister Dee Bee (IRE) 752
Mister Fantastic (GB) 387
Mister Green (FR) 1541
Mister Standfast 490
Mister Tinktastic (IRE) 388
Misty Glade 999
Mobaghit (USA) 1506
Mohalhal (IRE) 1414
Mohanad (IRE) 260
Mojeerr 1507
Monaco Dream (IRE) 832
Monaco Mistress (IRE) 709
Moneycantbuymelove 90
Monitor Closely (IRE) 298
Mons Calpe 351
Mooakada 544
Moonburst 415
Mootriba 612
Moral Maze (IRE) 545
Moss Mojito (IRE) 780
Mossy Rose 119
Mount Acclaim 1180
Mount Ella 1181

Moving Heart (IRE) 1580
Mr Clearview 1035
Mr Deal 847
Mr Melodious 753
Mr Mistoffelees (USA) 1153
Mr Prolific 754
Mrs Kipling 188
Mr Udagawa 58
Mt Kintyre (IRE) 1478
Mullionmileanhour 112
Multiplication 332
Munnings 1154
Muraweg (IRE) 546
Mustaqer (IRE) 755
Mutamaashi 613
Mutaraami 1508
Mutawarath (IRE) 614
Muzo (USA) 1104
My Boy Jack (IRE) 1377
My Girl Jode 1479
My Kingdom 1051
Myshkin 813
Mysteria (IRE) 814
Mystic Prince 1000
Mystika (IRE) 1378
My Sweet Georgia (IRE) 756
Mythicism 1357
My Topaz (IRE) 1581
Myttons Maid 10

My Vision (USA) 1452
Nafaath (IRE) 1269
Naiazek 1582
Naizak 458
Nancy Rock (IRE) 135
Naseehah (USA) 1453
Nasemah (IRE) 416
Nation (IRE) 1155
Nehaam 547
Nellie Finlay (IRE) 136
Nemorosa 615
Nethaam (IRE) 1583
Newlyn Art 478
Newsforyou 1415
Nicky Nutjob 299
Night Knight 91
Night Of Fortune 1295
Noble Dictator 1523
Noble Heart (IRE) 44
Noble Jack (IRE) 672
No Brainer 548
Non Dom (IRE) 1052
Northern Hero (IRE) 417
Norwegian Dancer (UAE) 969
Nothing To Worry (IRE) 261
Nubar Lady (IRE) 1379
Nuwaith 871

Oasis Knight (IRE) 1509

Oceanic Dancer (IRE) 1083
Ohiyesa (IRE) 949
Olaudah Equiano 1480
Olive Green (USA) 467
Olynard (IRE) 59
Omega Wolf (IRE) 11
Omnium Duke (IRE) 781
On Our Way 223
Optimal Power (IRE) 933
Oratory (IRE) 673
Orthology (IRE) 1481
Ostaadi 815
Ottoman Empire (FR) 915
Oui Say Oui (IRE) 1380
Ouqba 757
Our Day Will Come 674
Our Wee Girl 896 ·
Ouster 479
Overachiever (IRE) 468

Pachakutek (USA) 1524
Pacific Bay (IRE) 393
Pagan Flight (IRE) 1001
Pagan Force (IRE) 1238
Paisley 373
Pallas Athena (IRE) 1201
Pallazone (IRE) 950
Pampered King (USA) 1296
Pansy Potter 1002
Papyrian 833
Parabola 934
Park Lane 758
Park Melody (IRE) 1003
Parthenon 873
Partner Shift (IRE) 418
Party Cat (IRE) 675
Pasar Silbano (IRE) 951
Passage To India 1182
Passkey 1297
Patronne 1298
Pelinnore 1525
Peninsula Girl (IRE) 262
Penitent 616
Penny's Gift 676
Penperth 491
Penzina 910
Perception (IRE) 333
Perfect Affair (USA) 60
Perfect Secret 26
Pergamon (IRE) 549
Peter Grimes (IRE) 439
Peter Tchaikovsky 1156
Pether's Dancer (IRE) 1068
Photographic 759
Pick A Purse 61
Pictorial (USA) 1416
Pied Piper 1417
Pinocchio 874
Piquante 92
Piste 1004

Sri Putra 821
Stage Performance (IRE) 561
Standpoint 1421
Stan's Cool Cat (IRE) 352
Stan's Smarty Girl (USA) 353
Star Addition 3
Star Approval (IRE) 562
Star Of Sophia (IRE) 395
Starry Sky 1304
State Of War (USA) 563
Steel Free (IRE) 98
Step At A Time 879
Step Fast (USA) 880
Sterling Sound (USA) 1511
Stoic 1109
Storm Mist (IRE) 354
Straight Laced 912
Strawberrydaiquiri 1422
Street Of Hope (USA) 785
Strevelyn 396
Suakin Dancer (IRE) 1057
Suba (USA) 1456
Sub Prime 1187
Sugar Baby Love (IRE) 936
Sugar Free (IRE) 1384
Sultan's Way (IRE) 355
Sumbe (USA) 1512
Sunset Crest 397
Sunshine Always (IRE) 306
Sun Ship (IRE) 693
Super Flight 307
Super Fourteen 694
Super Midge 1011
Sutton Veny (IRE) 496
Sway Me Now (USA) 144
Sweet Smile (IRE) 1327
Swift Chap 1038
Swift Flight 377
Swindler 33
Swiss Diva 484
Swiss Guard 1164
Swiss Lake Sweetie (USA) 784

Ta Aleem 1513
Taameer 1514
Taarab 1457
Taazur 881
Tactic 462
Tae Kwon Do (USA) 426
Tagseed (IRE) 628
Takaatuf 882
Takasima (IRE) 1207
Take The Hint 564
Talking Hands 899

Tanoura (IRE) 1208
Taqarub 766
Tarqua (IRE) 695
Tarrip (USA) 145
Tartan Gunna 883
Tartan Turban (IRE) 696
Tartaria 1110
Tarzan (IRE) 884
Tasman Gold 34
Tejime 565
Telescopic Vision (IRE) 1593
Test Match 1515
That Boy Ronaldo 105
Theatrikos (IRE) 1209
Thecreditcrunchie (IRE) 1385
The Desert Saint 35
The Dial House 1188
The Fonz 1423
The Hague 566
The Magic Of Rio 629
The Miniver Rose (IRE) 697
The Proper Guru 398
The Saucy Snipe 1599
Thewaytosanjose (IRE) 900
Thief 378
Thousand Knights 1111
Three Moons (IRE) 440
Three Steps To Heaven 767
Thunderous Mood (USA) 356
Tiantai (USA) 226
Tiger Eye 308
Time And Tide (IRE) 1386
Timeless Dream 309
Tinar (USA) 227
Tinseltown 1165
Tishtar 698
Tito Gobbi 711
Titus Andronicus (IRE) 1328
Today's The Day 823
Toll Road 427
Tomintoul Star 228
Too Many Tears (IRE) 157
Too Much Trouble 272
Too Tall 379
Top Tinker 1484
Top Town Girl 66
To The Point 971
Towanda (USA) 567
Towering Habab (IRE) 1424
Trading Nation (USA) 337
Transformer (IRE) 913
Tressway (IRE) 357
Tribal Squaw 1189
Tricky Situation 514

Trigger McCann 1041
Trip Switch 1071
Troopingthecolour 568
Tropical Paradise (IRE) 1600
Trueblue Wizard (IRE) 1072
True Decision 901
Truly Asia 338
Tudor Key (IRE) 1244
Turkish Lokum 492
Twisted 569

Uncle Keef (IRE) 1516
Undaunted Affair (IRE) 1329
Union Island (IRE) 1330
United States (USA) 1166
Unwavering (IRE) 229

Valid Point (IRE) 1305
Veiled 1306
Venetian Lady 399
Verinco 1362
Verlegen (IRE) 699
Veroon (IRE) 515
Versaki (IRE) 700
Very Distinguished 1310
Viceroy Of India 1167
Vilasol (IRE) 1276
Vocalised (USA) 146
Von Jewlensky (IRE) 1168
Voveen 1363

Waahej 463
Wabi Sabi (IRE) 768
Waffle 1112
Wajaha (IRE) 570
Wanna (IRE) 1387
Wardati 822
War Native 1113
Warrant's Attention (IRE) 36
Warrior Chant (USA) 937
Wartime 571
Watergate (IRE) 1307
Waterstown (IRE) 1085
Wave Aside 1012
Way To Finish 1425
Weald Park (USA) 701
Wee Giant 1331
Well Of Echoes 959
Wemyss Bay 230
West Kirk 837
West Leake (IRE) 769
West With The Wind (USA) 310
Wetherby Place (IRE) 67
What A Fella 400
Whatagoodcatch (IRE) 1210

Whispering Angel 1013
Whooska (USA) 311
Wicklows Call (IRE) 1388
Wilbury Star (IRE) 702
Wilfred Pickles (IRE) 1245
Winged Harriet (IRE) 630
Wingwalker 231
Winner's Call 1114
Winterbourne 120
Wohaida (IRE) 273
Woodlark Island (IRE) 1517
Wrong Way Round (IRE) 572

Yaldas Girl (USA) 113
Yankee Doodle 1169
Yeoman Blaze 37
Yirga 1458
Yokozuna 428
Young Star Gazer 232

Zaaqya 464
Zacinto 1426
Zaffaan 429
Zavaala (IRE) 147
Za Za 233
Zelos Diktator 516
Zero Money 339
Zuzu 824

UNNAMED: 7, 12, 38-40, 46, 68, 69, 99-102, 106, 114-116, 155, 158-173, 178-181, 192-204, 234-237, 274-283, 312-319, 380, 389, 430-432, 441, 472, 485, 486, 497-501, 517, 518, 573-579, 582-587, 592-595, 631, 703, 704, 712, 770-773, 786-792, 825, 826, 838, 839, 849, 885, 902, 916-924, 938-941, 952, 954-957, 960-962, 1014-1029, 1042-1045, 1058-1061, 1073, 1074, 1115-1124, 1170, 1171, 1190-1196, 1211-1223, 1246, 1252, 1311-1314, 1332, 1334-1338, 1344-1355, 1364-1368, 1389, 1390, 1463-1466, 1485-1488, 1529-1531, 1534, 1535, 1545-1550, 1594-1596